CCNA: Cisco Certified Network Guide

CCNA Exam 640-802 Objectives

OBJECTIVE	CHAPTER
Describe how a network works	
Describe the purpose and functions of various network devices	1
Select the components required to meet a network specification	1
Use the OSI and TCP/IP models and their associated protocols to explain how data flows in a network	1
Describe common networked applications including web applications	1
Describe the purpose and basic operation of the protocols in the OSI and TCP models	1, 2
Describe the impact of applications (Voice Over IP and Video Over IP) on a network	1, 9
Interpret network diagrams	1, 3
Determine the path between two hosts across a network	6
Describe the components required for network and Internet communications	1
Identify and correct common network problems at layers 1, 2, 3 and 7 using a layered model approach	1, 2
Differentiate between LAN/WAN operation and features	1, 14
Configure, verify and troubleshoot a switch with VLANs and interswitch communications	
Select the appropriate media, cables, ports, and connectors to connect switches to other network devices and hosts	1, 8
Explain the technology and media access control method for Ethernet networks	
Explain network segmentation and basic traffic management concepts	1, 8
Explain basic switching concepts and the operation of Cisco switches	8
Perform and verify initial switch configuration tasks including remote access management	8
Verify network status and switch operation using basic utilities (including: ping, traceroute, telnet, SSH, arp, ipconfig), SHOW & DEBUG commands	8, 9
Identify, prescribe, and resolve common switched network media issues, configuration issues, auto negotiation, and switch hardware failures	8, 9
Describe enhanced switching technologies (including: VTP, RSTP, VLAN, PVSTP, 802.1q)	9

Sybex®
An Imprint of
WILEY

OBJECTIVE	CHAPTER

Sybex®
An Imprint of
WILEY

OBJECTIVE	CHAPTER
Select the appropriate media, cables, ports, and connectors to connect routers to other network devices and hosts	1
Configure, verify, and troubleshoot RIPv2	6
Access and utilize the router to set basic parameters (including: CLI/SDM)	4, 6, 7
Connect, configure, and verify operation status of a device interface	4, 6, 7
Verify device configuration and network connectivity using ping, traceroute, telnet, SSH or other utilities	4, 6, 7
Perform and verify routing configuration tasks for a static or default route given specific routing requirements	6, 7
Manage IOS configuration files (including: save, edit, upgrade, restore)	5
Manage Cisco IOS	5
Compare and contrast methods of routing and routing protocols	6, 7
Configure, verify, and troubleshoot OSPF	6, 7
Configure, verify, and troubleshoot EIGRP	6, 7
Verify network connectivity (including: using ping, traceroute, and telnet or SSH)	4, 5, 6, 7
Troubleshoot routing issues	4, 6, 7
Verify router hardware and software operation using SHOW & DEBUG commands	4, 6, 7
Implement basic router security	6, 7, 10
Explain and select the appropriate administrative tasks required for a WLAN	
Describe standards associated with wireless media (including: IEEE WI-FI Alliance, ITU/FCC)	12
Identify and describe the purpose of the components in a small wireless network (Including: SSID, BSS, ESS)	12
Identify the basic parameters to configure on a wireless network to ensure that devices connect to the correct access point	12
Compare and contrast wireless security features and capabilities of WPA security (including: open, WEP, WPA-1/2)	12
Identify common issues with implementing wireless networks (Including: Interface, Miss configuration)	12

OBJECTIVE	CHAPTER
Describe how VLANs create logically separate networks and the need for routing between them	9
Configure, verify, and troubleshoot VLANs	9
Configure, verify, and troubleshoot trunking on Cisco switches	9
Configure, verify, and troubleshoot interVLAN routing	9
Configure, verify, and troubleshoot VTP	9
Configure, verify, and troubleshoot RSTP operation	9
Interpret the output of various show and debug commands to verify the operational status of a Cisco switched network	9
Implement basic switch security (including: port security, trunk access, management vlan other than vlan1, etc.	9
Implement an IP addressing scheme and IP Services to meet network requirements in a medium-size Enterprise branch office network	
Describe the operation and benefits of using private and public IP addressing	2, 3
Explain the operation and benefits of using DHCP and DNS	1
Configure, verify and troubleshoot DHCP and DNS operation on a router (including: CLI/SDM)	4
Implement static and dynamic addressing services for hosts in a LAN environment	3
Calculate and apply an addressing scheme including VLSM IP addressing design to a network	3
Determine the appropriate classless addressing scheme using VLSM and summarization to satisfy addressing requirements in a LAN/WAN environment	3
Describe the technological requirements for running IPv6 in conjunction with IPv4 (including: protocols, dual stack, tunneling, etc)	13
Describe IPv6 addresses	13
Identify and correct common problems associated with IP addressing and host configurations	3
Configure, verify, and troubleshoot basic router operation and routing on Cisco devices	
Describe basic routing concepts (including: packet forwarding, router lookup process	6
Describe the operation of Cisco routers (including: router bootup process, POST, router components)	4

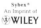

Sybex®
An Imprint of
WILEY

Advance Praise

"Todd's methods of discussing topics are tactfully approached so they are not confusing to the reader, and his explanations are clear and easy to understand."
—Amazon Reader Review

"I passed my CCNA on the first try after reading this book thoroughly. …If you read the book and do all the review questions and written labs at the end of each chapter, you will be well prepared for the exam."
—Amazon Reader Review

"This is a great book! Todd Lammle has the ability to make complex topics simple. Cisco books are essential once you've mastered networking basics, but there is nothing like Sybex for learning the concepts from A to Z."
—Amazon Reader Review

"Todd has been an authority in this field for as long as I can remember. His style of writing keeps the book from becoming a sleep aid and provides nuts and bolts information that is both excellent real-world reference and directly relevant to exam objectives. If you are considering taking the CCNA exam, you would be ill advised to not give this book a thorough read."
—Amazon Reader Review

"This is the first book review I have ever written on Amazon. I've been in the computer/network support field for many years, but had almost no contact with Cisco equipment. I basically knew the 'enable' and 'config' Cisco commands. I had originally planned on shelling out the $3000 to take a CCNA boot camp, but decided that that was way too much money. So I bought this book instead … took a week off from work (which I would have done anyway for the class), and went at it … My homegrown boot camp paid off because I passed the exam on the first try, saving almost $2900!"
—Amazon Reader Review

"This is the best technical book I have ever read!!"
—Amazon Reader Review

"This book is excellent resource for preparation for CCNA certification. It has needed information regarding the Cisco's objective. Sample test and Bonus Test give extra knowledge for exam's question. Users have more knowledge and practice of test exams. I will recommend this book for anyone who does not have any knowledge of CCNA material."
—Amazon Reader Review

"I've recently passed the CCNA exam with 985 out of 1000 points and Todd Lammle's book was my only study material (along with a Cisco 2500 router).

"It covers all relevant topics in such an easy-to-understand way and gives you a great networking/Cisco knowledge to build upon. Even now, while I'm pursuing other certifications, it serves as an irreplaceable reference. Every chapter concludes with review questions, hands-on exercises or labs to give you the opportunity of applying your new skills in real-world scenarios and the CD provides additional sample tests and flashcards to consolidate your knowledge.

"By reading the book twice and doing all the exercises you will be able to answer just about any question you may encounter on the exam. Highly recommended!"
—Amazon Reader Review

"I had made three previous attempts using Cisco Press but could not get over the hump. Needless to say I was getting pretty discouraged. However, I had heard good things about the Sybex book by Todd Lammle and decided to give it a try. It was the best thing I could have done. The book read great and it explained the required concepts and topics very well. The review questions and Hand-on Labs at the end of each chapter were also very helpful.

"I took the test last weekend and passed!!

"Thank you!!"
—Amazon Reader Review

"Good exam prep. I read this book and with only slight network experience was able to pass the CCNA."
—Amazon Reader Review

"There isn't much more I can say about this book than has already been said. I used Todd's guide to help me pass the CCNA in 2000 and am using him again to recertify. Just an excellent book. Period."
—Amazon Reader Review

"This book covered everything I needed to pass the exam, with hands-on experience, and the bonus material. What a great written book this is. The best I have ever read.

"I recommend this book highly!!"
—Amazon Reader Review

CCNA®:
Cisco® Certified
Network Associate
Study Guide
Sixth Edition

Todd Lammle

BICENTENNIAL
1807
WILEY
2007
BICENTENNIAL

Wiley Publishing, Inc.

Acquisitions Editor: Jeff Kellum
Development Editor: Toni Zuccarini Ackley
Technical Editor: Patrick J. Conlan
Production Editor: Sarah Groff-Palermo
Copy Editor: Judy Flynn
Production Manager: Tim Tate
Vice President and Executive Group Publisher: Richard Swadley
Vice President and Executive Publisher: Joseph B. Wikert
Vice President and Publisher: Neil Edde
Media Project Supervisor: Laura Atkinson
Media Development Specialist: Josh Frank
Media Quality Assurance: Angie Denny
Book Designers: Judy Fung and Bill Gibson
Compositor: Craig Woods, Happenstance Type-O-Rama
Proofreader: Nancy Riddiough
Indexer: Ted Laux
Anniversary Logo Design: Richard Pacifico
Cover Designer: Ryan Sneed

Sybex®
An Imprint of
WILEY

To Our Valued Readers:

Thank you for looking to Sybex for your CCNA exam prep needs. We at Sybex are proud of our reputation for providing certification candidates with the practical knowledge and skills needed to succeed in the highly competitive IT marketplace. This latest edition of the best-selling *CCNA: Cisco Certified Network Associate Study Guide* reflects our commitment to provide CCNA candidates with the most up-to-date, accurate, and accessible instructional material on the market.

As with previous editions, Todd and the editors have worked hard to ensure that the study guide you hold in your hands is comprehensive, in-depth, and pedagogically sound. We're confident that this book will exceed the demanding standards of the certification marketplace and help you, the CCNA certification candidate, succeed in your endeavors.

As always, your feedback is important to us. If you believe you've identified an error in the book, please visit the Customer Support section of the Wiley website. And if you have general comments or suggestions, feel free to drop me a line directly at nedde@wiley.com. At Sybex, we're continually striving to meet the needs of individuals preparing for certification exams.

Good luck in pursuit of your CCNA certification!

Neil Edde
Publisher—Certification
Sybex, an Imprint of Wiley

Acknowledgments

Monica Lammle's writing style and voice, editing ability, encouragement, and dedication to ensuring that my books are concise yet highly readable has been invaluable to the success of this and many other projects. She brings clarity and life to what can truly be some very arcane and difficult material!

Mr. Patrick Conlan has got to be the personification of perseverance—he's a rock! Patrick literally hashed and rehashed each topic in this guide with me at all hours of the day and night—scrutinizing the material until we both agreed it was verifiably solid. He was so instrumental in the development of this book that I hired him at GlobalNet Training to work as a course developer and trainer! You're going to be hearing a lot more from Mr. Conlan in the technical instruction and writing arena in the future for sure.

Daniel Aguilera, who has worked with me at GlobalNet Training for seven years, also worked diligently, helping me put together the bonus exams you'll find on the CD (so be sure to give him a call if you happen to find a problem <G>). Dan possesses both the intelligence and optimism required to be a great source of encouragement and a deep reservoir of problem-solving ability whenever I found myself discouraged or burned out.

Toni Zuccarini Ackley was the main editor of this—the newest book in the Sybex Cisco series. Thank you Toni for having the patience of Job, and for working so hard on this book with me. I'm so happy (and relieved) that you took on the job and, most of all, that you didn't run screaming from the room the next day!

Jeff Kellum is instrumental to my success in the Cisco world and is my acquisitions editor. Jeff, thanks for your guidance and continued patience. Although we work well together and put out fantastic material, I am sure he groans when he sees my name on caller ID!

In addition, Sarah Groff-Palermo was an excellent production editor and she worked really hard to get the book done as quickly as possible, without missing the small mistakes that are so easy to over look. Judy Flynn was the copy editor and she showed me that you can actually write a book and still have patience, be helpful but yet work extremely hard to get this book out on the shelves as fast as possible, and for that I thank you tremendously. Both Sarah and Judy worked very hard editing the book for what will hopefully turn out to be a great guide to lead you on your journey toward becoming a CCNA.

Finally a big thanks to Craig Woods and Happenstance-Type-O-Rama, and the CD team: Laura Atkinson, Josh Frank, and Angie Denny.

Contents at a Glance

Table of Contents

Introduction

Welcome to the exciting world of Cisco certification! You have picked up this book because you want something better—namely, a better job with more satisfaction. Rest assured that you have made a good decision. Cisco certification can help you get your first networking job or more money and a promotion if you are already in the field.

Cisco certification can also improve your understanding of the internetworking of more than just Cisco products: You will develop a complete understanding of networking and how different network topologies work together to form a network. This is beneficial to every networking job and is the reason Cisco certification is in such high demand, even at companies with few Cisco devices.

Cisco is the king of routing, switching, and security, the Microsoft of the internetworking world. The Cisco certifications reach beyond the popular certifications, such as the MCSE, to provide you with an indispensable factor in understanding today's network—insight into the Cisco world of internetworking. By deciding that you want to become Cisco certified, you are saying that you want to be the best—the best at routing and the best at switching. This book will lead you in that direction.

For up-to-the minute updates covering additions or modifications to the CCNA certification exams, as well as additional study tools and review questions, be sure to visit the Todd Lammle forum and website at www.lammle.com and/or www.sybex.com.

Cisco's Network Support Certifications

Initially, to secure the coveted Cisco CCIE certification, you took only one test and then you were faced with the (extremely difficult) hands-on lab, an all-or-nothing approach that made it tough to succeed.

In response, Cisco created a series of new certifications to help you get the coveted CCIE as well as aid prospective employers in measuring skill levels. With these new certifications, which make for a better approach to preparing for that almighty lab, Cisco opened doors that few were allowed through before.

This book covers everything CCNA related. For up-to-date information on Todd Lammle Cisco Authorized CCNA CCNP, CCSP, CCVP, and CCIE boot-camps, please see www.lammle.com and/or www.globalnettraining.com.

Cisco Certified Network Associate (CCNA)

The CCNA certification was the first in the new line of Cisco certifications and was the precursor to all current Cisco certifications. Now you can become a Cisco Certified Network Associate for the meager cost of this book and either one test at $150 or two tests at $125 each—although the CCNA exams are extremely hard and cover a lot of material, so you have to really know your stuff! Taking a Cisco class or spending months with hands-on experience is not out of the norm.

And once you have your CCNA, you don't have to stop there—you can choose to continue with your studies and achieve a higher certification, called the Cisco Certified Network Professional (CCNP). Someone with a CCNP has all the skills and knowledge he or she needs to attempt the Routing and Switching CCIE lab. But just becoming a CCNA can land you that job you've dreamed about.

Why Become a CCNA?

Cisco, not unlike Microsoft and Novell (Linux), has created the certification process to give administrators a set of skills and to equip prospective employers with a way to measure skills or match certain criteria. Becoming a CCNA can be the initial step of a successful journey toward a new, highly rewarding, and sustainable career.

The CCNA program was created to provide a solid introduction not only to the Cisco Internetwork Operating System (IOS) and Cisco hardware, but also to internetworking in general, making it helpful to you in areas that are not exclusively Cisco's. At this point in the certification process, it's not unrealistic that network managers—even those without Cisco equipment—require Cisco certifications for their job applicants.

If you make it through the CCNA and are still interested in Cisco and internetworking, you're headed down a path to certain success.

What Skills Do You Need to Become a CCNA?

To meet the CCNA certification skill level, you must be able to understand or do the following:

- A CCNA certified professional can install, configure, and operate LAN, WAN, and wireless access services securely, as well as troubleshoot and configure small to medium networks (500 nodes or fewer) for performance.

- This knowledge includes, but is not limited to, use of these protocols: IP, IPv6, EIGRP, RIP, RIPv2, OSPF, serial connections, Frame Relay, cable, DSL, PPPoE, LAN switching, VLANs, Ethernet, security, and access lists.

Be sure and check my web site and/or Cisco's web site for the latest Cisco CCNA objectives and other Cisco exams, objectives, and certifications that can change on a moment's notice

How Do You Become a CCNA?

The way to become a CCNA is to pass one little test (CCNA Composite exam 640-802). Then—poof!—you're a CCNA. (Don't you wish it were that easy?) True, it can be just one test, but you still have to possess enough knowledge to understand what the test writers are saying.

However, Cisco has a two-step process that you can take in order to become a CCNA that may or may not be easier than taking one longer exam (this book is based on the one-step method 640-802); however, this book has all the information you need to pass all three exams.

The two-step method involves passing the following:

- Exam 640-822: Interconnecting Cisco Networking Devices 1(ICND1)
- Exam 640-816: Introduction to Cisco Networking Devices 2 (ICND2)

I can't stress this enough: It's critical that you have some hands-on experience with Cisco routers. If you can get ahold of some 1841 or 2800 series routers, you're set. But if you can't, I've worked hard to provide hundreds of configuration examples throughout this book to help network administrators (or people who want to become network administrators) learn what they need to know to pass the CCNA exam.

Since the new 640-802 exam is so hard, Cisco wants to reward you for taking the two-test approach. Or so it seems. If you take the ICND1 exam, you actually receive a certification called the CCENT (Cisco Certified Entry Networking Technician). This is one step toward your CCNA. To achieve your CCNA, you must still pass your ICND2 exam.

Again, this book was written for the CCNA 640-802 Composite exam—one exam and you get your certification.

For Cisco Authorized hands-on training with CCSI Todd Lammle, please see www.globalnettraining.com. Each student will get hands-on experience by configuring at least three routers and two switches—no sharing of equipment!

What Does This Book Cover?

This book covers everything you need to know in order to pass the CCNA 640-802 exam. However, taking the time to study and practice with routers or a router simulator is the real key to success.

You will learn the following information in this book:

- Chapter 1 introduces you to internetworking. You will learn the basics of the Open Systems Interconnection (OSI) model the way Cisco wants you to learn it. Ethernet networking and standards are discussed in detail in this chapter as well. There are written labs and plenty of review questions to help you. Do not skip the written labs in this chapter!

- Chapter 2 provides you with the background necessary for success on the exam as well as in the real world by discussing TCP/IP. This in-depth chapter covers the very beginnings of the Internet Protocol stack and then goes all the way to IP addressing and understanding the difference between a network address and a broadcast address before finally ending with network troubleshooting.

- Chapter 3 introduces you to subnetting. You will be able to subnet a network in your head after reading this chapter. In addition, you'll learn about Variable Length Subnet Masks (VLSMs) and how to design a network using VLSMs. This chapter will finish with summarization techniques and configurations. Plenty of help is found in this chapter if you do not skip the Written Lab and Review Questions.

- Chapter 4 introduces you to the Cisco Internetwork Operating System (IOS) and command-line interface (CLI). In this chapter you will learn how to turn on a router and configure the basics of the IOS, including setting passwords, banners, and more. IP configuration using the Secure Device Manager (SDM) will be discussed and Hands-on Labs will help you gain a firm grasp of the concepts taught in the chapter. Before you go through the Hands-on Labs, be sure to complete the Written Lab and Review Questions.

- Chapter 5 provides you with the management skills needed to run a Cisco IOS network. Backing up and restoring the IOS, as well as router configuration, is covered, as are the trouble-shooting tools necessary to keep a network up and running. Before performing the Hands-on Labs in this chapter, complete the Written Lab and Review Questions.

- Chapter 6 teaches you about IP routing. This is a fun chapter, because you will begin to build your network, add IP addresses, and route data between routers. You will also learn about static, default, and dynamic routing using RIP and RIPv2 (with a small touch of IGRP). Written and Hands-on Labs will help you understand IP routing to the fullest.

- Chapter 7 dives into more complex dynamic routing with Enhanced IGRP and OSPF routing. The Written Lab, Hands-on Labs, and Review Questions will help you master these routing protocols.

- Chapter 8 gives you a background on layer 2 switching and how switches perform address learning and make forwarding and filtering decisions. Network loops and how to avoid them with the Spanning Tree Protocol (STP) will be discussed, as well as the 802.1w STP version. Go through the Written Lab and Review Questions to help you really understand the basic layer 2 switching on an internetwork.

- Chapter 9 covers virtual LANs and how you can use them in your internetwork. This chapter also covers the nitty-gritty of VLANs and the different concepts and protocols used with VLANs, as well as troubleshooting. The Written Lab and Review Questions will reinforce the VLAN material.

- Chapter 10 covers security and access lists, which are created on routers to filter the network. IP standard, extended, and named access lists are covered in detail. Written and Hands-on Labs, along with Review Questions, will help you study for the security and access-list portion of the CCNA Composite exam.

- Chapter 11 covers Network Address Translation (NAT). This chapter has been on the Sybex website for a few years as an update to my last CCNA book, but I updated it and added it to this edition. New information, commands, troubleshooting, and labs will help you nail the NAT CCNA objectives.

- Chapter 12 covers wireless technologies. This is an introductory chapter regarding wireless technologies as Cisco sees them. However, I also added some advanced wireless topics that cover Cisco's newest gear. At this time, advanced wireless is not covered within the Cisco CCNA objectives, but that can change on any given day. Make sure you understand your basic wireless technologies like access points and clients, as well as the difference between 802.11a, b, and g.

▪ Chapter 13 covers IPv6. This is a fun chapter and has some great information. IPv6 is not the big, bad scary monster that most people think it is. IPv6 is an objective on this new exam, so study this chapter carefully. Keep an eye out at www.lammle.com for late-breaking updates.

▪ Chapter 14 concentrates on Cisco wide area network (WAN) protocols. This chapter covers HDLC, PPP, and Frame Relay in depth, as well as other protocols we use on a daily basis like Cable, DSL and PPPoE. You must be proficient in all these protocols to be successful on the CCNA exam. Do not skip the Written Lab, Review Questions, or Hands-on Labs found in this chapter.

How to Use This Book

If you want a solid foundation for the serious effort of preparing for the Cisco Certified Network Associate (CCNA Composite) 640-802 exam, then look no further. I have spent hundreds of hours putting together this book with the sole intention of helping you to pass the CCNA exam and learn how to configure Cisco routers and switches (among hundreds of other things!).

This book is loaded with valuable information, and you will get the most out of your studying time if you understand how I put the book together.

To best benefit from this book, I recommend the following study method:

1. Take the assessment test immediately following this introduction. (The answers are at the end of the test.) It's okay if you don't know any of the answers; that is why you bought this book! Carefully read over the explanations for any question you get wrong and note the chapters in which the material is covered. This information should help you plan your study strategy. Honestly, my recommendation is to just start reading from Chapter 1 and don't stop until you're all the way through Chapter 14.

2. Study each chapter carefully, making sure that you fully understand the information and the test objectives listed at the beginning of each one. Pay extra-close attention to any chapter that includes material covered in questions you missed in the assessment test.

3. Complete each Written Lab at the end of each chapter. Do *not* skip these written exercises because they directly relate to the CCNA Composite objectives and what you must glean from the chapters in which they appear. Do not just skim these labs! Make sure you understand completely the reason for each answer.

4. Complete all Hands-on Labs in the chapter (not all chapters have hands-on labs, referring to the text of the chapter so that you understand the reason for each step you take. If you do not have Cisco equipment available, go to www.routersim.com for a router simulator that will cover all the hands-on labs needed for all your Cisco certification needs.

5. Answer all of the Review Questions related to each chapter. (The answers appear at the end of the chapters.) Note the questions that confuse you and study those sections of the book again. Do not just skim these questions! Make sure you understand completely the reason for each answer. Remember that these will not be the exact questions you find on the exam; they are written to help you understand the chapter material.

6. Try your hand at the bonus exams that are included on the companion CD. The questions in these exams appear only on the CD. Check out www.lammle.com for more Cisco exam prep questions. The questions found at www.lammle.com will be updated at least monthly, if not weekly or even daily! Before you take your test, be sure and visit my web site for questions, videos, audios and other useful information.

7. Also on the companion CD is the first module from my complete CCNA video series, which covers internetworking and basic networking. This is critical for the CCNA exam. In addition, as an added bonus, I have included an audio section from my CCNA audio program. Do not skip the video and audio section!

> Just a note to let you know that I mention the test number 640-801 in the video and audio sections. This is nothing to be concerned about as the information presented is valid for both the 640-801 and 640-802 exam.

8. Test yourself using all the flashcards on the CD. These are brand new and updated flashcard programs to help you prepare for the CCNA exam. These are a great study tool!

To learn every bit of the material covered in this book, you'll have to apply yourself regularly, and with discipline. Try to set aside the same time period every day to study, and select a comfortable and quiet place to do so. If you work hard, you will be surprised at how quickly you learn this material.

If you follow the steps listed above and really study and practice the Review Questions, bonus exams, the Todd Lammle video/audio sections, and the electronic flashcards, as well as all the Written and Hands-on Labs, it would be hard to fail the CCNA Composite exam. However, studying for the CCNA exam is like trying to get in shape—if you do not go to the gym every day, you won't get in shape.

What's on the CD?

We worked hard to provide some really great tools to help you with your certification process. All of the following tools should be loaded on your workstation when you're studying for the test. As a fantastic bonus, I was able to add a section from both my CCNA video and audio series to the CD included with this book!

The Sybex Test Preparation Software

The test preparation software prepares you to pass the CCNA exam. In this test engine, you will find all the review and assessment questions from the book, plus two additional bonus exams that appear exclusively on the CD.

Electronic Flashcards for PC, Pocket PC, and Palm Devices

To prepare for the exam, you can read this book, study the Review Questions at the end of each chapter, and work through the practice exams included in the book and on the companion CD. But wait, there's more! You can also test yourself with the flashcards included on the

CD. If you can get through these difficult questions and understand the answers, you'll know you're ready for the CCNA exam.

The flashcards include over 250 questions specifically written to hit you hard and make sure you are ready for the exam. Between the review questions, bonus exams, and flashcards on the CD, you'll be more than prepared for the exam.

CCNA: Cisco Certified Network Associate Study Guide in PDF

Sybex offers the *CCNA Exam 640-802 Study Guide* in PDF on the CD so you can read the book on your PC or laptop. (Acrobat Reader 7 is also included on the CD.)

Todd Lammle Videos

I have created a full CCNA series of videos that can be purchased in either DVD or downloadable format. However, as a bonus included with this book, the first module of this series is included on the CD in its entirety. The video is over one hour of informative CCNA information. This is a $149 value! Do not skip this video as it covers the internetworking objectives, which are very important to the CCNA exam.

Todd Lammle Audios

In addition to the videos included for free on the CD, I have also included a full section from my CCNA audio series. The CCNA audio series is a $199 value! This is a great tool to add to your arsenal of study material to help you pass the CCNA exam.

 To find more Todd Lammle videos and audios, as well as other Cisco study material, please see www.lammle.com. And well you're there, sign up for my forum. There is a lot of useful information that can found in the forum, plus you can ask me questions directly related to your studies.

Where Do You Take the Exams?

You may take the CCNA Composite exam at any Pearson VUE authorized testing centers (www.vue.com) or call 877-404-EXAM (3926).

To register for a Cisco Certified Network Associate exam:

1. Determine the number of the exam you want to take. (The CCNA Composite exam number is 640-802.)

2. Register with the nearest Pearson VUE testing center. At this point, you will be asked to pay in advance for the exam. At the time of this writing, the exam is $150 and must be taken within one year of payment. You can schedule exams up to six weeks in advance or as late as the same day you want to take it—but if you fail a Cisco exam, you must wait five days before you will be allowed to retake the exam. If something comes up and you need to cancel or reschedule your exam appointment, contact Prometric or Pearson VUE at least 24 hours in advance.

3. When you schedule the exam, you'll get instructions regarding all appointment and cancellation procedures, the ID requirements, and information about the testing-center location.

Tips for Taking Your CCNA Composite Exam

The CCNA Composite exam test contains about 55 to 60 questions and must be completed in 75 to 90 minutes or less. This information can change per exam. You must get a score of about 85% to pass this exam, but again, each exam can be different.

Many questions on the exam have answer choices that at first glance look identical—especially the syntax questions! Remember to read through the choices carefully because close doesn't cut it. If you get commands in the wrong order or forget one measly character, you'll get the question wrong. So, to practice, do the hands-on exercises at the end of this book's chapters over and over again until they feel natural to you.

Also, never forget that the right answer is the Cisco answer. In many cases, more than one appropriate answer is presented, but the *correct* answer is the one that Cisco recommends. On the exam, you're always instructed to pick one, two, or three, never "choose all that apply." The CCNA Composite 640-802 exam may include the following test formats:

- Multiple-choice single answer
- Multiple-choice multiple answer
- Drag-and-drop
- Fill-in-the-blank
- Router simulations

In addition to multiple choice and fill-in response questions, Cisco Career Certifications exams may include performance simulation exam items.

Check out the software at www.routersim.com that lets you design and configure an unlimited number of Cisco routers and switches running multiple routing protocols!

The software on the CD and at RouterSim.com provides step-by-step instruction on how to configure both Cisco routers and switches. However, router simulations in Cisco proctored exams will not show the steps to follow in completing a router interface configuration. They do allow partial command responses. For example, show config or sho config or sh conf would be acceptable. Router#show ip protocol or router#show ip prot would be acceptable.

Here are some general tips for exam success:

- Arrive early at the exam center so you can relax and review your study materials.

- Read the questions *carefully*. Don't jump to conclusions. Make sure you're clear about *exactly* what each question asks.

- When answering multiple-choice questions that you're not sure about, use the process of elimination to get rid of the obviously incorrect answers first. Doing this greatly improves your odds if you need to make an educated guess.

- You can no longer move forward and backward through the Cisco exams, so double-check your answer before clicking Next since you can't change your mind.

After you complete an exam, you'll get immediate, online notification of your pass or fail status, a printed Examination Score Report that indicates your pass or fail status, and your exam results by section. (The test administrator will give you the printed score report.) Test scores are automatically forwarded to Cisco within five working days after you take the test, so you don't need to send your score to them. If you pass the exam, you'll receive confirmation from Cisco, typically within two to four weeks, sometimes longer.

How to Contact the Author

You can reach Todd Lammle through his forum at www.lammle.com.

Assessment Test

1. What protocol does PPP use to identify the Network layer protocol?

   A. NCP

   B. ISDN

   C. HDLC

   D. LCP

2. You have 10 users plugged into a hub running 10Mbps half-duplex. There is a server connected to the switch running 10Mbps half-duplex as well. How much bandwidth does each host have to the server?

   A. 100kbps

   B. 1Mbps

   C. 2Mbps

   D. 10Mbps

3. In a network with dozens of switches, how many root bridges would you have?

   A. 1

   B. 2

   C. 5

   D. 12

4. What does the command `routerA(config)#line cons 0` allow you to perform next?

   A. Set the Telnet password.

   B. Shut down the router.

   C. Set your console password.

   D. Disable console connections.

5. How long is an IPv6 address?

   A. 32 bits

   B. 128 bytes

   C. 64 bits

   D. 128 bits

6. What PPP protocol provides dynamic addressing, authentication, and multilink?

   A. NCP

   B. HDLC

   C. LCP

   D. X.25

7. What command will display the line, protocol, DLCI, and LMI information of an interface?

   A. `sh pvc`

   B. `show interface`

   C. `show frame-relay pvc`

   D. `sho runn`

8. Which of the following is the valid host range for the subnet on which the IP address 192.168.168.188 255.255.255.192 resides?

   A. 192.168.168.129–190

   B. 192.168.168.129–191

   C. 192.168.168.128–190

   D. 192.168.168.128–192

9. What does the `passive` command provide to dynamic routing protocols?

   A. Stops an interface from sending or receiving periodic dynamic updates

   B. Stops an interface from sending periodic dynamic updates but not from receiving updates

   C. Stops the router from receiving any dynamic updates

   D. Stops the router from sending any dynamic updates

10. Which protocol does Ping use?

   A. TCP

   B. ARP

   C. ICMP

   D. BootP

11. How many collision domains are created when you segment a network with a 12-port switch?

   A. 1

   B. 2

   C. 5

   D. 12

12. Which of the following commands will allow you to set your Telnet password on a Cisco router?

   A. `line telnet 0 4`

   B. `line aux 0 4`

   C. `line vty 0 4`

   D. `line con 0`

13. Which router command allows you to view the entire contents of all access lists?

   A. `show all access-lists`

   B. `show access-lists`

   C. `show ip interface`

   D. `show interface`

14. What does a VLAN do?

   A. Acts as the fastest port to all servers

   B. Provides multiple collision domains on one switch port

   C. Breaks up broadcast domains in a layer 2 switch internetwork

   D. Provides multiple broadcast domains within a single collision domain

15. If you wanted to delete the configuration stored in NVRAM, what would you type?

   A. `erase startup`

   B. `erase nvram`

   C. `delete nvram`

   D. `erase running`

16. Which protocol is used to send a destination network unknown message back to originating hosts?

   A. TCP

   B. ARP

   C. ICMP

   D. BootP

17. Which class of IP address has the most host addresses available by default?

   A. A

   B. B

   C. C

   D. A and B

18. How often are BPDUs sent from a layer 2 device?

   A. Never

   B. Every 2 seconds

   C. Every 10 minutes

   D. Every 30 seconds

19. Which one of the following is true regarding VLANs?

   A. Two VLANs are configured by default on all Cisco switches.

   B. VLANs only work if you have a complete Cisco switched internetwork. No off-brand switches are allowed.

   C. You should not have more than 10 switches in the same VTP domain.

   D. VTP is used to send VLAN information to switches in a configured VTP domain.

20. Which WLAN IEEE specification allows up to 54Mbps at 2.4GHz?

   A. A

   B. B

   C. G

   D. N

21. How many broadcast domains are created when you segment a network with a 12-port switch?

A. 1

B. 2

C. 5

D. 12

22. What flavor of Network Address Translation can be used to have one IP address allow many users to connect to the global Internet?

A. NAT

B. Static

C. Dynamic

D. PAT

23. What protocols are used to configure trunking on a switch? (Choose two.)

A. VLAN Trunking Protocol

B. VLAN

C. 802.1Q

D. ISL

24. What is a stub network?

A. A network with more than one exit point

B. A network with more than one exit and entry point

C. A network with only one entry and no exit point

D. A network that has only one entry and exit point

25. Where is a hub specified in the OSI model?

A. Session layer

B. Physical layer

C. Data Link layer

D. Application layer

26. What are the two main types of access control lists (ACLs)?

A. Standard

B. IEEE

C. Extended

D. Specialized

27. To back up an IOS, what command will you use?

A. `backup IOS disk`

B. `copy ios tftp`

C. `copy tftp flash`

D. `copy flash tftp`

28. What command is used to create a backup configuration?

   A. `copy running backup`

   B. `copy running-config startup-config`

   C. `config mem`

   D. `wr mem`

29. What is the main reason the OSI model was created?

   A. To create a layered model larger than the DoD model

   B. So application developers can change only one layer's protocols at a time

   C. So different networks could communicate

   D. So Cisco could use the model

30. Which protocol does DHCP use at the Transport layer?

   A. IP

   B. TCP

   C. UDP

   D. ARP

31. If your router is facilitating a CSU/DSU, which of the following commands do you need to use to provide the router with a 64000bps serial link?

   A. `RouterA(config)#`**`bandwidth 64`**

   B. `RouterA(config-if)#`**`bandwidth 64000`**

   C. `RouterA(config)#`**`clockrate 64000`**

   D. `RouterA(config-if)#`**`clock rate 64`**

   E. `RouterA(config-if)#`**`clock rate 64000`**

32. Which command is used to determine if an IP access list is enabled on a particular interface?

   A. `show access-lists`

   B. `show interface`

   C. `show ip interface`

   D. `show interface access-lists`

33. Which command is used to upgrade an IOS on a Cisco router?

   A. `copy tftp run`

   B. `copy tftp start`

   C. `config net`

   D. `copy tftp flash`

Answers to Assessment Test

1. A. Network Control Protocol is used to help identify the Network layer protocol used in the packet. See Chapter 14 for more information.

2. D. Each device has 10Mpbs to the server. See Chapter 8 for more information.

3. A. You should have only one root bridge per network. See Chapter 8 for more information.

4. C. The command `line console 0` places you at a prompt where you can then set your console user-mode password. See Chapter 4 for more information.

5. D. An IPv6 address is 128 bits long, compared to an IPv4 address, which is only 32 bits long. See Chapter 13 for more information.

6. C. Link Control Protocol in the PPP stack provides dynamic addressing, authentication, and multilink. See Chapter 14 for more information.

7. B. The `show interface` command shows the line, protocol, DLCI, and LMI information of an interface. See Chapter 14 for more information.

8. A. 256 – 192 = 64. 64 + 64 = 128. 128 + 64 = 192. The subnet is 128, the broadcast address is 191, and the valid host range is the numbers in between, or 129–190. See Chapter 3 for more information.

9. B. The `passive` command, short for `passive-interface`, stops regular updates from being sent out an interface. However, the interface can still receive updates. See Chapter 6 for more information.

10. C. ICMP is the protocol at the Network layer that is used to send echo requests and replies. See Chapter 2 for more information.

11. D. Layer 2 switching creates individual collision domains. See Chapter 1 for more information.

12. C. The command `line vty 0 4` places you in a prompt that will allow you to set or change your Telnet password. See Chapter 4 for more information.

13. B. To see the contents of all access lists, use the `show access-lists` command. See Chapter 10 for more information.

14. C. VLANs break up broadcast domains at layer 2. See Chapter 9 for more information.

15. A. The command `erase startup-config` deletes the configuration stored in NVRAM. See Chapter 4 for more information.

16. C. ICMP is the protocol at the Network layer that is used to send messages back to an originating router. See Chapter 2 for more information.

17. A. Class A addressing provides 24 bits for host addressing. See Chapter 3 for more information.

18. B. Every 2 seconds, BPDUs are sent out from all active bridge ports by default. See Chapter 7 for more information.

19. D. Switches do not propagate VLAN information by default; you must configure the VTP domain. VLAN Trunking Protocol (VTP) is used to propagate VLAN information across a trunk link. See Chapter 9 for more information.

20. C. IEEE 802.11B is 2.4GHz, but with a maximum of only 11Mbps. IEEE 802.11G is in the 2.4GHz range, with a top speed of 54Mbps. See Chapter 12 for more information.

21. A. By default, switches break up collision domains but are one large broadcast domain. See Chapter 1 for more information.

22. D. Port Address Translation (PAT) allows a one-to-many approach to network address translation. See Chapter 11 for more information.

23. C, D. VTP is not right because it has nothing to do with trunking except that it sends VLAN information across a trunk link. 802.1Q and ISL are used to configure trunking on a port. See Chapter 9 for more information.

24. D. Stub networks have only one connection to an internetwork. Only default routes can be set on a stub network or network loops may occur. See Chapter 7 for more information.

25. B. Hubs regenerate electrical signals, which are specified at the Physical layer. See Chapter 1 for more information.

26. A, C. Standard and extended access control lists (ACLs) are used to configure security on a router. See Chapter 10 for more information.

27. D. The command `copy flash tftp` will prompt you to back up an existing IOS in flash to a TFTP host. See Chapter 5 for more information.

28. B. The command to back up the configuration on a router is `copy running-config startup-config`. See Chapter 5 for more information.

29. C. The primary reason the OSI model was created was so that different networks could interoperate. See Chapter 1 for more information.

30. C. User Datagram Protocol is a connection network service at the Transport layer, and DHCP uses this connectionless service. See Chapter 2 for more information.

31. E. The `clock rate` command is two words, and the speed of the line is in bps. See Chapter 4 for more information.

32. C. The `show ip interface` command will show you if any outbound or inbound interfaces have an access list set. See Chapter 10 for more information.

33. D. The `copy tftp flash` command places a new file in flash memory, which is the default location for the Cisco IOS in Cisco routers. See Chapter 5 for more information.

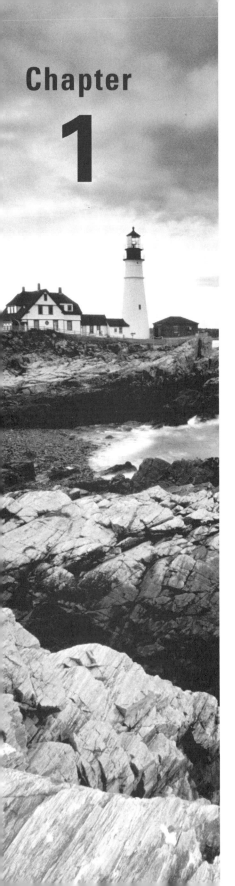

Chapter

1

Internetworking

THE CCNA EXAM TOPICS COVERED IN THIS CHAPTER INCLUDE THE FOLLOWING:

✓ **Describe how a network works**

- ▪ Describe the purpose and functions of various network devices
- ▪ Select the components required to meet a network specification
- ▪ Use the OSI and TCP/IP models and their associated protocols to explain how data flows in a network
- ▪ Describe common networked applications including web applications
- ▪ Describe the purpose and basic operation of the protocols in the OSI and TCP models
- ▪ Describe the impact of applications (Voice Over IP and Video Over IP) on a network
- ▪ Interpret network diagrams
- ▪ Describe the components required for network and Internet communications
- ▪ Identify and correct common network problems at layers 1, 2, 3 and 7 using a layered model approach
- ▪ Differentiate between LAN/WAN operation and features

✓ **Configure, verify and troubleshoot a switch with VLANs and interswitch communications**

- ▪ Select the appropriate media, cables, ports, and connectors to connect switches to other network devices and hosts
- ▪ Explain the technology and media access control method for Ethernet networks
- ▪ Explain network segmentation and basic traffic management concepts

✓ **Implement an IP addressing scheme and IP Services to meet network requirements in a medium-size Enterprise branch office network**

- Explain the operation and benefits of using DHCP and DNS

✓ **Configure, verify, and troubleshoot basic router operation and routing on Cisco devices**

- Select the appropriate media, cables, ports, and connectors to connect routers to other network devices and hosts

Welcome to the exciting world of internetworking. This first chapter will really help you understand the basics of internetworking by focusing on how to connect networks together using Cisco routers and switches. First, you need to know exactly what an internetwork is, right? You create an internetwork when you connect two or more LANs or WANs via a router and configure a logical network addressing scheme with a protocol such as IP.

I'll be covering these four topics in this chapter:

- Internetworking basics

- Network segmentation

- How bridges, switches, and routers are used to physically segment a network

- How routers are employed to create an internetwork

I'm also going to dissect the Open Systems Interconnection (OSI) model and describe each part to you in detail because you really need a good grasp of it for the solid foundation you'll build your networking knowledge upon. The OSI model has seven hierarchical layers that were developed to enable different networks to communicate reliably between disparate systems. Since this book is centering upon all things CCNA, it's crucial for you to understand the OSI model as Cisco sees it, so that's how I'll be presenting the seven layers to you.

Since there are a bunch of different types of devices specified at the different layers of the OSI model, it's also very important to understand the many types of cables and connectors used for connecting all those devices to a network. We'll go over cabling Cisco devices, discussing how to connect to a router or switch (along with Ethernet LAN technologies) and even how to connect a router or switch with a console connection.

We'll finish the chapter by discussing the three-layer hierarchical model that was developed by Cisco to help you design, implement, and troubleshoot internetworks.

After you finish reading this chapter, you'll encounter 20 review questions and four written labs. These are given to you to really lock the information from this chapter into your memory. So don't skip them!

To find up to the minute updates for this chapter, please see www.lammle.com and/or www.sybex.com.

Internetworking Basics

Before we explore internetworking models and the specifications of the OSI reference model, you've got to understand the big picture and learn the answer to the key question, Why is it so important to learn Cisco internetworking?

Networks and networking have grown exponentially over the last 15 years—understandably so. They've had to evolve at light speed just to keep up with huge increases in basic mission-critical user needs such as sharing data and printers as well as more advanced demands such as videoconferencing. Unless everyone who needs to share network resources is located in the same office area (an increasingly uncommon situation), the challenge is to connect the sometimes many relevant networks together so all users can share the networks' wealth.

Starting with a look at Figure 1.1, you get a picture of a basic LAN network that's connected together using a hub. This network is actually one collision domain and one broadcast domain—but no worries if you have no idea what this means because I'm going to talk about both collision and broadcast domains so much throughout this whole chapter, you'll probably even dream about them!

FIGURE 1.1   The basic network

Bob   Sally

(Hub)

The basic network allows devices to share information.
The term computer language refers to binary code (0s or 1s).
The two hosts above communicate using hardware or MAC addresses.

Okay, about Figure 1.1... How would you say the PC named Bob communicates with the PC named Sally? Well, they're both on the same LAN connected with a multiport repeater (a hub). So does Bob just send out a data message, "Hey Sally, you there?" or does Bob use Sally's IP address and put things more like, "Hey 192.168.0.3, are you there?" Hopefully, you picked the IP address option, but even if you did, the news is still bad—both answers are wrong! Why? Because Bob is actually going to use Sally's MAC address (known as a hardware address), which is burned right into the network card of Sally's PC, to get ahold of her.

Great, but how does Bob get Sally's MAC address since Bob knows only Sally's name and doesn't even have her IP address yet? Bob is going to start with name resolution (hostname to

IP address resolution), something that's usually accomplished using Domain Name Service (DNS). And of note, if these two are on the same LAN, Bob can just broadcast to Sally asking her for the information (no DNS needed)—welcome to Microsoft Windows (Vista included)!

Here's an output from a network analyzer depicting a simple name resolution process from Bob to Sally:

```
Time       Source      Destination   Protocol   Info
53.892794  192.168.0.2  192.168.0.255  NBNS   Name query NB SALLY<00>
```

As I already mentioned, since the two hosts are on a local LAN, Windows (Bob) will just broadcast to resolve the name Sally (the destination 192.168.0.255 is a broadcast address). Let's take a look at the rest of the information:

```
EthernetII,Src:192.168.0.2(00:14:22:be:18:3b),Dst:Broadcast (ff:ff:ff:ff:ff:ff)
```

What this output shows is that Bob knows his own MAC address and source IP address but not Sally's IP address or MAC address, so Bob sends a broadcast address of all *f*s for the MAC address (a Data Link layer broadcast) and an IP LAN broadcast of 192.168.0.255. Again, don't freak—you're going to learn all about broadcasts in Chapter 3, "Subnetting, Variable Length Subnet Masks (VLSMs), and Troubleshooting TCP/IP."

Before the name is resolved, the first thing Bob has to do is broadcast on the LAN to get Sally's MAC address so he can communicate to her PC and resolve her name to an IP address:

```
Time      Source      Destination Protocol Info
5.153054  192.168.0.2 Broadcast   ARP Who has 192.168.0.3? Tell 192.168.0.2
```

Next, check out Sally's response:

```
Time       Source      Destination   Protocol   Info
5.153403 192.168.0.3 192.168.0.2   ARP   192.168.0.3 is at 00:0b:db:99:d3:5e
5.53.89317  192.168.0.3 192.168.0.2 NBNS Name query response NB 192.168.0.3
```

Okay sweet— Bob now has both Sally's IP address and her MAC address! These are both listed as the source address at this point because this information was sent from Sally back to Bob. So, *finally*, Bob has all the goods he needs to communicate with Sally. And just so you know, I'm going to tell you all about ARP and show you exactly how Sally's IP address was resolved to a MAC address a little later in Chapter 6, "IP Routing."

By the way, I want you to understand that Sally still had to go through the same resolution processes to communicate back to Bob—sounds crazy, huh? Consider this a welcome to IPv4 and basic networking with Windows (and we haven't even added a router yet!).

To complicate things further, it's also likely that at some point you'll have to break up one large network into a bunch of smaller ones because user response will have dwindled to a slow crawl as the network grew and grew. And with all that growth, your LAN's traffic congestion has reached epic proportions. The answer to this is breaking up a really big network into a number of smaller ones—something called *network segmentation*. You do this by using devices like *routers*, *switches*, and *bridges*. Figure 1.2 displays a network that's been segmented with a switch so each network segment connected to the switch is now a separate collision domain. But make note of the fact that this network is still one broadcast domain.

FIGURE 1.2   A switch can replace the hub, breaking up collision domains.

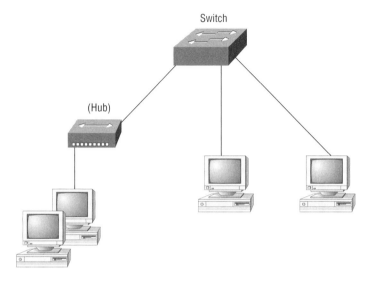

Keep in mind that the hub used in Figure 1.2 just extended the one collision domain from the switch port. Here's a list of some of the things that commonly cause LAN traffic congestion:

- Too many hosts in a broadcast domain
- Broadcast storms
- Multicasting
- Low bandwidth
- Adding hubs for connectivity to the network
- A bunch of ARP or IPX traffic (IPX is a Novell protocol that is like IP, but really, really chatty. Typically not used in today's networks.)

Take another look at Figure 1.2—did you notice that I replaced the main hub from Figure 1.1 with a switch? Whether you did or didn't, the reason I did that is because hubs don't segment a network; they just connect network segments together. So basically, it's an inexpensive way to connect a couple of PCs together, which is great for home use and troubleshooting, but that's about it!

Now routers are used to connect networks together and route packets of data from one network to another. Cisco became the de facto standard of routers because of its high-quality router products, great selection, and fantastic service. Routers, by default, break up a *broadcast domain*—the set of all devices on a network segment that hear all the broadcasts sent on that segment. Figure 1.3 shows a router in our little network that creates an internetwork and breaks up broadcast domains.

FIGURE 1.3 Routers create an internetwork.

A router creates an internetwork and
provides connections to WAN services.

The network in Figure 1.3 is a pretty cool network. Each host is connected to its own collision domain, and the router has created two broadcast domains. And don't forget that the router provides connections to WAN services as well! The router uses something called a serial interface for WAN connections, specifically, a V.35 physical interface on a Cisco router.

Breaking up a broadcast domain is important because when a host or server sends a network broadcast, every device on the network must read and process that broadcast—unless you've got a router. When the router's interface receives this broadcast, it can respond by basically saying, "Thanks, but no thanks," and discard the broadcast without forwarding it on to other networks. Even though routers are known for breaking up broadcast domains by default, it's important to remember that they break up collision domains as well.

There are two advantages of using routers in your network:

- They don't forward broadcasts by default.
- They can filter the network based on layer 3 (Network layer) information (e.g., IP address).

Four router functions in your network can be listed as follows:

- Packet switching
- Packet filtering
- Internetwork communication
- Path selection

Remember that routers are really switches; they're actually what we call layer 3 switches (we'll talk about layers later in this chapter). Unlike layer 2 switches, which forward or filter frames, routers (layer 3 switches) use logical addressing and provide what is called packet switching. Routers can also provide packet filtering by using access lists, and when routers connect two or more networks together and use logical addressing (IP or IPv6), this is called an internetwork. Last, routers use a routing table (map of the internetwork) to make path selections and to forward packets to remote networks.

Conversely, switches aren't used to create internetworks (they do not break up broadcast domains by default); they're employed to add functionality to a network LAN. The main purpose of a switch is to make a LAN work better—to optimize its performance—providing more bandwidth for the LAN's users. And switches don't forward packets to other networks as routers do. Instead, they only "switch" frames from one port to another within the switched network. Okay, you may be thinking, "Wait a minute, what are frames and packets?" I'll tell you all about them later in this chapter, I promise!

By default, switches break up *collision domains*. This is an Ethernet term used to describe a network scenario wherein one particular device sends a packet on a network segment, forcing every other device on that same segment to pay attention to it. At the same time, a different device tries to transmit, leading to a collision, after which both devices must retransmit, one at a time. Not very efficient! This situation is typically found in a hub environment where each host segment connects to a hub that represents only one collision domain and only one broadcast domain. By contrast, each and every port on a switch represents its own collision domain.

Switches create separate collision domains but a single broadcast domain. Routers provide a separate broadcast domain for each interface.

The term *bridging* was introduced before routers and hubs were implemented, so it's pretty common to hear people referring to bridges as switches. That's because bridges and switches basically do the same thing—break up collision domains on a LAN (in reality, you cannot buy a physical bridge these days, only LAN switches, but they use bridging technologies, so Cisco still calls them multiport bridges).

So what this means is that a switch is basically just a multiple-port bridge with more brainpower, right? Well, pretty much, but there are differences. Switches do provide this function, but they do so with greatly enhanced management ability and features. Plus, most of the time, bridges only had 2 or 4 ports. Yes, you could get your hands on a bridge with up to 16 ports, but that's nothing compared to the hundreds available on some switches!

You would use a bridge in a network to reduce collisions within broadcast domains and to increase the number of collision domains in your network. Doing this provides more bandwidth for users. And keep in mind that using hubs in your network can contribute to congestion on your Ethernet network. As always, plan your network design carefully!

Figure 1.4 shows how a network would look with all these internetwork devices in place. Remember that the router will not only break up broadcast domains for every LAN interface, it will break up collision domains as well.

FIGURE 1.4   Internetworking devices

When you looked at Figure 1.4, did you notice that the router is found at center stage and that it connects each physical network together? We have to use this layout because of the older technologies involved—bridges and hubs.

On the top internetwork in Figure 1.4, you'll notice that a bridge was used to connect the hubs to a router. The bridge breaks up collision domains, but all the hosts connected to both hubs are still crammed into the same broadcast domain. Also, the bridge only created two collision domains, so each device connected to a hub is in the same collision domain as every other device connected to that same hub. This is actually pretty lame, but it's still better than having one collision domain for all hosts.

Notice something else: The three hubs at the bottom that are connected also connect to the router, creating one collision domain and one broadcast domain. This makes the bridged network look much better indeed!

Although bridges/switches are used to segment networks, they will not isolate broadcast or multicast packets.

The best network connected to the router is the LAN switch network on the left. Why? Because each port on that switch breaks up collision domains. But it's not all good—all devices are still in the same broadcast domain. Do you remember why this can be a really bad thing? Because all devices must listen to all broadcasts transmitted, that's why. And if your broadcast domains are too large, the users have less bandwidth and are required to process more broadcasts, and network response time will slow to a level that could cause office riots.

Once we have only switches in our network, things change a lot! Figure 1.5 shows the network that is typically found today.

FIGURE 1.5   Switched networks creating an internetwork

Okay, here I've placed the LAN switches at the center of the network world so the routers are connecting only logical networks together. If I implemented this kind of setup, I've created virtual LANs (VLANs), something I'm going to tell you about in Chapter 9, "Virtual LANs (VLANs)." So don't stress. But it is really important to understand that even though you have a switched network, you still need a router to provide your inter-VLAN communication, or internetworking. Don't forget that!

Obviously, the best network is one that's correctly configured to meet the business requirements of the company it serves. LAN switches with routers, correctly placed in the network, are the best network design. This book will help you understand the basics of routers and switches so you can make tight, informed decisions on a case-by-case basis.

Let's go back to Figure 1.4 again. Looking at the figure, how many collision domains and broadcast domains are in this internetwork? Hopefully, you answered nine collision domains and three broadcast domains! The broadcast domains are definitely the easiest to see because only routers break up broadcast domains by default. And since there are three connections, that gives you three broadcast domains. But do you see the nine collision domains? Just in case that's a no, I'll explain. The all-hub network is one collision domain; the bridge network equals three collision domains. Add in the switch network of five collision domains—one for each switch port—and you've got a total of nine.

Now, in Figure 1.5, each port on the switch is a separate collision domain and each VLAN is a separate broadcast domain. But you still need a router for routing between VLANs. How many collision domains do you see here? I'm counting 10—remember that connections between the switches are considered a collision domain!

 Real World Scenario

Should I Just Replace All My Hubs with Switches?

You're a network administrator at a large company in San Jose. The boss comes to you and says that he got your requisition to buy a switch and is not sure about approving the expense; do you really need it?

Well, if you can, sure—why not? Switches really add a lot of functionality to a network that hubs just don't have. But most of us don't have an unlimited budget. Hubs still can create a nice network—that is, of course, if you design and implement the network correctly.

Let's say that you have 40 users plugged into four hubs, 10 users each. At this point, the hubs are all connected together so that you have one large collision domain and one large broadcast domain. If you can afford to buy just one switch and plug each hub into a switch port, as well as plug the servers into the switch, then you now have four collision domains and one broadcast domain. Not great, but for the price of one switch, your network is a much better thing. So, go ahead! Put that requisition in to buy all new switches. What do you have to lose?

So now that you've gotten an introduction to internetworking and the various devices that live in an internetwork, it's time to head into internetworking models.

Internetworking Models

When networks first came into being, computers could typically communicate only with computers from the same manufacturer. For example, companies ran either a complete DECnet solution or an IBM solution—not both together. In the late 1970s, the *Open Systems Interconnection (OSI) reference model* was created by the International Organization for Standardization (ISO) to break this barrier.

The OSI model was meant to help vendors create interoperable network devices and software in the form of protocols so that different vendor networks could work with each other. Like world peace, it'll probably never happen completely, but it's still a great goal.

The OSI model is the primary architectural model for networks. It describes how data and network information are communicated from an application on one computer through the network media to an application on another computer. The OSI reference model breaks this approach into layers.

In the following section, I am going to explain the layered approach and how we can use this approach to help us troubleshoot our internetworks.

The Layered Approach

A *reference model* is a conceptual blueprint of how communications should take place. It addresses all the processes required for effective communication and divides these processes into logical groupings called *layers*. When a communication system is designed in this manner, it's known as *layered architecture*.

Think of it like this: You and some friends want to start a company. One of the first things you'll do is sit down and think through what tasks must be done, who will do them, the order in which they will be done, and how they relate to each other. Ultimately, you might group these tasks into departments. Let's say you decide to have an order-taking department, an inventory department, and a shipping department. Each of your departments has its own unique tasks, keeping its staff members busy and requiring them to focus on only their own duties.

In this scenario, I'm using departments as a metaphor for the layers in a communication system. For things to run smoothly, the staff of each department will have to trust and rely heavily upon the others to do their jobs and competently handle their unique responsibilities. In your planning sessions, you would probably take notes, recording the entire process to facilitate later discussions about standards of operation that will serve as your business blueprint, or reference model.

Once your business is launched, your department heads, each armed with the part of the blueprint relating to their own department, will need to develop practical methods to implement their assigned tasks. These practical methods, or protocols, will need to be compiled into a standard operating procedures manual and followed closely. Each of the various procedures in your manual will have been included for different reasons and have varying degrees of importance and implementation. If you form a partnership or acquire another company, it will be imperative that its business protocols—its business blueprint—match yours (or at least be compatible with it).

Similarly, software developers can use a reference model to understand computer communication processes and see what types of functions need to be accomplished on any one layer. If they are developing a protocol for a certain layer, all they need to concern themselves with is that specific layer's functions, not those of any other layer. Another layer and protocol will handle the other functions. The technical term for this idea is *binding*. The communication processes that are related to each other are bound, or grouped together, at a particular layer.

Advantages of Reference Models

The OSI model is hierarchical, and the same benefits and advantages can apply to any layered model. The primary purpose of all such models, especially the OSI model, is to allow different vendors' networks to interoperate.

Advantages of using the OSI layered model include, but are not limited to, the following:

- It divides the network communication process into smaller and simpler components, thus aiding component development, design, and troubleshooting.

- It allows multiple-vendor development through standardization of network components.

- It encourages industry standardization by defining what functions occur at each layer of the model.

- It allows various types of network hardware and software to communicate.

- It prevents changes in one layer from affecting other layers, so it does not hamper development.

The OSI Reference Model

One of the greatest functions of the OSI specifications is to assist in data transfer between disparate hosts—meaning, for example, that they enable us to transfer data between a Unix host and a PC or a Mac.

The OSI isn't a physical model, though. Rather, it's a set of guidelines that application developers can use to create and implement applications that run on a network. It also provides a framework for creating and implementing networking standards, devices, and internetworking schemes.

The OSI has seven different layers, divided into two groups. The top three layers define how the applications within the end stations will communicate with each other and with users. The bottom four layers define how data is transmitted end to end. Figure 1.6 shows the three upper layers and their functions, and Figure 1.7 shows the four lower layers and their functions.

FIGURE 1.6   The upper layers

When you study Figure 1.6, understand that the user interfaces with the computer at the Application layer and also that the upper layers are responsible for applications communicating between hosts. Remember that none of the upper layers knows anything about networking or network addresses. That's the responsibility of the four bottom layers.

In Figure 1.7, you can see that it's the four bottom layers that define how data is transferred through a physical wire or through switches and routers. These bottom layers also determine how to rebuild a data stream from a transmitting host to a destination host's application.

FIGURE 1.7   The lower layers

Transport
- Provides reliable or unreliable delivery
- Performs error correction before retransmit

Network
- Provides logical addressing,
  which routers use for path determination

Data Link
- Combines packets into bytes and bytes into frames
- Provides access to media using MAC address
- Performs error detection not correction

Physical
- Moves bits between devices
- Specifies voltage, wire speed,
  and pin-out of cables

The following network devices operate at all seven layers of the OSI model:

- Network management stations (NMSs)
- Web and application servers
- Gateways (not default gateways)
- Network hosts

Basically, the ISO is pretty much the Emily Post of the network protocol world. Just as Ms. Post wrote the book setting the standards—or protocols—for human social interaction, the ISO developed the OSI reference model as the precedent and guide for an open network protocol set. Defining the etiquette of communication models, it remains today the most popular means of comparison for protocol suites.

The OSI reference model has seven layers:

- Application layer (layer 7)
- Presentation layer (layer 6)
- Session layer (layer 5)
- Transport layer (layer 4)
- Network layer (layer 3)
- Data Link layer (layer 2)
- Physical layer (layer 1)

Figure 1.8 shows a summary of the functions defined at each layer of the OSI model. With this in hand, you're now ready to explore each layer's function in detail.

FIGURE 1.8   Layer functions

The Application Layer

The *Application layer* of the OSI model marks the spot where users actually communicate to the computer. This layer only comes into play when it's apparent that access to the network is going to be needed soon. Take the case of Internet Explorer (IE). You could uninstall every trace of networking components from a system, such as TCP/IP, NIC card, and so on, and you could still use IE to view a local HTML document—no problem. But things would definitely get messy if you tried to do something like view an HTML document that must be retrieved using HTTP or nab a file with FTP or TFTP. That's because IE will respond to requests such as those by attempting to access the Application layer. And what's happening is that the Application layer is acting as an interface between the actual application program—which isn't at all a part of the layered structure—and the next layer down by providing ways for the application to send information down through the protocol stack. In other words, IE doesn't truly reside within the Application layer—it interfaces with Application layer protocols when it needs to deal with remote resources.

The Application layer is also responsible for identifying and establishing the availability of the intended communication partner and determining whether sufficient resources for the intended communication exist.

These tasks are important because computer applications sometimes require more than only desktop resources. Often, they'll unite communicating components from more than one network application. Prime examples are file transfers and email, as well as enabling remote access, network management activities, client/server processes, and information location. Many network applications provide services for communication over enterprise networks, but for present and future internetworking, the need is fast developing to reach beyond the limits of current physical networking.

> It's important to remember that the Application layer is acting as an interface between the actual application programs. This means that Microsoft Word, for example, does not reside at the Application layer but instead interfaces with the Application layer protocols. Chapter 2 will present some programs that actually reside at the Application layer—for example, FTP and TFTP.

The Presentation Layer

The *Presentation layer* gets its name from its purpose: It presents data to the Application layer and is responsible for data translation and code formatting.

This layer is essentially a translator and provides coding and conversion functions. A successful data-transfer technique is to adapt the data into a standard format before transmission. Computers are configured to receive this generically formatted data and then convert the data back into its native format for actual reading (for example, EBCDIC to ASCII). By providing translation services, the Presentation layer ensures that data transferred from the Application layer of one system can be read by the Application layer of another one.

The OSI has protocol standards that define how standard data should be formatted. Tasks like data compression, decompression, encryption, and decryption are associated with this layer. Some Presentation layer standards are involved in multimedia operations too.

The Session Layer

The *Session layer* is responsible for setting up, managing, and then tearing down sessions between Presentation layer entities. This layer also provides dialog control between devices, or nodes. It coordinates communication between systems and serves to organize their communication by offering three different modes: *simplex*, *half duplex*, and *full duplex*. To sum up, the Session layer basically keeps different applications' data separate from other applications' data.

The Transport Layer

The *Transport layer* segments and reassembles data into a data stream. Services located in the Transport layer segment and reassemble data from upper-layer applications and unite it into the same data stream. They provide end-to-end data transport services and can establish a logical connection between the sending host and destination host on an internetwork.

Some of you are probably familiar with TCP and UDP already. (But if you're not, no worries—I'll tell you all about them in Chapter 2.) If so, you know that both work at the Transport layer and that TCP is a reliable service and UDP is not. This means that application developers have more options because they have a choice between the two protocols when working with TCP/IP protocols.

The Transport layer is responsible for providing mechanisms for multiplexing upper-layer applications, establishing sessions, and tearing down virtual circuits. It also hides details of any network-dependent information from the higher layers by providing transparent data transfer.

> The term *reliable networking* can be used at the Transport layer. It means that acknowledgments, sequencing, and flow control will be used.

The Transport layer can be connectionless or connection-oriented. However, Cisco is mostly concerned with you understanding the connection-oriented portion of the Transport layer. The following sections will provide the skinny on the connection-oriented (reliable) protocol of the Transport layer.

Flow Control

Data integrity is ensured at the Transport layer by maintaining *flow control* and by allowing users to request reliable data transport between systems. Flow control prevents a sending host on one side of the connection from overflowing the buffers in the receiving host—an event that can result in lost data. Reliable data transport employs a connection-oriented communications session between systems, and the protocols involved ensure that the following will be achieved:

- The segments delivered are acknowledged back to the sender upon their reception.

- Any segments not acknowledged are retransmitted.

- Segments are sequenced back into their proper order upon arrival at their destination.

- A manageable data flow is maintained in order to avoid congestion, overloading, and data loss.

> The purpose of flow control is to provide a means for the receiver to govern the amount of data sent by the sender.

Connection-Oriented Communication

In reliable transport operation, a device that wants to transmit sets up a connection-oriented communication with a remote device by creating a session. The transmitting device first establishes a connection-oriented session with its peer system, which is called a *call setup* or a *three-way handshake*. Data is then transferred; when the transfer is finished, a call termination takes place to tear down the virtual circuit.

Figure 1.9 depicts a typical reliable session taking place between sending and receiving systems. Looking at it, you can see that both hosts' application programs begin by notifying their individual operating systems that a connection is about to be initiated. The two operating systems communicate by sending messages over the network confirming that the transfer is approved and that both sides are ready for it to take place. After all of this required synchronization takes place, a connection is fully established and the data transfer begins (this virtual circuit setup is called overhead!).

FIGURE 1.9   Establishing a connection-oriented session

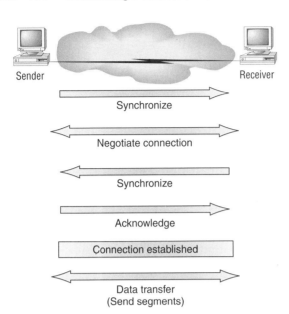

While the information is being transferred between hosts, the two machines periodically check in with each other, communicating through their protocol software to ensure that all is going well and that the data is being received properly.

Let me sum up the steps in the connection-oriented session—the three-way handshake—pictured in Figure 1.9:

- The first "connection agreement" segment is a request for synchronization.

- The second and third segments acknowledge the request and establish connection parameters—the rules—between hosts. These segments request that the receiver's sequencing is synchronized here as well so that a bidirectional connection is formed.

- The final segment is also an acknowledgment. It notifies the destination host that the connection agreement has been accepted and that the actual connection has been established. Data transfer can now begin.

Sounds pretty simple, but things don't always flow so smoothly. Sometimes during a transfer, congestion can occur because a high-speed computer is generating data traffic a lot faster than the network can handle transferring. A bunch of computers simultaneously sending datagrams through a single gateway or destination can also botch things up nicely. In the latter case, a gateway or destination can become congested even though no single source caused the problem. In either case, the problem is basically akin to a freeway bottleneck—too much traffic for too small a capacity. It's not usually one car that's the problem; there are simply too many cars on that freeway.

Okay, so what happens when a machine receives a flood of datagrams too quickly for it to process? It stores them in a memory section called a *buffer*. But this buffering action can solve the problem only if the datagrams are part of a small burst. If not, and the datagram deluge continues, a device's memory will eventually be exhausted, its flood capacity will be exceeded, and it will react by discarding any additional datagrams that arrive.

No huge worries here, though. Because of the transport function, network flood control systems really work quite well. Instead of dumping resources and allowing data to be lost, the transport can issue a "not ready" indicator to the sender, or source, of the flood (as shown in Figure 1.10). This mechanism works kind of like a stoplight, signaling the sending device to stop transmitting segment traffic to its overwhelmed peer. After the peer receiver processes the segments already in its memory reservoir—its buffer—it sends out a "ready" transport indicator. When the machine waiting to transmit the rest of its datagrams receives this "go" indicator, it resumes its transmission.

FIGURE 1.10   Transmitting segments with flow control

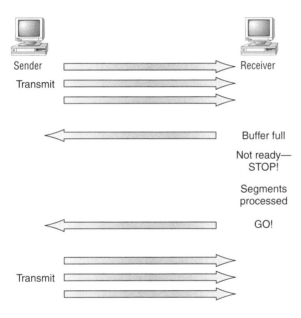

In fundamental, reliable, connection-oriented data transfer, datagrams are delivered to the receiving host in exactly the same sequence they're transmitted—and the transmission fails if this order is breached! If any data segments are lost, duplicated, or damaged along the way, a failure will transmit. This problem is solved by having the receiving host acknowledge that it has received each and every data segment.

A service is considered connection-oriented if it has the following characteristics:

- A virtual circuit is set up (e.g., a three-way handshake).

- It uses sequencing.

- It uses acknowledgments.

- It uses flow control.

The types of flow control are buffering, windowing, and congestion avoidance.

Windowing

Ideally, data throughput happens quickly and efficiently. And as you can imagine, it would be slow if the transmitting machine had to wait for an acknowledgment after sending each segment. But because there's time available *after* the sender transmits the data segment and *before* it finishes processing acknowledgments from the receiving machine, the sender uses the break as an opportunity to transmit more data. The quantity of data segments (measured in bytes) that the transmitting machine is allowed to send without receiving an acknowledgment for them is called a *window*.

 Windows are used to control the amount of outstanding, unacknowledged data segments.

So the size of the window controls how much information is transferred from one end to the other. While some protocols quantify information by observing the number of packets, TCP/IP measures it by counting the number of bytes.

As you can see in Figure 1.11, there are two window sizes—one set to 1 and one set to 3.

FIGURE 1.11 Windowing

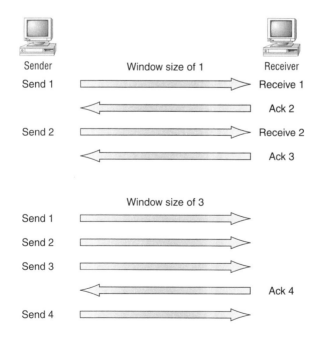

When you've configured a window size of 1, the sending machine waits for an acknowledgment for each data segment it transmits before transmitting another. If you've configured a window size of 3, it's allowed to transmit three data segments before an acknowledgment is received.

In our simplified example, both the sending and receiving machines are workstations. In reality this is not done in simple numbers but in the amount of bytes that can be sent.

> If a receiving host fails to receive all the segments that it should acknowledge, the host can improve the communication session by decreasing the window size.

Acknowledgments

Reliable data delivery ensures the integrity of a stream of data sent from one machine to the other through a fully functional data link. It guarantees that the data won't be duplicated or lost. This is achieved through something called *positive acknowledgment with retransmission*—a technique that requires a receiving machine to communicate with the transmitting source by sending an acknowledgment message back to the sender when it receives data. The sender documents each segment it sends and waits for this acknowledgment before sending the next segment. When it sends a segment, the transmitting machine starts a timer and retransmits if it expires before an acknowledgment is returned from the receiving end.

In Figure 1.12, the sending machine transmits segments 1, 2, and 3. The receiving node acknowledges it has received them by requesting segment 4. When it receives the acknowledgment, the sender then transmits segments 4, 5, and 6. If segment 5 doesn't make it to the destination, the receiving node acknowledges that event with a request for the segment to be resent. The sending machine will then resend the lost segment and wait for an acknowledgment, which it must receive in order to move on to the transmission of segment 7.

FIGURE 1.12   Transport layer reliable delivery

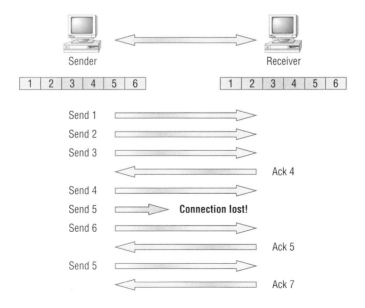

The Network Layer

The *Network layer* (also called layer 3) manages device addressing, tracks the location of devices on the network, and determines the best way to move data, which means that the Network layer must transport traffic between devices that aren't locally attached. Routers (layer 3 devices) are specified at the Network layer and provide the routing services within an internetwork.

It happens like this: First, when a packet is received on a router interface, the destination IP address is checked. If the packet isn't destined for that particular router, it will look up the destination network address in the routing table. Once the router chooses an exit interface, the packet will be sent to that interface to be framed and sent out on the local network. If the router can't find an entry for the packet's destination network in the routing table, the router drops the packet.

Two types of packets are used at the Network layer: data and route updates.

Data packets   Used to transport user data through the internetwork. Protocols used to support data traffic are called *routed protocols*; examples of routed protocols are IP and IPv6. You'll learn about IP addressing in Chapters 2 and 3 and IPv6 in Chapter 13 .

Route update packets   Used to update neighboring routers about the networks connected to all routers within the internetwork. Protocols that send route update packets are called routing protocols; examples of some common ones are RIP, RIPv2, EIGRP, and OSPF. Route update packets are used to help build and maintain routing tables on each router.

In Figure 1.13, I've given you an example of a routing table. The routing table used in a router includes the following information:

Network addresses   Protocol-specific network addresses. A router must maintain a routing table for individual routing protocols because each routing protocol keeps track of a network with a different addressing scheme (IP, IPv6, and IPX, for example). Think of it as a street sign in each of the different languages spoken by the residents that live on a particular street. So, if there were American, Spanish, and French folks on a street named Cat, the sign would read Cat/Gato/Chat.

FIGURE 1.13   Routing table used in a router

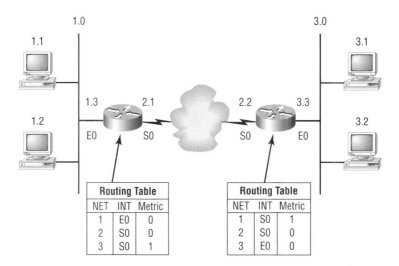

Interface   The exit interface a packet will take when destined for a specific network.

Metric   The distance to the remote network. Different routing protocols use different ways of computing this distance. I'm going to cover routing protocols in Chapters 6 and 7, but for now, know that some routing protocols (namely RIP) use something called a *hop count* (the number of routers a packet passes through en route to a remote network), while others use bandwidth, delay of the line, or even tick count (1/18 of a second).

And as I mentioned earlier, routers break up broadcast domains, which means that by default, broadcasts aren't forwarded through a router. Do you remember why this is a good thing? Routers also break up collision domains, but you can also do that using layer 2 (Data Link layer) switches. Because each interface in a router represents a separate network, it must be assigned unique network identification numbers, and each host on the network connected to that router must use the same network number. Figure 1.14 shows how a router works in an internetwork.

FIGURE 1.14   A router in an internetwork

Each router interface is a broadcast domain.
Routers break up broadcast domains by
default and provide WAN services.

Here are some points about routers that you should really commit to memory:

- Routers, by default, will not forward any broadcast or multicast packets.
- Routers use the logical address in a Network layer header to determine the next hop router to forward the packet to.
- Routers can use access lists, created by an administrator, to control security on the types of packets that are allowed to enter or exit an interface.
- Routers can provide layer 2 bridging functions if needed and can simultaneously route through the same interface.
- Layer 3 devices (routers in this case) provide connections between virtual LANs (VLANs).
- Routers can provide quality of service (QoS) for specific types of network traffic.

Switching and VLANs and are covered in Chapter 8, "LAN Switching and STP," and Chapter 9, "Virtual LANs (VLANs)."

The Data Link Layer

The *Data Link layer* provides the physical transmission of the data and handles error notification, network topology, and flow control. This means that the Data Link layer will ensure that messages are delivered to the proper device on a LAN using hardware addresses and will translate messages from the Network layer into bits for the Physical layer to transmit.

The Data Link layer formats the message into pieces, each called a *data frame*, and adds a customized header containing the hardware destination and source address. This added information forms a sort of capsule that surrounds the original message in much the same way that engines, navigational devices, and other tools were attached to the lunar modules of the Apollo project. These various pieces of equipment were useful only during certain stages of space flight and were stripped off the module and discarded when their designated stage was complete. Data traveling through networks is similar.

Figure 1.15 shows the Data Link layer with the Ethernet and IEEE specifications. When you check it out, notice that the IEEE 802.2 standard is used in conjunction with and adds functionality to the other IEEE standards.

FIGURE 1.15   Data Link layer

| 802.5 | 802.3 | 802.2 |

It's important for you to understand that routers, which work at the Network layer, don't care at all about where a particular host is located. They're only concerned about where networks are located and the best way to reach them—including remote ones. Routers are totally obsessive when it comes to networks. And for once, this is a good thing! It's the Data Link layer that's responsible for the actual unique identification of each device that resides on a local network.

For a host to send packets to individual hosts on a local network as well as transmit packets between routers, the Data Link layer uses hardware addressing. Each time a packet is sent between routers, it's framed with control information at the Data Link layer, but that information is stripped off at the receiving router and only the original packet is left completely intact. This framing of the packet continues for each hop until the packet is finally delivered to the correct receiving host. It's really important to understand that the packet itself is never altered along the route; it's only encapsulated with the type of control information required for it to be properly passed on to the different media types.

The IEEE Ethernet Data Link layer has two sublayers:

Media Access Control (MAC) 802.3 Defines how packets are placed on the media. Contention media access is "first come/first served" access where everyone shares the same bandwidth—hence the name. Physical addressing is defined here, as well as logical topologies. What's a logical topology? It's the signal path through a physical topology. Line discipline, error notification (not correction), ordered delivery of frames, and optional flow control can also be used at this sublayer.

Logical Link Control (LLC) 802.2 Responsible for identifying Network layer protocols and then encapsulating them. An LLC header tells the Data Link layer what to do with a packet once a frame is received. It works like this: A host will receive a frame and look in the LLC header to find out where the packet is destined—say, the IP protocol at the Network layer. The LLC can also provide flow control and sequencing of control bits.

The switches and bridges I talked about near the beginning of the chapter both work at the Data Link layer and filter the network using hardware (MAC) addresses. We will look at these in the following section.

Switches and Bridges at the Data Link Layer

Layer 2 switching is considered hardware-based bridging because it uses specialized hardware called an *application-specific integrated circuit (ASIC)*. ASICs can run up to gigabit speeds with very low latency rates.

NOTE Latency is the time measured from when a frame enters a port to the time it exits a port.

Bridges and switches read each frame as it passes through the network. The layer 2 device then puts the source hardware address in a filter table and keeps track of which port the frame was received on. This information (logged in the bridge's or switch's filter table) is what helps the machine determine the location of the specific sending device. Figure 1.16 shows a switch in an internetwork.

The real estate business is all about location, location, location, and it's the same way for both layer 2 and layer 3 devices. Though both need to be able to negotiate the network, it's crucial to remember that they're concerned with very different parts of it. Primarily, layer 3 machines (such as routers) need to locate specific networks, whereas layer 2 machines (switches and bridges) need to eventually locate specific devices. So, networks are to routers as individual devices are to switches and bridges. And routing tables that "map" the internetwork are for routers as filter tables that "map" individual devices are for switches and bridges.

After a filter table is built on the layer 2 device, it will forward frames only to the segment where the destination hardware address is located. If the destination device is on the same segment as the frame, the layer 2 device will block the frame from going to any other segments. If the destination is on a different segment, the frame can be transmitted only to that segment. This is called *transparent bridging*.

When a switch interface receives a frame with a destination hardware address that isn't found in the device's filter table, it will forward the frame to all connected segments. If the unknown device that was sent the "mystery frame" replies to this forwarding action, the switch updates its filter table regarding that device's location. But in the event the destination address of the transmitting frame is a broadcast address, the switch will forward all broadcasts to every connected segment by default.

FIGURE 1.16   A switch in an internetwork

Each segment has its own collision domain.
All segments are in the same broadcast domain.

All devices that the broadcast is forwarded to are considered to be in the same broadcast domain. This can be a problem; layer 2 devices propagate layer 2 broadcast storms that choke performance, and the only way to stop a broadcast storm from propagating through an internetwork is with a layer 3 device—a router.

The biggest benefit of using switches instead of hubs in your internetwork is that each switch port is actually its own collision domain. (Conversely, a hub creates one large collision domain.) But even armed with a switch, you still can't break up broadcast domains. Neither switches nor bridges will do that. They'll typically simply forward all broadcasts instead.

Another benefit of LAN switching over hub-centered implementations is that each device on every segment plugged into a switch can transmit simultaneously—at least, they can as long as there is only one host on each port and a hub isn't plugged into a switch port. As you might have guessed, hubs allow only one device per network segment to communicate at a time.

Binary to Decimal and Hexadecimal Conversion

Before we finish this chapter and move to discussing the TCP/IP protocol stack and IP addressing in Chapter 2, it's really important for you to truly understand the differences between binary, decimal, and hexadecimal numbers and how to convert one format into the other.

So we'll start with binary numbering. It's pretty simple, really. The digits used are limited to either a 1 (one) or a 0 (zero), and each digit is called 1 bit (short for *bi*nary dig*it*). Typically, you count either 4 or 8 bits together, with these being referred to as a nibble and a byte, respectively.

What interests us in binary numbering is the value represented in a decimal format—the typical decimal format being the base-10 number scheme that we've all used since kindergarten. The binary numbers are placed in a value spot: starting at the right and moving left, with each spot having double the value of the previous spot.

Table 1.1 shows the decimal values of each bit location in a nibble and a byte. Remember, a nibble is 4 bits and a byte is 8 bits.

TABLE 1.1 Binary Values

Nibble Values	Byte Values
8 4 2 1	128 64 32 16 8 4 2 1

What all this means is that if a one digit (1) is placed in a value spot, then the nibble or byte takes on that decimal value and adds it to any other value spots that have a 1. And if a zero (0) is placed in a bit spot, you don't count that value.

Let me clarify things. If we have a 1 placed in each spot of our nibble, we would then add up 8 + 4 + 2 + 1, to give us a maximum value of 15. Another example for our nibble values would be 1010; that means that the 8 bit and the 2 bit are turned on, which equals a decimal value of 10. If we have a nibble binary value of 0110, then our decimal value would be 6, because the 4 and 2 bits are turned on.

But the byte values can add up to a value that's significantly higher than 15. This is how: If we counted every bit as a one (1), then the byte binary value would look like this (remember, 8 bits equal a byte):

11111111

We would then count up every bit spot because each is turned on. It would look like this, which demonstrates the maximum value of a byte:

128 + 64 + 32 + 16 + 8 + 4 + 2 + 1 = 255

There are plenty of other decimal values that a binary number can equal. Let's work through a few examples:

10010110

Which bits are on? The 128, 16, 4, and 2 bits are on, so we'll just add them up: 128 + 16 + 4 + 2 = 150.

01101100

Which bits are on? The 64, 32, 8, and 4 bits are on, so we just need to add them up: 64 + 32 + 8 + 4 = 108.

11101000

Which bits are on? The 128, 64, 32, and 8 bits are on, so just add the values up: 128 + 64 + 32 + 8 = 232.

Table 1.2 is a table you should memorize before braving the IP sections in Chapters 2 and 3.

TABLE 1.2 Binary to Decimal Memorization Chart

Binary Value	Decimal Value
10000000	128
11000000	192
11100000	224
11110000	240
11111000	248
11111100	252
11111110	254
11111111	255

Hexadecimal addressing is completely different than binary or decimal—it's converted by reading nibbles, not bytes. By using a nibble, we can convert these bits to hex pretty simply. First, understand that the hexadecimal addressing scheme uses only the numbers 0 through 9. And since the numbers 10, 11, 12, and so on can't be used (because they are two-digit numbers), the letters *A*, *B*, *C*, *D*, *E*, and *F* are used to represent 10, 11, 12, 13, 14, and 15, respectively.

Hex is short for *hexadecimal*, which is a numbering system that uses the first six letters of the alphabet (*A* through *F*) to extend beyond the available 10 digits in the decimal system. Hexadecimal has a total of 16 digits.

Table 1.3 shows both the binary value and the decimal value for each hexadecimal digit.

TABLE 1.3 Hex to Binary to Decimal Chart

Hexadecimal Value	Binary Value	Decimal Value
0	0000	0
1	0001	1
2	0010	2

TABLE 1.3   Hex to Binary to Decimal Chart *(continued)*

Hexadecimal Value	Binary Value	Decimal Value
3	0011	3
4	0100	4
5	0101	5
6	0110	6
7	0111	7
8	1000	8
9	1001	9
A	1010	10
B	1011	11
C	1100	12
D	1101	13
E	1110	14
F	1111	15

Did you notice that the first 10 hexadecimal digits (0–9) are the same value as the decimal values? If not, look again. This handy fact makes those values super easy to convert.

So suppose you have something like this: 0x6A. (Sometimes Cisco likes to put *0x* in front of characters so you know that they are a hex value. It doesn't have any other special meaning.) What are the binary and decimal values? All you have to remember is that each hex character is one nibble and two hex characters together make a byte. To figure out the binary value, we need to put the hex characters into two nibbles and then put them together into a byte. 6 = 0110 and A (which is 10 in hex) = 1010, so the complete byte would be 01101010.

To convert from binary to hex, just take the byte and break it into nibbles. Here's what I mean.

Say you have the binary number 01010101. First, break it into nibbles—0101 and 0101—with the value of each nibble being 5 since the 1 and 4 bits are on. This makes the hex answer 0x55. And in decimal format, the binary number is 01010101, which converts to 64 + 16 + 4 + 1 = 85.

Here's another binary number:

11001100

Your answer would be 1100 = 12 and 1100 = 12 (therefore, it's converted to CC in hex). The decimal conversion answer would be 128 + 64 + 8 + 4 = 204.

One more example, then we need to get working on the Physical layer. Suppose you had the following binary number:

10110101

The hex answer would be 0xB5, since 1011 converts to B and 0101 converts to 5 in hex value. The decimal equivalent is 128 + 32 + 16 + 4 + 1 = 181.

   See Written Lab 1.4 for more practice with binary/hex/decimal conversion.

The Physical Layer

Finally arriving at the bottom, we find that the *Physical layer* does two things: It sends bits and receives bits. Bits come only in values of 1 or 0—a Morse code with numerical values. The Physical layer communicates directly with the various types of actual communication media. Different kinds of media represent these bit values in different ways. Some use audio tones, while others employ *state transitions*—changes in voltage from high to low and low to high. Specific protocols are needed for each type of media to describe the proper bit patterns to be used, how data is encoded into media signals, and the various qualities of the physical media's attachment interface.

The Physical layer specifies the electrical, mechanical, procedural, and functional requirements for activating, maintaining, and deactivating a physical link between end systems. This layer is also where you identify the interface between the *data terminal equipment (DTE)* and the *data communication equipment (DCE)*. (Some old phone-company employees still call DCE data circuit-terminating equipment.) The DCE is usually located at the service provider, while the DTE is the attached device. The services available to the DTE are most often accessed via a modem or *channel service unit/data service unit (CSU/DSU)*.

The Physical layer's connectors and different physical topologies are defined by the OSI as standards, allowing disparate systems to communicate. The CCNA objectives are only interested in the IEEE Ethernet standards.

Hubs at the Physical Layer

A *hub* is really a multiple-port repeater. A repeater receives a digital signal and reamplifies or regenerates that signal and then forwards the digital signal out all active ports without looking at any data. An active hub does the same thing. Any digital signal received from a segment on a hub port is regenerated or reamplified and transmitted out all ports on the hub. This means all devices plugged into a hub are in the same collision domain as well as in the same broadcast domain. Figure 1.17 shows a hub in a network.

FIGURE 1.17   A hub in a network

All devices in the same collision domain.
All devices in the same broadcast domain.
Devices share the same bandwidth.

Hubs, like repeaters, don't examine any of the traffic as it enters and is then transmitted out to the other parts of the physical media. Every device connected to the hub, or hubs, must listen if a device transmits. A physical star network—where the hub is a central device and cables extend in all directions out from it—is the type of topology a hub creates. Visually, the design really does resemble a star, whereas Ethernet networks run a logical bus topology, meaning that the signal has to run through the network from end to end.

Hubs and repeaters can be used to enlarge the area covered by a single LAN segment, although I do not recommend this. LAN switches are affordable for almost every situation.

Ethernet Networking

Ethernet is a contention media access method that allows all hosts on a network to share the same bandwidth of a link. Ethernet is popular because it's readily scalable, meaning that it's comparatively easy to integrate new technologies, such as Fast Ethernet and Gigabit Ethernet, into an existing network infrastructure. It's also relatively simple to implement in the first place, and with it, troubleshooting is reasonably straightforward. Ethernet uses both Data Link and Physical layer specifications, and this section of the chapter will give you both the Data Link layer and Physical layer information you need to effectively implement, trouble-shoot, and maintain an Ethernet network.

Ethernet networking uses *Carrier Sense Multiple Access with Collision Detection (CSMA/CD)*, a protocol that helps devices share the bandwidth evenly without having two devices transmit at the same time on the network medium. CSMA/CD was created to overcome the problem of those collisions that occur when packets are transmitted simultaneously from different nodes. And trust me—good collision management is crucial, because when a node transmits in a CSMA/CD network, all the other nodes on the network receive and examine that transmission. Only bridges and routers can effectively prevent a transmission from propagating throughout the entire network!

So, how does the CSMA/CD protocol work? Let's start by taking a look at Figure 1.18.

FIGURE 1.18   CSMA/CD

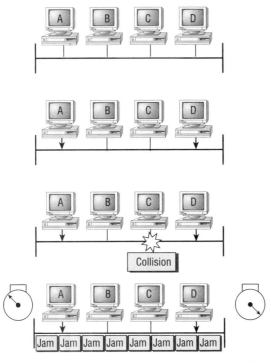

Carrier Sense Multiple Access with Collision Detection (CSMA/CD)

When a host wants to transmit over the network, it first checks for the presence of a digital signal on the wire. If all is clear (no other host is transmitting), the host will then proceed with its transmission. But it doesn't stop there. The transmitting host constantly monitors the wire to make sure no other hosts begin transmitting. If the host detects another signal on the wire, it sends out an extended jam signal that causes all nodes on the segment to stop sending data (think busy signal). The nodes respond to that jam signal by waiting a while before attempting to transmit again. Backoff algorithms determine when the colliding stations can retransmit. If collisions keep occurring after 15 tries, the nodes attempting to transmit will then timeout. Pretty clean!

When a collision occurs on an Ethernet LAN, the following happens:

- A jam signal informs all devices that a collision occurred.

- The collision invokes a random backoff algorithm.

- Each device on the Ethernet segment stops transmitting for a short time until the timers expire.

- All hosts have equal priority to transmit after the timers have expired.

The following are the effects of having a CSMA/CD network sustaining heavy collisions:

- Delay
- Low throughput
- Congestion

 Backoff on an 802.3 network is the retransmission delay that's enforced when a collision occurs. When a collision occurs, a host will resume transmission after the forced time delay has expired. After this backoff delay period has expired, all stations have equal priority to transmit data.

In the following sections, I am going to cover Ethernet in detail at both the Data Link layer (layer 2) and the Physical layer (layer 1).

Half- and Full-Duplex Ethernet

Half-duplex Ethernet is defined in the original 802.3 Ethernet; Cisco says it uses only one wire pair with a digital signal running in both directions on the wire. Certainly, the IEEE specifications discuss the process of half duplex somewhat differently, but what Cisco is talking about is a general sense of what is happening here with Ethernet.

It also uses the CSMA/CD protocol to help prevent collisions and to permit retransmitting if a collision does occur. If a hub is attached to a switch, it must operate in half-duplex mode because the end stations must be able to detect collisions. Half-duplex Ethernet—typically 10BaseT—is only about 30 to 40 percent efficient as Cisco sees it because a large 10BaseT network will usually only give you 3 to 4Mbps, at most.

But full-duplex Ethernet uses two pairs of wires instead of one wire pair like half duplex. And full duplex uses a point-to-point connection between the transmitter of the transmitting device and the receiver of the receiving device. This means that with full-duplex data transfer, you get a faster data transfer compared to half duplex. And because the transmitted data is sent on a different set of wires than the received data, no collisions will occur.

The reason you don't need to worry about collisions is because now it's like a freeway with multiple lanes instead of the single-lane road provided by half duplex. Full-duplex Ethernet is supposed to offer 100 percent efficiency in both directions—for example, you can get 20Mbps with a 10Mbps Ethernet running full duplex or 200Mbps for Fast Ethernet. But this rate is something known as an aggregate rate, which translates as "you're supposed to get" 100 percent efficiency. No guarantees, in networking as in life.

Full-duplex Ethernet can be used in three situations:

- With a connection from a switch to a host
- With a connection from a switch to a switch
- With a connection from a host to a host using a crossover cable

 Full-duplex Ethernet requires a point-to-point connection when only two nodes are present. You can run full-duplex with just about any device except a hub.

Now, if it's capable of all that speed, why wouldn't it deliver? Well, when a full-duplex Ethernet port is powered on, it first connects to the remote end and then negotiates with the other end of the Fast Ethernet link. This is called an *auto-detect mechanism*. This mechanism first decides on the exchange capability, which means it checks to see if it can run at 10 or 100Mbps. It then checks to see if it can run full duplex, and if it can't, it will run half duplex.

 Remember that half-duplex Ethernet shares a collision domain and provides a lower effective throughput than full-duplex Ethernet, which typically has a private collision domain and a higher effective throughput.

Lastly, remember these important points:

- There are no collisions in full-duplex mode.

- A dedicated switch port is required for each full-duplex node.

- The host network card and the switch port must be capable of operating in full-duplex mode.

Now let's take a look at how Ethernet works at the Data Link layer.

Ethernet at the Data Link Layer

Ethernet at the Data Link layer is responsible for Ethernet addressing, commonly referred to as hardware addressing or MAC addressing. Ethernet is also responsible for framing packets received from the Network layer and preparing them for transmission on the local network through the Ethernet contention media access method.

Ethernet Addressing

Here's where we get into how Ethernet addressing works. It uses the *Media Access Control (MAC) address* burned into each and every Ethernet network interface card (NIC). The MAC, or hardware, address is a 48-bit (6-byte) address written in a hexadecimal format.

Figure 1.19 shows the 48-bit MAC addresses and how the bits are divided.

FIGURE 1.19   Ethernet addressing using MAC addresses

The *organizationally unique identifier (OUI)* is assigned by the IEEE to an organization. It's composed of 24 bits, or 3 bytes. The organization, in turn, assigns a globally administered address (24 bits, or 3 bytes) that is unique (supposedly, again—no guarantees) to each and every adapter it manufactures. Look closely at the figure. The high-order bit is the Individual/Group (I/G) bit. When it has a value of 0, we can assume that the address is the MAC address of a device and may well appear in the source portion of the MAC header. When it is a 1, we can assume that the address represents either a broadcast or multicast address in Ethernet or a broadcast or functional address in TR and FDDI (who really knows about FDDI?).

The next bit is the global/local bit, or just G/L bit (also known as U/L, where U means *universal*).When set to 0, this bit represents a globally administered address (as by the IEEE). When the bit is a 1, it represents a locally governed and administered address (as in what DECnet used to do). The low-order 24 bits of an Ethernet address represent a locally administered or manufacturer-assigned code. This portion commonly starts with 24 0s for the first card made and continues in order until there are 24 1s for the last (16,777,216th) card made. You'll find that many manufacturers use these same six hex digits as the last six characters of their serial number on the same card.

Ethernet Frames

The Data Link layer is responsible for combining bits into bytes and bytes into frames. Frames are used at the Data Link layer to encapsulate packets handed down from the Network layer for transmission on a type of media access.

The function of Ethernet stations is to pass data frames between each other using a group of bits known as a MAC frame format. This provides error detection from a cyclic redundancy check (CRC). But remember—this is error detection, not error correction. The 802.3 frames and Ethernet frame are shown in Figure 1.20.

Encapsulating a frame within a different type of frame is called *tunneling*.

FIGURE 1.20   802.3 and Ethernet frame formats

Ethernet_II

Preamble 8 bytes	DA 6 bytes	SA 6 bytes	Type 2 bytes	Data	FCS 4 bytes

802.3_Ethernet

Preamble 8 bytes	DA 6 bytes	SA 6 bytes	Length 2 bytes	Data	FCS

Following are the details of the different fields in the 802.3 and Ethernet frame types:

Preamble   An alternating 1,0 pattern provides a 5MHz clock at the start of each packet, which allows the receiving devices to lock the incoming bit stream.

Start Frame Delimiter (SFD)/Synch   The preamble is seven octets and the SFD is one octet (synch). The SFD is 10101011, where the last pair of 1s allows the receiver to come into the alternating 1,0 pattern somewhere in the middle and still sync up and detect the beginning of the data.

Destination Address (DA)   This transmits a 48-bit value using the least significant bit (LSB) first. The DA is used by receiving stations to determine whether an incoming packet is addressed to a particular node. The destination address can be an individual address or a broadcast or multicast MAC address. Remember that a broadcast is all 1s (or Fs in hex) and is sent to all devices but a multicast is sent only to a similar subset of nodes on a network.

Source Address (SA)   The SA is a 48-bit MAC address used to identify the transmitting device, and it uses the LSB first. Broadcast and multicast address formats are illegal within the SA field.

Length or Type   802.3 uses a Length field, but the Ethernet frame uses a Type field to identify the Network layer protocol. 802.3 cannot identify the upper-layer protocol and must be used with a proprietary LAN—IPX, for example.

Data   This is a packet sent down to the Data Link layer from the Network layer. The size can vary from 64 to 1,500 bytes.

Frame Check Sequence (FCS)   FCS is a field at the end of the frame that's used to store the CRC.

Let's pause here for a minute and take a look at some frames caught on our trusty OmniPeek network analyzer. You can see that the frame below has only three fields: Destination, Source, and Type (shown as Protocol Type on this analyzer):

```
Destination:    00:60:f5:00:1f:27
Source:         00:60:f5:00:1f:2c
Protocol Type: 08-00 IP
```

This is an Ethernet_II frame. Notice that the type field is IP, or 08-00 (mostly just referred to as 0x800) in hexadecimal.

The next frame has the same fields, so it must be an Ethernet_II frame too:

```
Destination:    ff:ff:ff:ff:ff:ff Ethernet Broadcast
Source:         02:07:01:22:de:a4
Protocol Type: 08-00 IP
```

Did you notice that this frame was a broadcast? You can tell because the destination hardware address is all 1s in binary, or all Fs in hexadecimal.

Let's take a look at one more Ethernet_II frame. I'll talk about this next example again when we use IPv6 in Chapter 13, but you can see that the Ethernet frame is the same Ethernet_II frame we use with the IPv4 routed protocol but the type field has 0x86dd when we are carrying IPv6 data, and when we have IPv4 data, we use 0x0800 in the protocol field:

```
Destination: IPv6-Neighbor-Discovery_00:01:00:03 (33:33:00:01:00:03)
Source: Aopen_3e:7f:dd (00:01:80:3e:7f:dd)
Type: IPv6 (0x86dd)
```

This is the beauty of the Ethernet_II frame. Because of the protocol field, we can run any Network layer routed protocol and it will carry the data because it can identify the Network layer protocol.

Ethernet at the Physical Layer

Ethernet was first implemented by a group called DIX (Digital, Intel, and Xerox). They created and implemented the first Ethernet LAN specification, which the IEEE used to create the IEEE 802.3 Committee. This was a 10Mbps network that ran on coax and then eventually twisted-pair and fiber physical media.

The IEEE extended the 802.3 Committee to two new committees known as 802.3u (Fast Ethernet) and 802.3ab (Gigabit Ethernet on category 5) and then finally 802.3ae (10Gbps over fiber and coax).

Figure 1.21 shows the IEEE 802.3 and original Ethernet Physical layer specifications.

When designing your LAN, it's really important to understand the different types of Ethernet media available to you. Sure, it would be great to run Gigabit Ethernet to each desktop and 10Gbps between switches, and although this might happen one day, justifying the cost of that network today would be pretty difficult. But if you mix and match the different types of Ethernet media methods currently available, you can come up with a cost-effective network solution that works great.

FIGURE 1.21   Ethernet Physical layer specifications

The EIA/TIA (Electronic Industries Association and the newer Telecommunications Industry Alliance) is the standards body that creates the Physical layer specifications for Ethernet. The EIA/TIA specifies that Ethernet use a *registered jack (RJ) connector* with a 4 5 wiring sequence on *unshielded twisted-pair (UTP)* cabling (RJ45). However, the industry is moving toward calling this just an 8-pin modular connector.

Each Ethernet cable type that is specified by the EIA/TIA has inherent attenuation, which is defined as the loss of signal strength as it travels the length of a cable and is measured in decibels (dB). The cabling used in corporate and home markets is measured in categories. A higher-quality cable will have a higher-rated category and lower attenuation. For example, category 5 is better than category 3 because category 5 cables have more wire twists per foot and therefore less crosstalk. Crosstalk is the unwanted signal interference from adjacent pairs in the cable.

Here are the original IEEE 802.3 standards:

10Base2   10Mbps, baseband technology, up to 185 meters in length. Known as *thinnet* and can support up to 30 workstations on a single segment. Uses a physical and logical bus with AUI connectors. The 10 means 10Mbps, *Base* means baseband technology (which is a signaling method for communication on the network), and the 2 means almost 200 meters. 10Base2 Ethernet cards use BNC (British Naval Connector, Bayonet Neill Concelman, or Bayonet Nut Connector) and T-connectors to connect to a network.

10Base5   10Mbps, baseband technology, up to 500 meters in length. Known as *thicknet*. Uses a physical and logical bus with AUI connectors. Up to 2,500 meters with repeaters and 1,024 users for all segments.

10BaseT   10Mbps using category 3 UTP wiring. Unlike with the 10Base2 and 10Base5 networks, each device must connect into a hub or switch, and you can have only one host per segment or wire. Uses an RJ45 connector (8-pin modular connector) with a physical star topology and a logical bus.

Each of the 802.3 standards defines an Attachment Unit Interface (AUI), which allows a one-bit-at-a-time transfer to the Physical layer from the Data Link media access method. This allows the MAC to remain constant but means the Physical layer can support any existing and new technologies. The original AUI interface was a 15-pin connector, which allowed a transceiver (transmitter/receiver) that provided a 15-pin-to-twisted-pair conversion.

The thing is, the AUI interface cannot support 100Mbps Ethernet because of the high frequencies involved. So 100BaseT needed a new interface, and the 802.3u specifications created one called the Media Independent Interface (MII), which provides 100Mbps throughput. The MII uses a *nibble*, defined as 4 bits. Gigabit Ethernet uses a Gigabit Media Independent Interface (GMII) and transmits 8 bits at a time.

802.3u (Fast Ethernet) is compatible with 802.3 Ethernet because they share the same physical characteristics. Fast Ethernet and Ethernet use the same maximum transmission unit (MTU), use the same MAC mechanisms, and preserve the frame format that is used by 10BaseT Ethernet. Basically, Fast Ethernet is just based on an extension to the IEEE 802.3 specification, except that it offers a speed increase of 10 times that of 10BaseT.

Here are the expanded IEEE Ethernet 802.3 standards:

100BaseTX (IEEE 802.3u)   EIA/TIA category 5, 6, or 7 UTP two-pair wiring. One user per segment; up to 100 meters long. It uses an RJ45 connector with a physical star topology and a logical bus.

100BaseFX (IEEE 802.3u)   Uses fiber cabling 62.5/125-micron multimode fiber. Point-to-point topology; up to 412 meters long. It uses an ST or SC connector, which are media-interface connectors.

1000BaseCX (IEEE 802.3z)   Copper twisted-pair called twinax (a balanced coaxial pair) that can only run up to 25 meters.

1000BaseT (IEEE 802.3ab)   Category 5, four-pair UTP wiring up to 100 meters long.

1000BaseSX (IEEE 802.3z)   MMF using 62.5- and 50-micron core; uses an 850 nano-meter laser and can go up to 220 meters with 62.5-micron, 550 meters with 50-micron.

1000BaseLX (IEEE 802.3z)   Single-mode fiber that uses a 9-micron core and 1300 nano-meter laser and can go from 3 kilometers up to 10 kilometers.

If you want to implement a network medium that is not susceptible to electromagnetic interference (EMI), fiber-optic cable provides a more secure, long-distance cable that is not susceptible to EMI at high speeds.

Ethernet Cabling

Ethernet cabling is an important discussion, especially if you are planning on taking the Cisco exams. Three types of Ethernet cables are available:

- Straight-through cable
- Crossover cable
- Rolled cable

We will look at each in the following sections.

Straight-Through Cable

The *straight-through cable* is used to connect

- Host to switch or hub
- Router to switch or hub

Four wires are used in straight-through cable to connect Ethernet devices. It is relatively simple to create this type; Figure 1.22 shows the four wires used in a straight-through Ethernet cable.

Notice that only pins 1, 2, 3, and 6 are used. Just connect 1 to 1, 2 to 2, 3 to 3, and 6 to 6 and you'll be up and networking in no time. However, remember that this would be an Ethernet-only cable and wouldn't work with voice, Token Ring, ISDN, and so on.

FIGURE 1.22   Straight-through Ethernet cable

Hub/Switch		Host
1	⟷	1
2	⟷	2
3	⟷	3
6	⟷	6

Crossover Cable

The *crossover cable* can be used to connect

- Switch to switch
- Hub to hub
- Host to host
- Hub to switch
- Router direct to host

The same four wires are used in this cable as in the straight-through cable; we just connect different pins together. Figure 1.23 shows how the four wires are used in a crossover Ethernet cable.

Notice that instead of connecting 1 to 1, 2 to 2, and so on, here we connect pins 1 to 3 and 2 to 6 on each side of the cable.

FIGURE 1.23   Crossover Ethernet cable

Rolled Cable

Although *rolled cable* isn't used to connect any Ethernet connections together, you can use a rolled Ethernet cable to connect a host to a router console serial communication (com) port.

If you have a Cisco router or switch, you would use this cable to connect your PC running HyperTerminal to the Cisco hardware. Eight wires are used in this cable to connect serial devices, although not all eight are used to send information, just as in Ethernet networking. Figure 1.24 shows the eight wires used in a rolled cable.

FIGURE 1.24   Rolled Ethernet cable

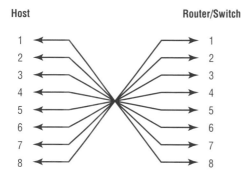

These are probably the easiest cables to make because you just cut the end off on one side of a straight-through cable, turn it over, and put it back on (with a new connector, of course).

Once you have the correct cable connected from your PC to the Cisco router or switch, you can start HyperTerminal to create a console connection and configure the device. Set the configuration as follows:

1. Open HyperTerminal and enter a name for the connection. It is irrelevant what you name it, but I always just use Cisco. Then click OK.

2. Choose the communications port—either COM1 or COM2, whichever is open on your PC.

3. Now set the port settings. The default values (2400bps and no flow control hardware) will not work; you must set the port settings as shown in Figure 1.25.

Notice that the bit rate is now set to 9600 and the flow control is set to None. At this point, you can click OK and press the Enter key and you should be connected to your Cisco device console port.

We've taken a look at the various RJ45 unshielded twisted pair (UTP) cables. Keeping this in mind, what cable is used between the switches in Figure 1.26?

In order for host A to ping host B, you need a crossover cable to connect the two switches together. But what types of cables are used in the network shown in Figure 1.27?

In Figure 1.27, there are a variety of cables in use. For the connection between the switches, we'd obviously use a crossover cable like we saw in Figure 1.23. The trouble is, we have a console connection that uses a rolled cable. Plus, the connection from the router to the switch is a straight-through cable, as is true for the hosts to the switches. Keep in mind that if we had a serial connection (which we don't), it would be a V.35 that we'd use to connect us to a WAN.

FIGURE 1.25 Port settings for a rolled cable connection

FIGURE 1.26 RJ45 UTP cable question #1

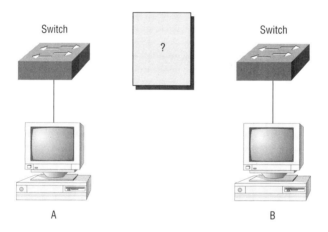

FIGURE 1.27 RJ45 UTP cable question #2

Data Encapsulation

When a host transmits data across a network to another device, the data goes through *encapsulation*: It is wrapped with protocol information at each layer of the OSI model. Each layer communicates only with its peer layer on the receiving device.

To communicate and exchange information, each layer uses *Protocol Data Units (PDUs)*. These hold the control information attached to the data at each layer of the model. They are usually attached to the header in front of the data field but can also be in the trailer, or end, of it.

Each PDU attaches to the data by encapsulating it at each layer of the OSI model, and each has a specific name depending on the information provided in each header. This PDU information is read only by the peer layer on the receiving device. After it's read, it's stripped off and the data is then handed to the next layer up.

Figure 1.28 shows the PDUs and how they attach control information to each layer. This figure demonstrates how the upper-layer user data is converted for transmission on the network. The data stream is then handed down to the Transport layer, which sets up a virtual circuit to the receiving device by sending over a synch packet. Next, the data stream is broken up into smaller pieces, and a Transport layer header (a PDU) is created and attached to the header of the data field; now the piece of data is called a segment. Each segment is sequenced so the data stream can be put back together on the receiving side exactly as it was transmitted.

Each segment is then handed to the Network layer for network addressing and routing through the internetwork. Logical addressing (for example, IP) is used to get each segment to the correct network. The Network layer protocol adds a control header to the segment handed down from the Transport layer, and what we have now is called a *packet* or *datagram*. Remember that the Transport and Network layers work together to rebuild a data stream on a receiving host, but it's not part of their work to place their PDUs on a local network segment—which is the only way to get the information to a router or host.

FIGURE 1.28   Data encapsulation

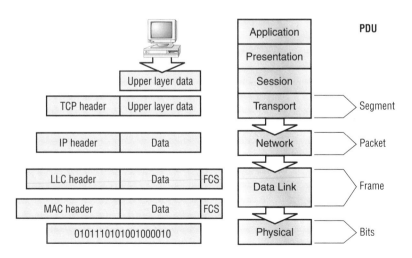

It's the Data Link layer that's responsible for taking packets from the Network layer and placing them on the network medium (cable or wireless). The Data Link layer encapsulates each packet in a *frame*, and the frame's header carries the hardware address of the source and destination hosts. If the destination device is on a remote network, then the frame is sent to a router to be routed through an internetwork. Once it gets to the destination network, a new frame is used to get the packet to the destination host.

To put this frame on the network, it must first be put into a digital signal. Since a frame is really a logical group of 1s and 0s, the Physical layer is responsible for encoding these digits into a digital signal, which is read by devices on the same local network. The receiving devices will synchronize on the digital signal and extract (decode) the 1s and 0s from the digital signal. At this point, the devices build the frames, run a CRC, and then check their answer against the answer in the frame's FCS field. If it matches, the packet is pulled from the frame and what's left of the frame is discarded. This process is called *de-encapsulation*. The packet is handed to the Network layer, where the address is checked. If the address matches, the segment is pulled from the packet and what's left of the packet is discarded. The segment is processed at the Transport layer, which rebuilds the data stream and acknowledges to the transmitting station that it received each piece. It then happily hands the data stream to the upper-layer application.

At a transmitting device, the data encapsulation method works like this:

1. User information is converted to data for transmission on the network.

2. Data is converted to segments and a reliable connection is set up between the transmitting and receiving hosts.

3. Segments are converted to packets or datagrams, and a logical address is placed in the header so each packet can be routed through an internetwork.

4. Packets or datagrams are converted to frames for transmission on the local network. Hardware (Ethernet) addresses are used to uniquely identify hosts on a local network segment.

5. Frames are converted to bits, and a digital encoding and clocking scheme is used.

6. To explain this in more detail using the layer addressing, I'll use Figure 1.29.

FIGURE 1.29   PDU and layer addressing

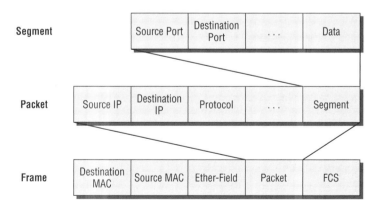

Bit   1011011100011110000

Remember that a data stream is handed down from the upper layer to the Transport layer. As technicians, we really don't care who the data stream comes from because that's really a programmer's problem. Our job is to rebuild the data stream reliably and hand it to the upper layers on the receiving device.

Before we go further in our discussion of Figure 1.29, let's discuss port numbers and make sure we understand them. The Transport layer uses port numbers to define both the virtual circuit and the upper-layer process, as you can see from Figure 1.30.

FIGURE 1.30   Port numbers at the Transport layer

The Transport layer takes the data stream, makes segments out of it, and establishes a reliable session by creating a virtual circuit. It then sequences (numbers) each segment and uses acknowledgments and flow control. If you're using TCP, the virtual circuit is defined by the source port number. Remember, the host just makes this up starting at port number 1024 (0 through 1023 are reserved for well-known port numbers). The destination port number defines the upper-layer process (application) that the data stream is handed to when the data stream is reliably rebuilt on the receiving host.

Now that you understand port numbers and how they are used at the Transport layer, let's go back to Figure 1.30. Once the Transport layer header information is added to the piece of data, it becomes a segment and is handed down to the Network layer along with the destination IP address. (The destination IP address was handed down from the upper layers to the Transport layer with the data stream, and it was discovered through a name resolution method at the upper layers—probably DNS.)

The Network layer adds a header, and adds the logical addressing (IP addresses), to the front of each segment. Once the header is added to the segment, the PDU is called a packet. The packet has a protocol field that describes where the segment came from (either UDP or TCP) so it can hand the segment to the correct protocol at the Transport layer when it reaches the receiving host.

The Network layer is responsible for finding the destination hardware address that dictates where the packet should be sent on the local network. It does this by using the Address Resolution Protocol (ARP)—something I'll talk about more in Chapter 2. IP at the Network layer looks at the destination IP address and compares that address to its own source IP address and subnet mask. If it turns out to be a local network request, the hardware address of the local host is requested via an ARP request. If the packet is destined for a remote host, IP will look for the IP address of the default gateway (router) instead.

The packet, along with the destination hardware address of either the local host or default gateway, is then handed down to the Data Link layer. The Data Link layer will add a header to the front of the packet and the piece of data then becomes a frame. (We call it a frame because both a header and a trailer are added to the packet, which makes the data resemble bookends or a frame, if you will.) This is shown in Figure 1.29. The frame uses an Ether-Type field to describe which protocol the packet came from at the Network layer. Now a cyclic redundancy check (CRC) is run on the frame, and the answer to the CRC is placed in the Frame Check Sequence field found in the trailer of the frame.

The frame is now ready to be handed down, one bit at a time, to the Physical layer, which will use bit timing rules to encode the data in a digital signal. Every device on the network segment will synchronize with the clock and extract the 1s and 0s from the digital signal and build a frame. After the frame is rebuilt, a CRC is run to make sure the frame is okay. If everything turns out to be all good, the hosts will check the destination address to see if the frame is for them.

If all this is making your eyes cross and your brain freeze, don't freak. I'll be going over exactly how data is encapsulated and routed through an internetwork in Chapter 6.

The Cisco Three-Layer Hierarchical Model

Most of us were exposed to hierarchy early in life. Anyone with older siblings learned what it was like to be at the bottom of the hierarchy. Regardless of where you first discovered hierarchy, today most of us experience it in many aspects of our lives. It is *hierarchy* that helps us understand where things belong, how things fit together, and what functions go where. It brings order and understandability to otherwise complex models. If you want a pay raise, for instance, hierarchy dictates that you ask your boss, not your subordinate. That is the person whose role it is to grant (or deny) your request. So basically, understanding hierarchy helps us discern where we should go to get what we need.

Hierarchy has many of the same benefits in network design that it does in other areas of life. When used properly, it makes networks more predictable. It helps us define which areas should perform certain functions. Likewise, you can use tools such as access lists at certain levels in hierarchical networks and avoid them at others.

Let's face it: Large networks can be extremely complicated, with multiple protocols, detailed configurations, and diverse technologies. Hierarchy helps us summarize a complex collection of details into an understandable model. Then, as specific configurations are needed, the model dictates the appropriate manner in which to apply them.

The Cisco hierarchical model can help you design, implement, and maintain a scalable, reliable, cost-effective hierarchical internetwork. Cisco defines three layers of hierarchy, as shown in Figure 1.31, each with specific functions.

FIGURE 1.31   The Cisco hierarchical model

The following are the three layers and their typical functions:

- The core layer: backbone
- The distribution layer: routing
- The access layer: switching

Each layer has specific responsibilities. Remember, however, that the three layers are logical and are not necessarily physical devices. Consider the OSI model, another logical hierarchy. The seven layers describe functions but not necessarily protocols, right? Sometimes a protocol maps to more than one layer of the OSI model, and sometimes multiple protocols communicate within a single layer. In the same way, when we build physical implementations of hierarchical networks, we may have many devices in a single layer, or we might have a single device performing functions at two layers. The definition of the layers is logical, not physical.

Now, let's take a closer look at each of the layers.

The Core Layer

The *core layer* is literally the core of the network. At the top of the hierarchy, the core layer is responsible for transporting large amounts of traffic both reliably and quickly. The only purpose of the network's core layer is to switch traffic as fast as possible. The traffic transported across the core is common to a majority of users. However, remember that user data is processed at the distribution layer, which forwards the requests to the core if needed.

If there is a failure in the core, *every single user* can be affected. Therefore, fault tolerance at this layer is an issue. The core is likely to see large volumes of traffic, so speed and latency are driving concerns here. Given the function of the core, we can now consider some design specifics. Let's start with some things we don't want to do:

- Don't do anything to slow down traffic. This includes using access lists, routing between virtual local area networks (VLANs), and implementing packet filtering.

- Don't support workgroup access here.

- Avoid expanding the core (i.e., adding routers) when the internetwork grows. If performance becomes an issue in the core, give preference to upgrades over expansion.

Now, there are a few things that we want to do as we design the core:

- Design the core for high reliability. Consider data-link technologies that facilitate both speed and redundancy, such as FDDI, Fast Ethernet (with redundant links), or even ATM.

- Design with speed in mind. The core should have very little latency.

- Select routing protocols with lower convergence times. Fast and redundant data-link connectivity is no help if your routing tables are shot!

The Distribution Layer

The *distribution layer* is sometimes referred to as the *workgroup layer* and is the communication point between the access layer and the core. The primary functions of the distribution layer are to provide routing, filtering, and WAN access and to determine how packets can access the core, if needed. The distribution layer must determine the fastest way that network service requests are handled—for example, how a file request is forwarded to a server. After the distribution layer determines the best path, it forwards the request to the core layer if necessary. The core layer then quickly transports the request to the correct service.

The distribution layer is the place to implement policies for the network. Here you can exercise considerable flexibility in defining network operation. There are several actions that generally should be done at the distribution layer:

- Routing

- Implementing tools (such as access lists), packet filtering, and queuing

- Implementing security and network policies, including address translation and firewalls

- Redistributing between routing protocols, including static routing

- Routing between VLANs and other workgroup support functions

- Defining broadcast and multicast domains

Things to avoid at the distribution layer are limited to those functions that exclusively belong to one of the other layers.

The Access Layer

The *access layer* controls user and workgroup access to internetwork resources. The access layer is sometimes referred to as the *desktop layer*. The network resources most users need will be available locally. The distribution layer handles any traffic for remote services. The following are some of the functions to be included at the access layer:

- Continued (from distribution layer) use of access control and policies
- Creation of separate collision domains (segmentation)
- Workgroup connectivity into the distribution layer

Technologies such as DDR and Ethernet switching are frequently seen in the access layer. Static routing (instead of dynamic routing protocols) is seen here as well.

As already noted, three separate levels does not imply three separate routers. There could be fewer, or there could be more. Remember, this is a *layered* approach.

Summary

Whew! I know this seemed like the chapter that wouldn't end, but it did—and you made it through! You're now armed with a ton of fundamental information; you're ready to build upon it and are well on your way to certification.

I started by discussing simple, basic networking and the differences between collision and broadcast domains. I also discussed the various devices used in an internetwork.

I then discussed the OSI model—the seven-layer model used to help application developers design applications that can run on any type of system or network. Each layer has its special jobs and select responsibilities within the model to ensure that solid, effective communications do, in fact, occur. I provided you with complete details of each layer and discussed how Cisco views the specifications of the OSI model.

In addition, each layer in the OSI model specifies different types of devices. I described the different devices, cables, and connectors used at each layer. Remember that hubs are Physical layer devices and repeat the digital signal to all segments except the one from which it was received. Switches segment the network using hardware addresses and break up collision domains. Routers break up broadcast domains (and collision domains) and use logical addressing to send packets through an internetwork.

Last, this chapter covered the Cisco three-layer hierarchical model. I described in detail the three layers and how each is used to help design and implement a Cisco internetwork. We are now going to move on to IP addressing in the next chapter.

Exam Essentials

Remember the possible causes of LAN traffic congestion.   Too many hosts in a broadcast domain, broadcast storms, multicasting, and low bandwidth are all possible causes of LAN traffic congestion.

Understand the difference between a collision domain and a broadcast domain. *Collision domain* is an Ethernet term used to describe a network collection of devices in which one particular device sends a packet on a network segment, forcing every other device on that same segment to pay attention to it. On a broadcast domain, a set of all devices on a network segment hear all broadcasts sent on that segment.

Understand the difference between a hub, a bridge, a switch, and a router. Hubs create one collision domain and one broadcast domain. Bridges break up collision domains but create one large broadcast domain. They use hardware addresses to filter the network. Switches are really just multiple port bridges with more intelligence. They break up collision domains but create one large broadcast domain by default. Switches use hardware addresses to filter the network. Routers break up broadcast domains (and collision domains) and use logical addressing to filter the network.

Remember the difference between connection-oriented and connectionless network services. Connection-oriented services use acknowledgments and flow control to create a reliable session. More overhead is used than in a connectionless network service. Connectionless services are used to send data with no acknowledgments or flow control. This is considered unreliable.

Remember the OSI layers. You must remember the seven layers of the OSI model and what function each layer provides. The Application, Presentation, and Session layers are upper layers and are responsible for communicating from a user interface to an application. The Transport layer provides segmentation, sequencing, and virtual circuits. The Network layer provides logical network addressing and routing through an internetwork. The Data Link layer provides framing and placing of data on the network medium. The Physical layer is responsible for taking 1s and 0s and encoding them into a digital signal for transmission on the network segment.

Remember the types of Ethernet cabling and when you would use them. The three types of cables that can be created from an Ethernet cable are straight-through (to connect a PC's or a router's Ethernet interface to a hub or switch), crossover (to connect hub to hub, hub to switch, switch to switch, or PC to PC), and rolled (for a console connection from a PC to a router or switch).

Understand how to connect a console cable from a PC to a router and start HyperTerminal. Take a rolled cable and connect it from the COM port of the host to the console port of a router. Start HyperTerminal and set the BPS to 9600 and flow control to None.

Remember the three layers in the Cisco three-layer model. The three layers in the Cisco hierarchical model are the core, distribution, and access layers.

Written Lab 1

In this section, you'll complete the following labs to make sure you've got the information and concepts contained within them fully dialed in:

- Lab 1.1: OSI Questions
- Lab 1.2: Defining the OSI Layers and Devices

- Lab 1.3: Identifying Collision and Broadcast Domains
- Lab 1.4: Binary/Decimal/Hexadecimal Conversion

(The answers to the written labs can be found following the answers to the review questions for this chapter.)

Written Lab 1.1: OSI Questions

Answer the following questions about the OSI model:

1. Which layer chooses and determines the availability of communicating partners along with the resources necessary to make the connection, coordinates partnering applications, and forms a consensus on procedures for controlling data integrity and error recovery?

2. Which layer is responsible for converting data packets from the Data Link layer into electrical signals?

3. At which layer is routing implemented, enabling connections and path selection between two end systems?

4. Which layer defines how data is formatted, presented, encoded, and converted for use on the network?

5. Which layer is responsible for creating, managing, and terminating sessions between applications?

6. Which layer ensures the trustworthy transmission of data across a physical link and is primarily concerned with physical addressing, line discipline, network topology, error notification, ordered delivery of frames, and flow control?

7. Which layer is used for reliable communication between end nodes over the network and provides mechanisms for establishing, maintaining, and terminating virtual circuits; transport-fault detection and recovery; and controlling the flow of information?

8. Which layer provides logical addressing that routers will use for path determination?

9. Which layer specifies voltage, wire speed, and pinout cables and moves bits between devices?

10. Which layer combines bits into bytes and bytes into frames, uses MAC addressing, and provides error detection?

11. Which layer is responsible for keeping the data from different applications separate on the network?

12. Which layer is represented by frames?

13. Which layer is represented by segments?

14. Which layer is represented by packets?

15. Which layer is represented by bits?

16. Put the following in order of encapsulation:

 - Packets
 - Frames

- ▪ Bits
- ▪ Segments

17. Which layer segments and reassembles data into a data stream?

18. Which layer provides the physical transmission of the data and handles error notification, network topology, and flow control?

19. Which layer manages device addressing, tracks the location of devices on the network, and determines the best way to move data?

20. What is the bit length and expression form of a MAC address?

Written Lab 1.2: Defining the OSI Layers and Devices

Fill in the blanks with the appropriate layer of the OSI or hub, switch, or router device.

Description	Device or OSI Layer
This device sends and receives information about the Network layer.	
This layer creates a virtual circuit before transmitting between two end stations.	
This layer uses service access points.	
This device uses hardware addresses to filter a network.	
Ethernet is defined at these layers.	
This layer supports flow control and sequencing.	
This device can measure the distance to a remote network.	
Logical addressing is used at this layer.	
Hardware addresses are defined at this layer.	
This device creates one big collision domain and one large broadcast domain.	
This device creates many smaller collision domains, but the network is still one large broadcast domain.	
This device can never run full duplex.	
This device breaks up collision domains and broadcast domains.	

Written Lab 1.3: Identifying Collision and Broadcast Domains

In the following exhibit, identify the number of collision domains and broadcast domains in each specified device. Each device is represented by a letter:

A.   Hub

B.   Bridge

C.   Switch

D.   Router

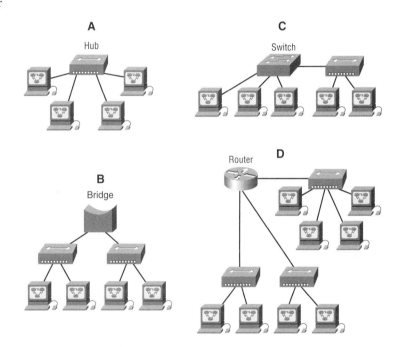

Written Lab 1.4: Binary/Decimal/Hexadecimal Conversion

1.   Convert from decimal IP address to binary format.

   Complete the following table to express 192.168.10.15 in binary format.

128	64	32	16	8	4	2	1	Binary

Complete the following table to express 172.16.20.55 in binary format.

128	64	32	16	8	4	2	1	Binary

Complete the following table to express 10.11.12.99 in binary format.

128	64	32	16	8	4	2	1	Binary

2. Convert the following from binary format to decimal IP address.

Complete the following table to express 11001100.00110011.10101010.01010101 in decimal IP address format.

128	64	32	16	8	4	2	1	Decimal

Complete the following table to express 11000110.11010011.00111001.11010001 in decimal IP address format.

128	64	32	16	8	4	2	1	Decimal

Complete the following table to express 10000100.11010010.10111000.10100110 in decimal IP address format.

128	64	32	16	8	4	2	1	Decimal

3. Convert the following from binary format to hexadecimal.

Complete the following table to express 11011000.00011011.00111101.01110110 in hexadecimal.

128	64	32	16	8	4	2	1	Hexadecimal

Complete the following table to express 11001010.11110101.10000011.11101011 in hexadecimal.

128	64	32	16	8	4	2	1	Hexadecimal

Complete the following table to express 10000100.11010010.01000011.10110011 in hexadecimal.

128	64	32	16	8	4	2	1	Hexadecimal

Review Questions

 The following questions are designed to test your understanding of this chapter's material. For more information on how to get additional questions, please see this book's Introduction.

1. A receiving host has failed to receive all of the segments that it should acknowledge. What can the host do to improve the reliability of this communication session?

    A. Send a different source port number.

    B. Restart the virtual circuit.

    C. Decrease the sequence number.

    D. Decrease the window size.

2. Which fields are contained within an IEEE Ethernet frame header? (Choose two.)

    A. Source and destination MAC address

    B. Source and destination network address

    C. Source and destination MAC address and source and destination network address

    D. FCS field

3. Which layer 1 devices can be used to enlarge the area covered by a single LAN segment? (Choose two.)

    A. Switch

    B. NIC

    C. Hub

    D. Repeater

    E. RJ45 transceiver

4. Segmentation of a data stream happens at which layer of the OSI model?

    A. Physical

    B. Data Link

    C. Network

    D. Transport

5. Which of the following describe router functions? (Choose four.)

    A. Packet switching

    B. Collision prevention

    C. Packet filtering

    D. Broadcast domain enlargement

    E. Internetwork communication

    F. Broadcast forwarding

    G. Path selection

6. Routers operate at layer __. LAN switches operate at layer __. Ethernet hubs operate at layer __. Word processing operates at layer __.

   A. 3, 3, 1, 7

   B. 3, 2, 1, none

   C. 3, 2, 1, 7

   D. 2, 3, 1, 7

   E. 3, 3, 2, none

7. When data is encapsulated, which is the correct order?

   A. Data, frame, packet, segment, bit

   B. Segment, data, packet, frame, bit

   C. Data, segment, packet, frame, bit

   D. Data, segment, frame, packet, bit

8. Why does the data communication industry use the layered OSI reference model? (Choose two.)

   A. It divides the network communication process into smaller and simpler components, thus aiding component development, design, and troubleshooting.

   B. It enables equipment from different vendors to use the same electronic components, thus saving research and development funds.

   C. It supports the evolution of multiple competing standards and thus provides business opportunities for equipment manufacturers.

   D. It encourages industry standardization by defining what functions occur at each layer of the model.

   E. It provides a framework by which changes in functionality in one layer require changes in other layers.

9. What are two purposes for segmentation with a bridge?

   A. To add more broadcast domains

   B. To create more collision domains

   C. To add more bandwidth for users

   D. To allow more broadcasts for users

10. Which of the following are unique characteristics of half-duplex Ethernet when compared to full-duplex Ethernet? (Choose two.)

   A. Half-duplex Ethernet operates in a shared collision domain.

   B. Half-duplex Ethernet operates in a private collision domain.

   C. Half-duplex Ethernet has higher effective throughput.

   D. Half-duplex Ethernet has lower effective throughput.

   E. Half-duplex Ethernet operates in a private broadcast domain.

11. You want to implement a network medium that is not susceptible to EMI. Which type of cabling should you use?

    A. Thicknet coax

    B. Thinnet coax

    C. Category 5 UTP cable

    D. Fiber-optic cable

12. Acknowledgments, sequencing, and flow control are characteristics of which OSI layer?

    A. Layer 2

    B. Layer 3

    C. Layer 4

    D. Layer 7

13. Which of the following are types of flow control? (Choose all that apply.)

    A. Buffering

    B. Cut-through

    C. Windowing

    D. Congestion avoidance

    E. VLANs

14. Which of the following types of connections can use full duplex? (Choose three.)

    A. Hub to hub

    B. Switch to switch

    C. Host to host

    D. Switch to hub

    E. Switch to host

15. What is the purpose of flow control?

    A. To ensure that data is retransmitted if an acknowledgment is not received

    B. To reassemble segments in the correct order at the destination device

    C. To provide a means for the receiver to govern the amount of data sent by the sender

    D. To regulate the size of each segment

16. Which three statements are true about the operation of a full-duplex Ethernet network?

    A. There are no collisions in full-duplex mode.

    B. A dedicated switch port is required for each full-duplex node.

    C. Ethernet hub ports are preconfigured for full-duplex mode.

    D. In a full-duplex environment, the host network card must check for the availability of the network media before transmitting.

    E. The host network card and the switch port must be capable of operating in full-duplex mode.

17. What type of RJ45 UTP cable is used between switches?

   A. Straight-through

   B. Crossover cable

   C. Crossover with a CSU/DSU

   D. Crossover with a router in between the two switches

18. How does a host on an Ethernet LAN know when to transmit after a collision has occurred? (Choose two.)

   A. In a CSMA/CD collision domain, multiple stations can successfully transmit data simultaneously.

   B. In a CSMA/CD collision domain, stations must wait until the media is not in use before transmitting.

   C. You can improve the CSMA/CD network by adding more hubs.

   D. After a collision, the station that detected the collision has first priority to resend the lost data.

   E. After a collision, all stations run a random backoff algorithm. When the backoff delay period has expired, all stations have equal priority to transmit data.

   F. After a collision, all stations involved run an identical backoff algorithm and then synchronize with each other prior to transmitting data.

19. What type of RJ45 UTP cable do you use to connect a PC's COM port to a router or switch console port?

   A. Straight-through

   B. Crossover cable

   C. Crossover with a CSU/DSU

   D. Rolled

20. You have the following binary number:

   10110111

   What are the decimal and hexadecimal equivalents?

   A. 69/0x2102

   B. 183/B7

   C. 173/A6

   D. 83/0xC5

Answers to Review Questions

1. D. A receiving host can control the transmitter by using flow control (TCP uses Windowing by default). By decreasing the window size, the receiving host can slow down the transmitting host so the receiving host does not overflow its buffers.

2. A, D. An Ethernet frame has source and destination MAC addresses, an Ether-Type field to identify the Network layer protocol, the data, and the FCS field that holds the answer to the CRC.

3. C, D. Not that you really want to enlarge a single collision domain, but a hub (multiport repeater) will provide this for you.

4. D. The Transport layer receives large data streams from the upper layers and breaks these up into smaller pieces called segments.

5. A, C, E, G. Routers provide packet switching, packet filtering, internetwork communication, and path selection.

6. B. Routers operate at layer 3. LAN switches operate at layer 2. Ethernet hubs operate at layer 1. Word processing applications communicate to the Application layer interface, but do not operate at layer 7, so the answer would be none.

7. C. The encapsulation method is data, segment, packet, frame, bit.

8. A, D. The main advantage of a layered model is that it can allow application developers to change aspects of a program in just one layer of the layer model's specifications. Advantages of using the OSI layered model include, but are not limited to, the following: It divides the network communication process into smaller and simpler components, thus aiding component development, design, and troubleshooting; it allows multiple-vendor development through standardization of network components; it encourages industry standardization by defining what functions occur at each layer of the model; it allows various types of network hardware and software to communicate; and it prevents changes in one layer from affecting other layers, so it does not hamper development.

9. B, C. Bridges break up collision domains, which allow more bandwidth for users.

10. A, D. Unlike full duplex, half-duplex Ethernet operates in a shared collision domain, and it has a lower effective throughput than full duplex.

11. D. Fiber-optic cable provides a more secure, long-distance cable that is not susceptible to EMI interference at high speeds.

12. C. A reliable Transport layer connection uses acknowledgments to make sure all data is transmitted and received reliably. A reliable connection is defined by a virtual circuit that uses acknowledgments, sequencing, and flow control, which are characteristics of the Transport layer (layer 4).

13. A, C, D. The common types of flow control are buffering, windowing, and congestion avoidance.

14. B, C, E. Hubs cannot run full-duplex Ethernet. Full duplex must be used on a point-to-point connection between two devices capable of running full duplex. Switches and hosts can run full duplex between each other, but a hub can never run full duplex.

15. C. Flow control allows the receiving device to control the transmitter so the receiving device's buffer does not overflow.

16. A, B, E. Full-duplex means you are using both wire pairs simultaneously to send and receive data. You must have a dedicated switch port for each node, which means you will not have collisions. Both the host network card and the switch port must be capable and set to work in full-duplex mode.

17. B. To connect two switches together, you would use a RJ45 UTP crossover cable.

18. B, E. Once transmitting stations on an Ethernet segment hear a collision, they send an extended jam signal to ensure that all stations recognize the collision. After the jamming is complete, each sender waits a predetermined amount of time, plus a random time. After both timers expire, they are free to transmit, but they must make sure the media is clear before transmitting and that they all have equal priority.

19. D. To connect to a router or switch console port, you would use an RJ45 UTP rolled cable.

20. B. You must be able to take a binary number and convert it into both decimal and hexadecimal. To convert to decimal, just add up the 1s using their values. The values that are turned on with the binary number of 10110111 are $128 + 32 + 16 + 4 + 2 + 1 = 183$. To get the hexadecimal equivalent, you need to break the eight binary digits into nibbles (4 bits), 1011 and 0111. By adding up these values, you get 11 and 7. In hexadecimal, 11 is B, so the answer is 0xB7.

Answers to Written Lab 1

1. The Application layer is responsible for finding the network resources broadcast from a server and adding flow control and error control (if the application developer chooses).

2. The Physical layer takes frames from the Data Link layer and encodes the 1s and 0s into a digital signal for transmission on the network medium.

3. The Network layer provides routing through an internetwork and logical addressing.

4. The Presentation layer makes sure that data is in a readable format for the Application layer.

5. The Session layer sets up, maintains, and terminates sessions between applications.

6. PDUs at the Data Link layer are called frames. As soon as you see *frame* in a question, you know the answer.

7. The Transport layer uses virtual circuits to create a reliable connection between two hosts.

8. The Network layer provides logical addressing, typically IP addressing and routing.

9. The Physical layer is responsible for the electrical and mechanical connections between devices.

10. The Data Link layer is responsible for the framing of data packets.

11. The Session layer creates sessions between different hosts' applications.

12. The Data Link layer frames packets received from the Network layer.

13. The Transport layer segments user data.

14. The Network layer creates packets out of segments handed down from the Transport layer.

15. The Physical layer is responsible for transporting 1s and 0s in a digital signal.

16. Segments, packets, frames, bits

17. Transport

18. Data Link

19. Network

20. 48 bits (6 bytes) expressed as a hexadecimal number

Answer to Written Lab 1.2

Description	Device or OSI Layer
This device sends and receives information about the Network layer.	Router
This layer creates a virtual circuit before transmitting between two end stations.	Transport
This layer uses service access points.	Data Link (LLC sublayer)
This device uses hardware addresses to filter a network.	Bridge or switch
Ethernet is defined at these layers.	Data Link and Physical
This layer supports flow control and sequencing.	Transport
This device can measure the distance to a remote network.	Router
Logical addressing is used at this layer.	Network
Hardware addresses are defined at this layer.	Data Link (MAC sublayer)
This device creates one big collision domain and one large broadcast domain.	Hub
This device creates many smaller collision domains, but the network is still one large broadcast domain.	Switch or bridge
This device can never run full duplex	Hub
This device breaks up collision domains and broadcast domains.	Router

Answers to Written Lab 1.3

1. Hub: One collision domain, one broadcast domain
2. Bridge: Two collision domains, one broadcast domain
3. Switch: Four collision domains, one broadcast domain
4. Router: Three collision domains, three broadcast domains

Answers to Written Lab 1.4

1. Convert from decimal IP address to binary format.

   Complete the following table to express 192.168.10.15 in binary format.

Decimal	128	64	32	16	8	4	2	1	Binary
192	1	1	0	0	0	0	0	0	11000000
168	1	0	1	0	1	0	0	0	10101000
10	0	0	0	0	1	0	1	0	00001010
15	0	0	0	0	1	1	1	1	00001111

   Complete the following table to express 172.16.20.55 in binary format.

Decimal	128	64	32	16	8	4	2	1	Binary
172ˇ	1	0	1	0	1	1	0	0	10101100
16	0	0	0	1	0	0	0	0	00010000
20	0	0	0	1	0	1	0	0	00010100
55	0	0	1	1	0	1	1	1	00110111

   Complete the following table to express 10.11.12.99 in binary format.

Decimal	128	64	32	16	8	4	2	1	Binary
10	0	0	0	0	1	0	1	0	00001010
11	0	0	0	0	1	0	1	1	00001011
12	0	0	0	0	1	1	0	0	00001100
99	0	1	1	0	0	0	1	1	01100011

2. Convert the following from binary format to decimal IP address.

   Complete the following table to express 11001100.00110011.10101010.01010101 in decimal IP address format.

Binary	128	64	32	16	8	4	2	1	Decimal
11001100	1	1	0	0	1	1	0	0	204
00110011	0	0	1	1	0	0	1	1	51
10101010	1	0	1	0	1	0	1	0	170
01010101	0	1	0	1	0	1	0	1	85

Complete the following table to express 11000110.11010011.00111001.11010001 in decimal IP address format.

Binary	128	64	32	16	8	4	2	1	Decimal
11000110	1	1	0	0	0	1	1	0	198
11010011	1	1	0	1	0	0	1	1	211
00111001	0	0	1	1	1	0	0	1	57
11010001	1	1	0	1	0	0	0	1	209

Complete the following table to express 10000100.11010010.10111000.10100110 in decimal IP address format.

Binary	128	64	32	16	8	4	2	1	Decimal
10000100	1	0	0	0	0	1	0	0	132
11010010	1	1	0	1	0	0	1	0	210
10111000	1	0	1	1	1	0	0	0	184
10100110	1	0	1	0	0	1	1	0	166

3. Convert the following from binary format to hexadecimal.

Complete the following table to express 11011000.00011011.00111101.01110110 in hexadecimal.

Binary	128	64	32	16	8	4	2	1	Hexadecimal
11011000	1	1	0	1	1	0	0	0	D8
00011011	0	0	0	1	1	0	1	1	1B
00111101	0	0	1	1	1	1	0	1	3D
01110110	0	1	1	1	0	1	1	0	76

Complete the following table to express 11001010.11110101.10000011.11101011 in hexadecimal.

Binary	128	64	32	16	8	4	2	1	Hexadecimal
11001010	1	1	0	0	1	0	1	0	CA
11110101	1	1	1	1	0	1	0	1	F5
10000011	1	0	0	0	0	0	1	1	83
11101011	1	1	1	0	1	0	1	1	EB

Complete the following table to express 10000100.11010010.01000011.10110011 in hexadecimal.

Binary	128	64	32	16	8	4	2	1	Hexadecimal
10000100	1	0	0	0	0	1	0	0	84
11010010	1	1	0	1	0	0	1	0	D2
01000011	0	1	0	0	0	0	1	1	43
10110011	1	0	1	1	0	0	1	1	B3

Chapter

2

Introduction to TCP/IP

THE CCNA EXAM TOPICS COVERED IN THIS CHAPTER INCLUDE THE FOLLOWING:

✓ **Describe how a network works**

    ▪ Describe the purpose and basic operation of the protocols in the OSI and TCP models

    ▪ Identify and correct common network problems at layers 1, 2, 3 and 7 using a layered model approach

✓ **Implement an IP addressing scheme and IP Services to meet network requirements in a medium-size Enterprise branch office network**

    ▪ Describe the operation and benefits of using private and public IP addressing

The *Transmission Control Protocol/Internet Protocol (TCP/IP)* suite was created by the Department of Defense (DoD) to ensure and preserve data integrity, as well as maintain communications in the event of catastrophic war. So it follows that if designed and implemented correctly, a TCP/IP network can be a truly dependable and resilient one. In this chapter, I'll cover the protocols of TCP/IP, and throughout this book, you'll learn how to create a marvelous TCP/IP network—using Cisco routers, of course.

We'll begin by taking a look at the DoD's version of TCP/IP and then compare this version and its protocols with the OSI reference model discussed in Chapter 1, "Internetworking."

Once you understand the protocols used at the various levels of the DoD model, I'll cover IP addressing and the different classes of addresses used in networks today.

 Subnetting will be covered in Chapter 3, "IP Subnetting, Variable Length Subnet Masks (VLSMs), and Troubleshooting TCP/IP."

Last, because broadcast addresses are so important to understanding IP addressing, as well as subnetting, and VLSM, an understanding of the various flavors of broadcast addresses is critical. I'll finish with the various types of broadcast addresses that you just must know.

Internet Protocol version 6 will not be discussed in this chapter; this chapter will focus solely on IPv4. IPv6 will be covered in Chapter 13, "IP Version 6 (IPv6)." Also, when discussing Internet Protocol Version 4, you'll see it written as just IP, not typically IPv4.

 For up-to-the-minute updates for this chapter, please see www.lammle.com and/or www.sybex.com.

TCP/IP and the DoD Model

The DoD model is basically a condensed version of the OSI model—it's composed of four, instead of seven, layers:

- Process/Application layer
- Host-to-Host layer
- Internet layer
- Network Access layer

Figure 2.1 shows a comparison of the DoD model and the OSI reference model. As you can see, the two are similar in concept, but each has a different number of layers with different names.

FIGURE 2.1   The DoD and OSI models

 When the different protocols in the IP stack are discussed, the layers of the OSI and DoD models are interchangeable. In other words, the Internet layer and the Network layer describe the same thing, as do the Host-to-Host layer and the Transport layer.

A vast array of protocols combine at the DoD model's *Process/Application layer* to integrate the various activities and duties spanning the focus of the OSI's corresponding top three layers (Application, Presentation, and Session). We'll be looking closely at those protocols in the next part of this chapter. The Process/Application layer defines protocols for node-to-node application communication and also controls user-interface specifications.

The *Host-to-Host layer* parallels the functions of the OSI's Transport layer, defining protocols for setting up the level of transmission service for applications. It tackles issues such as creating reliable end-to-end communication and ensuring the error-free delivery of data. It handles packet sequencing and maintains data integrity.

The *Internet layer* corresponds to the OSI's Network layer, designating the protocols relating to the logical transmission of packets over the entire network. It takes care of the addressing of hosts by giving them an IP (Internet Protocol) address, and it handles the routing of packets among multiple networks.

At the bottom of the DoD model, the *Network Access layer* monitors the data exchange between the host and the network. The equivalent of the Data Link and Physical layers of the OSI model, the Network Access layer oversees hardware addressing and defines protocols for the physical transmission of data.

The DoD and OSI models are alike in design and concept and have similar functions in similar layers. Figure 2.2 shows the TCP/IP protocol suite and how its protocols relate to the DoD model layers.

FIGURE 2.2   The TCP/IP protocol suite

DoD Model

In the following sections, we will look at the different protocols in more detail, starting with the Process/Application layer protocols.

The Process/Application Layer Protocols

In this section, I'll describe the different applications and services typically used in IP networks. The following protocols and applications are covered in this section:

- Telnet
- FTP
- TFTP
- NFS
- SMTP
- LPD
- X Window
- SNMP
- DNS
- DHCP/BootP

Telnet

Telnet is the chameleon of protocols—its specialty is terminal emulation. It allows a user on a remote client machine, called the Telnet client, to access the resources of another machine, the Telnet server. Telnet achieves this by pulling a fast one on the Telnet server and making the client machine appear as though it were a terminal directly attached to the local network. This projection is actually a software image—a virtual terminal that can interact with the chosen remote host.

These emulated terminals are of the text-mode type and can execute refined procedures such as displaying menus that give users the opportunity to choose options and access the applications on the duped server. Users begin a Telnet session by running the Telnet client software and then logging into the Telnet server.

File Transfer Protocol (FTP)

File Transfer Protocol (FTP) is the protocol that actually lets us transfer files, and it can accomplish this between any two machines using it. But FTP isn't just a protocol; it's also a program. Operating as a protocol, FTP is used by applications. As a program, it's employed by users to perform file tasks by hand. FTP also allows for access to both directories and files and can accomplish certain types of directory operations, such as relocating into different ones. FTP teams up with Telnet to transparently log you into the FTP server and then provides for the transfer of files.

Accessing a host through FTP is only the first step, though. Users must then be subjected to an authentication login that's probably secured with passwords and usernames implemented by system administrators to restrict access. You can get around this somewhat by adopting the username *anonymous*—though what you'll gain access to will be limited.

Even when employed by users manually as a program, FTP's functions are limited to listing and manipulating directories, typing file contents, and copying files between hosts. It can't execute remote files as programs.

Trivial File Transfer Protocol (TFTP)

Trivial File Transfer Protocol (TFTP) is the stripped-down, stock version of FTP, but it's the protocol of choice if you know exactly what you want and where to find it, plus it's so easy to use and it's fast too! It doesn't give you the abundance of functions that FTP does, though. TFTP has no directory-browsing abilities; it can do nothing but send and receive files. This compact little protocol also skimps in the data department, sending much smaller blocks of data than FTP, and there's no authentication as with FTP, so it's insecure. Few sites support it because of the inherent security risks.

Network File System (NFS)

Network File System (NFS) is a jewel of a protocol specializing in file sharing. It allows two different types of file systems to interoperate. It works like this: Suppose the NFS server software is running on an NT server and the NFS client software is running on a Unix host. NFS allows for a portion of the RAM on the NT server to transparently store Unix files, which can, in turn, be used by Unix users. Even though the NT file system and Unix file system are unlike—they have different case sensitivity, filename lengths, security, and so on—both Unix users and NT users can access that same file with their normal file systems, in their normal way.

Real World Scenario

When Should You Use FTP?

The folks at your San Francisco office needs a 50MB file emailed to them right away. What do you do? Most email servers would reject the email because they have size limits. Even if there's no size limit on the server, it still would take a while to send this big file to SF. FTP to the rescue!

If you need to give someone a large file or you need to get a large file from someone, FTP is a nice choice. Smaller files (less than 5MB) can just be sent via email if you have the bandwidth of DSL or a cable modem. However, most ISPs don't allow files larger then 5MB to be emailed, so FTP is an option you should consider if you are in need of sending and receiving large files. (Who isn't these days?) To use FTP, you will need to set up an FTP server on the Internet so that the files can be shared.

Besides, FTP is faster than email, which is another reason to use FTP for sending or receiving large files. In addition, because it uses TCP and is connection-oriented, if the session dies, FTP can sometimes start up where it left off. Try that with your email client!

Simple Mail Transfer Protocol (SMTP)

Simple Mail Transfer Protocol (SMTP), answering our ubiquitous call to email, uses a spooled, or queued, method of mail delivery. Once a message has been sent to a destination, the message is spooled to a device—usually a disk. The server software at the destination posts a vigil, regularly checking the queue for messages. When it detects them, it proceeds to deliver them to their destination. SMTP is used to send mail; POP3 is used to receive mail.

Line Printer Daemon (LPD)

The Line Printer Daemon (LPD) protocol is designed for printer sharing. The LPD, along with the Line Printer (LPR) program, allows print jobs to be spooled and sent to the network's printers using TCP/IP.

X Window

Designed for client/server operations, *X Window* defines a protocol for writing client/server applications based on a graphical user interface (GUI). The idea is to allow a program, called a client, to run on one computer and have it display things through a window server on another computer.

Simple Network Management Protocol (SNMP)

Simple Network Management Protocol (SNMP) collects and manipulates valuable network information. It gathers data by polling the devices on the network from a management station at fixed or random intervals, requiring them to disclose certain information. When all is well,

SNMP receives something called a *baseline*—a report delimiting the operational traits of a healthy network. This protocol can also stand as a watchdog over the network, quickly notifying managers of any sudden turn of events. These network watchdogs are called *agents*, and when aberrations occur, agents send an alert called a *trap* to the management station.

Domain Name Service (DNS)

Domain Name Service (DNS) resolves hostnames—specifically, Internet names, such as www.routersim.com. You don't have to use DNS; you can just type in the IP address of any device you want to communicate with. An IP address identifies hosts on a network and the Internet as well. However, DNS was designed to make our lives easier. Think about this: What would happen if you wanted to move your web page to a different service provider? The IP address would change and no one would know what the new one was. DNS allows you to use a domain name to specify an IP address. You can change the IP address as often as you want and no one will know the difference.

DNS is used to resolve a *fully qualified domain name (FQDN)*—for example, www.lammle .com or todd.lammle.com. An FQDN is a hierarchy that can logically locate a system based on its domain identifier.

If you want to resolve the name *todd*, you either must type in the FQDN of todd.lammle .com or have a device such as a PC or router add the suffix for you. For example, on a Cisco router, you can use the command ip domain-name lammle.com to append each request with the lammle.com domain. If you don't do that, you'll have to type in the FQDN to get DNS to resolve the name.

> An important thing to remember about DNS is that if you can ping a device with an IP address but cannot use its FQDN, then you might have some type of DNS configuration failure.

Dynamic Host Configuration Protocol (DHCP)/Bootstrap Protocol (BootP)

Dynamic Host Configuration Protocol (DHCP) assigns IP addresses to hosts. It allows easier administration and works well in small to even very large network environments. All types of hardware can be used as a DHCP server, including a Cisco router.

DHCP differs from BootP in that BootP assigns an IP address to a host but the host's hardware address must be entered manually in a BootP table. You can think of DHCP as a dynamic BootP. But remember that BootP is also used to send an operating system that a host can boot from. DHCP can't do that.

But there is a lot of information a DHCP server can provide to a host when the host is requesting an IP address from the DHCP server. Here's a list of the information a DHCP server can provide:

▪ IP address

▪ Subnet mask

- Domain name
- Default gateway (routers)
- DNS
- WINS information

A DHCP server can give us even more information than this, but the items in the list are the most common.

A client that sends out a DHCP Discover message in order to receive an IP address sends out a broadcast at both layer 2 and layer 3. The layer 2 broadcast is all *F*s in hex, which looks like this: FF:FF:FF:FF:FF:FF. The layer 3 broadcast is 255.255.255.255, which means all networks and all hosts. DHCP is connectionless, which means it uses User Datagram Protocol (UDP) at the Transport layer, also known as the Host-to-Host layer, which we'll talk about next.

In case you don't believe me, here's an example of output from my trusty Ethereal analyzer:

```
Ethernet II, Src: 192.168.0.3 (00:0b:db:99:d3:5e), Dst: Broadcast➡
 (ff:ff:ff:ff:ff:ff)
Internet Protocol, Src: 0.0.0.0 (0.0.0.0), Dst: 255.255.255.255➡
 (255.255.255.255)
```

The Data Link and Network layers are both sending out "all hands" broadcasts saying, "Help—I don't know my IP address!"

Broadcast addresses will be discussed in more detail at the end of this chapter.

The Host-to-Host Layer Protocols

The main purpose of the Host-to-Host layer is to shield the upper-layer applications from the complexities of the network. This layer says to the upper layer, "Just give me your data stream, with any instructions, and I'll begin the process of getting your information ready to send."

The following sections describe the two protocols at this layer:

- Transmission Control Protocol (TCP)
- User Datagram Protocol (UDP)

In addition, we'll look at some of the key host-to-host protocol concepts, as well as the port numbers.

Remember, this is still considered layer 4, and Cisco really likes the way layer 4 can use acknowledgments, sequencing, and flow control.

Transmission Control Protocol (TCP)

Transmission Control Protocol (TCP) takes large blocks of information from an application and breaks them into segments. It numbers and sequences each segment so that the destination's TCP stack can put the segments back into the order the application intended. After these segments are sent, TCP (on the transmitting host) waits for an acknowledgment of the receiving end's TCP virtual circuit session, retransmitting those that aren't acknowledged.

Before a transmitting host starts to send segments down the model, the sender's TCP stack contacts the destination's TCP stack to establish a connection. What is created is known as a *virtual circuit*. This type of communication is called *connection-oriented*. During this initial handshake, the two TCP layers also agree on the amount of information that's going to be sent before the recipient's TCP sends back an acknowledgment. With everything agreed upon in advance, the path is paved for reliable communication to take place.

TCP is a full-duplex, connection-oriented, reliable, and accurate protocol, but establishing all these terms and conditions, in addition to error checking, is no small task. TCP is very complicated and, not surprisingly, costly in terms of network overhead. And since today's networks are much more reliable than those of yore, this added reliability is often unnecessary.

TCP Segment Format

Since the upper layers just send a data stream to the protocols in the Transport layers, I'll demonstrate how TCP segments a data stream and prepares it for the Internet layer. When the Internet layer receives the data stream, it routes the segments as packets through an internetwork. The segments are handed to the receiving host's Host-to-Host layer protocol, which rebuilds the data stream to hand to the upper-layer applications or protocols.

Figure 2.3 shows the TCP segment format. The figure shows the different fields within the TCP header.

FIGURE 2.3   TCP segment format

The TCP header is 20 bytes long, or up to 24 bytes with options. You need to understand what each field in the TCP segment is:

Source port   The port number of the application on the host sending the data. (Port numbers will be explained a little later in this section.)

Destination port   The port number of the application requested on the destination host.

Sequence number   A number used by TCP that puts the data back in the correct order or retransmits missing or damaged data, a process called *sequencing*.

Acknowledgment number   The TCP octet that is expected next.

Header length   The number of 32-bit words in the TCP header. This indicates where the data begins. The TCP header (even one including options) is an integral number of 32 bits in length.

Reserved   Always set to zero.

Code bits   Control functions used to set up and terminate a session.

Window   The window size the sender is willing to accept, in octets.

Checksum   The cyclic redundancy check (CRC), because TCP doesn't trust the lower layers and checks everything. The CRC checks the header and data fields.

Urgent   A valid field only if the Urgent pointer in the code bits is set. If so, this value indicates the offset from the current sequence number, in octets, where the first segment of non-urgent data begins.

Options   May be 0 or a multiple of 32 bits, if any. What this means is that no options have to be present (option size of 0). However, if any options are used that do not cause the option field to total a multiple of 32 bits, padding of 0s must be used to make sure the data begins on a 32-bit boundary.

Data   Handed down to the TCP protocol at the Transport layer, which includes the upper-layer headers.

Let's take a look at a TCP segment copied from a network analyzer:

```
TCP - Transport Control Protocol
 Source Port:      5973
 Destination Port: 23
 Sequence Number:  1456389907
 Ack Number:       1242056456
 Offset:           5
 Reserved:         %000000
 Code:             %011000
     Ack is valid
     Push Request
 Window:           61320
 Checksum:         0x61a6
```

```
Urgent Pointer:   0
No TCP Options
TCP Data Area:
vL.5.+.5.+.5.+.5   76 4c 19 35 11 2b 19 35 11 2b 19 35 11
  2b 19 35 +. 11 2b 19
Frame Check Sequence: 0x0d00000f
```

Did you notice that everything I talked about earlier is in the segment? As you can see from the number of fields in the header, TCP creates a lot of overhead. Application developers may opt for efficiency over reliability to save overhead, so User Datagram Protocol was also defined at the Transport layer as an alternative.

User Datagram Protocol (UDP)

If you were to compare *User Datagram Protocol (UDP)* with TCP, the former is basically the scaled-down economy model that's sometimes referred to as a thin protocol. Like a thin person on a park bench, a thin protocol doesn't take up a lot of room—or in this case, much bandwidth on a network.

UDP doesn't offer all the bells and whistles of TCP either, but it does do a fabulous job of transporting information that doesn't require reliable delivery—and it does so using far fewer network resources. (UDP is covered thoroughly in Request for Comments 768.)

The Requests for Comments (RFCs) form a series of notes, started in 1969, about the Internet (originally the ARPAnet). The notes discuss many aspects of computer communication; they focus on networking protocols, procedures, programs, and concepts but also include meeting notes, opinion, and sometimes humor.

There are some situations in which it would definitely be wise for developers to opt for UDP rather than TCP. Remember the watchdog SNMP up there at the Process/Application layer? SNMP monitors the network, sending intermittent messages and a fairly steady flow of status updates and alerts, especially when running on a large network. The cost in overhead to establish, maintain, and close a TCP connection for each one of those little messages would reduce what would be an otherwise healthy, efficient network to a dammed-up bog in no time!

Another circumstance calling for UDP over TCP is when reliability is already handled at the Process/Application layer. Network File System (NFS) handles its own reliability issues, making the use of TCP both impractical and redundant. But ultimately, it's up to the application developer to decide whether to use UDP or TCP, not the user who wants to transfer data faster.

UDP does *not* sequence the segments and does not care in which order the segments arrive at the destination. But after that, UDP sends the segments off and forgets about them. It doesn't follow through, check up on them, or even allow for an acknowledgment of safe arrival—complete abandonment. Because of this, it's referred to as an unreliable protocol. This does not mean that UDP is ineffective, only that it doesn't handle issues of reliability.

Further, UDP doesn't create a virtual circuit, nor does it contact the destination before delivering information to it. Because of this, it's also considered a *connectionless* protocol. Since UDP assumes that the application will use its own reliability method, it doesn't use any. This gives an application developer a choice when running the Internet Protocol stack: TCP for reliability or UDP for faster transfers.

So if you're using Voice over IP (VoIP), for example, you really don't want to use UDP, because if the segments arrive out of order (very common in IP networks), they'll just be passed up to the next OSI (DoD) layer in whatever order they're received, resulting in some seriously garbled data. On the other hand, TCP sequences the segments so they get put back together in exactly the right order—something UDP just can't do.

UDP Segment Format

Figure 2.4 clearly illustrates UDP's markedly low overhead as compared to TCP's hungry usage. Look at the figure carefully—can you see that UDP doesn't use windowing or provide for acknowledgments in the UDP header?

FIGURE 2.4   UDP segment

It's important for you to understand what each field in the UDP segment is:

Source port   Port number of the application on the host sending the data

Destination port   Port number of the application requested on the destination host

Length   Length of UDP header and UDP data

Checksum   Checksum of both the UDP header and UDP data fields

Data   Upper-layer data

UDP, like TCP, doesn't trust the lower layers and runs its own CRC. Remember that the Frame Check Sequence (FCS) is the field that houses the CRC, which is why you can see the FCS information.

The following shows a UDP segment caught on a network analyzer:

```
UDP - User Datagram Protocol
 Source Port:      1085
 Destination Port: 5136
 Length:           41
 Checksum:         0x7a3c
```

```
UDP Data Area:
..Z......00 01 5a 96 00 01 00 00 00 00 00 11 0000 00
...C..2._C._C  2e 03 00 43 02 1e 32 0a 00 0a 00 80 43 00 80
Frame Check Sequence: 0x00000000
```

Notice that low overhead! Try to find the sequence number, ack number, and window size in the UDP segment. You can't because they just aren't there!

Key Concepts of Host-to-Host Protocols

Since you've seen both a connection-oriented (TCP) and connectionless (UDP) protocol in action, it would be good to summarize the two here. Table 2.1 highlights some of the key concepts that you should keep in mind regarding these two protocols. You should memorize this table.

TABLE 2.1   Key Features of TCP and UDP

TCP	UDP
Sequenced	Unsequenced
Reliable	Unreliable
Connection-oriented	Connectionless
Virtual circuit	Low overhead
Acknowledgments	No acknowledgment
Windowing flow control	No windowing or flow control

A telephone analogy could really help you understand how TCP works. Most of us know that before you speak to someone on a phone, you must first establish a connection with that other person—wherever they are. This is like a virtual circuit with the TCP protocol. If you were giving someone important information during your conversation, you might say, "You know?" or ask, "Did you get that?" Saying something like this is a lot like a TCP acknowledgment—it's designed to get you verification. From time to time (especially on cell phones), people also ask, "Are you still there?" They end their conversations with a "Goodbye" of some kind, putting closure on the phone call. TCP also performs these types of functions.

Alternately, using UDP is like sending a postcard. To do that, you don't need to contact the other party first. You simply write your message, address the postcard, and mail it. This is analogous to UDP's connectionless orientation. Since the message on the postcard is probably not a matter of life or death, you don't need an acknowledgment of its receipt. Similarly, UDP does not involve acknowledgments.

Let's take a look at another figure, one that includes TCP, UDP, and the applications associated to each protocol, Figure 2.5.

Port Numbers

TCP and UDP must use *port numbers* to communicate with the upper layers because they're what keep track of different conversations crossing the network simultaneously. Originating-source port numbers are dynamically assigned by the source host and will equal some number starting at 1024. 1023 and below are defined in RFC 3232 (or just see www.iana.org), which discusses what are called well-known port numbers.

Virtual circuits that don't use an application with a well-known port number are assigned port numbers randomly from a specific range instead. These port numbers identify the source and destination application or process in the TCP segment.

Figure 2.5 illustrates how both TCP and UDP use port numbers.

FIGURE 2.5   Port numbers for TCP and UDP

The different port numbers that can be used are explained next:

- Numbers below 1024 are considered well-known port numbers and are defined in RFC 3232.
- Numbers 1024 and above are used by the upper layers to set up sessions with other hosts and by TCP to use as source and destination addresses in the TCP segment.

In the following sections, we'll take a look at an analyzer output showing a TCP session.

TCP Session: Source Port

The following listing shows a TCP session captured with OmniPeek analyzer software:

```
TCP - Transport Control Protocol
  Source Port:      5973
  Destination Port: 23
  Sequence Number:  1456389907
  Ack Number:       1242056456
  Offset:           5
  Reserved:         %000000
  Code:             %011000
      Ack is valid
      Push Request
  Window:           61320
```

```
Checksum:           0x61a6
Urgent Pointer:     0
No TCP Options
TCP Data Area:
vL.5.+.5.+.5.+.5  76 4c 19 35 11 2b 19 35 11 2b 19 35 11
  2b 19 35 +. 11 2b 19
Frame Check Sequence: 0x0d00000f
```

Notice that the source host makes up the source port, which in this case is 5973. The destination port is 23, which is used to tell the receiving host the purpose of the intended connection (Telnet).

By looking at this session, you can see that the source host makes up the source port by using numbers from 1024 to 65535. But why does the source make up a port number? To differentiate between sessions with different hosts, my friend. How would a server know where information is coming from if it didn't have a different number from a sending host? TCP and the upper layers don't use hardware and logical addresses to understand the sending host's address as the Data Link and Network layer protocols do. Instead, they use port numbers. And it's easy to imagine the receiving host getting thoroughly confused if all the hosts used the same source port number to get to FTP!

TCP Session: Destination Port

You'll sometimes look at an analyzer and see that only the source port is above 1024 and the destination port is a well-known port, as shown in the following trace:

```
TCP - Transport Control Protocol
 Source Port:       1144
 Destination Port: 80 World Wide Web HTTP
 Sequence Number:   9356570
 Ack Number:        0
 Offset:            7
 Reserved:          %000000
 Code:              %000010
      Synch Sequence
 Window:            8192
 Checksum:          0x57E7
 Urgent Pointer:    0
 TCP Options:
  Option Type: 2 Maximum Segment Size
    Length:    4
    MSS:       536
  Option Type: 1 No Operation
  Option Type: 1 No Operation
  Option Type: 4
```

```
  Length:    2
  Opt Value:
 No More HTTP Data
Frame Check Sequence: 0x43697363
```

And sure enough, the source port is over 1024, but the destination port is 80, or HTTP service. The server, or receiving host, will change the destination port if it needs to.

In the preceding trace, a "syn" packet is sent to the destination device. The syn sequence is what's telling the remote destination device that it wants to create a session.

TCP Session: Syn Packet Acknowledgment

The next trace shows an acknowledgment to the syn packet:

```
TCP - Transport Control Protocol
 Source Port:       80 World Wide Web HTTP
 Destination Port: 1144
 Sequence Number:  2873580788
 Ack Number:       9356571
 Offset:           6
 Reserved:         %000000
 Code:             %010010
      Ack is valid
      Synch Sequence
 Window:           8576
 Checksum:         0x5F85
 Urgent Pointer:   0
 TCP Options:
  Option Type: 2 Maximum Segment Size
    Length:    4
    MSS:       1460
  No More HTTP Data
Frame Check Sequence: 0x6E203132
```

Notice the *Ack is valid*, which means that the source port was accepted and the device agreed to create a virtual circuit with the originating host.

And here again, you can see that the response from the server shows the source is 80 and the destination is the 1144 sent from the originating host—all's well.

Table 2.2 gives you a list of the typical applications used in the TCP/IP suite, their well-known port numbers, and the Transport layer protocols used by each application or process. It's important that you study and memorize this table.

Notice that DNS uses both TCP and UDP. Whether it opts for one or the other depends on what it's trying to do. Even though it's not the only application that can use both protocols, it's certainly one that you should remember in your studies.

TABLE 2.2   Key Protocols That Use TCP and UDP

TCP	UDP
Telnet 23	SNMP 161
SMTP 25	TFTP 69
HTTP 80	DNS 53
FTP 21	
DNS 53	
HTTPS 443	

What makes TCP reliable is sequencing, acknowledgments, and flow control (windowing). UDP does not have reliability.

The Internet Layer Protocols

In the DoD model, there are two main reasons for the Internet layer's existence: routing and providing a single network interface to the upper layers.

None of the other upper- or lower-layer protocols have any functions relating to routing—that complex and important task belongs entirely to the Internet layer. The Internet layer's second duty is to provide a single network interface to the upper-layer protocols. Without this layer, application programmers would need to write "hooks" into every one of their applications for each different Network Access protocol. This would not only be a pain in the neck, but it would lead to different versions of each application—one for Ethernet, another one for Token Ring, and so on. To prevent this, IP provides one single network interface for the upper-layer protocols. That accomplished, it's then the job of IP and the various Network Access protocols to get along and work together.

All network roads don't lead to Rome—they lead to IP. And all the other protocols at this layer, as well as all those at the upper layers, use it. Never forget that. All paths through the DoD model go through IP. The following sections describe the protocols at the Internet layer:

- Internet Protocol (IP)
- Internet Control Message Protocol (ICMP)
- Address Resolution Protocol (ARP)
- Reverse Address Resolution Protocol (RARP)
- Proxy ARP

Internet Protocol (IP)

Internet Protocol (IP) essentially is the Internet layer. The other protocols found here merely exist to support it. IP holds the big picture and could be said to "see all," in that it's aware of all the interconnected networks. It can do this because all the machines on the network have a software, or logical, address called an IP address, which I'll cover more thoroughly later in this chapter.

IP looks at each packet's address. Then, using a routing table, it decides where a packet is to be sent next, choosing the best path. The protocols of the Network Access layer at the bottom of the DoD model don't possess IP's enlightened scope of the entire network; they deal only with physical links (local networks).

Identifying devices on networks requires answering these two questions: Which network is it on? And what is its ID on that network? The first answer is the *software address*, or *logical address* (the correct street). The second answer is the hardware address (the correct mailbox). All hosts on a network have a logical ID called an IP address. This is the software, or logical, address and contains valuable encoded information, greatly simplifying the complex task of routing. (IP is discussed in RFC 791.)

IP receives segments from the Host-to-Host layer and fragments them into datagrams (packets) if necessary. IP then reassembles datagrams back into segments on the receiving side. Each datagram is assigned the IP address of the sender and of the recipient. Each router (layer 3 device) that receives a datagram makes routing decisions based on the packet's destination IP address.

Figure 2.6 shows an IP header. This will give you an idea of what the IP protocol has to go through every time user data is sent from the upper layers and is to be sent to a remote network.

FIGURE 2.6   IP header

The following fields make up the IP header:

Version   IP version number.

Header length   Header length (HLEN) in 32-bit words.

Priority and Type of Service   Type of Service tells how the datagram should be handled. The first 3 bits are the priority bits.

Total length   Length of the packet including header and data.

Identification   Unique IP-packet value.

Flags   Specifies whether fragmentation should occur.

Fragment offset   Provides fragmentation and reassembly if the packet is too large to put in a frame. It also allows different maximum transmission units (MTUs) on the Internet.

Time to Live   The time to live is set into a packet when it is originally generated. If it doesn't get to where it wants to go before the TTL expires, boom—it's gone. This stops IP packets from continuously circling the network looking for a home.

Protocol   Port of upper-layer protocol (TCP is port 6 or UDP is port 17 [hex]). Also supports Network layer protocols, like ARP and ICMP. Can be called Type field in some analyzers. We'll talk about this field in more detail in a minute.

Header checksum   Cyclic redundancy check (CRC) on header only.

Source IP address   32-bit IP address of sending station.

Destination IP address   32-bit IP address of the station this packet is destined for.

Options   Used for network testing, debugging, security, and more.

Data   After the IP option field will be the upper-layer data.

Here's a snapshot of an IP packet caught on a network analyzer (notice that all the header information discussed previously appears here):

```
IP Header - Internet Protocol Datagram
 Version:               4
 Header Length:         5
 Precedence:            0
 Type of Service:       %000
 Unused:                %00
 Total Length:          187
 Identifier:            22486
 Fragmentation Flags:   %010 Do Not Fragment
 Fragment Offset:       0
 Time To Live:          60
 IP Type:               0x06 TCP
 Header Checksum:       0xd031
 Source IP Address:     10.7.1.30
```

```
Dest. IP Address:      10.7.1.10
No Internet Datagram Options
```

The Type field—it's typically a Protocol field, but this analyzer sees it as an IP Type field—is important. If the header didn't carry the protocol information for the next layer, IP wouldn't know what to do with the data carried in the packet. The preceding example tells IP to hand the segment to TCP.

Figure 2.7 demonstrates how the Network layer sees the protocols at the Transport layer when it needs to hand a packet to the upper-layer protocols.

FIGURE 2.7   The Protocol field in an IP header

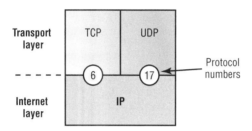

In this example, the Protocol field tells IP to send the data to either TCP port 6 or UDP port 17 (both hex addresses). But it will only be UDP or TCP if the data is part of a data stream headed for an upper-layer service or application. It could just as easily be destined for Internet Control Message Protocol (ICMP), Address Resolution Protocol (ARP), or some other type of Network layer protocol.

Table 2.3 is a list of some other popular protocols that can be specified in the Protocol field.

TABLE 2.3   Possible Protocols Found in the Protocol Field of an IP Header

Protocol	Protocol Number
ICMP	1
IP in IP (tunneling)	4
IGRP	9
EIGRP	88
OSPF	89
IPv6	41
GRE	47
Layer 2 tunnel (L2TP)	115

You can find a complete list of protocol field numbers at www.iana.org/assignments/protocol-numbers.

Internet Control Message Protocol (ICMP)

Internet Control Message Protocol (ICMP) works at the Network layer and is used by IP for many different services. ICMP is a management protocol and messaging service provider for IP. Its messages are carried as IP datagrams. RFC 1256 is an annex to ICMP, which affords host's extended capability in discovering routes to gateways.

ICMP packets have the following characteristics:

- They can provide hosts with information about network problems.
- They are encapsulated within IP datagrams.

The following are some common events and messages that ICMP relates to:

Destination Unreachable If a router can't send an IP datagram any further, it uses ICMP to send a message back to the sender, advising it of the situation. For example, take a look at Figure 2.8, which shows that interface E0 of the Lab_B router is down.

FIGURE 2.8 ICMP error message is sent to the sending host from the remote router.

E0 on Lab B is down. Host A is trying to communicate to Host B. What happens?

When Host A sends a packet destined for Host B, the Lab_B router will send an ICMP destination unreachable message back to the sending device (Host A in this example).

Buffer Full If a router's memory buffer for receiving incoming datagrams is full, it will use ICMP to send out this message until the congestion abates.

Hops Each IP datagram is allotted a certain number of routers, called hops, to pass through. If it reaches its limit of hops before arriving at its destination, the last router to receive that datagram deletes it. The executioner router then uses ICMP to send an obituary message, informing the sending machine of the demise of its datagram.

Ping   Packet Internet Groper (Ping) uses ICMP echo request and reply messages to check the physical and logical connectivity of machines on an internetwork.

Traceroute   Using ICMP time-outs, Traceroute is used to discover the path a packet takes as it traverses an internetwork.

 Both Ping and Traceroute (also just called Trace; Microsoft Windows uses tracert) allow you to verify address configurations in your internetwork.

The following data is from a network analyzer catching an ICMP echo request:

```
Flags:          0x00
 Status:         0x00
 Packet Length: 78
 Timestamp:      14:04:25.967000 12/20/03
Ethernet Header
 Destination: 00:a0:24:6e:0f:a8
 Source:        00:80:c7:a8:f0:3d
 Ether-Type:  08-00 IP
IP Header - Internet Protocol Datagram
 Version:             4
 Header Length:       5
 Precedence:          0
 Type of Service:     %000
 Unused:              %00
 Total Length:        60
 Identifier:          56325
 Fragmentation Flags: %000
 Fragment Offset:     0
 Time To Live:        32
 IP Type:             0x01 ICMP
 Header Checksum:     0x2df0
 Source IP Address:   100.100.100.2
 Dest. IP Address:    100.100.100.1
 No Internet Datagram Options
ICMP - Internet Control Messages Protocol
 ICMP Type:       8 Echo Request
 Code:            0
 Checksum:        0x395c
 Identifier:      0x0300
 Sequence Number: 4352
```

```
ICMP Data Area:
abcdefghijklmnop  61 62 63 64 65 66 67 68 69 6a 6b 6c 6d
qrstuvwabcdefghi  71 72 73 74 75 76 77 61 62 63 64 65 66
Frame Check Sequence: 0x00000000
```

Notice anything unusual? Did you catch the fact that even though ICMP works at the Internet (Network) layer, it still uses IP to do the Ping request? The Type field in the IP header is 0x01, which specifies that the data we're carrying is owned by the ICMP protocol. Remember, just as all roads lead to Rome, all segments or data *must* go through IP!

The Ping program uses the alphabet in the data portion of the packet as just a payload, 100 bytes by default, unless, of course, you are pinging from a Windows device, which thinks the alphabet stops at the letter *W* and doesn't' include *X*, *Y*, or *Z* and then starts at *A* again. Go figure!

If you remember reading about the Data Link layer and the different frame types in Chapter 1, you should be able to look at the preceding trace and tell what type of Ethernet frame this is. The only fields are destination hardware address, source hardware address, and Ether-Type. The only frame that uses an Ether-Type field exclusively is an Ethernet_II frame.

But before we get into the ARP protocol, let's take another look at ICMP in action. Figure 2.9 shows an internetwork (it has a router, so it's an internetwork, right?).

FIGURE 2.9   ICMP in action

Server1 (10.1.2.2) telnets to 10.1.1.5 from a DOS prompt. What do you think Server1 will receive as a response? Since Server1 will send the Telnet data to the default gateway, which is the router, the router will drop the packet because there isn't a network 10.1.1.0 in the routing table. Because of this, Server1 will receive a destination unreachable back from ICMP.

Address Resolution Protocol (ARP)

Address Resolution Protocol (ARP) finds the hardware address of a host from a known IP address. Here's how it works: When IP has a datagram to send, it must inform a Network Access protocol, such as Ethernet or Token Ring, of the destination's hardware address on the local network. (It has already been informed by upper-layer protocols of the destination's IP address.) If IP doesn't find the destination host's hardware address in the ARP cache, it uses ARP to find this information.

As IP's detective, ARP interrogates the local network by sending out a broadcast asking the machine with the specified IP address to reply with its hardware address. So basically, ARP translates the software (IP) address into a hardware address—for example, the destination machine's Ethernet board address—and from it, deduces its whereabouts on the LAN by broadcasting for this address. Figure 2.10 shows how an ARP looks to a local network.

 ARP resolves IP addresses to Ethernet (MAC) addresses.

FIGURE 2.10   Local ARP broadcast

The following trace shows an ARP broadcast—notice that the destination hardware address is unknown and is all *F*s in hex (all 1s in binary)—and is a hardware address broadcast:

```
Flags:        0x00
Status:       0x00
```

```
Packet Length: 64
Timestamp:       09:17:29.574000 12/06/03
Ethernet Header
 Destination:    FF:FF:FF:FF:FF:FF Ethernet Broadcast
 Source:         00:A0:24:48:60:A5
 Protocol Type: 0x0806 IP ARP
ARP - Address Resolution Protocol
 Hardware:                   1 Ethernet (10Mb)
 Protocol:                   0x0800 IP
 Hardware Address Length: 6
 Protocol Address Length: 4
 Operation:                  1 ARP Request
 Sender Hardware Address: 00:A0:24:48:60:A5
 Sender Internet Address: 172.16.10.3
 Target Hardware Address: 00:00:00:00:00:00 (ignored)
 Target Internet Address: 172.16.10.10
Extra bytes (Padding):
 ............... 0A 0A 0A 0A 0A 0A 0A 0A 0A 0A 0A 0A 0A
  0A 0A 0A 0A 0A
Frame Check Sequence: 0x00000000
```

Reverse Address Resolution Protocol (RARP)

When an IP machine happens to be a diskless machine, it has no way of initially knowing its IP address. But it does know its MAC address. *Reverse Address Resolution Protocol (RARP)* discovers the identity of the IP address for diskless machines by sending out a packet that includes its MAC address and a request for the IP address assigned to that MAC address. A designated machine, called a *RARP server*, responds with the answer and the identity crisis is over. RARP uses the information it does know about the machine's MAC address to learn its IP address and complete the machine's ID portrait.

Figure 2.11 shows a diskless workstation asking for its IP address with a RARP broadcast.

RARP resolves Ethernet (MAC) addresses to IP addresses.

Proxy Address Resolution Protocol (Proxy ARP)

On a network, your hosts can't have more then one default gateway configured. Think about this...What if the default gateway (router) happens to go down? The host won't just start sending to another router automatically—you've got to reconfigure that host. But Proxy ARP can actually help machines on a subnet reach remote subnets without configuring routing or even a default gateway.

FIGURE 2.11   RARP broadcast example

One advantage of using Proxy ARP is that it can be added to a single router on a network without disturbing the routing tables of all the other routers that live there too. But there's a serious downside to using Proxy ARP. Using Proxy ARP will definitely increase the amount of traffic on your network segment, and hosts will have a larger ARP table than usual in order to handle all the IP-to-MAC-address mappings. And Proxy ARP is configured on all Cisco routers by default—you should disable it if you don't think you're going to use it.

One last thought on Proxy ARP: Proxy ARP isn't really a separate protocol. It is a service run by routers on behalf of other devices (usually PC's) that are separated from their query to another device by a router, although they think they share the subnet with the remote device.

If you can afford it, use Cisco's Hot Standby Router Protocol (HSRP) instead. It means you have to buy two or more of your Cisco device(s), but it is well worth it. Check out the Cisco website for more information on HSRP.

IP Addressing

One of the most important topics in any discussion of TCP/IP is IP addressing. An *IP address* is a numeric identifier assigned to each machine on an IP network. It designates the specific location of a device on the network.

An IP address is a software address, not a hardware address—the latter is hard-coded on a network interface card (NIC) and used for finding hosts on a local network. IP addressing was designed to allow hosts on one network to communicate with a host on a different network regardless of the type of LANs the hosts are participating in.

Before we get into the more complicated aspects of IP addressing, you need to understand some of the basics. First I'm going to explain some of the fundamentals of IP addressing and its terminology. Then you'll learn about the hierarchical IP addressing scheme and private IP addresses.

IP Terminology

Throughout this chapter you'll learn several important terms vital to your understanding of the Internet Protocol. Here are a few to get you started:

Bit   A *bit* is one digit, either a 1 or a 0.

Byte   A *byte* is 7 or 8 bits, depending on whether parity is used. For the rest of this chapter, always assume a byte is 8 bits.

Octet   An octet, made up of 8 bits, is just an ordinary 8-bit binary number. In this chapter, the terms *byte* and *octet* are completely interchangeable.

Network address   This is the designation used in routing to send packets to a remote network—for example, 10.0.0.0, 172.16.0.0, and 192.168.10.0.

Broadcast address   The address used by applications and hosts to send information to all nodes on a network is called the *broadcast address*. Examples include 255.255.255.255, which is all networks, all nodes; 172.16.255.255, which is all subnets and hosts on network 172.16.0.0; and 10.255.255.255, which broadcasts to all subnets and hosts on network 10.0.0.0.

The Hierarchical IP Addressing Scheme

An IP address consists of 32 bits of information. These bits are divided into four sections, referred to as *octets* or bytes, each containing 1 byte (8 bits). You can depict an IP address using one of three methods:

- Dotted-decimal, as in 172.16.30.56

- Binary, as in 10101100.00010000.00011110.00111000

- Hexadecimal, as in AC.10.1E.38

All these examples truly represent the same IP address. Hexadecimal isn't used as often as dotted-decimal or binary when IP addressing is discussed, but you still might find an IP address stored in hexadecimal in some programs. The Windows Registry is a good example of a program that stores a machine's IP address in hex.

The 32-bit IP address is a structured or hierarchical address, as opposed to a flat or nonhierarchical address. Although either type of addressing scheme could have been used, *hierarchical addressing* was chosen for a good reason. The advantage of this scheme is that it can handle a large number of addresses, namely 4.3 billion (a 32-bit address space with two possible values for each position—either 0 or 1—gives you 2^{32}, or 4,294,967,296). The disadvantage of the flat addressing scheme, and the reason it's not used for IP addressing, relates to routing. If every address were unique, all routers on the Internet would need to store the address of each and every machine on the Internet. This would make efficient routing impossible, even if only a fraction of the possible addresses were used.

The solution to this problem is to use a two- or three-level hierarchical addressing scheme that is structured by network and host or by network, subnet, and host.

This two- or three-level scheme is comparable to a telephone number. The first section, the area code, designates a very large area. The second section, the prefix, narrows the scope to a local calling area. The final segment, the customer number, zooms in on the specific connection. IP addresses use the same type of layered structure. Rather than all 32 bits being treated as a unique identifier, as in flat addressing, a part of the address is designated as the network address and the other part is designated as either the subnet and host or just the node address.

In the following sections, I'm going to discuss IP network addressing and the different classes of address we can use to address our networks.

Network Addressing

The *network address* (which can also be called the network number) uniquely identifies each network. Every machine on the same network shares that network address as part of its IP address. In the IP address 172.16.30.56, for example, 172.16 is the network address.

The *node address* is assigned to, and uniquely identifies, each machine on a network. This part of the address must be unique because it identifies a particular machine—an individual—as opposed to a network, which is a group. This number can also be referred to as a *host address*. In the sample IP address 172.16.30.56, the 30.56 is the node address.

The designers of the Internet decided to create classes of networks based on network size. For the small number of networks possessing a very large number of nodes, they created the rank *Class A network*. At the other extreme is the *Class C network*, which is reserved for the numerous networks with a small number of nodes. The class distinction for networks between very large and very small is predictably called the *Class B network*.

Subdividing an IP address into a network and node address is determined by the class designation of one's network. Figure 2.12 summarizes the three classes of networks—a subject I'll explain in much greater detail throughout this chapter.

FIGURE 2.12   Summary of the three classes of networks

	8 bits	8 bits	8 bits	8 bits
Class A:	Network	Host	Host	Host
Class B:	Network	Network	Host	Host
Class C:	Network	Network	Network	Host
Class D:	Multicast			
Class E:	Research			

To ensure efficient routing, Internet designers defined a mandate for the leading-bits section of the address for each different network class. For example, since a router knows that a Class A network address always starts with a 0, the router might be able to speed a packet on its way after reading only the first bit of its address. This is where the address schemes define the difference between a Class A, a Class B, and a Class C address. In the next sections, I'll discuss the differences between these three classes, followed by a discussion of the Class D and Class E addresses (Classes A, B, and C are the only ranges that are used to address hosts in our networks).

Network Address Range: Class A

The designers of the IP address scheme said that the first bit of the first byte in a Class A network address must always be off, or 0. This means a Class A address must be between 0 and 127 in the first byte, inclusive.

Consider the following network address:

0xxxxxxx

If we turn the other 7 bits all off and then turn them all on, we'll find the Class A range of network addresses:

00000000 = 0
01111111 = 127

So, a Class A network is defined in the first octet between 0 and 127, and it can't be less or more. (Yes, I know 0 and 127 are not valid in a Class A network. I'll talk about reserved addresses in a minute.)

Network Address Range: Class B

In a Class B network, the RFCs state that the first bit of the first byte must always be turned on but the second bit must always be turned off. If you turn the other 6 bits all off and then all on, you will find the range for a Class B network:

10000000 = 128
10111111 = 191

As you can see, a Class B network is defined when the first byte is configured from 128 to 191.

Network Address Range: Class C

For Class C networks, the RFCs define the first 2 bits of the first octet as always turned on, but the third bit can never be on. Following the same process as the previous classes, convert from binary to decimal to find the range. Here's the range for a Class C network:

11000000 = 192
11011111 = 223

So, if you see an IP address that starts at 192 and goes to 223, you'll know it is a Class C IP address.

Network Address Ranges: Classes D and E

The addresses between 224 to 255 are reserved for Class D and E networks. Class D (224–239) is used for multicast addresses and Class E (240–255) for scientific purposes, but I'm not going into these types of addresses in this book (and you don't need to know them).

Network Addresses: Special Purpose

Some IP addresses are reserved for special purposes, so network administrators can't ever assign these addresses to nodes. Table 2.4 lists the members of this exclusive little club and the reasons why they're included in it.

TABLE 2.4   Reserved IP Addresses

Address	Function
Network address of all 0s	Interpreted to mean "this network or segment."
Network address of all 1s	Interpreted to mean "all networks."
Network 127.0.0.1	Reserved for loopback tests. Designates the local node and allows that node to send a test packet to itself without generating network traffic.
Node address of all 0s	Interpreted to mean "network address" or any host on specified network.
Node address of all 1s	Interpreted to mean "all nodes" on the specified network; for example, 128.2.255.255 means "all nodes" on network 128.2 (Class B address).
Entire IP address set to all 0s	Used by Cisco routers to designate the default route. Could also mean "any network."
Entire IP address set to all 1s (same as 255.255.255.255)	Broadcast to all nodes on the current network; sometimes called an "all 1s broadcast" or limited broadcast.

Class A Addresses

In a Class A network address, the first byte is assigned to the network address and the three remaining bytes are used for the node addresses. The Class A format is as follows:

network.*node*.*node*.*node*

For example, in the IP address 49.22.102.70, the 49 is the network address and 22.102.70 is the node address. Every machine on this particular network would have the distinctive network address of 49.

Class A network addresses are 1 byte long, with the first bit of that byte reserved and the 7 remaining bits available for manipulation (addressing). As a result, the maximum number of Class A networks that can be created is 128. Why? Because each of the 7 bit positions can be either a 0 or a 1, thus 2^7, or 128.

To complicate matters further, the network address of all 0s (0000 0000) is reserved to designate the default route (see Table 2.4 in the previous section). Additionally, the address 127, which is reserved for diagnostics, can't be used either, which means that you can really only use the numbers 1 to 126 to designate Class A network addresses. This means the actual number of usable Class A network addresses is 128 minus 2, or 126.

 The IP address 127.0.0.1 is used to test the IP stack on an individual node and cannot be used as a valid host address.

Each Class A address has 3 bytes (24-bit positions) for the node address of a machine. This means there are 2^{24}—or 16,777,216—unique combinations and, therefore, precisely that many possible unique node addresses for each Class A network. Because node addresses with the two patterns of all 0s and all 1s are reserved, the actual maximum usable number of nodes for a Class A network is 2^{24} minus 2, which equals 16,777,214. Either way, that's a huge amount of hosts on a network segment!

Class A Valid Host IDs

Here's an example of how to figure out the valid host IDs in a Class A network address:

- All host bits off is the network address: 10.0.0.0.
- All host bits on is the broadcast address: 10.255.255.255.

The valid hosts are the numbers in between the network address and the broadcast address: 10.0.0.1 through 10.255.255.254. Notice that 0s and 255s can be valid host IDs. All you need to remember when trying to find valid host addresses is that the host bits can't all be turned off or all be on at the same time.

Class B Addresses

In a Class B network address, the first 2 bytes are assigned to the network address and the remaining 2 bytes are used for node addresses. The format is as follows:

network.network.node.node

For example, in the IP address 172.16.30.56, the network address is 172.16 and the node address is 30.56.

With a network address being 2 bytes (8 bits each), there would be 2^{16} unique combinations. But the Internet designers decided that all Class B network addresses should start with the binary digit 1, then 0. This leaves 14 bit positions to manipulate, therefore 16,384 (that is, 2^{14}) unique Class B network addresses.

A Class B address uses 2 bytes for node addresses. This is 2^{16} minus the two reserved patterns (all 0s and all 1s), for a total of 65,534 possible node addresses for each Class B network.

Class B Valid Host IDs

Here's an example of how to find the valid hosts in a Class B network:

- All host bits turned off is the network address: 172.16.0.0.
- All host bits turned on is the broadcast address: 172.16.255.255.

The valid hosts would be the numbers in between the network address and the broadcast address: 172.16.0.1 through 172.16.255.254.

Class C Addresses

The first 3 bytes of a Class C network address are dedicated to the network portion of the address, with only 1 measly byte remaining for the node address. Here's the format:

network.network.network.node

Using the example IP address 192.168.100.102, the network address is 192.168.100 and the node address is 102.

In a Class C network address, the first three bit positions are always the binary 110. The calculation is as follows: 3 bytes, or 24 bits, minus 3 reserved positions leaves 21 positions. Hence, there are 2^{21}, or 2,097,152, possible Class C networks.

Each unique Class C network has 1 byte to use for node addresses. This leads to 2^8 or 256, minus the two reserved patterns of all 0s and all 1s, for a total of 254 node addresses for each Class C network.

Class C Valid Host IDs

Here's an example of how to find a valid host ID in a Class C network:

- All host bits turned off is the network ID: 192.168.100.0.
- All host bits turned on is the broadcast address: 192.168.100.255.

The valid hosts would be the numbers in between the network address and the broadcast address: 192.168.100.1 through 192.168.100.254.

Private IP Addresses

The people who created the IP addressing scheme also created what we call private IP addresses. These addresses can be used on a private network, but they're not routable through the Internet. This is designed for the purpose of creating a measure of well-needed security, but it also conveniently saves valuable IP address space.

If every host on every network had to have real routable IP addresses, we would have run out of IP addresses to hand out years ago. But by using private IP addresses, ISPs, corporations, and home users only need a relatively tiny group of bona fide IP addresses to connect their networks to the Internet. This is economical because they can use private IP addresses on their inside networks and get along just fine.

To accomplish this task, the ISP and the corporation—the end user, no matter who they are—need to use something called *Network Address Translation (NAT)*, which basically takes a private IP address and converts it for use on the Internet. (NAT is covered in Chapter 11, "Network Address Translation.") Many people can use the same real IP address to transmit out onto the Internet. Doing things this way saves megatons of address space—good for us all!

Real World Scenario

So, What Private IP Address Should I Use?

That's a really great question: Should you use Class A, Class B, or even Class C private addressing when setting up your network? Let's take Acme Corporation in SF as an example. This company is moving into a new building and needs a whole new network (what a treat this is!). It has 14 departments, with about 70 users in each. You could probably squeeze one or two Class C addresses to use, or maybe you could use a Class B, or even a Class A just for fun.

The rule of thumb in the consulting world is, when you're setting up a corporate network—regardless of how small it is—you should use a Class A network address because it gives you the most flexibility and growth options. For example, if you used the 10.0.0.0 network address with a /24 mask, then you'd have 65,536 networks, each with 254 hosts. Lots of room for growth with that network!

But if you're setting up a home network, you'd opt for a Class C address because it is the easiest for people to understand and configure. Using the default Class C mask gives you one network with 254 hosts—plenty for a home network.

With the Acme Corporation, a nice 10.1.*x*.0 with a /24 mask (the *x* is the subnet for each department) makes this easy to design, install, and troubleshoot.

The reserved private addresses are listed in Table 2.5.

TABLE 2.5 Reserved IP Address Space

Address Class	Reserved Address Space
Class A	10.0.0.0 through 10.255.255.255
Class B	172.16.0.0 through 172.31.255.255
Class C	192.168.0.0 through 192.168.255.255

You must know your private address space!

Broadcast Addresses

Most people use the term *broadcast* as a generic term, and most of the time, we understand what they mean. But not always. For example, you might say, "The host broadcasted through a router to a DHCP server," but, well, it's pretty unlikely that this would ever really happen. What you probably mean—using the correct technical jargon—is, "The host broadcasted for an IP address; a router then forwarded this as a unicast packet to the DHCP server." Oh, and remember that with IPv4, broadcasts are pretty important, but with IPv6, there aren't any broadcasts sent at all—now there's something to get you excited about when you get to Chapter 13!

Okay, I've referred to broadcast addresses throughout Chapters 1 and 2, and even showed you some examples. But I really haven't gone into the different terms and uses associated with them yet, and it's about time I did. So here are the four different broadcast (generic term *broadcast*) types that I'd like to define for you:

Layer 2 broadcasts   These are sent to all nodes on a LAN.

Broadcasts (layer 3)   These are sent to all nodes on the network.

Unicast   These are sent to a single destination host.

Multicast   These are packets sent from a single source and transmitted to many devices on different networks.

First, understand that layer 2 broadcasts are also known as hardware broadcasts—they only go out on a LAN, and they don't go past the LAN boundary (router). The typical hardware address is 6 bytes (48 bits) and looks something like 0c.43.a4.f3.12.c2. The broadcast would be all 1s in binary, which would be all *F*s in hexadecimal, as in FF.FF.FF.FF.FF.FF.

Then there's the plain old broadcast addresses at layer 3. Broadcast messages are meant to reach all hosts on a broadcast domain. These are the network broadcasts that have all host bits on. Here's an example that you're already familiar with: The network address of 172.16.0.0 255.255.0.0 would have a broadcast address of 172.16.255.255—all host bits on. Broadcasts can also be "all networks and all hosts," as indicated by 255.255.255.255. A good example of a broadcast message is an Address Resolution Protocol (ARP) request. When a host has a packet, it knows the logical address (IP) of the destination. To get the packet to the destination, the host needs to forward the packet to a default gateway if the destination resides on a different IP network. If the destination is on the local network, the source will forward the packet directly to the destination. Because the source doesn't have the MAC address to which it needs to forward the frame, it sends out a broadcast, something that every device in the local broadcast domain will listen to. This broadcast says, in essence, "If you are the owner of IP address 192.168.2.3, please forward your MAC address to me," with the source giving the appropriate information.

A unicast is different because it's a broadcast packet that goes from 255.255.255.255 to an actual destination IP address—in other words, it's directed to a specific host. A DHCP client request is a good example of how a unicast works. Here's an example: Your host on a LAN sends out an FF.FF.FF.FF.FF.FF layer 2 broadcast and 255.255.255.255 layer 3 destination broadcast looking for a DHCP server on the LAN. The router will see that this is a broadcast meant for the DHCP server because it has a destination port number of 67 (BootP server) and will forward the request to the IP address of the DHCP server on another LAN. So, basically, if your DHCP server IP address is 172.16.10.1, your host just sends out a 255.255.255.255 DHCP client broadcast request, and the router changes that broadcast to the specific destination address of 172.16.10.1. (In order for the router to provide this service, you need to configure the interfaces with the `ip helper-address` command—this is not a default service.)

Multicast is a different beast entirely. At first glance, it appears to be a hybrid of unicast and broadcast communication, but that isn't quite the case. Multicast does allow point-to-multipoint communication, which is similar to broadcasts, but it happens in a different manner. The crux of *multicast* is that it enables multiple recipients to receive messages without flooding the messages to all hosts on a broadcast domain.

Multicast works by sending messages or data to IP *multicast group* addresses. Routers then forward copies (unlike broadcasts, which are not forwarded) of the packet out every interface that has hosts *subscribed* to that group address. This is where multicast differs from broadcast messages—with multicast communication, copies of packets, in theory, are sent only to subscribed hosts. When I say in theory, this means that the hosts will receive, for example, a multicast packet destined for 224.0.0.9 (this is an EIGRP packet and only a router running the EIGRP protocol will read these). All hosts on the broadcast LAN (Ethernet is a broadcast multi-access LAN technology) will pick up the frame, read the destination address, and immediately discard the frame, unless they are in the multicast group. This saves PC processing, not LAN bandwidth. Multicasting can cause severe LAN congestion, in some instances, if not implemented carefully.

There are several different groups that users or applications can subscribe to. The range of multicast addresses starts with 224.0.0.0 and goes through 239.255.255.255. As you can see, this range of addresses falls within IP Class D address space based on classful IP assignment.

Summary

If you made it this far and understood everything the first time through, you should be proud of yourself. We really covered a lot of ground in this chapter, but understand that the information in this chapter is key to being able to navigate through the rest of this book. And even if you didn't get a complete understanding the first time around, don't stress. It really wouldn't hurt you to read this chapter more than once. There is still a lot of ground to cover, so make sure you've got it all down, and get ready for more. What we're doing is building a foundation, and you want a strong foundation, right?

After you learned about the DoD model, the layers, and associated protocols, you learned about the oh-so-important IP addressing. I discussed in detail the difference between each class of address and how to find a network address, broadcast address, and valid host range, which is critical information to understand before going on to Chapter 3.

Since you've already come this far, there's no reason to stop now and waste all those brainwaves and new neurons. So don't stop—go through the written lab and review questions at the end of this chapter and make sure you understand each answer's explanation. The best is yet to come!

Exam Essentials

Remember the Process/Application layer protocols.   Telnet is a terminal emulation program that allows you to log into a remote host and run programs. File Transfer Protocol (FTP) is a connection-oriented service that allows you to transfer files. Trivial FTP (TFTP) is a connectionless file transfer program. Simple Mail Transfer Protocol (SMTP) is a send-mail program.

Remember the Host-to-Host layer protocols.   Transmission Control Protocol (TCP) is a connection-oriented protocol that provides reliable network service by using acknowledgments and flow control. User Datagram Protocol (UDP) is a connectionless protocol that provides low overhead and is considered unreliable.

Remember the Internet layer protocols.   Internet Protocol (IP) is a connectionless protocol that provides network address and routing through an internetwork. Address Resolution Protocol (ARP) finds a hardware address from a known IP address. Reverse ARP (RARP) finds an IP address from a known hardware address. Internet Control Message Protocol (ICMP) provides diagnostics and destination unreachable messages.

Remember the Class A range.   The IP range for a Class A network is 1–126. This provides 8 bits of network addressing and 24 bits of host addressing by default.

Remember the Class B range.   The IP range for a Class B network is 128–191. Class B addressing provides 16 bits of network addressing and 16 bits of host addressing by default.

Remember the Class C range.   The IP range for a Class C network is 192–223. Class C addressing provides 24 bits of network addressing and 8 bits of host addressing by default.

Remember the Private IP ranges.   Class A private address range is 10.0.0.0 through 10.255.255.255.

Class B private address range is 172.16.0.0 through 172.31.255.255.

Class C private address range is 192.168.0.0 through 192.168.255.255.

Written Lab 2

Answer the following questions about TCP/IP:

1. What is the Class C address range in decimal and in binary?
2. What layer of the DoD model is equivalent to the Transport layer of the OSI model?
3. What is the valid range of a Class A network address?
4. What is the 127.0.0.1 address used for?
5. How do you find the network address from a listed IP address?
6. How do you find the broadcast address from a listed IP address?
7. What is the Class A private IP address space?

8. What is the Class B private IP address space?

9. What is the Class C private IP address space?

10. What are all the available characters that you can use in hexadecimal addressing?

(The answers to Written Lab 2 can be found following the answers to the review questions for this chapter.)

Review Questions

NOTE   The following questions are designed to test your understanding of this chapter's material. For more information on how to get additional questions, please see this book's Introduction.

1. What are the decimal and hexadecimal equivalents of the binary number 10011101? (Choose two.)

   A. 159

   B. 157

   C. 185

   D. 0x9D

   E. 0xD9

   F. 0x159

2. Which of the following allows a router to respond to an ARP request that is intended for a remote host?

   A. Gateway DP

   B. Reverse ARP (RARP)

   C. Proxy ARP

   D. Inverse ARP (IARP)

   E. Address Resolution Protocol (ARP)

3. You want to implement a mechanism that automates the IP configuration, including IP address, subnet mask, default gateway, and DNS information. Which protocol will you use to accomplish this?

   A. SMTP

   B. SNMP

   C. DHCP

   D. ARP

4. What protocol is used to find the hardware address of a local device?

   A. RARP

   B. ARP

   C. IP

   D. ICMP

   E. BootP

5. Which of the following are layers in the TCP/IP model? (Choose three.)

   A. Application

   B. Session

   C. Transport

   D. Internet

   E. Data Link

   F. Physical

6. Which class of IP address provides a maximum of only 254 host addresses per network ID?

   A. Class A

   B. Class B

   C. Class C

   D. Class D

   E. Class E

7. Which of the following describe the DHCP Discover message? (Choose two.)

   A. It uses FF:FF:FF:FF:FF:FF as a layer 2 broadcast.

   B. It uses UDP as the Transport layer protocol.

   C. It uses TCP as the Transport layer protocol.

   D. It does not use a layer 2 destination address.

8. Which layer 4 protocol is used for a Telnet connection?

   A. IP

   B. TCP

   C. TCP/IP

   D. UDP

   E. ICMP

9. Which statements are true regarding ICMP packets? (Choose two.)

   A. They acknowledge receipt of a TCP segment.

   B. They guarantee datagram delivery.

   C. They can provide hosts with information about network problems.

   D. They are encapsulated within IP datagrams.

   E. They are encapsulated within UDP datagrams.

10. Which of the following services use TCP? (Choose three.)

    A. DHCP

    B. SMTP

    C. SNMP

    D. FTP

    E. HTTP

    F. TFTP

11. Which of the following services use UDP? (Choose three.)

   A. DHCP

   B. SMTP

   C. SNMP

   D. FTP

   E. HTTP

   F. TFTP

12. Which of the following are TCP/IP protocols used at the Application layer of the OSI model? (Choose three.)

   A. IP

   B. TCP

   C. Telnet

   D. FTP

   E. TFTP

13. The following illustration shows a data structure header. What protocol is this header from?

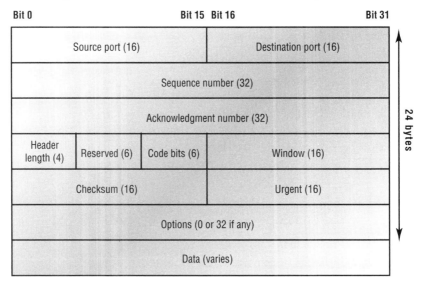

   A. IP

   B. ICMP

   C. TCP

   D. UDP

   E. ARP

   F. RARP

14. If you use either Telnet or FTP, which is the highest layer you are using to transmit data?

    A. Application

    B. Presentation

    C. Session

    D. Transport

15. The DoD model (also called the TCP/IP stack) has four layers. Which layer of the DoD model is equivalent to the Network layer of the OSI model?

    A. Application

    B. Host-to-Host

    C. Internet

    D. Network Access

16. Which two of the following are private IP addresses?

    A. 12.0.0.1

    B. 168.172.19.39

    C. 172.20.14.36

    D. 172.33.194.30

    E. 192.168.24.43

17. What layer in the TCP/IP stack is equivalent to the Transport layer of the OSI model?

    A. Application

    B. Host-to-Host

    C. Internet

    D. Network Access

18. Which statements are true regarding ICMP packets? (Choose two)

    A. ICMP guarantees datagram delivery.

    B. ICMP can provide hosts with information about network problems.

    C. ICMP is encapsulated within IP datagrams.

    D. ICMP is encapsulated within UDP datagrams.

19. What is the address range of a Class B network address in binary?

    A. 01*xxxxxx*

    B. 0*xxxxxxx*

    C. 10*xxxxxx*

    D. 110*xxxxx*

20. Which of the following protocols uses both TCP and UDP?

    A. FTP

    B. SMTP

    C. Telnet

    D. DNS

Answers to Review Questions

1. B, D. To turn a binary number into decimal, you just have to add the values of each bit that is a 1. The values of 10011101 are 128, 16, 8, 4, and 1. 128 + 16 + 8 + 4 + 1 = 157. Hexadecimal is a base-16 number system. The values of hexadecimal are 0, 1, 2, 3, 4, 5, 6, 7, 8, 9, A, B, C, D, E, F—16 characters total, from which to create all the numbers you'll ever need. So, if 1001 in binary is 9, then the hexadecimal equivalent is 9. Since we then have 1101, which is 13 in binary, the hexadecimal answer is D and the complete hexadecimal answer is 0x9D. Even though binary/hex numbers were discussed in Chapter 1, a good review is necessary here.

2. C. Proxy ARP can help machines on a subnet reach remote subnets without configuring routing or a default gateway.

3. C. Dynamic Host Configuration Protocol (DHCP) is used to provide IP information to hosts on your network. DHCP can provide a lot of information, but the most common is IP address, subnet mask, default gateway, and DNS information.

4. B. Address Resolution Protocol (ARP) is used to find the hardware address from a known IP address.

5. A, C, D. This seems like a hard question at first because it doesn't make sense. The listed answers are from the OSI model and the question asked about the TCP/IP protocol stack (DoD model). However, let's just look for what is wrong. First, the Session layer is not in the TCP/IP model; neither are the Data Link and Physical layers. This leaves us with the Transport layer (Host-to-Host in the DoD model), Internet layer (Network layer in the OSI), and Application layer (Application/Process in the DoD).

6. C. A Class C network address has only 8 bits for defining hosts: $2^8 - 2 = 254$.

7. A, B. A client that sends out a DHCP Discover message in order to receive an IP address sends out a broadcast at both layer 2 and layer 3. The layer 2 broadcast is all Fs in hex, or FF:FF:FF:FF:FF:FF. The layer 3 broadcast is 255.255.255.255, which means all networks and all hosts. DHCP is connectionless, which means it uses User Datagram Protocol (UDP) at the Transport layer, also called the Host-to-Host layer.

8. B. Although Telnet does use TCP and IP (TCP/IP), the question specifically asks about layer 4, and IP works at layer 3. Telnet uses TCP at layer 4.

9. C, D. Internet Control Message Protocol (ICMP) is used to send error messages through the network, but they do not work alone. Every segment or ICMP payload must be encapsulated within an IP datagram (or packet).

10. B, D, E. SMTP, FTP, and HTTP use TCP.

11. A, C, F. Explanation:DHCP, SNMP, and TFTP use UDP. SMTP, FTP, and HTTP use TCP.

12. C, D, E. Telnet, File Transfer Protocol (FTP), and Trivial FTP (TFTP) are all Application layer protocols. IP is a Network layer protocol. Transmission Control Protocol (TCP) is a Transport layer protocol.

13. C. First, you should know easily that only TCP and UDP work at the Transport layer, so now you have a 50/50 shot. However, since the header has sequencing, acknowledgment, and window numbers, the answer can only be TCP.

14. A. Both FTP and Telnet use TCP at the Transport layer; however, they both are Application layer protocols, so the Application layer is the best answer for this question.

15. C. The four layers of the DoD model are Application/Process, Host-to-Host, Internet, and Network Access. The Internet layer is equivalent to the Network layer of the OSI model.

16. C, E. Class A private address range is 10.0.0.0 through 10.255.255.255. Class B private address range is 172.16.0.0 through 172.31.255.255, and Class C private address range is 192.168.0.0 through 192.168.255.255.

17. B. The four layers of the TCP/IP stack (also called the DoD model) are Application/Process, Host-to-Host, Internet, and Network Access. The Host-to-Host layer is equivalent to the Transport layer of the OSI model.

18. B, C. ICMP is used for diagnostics and destination unreachable messages. ICMP is encapsulated within IP datagrams, and because it is used for diagnostics, it will provide hosts with information about network problems.

19. C. The range of a Class B network address is 128–191. This makes our binary range 10xxxxxx.

20. D. DNS uses TCP for zone exchanges between servers and UDP when a client is trying to resolve a hostname to an IP address.

Answers to Written Lab 2

1. 192–223, 110*xxxxx*
2. Host-to-Host
3. 1–126
4. Loopback or diagnostics
5. Turn all host bits off.
6. Turn all host bits on.
7. 10.0.0.0 through 10.255.255.255
8. 172.16.0.0 through 172.31.255.255
9. 192.168.0.0 through 192.168.255.255
10. 0–9 and *A*, *B*, *C*, *D*, *E*, and *F*

Chapter

3

Subnetting, Variable Length Subnet Masks (VLSMs), and Troubleshooting TCP/IP

THE CCNA EXAM TOPICS COVERED IN THIS CHAPTER INCLUDE THE FOLLOWING:

✓ **Describe how a network works**

- Interpret network

✓ **Implement an IP addressing scheme and IP Services to meet network requirements in a medium-size Enterprise branch office network**

- Describe the operation and benefits of using private and public IP addressing

- Implement static and dynamic addressing services for hosts in a LAN environment

- Calculate and apply an addressing scheme including VLSM IP addressing design to a network

- Determine the appropriate classless addressing scheme using VLSM and summarization to satisfy addressing requirements in a LAN/WAN environment

- Identify and correct common problems associated with IP addressing and host configurations

This chapter will pick up right where we left off in the last chapter. We will continue our discussion of IP addressing.

We'll start with subnetting an IP network. You're going to have to really apply yourself, because subnetting takes time and practice in order to nail it. So be patient. Do whatever it takes to get this stuff dialed in. This chapter truly is important—possibly the most important chapter in this book for you to understand.

I'll thoroughly cover IP subnetting from the very beginning. I know this might sound weird to you, but I think you'll be much better off if you can try to forget everything you've learned about subnetting before reading this chapter—especially if you've been to a Microsoft class!

After our discussion of IP subnetting, I'm going to tell you all about Variable Length Subnet Masks (VLSMs), as well as show you how to design and implement a network using VLSM networks.

Once you have mastered VLSM design and implementation, I'll show you how to summarize classful boundaries. We'll go into this further in Chapter 7, "Enhanced IGRP (EIGRP) and Open Shortest Path First (OSPF)," where I'll demonstrate summarizing using EIGRP and OSPF routing protocols.

I'll wrap up the chapter by going over IP address troubleshooting and take you through the steps Cisco recommends when troubleshooting an IP network.

So get psyched—you're about to go for quite a ride! This chapter will truly help you understand IP addressing and networking, so don't get discouraged or give up. If you stick with it, I promise that one day you'll look back on this and you'll be really glad you decided to hang on. It's one of those things that after you understand it, you'll wonder why you once thought it was so hard. Ready? Let's go!

For up-to-the-minute updates for this chapter, please see www.lammle.com and/or www.sybex.com.

Subnetting Basics

In Chapter 2, you learned how to define and find the valid host ranges used in a Class A, Class B, and Class C network address by turning the host bits all off and then all on. This is very good, but here's the catch: You were defining only one network. What happens if you wanted to take one network address and create six networks from it? You would have to do something called *subnetting*, because that's what allows you to take one larger network and break it into a bunch of smaller networks.

There are loads of reasons in favor of subnetting, including the following benefits:

Reduced network traffic   We all appreciate less traffic of any kind. Networks are no different. Without trusty routers, packet traffic could grind the entire network down to a near standstill. With routers, most traffic will stay on the local network; only packets destined for other networks will pass through the router. Routers create broadcast domains. The more broadcast domains you create, the smaller the broadcast domains and the less network traffic on each network segment.

Optimized network performance   This is a result of reduced network traffic.

Simplified management   It's easier to identify and isolate network problems in a group of smaller connected networks than within one gigantic network.

Facilitated spanning of large geographical distances   Because WAN links are considerably slower and more expensive than LAN links, a single large network that spans long distances can create problems in every area previously listed. Connecting multiple smaller networks makes the system more efficient.

In the following sections, I am going to move to subnetting a network address. This is the good part—ready?

IP Subnet-Zero

IP subnet-zero is not a new command, but in the past, Cisco courseware, and Cisco exam objectives, didn't cover it—but it certainly does now! This command allows you to use the first and last subnet in your network design. For example, the Class C mask of 192 provides subnets 64 and 128 (discussed thoroughly later in this chapter), but with the ip subnet-zero command, you now get to use subnets 0, 64, 128, and 192. That is two more subnets for every subnet mask we use.

Even though we don't discuss the command line interface (CLI) until the next chapter, "Cisco's Internetworking Operating System (IOS) and Security Device Manager (SDM)," it's important for you to be familiar with this command:

```
P1R1#sh running-config
Building configuration...
Current configuration : 827 bytes
!
hostname Pod1R1
!
ip subnet-zero
!
```

This router output shows that the command ip subnet-zero is enabled on the router. Cisco has turned this command on by default starting with Cisco IOS version 12.*x*.

When studying for your Cisco exams, make sure you read very carefully and understand if Cisco is asking you *not* to use ip subnet-zero. There are instances where this may happen.

How to Create Subnets

To create subnetworks, you take bits from the host portion of the IP address and reserve them to define the subnet address. This means fewer bits for hosts, so the more subnets, the fewer bits available for defining hosts.

Later in this chapter, you'll learn how to create subnets, starting with Class C addresses. But before you actually implement subnetting, you need to determine your current requirements as well as plan for future conditions.

Before we move on to designing and creating a subnet mask, you need to understand that in this first section, we will be discussing classful routing, which means that all hosts (all nodes) in the network use the exact same subnet mask. When we move on to Variable Length Subnet Masks (VLSMs), I'll discuss classless routing, which means that each network segment *can* use a different subnet mask.

To create a subnet follow these steps:

1. Determine the number of required network IDs:
   - One for each subnet
   - One for each wide area network connection

2. Determine the number of required host IDs per subnet:
   - One for each TCP/IP host
   - One for each router interface

3. Based on the above requirements, create the following:
   - One subnet mask for your entire network
   - A unique subnet ID for each physical segment
   - A range of host IDs for each subnet

Understanding the Powers of 2

Powers of 2 are important to understand and memorize for use with IP subnetting. To review powers of 2, remember that when you see a number with another number to its upper right (called an exponent), this means you should multiply the number by itself as many times as the upper number specifies. For example, 2^3 is $2 \times 2 \times 2$, which equals 8. Here's a list of powers of 2 that you should commit to memory:

$2^1 = 2$

$2^2 = 4$

$2^3 = 8$

$2^4 = 16$

$2^5 = 32$

$2^6 = 64$

$2^7 = 128$

$2^8 = 256$

$2^9 = 512$

$2^{10} = 1,024$

$2^{11} = 2,048$

$2^{12} = 4,096$

$2^{13} = 8,192$

$2^{14} = 16,384$

Before you get stressed out about knowing all these exponents, remember that it's helpful to know them, but it's not absolutely necessary. Here's a little trick since you're working with 2s: Each successive power of 2 is double the previous one.

For example, all you have to do to remember the value of 2^9 is to first know that $2^8 = 256$. Why? Because when you double 2 to the eighth power (256), you get 2^9 (or 512). To determine the value of 2^{10}, simply start at $2^8 = 256$, and then double it twice.

You can go the other way as well. If you needed to know what 2^6 is, for example, you just cut 256 in half two times: once to reach 2^7 and then one more time to reach 2^6.

Subnet Masks

For the subnet address scheme to work, every machine on the network must know which part of the host address will be used as the subnet address. This is accomplished by assigning a *subnet mask* to each machine. A subnet mask is a 32-bit value that allows the recipient of IP packets to distinguish the network ID portion of the IP address from the host ID portion of the IP address.

The network administrator creates a 32-bit subnet mask composed of 1s and 0s. The 1s in the subnet mask represent the positions that refer to the network or subnet addresses.

Not all networks need subnets, meaning they use the default subnet mask. This is basically the same as saying that a network doesn't have a subnet address. Table 3.1 shows the default subnet masks for Classes A, B, and C. These default masks cannot change. In other words, you can't make a Class B subnet mask read 255.0.0.0. If you try, the host will read that address as invalid and usually won't even let you type it in. For a Class A network, you can't change the first byte in a subnet mask; it must read 255.0.0.0 at a minimum. Similarly, you cannot assign 255.255.255.255, as this is all 1s—a broadcast address. A Class B address must start with 255.255.0.0, and a Class C has to start with 255.255.255.0.

TABLE 3.1   Default Subnet Mask

Class	Format	Default Subnet Mask
A	*network.node.node.node*	255.0.0.0
B	*network.network.node.node*	255.255.0.0
C	*network.network.network.node*	255.255.255.0

Classless Inter-Domain Routing (CIDR)

Another term you need to familiarize yourself with is *Classless Inter-Domain Routing (CIDR)*. It's basically the method that ISPs (Internet service providers) use to allocate a number of addresses to a company, a home—a customer. They provide addresses in a certain block size, something I'll be going into in greater detail later in this chapter.

When you receive a block of addresses from an ISP, what you get will look something like this: 192.168.10.32/28. This is telling you what your subnet mask is. The slash notation (/) means how many bits are turned on (1s). Obviously, the maximum could only be /32 because a byte is 8 bits and there are 4 bytes in an IP address: (4 × 8 = 32). But keep in mind that the largest subnet mask available (regardless of the class of address) can only be a /30 because you've got to keep at least 2 bits for host bits.

Take, for example, a Class A default subnet mask, which is 255.0.0.0. This means that the first byte of the subnet mask is all ones (1s), or 11111111. When referring to a slash notation, you need to count all the 1s bits to figure out your mask. The 255.0.0.0 is considered a /8 because it has 8 bits that are 1s—that is, 8 bits that are turned on.

A Class B default mask would be 255.255.0.0, which is a /16 because 16 bits are ones (1s): 11111111.11111111.00000000.00000000.

Table 3.2 has a listing of every available subnet mask and its equivalent CIDR slash notation.

TABLE 3.2   CIDR Values

Subnet Mask	CIDR Value
255.0.0.0	/8
255.128.0.0	/9
255.192.0.0	/10
255.224.0.0	/11
255.240.0.0	/12

TABLE 3.2   CIDR Values *(continued)*

Subnet Mask	CIDR Value
255.248.0.0	/13
255.252.0.0	/14
255.254.0.0	/15
255.255.0.0	/16
255.255.128.0	/17
255.255.192.0	/18
255.255.224.0	/19
255.255.240.0	/20
255.255.248.0	/21
255.255.252.0	/22
255.255.254.0	/23
255.255.255.0	/24
255.255.255.128	/25
255.255.255.192	/26
255.255.255.224	/27
255.255.255.240	/28
255.255.255.248	/29
255.255.255.252	/30

The /8 through /15 can only be used with Class A network addresses. /16 through /23 can be used by Class A and B network addresses. /24 through /30 can be used by Class A, B, and C network addresses. This is a big reason why most companies use Class A network addresses. Since they can use all subnet masks, they get the maximum flexibility in network design.

No, you cannot configure a Cisco router using this slash format. But wouldn't that be nice? Nevertheless, it's *really* important for you to know subnet masks in the slash notation (CIDR).

Subnetting Class C Addresses

There are many different ways to subnet a network. The right way is the way that works best for you. In a Class C address, only 8 bits are available for defining the hosts. Remember that subnet bits start at the left and go to the right, without skipping bits. This means that the only Class C subnet masks can be the following:

```
Binary      Decimal  CIDR
--------------------------------------------------------
00000000 = 0         /24
10000000 = 128       /25
11000000 = 192       /26
11100000 = 224       /27
11110000 = 240       /28
11111000 = 248       /29
11111100 = 252       /30
```

We can't use a /31 or /32 because we have to have at least 2 host bits for assigning IP addresses to hosts. In the past, I never discussed the /25 in a Class C network. Cisco always had been concerned with having at least 2 subnet bits, but now, because of Cisco recognizing the `ip subnet-zero` command in its curriculum and exam objectives, we can use just 1 subnet bit.

In the following sections, I'm going to teach you an alternate method of subnetting that makes it easier to subnet larger numbers in no time. Trust me, you need to be able to subnet fast!

Subnetting a Class C Address: The Fast Way!

When you've chosen a possible subnet mask for your network and need to determine the number of subnets, valid hosts, and broadcast addresses of a subnet that the mask provides, all you need to do is answer five simple questions:

- How many subnets does the chosen subnet mask produce?
- How many valid hosts per subnet are available?
- What are the valid subnets?
- What's the broadcast address of each subnet?
- What are the valid hosts in each subnet?

At this point, it's important that you both understand and have memorized your powers of 2. Please refer to the sidebar "Understanding the Powers of 2" earlier in this chapter if you need some help. Here's how you get the answers to those five big questions:

- *How many subnets?* 2^x = number of subnets. x is the number of masked bits, or the 1s. For example, in 11000000, the number of 1s gives us 2^2 subnets. In this example, there are 4 subnets.

- *How many hosts per subnet?* $2^y - 2$ = number of hosts per subnet. y is the number of unmasked bits, or the 0s. For example, in 11000000, the number of 0s gives us $2^6 - 2$ hosts. In this example, there are 62 hosts per subnet. You need to subtract 2 for the subnet address and the broadcast address, which are not valid hosts.

- *What are the valid subnets?* 256 − subnet mask = block size, or increment number. An example would be 256 − 192 = 64. The block size of a 192 mask is always 64. Start counting at zero in blocks of 64 until you reach the subnet mask value and these are your subnets. 0, 64, 128, 192. Easy, huh?

- *What's the broadcast address for each subnet?* Now here's the really easy part. Since we counted our subnets in the last section as 0, 64, 128, and 192, the broadcast address is always the number right before the next subnet. For example, the 0 subnet has a broadcast address of 63 because the next subnet is 64. The 64 subnet has a broadcast address of 127 because the next subnet is 128. And so on. And remember, the broadcast address of the last subnet is always 255.

- *What are the valid hosts?* Valid hosts are the numbers between the subnets, omitting the all 0s and all 1s. For example, if 64 is the subnet number and 127 is the broadcast address, then 65–126 is the valid host range—it's *always* the numbers between the subnet address and the broadcast address.

I know this can truly seem confusing. But it really isn't as hard as it seems to be at first—just hang in there! Why not try a few and see for yourself?

Subnetting Practice Examples: Class C Addresses

Here's your opportunity to practice subnetting Class C addresses using the method I just described. Exciting, isn't it! We're going to start with the first Class C subnet mask and work through every subnet that we can using a Class C address. When we're done, I'll show you how easy this is with Class A and B networks too!

Practice Example #1C: 255.255.255.128 (/25)

Since 128 is 10000000 in binary, there is only 1 bit for subnetting and 7 bits for hosts. We're going to subnet the Class C network address 192.168.10.0.

192.168.10.0 = Network address

255.255.255.128 = Subnet mask

Now, let's answer the big five:

- *How many subnets?* Since 128 is 1 bit on (1**0000000**), the answer would be $2^1 = 2$.

- *How many hosts per subnet?* We have 7 host bits off (1**0000000**), so the equation would be $2^7 - 2 = 126$ hosts.

- *What are the valid subnets?* 256 – 128 = 128. Remember, we'll start at zero and count in our block size, so our subnets are 0, 128.

- *What's the broadcast address for each subnet?* The number right before the value of the next subnet is all host bits turned on and equals the broadcast address. For the zero subnet, the next subnet is 128, so the broadcast of the 0 subnet is 127.

- *What are the valid hosts?* These are the numbers between the subnet and broadcast address. The easiest way to find the hosts is to write out the subnet address and the broadcast address. This way, the valid hosts are obvious. The following table shows the 0 and 128 subnets, the valid host ranges of each, and the broadcast address of both subnets:

Subnet	0	128
First host	1	129
Last host	126	254
Broadcast	127	255

Before moving on to the next example, take a look at Figure 3.1. Okay, looking at a Class C /25, it's pretty clear there are two subnets. But so what—why is this significant? Well actually, it's not, but that's not the right question. What you really want to know is what you would do with this information!

FIGURE 3.1   Implementing a Class C /25 logical network

```
Router#show ip route
[output cut]
C 192.168.10.0 is directly connected to Ethernet 0.
C 192.168.10.128 is directly connected to Ethernet 1.
```

I know this isn't exactly everyone's favorite pastime, but it's really important, so just hang in there; we're going to talk about subnetting—period. You need to know that the key to understanding subnetting is to understand the very reason you need to do it. And I'm going to demonstrate this by going through the process of building a physical network—and let's add a router. (We now have an internetwork, as I truly hope you already know!) All right, because we added that router, in order for the hosts on our internetwork to communicate, they must now have a logical network addressing scheme. We could use IPX or IPv6, but IPv4 is still the most popular, and it also just happens to be what we're studying at the moment, so that's what we're going with. Okay—now take a look back to Figure 3.1. There are two physical networks, so we're going to implement a logical addressing scheme that allows for two logical networks. As always, it's a really good idea to look ahead and consider likely growth scenarios—both short and long term, but for this example, a /25 will do the trick.

Practice Example #2C: 255.255.255.192 (/26)

In this second example, we're going to subnet the network address 192.168.10.0 using the subnet mask 255.255.255.192.

192.168.10.0 = Network address

255.255.255.192 = Subnet mask

Now, let's answer the big five:

- *How many subnets?* Since 192 is 2 bits on (**11**000000), the answer would be $2^2 = 4$ subnets.
- *How many hosts per subnet?* We have 6 host bits off (11**000000**), so the equation would be $2^6 - 2 = 62$ hosts.
- *What are the valid subnets?* 256 − 192 = 64. Remember, we start at zero and count in our block size, so our subnets are 0, 64, 128, and 192.
- *What's the broadcast address for each subnet?* The number right before the value of the next subnet is all host bits turned on and equals the broadcast address. For the zero subnet, the next subnet is 64, so the broadcast address for the zero subnet is 63.
- *What are the valid hosts?* These are the numbers between the subnet and broadcast address. The easiest way to find the hosts is to write out the subnet address and the broadcast address. This way, the valid hosts are obvious. The following table shows the 0, 64, 128, and 192 subnets, the valid host ranges of each, and the broadcast address of each subnet:

The subnets (do this first)	0	64	128	192
Our first host (perform host addressing last)	1	65	129	193
Our last host	62	126	190	254
The broadcast address (do this second)	63	127	191	255

Okay, again, before getting into the next example, you can see that we can now subnet a /26. And what are you going to do with this fascinating information? Implement it! We'll use Figure 3.2 to practice a /26 network implementation.

The /26 mask provides four subnetworks, and we need a subnet for each router interface. With this mask, in this example, we actually have room to add another router interface.

Practice Example #3C: 255.255.255.224 (/27)

This time, we'll subnet the network address 192.168.10.0 and subnet mask 255.255.255.224.

192.168.10.0 = Network address

255.255.255.224 = Subnet mask

- *How many subnets?* 224 is 11100000, so our equation would be $2^3 = 8$.
- *How many hosts?* $2^5 - 2 = 30$.
- *What are the valid subnets?* 256 − 224 = 32. We just start at zero and count to the subnet mask value in blocks (increments) of 32: 0, 32, 64, 96, 128, 160, 192, and 224.

- *What's the broadcast address for each subnet (always the number right before the next subnet)?*

- *What are the valid hosts (the numbers between the subnet number and the broadcast address)?*

FIGURE 3.2   Implementing a Class C /26 logical network

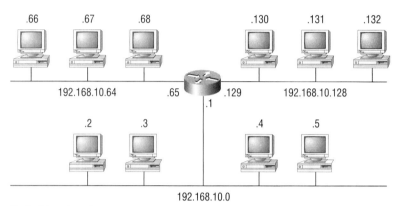

```
Router#show ip route
[output cut]
C 192.168.10.0 is directly connected to Ethernet 0
C 192.168.10.64 is directly connected to Ethernet 1
C 192.168.10.128 is directly connected to Ethernet 2
```

To answer the last two questions, first just write out the subnets, then write out the broadcast addresses—the number right before the next subnet. Last, fill in the host addresses. The following table gives you all the subnets for the 255.255.255.224 Class C subnet mask:

The subnet address	0	32	64	96	128	160	192	224
The first valid host	1	33	65	97	129	161	193	225
The last valid host	30	62	94	126	158	190	222	254
The broadcast address	31	63	95	127	159	191	223	255

Practice Example #4C: 255.255.255.240 (/28)

Let's practice on another one:

> 192.168.10.0 = Network address

> 255.255.255.240 = Subnet mask

- *Subnets?* 240 is 11110000 in binary. $2^4 = 16$.

- *Hosts?* 4 host bits, or $2^4 - 2 = 14$.

- *Valid subnets?* 256 − 240 = 16. Start at 0: 0 + 16 = 16. 16 + 16 = 32. 32 + 16 = 48. 48 + 16 = 64. 64 + 16 = 80. 80 + 16 = 96. 96 + 16 = 112. 112 + 16 = 128. 128 + 16 = 144. 144 + 16 = 160. 160 + 16 = 176. 176 + 16 = 192. 192 + 16 = 208. 208 + 16 = 224. 224 + 16 = 240.

- *Broadcast address for each subnet?*
- *Valid hosts?*

To answer the last two questions, check out the following table. It gives you the subnets, valid hosts, and broadcast addresses for each subnet. First, find the address of each subnet using the block size (increment). Second, find the broadcast address of each subnet increment (it's always the number right before the next valid subnet), then just fill in the host addresses. The following table shows the available subnets, hosts, and broadcast addresses provided from a Class C 255.255.255.240 mask:

Subnet	0	16	32	48	64	80	96	112	128	144	160	176	192	208	224	240
First host	1	17	33	49	65	81	97	113	129	145	161	177	193	209	225	241
Last host	14	30	46	62	78	94	110	126	142	158	174	190	206	222	238	254
Broadcast	15	31	47	63	79	95	111	127	143	159	175	191	207	223	239	255

Cisco has figured out that most people cannot count in 16s and therefore have a hard time finding valid subnets, hosts, and broadcast addresses with the Class C 255.255.255.240 mask. You'd be wise to study this mask.

Practice Example #5C: 255.255.255.248 (/29)

Let's keep practicing:

192.168.10.0 = Network address

255.255.255.248 = Subnet mask

- *Subnets?* 248 in binary = 11111000. $2^5 = 32$.
- *Hosts?* $2^3 - 2 = 6$.
- *Valid subnets?* $256 - 248 = 0, 8, 16, 24, 32, 40, 48, 56, 64, 72, 80, 88, 96, 104, 112, 120, 128, 136, 144, 152, 160, 168, 176, 184, 192, 200, 208, 216, 224, 232, 240,$ and 248.
- *Broadcast address for each subnet?*
- *Valid hosts?*

Take a look at the following table. It shows some of the subnets (first four and last four only), valid hosts, and broadcast addresses for the Class C 255.255.255.248 mask:

Subnet	0	8	16	24	...	224	232	240	248
First host	1	9	17	25	...	225	233	241	249
Last host	6	14	22	30	...	230	238	246	254
Broadcast	7	15	23	31	...	231	239	247	255

Practice Example #6C: 255.255.255.252 (/30)

Just one more:

192.168.10.0 = Network address

255.255.255.252 = Subnet mask

- *Subnets?* 64.

- *Hosts?* 2.

- *Valid subnets?* 0, 4, 8, 12, etc., all the way to 252.

- *Broadcast address for each subnet (always the number right before the next subnet)?*

- *Valid hosts (the numbers between the subnet number and the broadcast address)?*

The following table shows you the subnet, valid host, and broadcast address of the first four and last four subnets in the 255.255.255.252 Class C subnet:

Subnet	0	4	8	12	...	240	244	248	252
First host	1	5	9	13	...	241	245	249	253
Last host	2	6	10	14	...	242	246	250	254
Broadcast	3	7	11	15	...	243	247	251	255

> ⊕ **Real World Scenario**
>
> **Should We Really Use This Mask That Provides Only Two Hosts?**
>
> You are the network administrator for Acme Corporation in San Francisco, with dozens of WAN links connecting to your corporate office. Right now your network is a classful network, which means that the same subnet mask is on each host and router interface. You've read about classless routing where you can have different size masks but don't know what to use on your point-to-point WAN links. Is the 255.255.255.252 (/30) a helpful mask in this situation?
>
> Yes, this is a very helpful mask in wide area networks.
>
> If you use the 255.255.255.0 mask, then each network would have 254 hosts, but you only use 2 addresses with a WAN link! That is a waste of 252 hosts per subnet. If you use the 255.255.255.252 mask, then each subnet has only 2 hosts and you don't waste precious addresses. This is a really important subject, one that we'll address in a lot more detail in the section on VLSM network design later in this chapter.

Subnetting in Your Head: Class C Addresses

It really is possible to subnet in your head. Even if you don't believe me, I'll show you how. And it's not all that hard either—take the following example:

192.168.10.33 = Node address

255.255.255.224 = Subnet mask

First, determine the subnet and broadcast address of the above IP address. You can do this by answering question 3 of the big five questions: 256 – 224 = 32. 0, 32, 64. The address of 33 falls between the two subnets of 32 and 64 and must be part of the 192.168.10.32 subnet. The next subnet is 64, so the broadcast address of the 32 subnet is 63. (Remember that the broadcast address of a subnet is always the number right before the next subnet.) The valid host range is 33–62 (the numbers between the subnet and broadcast address). This is too easy!

Okay, let's try another one. We'll subnet another Class C address:

192.168.10.33 = Node address

255.255.255.240 = Subnet mask

What subnet and broadcast address is the above IP address a member of? 256 – 240 = 16. 0, 16, 32, 48. Bingo—the host address is between the 32 and 48 subnets. The subnet is 192.168.10.32, and the broadcast address is 47 (the next subnet is 48). The valid host range is 33–46 (the numbers between the subnet number and the broadcast address).

Okay, we need to do more, just to make sure you have this down.

You have a node address of 192.168.10.174 with a mask of 255.255.255.240. What is the valid host range?

The mask is 240, so we'd do a 256 – 240 = 16. This is our block size. Just keep adding 16 until we pass the host address of 174, starting at zero, of course: 0, 16, 32, 48, 64, 80, 96, 112, 128, 144, 160, 176. The host address of 174 is between 160 and 176, so the subnet is 160. The broadcast address is 175; the valid host range is 161–174. That was a tough one.

One more—just for fun. This is the easiest one of all Class C subnetting:

192.168.10.17 = Node address

255.255.255.252 = Subnet mask

What subnet and broadcast address is the above IP address a member of? 256 – 252 = 0 (always start at zero unless told otherwise), 4, 8, 12, 16, 20, etc. You've got it! The host address is between the 16 and 20 subnets. The subnet is 192.168.10.16, and the broadcast address is 19. The valid host range is 17–18.

Now that you're all over Class C subnetting, let's move on to Class B subnetting. But before we do, let's have a quick review.

What Do We Know?

Okay—here's where you can really apply what you've learned so far, and begin committing it all to memory. This is a very cool section that I've been using in my classes for years. It will really help you nail down subnetting!

When you see a subnet mask or slash notation (CIDR), you should know the following:

/25 What do we know about a /25?

- 128 mask
- 1 bits on and 7 bits off (10000000)
- Block size of 128
- 2 subnets, each with 126 hosts

/26   What do we know about a /26?

- 192 mask
- 2 bits on and 6 bits off (11000000)
- Block size of 64
- 4 subnets, each with 62 hosts

/27   What do we know about a /27?

- 224 mask
- 3 bits on and 5 bits off (11100000)
- Block size of 32
- 8 subnets, each with 30 hosts

/28   What do we know about a /28?

- 240 mask
- 4 bits on and 4 bits off
- Block size of 16
- 16 subnets, each with 14 hosts

/29   What do we know about a /29?

- 248 mask
- 5 bits on and 3 bits off
- Block size of 8
- 32 subnets, each with 6 hosts

/30   What do we know about a /30?

- 252 mask
- 6 bits on and 2 bits off
- Block size of 4
- 64 subnets, each with 2 hosts

Regardless of whether you have a Class A, Class B, or Class C address, the /30 mask will provide you with only two hosts, ever. This mask is suited almost exclusively—as well as suggested by Cisco—for use on point-to-point links.

If you can memorize this "What Do We Know?" section, you'll be much better off in your day-to-day job and in your studies. Try saying it out loud, which helps you memorize things—yes, your significant other and/or coworkers will think you've lost it, but they probably already do if you are in the networking field. And if you're not yet in the networking field but are studying all this to break into it, you might as well have people start thinking you're an odd bird now since they will eventually anyway.

It's also helpful to write these on some type of flashcards and have people test your skill. You'd be amazed at how fast you can get subnetting down if you memorize block sizes as well as this "What Do We Know?" section.

Subnetting Class B Addresses

Before we dive into this, let's look at all the possible Class B subnet masks first. Notice that we have a lot more possible subnet masks than we do with a Class C network address:

```
255.255.0.0     (/16)
255.255.128.0   (/17)      255.255.255.0    (/24)
255.255.192.0   (/18)      255.255.255.128  (/25)
255.255.224.0   (/19)      255.255.255.192  (/26)
255.255.240.0   (/20)      255.255.255.224  (/27)
255.255.248.0   (/21)      255.255.255.240  (/28)
255.255.252.0   (/22)      255.255.255.248  (/29)
255.255.254.0   (/23)      255.255.255.252  (/30)
```

We know the Class B network address has 16 bits available for host addressing. This means we can use up to 14 bits for subnetting (because we have to leave at least 2 bits for host addressing). Using a /16 means you are not subnetting with class B, but it is a mask you can use.

By the way, do you notice anything interesting about that list of subnet values—a pattern, maybe? Ah ha! That's exactly why I had you memorize the binary-to-decimal numbers at the beginning of this section. Since subnet mask bits start on the left and move to the right and bits can't be skipped, the numbers are always the same regardless of the class of address. Memorize this pattern.

The process of subnetting a Class B network is pretty much the same as it is for a Class C, except that you just have more host bits and you start in the third octet.

Use the same subnet numbers for the third octet with Class B that you used for the fourth octet with Class C, but add a zero to the network portion and a 255 to the broadcast section in the fourth octet. The following table shows you an example host range of two subnets used in a Class B 240 (/20) subnet mask:

First subnet	16.0	31.255
Second subnet	32.0	47.255

Just add the valid hosts between the numbers, and you're set!

The preceding example is true only until you get up to /24. After that, it's numerically exactly like Class C.

Subnetting Practice Examples: Class B Addresses

This section will give you an opportunity to practice subnetting Class B addresses. Again, I have to mention that this is the same as subnetting with Class C, except we start in the third octet—with the exact same numbers!

Practice Example #1B: 255.255.128.0 (/17)

> 172.16.0.0 = Network address
>
> 255.255.128.0 = Subnet mask

- *Subnets?* 2^1 = 2 (same as Class C).
- *Hosts?* 2^{15} – 2 = 32,766 (7 bits in the third octet, and 8 in the fourth).
- *Valid subnets?* 256 – 128 = 128. 0, 128. Remember that subnetting is performed in the third octet, so the subnet numbers are really 0.0 and 128.0, as shown in the next table. These are the exact numbers we used with Class C; we use them in the third octet and add a 0 in the fourth octet for the network address.
- *Broadcast address for each subnet?*
- *Valid hosts?*

The following table shows the two subnets available, the valid host range, and the broadcast address of each:

Subnet	0.0	128.0
First host	0.1	128.1
Last host	127.254	255.254
Broadcast	127.255	255.255

Okay, notice that we just added the fourth octet's lowest and highest values and came up with the answers. And again, it's done exactly the same way as for a Class C subnet. We just use the same numbers in the third octet and added 0 and 255 in the fourth octet—pretty simple huh! I really can't say this enough: It's just not hard; the numbers never change; we just use them in different octets!

Practice Example #2B: 255.255.192.0 (/18)

> 172.16.0.0 = Network address
>
> 255.255.192.0 = Subnet mask

- *Subnets?* 2^2 = 4.
- *Hosts?* 2^{14} – 2 = 16,382 (6 bits in the third octet, and 8 in the fourth).
- *Valid subnets?* 256 – 192 = 64. 0, 64, 128, 192. Remember that the subnetting is performed in the third octet, so the subnet numbers are really 0.0, 64.0, 128.0, and 192.0, as shown in the next table.
- *Broadcast address for each subnet?*
- *Valid hosts?*

The following table shows the four subnets available, the valid host range, and the broadcast address of each:

Subnet	0.0	64.0	128.0	192.0
First host	0.1	64.1	128.1	192.1
Last host	63.254	127.254	191.254	255.254
Broadcast	63.255	127.255	191.255	255.255

Again, it's pretty much the same as it is for a Class C subnet—we just added 0 and 255 in the fourth octet for each subnet in the third octet.

Practice Example #3B: 255.255.240.0 (/20)

172.16.0.0 = Network address

255.255.240.0 = Subnet mask

- *Subnets?* 2^4 = 16.
- *Hosts?* $2^{12} - 2$ = 4094.
- *Valid subnets?* 256 – 240 = 0, 16, 32, 48, etc., up to 240. Notice that these are the same numbers as a Class C 240 mask – we just put them in the third octet and add a 0 and 255 in the fourth octet.
- *Broadcast address for each subnet?*
- *Valid hosts?*

The following table shows the first four subnets, valid hosts, and broadcast addresses in a Class B 255.255.240.0 mask:

Subnet	0.0	16.0	32.0	48.0
First host	0.1	16.1	32.1	48.1
Last host	15.254	31.254	47.254	63.254
Broadcast	15.255	31.255	47.255	63.255

Practice Example #4B: 255.255.254.0 (/23)

172.16.0.0 = Network address

255.255.254.0 = Subnet mask

- *Subnets?* 2^7 = 128.
- *Hosts?* $2^9 - 2$ = 510.
- *Valid subnets?* 256 – 254 = 0, 2, 4, 6, 8, etc., up to 254.
- *Broadcast address for each subnet?*
- *Valid hosts?*

The following table shows the first five subnets, valid hosts, and broadcast addresses in a Class B 255.255.254.0 mask:

Subnet	0.0	2.0	4.0	6.0	8.0
First host	0.1	2.1	4.1	6.1	8.1
Last host	1.254	3.254	5.254	7.254	9.254
Broadcast	1.255	3.255	5.255	7.255	9.255

Practice Example #5B: 255.255.255.0 (/24)

Contrary to popular belief, 255.255.255.0 used with a Class B network address is not called a Class B network with a Class C subnet mask. It's amazing how many people see this mask used in a Class B network and think it's a Class C subnet mask. This is a Class B subnet mask with 8 bits of subnetting—it's considerably different from a Class C mask. Subnetting this address is fairly simple:

> 172.16.0.0 = Network address
>
> 255.255.255.0 = Subnet mask

- *Subnets?* 2^8 = 256.
- *Hosts?* $2^8 - 2$ = 254.
- *Valid subnets?* 256 − 255 = 1. 0, 1, 2, 3, etc., all the way to 255.
- *Broadcast address for each subnet?*
- *Valid hosts?*

The following table shows the first four and last two subnets, the valid hosts, and the broadcast addresses in a Class B 255.255.255.0 mask:

Subnet	0.0	1.0	2.0	3.0	...	254.0	255.0
First host	0.1	1.1	2.1	3.1	...	254.1	255.1
Last host	0.254	1.254	2.254	3.254	...	254.254	255.254
Broadcast	0.255	1.255	2.255	3.255	...	254.255	255.255

Practice Example #6B: 255.255.255.128 (/25)

This is one of the hardest subnet masks you can play with. And worse, it actually is a really good subnet to use in production because it creates over 500 subnets with 126 hosts for each subnet—a nice mixture. So, don't skip over it!

> 172.16.0.0 = Network address
>
> 255.255.255.128 = Subnet mask

- *Subnets?* $2^9 = 512$.

- *Hosts?* $2^7 - 2 = 126$.

- *Valid subnets?* Okay, now for the tricky part. $256 - 255 = 1$. 0, 1, 2, 3, etc. for the third octet. But you can't forget the one subnet bit used in the fourth octet. Remember when I showed you how to figure one subnet bit with a Class C mask? You figure this the same way. (Now you know why I showed you the 1-bit subnet mask in the Class C section—to make this part easier.) You actually get two subnets for each third octet value, hence the 512 subnets. For example, if the third octet is showing subnet 3, the two subnets would actually be 3.0 and 3.128.

- *Broadcast address for each subnet?*

- *Valid hosts?*

The following table shows how you can create subnets, valid hosts, and broadcast addresses using the Class B 255.255.255.128 subnet mask (the first eight subnets are shown, and then the last two subnets):

Subnet	0.0	0.128	1.0	1.128	2.0	2.128	3.0	3.128	...	255.0	255.128
First host	0.1	0.129	1.1	1.129	2.1	2.129	3.1	3.129	...	255.1	255.129
Last host	0.126	0.254	1.126	1.254	2.126	2.254	3.126	3.254	...	255.126	255.254
Broad-cast	0.127	0.255	1.127	1.255	2.127	2.255	3.127	3.255	...	255.127	255.255

Practice Example #7B: 255.255.255.192 (/26)

Now, this is where Class B subnetting gets easy. Since the third octet has a 255 in the mask section, whatever number is listed in the third octet is a subnet number. However, now that we have a subnet number in the fourth octet, we can subnet this octet just as we did with Class C subnetting. Let's try it out:

172.16.0.0 = Network address

255.255.255.192 = Subnet mask

- *Subnets?* $2^{10} = 1024$.

- *Hosts?* $2^6 - 2 = 62$.

- *Valid subnets?* $256 - 192 = 64$. The subnets are shown in the following table. Do these numbers look familiar?

- *Broadcast address for each subnet?*

- *Valid hosts?*

The following table shows the first eight subnet ranges, valid hosts, and broadcast addresses:

Subnet	0.0	0.64	0.128	0.192	1.0	1.64	1.128	1.192
First host	0.1	0.65	0.129	0.193	1.1	1.65	1.129	1.193
Last host	0.62	0.126	0.190	0.254	1.62	1.126	1.190	1.254
Broadcast	0.63	0.127	0.191	0.255	1.63	1.127	1.191	1.255

Notice that for each subnet value in the third octet, you get subnets 0, 64, 128, and 192 in the fourth octet.

Practice Example #8B: 255.255.255.224 (/27)

This is done the same way as the preceding subnet mask, except that we just have more subnets and fewer hosts per subnet available.

172.16.0.0 = Network address

255.255.255.224 = Subnet mask

- *Subnets?* 2^{11} = 2048.
- *Hosts?* $2^5 - 2$ = 30.
- *Valid subnets?* 256 − 224 = 32. 0, 32, 64, 96, 128, 160, 192, 224.
- *Broadcast address for each subnet?*
- *Valid hosts?*

The following table shows the first eight subnets:

Subnet	0.0	0.32	0.64	0.96	0.128	0.160	0.192	0.224
First host	0.1	0.33	0.65	0.97	0.129	0.161	0.193	0.225
Last host	0.30	0.62	0.94	0.126	0.158	0.190	0.222	0.254
Broadcast	0.31	0.63	0.95	0.127	0.159	0.191	0.223	0.255

This next table shows the last eight subnets:

Subnet	255.0	255.32	255.64	255.96	255.128	255.160	255.192	255.224
First host	255.1	255.33	255.65	255.97	255.129	255.161	255.193	255.225
Last host	255.30	255.62	255.94	255.126	255.158	255.190	255.222	255.254
Broadcast	255.31	255.63	255.95	255.127	255.159	255.191	255.223	255.255

Subnetting in Your Head: Class B Addresses

Are you nuts? Subnet Class B addresses in our heads? It's actually easier than writing it out—
I'm not kidding! Let me show you how:

Question: What subnet and broadcast address is the IP address 172.16.10.33
255.255.255.224 (/27) a member of?

Answer: The interesting octet is the fourth octet. 256 – 224 = 32. 32 + 32 = 64. Bingo: 33
is between 32 and 64. However, remember that the third octet is considered part of the
subnet, so the answer would be the 10.32 subnet. The broadcast is 10.63, since 10.64 is
the next subnet. That was a pretty easy one.

Question: What subnet and broadcast address is the IP address 172.16.66.10
255.255.192.0 (/18) a member of?

Answer: The interesting octet is the third octet instead of the fourth octet. 256 – 192 = 64.
0, 64, 128. The subnet is 172.16.64.0. The broadcast must be 172.16.127.255 since
128.0 is the next subnet.

Question: What subnet and broadcast address is the IP address 172.16.50.10
255.255.224.0 (/19) a member of?

Answer: 256 – 224 = 0, 32, 64 (remember, we always start counting at zero (0)). The subnet
is 172.16.32.0, and the broadcast must be 172.16.63.255 since 64.0 is the next subnet.

Question: What subnet and broadcast address is the IP address 172.16.46.255
255.255.240.0 (/20) a member of?

Answer: 256 – 240 = 16. The third octet is interesting to us. 0, 16, 32, 48. This subnet
address must be in the 172.16.32.0 subnet, and the broadcast must be 172.16.47.255
since 48.0 is the next subnet. So, yes, 172.16.46.255 is a valid host.

Question: What subnet and broadcast address is the IP address 172.16.45.14
255.255.255.252 (/30) a member of?

Answer: Where is the interesting octet? 256 – 252 = 0, 4, 8, 12, 16 (in the fourth octet).
The subnet is 172.16.45.12, with a broadcast of 172.16.45.15 because the next subnet is
172.16.45.16.

Question: What is the subnet and broadcast address of the host 172.16.88.255/20?

Answer: What is a /20? If you can't answer this, you can't answer this question, can you?
A /20 is 255.255.240.0, which gives us a block size of 16 in the third octet, and since no
subnet bits are on in the fourth octet, the answer is always 0 and 255 in the fourth octet.
0, 16, 32, 48, 64, 80, 96…bingo. 88 is between 80 and 96, so the subnet is 80.0 and the
broadcast address is 95.255.

Question: A router receives a packet on an interface with a destination address of
172.16.46.191/26. What will the router do with this packet?

Answer: Discard it. Do you know why? 172.16.46.191/26 is a 255.255.255.192 mask,
which gives us a block size of 64. Our subnets are then 0, 64, 128, 192. 191 is the broadcast address of the 128 subnet, so a router, by default, will discard any broadcast packets.

Subnetting Class A Addresses

Class A subnetting is not performed any differently than Classes B and C, but there are 24 bits to play with instead of the 16 in a Class B address and the 8 in a Class C address.

Let's start by listing all the Class A masks:

```
255.0.0.0      (/8)
255.128.0.0    (/9)        255.255.240.0  (/20)
255.192.0.0    (/10)       255.255.248.0  (/21)
255.224.0.0    (/11)       255.255.252.0  (/22)
255.240.0.0    (/12)       255.255.254.0  (/23)
255.248.0.0    (/13)       255.255.255.0  (/24)
255.252.0.0    (/14)       255.255.255.128  (/25)
255.254.0.0    (/15)       255.255.255.192  (/26)
255.255.0.0    (/16)       255.255.255.224  (/27)
255.255.128.0  (/17)       255.255.255.240  (/28)
255.255.192.0  (/18)       255.255.255.248  (/29)
255.255.224.0  (/19)       255.255.255.252  (/30)
```

That's it. You must leave at least 2 bits for defining hosts. And I hope you can see the pattern by now. Remember, we're going to do this the same way as a Class B or C subnet. It's just that, again, we simply have more host bits and we just use the same subnet numbers we used with Class B and C, but we start using these numbers in the second octet.

Subnetting Practice Examples: Class A Addresses

When you look at an IP address and a subnet mask, you must be able to distinguish the bits used for subnets from the bits used for determining hosts. This is imperative. If you're still struggling with this concept, please reread the section "IP Addressing" in Chapter 2. It shows you how to determine the difference between the subnet and host bits and should help clear things up.

Practice Example #1A: 255.255.0.0 (/16)

Class A addresses use a default mask of 255.0.0.0, which leaves 22 bits for subnetting since you must leave 2 bits for host addressing. The 255.255.0.0 mask with a Class A address is using 8 subnet bits.

- *Subnets?* $2^8 = 256$.

- *Hosts?* $2^{16} - 2 = 65,534$.

- *Valid subnets?* What is the interesting octet? $256 - 255 = 1$. 0, 1, 2, 3, etc. (all in the second octet). The subnets would be 10.0.0.0, 10.1.0.0, 10.2.0.0, 10.3.0.0, etc., up to 10.255.0.0.

- *Broadcast address for each subnet?*
- *Valid hosts?*

The following table shows the first two and last two subnets, valid host range, and broadcast addresses for the private Class A 10.0.0.0 network:

Subnet	10.0.0.0	10.1.0.0	...	10.254.0.0	10.255.0.0
First host	10.0.0.1	10.1.0.1	...	10.254.0.1	10.255.0.1
Last host	10.0.255.254	10.1.255.254	...	10.254.255.254	10.255.255.254
Broadcast	10.0.255.255	10.1.255.255	...	10.254.255.255	10.255.255.255

Practice Example #2A: 255.255.240.0 (/20)

255.255.240.0 gives us 12 bits of subnetting and leaves us 12 bits for host addressing.

- *Subnets?* $2^{12} = 4096$.
- *Hosts?* $2^{12} - 2 = 4094$.
- *Valid subnets?* What is your interesting octet? 256 – 240 = 16. The subnets in the second octet are a block size of 1 and the subnets in the third octet are 0, 16, 32, etc.
- *Broadcast address for each subnet?*
- *Valid hosts?*

The following table shows some examples of the host ranges—the first three and the last subnets:

Subnet	10.0.0.0	10.0.16.0	10.0.32.0	...	10.255.240.0
First host	10.0.0.1	10.0.16.1	10.0.32.1	...	10.255.240.1
Last host	10.0.15.254	10.0.31.254	10.0.47.254	...	10.255.255.254
Broadcast	10.0.15.255	10.0.31.255	10.0.47.255	...	10.255.255.255

Practice Example #3A: 255.255.255.192 (/26)

Let's do one more example using the second, third, and fourth octets for subnetting.

- *Subnets?* $2^{18} = 262,144$.
- *Hosts?* $2^{6} - 2 = 62$.
- *Valid subnets?* In the second and third octet, the block size is 1, and in the fourth octet, the block size is 64.
- *Broadcast address for each subnet?*
- *Valid hosts?*

The following table shows the first four subnets and their valid hosts and broadcast addresses in the Class A 255.255.255.192 mask:

Subnet	10.0.0.0	10.0.0.64	10.0.0.128	10.0.0.192
First host	10.0.0.1	10.0.0.65	10.0.0.129	10.0.0.193
Last host	10.0.0.62	10.0.0.126	10.0.0.190	10.0.0.254
Broadcast	10.0.0.63	10.0.0.127	10.0.0.191	10.0.0.255

The following table shows the last four subnets and their valid hosts and broadcast addresses:

Subnet	10.255.255.0	10.255.255.64	10.255.255.128	10.255.255.192
First host	10.255.255.1	10.255.255.65	10.255.255.129	10.255.255.193
Last host	10.255.255.62	10.255.255.126	10.255.255.190	10.255.255.254
Broadcast	10.255.255.63	10.255.255.127	10.255.255.191	10.255.255.255

Subnetting in Your Head: Class A Addresses

This sounds hard, but as with Class C and Class B, the numbers are the same; we just start in the second octet. What makes this easy? You only need to worry about the octet that has the largest block size (typically called the interesting octet; one that is something other than 0 or 255)—for example, 255.255.240.0 (/20) with a Class A network. The second octet has a block size of 1, so any number listed in that octet is a subnet. The third octet is a 240 mask, which means we have a block size of 16 in the third octet. If your host ID is 10.20.80.30, what is your subnet, broadcast address, and valid host range?

The subnet in the second octet is 20 with a block size of 1, but the third octet is in block sizes of 16, so we'll just count them out: 0, 16, 32, 48, 64, 80, 96...voilà! (By the way, you can count by 16s by now, right?) This makes our subnet 10.20.80.0, with a broadcast of 10.20.95.255 because the next subnet is 10.20.96.0. The valid host range is 10.20.80.1 through 10.20.95.254. And yes, no lie! You really can do this in your head if you just get your block sizes nailed!

Okay, let's practice on one more, just for fun!

Host IP: 10.1.3.65/23

First, you can't answer this question if you don't know what a /23, is. It's 255.255.254.0. The interesting octet here is the third one: 256 – 254 = 2. Our subnets in the third octet are 0, 2, 4, 6, etc. The host in this question is in subnet 2.0, and the next subnet is 4.0, so that makes the broadcast address 3.255. And any address between 10.1.2.1 and 10.1.3.254 is considered a valid host.

Variable Length Subnet Masks (VLSMs)

I could easily devote an entire chapter to *Variable Length Subnet Masks (VLSMs)*, but instead I'm going to show you a simple way to take one network and create many networks using subnet masks of different lengths on different types of network designs. This is called VLSM networking, and it does bring up another subject I mentioned at the beginning of this chapter: classful and classless networking.

Neither RIPv1 nor IGRP routing protocols have a field for subnet information, so the subnet information gets dropped. What this means is that if a router running RIP has a subnet mask of a certain value, it assumes that *all* interfaces within the classful address space have the same subnet mask. This is called classful routing, and RIP and IGRP are both considered classful routing protocols. (I'll be talking more about RIP and IGRP in Chapter 6, "IP Routing.") If you mix and match subnet mask lengths in a network running RIP or IGRP, that network just won't work!

Classless routing protocols, however, do support the advertisement of subnet information. Therefore, you can use VLSM with routing protocols such as RIPv2, EIGRP, and OSPF. (EIGRP and OSPF will be discussed in Chapter 7.) The benefit of this type of network is that you save a bunch of IP address space with it.

As the name suggests, with VLSMs we can have different subnet masks for different router interfaces. Look at Figure 3.3 to see an example of why classful network designs are inefficient.

Looking at this figure, you'll notice that we have two routers, each with two LANs and connected together with a WAN serial link. In a typical classful network design (RIP or IGRP routing protocols), you could subnet a network like this:

192.168.10.0 = Network

255.255.255.240 (/28) = Mask

FIGURE 3.3   Typical classful network

Our subnets would be (you know this part, right?) 0, 16, 32, 48, 64, 80, etc. This allows us to assign 16 subnets to our internetwork. But how many hosts would be available on each network? Well, as you probably know by now, each subnet provides only 14 hosts. This means that each LAN has 14 valid hosts available—one LAN doesn't even have enough addresses needed for all the hosts! But the point-to-point WAN link also has 14 valid hosts. It's too bad we can't just nick some valid hosts from that WAN link and give them to our LANs!

All hosts and router interfaces have the same subnet mask—again, this is called classful routing. And if we want this network to be more efficient, we definitely need to add different masks to each router interface.

But there's still another problem—the link between the two routers will never use more than two valid hosts! This wastes valuable IP address space, and it's the big reason I'm going to talk to you about VLSM network design.

VLSM Design

Let's take Figure 3.3 and use a classless design…which will become the new network shown in Figure 3.4. In the previous example, we wasted address space—one LAN didn't have enough addresses because every router interface and host used the same subnet mask. Not so good. What would be good is to provide only the needed number of hosts on each router interface. To do this, we use what are referred to as Variable Length Subnet Masks (VLSMs).

Now remember that we can use different size masks on each router interface. And if we use a /30 on our WAN links and a /27, /28, and /29 on our LANs, we'll get 2 hosts per WAN interface, and 30, 14, and 6 hosts per LAN interface—nice! This makes a huge difference—not only can we get just the right amount of hosts on each LAN, we still have room to add more WANs and LANs using this same network!

FIGURE 3.4   Classless network design

Remember, in order to implement a VLSM design on your network, you need to have a routing protocol that sends subnet mask information with the route updates. This would be RIPv2, EIGRP, and OSPF. RIPv1 and IGRP will not work in classless networks and are considered classful routing protocols.

Why Bother with VLSM Design?

You have just been hired by a new company and need to add on to the existing network. There is no problem with starting over with a new IP address scheme. Should you use a VLSM classless network or a classful network?

Let's just say you happen to have plenty of address space because you are using the Class A 10.0.0.0 private network address in your corporate environment and can't even come close to imagining that you'd ever run out of IP addresses. Why would you want to bother with the VLSM design process?

Good question. There's a good answer too!

Because by creating contiguous blocks of addresses to specific areas of your network, you can then easily summarize your network and keep route updates with a routing protocol to a minimum. Why would anyone want to advertise hundreds of networks between buildings when you can just send one summary route between buildings and achieve the same result?

If you're confused about what summary routes are, let me explain. Summarization, also called supernetting, provides route updates in the most efficient way possible by advertising many routes in one advertisement instead of individually. This saves a ton of bandwidth and minimizes router processing. As always, you use blocks of addresses (remember that block sizes are used in all sorts of networks) to configure your summary routes and watch your network's performance hum.

But know that summarization works only if you design your network carefully. If you carelessly hand out IP subnets to any location on the network, you'll notice straight away that you no longer have any summary boundaries. And you won't get very far with creating summary routes without those, so watch your step!

Implementing VLSM Networks

To create VLSMs quickly and efficiently, you need to understand how block sizes and charts work together to create the VLSM masks. Table 3.3 shows you the block sizes used when creating VLSMs with Class C networks. For example, if you need 25 hosts, then you'll need a block size of 32. If you need 11 hosts, you'll use a block size of 16. Need 40 hosts? Then you'll need a block of 64. You cannot just make up block sizes—they've got to be the block sizes shown in Table 3.3. So memorize the block sizes in this table—it's easy. They're the same numbers we used with subnetting!

TABLE 3.3   Block Sizes

Prefix	Mask	Hosts	Block Size
/25	128	126	128
/26	192	62	64
/27	224	30	32
/28	240	14	16
/29	248	6	8
/30	252	2	4

The next step is to create a VLSM table. Figure 3.5 shows you the table used in creating a VLSM network. The reason we use this table is so we don't accidentally overlap networks.

You'll find the sheet shown in Figure 3.5 very valuable because it lists every block size you can use for a network address. Notice that the block sizes are listed starting from a block size of 4 all the way to a block size of 128. If you have two networks with block sizes of 128, you'll quickly see that you can have only two networks. With a block size of 64, you can have only four networks, and so on, all the way to having 64 networks if you use only block sizes of 4. Remember that this takes into account that you are using the command `ip subnet-zero` in your network design.

Now, just fill in the chart in the lower-left corner, and then add the subnets to the worksheet and you're good to go.

So let's take what we've learned so far about our block sizes and VLSM table and create a VLSM using a Class C network address 192.168.10.0 for the network in Figure 3.6. Then fill out the VLSM table, as shown in Figure 3.7.

In Figure 3.6, we have four WAN links and four LANs connected together. We need to create a VLSM network that will allow us to save address space. Looks like we have two block sizes of 32, a block size of 16, and a block size of 8, and our WANs each have a block size of 4. Take a look and see how I filled out our VLSM chart in Figure 3.7.

FIGURE 3.5 The VLSM table

Variable Length Subnet Masks Worksheet

Subnet	Mask	Subnets	Hosts	Block
/25	128	2	126	128
/26	192	4	62	64
/27	224	8	30	32
/28	240	16	14	16
/29	248	32	6	8
/30	252	64	2	4

Class C Network   192.168.10.0

Network	Hosts	Block	Subnet	Mask
A				
B				
C				
D				
E				
F				
G				
H				
I				
J				
K				
L				

0
4
8
12
16
20
24
28
32
36
40
44
48
52
56
60
64
68
72
76
80
84
88
92
96
100
104
108
112
116
120
124
128
132
136
140
144
148
152
156
160
154
158
172
176
180
184
188
192
196
200
204
208
212
216
220
224
228
232
236
240
244
248
252
256

FIGURE 3.6   VLSM network example 1

We still have plenty of room for growth with this VLSM network design.

We never could accomplish that with one subnet mask using classful routing. Let's do another one. Figure 3.8 shows a network with 11 networks, two block sizes of 64, one of 32, five of 16, and three of 4.

First, create your VLSM table and use your block size chart to fill in the table with the subnets you need. Figure 3.9 shows a possible solution.

Notice that we filled in this entire chart and only have room for one more block size of 4! Only with a VLSM network can you provide this type of address space savings.

Keep in mind that it doesn't matter where you start your block sizes as long as you always count from zero. For example, if you had a block size of 16, you must start at 0 and count from there—0, 16, 32, 48, etc. You can't start a block size of 16 from, say, 40 or anything other than increments of 16.

Here's another example. If you had block sizes of 32, you must start at zero like this: 0, 32, 64, 96, etc. Just remember that you don't get to start wherever you want; you must always start counting from zero. In the example in Figure 3.9, I started at 64 and 128, with my two block sizes of 64. I didn't have much choice, because my options are 0, 64, 128, and 192. However, I added the block size of 32, 16, 8, and 4 wherever I wanted just as long as they were in the correct increments of that block size.

Okay—you have three locations you need to address, and the IP network you have received is 192.168.55.0 to use as the addressing for the entire network. You'll use `ip subnet-zero` and RIPv2 as the routing protocol. (RIPv2 supports VLSM networks, RIPv1 does not—both of them will be discussed in Chapter 6.) Figure 3.10 shows the network diagram and the IP address of the RouterA S0/0 interface.

FIGURE 3.7   A VLSM table, example one

Variable Length Subnet Masks Worksheet

Subnet	Mask	Subnets	Hosts	Block
/26	192	4	62	64
/27	224	8	30	32
/28	240	16	14	16
/29	248	32	6	8
/30	252	64	2	4

Class C Network   192.168.10.0

Network	Hosts	Block	Subnet	Mask
A	14	16	/28	240
B	30	32	/27	224
C	20	32	/27	224
D	6	8	/29	248
E	2	4	/30	252
F	2	4	/30	252
G	2	4	/30	252
H	2	4	/30	252

FIGURE 3.8   VLSM network example 2

From the list of IP addresses on the right of the figure, which IP address will be placed in each router's FastEthernet 0/0 interface and serial 0/1 of RouterB?

To answer this question, first look for clues in Figure 3.10. The first clue is that interface S0/0 on RouterA has IP address 192.168.55.2/30 assigned, which makes for an easy answer. A /30, as you know, is 255.255.255.252, which gives you a block size of 4. Your subnets are 0, 4, 8, etc. Since the known host has an IP address of 2, the only other valid host in the zero subnet is 1, so the third answer down is what you want for the s0/1 interface of RouterB.

The next clues are the listed number of hosts for each of the LANs. RouterA needs 7 hosts, a block size of 16 (/28); RouterB needs 90 hosts, a block size of 128 (/25); and RouterC needs 23 hosts, a block size of 32 (/27).

Figure 3.11 shows the answers to this question.

Once you figured out the block size needed for each LAN, this was actually a pretty simple question—all you need to do is look for the right clues and, of course, know your block sizes.

One last example of VLSM design before we move on to summarization. Figure 3.12 shows three routers, all running RIPv2. Which class C addressing scheme would you use to satisfy the needs of this network yet save as much address space as possible?

This is a really sweet network, just waiting for you to fill out the chart. There are block sizes of 64, 32, and 16 and two block sizes of 4. This should be a slam dunk for you. Take a look at my answer in Figure 3.13.

This is what I did: Starting at subnet 0, I used the block size of 64. (I didn't have to—I could have started with a block size of 4, but I usually like to start with the largest block size and move to the smallest.) Okay, then I added the block sizes of 32 and 16 and the two block sizes of 4. There's still a lot of room to add subnets to this network—very cool!

FIGURE 3.9   VLSM table example 2

Variable Length Subnet Masks Worksheet

Subnet	Mask	Subnets	Hosts	Block
/26	192	4	62	64
/27	224	8	30	32
/28	240	16	14	16
/29	248	32	6	8
/30	252	64	2	4

Class C Network   192.168.10.0

Network	Hosts	Block	Subnet	Mask
A	30	32	32	224
B	10	16	0	240
C	12	16	16	240
D	2	4	244	252
E	2	4	248	252
F	2	4	252	252
G	12	16	208	240
H	60	64	64	192
I	14	16	192	240
J	60	64	128	192
K	8	16	224	240

```
0
4
8       B - 192.168.10.0/28
12
16
20
24      C - 192.168.10.16/28
28
32
36
40
44
48      A - 192.168.10.32/27
52
56
60
64
68
72
76
80
84
88
92
96      H - 192.168.10.64/26
100
104
108
112
116
120
124
128
132
136
140
144
148
152
156
160     J - 192.168.10.128/26
154
158
172
176
180
184
188
192
196
200     I - 192.168.10.192/28
204
208
212
216     G - 192.168.10.208/28
220
224
228
232     K - 192.168.10.224/28
236
240
244
248     D - 192.168.10.244/30
252     E - 192.168.10.248/30
256     F - 192.168.10.252/30
```

FIGURE 3.10 VLSM design example 1

192.168.55.57/27
192.168.55.29/28
192.168.55.1/30
192.168.55.132/25
192.168.55.0/30
192.168.55.127/26

192.168.55.2/30

S0/1:

RouterA   RouterB   RouterC

S0/0

F0/0:   F0/0:   F0/0:

7 hosts   90 hosts   23 hosts

FIGURE 3.11 Solution to VLSM design example 1

192.168.55.2/30

S0/1: **192.168.55.1/30**

RouterA   RouterB   RouterC

S0/0

F0/0:
192.168.55.29/28

F0/0:
192.168.55.132/25

F0/0:
192.168.55.57/27

7 hosts   90 hosts   23 hosts

FIGURE 3.12 VLSM design example 2

4: Serial 1   5: Serial 2

60 hosts
Net 1

30 hosts
Net 2

12 hosts
Net 3

FIGURE 3.13   Solution to VLSM design example 2

Summarization

Summarization, also called route aggregation, allows routing protocols to advertise many networks as one address. The purpose of this is to reduce the size of routing tables on routers to save memory, which also shortens the amount of time for IP to parse the routing table and find the path to a remote network.

Figure 3.14 shows how a summary address would be used in an internetwork.

FIGURE 3.14   Summary address used in an internetwork

Summarization is actually somewhat simple because all you really need to have down are the block sizes that we just used in learning subnetting and VLSM design. For example, if you wanted to summarize the following networks into one network advertisement, you just have to find the block size first; then you can easily find your answer:

192.168.16.0 through network 192.168.31.0

What's the block size? There are exactly 16 Class C networks, so this neatly fits into a block size of 16.

Okay, now that you know the block size, you can find the network address and mask used to summarize these networks into one advertisement. The network address used to advertise the summary address is always the first network address in the block—in this example, 192.168.16.0. To figure out a summary mask, in this same example, what mask is used to get a block size of 16? Yes, 240 is correct. This 240 would be placed in the third octet—the octet where we are summarizing. So, the mask would be 255.255.240.0.

> You'll learn how to apply these summary addresses to a router in Chapter 7.

Here's another example:

Networks 172.16.32.0 through 172.16.50.0

This is not as clean as the previous example because there are two possible answers, and here's why: Since you're starting at network 32, your options for block sizes are 4, 8, 16, 32, 64, etc., and block sizes of 16 and 32 could work as this summary address.

- *Answer #1:* If you used a block size of 16, then the network address is 172.16.32.0 with a mask of 255.255.240.0 (240 provides a block of 16). However, this only summarizes from 32 to 47, which means that networks 48 through 50 would be advertised as single networks. This is probably the best answer, but that depends on your network design. Let's look at the next answer.

- *Answer #2:* If you used a block size of 32, then your summary address would still be 172.16.32.0, but the mask would be 255.255.224.0 (224 provides a block of 32). The possible problem with this answer is that it will summarize networks 32 to 63 and we only have networks 32 to 50. No worries if you're planning on adding networks 51 to 63 later into the same network, but you could have serious problems in your internetwork if somehow networks 51 to 63 were to show up and be advertised from somewhere else in your network! This is the reason why answer number one is the safest answer.

Let's take a look at another example, but let's look at it from a host's perspective.

Your summary address is 192.168.144.0/20—what's the range of host addresses that would be forwarded according to this summary? The /20 provides a summary address of 192.168.144.0 and mask of 255.255.240.0.

The third octet has a block size of 16, and starting at summary address 144, the next block of 16 is 160, so our network summary range is 144 to 159 in the third octet (again, you *must* be able to count in 16s!).

A router that has this summary address in the routing table will forward any packet with destination IP addresses of 192.168.144.1 through 192.168.159.254.

Only two more summarization examples, then we'll move on to troubleshooting.

In Figure 3.15, the Ethernet networks connected to router R1 are being summarized to R2 as 192.168.144.0/20. Which range of IP addresses will R2 forward to R1 according to this summary?

FIGURE 3.15   Summarization example 1

The Ethernet networks connected to router R1 are being
summarized to R2 as 192.168.144.0/20.
Which IP addresses will R2 forward to R1 according to
this summary?

192.168.144.0/20

No worries—this is really an easier question than it looks. The question actually has the summary address listed: 192.168.144.0/20. You already know that /20 is 255.255.240.0, which means you've got a block size of 16 in the third octet. Starting at 144 (this is also right there in the question), the next block size of 16 is 160, so you can't go above 159 in the third octet. The IP addresses that will be forwarded are 192.168.144.1 through 192.168.159.255. (Yes, the broadcast address is forwarded.)

Okay, last one. In Figure 3.16, there are five networks connected to router R1. What's the best summary address to R2?

FIGURE 3.16   Summarization example 2

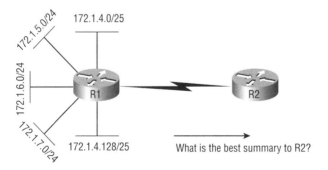

172.1.5.0/24
172.1.4.0/25
172.1.6.0/24
172.1.7.0/24
172.1.4.128/25
What is the best summary to R2?

I'm going to be honest—this is a much harder question than the one in Figure 3.15. You're going to have to look pretty hard to see the answer. The first thing to do with this is to write down all the networks and see if you can find anything in common with all six:

- 172.1.4.128/25
- 172.1.7.0/24
- 172.1.6.0/24
- 172.1.5.0/24
- 172.1.4.0/25

Do you see an octet that looks interesting to you? I do. It's the third octet. 4, 5, 6, 7, and yes, it's a block size of 4. So you can summarize 172.1.4.0 using a mask of 255.255.252.0, which means you will use a block size of 4 in the third octet. The IP addresses forwarded with this summary are 172.1.4.1 through 172.1.7.255.

Now to summarize this summarization section: Basically, if you've nailed down your block sizes, then finding and applying summary addresses and masks is actually fairly easy. But you're going to get bogged down pretty quickly if you don't know what a /20 is or if you can't count by 16s!

Troubleshooting IP Addressing

Troubleshooting IP addressing is obviously an important skill because running into trouble somewhere along the way is pretty much a sure thing, and it's going to happen to you. No— I'm not a pessimist; I'm just keeping it real. Because of this nasty fact, it will be great when you can save the day because you can both figure out (diagnose) the problem and fix it on an IP network whether you're at work or at home!

So this is where I'm going to show you the "Cisco way" of troubleshooting IP addressing. Let's use Figure 3.17 as an example of your basic IP trouble—poor Sally can't log in to the Windows server. Do you deal with this by calling the Microsoft team to tell them their server is a pile of junk and causing all your problems? Probably not such a great idea—let's first double-check our network instead.

FIGURE 3.17 Basic IP troubleshooting

E0
172.16.10.1

Sally
172.16.10.2

Server
172.16.20.2

Okay let's get started by going over the troubleshooting steps that Cisco follows. They're pretty simple, but important nonetheless. Pretend you're at a customer host and they're complaining that they can't communicate to a server that just happens to be on a remote network. Here are the four troubleshooting steps Cisco recommends:

1. Open a DOS window and ping 127.0.0.1. This is the diagnostic, or loopback, address, and if you get a successful ping, your IP stack is considered to be initialized. If it fails, then you have an IP stack failure and need to reinstall TCP/IP on the host.

```
C:\>ping 127.0.0.1
Pinging 127.0.0.1 with 32 bytes of data:
Reply from 127.0.0.1: bytes=32 time<1ms TTL=128
Reply from 127.0.0.1: bytes=32 time<1ms TTL=128
Reply from 127.0.0.1: bytes=32 time<1ms TTL=128
Reply from 127.0.0.1: bytes=32 time<1ms TTL=128
Ping statistics for 127.0.0.1:
    Packets: Sent = 4, Received = 4, Lost = 0 (0% loss),
Approximate round trip times in milli-seconds:
    Minimum = 0ms, Maximum = 0ms, Average = 0ms
```

2. From the DOS window, ping the IP address of the local host. If that's successful, your network interface card (NIC) is functioning. If it fails, there is a problem with the NIC. Success here doesn't mean that a cable is plugged into the NIC, only that the IP protocol stack on the host can communicate to the NIC (via the LAN driver).

```
C:\>ping 172.16.10.2
Pinging 172.16.10.2 with 32 bytes of data:
Reply from 172.16.10.2: bytes=32 time<1ms TTL=128
Reply from 172.16.10.2: bytes=32 time<1ms TTL=128
Reply from 172.16.10.2: bytes=32 time<1ms TTL=128
Reply from 172.16.10.2: bytes=32 time<1ms TTL=128
Ping statistics for 172.16.10.2:
    Packets: Sent = 4, Received = 4, Lost = 0 (0% loss),
Approximate round trip times in milli-seconds:
    Minimum = 0ms, Maximum = 0ms, Average = 0ms
```

3. From the DOS window, ping the default gateway (router). If the ping works, it means that the NIC is plugged into the network and can communicate on the local network. If it fails, you have a local physical network problem that could be anywhere from the NIC to the router.

```
C:\>ping 172.16.10.1
Pinging 172.16.10.1 with 32 bytes of data:
Reply from 172.16.10.1: bytes=32 time<1ms TTL=128
Reply from 172.16.10.1: bytes=32 time<1ms TTL=128
Reply from 172.16.10.1: bytes=32 time<1ms TTL=128
Reply from 172.16.10.1: bytes=32 time<1ms TTL=128
```

```
Ping statistics for 172.16.10.1:
    Packets: Sent = 4, Received = 4, Lost = 0 (0% loss),
Approximate round trip times in milli-seconds:
    Minimum = 0ms, Maximum = 0ms, Average = 0ms
```

4. If steps 1 through 3 were successful, try to ping the remote server. If that works, then you know that you have IP communication between the local host and the remote server. You also know that the remote physical network is working.

    C:\>**ping 172.16.20.2**

```
Pinging 172.16.20.2 with 32 bytes of data:
Reply from 172.16.20.2: bytes=32 time<1ms TTL=128
Reply from 172.16.20.2: bytes=32 time<1ms TTL=128
Reply from 172.16.20.2: bytes=32 time<1ms TTL=128
Reply from 172.16.20.2: bytes=32 time<1ms TTL=128
Ping statistics for 172.16.20.2:
    Packets: Sent = 4, Received = 4, Lost = 0 (0% loss),
Approximate round trip times in milli-seconds:
    Minimum = 0ms, Maximum = 0ms, Average = 0ms
```

If the user still can't communicate with the server after steps 1 through 4 are successful, you probably have some type of name resolution problem and need to check your Domain Name System (DNS) settings. But if the ping to the remote server fails, then you know you have some type of remote physical network problem and need to go to the server and work through steps 1 through 3 until you find the snag.

Before we move on to determining IP address problems and how to fix them, I just want to mention some basic DOS commands that you can use to help troubleshoot your network from both a PC and a Cisco router (the commands might do the same thing, but they are implemented differently).

Packet InterNet Groper (ping)   Uses ICMP echo request and replies to test if a node IP stack is initialized and alive on the network.

traceroute   Displays the list of routers on a path to a network destination by using TTL time-outs and ICMP error messages. This command will not work from a DOS prompt.

tracert   Same command as `traceroute`, but it's a Microsoft Windows command and will not work on a Cisco router.

arp -a   Displays IP-to-MAC-address mappings on a Windows PC.

show ip arp   Same command as `arp -a`, but displays the ARP table on a Cisco router. Like the commands `traceroute` and `tracert`, they are not interchangeable through DOS and Cisco.

ipconfig /all   Used only from a DOS prompt, shows you the PC network configuration.

Once you've gone through all these steps and used the appropriate DOS commands, if necessary, what do you do if you find a problem? How do you go about fixing an IP address configuration error? Let's move on and discuss how to determine the IP address problems and how to fix them.

Determining IP Address Problems

It's common for a host, router, or other network device to be configured with the wrong IP address, subnet mask, or default gateway. Because this happens way too often, I'm going to teach you how to both determine and fix IP address configuration errors.

Once you've worked through the four basic steps of troubleshooting and determined there's a problem, you obviously then need to find and fix it. It really helps to draw out the network and IP addressing scheme. If it's already done, consider yourself lucky and go buy a lottery ticket, because although it should be done, it rarely is. And if it is, it's usually outdated or inaccurate anyway. Typically it is not done, and you'll probably just have to bite the bullet and start from scratch.

I'll show you how to draw out your network using CDP in Chapter 5, "Managing the Cisco IOS."

Once you have your network accurately drawn out, including the IP addressing scheme, you need to verify each host's IP address, mask, and default gateway address to determine the problem. (I'm assuming that you don't have a physical problem or that if you did, you've already fixed it.)

Let's check out the example illustrated in Figure 3.18. A user in the sales department calls and tells you that she can't get to ServerA in the marketing department. You ask her if she can get to ServerB in the marketing department, but she doesn't know because she doesn't have rights to log on to that server. What do you do?

FIGURE 3.18 IP address problem 1

You ask the client to go through the four troubleshooting steps that you learned about in the preceding section. Steps 1 through 3 work, but step 4 fails. By looking at the figure, can you determine the problem? Look for clues in the network drawing. First, the WAN link between the Lab_A router and the Lab_B router shows the mask as a /27. You should already know that this mask is 255.255.255.224 and then determine that all networks are using this mask. The network address is 192.168.1.0. What are our valid subnets and hosts? 256 – 224 = 32, so this makes our subnets 32, 64, 96, 128, etc. So, by looking at the figure, you can see that subnet 32 is being used by the sales department, the WAN link is using subnet 96, and the marketing department is using subnet 64.

Now you've got to determine what the valid host ranges are for each subnet. From what you learned at the beginning of this chapter, you should now be able to easily determine the subnet address, broadcast addresses, and valid host ranges. The valid hosts for the Sales LAN are 33 through 62—the broadcast address is 63 because the next subnet is 64, right? For the Marketing LAN, the valid hosts are 65 through 94 (broadcast 95), and for the WAN link, 97 through 126 (broadcast 127). By looking at the figure, you can determine that the default gateway on the Lab_B router is incorrect. That address is the broadcast address of the 64 subnet, so there's no way it could be a valid host.

Did you get all that? Maybe we should try another one, just to make sure. Figure 3.19 shows a network problem. A user in the Sales LAN can't get to ServerB. You have the user run through the four basic troubleshooting steps and find that the host can communicate to the local network but not to the remote network. Find and define the IP addressing problem.

FIGURE 3.19   IP address problem 2

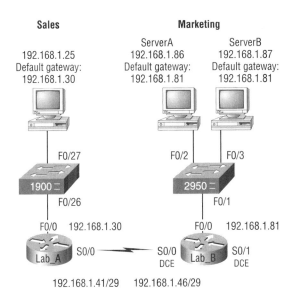

If you use the same steps used to solve the last problem, you can see first that the WAN link again provides the subnet mask to use— /29, or 255.255.255.248. You need to determine what the valid subnets, broadcast addresses, and valid host ranges are to solve this problem.

The 248 mask is a block size of 8 (256 – 248 = 8), so the subnets both start and increment in multiples of 8. By looking at the figure, you see that the Sales LAN is in the 24 subnet, the WAN is in the 40 subnet, and the Marketing LAN is in the 80 subnet. Can you see the problem yet? The valid host range for the Sales LAN is 25–30, and the configuration appears correct. The valid host range for the WAN link is 41–46, and this also appears correct. The valid host range for the 80 subnet is 81–86, with a broadcast address of 87 because the next subnet is 88. ServerB has been configured with the broadcast address of the subnet.

Okay, now that you can figure out misconfigured IP addresses on hosts, what do you do if a host doesn't have an IP address and you need to assign one? What you need to do is look at other hosts on the LAN and figure out the network, mask, and default gateway. Let's take a look at a couple of examples of how to find and apply valid IP addresses to hosts.

You need to assign a server and router IP addresses on a LAN. The subnet assigned on that segment is 192.168.20.24/29, and the router needs to be assigned the first usable address and the server the last valid host ID. What are the IP address, mask, and default gateway assigned to the server?

To answer this, you must know that a /29 is a 255.255.255.248 mask, which provides a block size of 8. The subnet is known as 24, the next subnet in a block of 8 is 32, so the broadcast address of the 24 subnet is 31, which makes the valid host range 25–30.

Server IP address: 192.168.20.30

Server mask: 255.255.255.248

Default gateway: 192.168.20.25 (router's IP address)

As another example, let's take a look at Figure 3.20 and solve this problem.

FIGURE 3.20   Find the valid host #1.

RouterA

E0: 192.168.10.33/27

HostA

Look at the router's IP address on Ethernet0. What IP address, subnet mask, and valid host range could be assigned to the host?

The IP address of the router's Ethernet0 is 192.168.10.33/27. As you already know, a /27 is a 224 mask with a block size of 32. The router's interface is in the 32 subnet. The next subnet is 64, so that makes the broadcast address of the 32 subnet 63 and the valid host range 33–62.

> Host IP address: 192.168.10.34–62 (any address in the range except for 33, which is assigned to the router)
>
> Mask: 255.255.255.224
>
> Default gateway: 192.168.10.33

Figure 3.21 shows two routers with Ethernet configurations already assigned. What are the host addresses and subnet masks of hosts A and B?

FIGURE 3.21   Find the valid host #2

RouterA has an IP address of 192.168.10.65/26 and RouterB has an IP address of 192.168.10.33/28. What are the host configurations? RouterA Ethernet0 is in the 192.168.10.64 subnet and RouterB Ethernet0 is in the 192.168.10.32 network.

> Host A IP address: 192.168.10.66–126
>
> Host A mask: 255.255.255.192
>
> Host A default gateway: 192.168.10.65
>
> Host B IP address: 192.168.10.34–46
>
> Host B mask: 255.255.255.240
>
> Host B default gateway: 192.168.10.33

Just a couple more examples and then this chapter is history. Hang in there!

Figure 3.22 shows two routers; you need to configure the S0/0 interface on RouterA. The network assigned to the serial link is 172.16.17.0/22. What IP address can be assigned?

First, you must know that a /22 CIDR is 255.255.252.0, which makes a block size of 4 in the third octet. Since 17 is listed, the available range is 16.1 through 19.254; so, for example, the IP address S0/0 could be 172.16.18.255 since that's within the range.

Okay, last one! You have one Class C network ID and you need to provide one usable subnet per city while allowing enough usable host addresses for each city specified in Figure 3.23. What is your mask?

FIGURE 3.22   Find the valid host address #3

172.16.17.0/22

RouterA   RouterB

S0/0   S0/0

Actually, this is probably the easiest thing you've done all day! I count 5 subnets needed and the Wyoming office needs 16 users (always look for the network that needs the most hosts). What block size is needed for the Wyoming office? 32. (Remember, you cannot use a block size of 16 because you always have to subtract 2!) What mask provides you with a block size of 32? 224. Bingo! This provides 8 subnets, each with 30 hosts.

You're done, the diva has sung, the chicken has crossed the road…whew! Okay, take a good break (but skip the shot and the beer for now), then come back and go through the written labs and review questions.

FIGURE 3.23   Find the valid subnet mask.

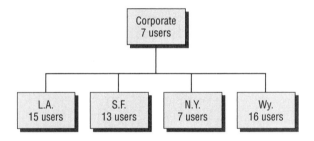

Summary

Did you read Chapters 2 and 3 and understand everything on the first pass? If so, that is fantastic—congratulations! The thing is, you probably got lost a couple of times—and as I told you, that's what usually happens, so don't stress. Don't feel bad if you have to read each chapter more than once, or even 10 times, before you're truly good to go.

This chapter provided you with an important understanding of IP subnetting. After reading this chapter, you should be able to subnet IP addresses in your head. You should also know how to design and implement simple VLSM networks.

You should also understand the Cisco troubleshooting methods. You must remember the four steps that Cisco recommends you take when trying to narrow down exactly where a network/IP addressing problem is and then know how to proceed systematically in order to fix it. In addition, you should be able to find valid IP addresses and subnet masks by looking at a network diagram.

Exam Essentials

Remember the steps to subnet in your head.   Understand how IP addressing and subnetting work. First, determine your block size by using the 256-subnet mask math. Then count your subnets and determine the broadcast address of each subnet—it is always the number right before the next subnet. Your valid hosts are the numbers between the subnet address and the broadcast address.

Understand the various block sizes.   This is an important part of understanding IP addressing and subnetting. The valid block sizes are always 4, 8, 16, 32, 64, 128, etc. You can determine your block size by using the 256-subnet mask math.

Remember the four diagnostic steps.   The four simple steps that Cisco recommends for trouble-shooting are ping the loopback address, ping the NIC, ping the default gateway, and ping the remote device.

You must be able to find and fix an IP addressing problem.   Once you go through the four troubleshooting steps that Cisco recommends, you must be able to determine the IP addressing problem by drawing out the network and finding the valid and invalid hosts addressed in your network.

Understand the troubleshooting tools that you can use from your host and a Cisco router   `ping 127.0.0.1` tests your local IP stack. `tracert` is a Windows DOS command to track the path a packet takes through an internetwork to a destination. Cisco routers use the command `traceroute`, or just `trace` for short. Don't confuse the Windows and Cisco commands. Although they produce the same output, they don't work from the same prompts. `ipconfig /all` will display your PC network configuration from a DOS prompt, and `arp -a` (again from a DOS prompt) will display IP-to-MAC-address mapping on a Windows PC.

Written Labs 3

In this section, you'll complete the following labs to make sure you've got the information and concepts contained within them fully dialed in:

- Lab 3.1: Written Subnet Practice #1
- Lab 3.2: Written Subnet Practice #2
- Lab 3.3: Written Subnet Practice #3

(The answers to the written labs can be found following the answers to the review questions for this chapter.)

Written Lab 3.1: Written Subnet Practice #1

Write the subnet, broadcast address, and valid host range for question 1 through question 6:

1. 192.168.100.25/30
2. 192.168.100.37/28
3. 192.168.100.66/27
4. 192.168.100.17/29
5. 192.168.100.99/26
6. 192.168.100.99/25
7. You have a Class B network and need 29 subnets. What is your mask?
8. What is the broadcast address of 192.168.192.10/29?
9. How many hosts are available with a Class C /29 mask?
10. What is the subnet for host ID 10.16.3.65/23?

Written Lab 3.2: Written Subnet Practice

Given a Class B network and the net bits identified (CIDR), complete the following table to identify the subnet mask and the number of host addresses possible for each mask.

Classful Address	Subnet Mask	Number of Hosts per Subnet ($2^x - 2$)
/16		
/17		
/18		
/19		
/20		
/21		
/22		
/23		
/24		
/25		
/26		
/27		
/28		
/29		
/30		

Written Lab 3.3: Written Subnet Practice

Decimal IP Address	Address Class	Number of Subnet and Host Bits	Number of Subnets (2^x)	Number of Hosts ($2^x - 2$)
10.25.66.154/23				
172.31.254.12/24				
192.168.20.123/28				
63.24.89.21/18				
128.1.1.254/20				
208.100.54.209/30				

(The answers to the written labs can be found following the answers to the review questions for this chapter.)

Review Questions

 The following questions are designed to test your understanding of this chapter's material. For more information on how to get additional questions, please see this book's Introduction.

1. What is the maximum number of IP addresses that can be assigned to hosts on a local subnet that uses the 255.255.255.224 subnet mask?

    A. 14

    B. 15

    C. 16

    D. 30

    E. 31

    F. 62

2. You have a network that needs 29 subnets while maximizing the number of host addresses available on each subnet. How many bits must you borrow from the host field to provide the correct subnet mask?

    A. 2

    B. 3

    C. 4

    D. 5

    E. 6

    F. 7

3. What is the subnetwork address for a host with the IP address 200.10.5.68/28?

    A. 200.10.5.56

    B. 200.10.5.32

    C. 200.10.5.64

    D. 200.10.5.0

4. The network address of 172.16.0.0/19 provides how many subnets and hosts?

    A. 7 subnets, 30 hosts each

    B. 7 subnets, 2,046 hosts each

    C. 7 subnets, 8,190 hosts each

    D. 8 subnets, 30 hosts each

    E. 8 subnets, 2,046 hosts each

    F. 8 subnets, 8,190 hosts each

5. Which two statements describe the IP address 10.16.3.65/23? (Choose two.)

    A. The subnet address is 10.16.3.0 255.255.254.0.

    B. The lowest host address in the subnet is 10.16.2.1 255.255.254.0.

    C. The last valid host address in the subnet is 10.16.2.254 255.255.254.0.

    D. The broadcast address of the subnet is 10.16.3.255 255.255.254.0.

    E. The network is not subnetted.

6. If a host on a network has the address 172.16.45.14/30, what is the subnetwork this host belongs to?

    A. 172.16.45.0

    B. 172.16.45.4

    C. 172.16.45.8

    D. 172.16.45.12

    E. 172.16.45.16

7. On a VLSM network, which mask should you use on point-to-point WAN links in order to reduce the waste of IP addresses?

    A. /27

    B. /28

    C. /29

    D. /30

    E. /31

8. What is the subnetwork number of a host with an IP address of 172.16.66.0/21?

    A. 172.16.36.0

    B. 172.16.48.0

    C. 172.16.64.0

    D. 172.16.0.0

9. You have an interface on a router with the IP address of 192.168.192.10/29. Including the router interface, how many hosts can have IP addresses on the LAN attached to the router interface?

    A. 6

    B. 8

    C. 30

    D. 62

    E. 126

10. You need to configure a server that is on the subnet 192.168.19.24/29. The router has the first available host address. Which of the following should you assign to the server?

    A. 192.168.19.0 255.255.255.0

    B. 192.168.19.33 255.255.255.240

    C. 192.168.19.26 255.255.255.248

    D. 192.168.19.31 255.255.255.248

    E. 192.168.19.34 255.255.255.240

11. You have an interface on a router with the IP address of 192.168.192.10/29. What is the broadcast address the hosts will use on this LAN?

    A. 192.168.192.15

    B. 192.168.192.31

    C. 192.168.192.63

    D. 192.168.192.127

    E. 192.168.192.255

12. You need to subnet a network that has 5 subnets, each with at least 16 hosts. Which classful subnet mask would you use?

    A. 255.255.255.192

    B. 255.255.255.224

    C. 255.255.255.240

    D. 255.255.255.248

13. A network administrator is connecting hosts A and B directly through their Ethernet interfaces, as shown in the illustration. Ping attempts between the hosts are unsuccessful. What can be done to provide connectivity between the hosts? (Choose two.)

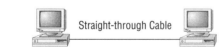

Straight-through Cable

IP Address: 192.168.1.20   IP Address: 192.168.1.201
Mask 255.255.255.240   Mask 255.255.255.240

    A. A crossover cable should be used in place of the straight-through cable.

    B. A rollover cable should be used in place of the straight-through cable.

    C. The subnet masks should be set to 255.255.255.192.

    D. A default gateway needs to be set on each host.

    E. The subnet masks should be set to 255.255.255.0.

14. If an Ethernet port on a router were assigned an IP address of 172.16.112.1/25, what would be the valid subnet address of this host?

   A. 172.16.112.0

   B. 172.16.0.0

   C. 172.16.96.0

   D. 172.16.255.0

   E. 172.16.128.0

15. Using the following illustration, what would be the IP address of E0 if you were using the eighth subnet? The network ID is 192.168.10.0/28 and you need to use the last available IP address in the range. The zero subnet should not be considered valid for this question.

   A. 192.168.10.142

   B. 192.168.10.66

   C. 192.168.100.254

   D. 192.168.10.143

   E. 192.168.10.126

16. Using the illustration from the previous question, what would be the IP address of S0 if you were using the first subnet? The network ID is 192.168.10.0/28 and you need to use the last available IP address in the range. Again, the zero subnet should not be considered valid for this question.

   A. 192.168.10.24

   B. 192.168.10.62

   C. 192.168.10.30

   D. 192.168.10.127

17. Which configuration command must be in effect to allow the use of 8 subnets if the Class C subnet mask is 255.255.255.224?

   A. Router(config)#`ip classless`

   B. Router(config)#`ip version 6`

   C. Router(config)#`no ip classful`

   D. Router(config)#`ip unnumbered`

   E. Router(config)#`ip subnet-zero`

   F. Router(config)#`ip all-nets`

18. You have a network with a subnet of 172.16.16.0/22. Which is the valid host address?

   A. 172.16.17.1 255.255.255.252

   B. 172.16.0.1 255.255.240.0

   C. 172.16.20.1 255.255.254.0

   D. 172.16.16.1 255.255.255.240

   E. 172.16.18.255 255.255.252.0

   F. 172.16.0.1 255.255.255.0

19. Your router has the following IP address on Ethernet0: 172.16.2.1/23. Which of the following can be valid host IDs on the LAN interface attached to the router? (Choose two.)

   A. 172.16.0.5

   B. 172.16.1.100

   C. 172.16.1.198

   D. 172.16.2.255

   E. 172.16.3.0

   F. 172.16.3.255

20. To test the IP stack on your local host, which IP address would you ping?

   A. 127.0.0.0

   B. 1.0.0.127

   C. 127.0.0.1

   D. 127.0.0.255

   E. 255.255.255.255

Answers to Review Questions

1. D. A /27 (255.255.255.224) is 3 bits on and 5 bits off. This provides 8 subnets, each with 30 hosts. Does it matter if this mask is used with a Class A, B, or C network address? Not at all. The number of host bits would never change.

2. D. A 240 mask is 4 subnet bits and provides 16 subnets, each with 14 hosts. We need more subnets, so let's add subnet bits. One more subnet bit would be a 248 mask. This provides 5 subnet bits (32 subnets) with 3 host bits (6 hosts per subnet). This is the best answer.

3. C. This is a pretty simple question. A /28 is 255.255.255.240, which means that our block size is 16 in the fourth octet. 0, 16, 32, 48, 64, 80, etc. The host is in the 64 subnet.

4. F. A CIDR address of /19 is 255.255.224.0. This is a Class B address, so that is only 3 subnet bits, but it provides 13 host bits, or 8 subnets, each with 8,190 hosts.

5. B, D. The mask 255.255.254.0 (/23) used with a Class A address means that there are 15 subnet bits and 9 host bits. The block size in the third octet is 2 (256 – 254). So this makes the subnets in the interesting octet 0, 2, 4, 6, etc., all the way to 254. The host 10.16.3.65 is in the 2.0 subnet. The next subnet is 4.0, so the broadcast address for the 2.0 subnet is 3.255. The valid host addresses are 2.1 through 3.254.

6. D. A /30, regardless of the class of address, has a 252 in the fourth octet. This means we have a block size of 4 and our subnets are 0, 4, 8, 12, 16, etc. Address 14 is obviously in the 12 subnet.

7. D. A point-to-point link uses only two hosts. A /30, or 255.255.255.252, mask provides two hosts per subnet.

8. C. A /21 is 255.255.248.0, which means we have a block size of 8 in the third octet, so we just count by 8 until we reach 66. The subnet in this question is 64.0. The next subnet is 72.0, so the broadcast address of the 64 subnet is 71.255.

9. A. A /29 (255.255.255.248), regardless of the class of address, has only 3 host bits. Six hosts is the maximum number of hosts on this LAN, including the router interface.

10. C. A /29 is 255.255.255.248, which is a block size of 8 in the fourth octet. The subnets are 0, 8, 16, 24, 32, 40, etc. 192.168.19.24 is the 24 subnet, and since 32 is the next subnet, the broadcast address for the 24 subnet is 31. 192.168.19.26 is the only correct answer.

11. A. A /29 (255.255.255.248) has a block size of 8 in the fourth octet. This means the subnets are 0, 8, 16, 24, etc. 10 is in the 8 subnet. The next subnet is 16, so 15 is the broadcast address.

12. B. You need 5 subnets, each with at least 16 hosts. The mask 255.255.255.240 provides 16 subnets with 14 hosts—this will not work. The mask 255.255.255.224 provides 8 subnets, each with 30 hosts. This is the best answer.

13. A, E. First, if you have two hosts directly connected, as shown in the graphic, then you need a crossover cable. A straight-through cable won't work. Second, the hosts have different masks, which puts them in different subnets. The easy solution is just to set both masks to 255.255.255.0 (/24).

14. A. A /25 mask is 255.255.255.128. Used with a Class B network, the third and fourth octets are used for subnetting with a total of 9 subnet bits, 8 bits in the third octet and 1 bit in the fourth octet. Since there is only 1 bit in the fourth octet, the bit is either off or on—which is a value of 0 or 128. The host in the question is in the 0 subnet, which has a broadcast address of 127 since 128 is the next subnet.

15. A. A /28 is a 255.255.255.240 mask. Let's count to the ninth subnet (we need to find the broadcast address of the eighth subnet, so we need to count to the ninth subnet). Starting at 16 (remember, the question stated that we will not use subnet zero, so we start at 16, not 0), 16, 32, 48, 64, 80, 96, 112, 128, 144. The eighth subnet is 128 and the next subnet is 144, so our broadcast address of the 128 subnet is 143. This makes the host range 129–142. 142 is the last valid host.

16. C. A /28 is a 255.255.255.240 mask. The first subnet is 16 (remember that the question stated not to use subnet zero) and the next subnet is 32, so our broadcast address is 31. This makes our host range 17–30. 30 is the last valid host.

17. E. A Class C subnet mask of 255.255.255.224 is 3 bits on and 5 bits off (11100000) and provides 8 subnets, each with 30 hosts. However, if the command `ip subnet-zero` is not used, then only 6 subnets would be available for use.

18. E. A Class B network ID with a /22 mask is 255.255.252.0, with a block size of 4 in the third octet. The network address in the question is in subnet 172.16.16.0 with a broadcast address of 172.16.19.255. Only option E even has the correct subnet mask listed, and 172.16.18.255 is a valid host.

19. D, E. The router's IP address on the E0 interface is 172.16.2.1/23, which is 255.255.254.0. This makes the third octet a block size of 2. The router's interface is in the 2.0 subnet, and the broadcast address is 3.255 because the next subnet is 4.0. The valid host range is 2.1 through 3.254. The router is using the first valid host address in the range.

20. C. To test the local stack on your host, ping the loopback interface of 127.0.0.1.

Answers to Written Lab 3.1

1. 192.168.100.25/30. A /30 is 255.255.255.252. The valid subnet is 192.168.100.24, broadcast is 192.168.100.27, and valid hosts are 192.168.100.25 and 26.

2. 192.168.100.37/28. A /28 is 255.255.255.240. The fourth octet is a block size of 16. Just count by 16s until you pass 37. 0, 16, 32, 48. The host is in the 32 subnet, with a broadcast address of 47. Valid hosts 33–46.

3. 192.168.100.66/27. A /27 is 255.255.255.224. The fourth octet is a block size of 32. Count by 32s until you pass the host address of 66. 0, 32, 64, 96. The host is in the 64 subnet, broadcast address of 95. Valid host range of 65-94.

4. 192.168.100.17/29. A /29 is 255.255.255.248. The fourth octet is a block size of 8. 0, 8, 16, 24. The host is in the 16 subnet, broadcast of 23. Valid hosts 17–22.

5. 192.168.100.99/26. A /26 is 255.255.255.192. The fourth octet has a block size of 64. 0, 64, 128. The host is in the 64 subnet, broadcast of 127. Valid hosts 65–126.

6. 192.168.100.99/25. A /25 is 255.255.255.128. The fourth octet is a block size of 128. 0, 128. The host is in the 0 subnet, broadcast of 127. Valid hosts 1–126.

7. A default Class B is 255.255.0.0. A Class B 255.255.255.0 mask is 256 subnets, each with 254 hosts. We need fewer subnets. If we used 255.255.240.0, this provides 16 subnets. Let's add one more subnet bit. 255.255.248.0. This is 5 bits of subnetting, which provides 32 subnets. This is our best answer, a /21.

8. A /29 is 255.255.255.248. This is a block size of 8 in the fourth octet. 0, 8, 16. The host is in the 8 subnet, broadcast is 15.

9. A /29 is 255.255.255.248, which is 5 subnet bits and 3 host bits. This is only 6 hosts per subnet.

10. A /23 is 255.255.254.0. The third octet is a block size of 2. 0, 2, 4. The host is in the 16.2.0 subnet; the broadcast address is 16.3.255.

Answers to Written Lab 3.2

Classful Address	Subnet Mask	Number of Hosts per Subnet ($2^h - 2$)
/16	255.255.0.0	65,534
/17	255.255.128.0	32,766
/18	255.255.192.0	16,382
/19	255.255.224.0	8,190
/20	255.255.240.0	4,094
/21	255.255.248.0	2,046
/22	255.255.252.0	1,022
/23	255.255.254.0	510
/24	255.255.255.0	254
/25	255.255.255.128	126
/26	255.255.255.192	62
/27	255.255.255.224	30
/28	255.255.255.240	14
/29	255.255.255.248	6
/30	255.255.255.252	2

Answers to Written Lab 3.3

Decimal IP Address	Address Class	Number of Subnet and Host Bits	Number of Subnets (2^x)	Number of Hosts ($2^x - 2$)
10.25.66.154/23	A	15/9	32768	510
172.31.254.12/24	B	8/8	256	254
192.168.20.123/28	C	4/4	16	14
63.24.89.21/18	A	10/14	1,024	16,382
128.1.1.254/20	B	4/12	16	4094
208.100.54.209/30	C	6/2	64	2

Chapter

4

Cisco's Internetworking Operating System (IOS) and Security Device Manager (SDM)

THE CCNA EXAM TOPICS COVERED IN THIS CHAPTER INCLUDE THE FOLLOWING:

✓ **Implement an IP addressing scheme and IP Services to meet network requirements in a medium-size Enterprise branch office network**

- Configure, verify and troubleshoot DHCP and DNS operation on a router (including: CLI/SDM)

✓ **Configure, verify, and troubleshoot basic router operation and routing on Cisco devices**

- Describe the operation of Cisco routers (including: router bootup process, POST, router components)
- Access and utilize the router to set basic parameters (including: CLI/SDM)
- Connect, configure, and verify operation status of a device interface
- Verify device configuration and network connectivity using ping, traceroute, telnet, SSH or other utilities
- Verify network connectivity (including: using ping, traceroute, and telnet or SSH)
- Troubleshoot routing issues
- Verify router hardware and software operation using SHOW & DEBUG commands

The time has come to introduce you to the Cisco Internetwork Operating System (IOS). The IOS is what runs Cisco routers as well as Cisco's switches, and it's what allows you to configure the devices as well.

So that's what you're going to learn about in this chapter. I'm going to show you how to configure a Cisco IOS router using the Cisco IOS command-line interface (CLI). When you become proficient with this interface, you'll be able to configure hostnames, banners, passwords, and more, as well as troubleshoot using the Cisco IOS.

From there, we'll take a peek at Cisco's Security Device Manager (SDM) and you'll find out how to set up an HTTPS session to a router to provide the same types of configurations. The SDM really becomes a much more powerful tool in later chapters because it makes configuring access lists, VPNs, and IPSec a snap, but first, you need to learn the basics of Cisco's IOS.

I'm also going to get you up to speed on the vital basics of router configurations and command verifications. Here's a list of the subjects we'll be covering in this chapter:

- Understanding and configuring the Cisco Internetwork Operating System (IOS)
- Connecting to a router
- Bringing up a router
- Logging into a router
- Understanding the router prompts
- Understanding the CLI prompts
- Performing editing and help features
- Gathering basic routing information
- Setting administrative functions
- Setting hostnames
- Setting banners
- Setting passwords
- Setting interface descriptions
- Performing interface configurations
- Viewing, saving, and erasing configurations
- Verifying routing configurations

And just as it was with preceding chapters, the fundamentals that you'll learn in this chapter are foundational building blocks that really need to be in place before you go on to the next chapters in the book.

For up-to-the-minute updates for this chapter, please see www.lammle.com and/or www.sybex.com.

The IOS User Interface

The *Cisco Internetwork Operating System (IOS)* is the kernel of Cisco routers and most switches. In case you didn't know, a kernel is the basic, indispensable part of an operating system that allocates resources and manages things such as low-level hardware interfaces and security.

In the following sections, I'll show you the Cisco IOS and how to configure a Cisco router using the command-line interface (CLI). We'll use Cisco's SDM toward the end of the chapter.

I'm going to save Cisco switch configurations for Chapter 8, "LAN Switching and Spanning Tree Protocol (STP)."

Cisco Router IOS

The Cisco IOS is a proprietary kernel that provides routing, switching, internetworking, and tele-communications features. The first IOS was written by William Yeager in 1986, and it enabled net-worked applications. It runs on most Cisco routers as well as an ever-increasing number of Cisco Catalyst switches, like the Catalyst 2950/2960 and 3550/3560 series switches.

These are some important things that the Cisco router IOS software is responsible for:

- Carrying network protocols and functions
- Connecting high-speed traffic between devices
- Adding security to control access and stop unauthorized network use
- Providing scalability for ease of network growth and redundancy
- Supplying network reliability for connecting to network resources

You can access the Cisco IOS through the console port of a router, from a modem into the auxiliary (or Aux) port, or even through Telnet. Access to the IOS command line is called an *EXEC session.*

Connecting to a Cisco Router

You can connect to a Cisco router to configure it, verify its configuration, and check statistics. There are different ways to do this, but most often, the first place you would connect to is the console port. The *console port* is usually an RJ-45 (8-pin modular) connection located at the back of the router—by default, there may or may not be a password set. The new ISR routers use cisco as the username and cisco as the password by default.

See Chapter 1, "Internetworking," for an explanation of how to configure a PC to connect to a router console port.

You can also connect to a Cisco router through an *auxiliary port*—which is really the same thing as a console port, so it follows that you can use it as one. But an auxiliary port also allows you to configure modem commands so that a modem can be connected to the router. This is a cool feature—it lets you dial up a remote router and attach to the auxiliary port if the router is down and you need to configure it *out-of-band* (meaning out of the network).

The third way to connect to a Cisco router is in-band, through the program *Telnet*. (*In-band* means configuring the router through the network, the opposite of "out-of-band.")Telnet is a terminal emulation program that acts as though it's a dumb terminal. You can use Telnet to connect to any active interface on a router, such as an Ethernet or serial port.

Figure 4.1 shows an illustration of a Cisco 2600 series modular router, which is a cut above routers populating the 2500 series because it has a faster processor and can handle many more interfaces. Both the 2500 and 2600 series routers are end of life (EOL), and you can only buy them used. However, many 2600 series routers are still found in production, so it's important to understand them. Pay close attention to all the different kinds of interfaces and connections.

FIGURE 4.1 A Cisco 2600 router

Cisco 2610 router

Ethernet 0/0
10BaseT port (RJ-45)   Console port (RJ-45)   Auxiliary port (RJ-45)

The 2600 series router can have multiple serial interfaces, which can be used for connecting a T1 or Frame Relay using a serial V.35 WAN connection. Multiple Ethernet or FastEthernet ports can be used on the router, depending on the model. This router also has one console and one auxiliary connection via RJ-45 connectors.

Another router I want to talk about is the 2800 series (shown in Figure 4.2). This router has replaced the 2600 series router series and is referred to as an Integrated Services Router (ISR). It gets its name because many of the services, like security, are built into it. It's a modular device like the 2600, but it's much faster and a lot more sleek—it's elegantly designed to support a broad new range of interface options.

FIGURE 4.2 A Cisco 2800 router

I mentioned that security is built in—the 2800 has the Security Device Manager (SDM) pre-installed. The SDM is a Web-based device-management tool for Cisco routers that can help you configure a router via a web console. I'll cover that later in this chapter. You need to keep in mind that for the most part, you get some serious bang for your buck with the 2800—unless you start adding a lot of interfaces to it. You've got to pony up for each one of those little beauties, and things can really start to add up—fast!

There are a couple of other series of routers that are less expensive then the 2800 series: the 1800 and 800 series. You may want to look into these routers if you're looking for a less-expensive alternative to the 2800 but still want to run the same 12.4 IOS and the latest SDM.

Figure 4.3 shows an 1841 router that holds most of the same interfaces as the 2800, but it's smaller and less expensive. The real reason you would opt for a 2800 instead of an 1800 series router comes down to the more advanced interfaces you can run on the 2800—things like the wireless controller and switching modules.

FIGURE 4.3   A Cisco 1841 router

As a heads up, I'm going to be using all new 2800, 1800, and 800 series routers throughout this book to demonstrate examples of router configurations. But understand that you can use the 2600, and even 2500 routers to practice routing principles.

 You can find more information about all Cisco routers at www.cisco.com/en/
US/products/hw/routers/index.html.

Bringing Up a Router

When you first bring up a Cisco router, it will run a power-on self-test (POST). If it passes, it will then look for and load the Cisco IOS from flash memory—if an IOS file is present. (Just in case you don't know, flash memory is electronically erasable programmable read-only memory—an EEPROM.) After that, the IOS loads and looks for a valid configuration—the startup-config—that's stored in nonvolatile RAM, or NVRAM.

The following messages appear when you first boot or reload a router (I am using my 2811 router):

```
System Bootstrap, Version 12.4(13r)T, RELEASE SOFTWARE (fc1)
Technical Support: http://www.cisco.com/techsupport
Copyright (c) 2006 by cisco Systems, Inc.
```

```
Initializing memory for ECC
c2811 platform with 262144 Kbytes of main memory
Main memory is configured to 64 bit mode with ECC enabled
Upgrade ROMMON initialized
program load complete, entry point: 0x8000f000, size: 0xcb80
program load complete, entry point: 0x8000f000, size: 0xcb80
```

This is the first part of the router boot process output. It's information about the bootstrap program that first runs the POST. It then tells the router how to load, which by default is to find the IOS in flash memory. It also lists the amount of RAM in the router.

The next part shows us that the IOS is being decompressed into RAM:

```
program load complete, entry point: 0x8000f000, size: 0x14b45f8
Self decompressing the image :
  #################################################################
  ############################################# [OK]
```

The pound signs are telling us that the IOS is being loaded into RAM. After it is decompressed into RAM, the IOS is loaded and starts running the router, as shown below. Notice that the IOS version is stated as advanced security version 12.4(12):

```
[some output cut]
Cisco IOS Software, 2800 Software (C2800NM-ADVSECURITYK9-M), Version
  12.4(12), RELEASE SOFTWARE (fc1)
Technical Support: http://www.cisco.com/techsupport
Copyright (c) 1986-2006 by Cisco Systems, Inc.
Compiled Fri 17-Nov-06 12:02 by prod_rel_team
Image text-base: 0x40093160, data-base: 0x41AA0000
```

A sweet new feature of the new ISR routers is that the IOS name is no longer cryptic. The filename actually tells you what the IOS can do, as in Advanced Security. Once the IOS is loaded, the information learned from the POST will be displayed next, as you can see here:

```
[some output cut]
Cisco 2811 (revision 49.46) with 249856K/12288K bytes of memory.
Processor board ID FTX1049A1AB
2 FastEthernet interfaces
4 Serial(sync/async) interfaces
1 Virtual Private Network (VPN) Module
DRAM configuration is 64 bits wide with parity enabled.
239K bytes of non-volatile configuration memory.
62720K bytes of ATA CompactFlash (Read/Write)
```

There are two FastEthernet interfaces, four serial interfaces, plus a VPN module. The amount of RAM, NVRAM, and flash are also displayed. The above router output shows us that there's 256MB of RAM, 239K of NVARM, and 64MB of flash.

When the IOS is loaded and up and running, a preconfiguration (called startup-config) will be copied from NVRAM into RAM. The copy of this file will be placed in RAM and called running-config.

My 1841 and 871W routers boot exactly the same as the 2811 router. The 1841 and 871W do show less memory and different interfaces, but other than that, they have the same bootup procedure and the same preconfigured startup-config file.

Bringing Up a Non-ISR Router (a 2600)

As you're about to see, the boot cycle is about the same for non-ISR routers as for the ISR routers. The following messages appear when you first boot or reload a 2600 router:

```
System Bootstrap, Version 11.3(2)XA4, RELEASE SOFTWARE (fc1)
Copyright (c) 1999 by cisco Systems, Inc.
TAC:Home:SW:IOS:Specials for info
C2600 platform with 65536 Kbytes of main memory
```

The next part shows us that the IOS is being decompressed into RAM:

```
program load complete, entry point:0x80008000, size:0x43b7fc
Self decompressing the image :
##############################################################################
##############################################################################
##############################################################################
##############################################################################
##############################################################################
##############################################################################
##############################################################################
## [OK]
```

So far, everything is pretty much the same. Notice below that the IOS version is stated as version 12.3(20):

```
Cisco Internetwork Operating System Software
IOS (tm) C2600 Software (C2600-IK9O3S3-M), Version 12.3(20), RELEASE
    SOFTWARE (fc2)
Technical Support: http://www.cisco.com/techsupport
Copyright (c) 1986-2006 by cisco Systems, Inc.
Compiled Tue 08-Aug-06 20:50 by kesnyder
Image text-base: 0x80008098, data-base: 0x81A0E7A8
```

Just as with the 2800 series, once the IOS is loaded, the information learned from the POST will be displayed:

```
cisco 2610 (MPC860) processor (revision 0x202) with 61440K/4096K bytes
   of memory.
Processor board ID JAD03348593 (1529298102)
M860 processor: part number 0, mask 49
Bridging software.
X.25 software, Version 3.0.0.
1 Ethernet/IEEE 802.3 interface(s)
1 Serial network interface(s)
2 Serial(sync/async) network interface(s)
32K bytes of non-volatile configuration memory.
16384K bytes of processor board System flash (Read/Write)
```

Okay—finally what we see here is one Ethernet interface and three serial interfaces. The amount of RAM and flash is also displayed, and the above router output shows there are 64MB of RAM and 16MB of flash.

And as I mentioned, when the IOS is loaded and up and running, a valid configuration called the startup-config will be loaded from NVRAM. But here's where it differs from the default bootup of the ISR routers—if there isn't a configuration in NVRAM, the router will broadcast looking for a valid one on a TFTP host. (This can only happen if the router senses carrier detect, or CD, on any interface.) If the broadcast fails, it will then go into what is called *setup mode*—a step-by-step process to help you configure the router. So you need to remember that if you plug any interface of your router into your network and then boot your router, you may have to wait a couple minutes while the router searches for the configuration.

 You can have your ISR routers perform this boot cycle by erasing the startup-config and reloading the router. This will give you a clean router with no default configuration. I'll show you how to do this a little later in the chapter.

You can also enter setup mode at any time from the command line by typing the command **setup** from something called privileged mode, which I'll get to in a minute. Setup mode covers only some global commands and is generally just unhelpful. Here is an example:

```
Would you like to enter the initial configuration dialog? [yes/no]: y

At any point you may enter a question mark '?' for help.
Use ctrl-c to abort configuration dialog at any prompt.
Default settings are in square brackets '[]'.

Basic management setup configures only enough connectivity
for management of the system, extended setup will ask you
```

```
to configure each interface on the system

Would you like to enter basic management setup? [yes/no]: y
Configuring global parameters:

  Enter host name [Router]:Ctrl+C
Configuration aborted, no changes made.
```

You can exit setup mode at any time by pressing Ctrl+C.

I highly recommend going through setup mode once, then never again. You should always use the CLI or SDM.

Command-Line Interface (CLI)

I sometimes refer to the CLI as "Cash Line Interface" because if you can create advanced configurations on Cisco routers and switches using the CLI, then you'll get the cash!

To use the CLI, press Enter after the router finishes booting up. After you do that, the router will respond with messages that tell you all about the status of each and every one of its interfaces and then display a banner and ask you to log in. Here's an example:

```
[some output cut]
*Feb 28 16:42:00.967: %VPN_HW-6-INFO_LOC: Crypto engine: onboard 0
    State changed to: Initialized
*Feb 28 16:42:00.971: %VPN_HW-6-INFO_LOC: Crypto engine: onboard 0
    State changed to: Enabled
*Feb 28 16:42:01.471: %LINK-3-UPDOWN: Interface FastEthernet0/0,
    changed state to up
*Feb 28 16:42:01.471: %LINK-3-UPDOWN: Interface FastEthernet0/1,
    changed state to up
*Feb 28 16:42:01.471: %LINK-3-UPDOWN: Interface Serial0/0/0, changed
    state to down
*Feb 28 16:42:01.471: %LINK-3-UPDOWN: Interface Serial0/0/1, changed
    state to down
*Feb 28 16:42:01.471: %LINK-3-UPDOWN: Interface Serial0/1/0, changed
    state to down
*Feb 28 16:42:01.471: %LINK-3-UPDOWN: Interface Serial0/2/0, changed
    state to down
```

```
[some output cut]
--------------------------------------------------------------------
Cisco Router and Security Device Manager (SDM) is installed on this
   device. This feature requires the one-time use of the username
   "cisco" with the password "cisco". The default username and password
   have a privilege level of 15.
Please change these publicly known initial credentials using SDM or the
   IOS CLI. Here are the Cisco IOS commands.
username <myuser>  privilege 15 secret 0 <mypassword>
no username cisco
Replace <myuser> and <mypassword> with the username and password you
   want to use.
For more information about SDM please follow the instructions in the
  QUICK START GUIDE for your router or go to http://www.cisco.com/go/sdm
--------------------------------------------------------------------
User Access Verification
Username: cisco
Password: cisco [this won't show on your screen]
yourname#
```

From here, just log in using cisco/cisco as the username/password and you will be in privilege mode—something I'll talk about next.

Now, the reason there's a configuration already installed on the router is so that you can connect with the SDM via HTTPS without having to configure the router. Again, I'll be going through the preconfigured startup-config a bit later in this chapter.

Entering the CLI from a Non-ISR Router

After the interface status messages appear and you press Enter, the Router> prompt will appear. This is called *user exec mode* (user mode), and it's mostly used to view statistics, but it's also a stepping stone to logging in to privileged mode.

You can only view and change the configuration of a Cisco router in *privileged exec mode* (privileged mode), which you can enter with the enable command.

Here's how:

```
Router>enable
Router#
```

You now end up with a Router# prompt, which indicates that you're in *privileged mode*, where you can both view and change the router's configuration. You can go back from privileged mode into user mode by using the disable command, as seen here:

```
Router#disable
Router>
```

At this point, you can type **logout** from either mode to exit the console:

```
Router>logout


Router con0 is now available
Press RETURN to get started.
```

 Remember, by deleting the default configuration of an ISR router and reloading, you'll get to these same prompts, and you won't be prompted for a username and password.

In the following sections, I am going to show you how to perform some basic administrative configurations.

Overview of Router Modes

To configure from a CLI, you can make global changes to the router by typing `configure terminal` (or `config t` for short), which puts you in global configuration mode and changes what's known as the running-config. A global command (a command run from global config) is set only once and affects the entire router.

You can type `config` from the privileged-mode prompt and then just press Enter to take the default of `terminal`, as seen here:

```
yourname#config
Configuring from terminal, memory, or network [terminal]? [press enter]
Enter configuration commands, one per line.  End with CNTL/Z.
yourname(config)#
```

At this point, you make changes that affect the router as a whole (globally), hence the term global configuration mode. To change the running-config—the current configuration running in dynamic RAM (DRAM)—you use the `configure terminal` command, as I just demonstrated.

To change the startup-config—the configuration stored in NVRAM—you use the `configure memory` command (or `config mem` for short), which merges the startup-config file into the running-config file in RAM. If you want to change a router configuration stored on a TFTP host (which is covered in Chapter 5, "Managing the Cisco IOS"), you use the `configure network` command (or `config net` for short), which also merges the file with the running-config file in RAM.

The `configure terminal`, `configure memory`, and `configure network` commands are all used to configure information into RAM on a router; however, typically only the `configure terminal` command is used. It is possible, though, that the commands `config mem` and `config net` can be useful if you screw up your running-config file and don't want to reboot your router.

Here are some of the other options under the `configure` command:

```
yourname(config)#exit or press cntl-z
yourname#config ?
  confirm             Confirm replacement of running-config with
a new config file
  memory              Configure from NV memory
  network             Configure from a TFTP network host
  overwrite-network   Overwrite NV memory from TFTP network host
  replace             Replace the running-config with a new config file
  terminal            Configure from the terminal
  <cr>
```

As you can see, Cisco has added a few more commands in the 12.4 IOS. We'll go through these commands in Chapter 5.

CLI Prompts

It's really important that you understand the different prompts you can find when configuring a router. Knowing these well will help you navigate and recognize where you are at any time within configuration mode. In this section, I'm going to demonstrate the prompts that are used on a Cisco router and discuss the various terms used. (Always check your prompts before making any changes to a router's configuration!)

I'm not going into every different command prompt offered, because doing that would be reaching beyond the scope of this book. Instead, I'm going to describe all the different prompts you'll see throughout this chapter and the rest of the book. These command prompts really are the ones you'll use most in real life anyway; plus, they're the ones you'll need to know for the exam.

Don't freak! It's not important that you understand what each of these command prompts accomplishes yet because I'm going to completely fill you in on all of them really soon. So right now, just relax and focus on becoming familiar with the different prompts available and all will be well!

Interfaces

To make changes to an interface, you use the `interface` command from global configuration mode:

```
yourname(config)#interface ?
  Async        Async interface
  BVI          Bridge-Group Virtual Interface
  CDMA-Ix      CDMA Ix interface
  CTunnel      CTunnel interface
```

```
Dialer               Dialer interface
FastEthernet         FastEthernet IEEE 802.3
Group-Async          Async Group interface
Lex                  Lex interface
Loopback             Loopback interface
MFR                  Multilink Frame Relay bundle interface
Multilink            Multilink-group interface
Null                 Null interface
Port-channel         Ethernet Channel of interfaces
Serial               Serial
Tunnel               Tunnel interface
Vif                  PGM Multicast Host interface
Virtual-PPP          Virtual PPP interface
Virtual-Template     Virtual Template interface
Virtual-TokenRing    Virtual TokenRing
range                interface range command
yourname(config)#interface fastEthernet 0/0
yourname(config-if)#
```

Did you notice that the prompt changed to yourname(config-if)#? This tells you that you're in *interface configuration mode.* And wouldn't it be nice if the prompt also gave you an indication of what interface you were configuring? Well, at least for now we'll have to live without the prompt information, because it doesn't. One thing is for sure: You really have to pay attention when configuring a router!

Subinterfaces

Subinterfaces allow you to create logical interfaces within the router. The prompt then changes to yourname(config-subif)#:

```
yourname(config-if)#interface f0/0.1
yourname(config-subif)#
```

You can read more about subinterfaces in Chapter 9, "Virtual LANs" and Chapter 14, "Wide Area Networks," but don't skip ahead just yet!

Line Commands

To configure user-mode passwords, use the line command. The prompt then becomes yourname(config-line)#:

```
yourname#config t
Enter configuration commands, one per line.  End with CNTL/Z.
```

```
yourname(config)#line ?
  <0-337>  First Line number
  aux      Auxiliary line
  console  Primary terminal line
  tty      Terminal controller
  vty      Virtual terminal
  x/y      Slot/Port for Modems
  x/y/z    Slot/Subslot/Port for Modems
```

The line console 0 command is known as a major command (also called a *global command*), and any command typed from the (config-line) prompt is known as a subcommand.

Routing Protocol Configurations

To configure routing protocols such as RIP and EIGRP, you'll use the prompt yourname(config-router#):

```
yourname#config t
Enter configuration commands, one per line.  End with CNTL/Z.
yourname(config)#router rip
yourname(config-router)#version 2
yourname(config-router)#
```

Defining Router Terms

Table 4.1 defines some of the terms we've used so far.

TABLE 4.1   Router Terms

Mode	Definition
User EXEC mode	Limited to basic monitoring commands
Privileged EXEC mode	Provides access to all other router commands
Global configuration mode	Commands that affect the entire system
Specific configuration modes	Commands that affect interfaces/processes only
Setup mode	Interactive configuration dialog

Editing and Help Features

You can use the Cisco advanced editing features to help you configure your router. If you type in a question mark (?) at any prompt, you'll be given a list of all the commands available from that prompt:

```
yourname#?
Exec commands:
  access-enable    Create a temporary Access-List entry
  access-profile   Apply user-profile to interface
  access-template  Create a temporary Access-List entry
  archive          manage archive files
  auto             Exec level Automation
  bfe              For manual emergency modes setting
  calendar         Manage the hardware calendar
  cd               Change current directory
  clear            Reset functions
  clock            Manage the system clock
  cns              CNS agents
  configure        Enter configuration mode
  connect          Open a terminal connection
  copy             Copy from one file to another
  crypto           Encryption related commands.
  ct-isdn          Run an ISDN component test command
  debug            Debugging functions (see also 'undebug')
  delete           Delete a file
  dir              List files on a filesystem
  disable          Turn off privileged commands
  disconnect       Disconnect an existing network connection
 --More--
```

Plus, at this point you can press the spacebar to get another page of information, or you can press Enter to go one command at a time. You can also press Q (or any other key, for that matter) to quit and return to the prompt.

Here's a shortcut: To find commands that start with a certain letter, use the letter and the question mark with no space between them:

```
yourname#c?
calendar  cd        clear    clock
cns       configure connect  copy
crypto    ct-isdn

yourname#c
```

By typing c?, we received a response listing all the commands that start with *c*. Also notice that the yourname#c prompt reappears after the list of commands is displayed. This can be helpful when you have long commands and need the next possible command. It would be pretty lame if you had to retype the entire command every time you used a question mark!

To find the next command in a string, type the first command and then a question mark:

```
yourname#clock ?
  read-calendar      Read the hardware calendar into the clock
  set                Set the time and date
  update-calendar    Update the hardware calendar from the clock
yourname#clock set ?
  hh:mm:ss   Current Time
yourname#clock set 11:15:11 ?
  <1-31>   Day of the month
  MONTH    Month of the year
yourname#clock set 11:15:11 25 aug ?
  <1993-2035>   Year
yourname#clock set 11:15:11 25 aug 2007 ?
  <cr>
yourname#clock set 11:15:11 25 aug 2007
*Aug 25 11:15:11.000: %SYS-6-CLOCKUPDATE: System clock has
been updated from 18:52:53 UTC Wed Feb 28 2007 to 11:15:11
UTC Sat Aug 25 2007, configured from console by cisco on console.
```

By typing the clock ? command, you'll get a list of the next possible parameters and what they do. Notice that you should just keep typing a command, a space, and then a question mark until <cr> (carriage return) is your only option.

If you're typing commands and receive

```
yourname#clock set 11:15:11
% Incomplete command.
```

you'll know that the command string isn't done yet. Just press the up arrow key to redisplay the last command entered, and then continue with the command by using your question mark.

And if you receive the error

```
yourname(config)#access-list 110 permit host 1.1.1.1
                                      ^
% Invalid input detected at '^' marker.
```

you've entered a command incorrectly. See that little caret—the ^? It's a very helpful tool that marks the exact point where you blew it and entered the command incorrectly. Here's another example of when you'll see the caret:

```
yourname#sh serial 0/0/0
           ^
% Invalid input detected at '^' marker.
```

This command looks right, but be careful! The problem is that the full command is show interface serial 0/0/0.

Now if you receive the error

yourname#**sh ru**
% Ambiguous command: "sh ru"

it means there are multiple commands that begin with the string you entered and it's not unique. Use the question mark to find the command you need:

yourname#**sh ru?**
rudpv1 running-config

As you can see, there are two commands that start with show ru.

Table 4.2 lists the enhanced editing commands available on a Cisco router.

TABLE 4.2   Enhanced Editing Commands

Command	Meaning
Ctrl+A	Moves your cursor to the beginning of the line
Ctrl+E	Moves your cursor to the end of the line
Esc+B	Moves back one word
Ctrl+B	Moves back one character
Ctrl+F	Moves forward one character
Esc+F	Moves forward one word
Ctrl+D	Deletes a single character
Backspace	Deletes a single character
Ctrl+R	Redisplays a line
Ctrl+U	Erases a line
Ctrl+W	Erases a word
Ctrl+Z	Ends configuration mode and returns to EXEC
Tab	Finishes typing a command for you

Another cool editing feature I want to show you is the automatic scrolling of long lines. In the following example, the command typed had reached the right margin and automatically moved 11 spaces to the left (the dollar sign [$] indicates that the line has been scrolled to the left):

```
yourname#config t
Enter configuration commands, one per line. End with CNTL/Z.
yourname(config)#$110 permit host 171.10.10.10 0.0.0.0 eq 23
```

You can review the router-command history with the commands shown in Table 4.3.

TABLE 4.3   Router-Command History

Command	Meaning
Ctrl+P or up arrow	Shows last command entered
Ctrl+N or down arrow	Shows previous commands entered
show history	Shows last 10 commands entered by default
show terminal	Shows terminal configurations and history buffer size
terminal history size	Changes buffer size (max 256)

The following example demonstrates the show history command and how to change the history size, as well as how to verify it with the show terminal command. First, use the show history command to see the last 20 commands that were entered on the router:

```
yourname#show history
 en
 sh history
 show terminal
 sh cdp neig
 sh ver
 sh flash
 sh int fa0
 sh history
 sh int s0/0
 sh int s0/1
```

Now use the show terminal command to verify the terminal history size:

```
yourname#show terminal
Line 0, Location: "", Type: ""
```

```
[output cut]
Modem type is unknown.
Session limit is not set.
Time since activation: 00:21:41
Editing is enabled.
History is enabled, history size is 20.
DNS resolution in show commands is enabled
Full user help is disabled
Allowed input transports are none.
Allowed output transports are pad telnet rlogin lapb-ta mop v120 ssh.
Preferred transport is telnet.
No output characters are padded
No special data dispatching characters
```

The terminal history size command, used from privileged mode, can change the size of the history buffer:

```
yourname#terminal history size ?
 <0-256> Size of history buffer
yourname#terminal history size 25
```

You verify the change with the show terminal command:

```
yourname#show terminal
Line 0, Location: "", Type: ""
[output cut]
Editing is enabled.
History is enabled, history size is 25.
Full user help is disabled
Allowed transports are lat pad v120 telnet mop rlogin
  nasi. Preferred is lat.
No output characters are padded
No special data dispatching characters
Group codes:  0
```

Gathering Basic Routing Information

The show version command will provide basic configuration for the system hardware as well as the software version and the boot images. Here's an example:

```
yourname#show version
Cisco IOS Software, 2800 Software (C2800NM-ADVSECURITYK9-M), Version
  12.4(12), RELEASE SOFTWARE (fc1)
```

Real World Scenario

When Do You Use the Cisco Editing Features?

A couple of editing features are used quite often and some not so much, if at all. Understand that Cisco didn't make these up; these are just old Unix commands. However, Ctrl+A is really helpful to negate a command.

For example, if you were to put in a long command and then decide you didn't want to use that command in your configuration after all, or if it didn't work, then you could just press your up arrow key to show the last command entered, press Ctrl+A, type **no** and then a space, press Enter—and poof! The command is negated. This doesn't work on every command, but it works on a lot of them.

```
Technical Support: http://www.cisco.com/techsupport
Copyright (c) 1986-2006 by Cisco Systems, Inc.
Compiled Fri 17-Nov-06 12:02 by prod_rel_team
```

The preceding section of output describes the Cisco IOS running on the router. The following section describes the read-only memory (ROM) used, which is used to boot the router and holds the POST:

```
ROM: System Bootstrap, Version 12.4(13r)T, RELEASE SOFTWARE (fc1)
```

The next section shows how long the router has been running, how it was restarted (if you see a system restarted by bus error, that is a very bad thing), the location from which the Cisco IOS was loaded, and the IOS name. Flash is the default:

```
yourname uptime is 2 hours, 30 minutes
System returned to ROM by power-on
System restarted at 09:04:07 UTC Sat Aug 25 2007
System image file is "flash:c2800nm-advsecurityk9-mz.124-12.bin"
```

This next section displays the processor, the amount of DRAM and flash memory, and the interfaces the POST found on the router:

```
[some output cut]
Cisco 2811 (revision 53.50) with 249856K/12288K bytes of memory.
Processor board ID FTX1049A1AB
2 FastEthernet interfaces
4 Serial(sync/async) interfaces
1 Virtual Private Network (VPN) Module
DRAM configuration is 64 bits wide with parity enabled.
239K bytes of non-volatile configuration memory.
```

```
62720K bytes of ATA CompactFlash (Read/Write)
Configuration register is 0x2102
```

The configuration register value is listed last—it's something I'll cover in Chapter 5.

In addition, the show interfaces and show ip interface brief commands are very useful in verifying and troubleshooting a router as well as network issues. These commands are covered later in this chapter. Don't miss it!

Router and Switch Administrative Configurations

Even though this section isn't critical to making a router or switch work on a network, it's still really important; in it, I'm going to lead you through configuring commands that will help you administer your network.

The administrative functions that you can configure on a router and switch are as follows:

- Hostnames
- Banners
- Passwords
- Interface descriptions

Remember, none of these will make your routers or switches work better or faster, but trust me, your life will be a whole lot better if you just take the time to set these configurations on each of your network devices. That's because doing this makes troubleshooting and maintaining your network sooooo much easier—seriously! In this next section, I'll be demonstrating commands on a Cisco router, but these commands are exactly the same on a Cisco switch.

Hostnames

You can set the identity of the router with the hostname command. This is only locally significant, which means that it has no bearing on how the router performs name lookups or how the router works on the internetwork. However, I'll use the hostname in Chapter 14 for authentication purposes when I discuss PPP.

Here's an example:

```
yourname#config t
Enter configuration commands, one per line. End with
  CNTL/Z.
yourname(config)#hostname Todd
Todd(config)#hostname Atlanta
Atlanta(config)#hostname Todd
Todd(config)#
```

Even though it's pretty tempting to configure the hostname after your own name, it's definitely a better idea to name the router something pertinent to the location. This is because giving it a hostname that's somehow relevant to where the device actually lives will make finding it a whole lot easier. And it also helps you confirm that you are, indeed, configuring the right device. For this chapter, we'll leave it at Todd for now.

Banners

A *banner* is more than just a little cool—one very good reason for having a banner is to give any and all who dare attempt to telnet or dial into your internetwork a little security notice. And you can create a banner to give anyone who shows up on the router exactly the information you want them to have.

Make sure you're familiar with these four available banner types: exec process creation banner, incoming terminal line banner, login banner, and message of the day banner (all illustrated in the following code):

```
Todd(config)#banner ?
  LINE           c banner-text c, where 'c' is a delimiting character
  exec           Set EXEC process creation banner
  incoming       Set incoming terminal line banner
  login          Set login banner
  motd           Set Message of the Day banner
  prompt-timeout Set Message for login authentication timeout
  slip-ppp       Set Message for SLIP/PPP
```

Message of the day (MOTD) is the most extensively used banner. It gives a message to every person dialing into or connecting to the router via Telnet or an auxiliary port, or even through a console port as seen here:

```
Todd(config)#banner motd ?
LINE c banner-text c, where 'c' is a delimiting character
Todd(config)#banner motd #
Enter TEXT message. End with the character '#'.
$ Acme.com network, then you must disconnect immediately.
#
Todd(config)#^Z
Todd#
00:25:12: %SYS-5-CONFIG_I: Configured from console by
  console
Todd#exit

Router con0 is now available
```

```
Press RETURN to get started.

If you are not authorized to be in Acme.com network, then you
must disconnect immediately.
Todd#
```

The preceding MOTD banner essentially tells anyone connecting to the router to get lost if they're not on the guest list! The part to understand is the delimiting character—the thing that's used to tell the router when the message is done. You can use any character you want for it, but (I hope this is obvious) you can't use the delimiting character in the message itself. Also, once the message is complete, press Enter, then the delimiting character, and then Enter again. It'll still work if you don't do that, but if you have more than one banner, they'll be combined as one message and put on a single line.

For example, you can set a banner on one line as shown:

```
Todd(config)#banner motd x Unauthorized access prohibited! x
```

This example will work just fine, but if you add another MOTD banner message, they would end up on a single line.

Here are some details of the other banners I mentioned:

Exec banner   You can configure a line-activation (exec) banner to be displayed when an EXEC process (such as a line activation or incoming connection to a VTY line) is created. By simply starting a user exec session through a console port, you'll activate the exec banner.

Incoming banner   You can configure a banner to be displayed on terminals connected to reverse Telnet lines. This banner is useful for providing instructions to users who use reverse Telnet.

Login banner   You can configure a login banner to be displayed on all connected terminals. This banner is displayed after the MOTD banner but before the login prompts. The login banner can't be disabled on a per-line basis, so to globally disable it, you've got to delete it with the no banner login command.

Here is an example of a login banner:

```
!
banner login ^C
----------------------------------------------------------------
Cisco Router and Security Device Manager (SDM) is installed on this device.
This feature requires the one-time use of the username "cisco"
with the password "cisco". The default username and password have a privilege
level of 15.
Please change these publicly known initial credentials using SDM or the IOS
CLI.
Here are the Cisco IOS commands.
username <myuser>  privilege 15 secret 0 <mypassword>
no username cisco
```

```
Replace <myuser> and <mypassword> with the username and password you want to
use.
For more information about SDM please follow the instructions in the QUICK
START
GUIDE for your router or go to http://www.cisco.com/go/sdm
-----------------------------------------------------------------
^C
!
```

The above login banner should look pretty familiar—it's the banner that Cisco has in its default configuration for its ISR routers. This banner is displayed before the login prompts but *after* the MOTD banner.

Setting Passwords

Five passwords are used to secure your Cisco routers: console, auxiliary, telnet (VTY), enable password, and enable secret. The enable secret and enable password are used to set the password that's used to secure privileged mode. This will prompt a user for a password when the `enable` command is used. The other three are used to configure a password when user mode is accessed through the console port, through the auxiliary port, or via Telnet.

Let's take a look at each of these now.

Enable Passwords

You set the enable passwords from global configuration mode like this:

```
Todd(config)#enable ?
 last-resort Define enable action if no TACACS servers
            respond
 password    Assign the privileged level password
 secret      Assign the privileged level secret
 use-tacacs  Use TACACS to check enable passwords
```

The following points describe the enable password parameters:

last-resort   Allows you to still enter the router if you set up authentication through a TACACS server and it's not available. But it isn't used if the TACACS server is working.

password   Sets the enable password on older, pre-10.3 systems, and isn't ever used if an enable secret is set.

secret   This is the newer, encrypted password that overrides the enable password if it's set.

use-tacacs   This tells the router to authenticate through a TACACS server. It's convenient if you have anywhere from a dozen to multitudes of routers because, well, would you like to face the fun task of changing the password on all those routers? If you're sane, no, you wouldn't. So instead, just go through the TACACS server and you only have to change the password once—yeah!

Here's an example of setting the enable passwords:

```
Todd(config)#enable secret todd
Todd(config)#enable password todd
The enable password you have chosen is the same as your
    enable secret. This is not recommended. Re-enter the
    enable password.
```

If you try to set the enable secret and enable passwords the same, the router will give you a nice, polite warning to change the second password. If you don't have older legacy routers, don't even bother to use the enable password.

User-mode passwords are assigned by using the `line` command:

```
Todd(config)#line ?
  <0-337>  First Line number
  aux      Auxiliary line
  console  Primary terminal line
  tty      Terminal controller
  vty      Virtual terminal
  x/y      Slot/Port for Modems
  x/y/z    Slot/Subslot/Port for Modems
```

Here are the lines to be concerned with:

aux   Sets the user-mode password for the auxiliary port. It's usually used for attaching a modem to the router, but it can be used as a console as well.

console   Sets a console user-mode password.

vty   Sets a Telnet password on the router. If this password isn't set, then Telnet can't be used by default.

To configure the user-mode passwords, you configure the line you want and use either the `login` or `no login` command to tell the router to prompt for authentication. The next sections will provide a line-by-line example of the configuration of each line configuration

Auxiliary Password

To configure the auxiliary password, go into global configuration mode and type **line aux ?**. You can see here that you only get a choice of 0–0 (that's because there's only one port):

```
Todd#config t
Enter configuration commands, one per line.  End with CNTL/Z.
Todd(config)#line aux ?
  <0-0>  First Line number
Todd(config)#line aux 0
Todd(config-line)#login
```

```
% Login disabled on line 1, until 'password' is set
Todd(config-line)#password aux
Todd(config-line)#login
```

It's important to remember the login command or the auxiliary port won't prompt for authentication.

Cisco has begun this process of not letting you set the login command before a password is set on a line because if you set the login command under a line and then don't set a password, the line won't be usable. And it will prompt for a password that doesn't exist. So this is a good thing—a feature, not a hassle!

 Definitely remember that although Cisco has this new "password feature" on its routers starting in its newer IOS (12.2 and above), it's not in all its IOSes.

Console Password

To set the console password, use the line console 0 command. But look at what happened when I tried to type **line console 0 ?** from the (config-line)# prompt—I received an error. You can still type **line console 0** and it will accept it, but the help screens just don't work from that prompt. Type **exit** to get back one level and you'll find that your help screens now work. This is a "feature." Really.

Here's the example:

```
Todd(config-line)#line console ?
% Unrecognized command
Todd(config-line)#exit
Todd(config)#line console ?
  <0-0>  First Line number
Todd(config-line)#password console
Todd(config-line)#login
```

Since there's only one console port, I can only choose line console 0. You can set all your line passwords to the same password, but for security reasons, I'd recommend that you make them different.

There are a few other important commands to know for the console port.

For one, the exec-timeout 0 0 command sets the time-out for the console EXEC session to zero, which basically means to never time out. The default time-out is 10 minutes. (If you're feeling mischievous, try this on people at work: Set it to 0 1. That will make the console time out in 1 second! And to fix it, you have to continually press the down arrow key while changing the time-out time with your free hand!)

logging synchronous is a very cool command, and it should be a default command, but it's not. It stops annoying console messages from popping up and disrupting the input you're trying to type. The messages still pop up, but you are returned to your router prompt without your input interrupted. This makes your input messages oh-so-much easier to read.

Here's an example of how to configure both commands:

```
Todd(config-line)#line con 0
Todd(config-line)#exec-timeout ?
  <0-35791>  Timeout in minutes
Todd(config-line)#exec-timeout 0 ?
  <0-2147483>  Timeout in seconds
  <cr>
Todd(config-line)#exec-timeout 0 0
Todd(config-line)#logging synchronous
```

You can set the console to go from never timing out (0 0) to timing out in 35,791 minutes and 2,147,483 seconds. The default is 10 minutes.

Telnet Password

To set the user-mode password for Telnet access into the router, use the `line vty` command. Routers that aren't running the Enterprise edition of the Cisco IOS default to five VTY lines, 0 through 4. But if you have the Enterprise edition, you'll have significantly more. The best way to find out how many lines you have is to use that question mark:

```
Todd(config-line)#line vty 0 ?
% Unrecognized command
Todd(config-line)#exit
Todd(config)#line vty 0 ?
  <1-1180>  Last Line number
  <cr>
Todd(config)#line vty 0 1180
Todd(config-line)#password telnet
Todd(config-line)#login
```

Remember, you cannot get help from your (`config-line`)# prompt. You must go back to privilege mode in order to use the question mark (?).

You may or may not have to set the `login` command before the password on the VTY lines—it depends on the IOS version. The result is the same either way.

So what will happen if you try to telnet into a router that doesn't have a VTY password set? You'll receive an error stating that the connection is refused because, well, the password isn't set. So, if you telnet into a router and receive the message

```
Todd#telnet SFRouter
Trying SFRouter (10.0.0.1)…Open
```

```
Password required, but none set
[Connection to SFRouter closed by foreign host]
Todd#
```

then the remote router (SFRouter in this example) does not have the VTY (Telnet) password set. But you can get around this and tell the router to allow Telnet connections without a password by using the no login command:

```
SFRouter(config-line)#line vty 0 4
SFRouter(config-line)#no login
```

 I do not recommend using the no login command to allow Telnet connections without a password unless you are in a testing or classroom environment! In a production network, you should always set your VTY password.

After your routers are configured with an IP address, you can use the Telnet program to configure and check your routers instead of having to use a console cable. You can use the Telnet program by typing **telnet** from any command prompt (DOS or Cisco). Anything Telnet is covered more thoroughly in Chapter 5.

Setting Up Secure Shell (SSH)

Instead of Telnet, you can use Secure Shell, which creates a more secure session than the Telnet application that uses an unencrypted data stream. Secure Shell (SSH) uses encrypted keys to send data so that your username and password are not sent in the clear.

Here are the steps to setting up SSH:

1. Set your hostname:

    ```
    Router(config)#hostname Todd
    ```

2. Set the domain name (both the hostname and domain name are required for the encryption keys to be generated):

    ```
    Todd(config)#ip domain-name Lammle.com
    ```

3. Generate the encryption keys for securing the session:

    ```
    Todd(config)#crypto key generate rsa general-keys modulus ?
      <360-2048>  size of the key modulus [360-2048]
    Todd(config)#crypto key generate rsa general-keys modulus 1024
    The name for the keys will be: Todd.Lammle.com
    % The key modulus size is 1024 bits
    % Generating 1024 bit RSA keys, keys will be non-exportable...[OK]
    *June 24 19:25:30.035: %SSH-5-ENABLED: SSH 1.99 has been enabled
    ```

4. Set the max idle timer for a SSH session:

    Todd(config)#**ip ssh time-out ?**
      <1-120> SSH time-out interval (secs)
    Todd(config)#**ip ssh time-out 60**

5. Set the max failed attempts for an SSH connection:

    Todd(config)#**ip ssh authentication-retries ?**
      <0-5> Number of authentication retries
    Todd(config)#**ip ssh authentication-retries 2**

6. Connect to the vty lines of the router:

    Todd(config)#**line vty 0 1180**

7. Last, configure SSH and then Telnet as access protocols:

    Todd(config-line)#**transport input ssh telnet**

If you do not use the keyword te1net at the end of the command string, then only SSH will work on the router. I am not suggesting you use either way, but just understand that SSH is more secure than Telnet.

Encrypting Your Passwords

Because only the enable secret password is encrypted by default, you'll need to manually configure the user-mode and enable passwords for encryption.

Notice that you can see all the passwords except the enable secret when performing a show running-config on a router:

```
Todd#sh running-config
Building configuration...
[output cut]
!
enable secret 5 $1$2R.r$DcRaVoOyBnUJBf7dbG9XE0
enable password todd
!
[output cut]
!
line con 0
 exec-timeout 0 0
 password console
 logging synchronous
 login
line aux 0
 password aux
```

```
 login
line vty 0 4
 access-class 23 in
 privilege level 15
 password telnet
 login
 transport input telnet ssh
line vty 5 15
 access-class 23 in
 privilege level 15
 password telnet
 login
 transport input telnet ssh
line vty 16 1180
 password telnet
 login
!
end
```

To manually encrypt your passwords, use the service password-encryption command. Here's an example of how to do it:

```
Todd#config t
Enter configuration commands, one per line.  End with CNTL/Z.
Todd(config)#service password-encryption
Todd(config)#exit
Todd#sh run
Building configuration...
[output cut]
!
enable secret 5 $1$2R.r$DcRaVoOyBnUJBf7dbG9XE0
enable password 7 131118160F
!
[output cut]
!
line con 0
 exec-timeout 0 0
 password 7 0605002F5F41051C
 logging synchronous
 login
line aux 0
```

```
 password 7 03054E13
 login
line vty 0 4
 access-class 23 in
 privilege level 15
 password 7 01070308550E12
 login
 transport input telnet ssh
line vty 5 15
 access-class 23 in
 privilege level 15
 password 7 01070308550E12
 login
 transport input telnet ssh
line vty 16 1180
 password 7 120D001B1C0E18
 login
!
end
```

```
Todd#config t
Todd(config)#no service password-encryption
Todd(config)#^Z
Todd#
```

There you have it! The passwords will now be encrypted. You just encrypt the passwords, perform a show run, and then turn off the command. You can see that the enable password and the line passwords are all encrypted.

But before I get into showing you all about setting descriptions on your routers, let's talk about encrypting passwords a bit more. As I said, if you set your passwords and then turn on the service password-encryption command, you have to perform a show running-config before you turn off the encryption service or your passwords won't be encrypted. You don't have to turn off the encryption service at all; you'd only do that if your router is running low on processes. And if you turn on the service before you set your passwords, then you don't even have to view them to get them encrypted.

Descriptions

Setting descriptions on an interface is helpful to the administrator and, as with the hostname, only locally significant. The description command is a helpful one because you can, for instance, use it to keep track of circuit numbers.

Here's an example:

```
Todd#config t
Todd(config)#int s0/0/0
Todd(config-if)#description Wan to SF circuit number 6fdda12345678
Todd(config-if)#int fa0/0
Todd(config-if)#description Sales VLAN
Todd(config-if)#^Z
Todd#
```

You can view the description of an interface with either the show running-config command or the show interface command:

```
Todd#sh run
[output cut]
!
interface FastEthernet0/0
 description Sales VLAN
 ip address 10.10.10.1 255.255.255.248
 duplex auto
 speed auto
!
interface Serial0/0/0
 description Wan to SF circuit number 6fdda 12345678
 no ip address
 shutdown
!
[output cut]
Todd#sh int f0/0
FastEthernet0/0 is up, line protocol is down
  Hardware is MV96340 Ethernet, address is 001a.2f55.c9e8 (bia 001a.2f55.c9e8)
  Description: Sales VLAN
 [output cut]


Todd#sh int s0/0/0
Serial0/0/0 is administratively down, line protocol is down
  Hardware is GT96K Serial
  Description: Wan to SF circuit number 6fdda12345678
```

description: A Helpful Command

Bob, a senior network administrator at Acme Corporation in San Francisco, has over 50 WAN links to various branches throughout the U.S. and Canada. Whenever an interface goes down, Bob spends a lot of time trying to figure out the circuit number as well as the phone number of the provider of the WAN link.

The interface description command would be very helpful to Bob because he can use this command on his LAN links to discern exactly where every router interface is connected. And Bob would benefit tremendously by adding circuit numbers to each and every WAN interface, along with the phone number of the responsible provider.

So by spending the few hours it would take to add this information to each and every router interface, Bob can save a huge amount of precious time when his WAN links go down—and you know they will!

Doing the *do* Command

Beginning with IOS version 12.3, Cisco has finally added a command to the IOS that allows you to view the configuration and statistics from within configuration mode. (In the examples I gave you in the previous section, all show commands were run from privileged mode.)

In fact, with a pre-12.3 router, you'd get the following error if you tried to view the configuration from global-config:

```
Router(config)#sh run
              ^
% Invalid input detected at '^' marker.
```

Compare that to the output I get from entering that same command on my router that's running the 12.4 IOS:

```
Enter configuration commands, one per line.  End with CNTL/Z.
Todd(config)#do show run
Building configuration...

Current configuration : 3276 bytes
!
[output cut]

Todd(config)#do sh int f0/0
FastEthernet0/0 is up, line protocol is down
```

```
Hardware is MV96340 Ethernet, address is 001a.2f55.c9e8 (bia
    001a.2f55.c9e8)
Description: Sales VLAN
[output cut]
```

So basically, you can pretty much run any command from any configuration prompt now—cool, huh? Going back to the example of encrypting our passwords, the do command would definitely have gotten the party started sooner—so, my friends, this is a very, very good thing indeed!

Router Interfaces

Interface configuration is one of the most important router configurations because without interfaces, a router is pretty much a completely useless object. Plus, interface configurations must be totally precise to enable communication with other devices. Network layer addresses, media type, bandwidth, and other administrator commands are all used to configure an interface.

Different routers use different methods to choose the interfaces used on them. For instance, the following command shows a Cisco 2522 router with 10 serial interfaces, labeled 0 through 9:

```
Router(config)#int serial ?
 <0-9> Serial interface number
```

Now it's time to choose the interface you want to configure. Once you do that, you will be in interface configuration for that specific interface. The following command would be used to choose serial port 5, for example:

```
Router(config)#int serial 5
Router(config-if)#
```

The 2522 router has one Ethernet 10BaseT port, and typing **interface ethernet 0** can configure that interface, as seen here:

```
Router(config)#int ethernet ?
 <0-0> Ethernet interface number
Router(config)#int ethernet 0
Router(config-if)#
```

As I showed you above, the 2500 router is a fixed-configuration router. This means that when you buy that model, you're stuck with that physical configuration—a huge reason why I don't use them much. I certainly never would use them in a production setting anymore.

To configure an interface, we always used the interface *type number* sequence, but with the 2600 and 2800 series routers (actually, any ISR router for that matter), there's a physical slot in the router, with a port number on the module plugged into that slot. So on a modular router, the configuration would be interface *type slot/port*, as seen here:

```
Router(config)#int fastethernet ?
  <0-1> FastEthernet interface number
Router(config)#int fastethernet 0
% Incomplete command.
Router(config)#int fastethernet 0?
/
Router(config)#int fastethernet 0/?
  <0-1> FastEthernet interface number
```

Make note of the fact that you can't just type **int fastethernet 0**. You must type the full command: ***type slot/port***, or **int fastethernet 0/0** (or **int fa 0/0**).

For the ISR series, it's basically the same, only you get even more options. For example, the built-in FastEthernet interfaces work with the same configuration we used with the 2600 series:

```
Todd(config)#int fastEthernet 0/?
  <0-1>  FastEthernet interface number
Todd(config)#int fastEthernet 0/0
Todd(config-if)#
```

But the rest of the modules are different—they use three numbers instead of two. The first 0 is the router itself, and then you choose the slot, and then the port. Here's an example of a serial interface on my 2811:

```
Todd(config)#interface serial ?
  <0-2>  Serial interface number
Todd(config)#interface serial 0/0/?
  <0-1>  Serial interface number
Todd(config)#interface serial 0/0/0
Todd(config-if)#
```

This can look a little dicey, I know, but I promise it's really not that hard! It helps to remember that you should always view a running-config output first so you know what interfaces you have to deal with. Here's my 2801 output:

```
Todd(config-if)#do show run
Building configuration...
[output cut]
!
interface FastEthernet0/0
 no ip address
 shutdown
```

```
 duplex auto
 speed auto
!
interface FastEthernet0/1
 no ip address
 shutdown
 duplex auto
 speed auto
!
interface Serial0/0/0
 no ip address
 shutdown
 no fair-queue
!
interface Serial0/0/1
 no ip address
 shutdown
!
interface Serial0/1/0
 no ip address
 shutdown
!
interface Serial0/2/0
 no ip address
 shutdown
 clock rate 2000000
!
 [output cut]
```

For the sake of brevity, I didn't include my complete running-config, but I've displayed all you need. You can see the two built-in FastEthernet interfaces, the two serial interface in slot 0 (0/0/0 and 0/0/1), the serial interface in slot 1 (0/1/0), and the serial interface in slot 2 (0/2/0). Once you see the interfaces like this, it makes it a lot easier for you to understand how the modules are inserted into the router.

Just understand that if you type **interface e0** on a 2500, **interface fastethernet 0/0** on a 2600, or **interface serial 0/1/0** on a 2800, all you're doing is choosing an interface to configure, and basically, they're all configured the same way after that.

I'm going to continue with our router interface discussion in the next sections, and I'll include how to bring up the interface and set an IP address on a router interface.

Bringing Up an Interface

You can disable an interface with the interface command shutdown and enable it with the no shutdown command.

If an interface is shut down, it'll display administratively down when you use the show interfaces command (sh int for short):

```
Todd#sh int f0/1
FastEthernet0/1 is administratively down, line protocol is down
[output cut]
```

Another way to check an interface's status is via the show running-config command. All interfaces are shut down by default. You can bring up the interface with the no shutdown command (no shut for short):

```
Todd#config t
Todd(config)#int f0/1
Todd(config-if)#no shutdown
Todd(config-if)#
*Feb 28 22:45:08.455: %LINK-3-UPDOWN: Interface FastEthernet0/1,
    changed state to up
Todd(config-if)#do show int f0/1
FastEthernet0/1 is up, line protocol is up
[output cut]
```

Configuring an IP Address on an Interface

Even though you don't have to use IP on your routers, it's most often what people actually do use. To configure IP addresses on an interface, use the ip address command from interface configuration mode:

```
Todd(config)#int f0/1
Todd(config-if)#ip address 172.16.10.2 255.255.255.0
```

Don't forget to enable the interface with the no shutdown command. Remember to look at the command show interface int to see if the interface is administratively shut down or not. show running-config will also give you this information.

> The ip address *address mask* command starts the IP processing on the interface.

If you want to add a second subnet address to an interface, you have to use the secondary parameter. If you type another IP address and press Enter, it will replace the existing IP address and mask. This is definitely a most excellent feature of the Cisco IOS.

So let's try it. To add a secondary IP address, just use the secondary parameter:

```
Todd(config-if)#ip address 172.16.20.2 255.255.255.0 ?
  secondary  Make this IP address a secondary address
  <cr>
```

```
Todd(config-if)#ip address 172.16.20.2 255.255.255.0 secondary
Todd(config-if)#^Z
Todd(config-if)#do sh run
Building configuration...
[output cut]

interface FastEthernet0/1
 ip address 172.16.20.2 255.255.255.0 secondary
 ip address 172.16.10.2 255.255.255.0
 duplex auto
 speed auto
!
```

I really wouldn't recommend having multiple IP addresses on an interface because it's ugly and inefficient, but I showed you anyway just in case you someday find yourself dealing with an MIS manager who's in love with really bad network design and makes you administer it! And who knows? Maybe someone will ask you about it someday and you'll get to seem really smart because you know this.

Using the Pipe

No, not that pipe. I mean the output modifier. (Although with some of the router configurations I've seen in my career, sometimes I wonder!) This pipe (|) allows us to wade through all the configurations or other long outputs and get straight to our goods fast. Here's an example:

```
Todd#sh run | ?
  append    Append redirected output to URL (URLs supporting append operation
            only)
  begin     Begin with the line that matches
  exclude   Exclude lines that match
  include   Include lines that match
  redirect  Redirect output to URL
  section   Filter a section of output
  tee       Copy output to URL

Todd#sh run | begin interface
interface FastEthernet0/0
 description Sales VLAN
 ip address 10.10.10.1 255.255.255.248
 duplex auto
 speed auto
!
interface FastEthernet0/1
```

```
ip address 172.16.20.2 255.255.255.0 secondary
ip address 172.16.10.2 255.255.255.0
duplex auto
speed auto
!
interface Serial0/0/0
 description Wan to SF circuit number 6fdda 12345678
 no ip address
!
```

So basically, the pipe symbol (output modifier) is what you need to help you get where you want to go light years faster than mucking around in a router's entire configuration. I use it a lot when I am looking at a large routing table to find out whether a certain route is in the routing table. Here's an example:

```
Todd#sh ip route | include 192.168.3.32
R        192.168.3.32 [120/2] via 10.10.10.8, 00:00:25, FastEthernet0/0
Todd#
```

First, you need to know that this routing table had over 100 entries, so without my trusty pipe, I'd probably still be looking through that output! It's a powerfully efficient tool that saves you major time and effort by quickly finding a line in a configuration—or as the preceding example shows, a single route in a huge routing table.

Give yourself a little time to play around with the pipe command; get the hang of it, and you'll be seriously high on your newfound ability to quickly parse through router output.

Serial Interface Commands

Wait! Before you just jump in and configure a serial interface, you need some key information—like knowing that the interface will usually be attached to a CSU/DSU type of device that provides clocking for the line to the router, as I've shown in Figure 4.4.

FIGURE 4.4   A typical WAN connection

Clocking is typically provided by DCE network to routers.
In nonproduction environments, a DCE network is not always present.

Here you can see that the serial interface is used to connect to a DCE network via a CSU/DSU that provides the clocking to the router interface. But if you have a back-to-back configuration (for example, one that's used in a lab environment like I've shown you in Figure 4.5), one end—the data communication equipment (DCE) end of the cable—must provide clocking!

FIGURE 4.5   Providing clocking on a nonproduction network

Set clock rate if needed.

Todd#config t
Todd(config)#interface serial 0
Todd(config-if)#clock rate 64000

DCE

DTE

DCE side determined by cable.
Add clocking to DCE side only.

show controllers will show the cable connection type.

By default, Cisco routers are all data terminal equipment (DTE) devices, which means that you must configure an interface to provide clocking if you need it to act like a DCE device. Again, you would not provide clocking on a production T1 connection, for example, because you would have a CSU/DSU connected to your serial interface, as Figure 4.4 shows.

You configure a DCE serial interface with the clock rate command:

```
Todd#config t
Enter configuration commands, one per line.  End with CNTL/Z.
Todd(config)#int s0/0/0
Todd(config-if)#clock rate ?
      Speed (bits per second)
  1200
  2400
  4800
  9600
  14400
  19200
  28800
  32000
  38400
  48000
  56000
  57600
```

```
64000
72000
115200
125000
128000
148000
192000
250000
256000
384000
500000
512000
768000
800000
1000000
2000000
4000000
5300000
8000000

<300-8000000>      Choose clockrate from list above
```

```
Todd(config-if)#clock rate 1000000
```

The clock rate command is set in bits per second. Besides looking at the cable end to check for a label of DCE or DTE, you can see if a router's serial interface has a DCE cable connected with the show controllers *int* command:

```
Todd#sh controllers s0/0/0
Interface Serial0/0/0
Hardware is GT96K
DTE V.35idb at 0x4342FCB0, driver data structure at 0x434373D4
```

Here is an example of an output that shows a DCE connection:

```
Todd#sh controllers s0/2/0
Interface Serial0/2/0
Hardware is GT96K
DCE V.35, clock rate 1000000
```

The next command you need to get acquainted with is the bandwidth command. Every Cisco router ships with a default serial link bandwidth of T1 (1.544Mbps). But this has nothing to do with how data is transferred over a link. The bandwidth of a serial link is used by routing protocols such as EIGRP and OSPF to calculate the best cost (path) to a remote network. So if you're using RIP routing, the bandwidth setting of a serial link is irrelevant since RIP uses only hop count to determine that. If you're rereading this part thinking, "Huh—what? Routing protocols? Metrics?"—don't freak! I'm going over all that soon in Chapter 6, "IP Routing."

Here's an example of using the bandwidth command:

```
Todd#config t
Todd(config)#int s0/0/0
Todd(config-if)#bandwidth ?
  <1-10000000>  Bandwidth in kilobits
  inherit       Specify that bandwidth is inherited
  receive       Specify receive-side bandwidth
Todd(config-if)#bandwidth 1000
```

Did you notice that, unlike the clock rate command, the bandwidth command is configured in kilobits?

 After going through all these configuration examples regarding the clock rate command, understand that the new ISR routers automatically detect DCE connections and set the clock rate to 2000000. However, you still need to understand the clock rate command, even though the new routers set it for you automatically!

Viewing, Saving, and Erasing Configurations

If you run through setup mode, you'll be asked if you want to use the configuration you just created. If you say yes, then it will copy the configuration running in DRAM (known as the running-config) into NVRAM and name the file startup-config. Hopefully, you always will use the CLI or SDM and not setup mode.

You can manually save the file from DRAM to NVRAM by using the copy running-config startup-config command (you can use the shortcut copy run start also):

```
Todd#copy running-config startup-config
Destination filename [startup-config]? [press enter]
Building configuration...
[OK]
Todd#
Building configuration...
```

When you see a question with an answer in [], it means that if you just press Enter, you're choosing the default answer.

Also, when the command asked for the destination filename, the default answer was startup-config. The reason it asks is because you can copy the configuration pretty much anywhere you want. Take a look:

Todd#**copy running-config ?**
```
  archive:       Copy to archive: file system
  flash:         Copy to flash: file system
  ftp:           Copy to ftp: file system
  http:          Copy to http: file system
  https:         Copy to https: file system
  ips-sdf        Update (merge with) IPS signature configuration
  null:          Copy to null: file system
  nvram:         Copy to nvram: file system
  rcp:           Copy to rcp: file system
  running-config Update (merge with) current system configuration
  scp:           Copy to scp: file system
  startup-config Copy to startup configuration
  syslog:        Copy to syslog: file system
  system:        Copy to system: file system
  tftp:          Copy to tftp: file system
  xmodem:        Copy to xmodem: file system
  ymodem:        Copy to ymodem: file system
```

We'll take a closer look at how and where to copy files in Chapter 5.

You can view the files by typing **show running-config** or **show startup-config** from privileged mode. The sh run command, which is a shortcut for show running-config, tells us that we are viewing the current configuration:

Todd#**show running-config**
```
Building configuration...

Current configuration : 3343 bytes
!
version 12.4
[output cut]
```

The sh start command—one of the shortcuts for the show startup-config command—shows us the configuration that will be used the next time the router is reloaded. It also tells us how much NVRAM is being used to store the startup-config file. Here's an example:

Todd#**show startup-config**
```
Using 1978 out of 245752 bytes
```

```
!
version 12.4
[output cut]
```

Deleting the Configuration and Reloading the Router

You can delete the startup-config file by using the `erase startup-config` command:

```
Todd#erase startup-config
Erasing the nvram filesystem will remove all configuration files!
    Continue? [confirm][enter]
[OK]
Erase of nvram: complete
Todd#
*Feb 28 23:51:21.179: %SYS-7-NV_BLOCK_INIT: Initialized the geometry of nvram
Todd#sh startup-config
startup-config is not present
Todd#reload
Proceed with reload? [confirm]System configuration has been modified.
    Save? [yes/no]: n
```

If you reload or power down and up the router after using the `erase startup-config` command, you'll be offered setup mode because there's no configuration saved in NVRAM. You can press Ctrl+C to exit setup mode at any time (the `reload` command can only be used from privileged mode).

At this point, you shouldn't use setup mode to configure your router. So just say no to setup mode, because it's there to help people who don't know how to use the Cash Line Interface (CLI), and this no longer applies to you. Be strong—you can do it!

Verifying Your Configuration

Obviously, `show running-config` would be the best way to verify your configuration and `show startup-config` would be the best way to verify the configuration that'll be used the next time the router is reloaded—right?

Well, once you take a look at the running-config, if all appears well, you can verify your configuration with utilities such as Ping and Traceroute. Ping is Packet Internet Groper, a program that uses ICMP echo requests and replies. (ICMP is discussed in Chapter 2, "Introduction to TCP/IP.") Ping sends a packet to a remote host, and if that host responds, you know that it is alive. But you don't know if it's alive and also *well*—just because you can ping a Microsoft server does not mean you can log in! Even so, Ping is an awesome starting point for troubleshooting an internetwork.

Did you know that you can ping with different protocols? You can, and you can test this by typing **ping ?** at either the router user-mode or privileged-mode prompt:

```
Router#ping ?
  WORD       Ping destination address or hostname
  appletalk  Appletalk echo
  clns       CLNS echo
  decnet     DECnet echo
  ip         IP echo
  ipv6       IPv6 echo
  ipx        Novell/IPX echo
  srb        srb echo
  tag        Tag encapsulated IP echo
  <cr>
```

If you want to find a neighbor's Network layer address, either you need to go to the router or switch itself or you can type **show cdp entry * protocol** to get the Network layer addresses you need for pinging.

Cisco Discovery Protocol (CDP) is covered in Chapter 5.

Traceroute uses ICMP with IP time to live (TTL) time-outs to track the path a packet takes through an internetwork, in contrast to Ping, which just finds the host and responds. And Traceroute can also be used with multiple protocols.

```
Router#traceroute ?
  WORD       Trace route to destination address or hostname
  appletalk  AppleTalk Trace
  clns       ISO CLNS Trace
  ip         IP Trace
  ipv6       IPv6 Trace
  ipx        IPX Trace
  <cr>
```

Telnet, FTP, and HTTP are really the best tools because they use IP at the Network layer and TCP at the Transport layer to create a session with a remote host. If you can telnet, ftp, or http into a device, your IP connectivity just has to be good.

```
Router#telnet ?
 WORD IP address or hostname of a remote system
  <cr>
```

From the router prompt, you just type a hostname or IP address and it will assume you want to telnet—you don't need to type the actual command, `telnet`.

In the following sections, I am going to show you how to verify the interface statistics.

Verifying with the *show interface* Command

Another way to verify your configuration is by typing `show interface` commands, the first of which is `show interface ?`. That will reveal all the available interfaces to configure.

The `show interfaces` command displays the configurable parameters and statistics of all interfaces on a router.

This command is very useful for verifying and troubleshooting router and network issues. The following output is from my freshly erased and rebooted 2811 router:

```
Router#sh int ?
  Async              Async interface
  BVI                Bridge-Group Virtual Interface
  CDMA-Ix            CDMA Ix interface
  CTunnel            CTunnel interface
  Dialer             Dialer interface
  FastEthernet       FastEthernet IEEE 802.3
  Loopback           Loopback interface
  MFR                Multilink Frame Relay bundle interface
  Multilink          Multilink-group interface
  Null               Null interface
  Port-channel       Ethernet Channel of interfaces
  Serial             Serial
  Tunnel             Tunnel interface
  Vif                PGM Multicast Host interface
  Virtual-PPP        Virtual PPP interface
  Virtual-Template   Virtual Template interface
  Virtual-TokenRing  Virtual TokenRing
  accounting         Show interface accounting
  counters           Show interface counters
  crb                Show interface routing/bridging info
  dampening          Show interface dampening info
  description        Show interface description
  etherchannel       Show interface etherchannel information
  irb                Show interface routing/bridging info
  mac-accounting     Show interface MAC accounting info
  mpls-exp           Show interface MPLS experimental accounting info
```

precedence	Show interface precedence accounting info
pruning	Show interface trunk VTP pruning information
rate-limit	Show interface rate-limit info
stats	Show interface packets & octets, in & out, by switching path
status	Show interface line status
summary	Show interface summary
switching	Show interface switching
switchport	Show interface switchport information
trunk	Show interface trunk information
|	Output modifiers
<cr>	

The only "real" physical interfaces are FastEthernet, Serial, and Async; the rest are all logical interfaces or commands to verify with.

The next command is show interface fastethernet 0/0. It reveals to us the hardware address, logical address, and encapsulation method as well as statistics on collisions, as seen here:

```
Router#sh int f0/0
FastEthernet0/0 is up, line protocol is up
  Hardware is MV96340 Ethernet, address is 001a.2f55.c9e8 (bia 001a.2f55.c9e8)
  Internet address is 192.168.1.33/27
MTU 1500 bytes, BW 100000 Kbit, DLY 100 usec,
    reliability 255/255, txload 1/255, rxload 1/255
  Encapsulation ARPA, loopback not set
  Keepalive set (10 sec)
  Auto-duplex, Auto Speed, 100BaseTX/FX
  ARP type: ARPA, ARP Timeout 04:00:00
  Last input never, output 00:02:07, output hang never
  Last clearing of "show interface" counters never
  Input queue: 0/75/0/0 (size/max/drops/flushes); Total output drops: 0
  Queueing strategy: fifo
  Output queue: 0/40 (size/max)
  5 minute input rate 0 bits/sec, 0 packets/sec
  5 minute output rate 0 bits/sec, 0 packets/sec
    0 packets input, 0 bytes
    Received 0 broadcasts, 0 runts, 0 giants, 0 throttles
    0 input errors, 0 CRC, 0 frame, 0 overrun, 0 ignored
    0 watchdog
    0 input packets with dribble condition detected
    16 packets output, 960 bytes, 0 underruns
    0 output errors, 0 collisions, 0 interface resets
```

```
    0 babbles, 0 late collision, 0 deferred
    0 lost carrier, 0 no carrier
    0 output buffer failures, 0 output buffers swapped out
Router#
```

As you probably guessed, we're going to discuss the important statistics from this output, but first, for fun (this is all fun, right?), I've got to ask you, What subnet is the FastEthernet 0/0 a member of and what's the broadcast address and valid host range?

And, my friend, you really have to be able to nail these things Nascar fast! Just in case you didn't, the address is 192.168.1.33/27. And I've gotta be honest—if you don't know what a /27 is at this point, you'll need a miracle to pass the exam. (A /27 is 255.255.255.224.) The fourth octet is a block size of 32. The subnets are 0, 32, 64, …; the FastEthernet interface is in the 32 subnet; the broadcast address is 63; and the valid hosts are 33–62.

If you struggled with any of this, please save yourself from certain doom and get yourself back into Chapter 3, "Subnetting, Variable Length Subnet Masks (VLSMs), and Troubleshooting TCP/IP," now! Read and reread it until you've got it dialed in!

The preceding interface is working and looks to be in good shape. The **show interfaces** command will show you if you are receiving errors on the interface, and it will show you the maximum transmission units (MTUs), bandwidth (BW), reliability (255/255 means perfect!), and load (1/255 means no load).

Continuing to use the previous output, what is the bandwidth of the interface? Well, other than the easy giveaway of the interface being called a "FastEthernet" interface, we can see the bandwidth is 100000Kbit, which is 100,000,000 (Kbit means to add three zeros), which is 100Mbits per second, or FastEthernet. Gigabit would be 1000000Kbits per second.

The most important statistic of the **show interface** command is the output of the line and data-link protocol status. If the output reveals that FastEthernet 0/0 is up and the line protocol is up, then the interface is up and running:

```
Router#sh int fa0/0
FastEthernet0/0 is up, line protocol is up
```

The first parameter refers to the Physical layer, and it's up when it receives carrier detect. The second parameter refers to the Data Link layer, and it looks for keepalives from the connecting end. (Keepalives are used between devices to make sure connectivity has not dropped.)

Here's an example of where the problem usually is found—on serial interfaces:

```
Router#sh int s0/0/0
Serial0/0 is up, line protocol is down
```

If you see that the line is up but the protocol is down, as shown above, you're experiencing a clocking (keepalive) or framing problem—possibly an encapsulation mismatch. Check the keepalives on both ends to make sure that they match; that the clock rate is set, if needed, and that the encapsulation type is the same on both ends. The output above would be considered a Data Link layer problem.

If you discover that both the line interface and the protocol are down, it's a cable or interface problem. The following output would be considered a Physical layer problem:

```
Router#sh int s0/0/0
Serial0/0 is down, line protocol is down
```

If one end is administratively shut down (as shown next), the remote end would present as down and down:

```
Router#sh int s0/0/0
Serial0/0 is administratively down, line protocol is down
```

To enable the interface, use the command no shutdown from interface configuration mode.

The next show interface serial 0/0/0 command demonstrates the serial line and the maximum transmission unit (MTU)—1,500 bytes by default. It also shows the default bandwidth (BW) on all Cisco serial links: 1.544Kbps. This is used to determine the bandwidth of the line for routing protocols such as EIGRP and OSPF. Another important configuration to notice is the keepalive, which is 10 seconds by default. Each router sends a keepalive message to its neighbor every 10 seconds, and if both routers aren't configured for the same keepalive time, it won't work.

```
Router#sh int s0/0/0
Serial0/0 is up, line protocol is up
 Hardware is HD64570
 MTU 1500 bytes, BW 1544 Kbit, DLY 20000 usec,
   reliability 255/255, txload 1/255, rxload 1/255
 Encapsulation HDLC, loopback not set, keepalive set
  (10 sec)
 Last input never, output never, output hang never
 Last clearing of "show interface" counters never
 Queueing strategy: fifo
 Output queue 0/40, 0 drops; input queue 0/75, 0 drops
 5 minute input rate 0 bits/sec, 0 packets/sec
 5 minute output rate 0 bits/sec, 0 packets/sec
   0 packets input, 0 bytes, 0 no buffer
   Received 0 broadcasts, 0 runts, 0 giants, 0 throttles
   0 input errors, 0 CRC, 0 frame, 0 overrun, 0 ignored,
   0 abort
   0 packets output, 0 bytes, 0 underruns
   0 output errors, 0 collisions, 16 interface resets
   0 output buffer failures, 0 output buffers swapped out
   0 carrier transitions
   DCD=down DSR=down DTR=down RTS=down CTS=down
```

You can clear the counters on the interface by typing the command **clear counters**:

```
Router#clear counters ?
  Async             Async interface
  BVI               Bridge-Group Virtual Interface
  CTunnel           CTunnel interface
  Dialer            Dialer interface
  FastEthernet      FastEthernet IEEE 802.3
  Group-Async       Async Group interface
  Line              Terminal line
  Loopback          Loopback interface
  MFR               Multilink Frame Relay bundle interface
  Multilink         Multilink-group interface
  Null              Null interface
  Serial            Serial
  Tunnel            Tunnel interface
  Vif               PGM Multicast Host interface
  Virtual-Template  Virtual Template interface
  Virtual-TokenRing Virtual TokenRing
  <cr>
```

```
Router#clear counters s0/0/0
Clear "show interface" counters on this interface
  [confirm][enter]
Router#
00:17:35: %CLEAR-5-COUNTERS: Clear counter on interface
  Serial0/0/0 by console
Router#
```

Verifying with the *show ip interface* Command

The show ip interface command will provide you with information regarding the layer 3 configurations of a router's interfaces:

```
Router#sh ip interface
FastEthernet0/0 is up, line protocol is up
  Internet address is 1.1.1.1/24
  Broadcast address is 255.255.255.255
  Address determined by setup command
  MTU is 1500 bytes
  Helper address is not set
  Directed broadcast forwarding is disabled
  Outgoing access list is not set
```

```
  Inbound  access list is not set
  Proxy ARP is enabled
  Security level is default
  Split horizon is enabled
[output cut]
```

The status of the interface, the IP address and mask, information on whether an access list is set on the interface, and basic IP information are included in this output.

Using the *show ip interface brief* Command

The show ip interface brief command is probably one of the most helpful commands that you can ever use on a Cisco router. This command provides a quick overview of the router's interfaces, including the logical address and status:

```
Router#sh ip int brief
Interface        IP-Address     OK? Method Status  Protocol
FastEthernet0/0  unassigned      YES unset  up        up
FastEthernet0/1  unassigned      YES unset  up        up
Serial0/0/0      unassigned      YES unset  up        down
Serial0/0/1      unassigned      YES unset  administratively down down
Serial0/1/0      unassigned      YES unset  administratively down down
Serial0/2/0      unassigned      YES unset  administratively down down
```

Remember, administratively down means that you need to type no shutdown under the interface. Notice that Serial0/0/0 is up/down, which means that the physical layer is good and carrier detect is sensed but no keepalives are being received from the remote end. In a nonproduction network, like the one I am working with, the clock rate isn't set.

Verifying with the *show protocols* Command

The show protocols command is a really helpful command you'd use in order to quickly see the status of layers 1 and 2 of each interface as well as the IP addresses used.

Here's a look at one of my production routers:

```
Router#sh protocols
Global values:
  Internet Protocol routing is enabled
Ethernet0/0 is administratively down, line protocol is down
Serial0/0 is up, line protocol is up
  Internet address is 100.30.31.5/24
Serial0/1 is administratively down, line protocol is down
Serial0/2 is up, line protocol is up
  Internet address is 100.50.31.2/24
Loopback0 is up, line protocol is up
  Internet address is 100.20.31.1/24
```

Using the *show controllers* Command

The show controllers command displays information about the physical interface itself. It'll also give you the type of serial cable plugged into a serial port. Usually, this will only be a DTE cable that plugs into a type of data service unit (DSU).

Router#**sh controllers serial 0/0**
HD unit 0, idb = 0x1229E4, driver structure at 0x127E70
buffer size 1524 HD unit 0, **V.35 DTE cable**
cpb = 0xE2, eda = 0x4140, cda = 0x4000

Router#**sh controllers serial 0/1**
HD unit 1, idb = 0x12C174, driver structure at 0x131600
buffer size 1524 HD unit 1, **V.35 DCE cable**
cpb = 0xE3, eda = 0x2940, cda = 0x2800

Notice that serial 0/0 has a DTE cable, whereas the serial 0/1 connection has a DCE cable. Serial 0/1 would have to provide clocking with the clock rate command. Serial 0/0 would get its clocking from the DSU.

Let's look at this command again. In Figure 4.5, see the DTE/DCE cable between the two routers? Know that you will not see this in production networks!

FIGURE 4.6   The show controllers Command

Router R1 has a DTE connection—the default for all Cisco routers. Routers R1 and R2 can't communicate. Check out the output of the show controllers s0/0 command here:

R1#**sh controllers serial 0/0**
HD unit 0, idb = 0x1229E4, driver structure at 0x127E70
buffer size 1524 HD unit 0, **V.35 DCE cable**
cpb = 0xE2, eda = 0x4140, cda = 0x4000

The **show controllers s0/0** command shows that the interface is a V.35 DCE cable. This means that R1 needs to provide clocking of the line to router R2. Basically, the interface has the wrong label on the cable on the R1 router's serial interface. But if you add clocking on the R1 router's serial interface, the network should come right up.

Let's check out another issue, shown in Figure 4.6, that you can solve by using the show controllers command. Again, routers R1 and R2 can't communicate.

FIGURE 4.7   The show controllers command used with the show ip interface command

Here's the output of R1's show controllers s0/0 command and show ip interface s0/0:

R1#**sh controllers s0/0**
HD unit 0, idb = 0x1229E4, driver structure at 0x127E70
buffer size 1524 HD unit 0,
DTE V.35 clocks stopped
cpb = 0xE2, eda = 0x4140, cda = 0x4000

R1#**sh ip interface s0/0**
Serial0/0 is up, line protocol is down
  Internet address is 192.168.10.2/24
  Broadcast address is 255.255.255.255

If you use the show controllers command and the show ip interface command, you'll see that router R1 isn't receiving clocking of the line. This network is a nonproduction network, so no CSU/DSU is connected to provide clocking of the line. This means the DCE end of the cable will be providing the clock rate—in this case, the R2 router. The show ip interface indicates that the interface is up but the protocol is down, which means that no keepalives are being received from the far end. In this example, the likely culprit is the result of bad cable, or no clocking.

Cisco's Security Device Manager (SDM)

So finally, here it is… the part about Cisco's SDM. This beauty is used to help you configure a router from an HTTP or HTTPS interface. Actually, to be real, Cisco did produce something like this in the past, but honestly, it just didn't work all that well. But this one does—really! And by the way, SDM is available on Cisco router models from Cisco 830 Series to 7301. Plus, it's preinstalled on all new 850, 870, 1800, 2800, and 3800 series routers. It's all good!

    For the Cisco PIX product, use the Pix Device Manager (PDM), not the SDM.

But there is a catch. Although the SDM is a really great tool, it's best if you pull it out just for advanced configurations—not the super small, simple configurations like those we used in this chapter. Let me explain. Let's say you wanted to set up an advanced access list, VPN with IPSec, and intrusion protection on your router. If so, then SDM is your baby. You don't even have to know what IPSec means to configure it and make it work.

But again, there's both good news and bad news with this. Of course, we can now handle advanced configurations much more easily, but at the same time, it's not so good because, well, literally anyone can do the same thing!

What I'm going to do is show you how to log in using SDM; set your hostname, banner, and enable secret password; and assign a DHCP pool on a router and an IP address to an interface. And if it all goes well, after this section you'll find that SDM will turn out to be much more of a good thing because it will prove to be so much more helpful to you when you're reading the chapters on the IOS, NAT, wireless technologies, and security than the way it used to be when we were all mired down in basic IOS router configuration. I'll use it a little in every chapter both to show you the ease you'll gain and to explain its complexity. But I promise to truly expose the limitations of SDM as well.

Honestly, I could write a whole book about SDM, but I don't need to because Cisco did it already. To find more details about SDM, go to www.cisco.com/go/sdm. Plus, a new router will typically come with a CD that walks you through physically connecting your router and configuring it step by step (overkill in my opinion), but you truly don't need this CD to connect to your router and use SDM.

All you need is a supported ISR router (1800/2800, etc.) and you can download the latest version of SDM complete with instructions for installing it on your computer and your router from the following location: www.cisco.com/pcgi-bin/tablebuild.pl/sdm.

> To download this software, you need a Cisco Connection Online (CCO) login. However, this is free and only takes a minute or less to set up. Go to www.cisco.com and click on Register in the top-right corner. Fill in the short form, add the username and password you want to use, and you can now download the SDM and the SDM demo.

From this site, you can not only install the SDM on your computer to help the SDM pages load faster when connecting to your router, you can also enable the use of the Cisco SDM demo itself.

> I highly recommend downloading and running through the SDM demo if you don't have an ISR router to play with. First, install SDM on your computer, and then download the demo at www.cisco.com/pcgi-bin/tablebuild.pl/ sdm-tool-demo. Read the install instructions, or run through Hands-on Lab 4.6 at the end of this chapter to get you set up and going strong with SDM.

You need to know this though—to set up your host to log in using the SDM, you have to make sure your router is configured first. In the preceding section, I had deleted my configurations and reloaded the router, so I had to start from scratch. But doing that really isn't all that hard. You can just choose a LAN interface of the router and then connect a host directly to the router using a crossover cable—not so bad!

```
Would you like to enter the initial configuration dialog? [yes/no]: n
Press RETURN to get started!
```

```
Router>en
Router#config t
Enter configuration commands, one per line.  End with CNTL/Z.
Router(config)#int f0/0
Router(config-if)#ip address 1.1.1.1 255.255.255.0
Router(config-if)#no shut
Router(config-if)#do ping 1.1.1.2
Type escape sequence to abort.
Sending 5, 100-byte ICMP Echos to 1.1.1.2, timeout is 2 seconds:
!!!!!
Success rate is 100 percent (5/5), round-trip min/avg/max = 1/1/4 ms
```

So what's this all about? In the preceding configuration, I configured the FastEthernet interface with an IP address and enabled it with the **no shutdown** command. I then tested my connection by pinging my directly connected host from the router prompt. (This would be a minimum configuration and will allow you to connect via SDM.) From here, you just open a browser, with pop-ups enabled, type **http://1.1.1.1**, and follow the easy prompts once connected.

It's different if you want to set the router to use HTTPS, which allows you access into privileged mode upon connection (meaning we're setting the router back to the original default configuration). And you need to add a few more commands.

First, enable the HTTP/HTTPS server (your router won't support HTTPS if it doesn't have the advanced services IOS):

```
Router(config)#ip http server
Router(config)#ip http secure-server
% Generating 1024 bit RSA keys, keys will be non-exportable...[OK]
Router(config)#ip http authentication local
```

Second, create a user account using privilege level 15 (the highest level):

```
Router(config)#username cisco privilege ?
  <0-15>  User privilege level

Router(config)#username cisco privilege 15 password ?
  0     Specifies an UNENCRYPTED password will follow
  7     Specifies a HIDDEN password will follow
  LINE  The UNENCRYPTED (cleartext) user password
Router(config)#username cisco privilege 15 password 0 cisco
```

Last, configure the console, SSH, and Telnet to provide local login authentication at privilege level access:

```
Router(config)#line console 0
Router(config-line)#login local
```

```
Router(config-line)#exit
Router(config)#line vty 0 ?
  <1-1180>  Last Line number
  <cr>
Router(config)#line vty 0 1180
Router(config-line)#privilege level 15
Router(config-line)#login local
Router(config-line)#transport input telnet
Router(config-line)#transport input telnet ssh
Router(config-line)#^Z
```

Voilà! Now let's connect to my 2811 using HTTPS!

Okay—as soon as I connected via https://1.1.1.1, I received a security alert message.

I was then prompted to log in with the username/password I created. SDM started loading and told me to hold on, which means it needs a bit of time to load another window. *Do not* close this window.

The certificate that I created with the `ip http secure-server` command was loaded onto the router. I chose to click on Always Trust Content from this Publisher and then clicked Yes.

Of course, the certificate would not match any site name, so I then had to verify that I wanted to run it.

I then had to log in again and then wait for SDM to load, during which time the router had me change my default username and password.

Finally—yes! I am connected to SDM!

Clicking the Configure button at the top of the page, I chose to go step by step through interface configuration by first choosing the type of interface I wanted to configure and then clicking the Create New Connection button at the bottom of the page. This opens the LAN or WAN wizard, depending on which interface you choose to configure. (We'll configure our router interfaces with the Interface Wizard in Chapter 6.)

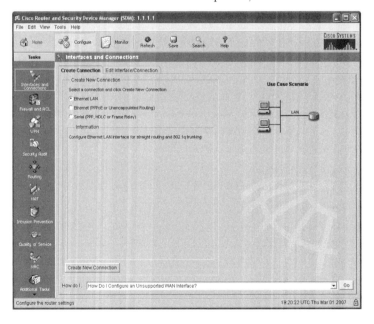

By clicking the Edit Interface/Connection tab, you get to see your interface status.

That's not all—just double-click on an interface to edit it. (You can only do this after you've gone through the LAN or WAN wizard and configured the interface.)

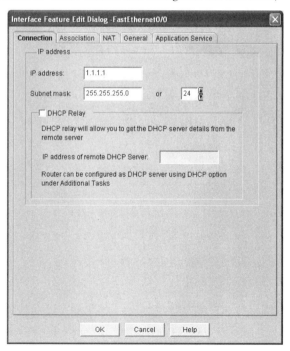

Look down at the bottom left portion of the wizard page and click the Additional Tasks button. From there, just click the Router Properties icon.

Here, you can set the hostname, MOTD banner, and enable secret password. Last, I clicked on the DHCP folder, then the DHCP pool icon. I then clicked Add and created a DHCP pool on my router.

Now, let's take a look at the configuration on the router:

```
Todd#sh run
Building configuration...
[output cut]
hostname Todd
!
ip domain name lammle.com
[output cut]
ip dhcp excluded-address 172.16.10.1
ip dhcp excluded-address 172.16.10.11 172.16.10.254
!
ip dhcp pool Todd's_LAN
   import all
   network 172.16.10.0 255.255.255.0
!
crypto pki trustpoint TP-self-signed-2645776477
 enrollment selfsigned
 subject-name cn=IOS-Self-Signed-Certificate-2645776477
 revocation-check none
 rsakeypair TP-self-signed-2645776477
!
crypto pki certificate chain TP-self-signed-2645776477
 certificate self-signed 01
  3082023E 308201A7 A0030201 02020101 300D0609 2A864886 F70D0101
   04050030 31312F30 2D060355 04031326 494F532D 53656C66 2D536967
   6E65642D 43657274 69666963 6174652D 32363435 37373634 3737301E
   170D3037 30333031 3139313 33335A17 0D323030 31303130 30303030
   305A3031 312F302D 06035504 03132649 4F532D53 656C662D 5369676E
   65642D43 65727469 66696361 74652D32 36343537 37363437 3730819F
   300D0609 2A864886 F70D0101 01050003 818D0030 81890281 8100BB24
   [output cut]
  quit
username todd privilege 15 secret 5 $1$nvgs$QRNCWKJ7rfmtNNkD2xvGq/
[output cut]
!
line con 0
 login local
line aux 0
line vty 0 4
 privilege level 15
```

```
 login local
 transport input telnet ssh
line vty 5 1180
 privilege level 15
 login local
 transport input telnet ssh
!
```

So what we can see here is that the router created the hostname, DHCP pool, and certificate. We went through a lot of setup because we were using HTTPS—it's so much easier and unencumbered with less setup to just use HTTP. But remember, what we used was an ISR default configuration to connect using SDM. We'll continue to use SDM throughout this book, but I seriously encourage you to get SDM for yourself and start getting familiar with it!

Summary

This was a fun chapter! I showed you a lot about the Cisco IOS and I really hope you gained a lot of insight into the Cisco router world. This chapter started off by explaining the Cisco Internetwork Operating System (IOS) and how you can use the IOS to run and configure Cisco routers. You learned how to bring a router up and what setup mode does. Oh, and by the way, since you can now basically configure Cisco routers, you should never use setup mode, right?

After I discussed how to connect to a router with a console and LAN connection, I covered the Cisco help features and how to use the CLI to find commands and command parameters. In addition, I discussed some basic show commands to help you verify your configurations.

Administrative functions on a router help you administer your network and verify that you are configuring the correct device. Setting router passwords is one of the most important configurations you can perform on your routers. I showed you the five passwords to set. In addition, I used the hostname, interface description, and banners to help you administer your router.

Last, I showed you how to configure the router so you can connect using the Secure Device Manager and configure your router. Again, it's a whole lot easier to use the CLI to configure basic router functions, but I'll show you how SDM can really help with the more advanced configurations coming up soon.

Well, that concludes your introduction to the Cisco IOS. And, as usual, it's super-important for you to have the basics that we went over in this chapter before you move on to the following chapters.

Exam Essentials

Understand what happens (and the sequence in which it happens) when you power on a router. When you first bring up a Cisco router, it will run a power-on self-test (POST), and if that passes, it will look for and load the Cisco IOS from flash memory, if a file is present. The IOS then proceeds to load and looks for a valid configuration in NVRAM called the startup-config. If no file is present in NVRAM, the router will go into setup mode.

Remember what setup mode provides. Setup mode is automatically started if a router boots and no startup-config is in NVRAM. You can also bring up setup mode by typing **setup** from privileged mode. Setup provides a minimum amount of configuration in an easy format for someone who does not understand how to configure a Cisco router from the command line.

Understand the difference between user mode and privileged mode. User mode provides a command-line interface with very few available commands by default. User mode does not allow the configuration to be viewed or changed. Privileged mode allows a user to both view and change the configuration of a router. You can enter privileged mode by typing the command **enable** and entering the enable password or enable secret password, if set.

Remember what the command `show version` provides. The `show version` command will provide basic configuration for the system hardware as well as the software version, the names and sources of configuration files, the `config-register` setting, and the boot images.

Remember how to set the hostname of a router. The command sequence to set the hostname of a router is as follows:

```
enable
config t
hostname Todd
```

Remember the difference between the enable password and enable secret password. Both of these passwords are used to gain access into privileged mode. However, the enable secret password is newer and is always encrypted by default. Also, if you set the enable password and then set the enable secret, only the enable secret will be used.

Remember how to set the enable secret on a router. To set the enable secret, you use the command `enable secret`. Do not use `enable secret password` *password* or you will set your password to *password password*. Here is an example:

```
enable
config t
enable secret todd
```

Remember how to set the console password on a router. To set the console password, use the following sequence:

```
enable
config t
```

```
line console 0
login
password todd
```

Remember how to set the Telnet password on a router.   To set the Telnet password, the sequence is as follows:

```
enable
config t
line vty 0 4
password todd
login
```

Understand how to troubleshoot a serial link problem.   If you type **show interface serial 0** and see down, line protocol is down, this will be considered a Physical layer problem. If you see it as up, line protocol is down, then you have a Data Link layer problem.

Understand how to verify your router with the show interfaces command   If you type **show interfaces**, you can view the statistics for the interfaces on the router, verify whether the interfaces are shut down, and see the IP address of each interface.

Written Lab 4

Write out the command or commands for the following questions:

1. What command is used to set a serial interface to provide clocking to another router at 64Kb?

2. If you telnet into a router and get the response connection refused, password not set, what would you do on the destination router to stop receiving this message and not be prompted for a password?

3. If you type **show inter et 0** and notice the port is administratively down, what would you do?

4. If you wanted to delete the configuration stored in NVRAM, what would you type?

5. If you wanted to set a user-mode password for the console port, what would you type?

6. If you wanted to set the enable secret password to *cisco*, what would you type?

7. If you wanted to see if a serial interface needed to provide clocking, what command would you use?

8. What command would you use to see the terminal history size?

9. You want to reinitialize the router and totally replace the running-config with the current startup-config. What command will you use?

10. How would you set the name of a router to *Chicago*?

(The answers to Written Lab 4 can be found following the answers to the review questions for this chapter.)

Hands-on Labs

In this section, you will perform commands on a Cisco router that will help you understand what you learned in this chapter.

You'll need at least one Cisco router—two would be better, three would be outstanding. The hands-on labs in this section are included for use with real Cisco routers. If you are using software from RouterSim.com or Sybex, please use the hands-on labs found in those programs. It doesn't matter what series type router you use with these labs (i.e., 2500, 2600, 800, 1800, or 2800).

This chapter includes the following six labs:

Lab 4.1: Logging into a Router

Lab 4.2: Using the Help and Editing Features

Lab 4.3: Saving a Router Configuration

Lab 4.4: Setting Your Passwords

Lab 4.5: Setting the Hostname, Descriptions, IP Address, and Clock Rate

Lab 4.6: Installing SDM on Your Computer

Hands-on Lab 4.1: Logging into a Router

1. Press Enter to connect to your router. This will put you into user mode.

2. At the Router> prompt, type a question mark (**?**).

3. Notice the -more- at the bottom of the screen.

4. Press the Enter key to view the commands line by line. Press the spacebar to view the commands a full screen at a time. You can type **q** at any time to quit.

5. Type **enable** or **en** and press Enter. This will put you into privileged mode where you can change and view the router configuration.

6. At the Router# prompt, type a question mark (**?**). Notice how many options are available to you in privileged mode.

7. Type **q** to quit.

8. Type **config** and press Enter.

9. Press Enter to configure your router using your terminal.

10. At the Router(config)# prompt, type a question mark (**?**), then **q** to quit, or hit the spacebar to view the commands.

11. Type **interface e0** or **int e0** (or even **int fa0/0**) and press Enter. This will allow you to configure interface Ethernet 0.

12. At the Router(config-if)# prompt, type a question mark (**?**).

13. Type **int s0 (int s0/0)** or **interface s0** (same as the interface serial 0 command) and press Enter. This will allow you to configure interface serial 0. Notice that you can go from interface to interface easily.

14. Type **encapsulation** ?.

15. Type **exit**. Notice how this brings you back one level.

16. Press Ctrl+Z. Notice how this brings you out of configuration mode and places you back into privileged mode.

17. Type **disable**. This will put you into user mode.

18. Type **exit**, which will log you out of the router.

Hands-on Lab 4.2: Using the Help and Editing Features

1. Log into the router and go to privileged mode by typing **en** or **enable**.

2. Type a question mark (**?**).

3. Type **cl?** and then press Enter. Notice that you can see all the commands that start with *cl*.

4. Type **clock** ? and press Enter.

 Notice the difference between steps 3 and 4. Step 3 has you type letters with no space and a question mark, which will give you all the commands that start with *cl*. Step 4 has you type a command, space, and question mark. By doing this, you will see the next available parameter.

5. Set the router's clock by typing **clock** ? and, following the help screens, setting the router's time and date.

6. Type **clock** ?.

7. Type **clock set** ?.

8. Type **clock set 10:30:30** ?.

9. Type **clock set 10:30:30 14 March** ?.

10. Type **clock set 10:30:30 14 March 2002**.

11. Press Enter.

12. Type **show clock** to see the time and date.

13. From privileged mode, type **show access-list 10**. Don't press Enter.

14. Press Ctrl+A. This takes you to the beginning of the line.

15. Press Ctrl+E. This should take you back to the end of the line.

16. Press Ctrl+A, then Ctrl+F. This should move you forward one character.

17. Press Ctrl+B, which will move you back one character.

18. Press Enter, then press Ctrl+P. This will repeat the last command.

19. Press the up arrow key on your keyboard. This will also repeat the last command.

20. Type **sh history**. This shows you the last 10 commands entered.

21. Type **terminal history size** ?. This changes the history entry size. The ? is the number of allowed lines.

22. Type **show terminal** to gather terminal statistics and history size.

23. Type **terminal no editing**. This turns off advanced editing. Repeat steps 14 through 18 to see that the shortcut editing keys have no effect until you type **terminal editing**.

24. Type **terminal editing** and press Enter to re-enable advanced editing.

25. Type **sh run**, then press your Tab key. This will finish typing the command for you.

26. Type **sh start**, then press your Tab key. This will finish typing the command for you.

Hands-on Lab 4.3: Saving a Router Configuration

1. Log into the router and go into privileged mode by typing **en** or **enable**, then press Enter.

2. To see the configuration stored in NVRAM, type **sh start** and press Tab and Enter, or type **show startup-config** and press Enter. However, if no configuration has been saved, you will get an error message.

3. To save a configuration to NVRAM, which is known as startup-config, you can do one of the following:
    - Type **copy run start** and press Enter.
    - Type **copy running**, press Tab, type **start**, press Tab, and press Enter.
    - Type **copy running-config startup-config** and press Enter.

4. Type **sh start**, press Tab, then press Enter.

5. Type **sh run**, press Tab, then press Enter.

6. Type **erase start**, press Tab, then press Enter.

7. Type **sh start**, press Tab, then press Enter. You should get an error message.

8. Type **reload**, then press Enter. Acknowledge the reload by pressing Enter. Wait for the router to reload.

9. Say no to entering setup mode, or just press Ctrl+C.

Hands-on Lab 4.4: Setting Your Passwords

1. Log into the router and go into privileged mode by typing **en** or **enable**.

2. Type **config t** and press Enter.

3. Type **enable** ?.

4. Set your enable secret password by typing **enable secret *password*** (the third word should be your own personalized password) and pressing Enter. Do not add the parameter password after the parameter secret (this would make your password the word *password*). An example would be enable secret todd.

5. Now let's see what happens when you log all the way out of the router and then log in. Log out by pressing Ctrl+Z, and then type **exit** and press Enter. Go to privileged mode. Before you are allowed to enter privileged mode, you will be asked for a password. If you successfully enter the secret password, you can proceed.

6. Remove the secret password. Go to privileged mode, type **config t**, and press Enter. Type **no enable secret** and press Enter. Log out and then log back in again; now you should not be asked for a password.

7. One more password used to enter privileged mode is called the enable password. It is an older, less secure password and is not used if an enable secret password is set. Here is an example of how to set it:

```
config t
enable password toddl
```

8. Notice that the enable secret and enable passwords are different. They cannot be the same.

9. Type **config t** to be at the right level to set your console and auxiliary passwords, then type **line ?**.

10. Notice that the parameters for the line commands are auxiliary, vty, and console. You will set all three.

11. To set the Telnet or VTY password, type **line vty 0 4** and then press Enter. The 0 4 is the range of the five available virtual lines used to connect with Telnet. If you have an enterprise IOS, the number of lines may vary. Use the question mark to determine the last line number available on your router.

12. The next command is used to set the authentication on or off. Type **login** and press Enter to prompt for a user-mode password when telnetting into the router. You will not be able to telnet into a router if the password is not set.

You can use the no login command to disable the user-mode password prompt when using Telnet.

13. One more command you need to set for your VTY password is password. Type **password** *password* to set the password. (*password* is your password.)

14. Here is an example of how to set the VTY password:

```
config t
line vty 0 4
login
password todd
```

15. Set your auxiliary password by first typing **line auxiliary 0** or **line aux 0**.

16. Type **login**.

17. Type **password** *password*.

18. Set your console password by first typing **line console 0** or **line con 0**.

19. Type **login**.

20. Type **password *password***. Here is an example of the last two commands:

```
config t
line con 0
login
password todd1
line aux 0
login
password todd
```

21. You can add the Exec-timeout 0 0 command to the console 0 line. This will stop the console from timing out and logging you out. The command will now look like this:

```
config t
line con 0
login
password todd2
exec-timeout 0 0
```

22. Set the console prompt to not overwrite the command you're typing with console messages by using the command logging synchronous.

```
config t
line con 0
logging synchronous
```

Hands-on Lab 4.5: Setting the Hostname, Descriptions, IP Address, and Clock Rate

1. Log into the router and go into privileged mode by typing **en** or **enable**.

2. Set your hostname on your router by using the hostname command. Notice that it is one word. Here is an example of setting your hostname:

```
Router#config t
Router(config)#hostname RouterA
RouterA(config)#
```

Notice that the hostname of the router changed as soon as you pressed Enter.

3. Set a banner that the network administrators will see by using the banner command.

4. Type **config t**, then **banner ?**.

5. Notice that you can set four different banners. For this lab we are only interested in the login and message of the day (MOTD) banners.

6. Set your MOTD banner, which will be displayed when a console, auxiliary, or Telnet connection is made to the router, by typing

```
config t
banner motd #
This is an motd banner
#
```

7. The preceding example used a # sign as a delimiting character. This tells the router when the message is done. You cannot use the delimiting character in the message itself.

8. You can remove the MOTD banner by typing

```
config t
no banner motd
```

9. Set the login banner by typing

```
config t
banner login #
This is a login banner
#
```

10. The login banner will display immediately after the MOTD but before the user-mode password prompt. Remember that you set your user-mode passwords by setting the console, auxiliary, and VTY line passwords.

11. You can remove the login banner by typing

```
config t
no banner login
```

12. You can add an IP address to an interface with the `ip address` command. You need to get into interface configuration mode first; here is an example of how you do that:

```
config t
int e0 (you can use int Ethernet 0 too)
ip address 1.1.1.1 255.255.0.0
no shutdown
```

Notice that the IP address (1.1.1.1) and subnet mask (255.255.0.0) are configured on one line. The `no shutdown` (or `no shut` for short) command is used to enable the interface. All interfaces are shut down by default.

13. You can add identification to an interface by using the `description` command. This is useful for adding information about the connection. Only administrators see this, not users. Here is an example:

```
config t
int s0
ip address 1.1.1.2 255.255.0.0
no shut
description Wan link to Miami
```

14. You can add the bandwidth of a serial link as well as the clock rate when simulating a DCE WAN link. Here is an example:

```
config t
int s0
bandwidth 64
clock rate 64000
```

Hands-on Lab 4.6: Installing SDM on Your Computer

This lab will have you download and install the full SDM program on your computer and then add the demo program inside the program. The links included in this lab were current as of this writing, but they could change at any time.

1. Download and install the latest SDM program from Cisco at the following location: www.cisco.com/pcgi-bin/tablebuild.pl/sdm.

2. After the SDM program is installed on your computer, download the SDM demo at www.cisco.com/pcgi-bin/tablebuild.pl/sdm-tool-demo.

3. Unzip the demo program into a folder of your choice.

4. Copy the dataFile.zip file to C:\.

5. Make sure you disable your pop-up blockers on your browser.

6. When SDM is installed on a PC, Internet Explorer may display HTML source code when you attempt to launch SDM. To fix this problem, choose **Tools** ➤ **Internet Options** ➤ **Advanced**. Then scroll to the Security section, check Allow Active Content to Run in Files on My Computer, and click Apply. Then relaunch SDM.

7. Click the Cisco SDM icon on your desktop to launch the SDM demo version. Enter the loopback address 127.0.0.1 and click the Launch button to start the SDM demo application. You can choose to use HTTPS if you want, and if you do, accept any security certificate notification messages that pop up.

8. The SDM demo will tell you there is debugging running on the router and to disable it because of possible performance degrading, but leave debugging running on the "simulation." You're not degrading any router performance.

9. Run through all the tabs: Configure Interfaces, Routing Protocols, Create a DHCP Pool, and so on—everything you can find. Spend some time getting to know SDM.

10. Understand that not all features are supported on the demo, but it is better than not having SDM and the demo actually works pretty well.

11. If you want to practice using certificates, use the ca.cer and router.cer certificates to demonstrate importing certificate authority (CA) and router certificates. You could get these certificates from SDM_demo_tool.zip.

Review Questions

The following questions are designed to test your understanding of this chapter's material. For more information on how to get additional questions, please see this book's Introduction.

1. You type **show running-config** and get this output:

   ```
   [output cut]
   Line console 0
         Exec-timeout 1 44
         Password 7098COBQR
         Login
   [output cut]
   ```

   What do the two numbers following the **exec-timeout** command mean?

   A. If no command has been typed in 44 seconds, the console connection will be closed.

   B. If no router activity has been detected in 1 hour and 44 minutes, the console will be locked out.

   C. If no commands have been typed in 1 minute and 44 seconds, the console connection will be closed.

   D. If you're connected to the router by a Telnet connection, input must be detected within 1 minute and 44 seconds or the connection will be closed.

2. You need to find the broadcast address used on a LAN on your router. What command will you type into the router from user mode to find the broadcast address?

   A. show running-config

   B. show startup-config

   C. show interfaces

   D. show protocols

3. You want to totally reinitialize the router and replace the current running-config with the current startup-config. What command will you use?

   A. replace run start

   B. copy run start

   C. copy start run

   D. reload

4. Which command will show you whether a DTE or a DCE cable is plugged into serial 0?

   A. `sh int s0`

   B. `sh int serial 0`

   C. `show controllers s 0`

   D. `show serial 0 controllers`

5. What keystroke will terminate setup mode?

   A. Ctrl+Z

   B. Ctrl+^

   C. Ctrl+C

   D. Ctrl+Shift+^

6. You set the console password, but when you display the configuration, the password doesn't show up; it looks like this:

```
[output cut]
Line console 0
      Exec-timeout 1 44
      Password 7098C0BQR
      Login
[output cut]
```

What cause the password to be stored like this?

   A. `encrypt password`

   B. `service password-encryption`

   C. `service-password-encryption`

   D. `exec-timeout 1 44`

7. Which of the following commands will configure all the default VTY ports on a router?

   A. `Router#line vty 0 4`

   B. `Router(config)#line vty 0 4`

   C. `Router(config-if)#line console 0`

   D. `Router(config)#line vty all`

8. Which of the following commands sets the secret password to Cisco?

   A. `enable secret password Cisco`

   B. `enable secret cisco`

   C. `enable secret Cisco`

   D. `enable password Cisco`

9. If you wanted administrators to see a message when logging into the router, which command would you use?

    A. message banner motd

    B. banner message motd

    C. banner motd

    D. message motd

10. How many simultaneous Telnet sessions does a Cisco router support by default?

    A. 1

    B. 2

    C. 3

    D. 4

    E. 5

    F. 6

11. What command do you type to save the configuration stored in RAM to NVRAM?

    A. Router(config)#**copy current to starting**

    B. Router#**copy starting to running**

    C. Router(config)#**copy running-config startup-config**

    D. Router#**copy run startup**

12. You try to telnet into SFRouter from router Corp and receive this message:

Corp#**telnet SFRouter**
Trying SFRouter (10.0.0.1)…Open

Password required, but none set
[Connection to SFRouter closed by foreign host]
Corp#

Which of the following sequences will address this problem correctly?

    A. Corp(config)#line console 0

    B. SFRemote(config)#line console 0

    C. Corp(config)#line vty 0 4

    D. SFRemote(config)#line vty 0 4

13. Which command will delete the contents of NVRAM on a router?

    A. delete NVRAM

    B. delete startup-config

    C. erase NVRAM

    D. erase start

14. What is the problem with an interface if you type **show interface serial 0** and receive the following message?

`Serial0 is administratively down, line protocol is down`

   A. The keepalives are different times.

   B. The administrator has the interface shut down.

   C. The administrator is pinging from the interface.

   D. No cable is attached.

15. Which of the following commands displays the configurable parameters and statistics of all interfaces on a router?

   A. `show running-config`

   B. `show startup-config`

   C. `show interfaces`

   D. `show versions`

16. If you delete the contents of NVRAM and reboot the router, what mode will you be in?

   A. Privileged mode

   B. Global mode

   C. Setup mode

   D. NVRAM loaded mode

17. You type the following command into the router and receive the following output:

`Router#show serial 0/0`
`          ^`

`% Invalid input detected at '^' marker.`

Why was this error message displayed?

   A. You need to be in privileged mode.

   B. You cannot have a space between serial and 0/0.

   C. The router does not have a serial0/0 interface.

   D. Part of the command is missing.

18. You type `Router#sh ru` and receive an `% ambiguous command` error. Why did you receive this message?

   A. The command requires additional options or parameters.

   B. There is more than one show command that starts with the letters *ru*.

   C. There is no show command that starts with *ru*.

   D. The command is being executed from the wrong router mode.

19. Which of the following commands will display the current IP addressing and the layer 1 and 2 status of an interface? (Choose three.)

   A. show version

   B. show protocols

   C. show interfaces

   D. show controllers

   E. show ip interface

   F. show running-config

20. What layer of the OSI model would you assume the problem is in if you type show interface serial 1 and receive the following message?

   Serial1 is down, line protocol is down

   A. Physical layer

   B. Data Link layer

   C. Network layer

   D. None; it is a router problem.

Answers to Review Questions

1. C. The `exec-timeout` command is set in minutes and seconds.

2. C. The command `show ip protocols` will actually show you the broadcast address for each interface—too bad it isn't a possible answer. Your best answer is `show interfaces`, which will provide the IP address and mask for each interface. You can then determine the mask from the vast subnetting knowledge you gained in Chapter 3.

3. D. You may have picked option C, which isn't a bad answer. Remember, though, it doesn't replace the configuration, it appends it. To completely replace the running-config with the startup-config, you must reload the router.

4. C. The `show controllers serial 0` command will show you whether either a DTE or DCE cable is connected to the interface. If it is a DCE connection, you need to add clocking with the `clock rate` command.

5. C. You can exit setup mode at any time by using the keystroke Ctrl+C.

6. B. The command `service password-encryption`, from global configuration mode, will encrypt the passwords.

7. B. From global configuration mode, use the `line vty 0 4` command to set all five default VTY lines.

8. C. The enable secret password is case sensitive, so the second option is wrong. To set the enable secret password, use the `enable secret` *password* command from global configuration mode.

9. C. The typical banner is a message of the day (MOTD) and is set by using the global configuration mode command `banner motd`.

10. E. Cisco routers, if they do not have the Enterprise edition of the IOS, will default to five simultaneous Telnet sessions.

11. D. To copy the running-config to NVRAM so that it will be used if the router is restarted, use the `copy running-config startup-config` command (`copy run start` for short).

12. D. To allow a VTY (Telnet) session into your router, you must set the VTY password. Option C is wrong because it is setting the password on the wrong router. Notice that the answers have you set the login command before you set the password. Remember, Cisco may have you set the password before the login command.

13. D. The `erase startup-config` command erases the contents of NVRAM and will put you in setup mode if the router is restarted.

14. B. If an interface is shut down, the `show interface` command will show the interface as administratively shut down. (It is possible that no cable is attached, but you can't tell that from this message.)

15. C. With the show interfaces command, you can view the configurable parameters, get statistics for the interfaces on the router, verify if the interfaces are shut down, and see the IP address of each interface.

16. C. If you delete the startup-config and reload the router, the router will automatically enter setup mode. You can also type **setup** from privileged mode at any time.

17. D. You can view the interface statistics from user mode, but the command is show interface serial 0/0.

18. B. The % ambiguous command error means that there is more then one possible command that starts with *ru*. Use a question mark to find the correct command.

19. B, C, E. The commands show protocols, show interfaces, and show ip interface will show you the layer 1 and 2 status and the IP addresses of your router's interfaces.

20. A. If you see that a serial interface and the protocol are both down, then you have a Physical layer problem. If you see serial1 is up, line protocol is down, then you are not receiving (Data Link) keepalives from the remote end.

Answers to Written Lab 4

1. `clock rate 64000`
2. `config t, line vty 0 4, no login`
3. `config t, int e0, no shut`
4. `erase startup-config`
5. `config t, line console 0, login, password todd`
6. `config t, enable secret cisco`
7. `show controllers` *int*
8. `show terminal`
9. `Router#reload`
10. `config t, hostname Chicago`

Chapter

5

Managing a Cisco Internetwork

THE CCNA EXAM TOPICS COVERED IN THIS CHAPTER INCLUDE THE FOLLOWING:

✓ **Configure, verify, and troubleshoot basic router operation and routing on Cisco devices**

- Manage IOS configuration files (including: save, edit, upgrade, restore)

- Manage Cisco IOS

- Verify network connectivity (including: using ping, traceroute, and telnet or SSH)

Here in Chapter 5, I'm going to show you how to manage Cisco routers on an internetwork. The Internetwork Operating System (IOS) and configuration files reside in different locations in a Cisco device, so it's really important to understand both where these files are located and how they work.

You'll be learning about the main components of a router, the router boot sequence, and the configuration register, including how to use the configuration register for password recovery. After that, you'll find out how to manage routers by using the copy command with a TFTP host when using the Cisco IOS File System (IFS) and the Cisco SDM.

We'll wrap up the chapter with an exploration of the Cisco Discovery Protocol, and you'll learn how to resolve hostnames and some important Cisco IOS troubleshooting techniques.

For up-to-the-minute updates for this chapter, please see www.lammle.com and/or www.sybex.com.

The Internal Components of a Cisco Router

To configure and troubleshoot a Cisco internetwork, you need to know the major components of Cisco routers and understand what each one does. Table 5.1 describes the major Cisco router components.

TABLE 5.1   Cisco Router Components

Component	Description
Bootstrap	Stored in the microcode of the ROM, the bootstrap is used to bring a router up during initialization. It will boot the router and then load the IOS.
POST (power-on self-test)	Stored in the microcode of the ROM, the POST is used to check the basic functionality of the router hardware and determines which interfaces are present.
ROM monitor	Stored in the microcode of the ROM, the ROM monitor is used for manufacturing, testing, and troubleshooting.

TABLE 5.1   Cisco Router Components *(continued)*

Component	Description
Mini-IOS	Called the RXBOOT or bootloader by Cisco, the mini-IOS is a small IOS in ROM that can be used to bring up an interface and load a Cisco IOS into flash memory. The mini-IOS can also perform a few other maintenance operations.
RAM (random access memory)	Used to hold packet buffers, ARP cache, routing tables, and also the software and data structures that allow the router to function. Running-config is stored in RAM, and most routers expand the IOS from flash into RAM upon boot.
ROM (read-only memory)	Used to start and maintain the router. Holds the POST and the bootstrap program, as well as the mini-IOS.
Flash memory	Stores the Cisco IOS by default. Flash memory is not erased when the router is reloaded. It is EEPROM (electronically erasable programmable read-only memory) created by Intel.
NVRAM (nonvolatile RAM)	Used to hold the router and switch configuration. NVRAM is not erased when the router or switch is reloaded. Does not store an IOS. The configuration register is stored in NVRAM.
Configuration register	Used to control how the router boots up. This value can be found as the last line of the show version command output and by default is set to 0x2102, which tells the router to load the IOS from flash memory as well as to load the configuration from NVRAM.

The Router Boot Sequence

When a router boots up, it performs a series of steps, called the *boot sequence*, to test the hardware and load the necessary software. The boot sequence consists of the following steps:

1. The router performs a POST. The POST tests the hardware to verify that all components of the device are operational and present. For example, the POST checks for the different interfaces on the router. The POST is stored in and run from *ROM (read-only memory)*.

2. The bootstrap then looks for and loads the Cisco IOS software. The bootstrap is a program in ROM that is used to execute programs. The bootstrap program is responsible for finding where each IOS program is located and then loading the file. By default, the IOS software is loaded from flash memory in all Cisco routers.

 The default order of an IOS loading from a router is Flash, TFTP server, then ROM.

3. The IOS software looks for a valid configuration file stored in NVRAM. This file is called startup-config and is only there if an administrator copies the running-config file into NVRAM. (As you already know, the new ISR routers have a small startup-config file preloaded.)

4. If a startup-config file is in NVRAM, the router will copy this file and place it in RAM and call the file running-config. The router will use this file to run the router. The router should now be operational. If a startup-config file is not in NVRAM, the router will broadcast out any interface that detects carrier detect (CD) for a TFTP host looking for a configuration, and when that fails (typically it will fail—most people won't even realize the router has attempted this process), it will start the setup mode configuration process.

Managing Configuration Register

All Cisco routers have a 16-bit software register that's written into NVRAM. By default, the *configuration register* is set to load the Cisco IOS from *flash memory* and to look for and load the startup-config file from NVRAM. In the following sections, I am going to discuss the configuration register settings and how to use these settings to provide password recovery on your routers.

Understanding the Configuration Register Bits

The 16 bits (2 bytes) of the configuration register are read from 15 to 0, from left to right. The default configuration setting on Cisco routers is 0x2102. This means that bits 13, 8, and 1 are on, as shown in Table 5.2. Notice that each set of 4 bits (called a nibble) is read in binary with a value of 8, 4, 2, 1.

TABLE 5.2   The Configuration Register Bit Numbers

Configuration Register			2					1				0			2	
Bit number	15	14	13	12	11	10	9	8	7	6	5	4	3	2	1	0
Binary	0	0	1	0	0	0	0	1	0	0	0	0	0	0	1	0

 Add the prefix *0x* to the configuration register address. The *0x* means that the digits that follow are in hexadecimal.

Table 5.3 lists the software configuration bit meanings. Notice that bit 6 can be used to ignore the NVRAM contents. This bit is used for password recovery—something I'll go over with you soon in the section "Recovering Passwords" later in this chapter.

Remember that in hex, the scheme is 0–9 and A–F (A = 10, B = 11, C = 12, D = 13, E = 14, and F = 15). This means that a 210F setting for the configuration register is actually 210(15), or 1111 in binary.

TABLE 5.3   Software Configuration Meanings

Bit	Hex	Description
0–3	0x0000–0x000F	Boot field (see Table 5.4).
6	0x0040	Ignore NVRAM contents.
7	0x0080	OEM bit enabled.
8	0x101	Break disabled.
10	0x0400	IP broadcast with all zeros.
5, 11–12	0x0800–0x1000	Console line speed.
13	0x2000	Boot default ROM software if network boot fails.
14	0x4000	IP broadcasts do not have net numbers.
15	0x8000	Enable diagnostic messages and ignore NVRAM contents.

The boot field, which consists of bits 0–3 in the configuration register, controls the router boot sequence. Table 5.4 describes the boot field bits.

TABLE 5.4   The Boot Field (Configuration Register Bits 00–03)

Boot Field	Meaning	Use
00	ROM monitor mode	To boot to ROM monitor mode, set the configuration register to 2100. You must manually boot the router with the b command. The router will show the rommon> prompt.
01	Boot image from ROM	To boot an IOS image stored in ROM, set the configuration register to 2101. The router will show the Router(boot)> prompt.
02–F	Specifies a default boot file name	Any value from 2102 through 210F tells the router to use the boot commands specified in NVRAM.

Checking the Current Configuration Register Value

You can see the current value of the configuration register by using the show version command (sh version or show ver for short), as demonstrated here:

```
Router#sh version
Cisco IOS Software, 2800 Software (C2800NM-ADVSECURITYK9-M), Version
    12.4(12), RELEASE SOFTWARE (fc1)
[output cut]
Configuration register is 0x2102
```

The last information given from this command is the value of the configuration register. In this example, the value is 0x2102—the default setting. The configuration register setting of 0x2102 tells the router to look in NVRAM for the boot sequence.

Notice that the show version command also provides the IOS version, and in the preceding example, it shows the IOS version as 12.4(12).

The show version command will display system hardware configuration information, software version, and the names of the boot images on a router.

Changing the Configuration Register

You can change the configuration register value to modify how the router boots and runs. These are the main reasons you would want to change the configuration register:

- To force the system into the ROM monitor mode
- To select a boot source and default boot filename
- To enable or disable the Break function
- To control broadcast addresses
- To set the console terminal baud rate
- To load operating software from ROM
- To enable booting from a Trivial File Transfer Protocol (TFTP) server

Before you change the configuration register, make sure you know the current configuration register value. Use the show version command to get this information.

You can change the configuration register by using the config-register command. Here's an example. The following commands tell the router to boot a small IOS from ROM and then show the current configuration register value:

```
Router(config)#config-register 0x2101
Router(config)#^Z
```

```
Router#sh ver
[output cut]
Configuration register is 0x2102 (will be 0x2101 at next
  reload)
```

Notice that the show version command displays the current configuration register value and also what that value will be when the router reboots. Any change to the configuration register won't take effect until the router is reloaded. The 0x2101 will load the IOS from ROM the next time the router is rebooted. You may see it listed as 0x101—that's basically the same thing, and it can be written either way.

Here is our router after setting the configuration register to 0x2101 and reloading:

```
Router(boot)#sh ver
Cisco IOS Software, 2800 Software (C2800NM-ADVSECURITYK9-M), Version
    12.4(12), RELEASE SOFTWARE (fc1)
[output cut]

ROM: System Bootstrap, Version 12.4(13r)T, RELEASE SOFTWARE (fc1)

Router uptime is 3 minutes
System returned to ROM by power-on
System image file is "flash:c2800nm-advsecurityk9-mz.124-12.bin"
[output cut]

Configuration register is 0x2101
```

At this point, if you typed **show flash**, you'd still see the IOS in flash memory ready to go. But we told our router to load from ROM, which is why the hostname shows up with (boot).

```
Router(boot)#sh flash
-#- --length-- -----date/time------ path
1    21710744 Jan 2 2007 22:41:14 +00:00 c2800nm-advsecurityk9-mz.124-12.bin
2        1823 Dec 5 2006 14:46:26 +00:00 sdmconfig-2811.cfg
3     4734464 Dec 5 2006 14:47:12 +00:00 sdm.tar
4      833024 Dec 5 2006 14:47:38 +00:00 es.tar
5     1052160 Dec 5 2006 14:48:10 +00:00 common.tar
6        1038 Dec 5 2006 14:48:32 +00:00 home.shtml
7      102400 Dec 5 2006 14:48:54 +00:00 home.tar
8      491213 Dec 5 2006 14:49:22 +00:00 128MB.sdf
9     1684577 Dec 5 2006 14:50:04 +00:00 securedesktop-ios-3.1.1.27-k9.pkg
10     398305 Dec 5 2006 14:50:34 +00:00 sslclient-win-1.1.0.154.pkg

32989184 bytes available (31027200 bytes used)
```

So even though we have our full IOS in flash, we changed the default loading of the router's software by changing the configuration register. If you want to set the configuration register back to the default, just type this:

```
Router(boot)#config t
Router(boot)(config)#config-register 0x2102
Router(boot)(config)#^Z
Router(boot)#reload
```

In the next section, I'll show you how to load the router into ROM monitor mode so you can perform password recovery.

Recovering Passwords

If you're locked out of a router because you forgot the password, you can change the configuration register to help you get back on your feet. As I said earlier, bit 6 in the configuration register is used to tell the router whether to use the contents of NVRAM to load a router configuration.

The default configuration register value is 0x2102, meaning that bit 6 is off. With the default setting, the router will look for and load a router configuration stored in NVRAM (startup-config). To recover a password, you need to turn on bit 6. Doing this will tell the router to ignore the NVRAM contents. The configuration register value to turn on bit 6 is 0x2142.

Here are the main steps to password recovery:

1. Boot the router and interrupt the boot sequence by performing a break, which will take the router into ROM monitor mode.

2. Change the configuration register to turn on bit 6 (with the value 0x2142).

3. Reload the router.

4. Enter privileged mode.

5. Copy the startup-config file to running-config.

6. Change the password.

7. Reset the configuration register to the default value.

8. Save the router configuration.

9. Reload the router (optional).

I'm going to cover these steps in more detail in the following sections. I'll also show you the commands to restore access to ISR, 2600, and even 2500 series routers. (You can still use 2500s (kinda) and you never know when you might need this information!)

As I said, you can enter ROM monitor mode by pressing Ctrl+Break during router bootup. But if the IOS is corrupt or missing, if there's no network connectivity available to find a TFTP host, or if the mini-IOS from ROM doesn't load (meaning the default router fallback failed), the router will enter ROM monitor mode by default.

Interrupting the Router Boot Sequence

Your first step is to boot the router and perform a break. This is usually done by pressing the Ctrl+Break key combination when using HyperTerminal (personally, I use SecureCRT) while the router first reboots.

After you've performed a break, you should see something like this for a 2600 series router (it is pretty much the same output for the ISR series):

```
System Bootstrap, Version 11.3(2)XA4, RELEASE SOFTWARE (fc1)
Copyright (c) 1999 by cisco Systems, Inc.
TAC:Home:SW:IOS:Specials for info
PC = 0xfff0a530, Vector = 0x500, SP = 0x680127b0
C2600 platform with 32768 Kbytes of main memory
PC = 0xfff0a530, Vector = 0x500, SP = 0x80004374
monitor: command "boot" aborted due to user interrupt
rommon 1 >
```

Notice the line `monitor: command "boot" aborted due to user interrupt`. At this point, you will be at the `rommon 1>` prompt, which is called ROM monitor mode.

Changing the Configuration Register

As I explained earlier, you can change the configuration register by using the `config-register` command. To turn on bit 6, use the configuration register value 0x2142.

Remember that if you change the configuration register to 0x2142, the startup-config will be bypassed and the router will load into setup mode.

Cisco ISR/2600 Series Commands

To change the bit value on a Cisco ISR/2600 series router, you just enter the command at the `rommon 1>` prompt:

```
rommon 1 >confreg 0x2142
You must reset or power cycle for new config to take effect
rommon 2 >reset
```

Cisco 2500 Series Commands

To change the configuration register on a 2500 series router, type **o** after creating a break sequence on the router. This brings up a menu of configuration register option settings. To change the configuration register, enter the command **o/r**, followed by the new register value. Here's an example of turning on bit 6 on a 2501 router:

```
System Bootstrap, Version 11.0(10c), SOFTWARE
Copyright (c) 1986-1996 by cisco Systems
```

```
2500 processor with 14336 Kbytes of main memory
Abort at 0x1098FEC (PC)
>o
Configuration register = 0x2102 at last boot
Bit#    Configuration register option settings:
15      Diagnostic mode disabled
14      IP broadcasts do not have network numbers
13      Boot default ROM software if network boot fails
12-11   Console speed is 9600 baud
10      IP broadcasts with ones
08      Break disabled
07      OEM disabled
06      Ignore configuration disabled
03-00   Boot file is cisco2-2500 (or 'boot system' command)
>o/r 0x2142
```

Notice that the last entry in the router output is 03-00. This tells the router what the IOS boot file is. By default, the router will use the first file found in the flash memory, so if you want to boot a different filename, you can either change the configuration register or use the boot system flash:ios_name command. (I'll show you the boot system command in a minute.)

Reloading the Router and Entering Privileged Mode

At this point, you need to reset the router like this:

- From the ISR/2600 series router, type **I** (for initialize) or **reset**.

- From the 2500 series router, type **I**.

The router will reload and ask if you want to use setup mode (because no startup-config is used). Answer no to entering setup mode, press Enter to go into user mode, and then type **enable** to go into privileged mode.

Viewing and Changing the Configuration

Now you're past the point where you would need to enter the user-mode and privileged-mode passwords in a router. Copy the startup-config file to the running-config file:

```
copy startup-config running-config
```

Or use the shortcut:

```
copy start run
```

The configuration is now running in *random access memory (RAM)*, and you're in privileged mode, meaning that you can now view and change the configuration. But you can't view the **enable secret** setting for the password since it is encrypted. To change the password, do this:

```
config t
enable secret todd
```

Resetting the Configuration Register and Reloading the Router

After you're finished changing passwords, set the configuration register back to the default value with the `config-register` command:

```
config t
config-register 0x2102
```

Finally, save the new configuration with a `copy running-config startup-config` and `reload` the router.

> If you save your configuration and reload the router and it comes up in setup mode, the configuration register setting is probably incorrect.

Boot System Commands

Did you know that you can configure your router to boot another IOS if the flash is corrupted? Well, you can. In fact, you just might want all your routers to boot from a TFTP host each time anyway because that way, you'll never have to upgrade each router individually. This may be a smooth way to go because it allows you to just change one file on a TFTP host to perform an upgrade.

There are some boot commands you can play with that will help you manage the way your router boots the Cisco IOS—but remember, we're talking about the router's IOS here, *not* the router's configuration!

```
Router>en
Router#config t
Enter configuration commands, one per line.  End with CNTL/Z.
Router(config)#boot ?
  bootstrap  Bootstrap image file
  config     Configuration file
  host       Router-specific config file
  network    Network-wide config file
  system     System image file
```

The boot command truly gives you a wealth of options, but first, I'll show you the typical settings that Cisco recommends. So let's get started—the boot system command will allow you to tell the router which file to boot from flash memory. Remember that the router, by default, boots the first file found in flash. You can change that with the following commands:

```
Router(config)#boot system ?
  WORD   TFTP filename or URL
  flash  Boot from flash memory
```

```
ftp    Boot from a server via ftp
mop    Boot from a Decnet MOP server
rcp    Boot from a server via rcp
rom    Boot from rom
tftp   Boot from a tftp server
Router(config)#boot system flash c2800nm-advsecurityk9-mz.124-12.bin
```

The above command configures the router to boot the IOS listed in it. This is a helpful command for when you load a new IOS into flash and want to test it, or even when you want to totally change which IOS is loading by default.

The next command is considered a fall-back routine, but as I said, you can make it a permanent way to have your routers boot from a TFTP host. Personally, I wouldn't necessarily recommend doing this (single point of failure); I'm just showing you it's possible:

```
Router(config)#boot system tftp ?
  WORD   System image filename
Router(config)#boot system tftp c2800nm-advsecurityk9-mz.124-12.bin ?
  Hostname or A.B.C.D  Address from which to download the file
  <cr>
Router(config)#boot system tftp c2800nm-advsecurityk9-mz.124-12.bin 1.1.1.2
Router(config)#
```

As your last recommended fall-back option—the one to go to if the IOS in flash doesn't load and the TFTP host does not produce the IOS—load the mini-IOS from ROM like this:

```
Router(config)#boot system rom
Router(config)#do show run | include boot system
boot system flash c2800nm-advsecurityk9-mz.124-12.bin
boot system tftp c2800nm-advsecurityk9-mz.124-12.bin 1.1.1.2
boot system rom
Router(config)#
```

To sum this up, we now have Cisco's suggested IOS backup routine configured on our router: flash, TFTP host, ROM.

Backing Up and Restoring the Cisco IOS

Before you upgrade or restore a Cisco IOS, you really should copy the existing file to a *TFTP host* as a backup just in case the new image crashes and burns.

And you can use any TFTP host to accomplish this. By default, the flash memory in a router is used to store the Cisco IOS. In the following sections, I'll describe how to check the amount of flash memory, how to copy the Cisco IOS from flash memory to a TFTP host, and how to copy the IOS from a TFTP host to flash memory.

You'll learn how to use the Cisco IFS and SDM to manage your IOS files after first learning how to manage them with a TFTP host.

But before you back up an IOS image to a network server on your intranet, you've got to do these three things:

- Make sure you can access the network server.
- Ensure that the network server has adequate space for the code image.
- Verify the file naming and path requirement.

And if you have a laptop or workstation's Ethernet port directly connected to a router's Ethernet interface, as shown in Figure 5.1, you need to verify the following before attempting to copy the image to or from the router:

- TFTP server software must be running on the administrator's workstation.
- The Ethernet connection between the router and the workstation must be made with a crossover cable.
- The workstation must be on the same subnet as the router's Ethernet interface.
- The copy flash tftp command must be supplied the IP address of the workstation if you are copying from the router flash.
- And if you're copying "into" flash, you need to verify that there's enough room in flash memory to accommodate the file to be copied.

FIGURE 5.1   Copying an IOS from a workstation to a router

Verifying Flash Memory

Before you attempt to upgrade the Cisco IOS on your router with a new IOS file, it's a good idea to verify that your flash memory has enough room to hold the new image. You verify the amount of flash memory and the file or files being stored in flash memory by using the show flash command (sh flash for short):

```
Router#sh flash
-#- --length-- -----date/time------ path
1    21710744 Jan 2 2007 22:41:14 +00:00 c2800nm-advsecurityk9-mz.124-12.bin
[output cut]
32989184 bytes available (31027200 bytes used)
```

The ISR router above has 64MB of RAM, and roughly half of the memory is in use.

The show flash command will display the amount of memory consumed by the current IOS image as well as tell you if there's enough room available to hold both current and new images. You should know that if there's not enough room for both the old and new image you want to load, the old image will be erased!

The amount of flash is actually easier to tally using the show version command on the ISR routers:

```
Router#show version
[output cut]
Cisco 2811 (revision 49.46) with 249856K/12288K bytes of memory.
Processor board ID FTX1049A1AB
2 FastEthernet interfaces
4 Serial(sync/async) interfaces
1 Virtual Private Network (VPN) Module
DRAM configuration is 64 bits wide with parity enabled.
239K bytes of non-volatile configuration memory.
62720K bytes of ATA CompactFlash (Read/Write)
```

You can see that the amount of flash shows up on the last line. By averaging up, we get the amount of flash to 64MB.

Notice that the filename in this example is c2800nm-advsecurityk9-mz.124-12.bin. The main difference in the output of the show flash and show version commands is that the show flash command displays all files in flash and the show version command shows the actual name of the file that the router is using to run the router.

Backing Up the Cisco IOS

To back up the Cisco IOS to a TFTP server, you use the copy flash tftp command. It's a straightforward command that requires only the source filename and the IP address of the TFTP server.

The key to success in this backup routine is to make sure you've got good, solid connectivity to the TFTP server. Check this by pinging the TFTP device from the router console prompt like this:

```
Router#ping 1.1.1.2
Type escape sequence to abort.
Sending 5, 100-byte ICMP Echos to 1.1.1.2, timeout
  is 2 seconds:
!!!!!
Success rate is 100 percent (5/5), round-trip min/avg/max
  = 4/4/8 ms
```

The *Packet Internet Groper (Ping)* utility is used to test network connectivity, and I use it in some of the examples in this chapter. I'll be talking about it in more detail in the section "Checking Network Connectivity and Troubleshooting" later in the chapter.

After you ping the TFTP server to make sure that IP is working, you can use the `copy flash tftp` command to copy the IOS to the TFTP server as shown next:

```
Router#copy flash tftp
Source filename []?c2800nm-advsecurityk9-mz.124-12.bin
Address or name of remote host []?1.1.1.2
Destination filename [c2800nm-advsecurityk9-mz.124-12.bin]?[enter]
!!!!!!!!!!!!!!!!!!!!!!!!!!!!!!!!!!!!!!!!!!!!!!!!!!!!!!!!!!!!!!!!!!!!!!!!!!!!!!!!!!!!!
!!!!!!!!
21710744 bytes copied in 60.724 secs (357532 bytes/sec)
Router#
```

Just copy the IOS filename from either the `show flash` or `show version` command and then paste it when prompted for the source filename.

In the preceding example, the contents of flash memory were copied successfully to the TFTP server. The address of the remote host is the IP address of the TFTP host, and the source filename is the file in flash memory.

The `copy flash tftp` command won't prompt you for the location of any file or ask you where to put the file. TFTP is just a "grab it and place it" program in this situation. This means that the TFTP server must have a default directory specified or it won't work!

Restoring or Upgrading the Cisco Router IOS

What happens if you need to restore the Cisco IOS to flash memory to replace an original file that has been damaged or if you want to upgrade the IOS? You can download the file from a TFTP server to flash memory by using the `copy tftp flash` command. This command requires the IP address of the TFTP host and the name of the file you want to download.

But before you begin, make sure the file you want to place in flash memory is in the default TFTP directory on your host. When you issue the command, TFTP won't ask you where the file is, so if the file you want to use isn't in the default directory of the TFTP host, this just won't work.

```
Router#copy tftp flash
Address or name of remote host []?1.1.1.2
Source filename []?c2800nm-advsecurityk9-mz.124-12.bin
```

```
Destination filename [c2800nm-advsecurityk9-mz.124-12.bin]?[enter]
%Warning:There is a file already existing with this name
Do you want to over write? [confirm][enter]
Accessing tftp://1.1.1.2/c2800nm-advsecurityk9-mz.124-12.bin...
Loading c2800nm-advsecurityk9-mz.124-12.bin from 1.1.1.2 (via
   FastEthernet0/0):
!!!!!!!!!!!!!!!!!!!!!!!!!!!!!!!!!!!!!!!!!!!!!!!!!!!!!!!!!!!!!!!!!!!!!!!!!!!
[OK - 21710744 bytes]

21710744 bytes copied in 82.880 secs (261954 bytes/sec)
Router#
```

In the above example, I copied the same file into flash memory, so it asked me if I wanted to overwrite it. Remember that we are "playing" with files in flash memory. If I had just corrupted my file by overwriting it, I won't know until I reboot the router. Be careful with this command! If the file is corrupted, you'll need to do an IOS restore from ROM monitor mode.

If you are loading a new file and you don't have enough room in flash memory to store both the new and existing copies, the router will ask to erase the contents of flash memory before writing the new file into flash memory.

A Cisco router can become a TFTP server host for a router system image that's run in flash memory. The global configuration command is `tftp-server flash: ios_name`.

Using the Cisco IOS File System (Cisco IFS)

Cisco has created a file system called Cisco IFS that allows you to work with files and directories just as you would from a Windows DOS prompt. The commands you use are `dir`, `copy`, `more`, `delete`, `erase` or `format`, `cd` and `pwd`, and `mkdir` and `rmdir`.

Working with IFS gives you the ability to view and classify all files—even those on remote servers. And you definitely want to find out if an image on one of your remote servers is valid before you copy it, right? You also need to know how big it is—size matters here! It's also a really good idea to take a look at the remote server's configuration and make sure it's all good before loading that file on your router.

It's very cool that IFS makes the file system user interface universal—it's not platform specific anymore. You now get to use the same syntax for all your commands on all of your routers, no matter the platform!

Sound too good to be true? Well, it kind of is because you'll find out that support for all commands on each file system and platform just isn't there. But it's really no big deal since various file systems differ in the actions they perform; the commands that aren't relevant to a particular file system are the very ones that aren't supported. Be assured that any file system or platform will fully support all the commands you need to manage it.

Another cool IFS feature is that it cuts down on all those obligatory prompts for a lot of the commands. If you want to enter a command, all you have to do is type all the necessary info straight into the command line—no more jumping through hoops of prompts! So, if you want to copy a file to an FTP server, all you'd do is first indicate where the desired source file is on your router, pinpoint where the destination file is on the FTP server, determine the username and password you're going to use when you want to connect to that server, and type it all in on one line—sleek! And for those of you resistant to change, you can still have the router prompt you for all the information it needs and enjoy entering a more elegantly minimized version of the command than you did before.

But even in spite of all this, your router might still prompt you—even if you did everything right in your command line. It comes down to how you've got the `file prompt` command configured and which command you're trying to use. But no worries—if that happens, the default value will be entered right there in the command, and all you have to do is hit Enter to verify the correct values.

IFS also lets you explore various directories and inventory files in any directory you want. Plus, you can make subdirectories in flash memory or on a card, but you only get to do that if you're working on one of the more recent platforms.

And get this—the new file system interface uses URLs to determine the whereabouts of a file. So just as they pinpoint places on the Web, URLs now indicate where files are on your Cisco router, or even on a remote file server! You just type URLs right into your commands to identify where the file or directory is. It's really that easy—to copy a file from one place to another, you simply enter the `copy source-url destination-url` command—sweet! IFS URLs are a tad different than what you're used to though, and there's an array of formats to use that vary depending on where, exactly, the file is that you're after.

We're going to use Cisco IFS commands pretty much the same way that we used the **copy** command in the IOS section earlier:

- For backing up the IOS

- For upgrading the IOS

- For viewing text files

Okay—with all that down, let's take a look at the common IFS commands available to us for managing the IOS. I'll get into configuration files soon, but for now I'm going to get you started with going over the basics used to manage the new Cisco IOS.

dir   Same as with Windows, this command lets you view files in a directory. Type **dir**, hit Enter, and by default you get the contents of the `flash:/` directory output.

copy   This is one popular command, often used to upgrade, restore, or back up an IOS. But as I said, when you use it, it's really important to focus on the details—what you're copying, where it's coming from, and where it's going to land.

more   Same as with Unix, this will give you a text file and let you look at it on a card. You can use it to check out your configuration file or your backup configuration file. I'll go over it more when we get into actual configuration.

show file   This command will give you the skinny on a specified file or file system, but it's kind of obscure because people don't use it a lot.

delete   Three guesses—yep, it deletes stuff. But with some types of routers, not as well as you'd think. That's because even though it whacks the file, it doesn't always free up the space it was using. To actually get the space back, you have to use something called the `squeeze` command too.

erase/format   Use these with care—make sure that when you're copying files, you say no to the dialog that asks you if you want to erase the file system! The type of memory you're using determines if you can nix the flash drive or not.

cd/pwd   Same as with Unix and DOS, `cd` is the command you use to change directories. Use the `pwd` command to print (show) the working directory.

mkdir/rmdir   Use these commands on certain routers and switches to create and delete directories—the `mkdir` command for creation and the `rmdir` command for deletion. Use the `cd` and `pwd` commands to change into these directories.

Using the Cisco IFS to Upgrade an IOS

Let's take a look at some of these Cisco IFS commands on my ISR router (1841 series) with a hostname of R1.

We'll start with the `pwd` command to verify our default directory and then use the `dir` command to verify the contents of the default directory (`flash:/`):

```
R1#pwd
flash:
R1#dir
Directory of flash:/
    1  -rw-    13937472  Dec 20 2006 19:58:18 +00:00  c1841-ipbase-
    mz.124-1c.bin
    2  -rw-        1821  Dec 20 2006 20:11:24 +00:00  sdmconfig-18xx.cfg
    3  -rw-     4734464  Dec 20 2006 20:12:00 +00:00  sdm.tar
    4  -rw-      833024  Dec 20 2006 20:12:24 +00:00  es.tar
    5  -rw-     1052160  Dec 20 2006 20:12:50 +00:00  common.tar
    6  -rw-        1038  Dec 20 2006 20:13:10 +00:00  home.shtml
    7  -rw-      102400  Dec 20 2006 20:13:30 +00:00  home.tar
    8  -rw-      491213  Dec 20 2006 20:13:56 +00:00  128MB.sdf
    9  -rw-     1684577  Dec 20 2006 20:14:34 +00:00  securedesktop-
    ios-3.1.1.27-k9.pkg
   10  -rw-      398305  Dec 20 2006 20:15:04 +00:00  sslclient-win-
    1.1.0.154.pkg

32071680 bytes total (8818688 bytes free)
```

What we can see here is that we have the basic IP IOS (`c1841-ipbase-mz.124-1c.bin`). Looks like we need to upgrade our 1841. You've just got to love how Cisco puts the IOS type in the filename now! First, let's check the size of the file that's in flash with the show file command (show flash would also work):

```
R1#show file info flash:c1841-ipbase-mz.124-1c.bin
flash:c1841-ipbase-mz.124-1c.bin:
  type is image (elf) []
  file size is 13937472 bytes, run size is 14103140 bytes
  Runnable image, entry point 0x8000F000, run from ram
```

With a file that size, the existing IOS will have to be erased before we can add our new IOS file (c1841-advipservicesk9-mz.124-12.bin), which is over 21MB. We'll use the delete command, but remember, we can play with any file in flash memory and nothing serious will happen until we reboot—that is, if we made a mistake. So obviously, and as I pointed out earlier, we need to be majorly careful here!

```
R1#delete flash:c1841-ipbase-mz.124-1c.bin
Delete filename [c1841-ipbase-mz.124-1c.bin]?[enter]
Delete flash:c1841-ipbase-mz.124-1c.bin? [confirm][enter]
R1#sh flash
-#- --length-- -----date/time------ path
1          1821 Dec 20 2006 20:11:24 +00:00 sdmconfig-18xx.cfg
2       4734464 Dec 20 2006 20:12:00 +00:00 sdm.tar
3        833024 Dec 20 2006 20:12:24 +00:00 es.tar
4       1052160 Dec 20 2006 20:12:50 +00:00 common.tar
5          1038 Dec 20 2006 20:13:10 +00:00 home.shtml
6        102400 Dec 20 2006 20:13:30 +00:00 home.tar
7        491213 Dec 20 2006 20:13:56 +00:00 128MB.sdf
8       1684577 Dec 20 2006 20:14:34 +00:00 securedesktop-ios-3.1.1.27-k9.pkg
9        398305 Dec 20 2006 20:15:04 +00:00 sslclient-win-1.1.0.154.pkg
22757376 bytes available (9314304 bytes used)
R1#sh file info flash:c1841-ipbase-mz.124-1c.bin
%Error opening flash:c1841-ipbase-mz.124-1c.bin (File not found)
R1#
```

So with the above commands, I deleted the existing file and then verified the deletion by using both the show flash and show file commands. Let's add the new file with the copy command, but again, I'm going to make sure I'm careful because this doesn't make it safer than the first method I showed you earlier:

```
R1#copy tftp://1.1.1.2//c1841-advipservicesk9-mz.124-12.bin/ flash:/
    c1841-advipservicesk9-mz.124-12.bin
Source filename [/c1841-advipservicesk9-mz.124-12.bin/]?[enter]
Destination filename [c1841-advipservicesk9-mz.124-12.bin]?[enter]
Loading /c1841-advipservicesk9-mz.124-12.bin/ from 1.1.1.2 (via
```

```
    FastEthernet0/0): !!!!!!!!!!!!!!!!!!!!!!!!!!!!!!!!!!!!!!!!!!!!!
[output cut]
!!!!!!!!!!!!!!!!!!!!!!!!!!!!!!!!!!!!!!!!!!!!!!!!!!!!!!!!!
[OK - 22103052 bytes]
22103052 bytes copied in 72.008 secs (306953 bytes/sec)
R1#sh flash
-#- --length-- -----date/time------ path
1         1821 Dec 20 2006 20:11:24 +00:00 sdmconfig-18xx.cfg
2      4734464 Dec 20 2006 20:12:00 +00:00 sdm.tar
3       833024 Dec 20 2006 20:12:24 +00:00 es.tar
4      1052160 Dec 20 2006 20:12:50 +00:00 common.tar
5         1038 Dec 20 2006 20:13:10 +00:00 home.shtml
6       102400 Dec 20 2006 20:13:30 +00:00 home.tar
7       491213 Dec 20 2006 20:13:56 +00:00 128MB.sdf
8      1684577 Dec 20 2006 20:14:34 +00:00 securedesktop-ios-3.1.1.27-k9.pkg
9       398305 Dec 20 2006 20:15:04 +00:00 sslclient-win-1.1.0.154.pkg
10    22103052 Mar 10 2007 19:40:50 +00:00 c1841-advipservicesk9-mz.124-12.bin
651264 bytes available (31420416 bytes used)
R1#
```

We can check the file information as well with the **show file** command:

```
R1#sh file information flash:c1841-advipservicesk9-mz.124-12.bin
flash:c1841-advipservicesk9-mz.124-12.bin:
  type is image (elf) []
  file size is 22103052 bytes, run size is 22268736 bytes
  Runnable image, entry point 0x8000F000, run from ram
```

Remember that the IOS is expanded into RAM when the router boots, so the new IOS will not run until you reload the router. So now let's take a look at how to use the Cisco SDM to upgrade a router's IOS.

 I really recommend that you play with the Cisco IFS commands on a router just to get a good feel for them because, as I've said, they can definitely give you some grief at first!

Using the SDM to Manage the Flash Memory

I was going to call this section "Using SDM to Upgrade/Restore/Back Up the IOS on Your Router," but the SDM allows management of *all* the files in flash memory (as well as NVRAM), not just the IOS. It can be an easier method of flash file management, but for what it's worth, you won't find it safer to do it this way. It *is* a way to manage your files though. Let's check it out.

I mention "safer methods" a lot in this chapter. Clearly, I've caused myself some serious pain not being careful enough when working in flash memory! I cannot tell you enough—pay attention when messing around with flash memory!

I'm going to connect to my other 1841 router (named R3) and upgrade that IOS using the SDM. Let's connect and see what's in flash. Looking at the first screen, we can see that IP is the only feature available and that Firewall, VPN, IPS, and NAC are "X'd" out. Let's fix that!

The next screen shows how to open the file management for flash. Chose File ➢ File Management.

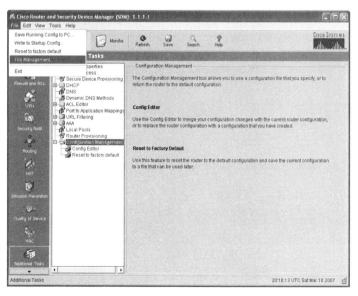

At this point, the screen shows all the files in flash, and we can see that we have the "ipbase" IOS.

Click Load file from PC on the top of the screen to add a new file. When I tried to load the new IOS, I received the message shown in the next screen shot.

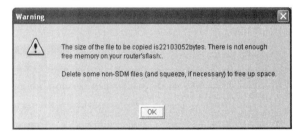

I clicked OK, tried to delete the existing file, and then received this message.

I chose yes, and then looked at the File Management window again to verify that the file was deleted.

I then chose Load File from PC again and the file started uploading into flash memory.

Woo-hoo—finally, success!

After rebooting, we can see that IP, Firewall, VPN, IPS, and NAC are all available with this new IOS!

 One of the brilliant features of the ISR routers is that they use the physical flash cards that are accessible from the front or back of any router. You can pull these flash cards out, put them in an appropriate slot in your PC, and the card will show up as a drive. You can then add, change, and delete files. Just put the flash card back in your router and power up—instant upgrade. Nice!

Backing Up and Restoring the Cisco Configuration

Any changes that you make to the router configuration are stored in the running-config file. And if you don't enter a `copy run start` command after you make a change to running-config, that change will go poof if the router reboots or gets powered down. So you probably want to make another backup of the configuration information just in case the router or switch completely dies on you. Even if your machine is healthy and happy, it's good to have for reference and documentation reasons.

In the following sections, I'll describe how to copy the configuration of a router to a TFTP server and how to restore that configuration.

Backing Up the Cisco Router Configuration

To copy the router's configuration from a router to a TFTP server, you can use either the `copy running-config tftp` or the `copy startup-config tftp` command. Either one will back up the router configuration that's currently running in DRAM or that's stored in NVRAM.

Verifying the Current Configuration

To verify the configuration in DRAM, use the `show running-config` command (`sh run` for short) like this:

```
Router#show running-config
Building configuration...

Current configuration : 776 bytes
!
version 12.4
```

The current configuration information indicates that the router is running version 12.4 of the IOS.

Verifying the Stored Configuration

Next, you should check the configuration stored in NVRAM. To see this, use the `show startup-config` command (`sh start` for short) like this:

```
Router#show startup-config
Using 776 out of 245752 bytes
!
version 12.4
```

The second line shows you how much room your backup configuration is using. Here, we can see that NVRAM is 239KB (again, memory is easier to see with the `show version` command when you're using an ISR router) and that only 776 bytes of it are used.

If you're not sure that the files are the same and the running-config file is what you want to use, then use the `copy running-config startup-config`. This will help you verify that both files are in fact the same. I'll go through this with you in the next section.

Copying the Current Configuration to NVRAM

By copying running-config to NVRAM as a backup, as shown in the following output, you're assured that your running-config will always be reloaded if the router gets rebooted. In the new IOS version 12.0, you're prompted for the filename you want to use:

```
Router#copy running-config startup-config
Destination filename [startup-config]?[enter]
Building configuration...
[OK]
Router#
```

The reason the filename prompt appears is that there are now so many options you can use when using the copy command:

```
Router#copy running-config ?
  archive:       Copy to archive: file system
  flash:         Copy to flash: file system
  ftp:           Copy to ftp: file system
  http:          Copy to http: file system
  https:         Copy to https: file system
  ips-sdf        Update (merge with) IPS signature configuration
  null:          Copy to null: file system
  nvram:         Copy to nvram: file system
  rcp:           Copy to rcp: file system
  running-config Update (merge with) current system configuration
  scp:           Copy to scp: file system
  startup-config Copy to startup configuration
  syslog:        Copy to syslog: file system
  system:        Copy to system: file system
  tftp:          Copy to tftp: file system
  xmodem:        Copy to xmodem: file system
  ymodem:        Copy to ymodem: file system
```

We'll go over the copy command again in a minute.

Copying the Configuration to a TFTP Server

Once the file is copied to NVRAM, you can make a second backup to a TFTP server by using the copy running-config tftp command (copy run tftp for short), like this:

```
Router#copy running-config tftp
Address or name of remote host []?1.1.1.2
Destination filename [router-confg]?todd-confg
!!
776 bytes copied in 0.800 secs (970 bytes/sec)
Router#
```

In the preceding example, I named the file todd-confg because I had not set a hostname for the router. If you have a hostname already configured, the command will automatically use the hostname plus the extension -confg as the name of the file.

Restoring the Cisco Router Configuration

If you've changed your router's running-config file and want to restore the configuration to the version in the startup-config file, the easiest way to do this is to use the copy startup-config running-config command (copy start run for short). You can also use the older Cisco command config mem to restore a configuration. Of course, this will work only if you copied running-config into NVRAM before making any changes!

If you did copy the router's configuration to a TFTP server as a second backup, you can restore the configuration using the copy tftp running-config command (copy tftp run for short) or the copy tftp startup-config command (copy tftp start for short), as shown here (the old command that provides this function is config net):

```
Router#copy tftp running-config
Address or name of remote host []?1.1.1.2
Source filename []?todd-confg
Destination filename[running-config]?[enter]
Accessing tftp://1.1.1.2/todd-confg...
Loading todd-confg from 1.1.1.2 (via FastEthernet0/0): !
[OK - 776 bytes]
776 bytes copied in 9.212 secs (84 bytes/sec)
Router#
*Mar  7 17:53:34.071: %SYS-5-CONFIG_I: Configured from
    tftp://1.1.1.2/todd-confg by console
Router#
```

The configuration file is an ASCII text file, meaning that before you copy the configuration stored on a TFTP server back to a router, you can make changes to the file with any text editor. Last, notice that the command was changed to a URL of tftp://1.1.1.2/todd-config. This is the Cisco IOS File System (IFS)—as discussed earlier—and we'll use that to back up and restore our configuration in a minute.

 It is important to remember that when you copy or merge a configuration from a TFTP server to a router's RAM, the interfaces are shut down by default and you must manually go and enable each interface with the no shutdown command.

Erasing the Configuration

To delete the startup-config file on a Cisco router, use the command erase startup-config, like this:

```
Router#erase startup-config
Erasing the nvram filesystem will remove all configuration files!
    Continue? [confirm][enter]
[OK]
Erase of nvram: complete
```

```
*Mar  7 17:56:20.407: %SYS-7-NV_BLOCK_INIT: Initialized the geometry of nvram
Router#reload
System configuration has been modified. Save? [yes/no]:n
Proceed with reload? [confirm][enter]
 *Mar  7 17:56:31.059: %SYS-5-RELOAD: Reload requested by console.
   Reload Reason: Reload Command.
```

This command deletes the contents of NVRAM on the router. If you type **reload** at privileged mode and say no to saving changes, the router will reload and come up into setup mode.

Using the Cisco IOS File System to Manage Your Router's Configuration (Cisco IFS)

Using the old, faithful copy command is still useful and I recommend it. However, you still need to know about the Cisco IFS. The first thing we'll do is use the show file command to see the contents of NVRAM and RAM:

```
R3#show file information nvram:startup-config
nvram:startup-config:
  type is config
R3#cd nvram:
R3#pwd
nvram:/
R3#dir
Directory of nvram:/

  190  -rw-         830                 <no date>  startup-config
  191  ----           5                 <no date>  private-config
  192  -rw-         830                 <no date>  underlying-config
    1  -rw-           0                 <no date>  ifIndex-table
196600 bytes total (194689 bytes free)
```

There really are no other commands that will actually show us the contents of NVRAM. However, I am not sure how helpful it is to see them either. Let's look at the contents of RAM:

```
R3#cd system:
R3#pwd
system:/
R3#dir ?
  /all            List all files
  /recursive      List files recursively
  all-filesystems List files on all filesystems
  archive:        Directory or file name
```

```
    cns:           Directory or file name
    flash:         Directory or file name
    null:          Directory or file name
    nvram:         Directory or file name
    system:        Directory or file name
    xmodem:        Directory or file name
    ymodem:        Directory or file name
    <cr>
R3#dir
Directory of system:/

    3  dr-x         0             <no date> lib
   33  dr-x         0             <no date> memory
    1  -rw-       750             <no date> running-config
    2  dr-x         0             <no date> vfiles
```

Again, not too exciting. Let's use the copy command with the Cisco IFS to copy a file from a TFTP host to RAM. First, let's try the old command config net that was used for the last 10 years or so to accomplish this same feat:

```
R3#config net
Host or network configuration file [host]?[enter]
This command has been replaced by the command:
        'copy <url> system:/running-config'
Address or name of remote host [255.255.255.255]?
```

Although the command tells us that the command has been replaced with the new URL command, the old command will still work. Let's try it with the Cisco IFS:

```
R3#copy tftp://1.1.1.2/todd-confg system://running-config
Destination filename [running-config]?[enter]
Accessing tftp://1.1.1.2/todd-confg...Loading todd-confg from 1.1.1.2
   (via FastEthernet0/0): !
[OK - 776 bytes]
[OK]
776 bytes copied in 13.816 secs (56 bytes/sec)
R3#
*Mar 10 22:12:59.819: %SYS-5-CONFIG_I:
Configured from tftp://1.1.1.2/todd-confg by console
```

I guess we can say that this was easier than using the copy tftp run command—Cisco says it is, so who am I to argue? Maybe it just takes some getting used to. Let's see if we can make this a bit easier by connecting to our router through HTTP or HTTPS and using the SDM to manage our configuration files.

Using the SDM to Back Up/Restore and Edit the Router's Configuration

Honestly, there really isn't anything special about how the SDM handles configurations on a router. Basically, if you were to telnet to a router, perform a show run, and copy this output to a text file on your PC, you've just performed (more or less) what SDM and its configuration management tools can do. But this is still a less confusing way to manage files than doing so through the Cisco IFS.

Why? Well, what's easier about using the SDM rather than the copy command we covered earlier in this chapter is that no TFTP host is needed. By using the SDM, you can http or https to a router and keep all files local on your PC instead of having to configure a TFTP host. As I mentioned in Chapter 4, SDM is best used for advanced configurations like security, IPS, QOS, and NAT. As you can tell by now, I am a command-line interface (CLI) guy. What can I say? Old habits die hard!

Let's take a quick look at how the SDM can back up and restore your configuration from your host. From the main menu, choose File ≻ Write to Startup Config to back up your configuration to NVRAM.

Then choose File ➢ Save Running Config to PC.

One last option for managing your files is to use the Configuration Management screens under Additional Tasks.

The Config Editor allows you to change the running-config, but before it will let you do that, you have to agree that you can screw up your router's configuration and that this is okay with you!

It's best to click the Save Running Configuration button. You can then choose to import the file from RAM or from your PC.

Last, from Configuration Management, you can choose Reset to Factory Default. This will place the HTTPS management back on the router.

As you can see, there are many different ways to screw up, umm, I mean, change the files in flash, NVRAM, and even RAM. Practice on the SDM demo I showed you in Chapter 4, or try to borrow a friend's router. (You don't want to practice these commands on your own router, do you?)

Using Cisco Discovery Protocol (CDP)

Cisco Discovery Protocol (CDP) is a proprietary protocol designed by Cisco to help administrators collect information about both locally attached and remote devices. By using CDP, you can gather hardware and protocol information about neighbor devices, which is useful info for troubleshooting and documenting the network.

In the following sections, I am going to discuss the CDP timer and CDP commands used to verify your network.

Getting CDP Timers and Holdtime Information

The show cdp command (sh cdp for short) gives you information about two CDP global parameters that can be configured on Cisco devices:

- *CDP timer* is how often CDP packets are transmitted out all active interfaces.
- *CDP holdtime* is the amount of time that the device will hold packets received from neighbor devices.

Both Cisco routers and Cisco switches use the same parameters.

 For this section and the rest of this chapter, my 2811 will have a hostname of Corp, and it will have four serial connections to ISR routers named R1, R2, and R3 (there are two connections to R1) and one FastEthernet connection to a 1242 access point with a hostname of just ap.

The output on the Corp router looks like this:

```
Corp#sh cdp
Global CDP information:
        Sending CDP packets every 60 seconds
        Sending a holdtime value of 180 seconds
        Sending CDPv2 advertisements is  enabled
```

Use the global commands cdp holdtime and cdp timer to configure the CDP holdtime and timer on a router:

```
Corp(config)#cdp ?
  advertise-v2     CDP sends version-2 advertisements
  holdtime         Specify the holdtime (in sec) to be sent in packets
  log              Log messages generated by CDP
  run              Enable CDP
  source-interface Insert the interface's IP in all CDP packets
  timer            Specify rate (in sec) at which CDP packets are sent  run
Corp(config)#cdp holdtime ?
  <10-255> Length  of time  (in sec) that receiver must keep this packet
Corp(config)#cdp timer ?
  <5-254>  Rate at which CDP packets are sent (in  sec)
```

You can turn off CDP completely with the no cdp run command from the global configuration mode of a router. To turn CDP off or on for an interface, use the no cdp enable and cdp enable commands. Be patient—I'll work through these with you in a second.

Gathering Neighbor Information

The show cdp neighbor command (sh cdp nei for short) delivers information about directly connected devices. It's important to remember that CDP packets aren't passed through a Cisco switch and that you only see what's directly attached. So this means that if your router is connected to a switch, you won't see any of the devices hooked up to that switch.

The following output shows the show cdp neighbor command used on my ISR router:

```
Corp#sh cdp neighbors
Capability Codes: R - Router, T - Trans Bridge, B - Source Route Bridge
```

```
                  S - Switch, H - Host, I - IGMP, r - Repeater
Device ID    Local Intrfce    Holdtme    Capability   Platform   Port ID
ap           Fas 0/1            165          T I       AIR-AP124  Fas 0
R2           Ser 0/1/0          140         R S I      2801       Ser 0/2/0
R3           Ser 0/0/1          157         R S I      1841       Ser 0/0/1
R1           Ser 0/2/0          154         R S I      1841       Ser 0/0/1
R1           Ser 0/0/0          154         R S I      1841       Ser 0/0/0
Corp#
```

Okay, we are directly connected with a console cable to the Corp ISR router, and the router is directly connected to four devices. We have two connections to the R1 router. The device ID shows the configured hostname of the connected device, the local interface is our interface, and the port ID is the remote devices' directly connected interface. All you get to view are directly connected devices.

Table 5.5 summarizes the information displayed by the show cdp neighbor command for each device.

TABLE 5.5   Output of the *show cdp neighbor* Command

Field	Description
Device ID	The hostname of the device directly connected.
Local Interface	The port or interface on which you are receiving the CDP packet.
Holdtime	The amount of time the router will hold the information before discarding it if no more CDP packets are received.
Capability	The capability of the neighbor, such as the router, switch, or repeater. The capability codes are listed at the top of the command output.
Platform	The type of Cisco device directly connected. In the previous output, the Corp router is directly connected to a 1242 Access point, a Cisco 2801 and two 1841 routers.
Port ID	The neighbor device's port or interface on which the CDP packets are multicast.

 It is imperative that you can look at the output of a show cdp neighbors command and decipher the neighbor's device (capability, i.e., router or switch), model number (platform), your port connecting to that device (local interface), and the port of the neighbor connecting to you (port ID).

Another command that'll deliver the goods on neighbor information is the show cdp neighbors detail command (show cdp nei de for short). This command can be run on both routers and switches, and it displays detailed information about each device connected to the device you're running the command on. Check out this router output for an example:

```
Corp#sh cdp neighbors detail
-------------------------
Device ID: ap
Entry address(es): 10.1.1.2
Platform: cisco AIR-AP1242AG-A-K9   , Capabilities: Trans-Bridge IGMP
Interface: FastEthernet0/1,  Port ID (outgoing port): FastEthernet0
Holdtime : 122 sec

Version :
Cisco IOS Software, C1240 Software (C1240-K9W7-M), Version 12.3(8)JEA,
    RELEASE SOFTWARE (fc2)
Technical Support: http://www.cisco.com/techsupport
Copyright (c) 1986-2006 by Cisco Systems, Inc.
Compiled Wed 23-Aug-06 16:45 by kellythw

advertisement version: 2
Duplex: full
Power drawn: 15.000 Watts
-------------------------
Device ID: R2
Entry address(es):
  IP address: 10.4.4.2
Platform: Cisco 2801,  Capabilities: Router Switch IGMP
Interface: Serial0/1/0,  Port ID (outgoing port): Serial0/2/0
Holdtime : 135 sec

Version :
Cisco IOS Software, 2801 Software (C2801-ADVENTERPRISEK9-M),
    Experimental Version 12.4(20050525:193634) [jezhao-ani 145]
Copyright (c) 1986-2005 by Cisco Systems, Inc.
Compiled Fri 27-May-05 23:53 by jezhao

advertisement version: 2
VTP Management Domain: ''
-------------------------
Device ID: R3
```

```
Entry address(es):
  IP address: 10.5.5.1
Platform: Cisco 1841,  Capabilities: Router Switch IGMP
Interface: Serial0/0/1,  Port ID (outgoing port): Serial0/0/1
Holdtime : 152 sec

Version :
Cisco IOS Software, 1841 Software (C1841-IPBASE-M), Version 12.4(1c),
    RELEASE SOFTWARE (fc1)
Technical Support: http://www.cisco.com/techsupport
Copyright (c) 1986-2005 by Cisco Systems, Inc.
Compiled Tue 25-Oct-05 17:10 by evmiller

advertisement version: 2
VTP Management Domain: ''
-------------------------
[output cut]
Corp#
```

What are we being shown here? First, we're given the hostname and IP address of all
directly connected devices. In addition to the same information displayed by the show cdp
neighbor command (see Table 5.5), the show cdp neighbor detail command gives us the
IOS version of the neighbor device.

 Remember that you can see the IP address of only directly connected devices.

The show cdp entry * command displays the same information as the show cdp neighbors
detail command. Here's an example of the router output using the show cdp entry * command:

```
Corp#sh cdp entry *
-------------------------
Device ID: ap
Entry address(es):
Platform: cisco AIR-AP1242AG-A-K9   ,  Capabilities: Trans-Bridge IGMP
Interface: FastEthernet0/1,  Port ID (outgoing port): FastEthernet0
Holdtime : 160 sec

Version :
Cisco IOS Software, C1240 Software (C1240-K9W7-M), Version 12.3(8)JEA,
    RELEASE SOFTWARE (fc2)
```

```
Technical Support: http://www.cisco.com/techsupport
Copyright (c) 1986-2006 by Cisco Systems, Inc.
Compiled Wed 23-Aug-06 16:45 by kellythw

advertisement version: 2
Duplex: full
Power drawn: 15.000 Watts
------------------------
Device ID: R2
Entry address(es):
  IP address: 10.4.4.2
Platform: Cisco 2801,  Capabilities: Router Switch IGMP
 --More-
[output cut]
```

There isn't any difference between the show cdp neighbors detail and show cdp entry *
commands. However, the sh cdp entry * command has two options that the show cdp
neighbors detail command does not:

```
Corp#sh cdp entry * ?
  protocol  Protocol information
  version   Version information
  |         Output modifiers
  <cr>
Corp#show cdp entry * protocols
Protocol information for ap :
  IP address: 10.1.1.2
Protocol information for R2 :
  IP address: 10.4.4.2
Protocol information for R3 :
  IP address: 10.5.5.1
Protocol information for R1 :
  IP address: 10.3.3.2
Protocol information for R1 :
  IP address: 10.2.2.2
```

The preceding output of the show cdp entry * protocols command can show you just
the IP addresses of each directly connected neighbor. The show cdp entry * version will
show you only the IOS version of your directly connected neighbors:

```
Corp#show cdp entry * version
Version information for ap :
  Cisco IOS Software, C1240 Software (C1240-K9W7-M), Version
  12.3(8)JEA, RELEASE SOFTWARE (fc2)
```

Technical Support: http://www.cisco.com/techsupport
Copyright (c) 1986-2006 by Cisco Systems, Inc.
Compiled Wed 23-Aug-06 16:45 by kellythw

Version information for R2 :
  Cisco IOS Software, 2801 Software (C2801-ADVENTERPRISEK9-M),
   Experimental Version 12.4(20050525:193634) [jezhao-ani 145]
Copyright (c) 1986-2005 by Cisco Systems, Inc.
Compiled Fri 27-May-05 23:53 by jezhao

Version information for R3 :
  Cisco IOS Software, 1841 Software (C1841-IPBASE-M), Version 12.4(1c),
   RELEASE SOFTWARE (fc1)
Technical Support: http://www.cisco.com/techsupport
Copyright (c) 1986-2005 by Cisco Systems, Inc.
Compiled Tue 25-Oct-05 17:10 by evmiller

 --More-
[output cut]

Although the show cdp neighbors detail and show cdp entry commands are very similar, the show cdp entry command allows you to display only one line of output for each directly connected neighbor, whereas the show cdp neighbor detail command does not. Next, let's look at the show cdp traffic command.

Gathering Interface Traffic Information

The show cdp traffic command displays information about interface traffic, including the number of CDP packets sent and received and the errors with CDP.

The following output shows the show cdp traffic command used on the Corp router:

Corp#**sh cdp traffic**
CDP counters :
        Total packets output: 911, Input: 524
        Hdr syntax: 0, Chksum error: 0, Encaps failed: 2
        No memory: 0, Invalid packet: 0, Fragmented: 0
        CDP version 1 advertisements output: 0, Input: 0
        CDP version 2 advertisements output: 911, Input: 524
Corp#

This is not really the most important information you can gather from a router, but it does show how many CDP packets are sent and received on a device.

Gathering Port and Interface Information

The show cdp interface command gives you the CDP status on router interfaces or switch ports.

As I said earlier, you can turn off CDP completely on a router by using the no cdp run command. But remember that you can also turn off CDP on a per-interface basis with the no cdp enable command. You enable a port with the cdp enable command. All ports and interfaces default to cdp enable.

On a router, the show cdp interface command displays information about each interface using CDP, including the encapsulation on the line, the timer, and the holdtime for each interface. Here's an example of this command's output on the ISR router:

```
Corp#sh cdp interface
FastEthernet0/0 is administratively down, line protocol is down
  Encapsulation ARPA
  Sending CDP packets every 60 seconds
  Holdtime is 180 seconds
FastEthernet0/1 is up, line protocol is up
  Encapsulation ARPA
  Sending CDP packets every 60 seconds
  Holdtime is 180 seconds
Serial0/0/0 is up, line protocol is up
  Encapsulation HDLC
  Sending CDP packets every 60 seconds
  Holdtime is 180 seconds
Serial0/0/1 is up, line protocol is up
  Encapsulation HDLC
  Sending CDP packets every 60 seconds
  Holdtime is 180 seconds
Serial0/1/0 is up, line protocol is up
  Encapsulation HDLC
  Sending CDP packets every 60 seconds
  Holdtime is 180 seconds
Serial0/2/0 is up, line protocol is up
  Encapsulation HDLC
  Sending CDP packets every 60 seconds
  Holdtime is 180 seconds
```

The above output is nice because it always tells you the interface's status. To turn off CDP on one interface on a router, use the no cdp enable command from interface configuration mode:

```
Corp#config t
Corp(config)#int s0/0/0
Corp(config-if)#no cdp enable
```

```
Corp(config-if)#do show cdp interface
FastEthernet0/0 is administratively down, line protocol is down
  Encapsulation ARPA
  Sending CDP packets every 60 seconds
  Holdtime is 180 seconds
FastEthernet0/1 is up, line protocol is up
  Encapsulation ARPA
  Sending CDP packets every 60 seconds
  Holdtime is 180 seconds
Serial0/0/1 is up, line protocol is up
  Encapsulation HDLC
  Sending CDP packets every 60 seconds
  Holdtime is 180 seconds
Serial0/1/0 is up, line protocol is up
  Encapsulation HDLC
  Sending CDP packets every 60 seconds
  Holdtime is 180 seconds
Serial0/2/0 is up, line protocol is up
  Encapsulation HDLC
  Sending CDP packets every 60 seconds
  Holdtime is 180 seconds
Corp(config-if)#
```

Notice that serial 0/0/0 isn't listed in the router output. To get that output, you'd have to perform a cdp enable on serial 0/0/0. It would then show up in the output:

```
Corp(config-if)#cdp enable
Corp(config-if)#^Z
Corp#
```

 Real World Scenario

CDP Can Save Lives!

Karen has just been hired as a senior network consultant at a large hospital in Dallas, Texas. She is expected to be able to take care of any problem that comes up. No stress here—she only has to worry about people possibly not getting the right health care if the network goes down. Talk about a potential life-or-death situation!

Karen starts her job happily. Soon, of course, the network has some problems. She asks one of the junior administrators for a network map so she can troubleshoot the network. This person tells her that the old senior administrator (who just got fired) had them with him and now no one can find them—ouch!

Doctors are calling every couple of minutes because they can't get the necessary information they need to take care of their patients. What should she do?

CDP to the rescue! Thank God this hospital has all Cisco routers and switches and that CDP is enabled by default on all Cisco devices. Also, luckily, the disgruntled administrator who just got fired didn't turn off CDP on any devices before he left.

All Karen has to do now is to use the show cdp neighbor detail command to find all the information she needs about each device to help draw out the hospital network and save lives!

The only snag for you nailing this in your own network is if you don't know the passwords of all those devices. Your only hope then is to somehow find out the access passwords or to perform password recovery on them.

So, use CDP— you never know when you may end up saving someone's life.

This is a true story.

Documenting a Network Topology Using CDP

As the title of this section implies, I'm now going to show you how to document a sample network by using CDP. You'll learn to determine the appropriate router types, interface types, and IP addresses of various interfaces using only CDP commands and the show running-config command. And you can only console into the Lab_A router to document the network. You'll have to assign any remote routers the next IP address in each range. Figure 5.2 is what you'll use to complete the documentation.

FIGURE 5.2 Documenting a network topology using CDP

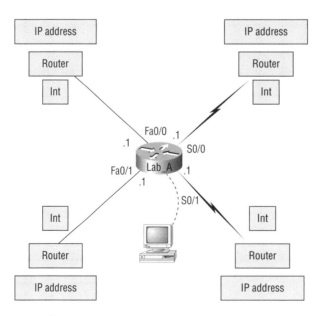

In this output, you can see that you have a router with four interfaces: two FastEthernet and two serial. First, determine the IP addresses of each interface by using the show running-config command:

```
Lab_A#sh running-config
Building configuration...

Current configuration : 960 bytes
!
version 12.2
service timestamps debug uptime
service timestamps log uptime
no service password-encryption
!
hostname Lab_A
!
ip subnet-zero
!
!
interface FastEthernet0/0
 ip address 192.168.21.1 255.255.255.0
 duplex auto
!
interface FastEthernet0/1
 ip address 192.168.18.1 255.255.255.0
 duplex auto
!
interface Serial0/0
ip address 192.168.23.1 255.255.255.0
!
interface Serial0/1
ip address 192.168.28.1 255.255.255.0
!
ip classless
!
line con 0
line aux 0
line vty 0 4
!
end
```

With this step completed, you can now write down the IP addresses of the Lab_A router's four interfaces. Next, you need to determine the type of device on the other end of each of these interfaces. It's easy to do this—just use the show cdp neighbors command:

```
Lab_A#sh cdp neighbors
Capability Codes: R - Router, T - Trans Bridge, B - Source Route Bridge
S - Switch, H - Host, I - IGMP, r - Repeater
Device ID   Local Intrfce    Holdtme    Capability Platform   Port ID
Lab_B       Fas 0/0            178         R         2501      E0
Lab_C       Fas 0/1            137         R         2621      Fa0/0
Lab_D       Ser 0/0            178         R         2514      S1
Lab_E       Ser 0/1            137         R         2620      S0/1
Lab_A#
```

You've got a good deal of information now! By using both the show running-config and show cdp neighbors commands, you know about all the IP addresses of the Lab_A router plus the types of routers connected to each of the Lab_A router's links and all the interfaces of the remote routers.

And by using all the information gathered from show running-config and show cdp neighbors, we can now create the topology in Figure 5.3.

If we needed to, we could've also used the show cdp neighbors detail command to view the neighbor's IP addresses. But since we know the IP addresses of each link on the Lab_A router, we already know what the next available IP address is going to be.

FIGURE 5.3 Network topology documented

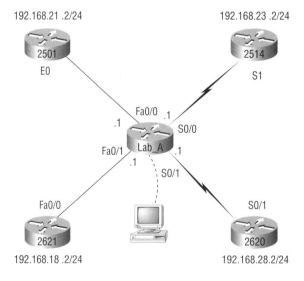

Using Telnet

Telnet, part of the TCP/IP protocol suite, is a virtual terminal protocol that allows you to make connections to remote devices, gather information, and run programs.

After your routers and switches are configured, you can use the Telnet program to reconfigure and/or check up on your routers and switches without using a console cable. You run the Telnet program by typing **telnet** from any command prompt (DOS or Cisco). You need to have VTY passwords set on the routers for this to work.

Remember, you can't use CDP to gather information about routers and switches that aren't directly connected to your device. But you can use the Telnet application to connect to your neighbor devices and then run CDP on those remote devices to get information on them.

You can issue the telnet command from any router prompt like this:

```
Corp#telnet 10.2.2.2
Trying 10.2.2.2 ... Open

Password required, but none set

[Connection to 10.2.2.2 closed by foreign host]
Corp#
```

As you can see, I didn't set my passwords—how embarrassing! Remember that the VTY ports on a router are configured as login, meaning that we have to either set the VTY passwords or use the no login command. (You can review setting passwords in Chapter 4, "Cisco's Internetworking Operating System (IOS) and Security Device Manager (SDM)," if you need to.)

 If you find you can't telnet into a device, it could be that the password on the remote device hasn't been set. It's also possible that an access control list is filtering the Telnet session.

On a Cisco router, you don't need to use the telnet command; you can just type in an IP address from a command prompt and the router will assume that you want to telnet to the device. Here's how that looks using just the IP address:

```
Corp#10.2.2.2
Trying 10.2.2.2 ... Open

Password required, but none set

[Connection to 10.2.2.2 closed by foreign host]
Corp#
```

At this point, it would be a great idea to set those VTY passwords on the router I want to telnet into. Here's what I did on the remote router named R1:

```
R1#config t
Enter configuration commands, one per line.  End with CNTL/Z.
R1(config)#line vty 0 ?
  <1-807>  Last Line number
  <cr>
R1(config)#line vty 0 807
R1(config-line)#password telnet
R1(config-line)#login
R1(config-line)#^Z
```

Now let's try this again. Here I'm connecting to the router from the Corp ISR console:

```
Corp#10.2.2.2
Trying 10.2.2.2 ... Open

User Access Verification

Password:
R1>
```

Remember that the VTY password is the user-mode password, not the enable-mode password. Watch what happens when I try to go into privileged mode after telnetting into router R1:

```
R1>en
% No password set
R1>
```

It is basically saying, "No way!" This is a really good security feature because you don't want anyone telnetting into your device and being able to just type the **enable** command to get into privileged mode. You've got to set your enable-mode password or enable secret password to use Telnet to configure remote devices!

 When you telnet into a remote device, you will not see console messages by default. For example, you will not see debugging output. To allow console messages to be sent to your Telnet session, use the `terminal monitor` command.

In the following examples, I am going to show you how to telnet into multiple devices simultaneously and then show you how to use hostnames instead of IP addresses.

Telnetting into Multiple Devices Simultaneously

If you telnet to a router or switch, you can end the connection by typing **exit** at any time. But what if you want to keep your connection to a remote device but still come back to your original router console? To do that, you can press the Ctrl+Shift+6 key combination, release it, and then press X.

Here's an example of connecting to multiple devices from my Corp router console:

```
Corp#10.2.2.2
Trying 10.2.2.2 ... Open

User Access Verification

Password:
R1>Ctrl+Shift+6
Corp#
```

In this example, I telnetted to the R1 router and then typed the password to enter user mode. I next pressed Ctrl+Shift+6, then X (but you can't see that because it doesn't show on the screen output). Notice that my command prompt is now back at the Corp router.

Let's run through some verification commands..

Checking Telnet Connections

To see the connections made from your router to a remote device, use the show sessions command:

```
Corp#sh sessions
Conn Host              Address          Byte  Idle Conn Name
   1 10.2.2.2          10.2.2.2            0     0 10.2.2.2
*  2 10.1.1.2          10.1.1.2            0     0 10.1.1.2
Corp#
```

See that asterisk (*) next to connection 2? It means that session 2 was your last session. You can return to your last session by pressing Enter twice. You can also return to any session by typing the number of the connection and pressing Enter.

Checking Telnet Users

You can list all active consoles and VTY ports in use on your router with the show users command:

```
Corp#sh users
    Line       User       Host(s)          Idle        Location
*   0 con 0               10.1.1.2         00:00:01
                          10.2.2.2         00:01:06
```

In the command's output, con represents the local console. In this example, the console is connected to two remote IP addresses, or in other words, two devices. In the next example, I typed sh users on the ap device that the Corp router had telnetted into and is connected to via line 1:

```
Corp#sh sessions
Conn Host               Address            Byte  Idle Conn Name
    1 10.1.1.2          10.1.1.2              0     0 10.1.1.2
*   2 10.2.2.2          10.2.2.2              0     0 10.2.2.2
Corp#1
[Resuming connection 1 to 10.1.1.2 ... ]
ap>sh users
     Line       User      Host(s)            Idle       Location
*   1 vty 0               idle            00:00:00 10.1.1.1
ap>
```

This output shows that the console is active and that VTY port 1 is being used. The asterisk represents the current terminal session from which the show user command was entered.

Closing Telnet Sessions

You can end Telnet sessions a few different ways—typing exit or disconnect is probably the easiest and quickest.

To end a session from a remote device, use the exit command:

```
ap>exit
[Connection to 10.1.1.2 closed by foreign host]
Corp#
```

Since the ap device was my last session, I just pressed Enter twice to return to that session.

To end a session from a local device, use the disconnect command:

```
Corp#sh session
Conn Host               Address            Byte  Idle Conn Name
    2 10.2.2.2          10.2.2.2              0     0 10.2.2.2
Corp#disconnect ?
  <0-0>  The number of an active network connection
  qdm    Disconnect QDM web-based clients
  ssh    Disconnect an active SSH connection
Corp#disconnect 2
Closing connection to 10.2.2.2 [confirm][enter]
Corp#
```

In this example, I used the session number 2 because that was the connection to the R1 router that I wanted to end. As I showed, you can use the show sessions command to see the connection number.

If you want to end a session of a device attached to your local device through Telnet, you should first check to see if any devices are telnetted into your router. To get that information, use the show users command like this:

```
R1#sh users
    Line        User        Host(s)            Idle       Location
*   0 con 0                 idle               00:00:00
    vty 194                 idle               00:00:21 10.2.2.1
```

This output shows that VTY has IP address 10.2.2.1 connected. That's the Corp router. Also notice that the Corp router connected to line 194—remember, you cannot choose which line you connect to! This is why we set the same password on all lines.

To clear the connection, use the clear line # command:

```
R1#clear line 194
[confirm][enter]
 [OK]
R1#sh users
    Line        User        Host(s)            Idle       Location
*   0 con 0                 idle               00:00:00
```

This output confirms that the line has been cleared.

Using SDM to Telnet into Your Router

There is not too much to tell you regarding Telnet services when using SDM. You don't get a menu or options, just a pop-up DOS screen that telnets into the router you are already connected to via HTTP or HTTPS.

Click the Tools menu, and then choose Telnet.

Once you choose Telnet, a DOS screen pops up and you will be in user mode (once you enter the telnet password, of course).

It would be nice if you had other options with Telnet when using SDM, but that is not to be at this time.

Resolving Hostnames

To use a hostname rather than an IP address to connect to a remote device, the device that you are using to make the connection must be able to translate the hostname to an IP address.

There are two ways to resolve hostnames to IP addresses: building a host table on each router or building a Domain Name System (DNS) server, which is similar to a dynamic host table.

Building a Host Table

A host table provides name resolution only on the router that it was built upon. The command to build a host table on a router is as follows:

```
ip host host_name tcp_port_number ip_address
```

The default is TCP port number 23, but you can create a session using Telnet with a different TCP port number if you want. You can also assign up to eight IP addresses to a hostname.

Here's an example of configuring a host table on the Corp router with two entries to resolve the names for the R1 router and the ap device:

```
Corp#config t
Corp(config)#ip host R1 ?
  <0-65535>   Default telnet port number
  A.B.C.D     Host IP address
  additional  Append addresses
  mx          Configure a MX record
  ns          Configure an NS record
  srv         Configure a SRV record
```

```
Corp(config)#ip host R1 10.2.2.2 ?
  A.B.C.D  Host IP address
  <cr>
Corp(config)#ip host R1 10.2.2.2
Corp(config)#ip host ap 10.1.1.2
```

Notice in the above router configuration that I can just keep adding IP addresses to reference a host, one after another, up to eight IP address. And to see the newly built host table, just use the show hosts command:

```
Corp(config)#do show hosts
Default domain is not set
Name/address lookup uses domain service
Name servers are 255.255.255.255

Codes: UN - unknown, EX - expired, OK - OK, ?? - revalidate
       temp - temporary, perm - permanent
       NA - Not Applicable None - Not defined
Host                    Port  Flags      Age Type  Address(es)
ap                      None  (perm, OK)  0   IP    10.1.1.2
R1                      None  (perm, OK)  0   IP    10.2.2.2
Corp(config)#^Z
Corp#
```

You can see the two hostnames plus their associated IP addresses in the preceding router output. The perm in the Flags column means that the entry is manually configured. If it said temp, it would be an entry that was resolved by DNS.

The show hosts command provides information on temporary DNS entries and permanent name-to-address mappings created using the ip host command.

To verify that the host table resolves names, try typing the hostnames at a router prompt. Remember that if you don't specify the command, the router assumes you want to telnet.

In the following example, I'll use the hostnames to telnet into the remote devices and press Ctrl+Shift+6 and then X to return to the main console of the Corp router:

```
Corp#r1
Trying R1 (10.2.2.2)... Open

User Access Verification

Password:
R1>Ctrl+Shift+6
```

```
Corp#ap
Trying ap (10.1.1.2)... Open

User Access Verification

Password:
ap>Ctrl+Shift+6
Corp#
```

I successfully used entries in the host table to create a session to two devices and used the names to telnet into both devices. Names in the host table are not case sensitive.

Notice that the entries in the following show sessions output now display the hostnames and IP addresses instead of just the IP addresses:

```
Corp#sh sessions
Conn Host            Address           Byte  Idle Conn Name
   1 r1              10.2.2.2              0     1 r1
*  2 ap              10.1.1.2              0     0 ap
Corp#
```

If you want to remove a hostname from the table, just use the no ip host command like this:

```
RouterA(config)#no ip host R1
```

The problem with the host table method is that you would need to create a host table on each router to be able to resolve names. And if you have a whole bunch of routers and want to resolve names, using DNS is a much better choice!

Using DNS to Resolve Names

If you have a lot of devices and don't want to create a host table in each device, you can use a DNS server to resolve hostnames.

Any time a Cisco device receives a command it doesn't understand, it will try to resolve it through DNS by default. Watch what happens when I type the special command todd at a Cisco router prompt:

```
Corp#todd
Translating "todd"...domain server (255.255.255.255)
Translating "todd"...domain server (255.255.255.255)
Translating "todd"...domain server (255.255.255.255)
% Unknown command or computer name, or unable to find
  computer address
Corp#
```

It doesn't know my name or what command I am trying to type, so it tries to resolve this through DNS. This is really annoying for two reasons: first, because it doesn't know my name <grin>, and second, because I need to hang out and wait for the name lookup to time out. You can get around this and prevent a time-consuming DNS lookup by using the no ip domain-lookup command on your router from global configuration mode.

If you have a DNS server on your network, you need to add a few commands to make DNS name resolution work:

- The first command is ip domain-lookup, which is turned on by default. It needs to be entered only if you previously turned it off (with the no ip domain-lookup command). The command can be used without the hyphen as well (ip domain lookup).

- The second command is ip name-server. This sets the IP address of the DNS server. You can enter the IP addresses of up to six servers.

- The last command is ip domain-name. Although this command is optional, it really should be set. It appends the domain name to the hostname you type in. Since DNS uses a fully qualified domain name (FQDN) system, you must have a full DNS name, in the form domain.com.

Here's an example of using these three commands:

```
Corp#config t
Corp(config)#ip domain-lookup
Corp(config)#ip name-server ?
  A.B.C.D  Domain server IP address (maximum of 6)
Corp(config)#ip name-server 192.168.0.70
Corp(config)#ip domain-name lammle.com
Corp(config)#^Z
Corp#
```

After the DNS configurations are set, you can test the DNS server by using a hostname to ping or telnet a device like this:

```
Corp#ping R1
Translating "R1"...domain server (192.168.0.70) [OK]
Type escape sequence to abort.
Sending 5, 100-byte ICMP Echos to 10.2.2.2, timeout is
  2 seconds:
!!!!!
Success rate is 100 percent (5/5), round-trip min/avg/max
  = 28/31/32 ms
```

Notice that the router uses the DNS server to resolve the name.

After a name is resolved using DNS, use the `show hosts` command to see that the device cached this information in the host table:

```
Corp#sh hosts
Default domain is lammle.com
Name/address lookup uses domain service
Name servers are 192.168.0.70
Host                   Flags      Age Type   Address(es)
R1                     (temp, OK)  0   IP     10.2.2.2
ap                     (perm, OK)  0   IP     10.1.1.2
Corp#
```

The entry that was resolved is shown as `temp`, but the ap device is still `perm`, meaning that it's a static entry. Notice that the hostname is a full domain name. If I hadn't used the `ip domain-name lammle.com` command, I would have needed to type in `ping r1.lammle.com`, which is a pain.

 Real World Scenario

Should You Use a Host Table or a DNS Server?

Karen has finally finished drawing out her network by using CDP and the doctors are much happier. However, Karen is having a difficult time administering the network because she has to look at the network drawing to find an IP address every time she needs to telnet to a remote router.

Karen was thinking about putting host tables on each router, but with literally hundreds of routers, this is a daunting task.

Most networks have a DNS server now anyway, so adding a hundred or so hostnames into it would be an easy way to go—certainly easier than adding these hostnames to each and every router! She can just add the three commands on each router and blammo—she's resolving names.

Using a DNS server makes it easy to update any old entries too—remember, even one little change and off she goes to each and every router to manually update its table if she's using static host tables.

Keep in mind that this has nothing to do with name resolution on the network and nothing to do with what a host on the network is trying to accomplish. This is only used when you're trying to resolve names from the router console.

Checking Network Connectivity and Troubleshooting

You can use the `ping` and `traceroute` commands to test connectivity to remote devices, and both of them can be used with many protocols, not just IP. But don't forget that the `show ip route` command is a good troubleshooting command for verifying your routing table and the `show interfaces` command will show you the status of each interface.

I'm not going to get into the `show interfaces` commands here because we've already been over that in Chapter 4. But I am going to go over both the `debug` command and the `show processes` command you need to troubleshoot a router.

Using the *ping* Command

So far, you've seen many examples of pinging devices to test IP connectivity and name resolution using the DNS server. To see all the different protocols that you can use with the *Ping* program, type **ping ?**:

```
Corp#ping ?
  WORD  Ping destination address or hostname
  clns  CLNS echo
  ip    IP echo
  srb   srb echo
  tag   Tag encapsulated IP echo
  <cr>
```

The `ping` output displays the minimum, average, and maximum times it takes for a ping packet to find a specified system and return. Here's an example:

```
Corp#ping R1
Translating "R1"...domain server (192.168.0.70)[OK]
Type escape sequence to abort.
Sending 5, 100-byte ICMP Echos to 10.2.2.2, timeout
  is 2 seconds:
!!!!!
Success rate is 100 percent (5/5), round-trip min/avg/max
  = 1/2/4 ms
Corp#
```

You can see that the DNS server was used to resolve the name, and the device was pinged in 1 ms (milliseconds), an average of 2 ms, and up to 4 ms.

The `ping` command can be used in user and privileged mode but not configuration mode.

Pinging with SDM

Unlike with the Telnet option in SDM, we at least have a screen we can use to choose an option or two.

Once you choose Tools➢ Ping, the Ping screen appears.

From here you can choose the source interface to ping from, which is a nice option. Enter your destination and then click Ping.

Using the *traceroute* Command

Traceroute (the `traceroute` command, or `trace` for short) shows the path a packet takes to get to a remote device. It uses time to live (TTL) time-outs and ICMP error messages to outline the path a packet takes through an internetwork to arrive at remote host.

Trace (the `trace` command), which can be used from either user mode or privileged mode, allows you to figure out which router in the path to an unreachable network host should be examined more closely for the cause of the network's failure.

To see the protocols that you can use with the `traceroute` command, type **traceroute ?**:

```
Corp#traceroute ?
  WORD      Trace route to destination address or hostname
  appletalk AppleTalk Trace
  clns      ISO CLNS Trace
  ip        IP Trace
  ipv6      IPv6 Trace
  ipx       IPX Trace
  <cr>
```

The `trace` command shows the hop or hops that a packet traverses on its way to a remote device. Here's an example:

```
Corp#traceroute r1

Type escape sequence to abort.
Tracing the route to R1 (10.2.2.2)

  1 R1 (10.2.2.2) 4 msec *  0 msec
Corp#
```

You can see that the packet went through only one hop to find the destination.

Do not get confused! You can't use the `tracert` command—it's a Windows command. For a router, use the `traceroute` command!

Here's an example of using `tracert` from a Windows DOS prompt (notice the command `tracert`!):

```
C:\>tracert www.whitehouse.gov

Tracing route to a1289.g.akamai.net [69.8.201.107]
over a maximum of 30 hops:
```

```
1    *        *        *      Request timed out.
2   53 ms    61 ms    53 ms  hlrn-dsl-gw15-207.hlrn.qwest.net
       [207.225.112.207]
3   53 ms    55 ms    54 ms  hlrn-agw1.inet.qwest.net [71.217.188.113]
4   54 ms    53 ms    54 ms  hlr-core-01.inet.qwest.net [205.171.253.97]
5   54 ms    53 ms    54 ms  apa-cntr-01.inet.qwest.net [205.171.253.26]
6   54 ms    53 ms    53 ms  63.150.160.34
7   54 ms    54 ms    53 ms  www.whitehouse.gov [69.8.201.107]
```

Trace complete.

Okay, let's move on now and talk about how to troubleshoot your network using the debug command.

Debugging

Debug is a troubleshooting command that's available from the privileged exec mode of Cisco IOS. It's used to display information about various router operations and the related traffic generated or received by the router, plus any error messages.

It's a useful and informative tool, but you really need to understand some important facts about its use. Debug is regarded as a very high-priority task because it can consume a huge amount of resources and the router is forced to process-switch the packets being debugged. So you don't just use debug as a monitoring tool—it's meant to be used for a short period of time and only as a troubleshooting tool. By using it, you can really find out some truly significant facts about both working and faulty software and/or hardware components.

Because debugging output takes priority over other network traffic, and because the debug all command generates more output than any other debug command, it can severely diminish the router's performance—even render it unusable. So in virtually all cases, it's best to use more-specific debug commands.

As you can see from the following output, you can't enable debugging from user mode, only privileged mode:

```
Corp>debug ?
% Unrecognized command
Corp>en
Corp#debug ?
  aaa                 AAA Authentication, Authorization and Accounting
  access-expression   Boolean access expression
  adjacency           adjacency
  all                 Enable all debugging
[output cut]
```

If you've got the freedom to pretty much take out a router and you really want to have some fun with debugging, use the debug all command:

```
Corp#debug all
```

```
This may severely impact network performance. Continue? (yes/[no]):yes
```

```
All possible debugging has been turned on
```

```
2d20h: SNMP: HC Timer 824AE5CC fired
2d20h: SNMP: HC Timer 824AE5CC rearmed, delay = 20000
2d20h: Serial0/0: HDLC myseq 4, mineseen 0, yourseen 0, line down
2d20h:
2d20h: Rudpv1 Sent: Pkts 0,  Data Bytes 0,  Data Pkts 0
2d20h: Rudpv1 Rcvd: Pkts 0,  Data Bytes 0,  Data Pkts 0
2d20h: Rudpv1 Discarded: 0,  Retransmitted 0
2d20h:
2d20h: RIP-TIMER: periodic timer expired
2d20h: Serial0/0: HDLC myseq 5, mineseen 0, yourseen 0, line down
2d20h: Serial0/0: attempting to restart
2d20h: PowerQUICC(0/0): DCD is up.
2d20h: is_up: 0 state: 4 sub state: 1 line: 0
2d20h:
2d20h: Rudpv1 Sent: Pkts 0,  Data Bytes 0,  Data Pkts 0
2d20h: Rudpv1 Rcvd: Pkts 0,  Data Bytes 0,  Data Pkts 0
2d20h: Rudpv1 Discarded: 0,  Retransmitted 0
2d20h: un all
All possible debugging has been turned off
Corp#
```

To disable debugging on a router, just use the command no in front of the debug command:

```
Corp#no debug all
```

But I typically just use the undebug all command since it is so easy when using the shortcut:

```
Corp#un all
```

Remember that instead of using the debug all command, it's almost always better to use specific commands—and only for short periods of time. Here's an example of deploying debug ip rip that will show you RIP updates being sent and received on a router:

```
Corp#debug ip rip
RIP protocol debugging is on
```

```
Corp#
1w4d: RIP: sending v2 update to 224.0.0.9 via Serial0/0 (192.168.12.1)
1w4d: RIP: build update entries
1w4d:    10.10.10.0/24 via 0.0.0.0, metric 2, tag 0
1w4d:    171.16.125.0/24 via 0.0.0.0, metric 3, tag 0
1w4d:    172.16.12.0/24 via 0.0.0.0, metric 1, tag 0
1w4d:    172.16.125.0/24 via 0.0.0.0, metric 3, tag 0
1w4d: RIP: sending v2 update to 224.0.0.9 via Serial0/2 (172.16.12.1)
1w4d: RIP: build update entries
1w4d:    192.168.12.0/24 via 0.0.0.0, metric 1, tag 0
1w4d:    192.168.22.0/24 via 0.0.0.0, metric 2, tag 0
1w4d: RIP: received v2 update from 192.168.12.2 on Serial0/0
1w4d:    192.168.22.0/24 via 0.0.0.0 in 1 hops
Corp#un all
```

I'm sure you can see that the **debug** command is one powerful command. And because of this, I'm also sure you realize that before you use any of the debugging commands, you should make sure you check the utilization of your router. This is important because in most cases, you don't want to negatively impact the device's ability to process the packets through on your internetwork. You can determine a specific router's utilization information by using the **show processes** command.

Remember, when you telnet into a remote device, you will not see console messages by default! For example, you will not see debugging output. To allow console messages to be sent to your Telnet session, use the **terminal monitor** command.

Using the *show processes* Command

As mentioned in the previous section, you've really got to be careful when using the **debug** command on your devices. If your router's CPU utilization is consistently at 50 percent or more, it's probably not a good idea to type in the **debug all** command unless you want to see what a router looks like when it crashes!

So what other approaches can you use? Well, the **show processes** (or **show processes cpu**) is a good tool for determining a given router's CPU utilization. Plus, it'll give you a list of active processes along with their corresponding process ID, priority, scheduler test (status), CPU time used, number of times invoked, and so on. Lots of great stuff! Plus, this command is super handy when you want to evaluate your router's performance and CPU utilization—for instance, when you find yourself otherwise tempted to reach for the **debug** command.

Okay—what do you see in the output below? The first line shows the CPU utilization output for the last 5 seconds, 1 minute, and 5 minutes. The output provides 2%/0% in front of the CPU utilization for the last 5 seconds. The first number equals the total utilization and the second one delimits the utilization due to interrupt routines:

```
Corp#sh processes
CPU utilization for five seconds: 2%/0%; one minute: 0%; five minutes: 0%
 PID QTy PC Runtime (ms)    Invoked   uSecs    Stacks TTY Process
   1 Cwe 8034470C   0         1        0 5804/6000   0 Chunk Manager
   2 Csp 80369A88   4         1856     2 2616/3000 0 Load Meter
   3 M*          0  112       14    800010656/12000  0 Exec
   5 Lst 8034FD9C   268246    52101 5148 5768/6000   0 Check heaps
   6 Cwe 80355E5C   20        3     6666 5704/6000   0 Pool Manager
   7 Mst 802AC3C4   0         2        0 5580/6000   0 Timers
[output cut]
```

So basically, the output from the **show processes** command shows that our router is happily able to process debugging commands without being overloaded.

Summary

In this chapter, you learned how Cisco routers are configured and how to manage those configurations.

This chapter covered the internal components of a router, which included ROM, RAM, NVRAM, and flash.

In addition, I covered what happens when a router boots and which files are loaded. The configuration register tells the router how to boot and where to find files, and you learned how to change and verify the configuration register settings for password recovery purposes.

Next, you learned how to back up and restore a Cisco IOS image, as well as how to back up and restore the configuration of a Cisco router. I showed you how to manage these files using the CLI, IFS, and SDM.

Then you learned how to use CDP and Telnet to gather information about remote devices. Finally, the chapter covered how to resolve hostnames and use the ping and trace commands to test network connectivity, as well as how to use the debug and show processes commands.

Exam Essentials

Remember the various configuration register commands and settings. The 0x2102 setting is the default on all Cisco routers and tells the router to look in NVRAM for the boot sequence. 0x2101 tells the router to boot from ROM, and 0x2142 tells the router to not load the startup-config in NVRAM to provide password recovery.

Remember how to back up an IOS image.   By using the privileged-mode command `copy flash tftp`, you can back up a file from flash memory to a TFTP (network) server.

Remember how to restore or upgrade an IOS image.   By using the privileged-mode command `copy tftp flash`, you can restore or upgrade a file from a TFTP (network) server to flash memory.

Remember what you must complete before you back up an IOS image to a network server. Make sure that you can access the network server, ensure that the network server has adequate space for the code image, and verify the file naming and path requirement.

Remember how to save the configuration of a router.   There are a couple of ways to do this, but the most common, as well as most tested, method is `copy running-config startup-config`.

Remember how to erase the configuration of a router.   Type the privileged-mode command `erase startup-config` and reload the router.

Understand when to use CDP.   Cisco Discovery Protocol can be used to help you document as well as troubleshoot your network.

Remember what the output from the `show cdp neighbors` command shows.   The `show cdp neighbors` command provides the following information: device ID, local interface, holdtime, capability, platform, and port ID (remote interface).

Understand how to telnet into a router and keep your connection but return to your originating console.   If you telnet to a router or switch, you can end the connection by typing `exit` at any time. However, if you want to keep your connection to a remote device but still come back to your original router console, you can press the Ctrl+Shift+6 key combination, release it, and then press X.

Remember the command to verify your Telnet sessions.   The command `show sessions` will provide you with information about all the sessions your router has with other routers.

Remember how to build a static host table on a router.   By using the global configuration command `ip host host_name ip_address`, you can build a static host table on your router. You can apply multiple IP addresses against the same host entry.

Remember how to verify your host table on a router.   You can verify the host table with the `show hosts` command.

Understand when to use the `ping` command.   Packet Internet Groper (Ping) uses ICMP echo request and ICMP echo replies to verify an active IP address on a network.

Remember how to ping a valid host ID.   You can ping an IP address from a router's user mode or privileged mode but not from configuration mode. You must ping a valid address, such as 1.1.1.1.

Written Lab 5

Write the answers to the following questions:

1. What is the command to copy a Cisco IOS to a TFTP server?

2. What is the command to copy a Cisco startup-config file to a TFTP server?

3. What is the command to copy the startup-config file to DRAM?

4. What is an older command that you can use to copy the startup-config file to DRAM?

5. What command can you use to see the neighbor router's IP address from your router prompt?

6. What command can you use to see the hostname, local interface, platform, and remote port of a neighbor router?

7. What keystrokes can you use to telnet into multiple devices simultaneously?

8. What command will show you your active Telnet connections to neighbor and remote devices?

9. What command can you use to upgrade a Cisco IOS?

10. What command can you use to merge a backup configuration with the configuration in RAM?

(The answers to Written Lab 5 can be found following the answers to the review questions for this chapter.)

Hands-on Labs

To complete the labs in this section, you need at least one router (three would be best) and at least one PC running as a TFTP server. Remember that the labs listed here were created for use with real routers.

 You can always run the first two labs by using the SDM demo (mostly) and skip the TFTP host sections of these labs; however, you need to know how to use both methods.

Here is a list of the labs in this chapter:

Lab 5.1: Backing Up Your Router IOS

Lab 5.2: Upgrading or Restoring Your Router IOS

Lab 5.3: Backing Up the Router Configuration

Lab 5.4: Using the Cisco Discovery Protocol (CDP)

Lab 5.5: Using Telnet

Lab 5.6: Resolving Hostnames

Hands-on Lab 5.1: Backing Up Your Router IOS

1. Log into your router and go into privileged mode by typing **en** or **enable**.

2. Make sure you can connect to the TFTP server that is on your network by pinging the IP address from the router console.

3. Type **show flash** to see the contents of flash memory.

4. Type **show version** at the router privileged-mode prompt to get the name of the IOS currently running on the router. If there is only one file in flash memory, the show flash and show version commands show the same file. Remember that the show version command shows you the file that is currently running and the show flash command shows you all of the files in flash memory.

5. Once you know you have good Ethernet connectivity to the TFTP server and you also know the IOS filename, back up your IOS by typing **copy flash tftp**. This command tells the router to copy the contents of flash memory (this is where the IOS is stored by default) to a TFTP server.

6. Enter the IP address of the TFTP server and the source IOS filename. The file is now copied and stored in the TFTP server's default directory.

Hands-on Lab 5.2: Upgrading or Restoring Your Router IOS

1. Log into your router and go into privileged mode by typing **en** or **enable**.

2. Make sure you can connect to the TFTP server by pinging the IP address of the server from the router console.

3. Once you know you have good Ethernet connectivity to the TFTP server, issue the copy tftp flash command.

4. Confirm that the router is not functioning during the restore or upgrade by following the prompts provided on the router console.

5. Enter the IP address of the TFTP server.

6. Enter the name of the IOS filename you want to restore or upgrade.

7. Confirm that you understand that the contents of flash memory will be erased.

8. Watch in amazement as your IOS is deleted out of flash memory and your new IOS is copied to flash memory.

If the file that was in flash memory is deleted but the new version wasn't copied to flash memory, the router will boot from ROM monitor mode. You'll need to figure out why the copy operation did not take place.

Hands-on Lab 5.3: Backing Up the Router Configuration

1. Log into your router and go into privileged mode by typing **en** or **enable**.

2. Ping the TFTP server to make sure you have IP connectivity.

3. From RouterB, type **copy run tftp**.

4. Type the IP address of the TFTP server (for example, 172.16.30.2) and press Enter.

5. The router will prompt you for a filename. The hostname of the router is followed by the suffix -confg (yes, I spelled that correctly). You can use any name you want.

```
Name of configuration file to write [RouterB-confg]?
```

Press Enter to accept the default name.

```
Write file RouterB-confg on host 172.16.30.2? [confirm]
```

Press Enter.

Hands-on Lab 5.4: Using the Cisco Discovery Protocol (CDP)

1. Log into your router and go into privileged mode by typing **en** or **enable**.

2. From the router, type **sh cdp** and press Enter. You should see that CDP packets are being sent out to all active interfaces every 60 seconds and the holdtime is 180 seconds (these are the defaults).

3. To change the CDP update frequency to 90 seconds, type **cdp timer 90** in global configuration mode.

```
RouterC#config t
Enter configuration commands, one per line.  End with
  CNTL/Z.
RouterC(config)#cdp timer ?
  <5-900>  Rate at which CDP packets are sent (in sec)
RouterC(config)#cdp timer 90
```

4. Verify that your CDP timer frequency has changed by using the command show cdp in privileged mode.

```
RouterC#sh cdp
Global CDP information:
Sending CDP packets every 90 seconds
Sending a holdtime value of 180 seconds
```

5. Now use CDP to gather information about neighbor routers. You can get the list of available commands by typing **sh cdp ?**.

```
RouterC#sh cdp ?
  entry     Information for specific neighbor entry
  interface CDP interface status and configuration
  neighbors CDP neighbor entries
  traffic   CDP statistics
  <cr>
```

6. Type **sh cdp int** to see the interface information plus the default encapsulation used by the interface. It also shows the CDP timer information.

7. Type **sh cdp entry** * to see the CDP information received from all devices.

8. Type **show cdp neighbors** to gather information about all connected neighbors. (You should know the specific information output by this command.)

9. Type **show cdp neighbors detail**. Notice that it produces the same output as show cdp entry *.

Hands-on Lab 5.5: Using Telnet

1. Log into your router and go into privileged mode by typing **en** or **enable**.

2. From RouterA, telnet into your remote router by typing **telnet ip_address** from the command prompt.

3. Type in RouterB's IP address from RouterA's command prompt. Notice that the router automatically tries to telnet to the IP address you specified. You can use the **telnet** command or just type in the IP address.

4. From RouterB, press Ctrl+Shift+6 and then X to return to RouterA's command prompt. Now telnet into your third router, RouterC. Press Ctrl+Shift+6 and then X to return to RouterA.

5. From RouterA, type **show sessions**. Notice your two sessions. You can press the number displayed to the left of the session and press Enter twice to return to that session. The asterisk shows the default session. You can press Enter twice to return to that session.

6. Go to the session for your RouterB. Type **show users**. This shows the console connection and the remote connection. You can use the **disconnect** command to clear the session or just type **exit** from the prompt to close your session with RouterB.

7. Go to the RouterC's console port by typing **show sessions** on the first router and using the connection number to return to RouterC. Type **show user** and notice the connection to your first router, RouterA.

8. Type **clear line** to disconnect the Telnet session.

Hands-on Lab 5.6: Resolving Hostnames

1. Log into your router and go into privileged mode by typing **en** or **enable**.

2. From RouterA, type **todd** and press Enter at the command prompt. Notice the error you receive and the delay. The router is trying to resolve the hostname to an IP address by looking for a DNS server. You can turn this feature off by using the no ip domain-lookup command from global configuration mode.

3. To build a host table, you use the ip host command. From RouterA, add a host table entry for RouterB and RouterC by entering the following commands:

```
ip host routerb ip_address
ip host routerc ip_address
```

Here is an example:

```
ip host routerb 172.16.20.2
ip host routerc 172.16.40.2
```

4. Test your host table by typing **ping routerb** from the command prompt (not the config prompt).

```
RouterA#ping routerb
Type escape sequence to abort.
Sending 5, 100-byte ICMP Echos to 172.16.20.2, timeout
  is 2 seconds:
!!!!!
Success rate is 100 percent (5/5), round-trip
  min/avg/max = 4/4/4 ms
```

5. Test your host table by typing **ping routerc**.

```
RouterA#ping routerc
Type escape sequence to abort.
Sending 5, 100-byte ICMP Echos to 172.16.40.2, timeout
  is 2 seconds:
!!!!!
Success rate is 100 percent (5/5), round-trip
  min/avg/max = 4/6/8 ms
```

6. Keep your session to RouterB open, and then return to RouterA by pressing Ctrl+Shift+6, then X.

7. Telnet to RouterC by typing **routerc** at the command prompt.

8. Return to RouterA and keep the session to RouterC open by pressing Ctrl+Shift+6, then X.

9. View the host table by typing **show hosts** and pressing Enter.

```
Default domain is not set
Name/address lookup uses domain service
Name servers are 255.255.255.255
Host               Flags        Age Type   Address(es)
routerb            (perm, OK)   0   IP     172.16.20.2
routerc            (perm, OK)   0   IP     172.16.40.2
```

Review Questions

 The following questions are designed to test your understanding of this chapter's material. For more information on how to get additional questions, please see this book's Introduction.

1. What does the command o/r 0x2142 provide?

   A. It is used to restart the router.

   B. It is used to bypass the configuration in NVRAM.

   C. It is used to enter ROM Monitor mode.

   D. It is used to view the lost password.

2. Which command will copy the IOS to a backup host on your network?

   A. transfer IOS to 172.16.10.1

   B. copy run start

   C. copy tftp flash

   D. copy start tftp

   E. copy flash tftp

3. You are troubleshooting a connectivity problem in your corporate network and want to isolate the problem. You suspect that a router on the route to an unreachable network is at fault. What IOS user exec command should you issue?

   A. Router>ping

   B. Router>trace

   C. Router>show ip route

   D. Router>show interface

   E. Router>show cdp neighbors

4. You copy a configuration from a network host to a router's RAM. The configuration looks correct, yet it is not working at all. What could the problem be?

   A. You copied the wrong configuration into RAM.

   B. You copied the configuration into flash memory instead.

   C. The copy did not override the shutdown command in running-config.

   D. The IOS became corrupted after the copy command was initiated.

5. A network administrator wants to upgrade the IOS of a router without removing the image currently installed. What command will display the amount of memory consumed by the current IOS image and indicate whether there is enough room available to hold both the current and new images?

   A. show version

   B. show flash

   C. show memory

   D. show buffers

   E. show running-config

6. The corporate office sends you a new router to connect, but upon connecting the console cable, you see that there is already a configuration on the router. What should be done before a new configuration is entered in the router?

   A. RAM should be erased and the router restarted.

   B. Flash should be erased and the router restarted.

   C. NVRAM should be erased and the router restarted.

   D. The new configuration should be entered and saved.

7. Which command loads a new version of the Cisco IOS into a router?

   A. copy flash ftp

   B. copy ftp flash

   C. copy flash tftp

   D. copy tftp flash

8. Which command will show you the IOS version running on your router?

   A. sh IOS

   B. sh flash

   C. sh version

   D. sh running-config

9. What should the configuration register value be after you successfully complete the password recovery procedure and return the router to normal operation?

   A. 0x2100

   B. 0x2101

   C. 0x2102

   D. 0x2142

10. You save the configuration on a router with the `copy running-config startup-config` command and reboot the router. The router, however, comes up with a blank configuration. What can the problem be?

    A. You didn't boot the router with the correct command.

    B. NVRAM is corrupted.

    C. The configuration register setting is incorrect.

    D. The newly upgraded IOS is not compatible with the hardware of the router.

    E. The configuration you save is not compatible with the hardware.

11. If you want to have more than one Telnet session open at the same time, what keystroke combination would you use?

    A. Tab+spacebar

    B. Ctrl+X, then 6

    C. Ctrl+Shift+X, then 6

    D. Ctrl+Shift+6, then X

12. You are unsuccessful in telnetting into a remote device. What could the problem be? (Choose two.)

    A. IP addresses are incorrect.

    B. Access control list is filtering Telnet.

    C. There is a defective serial cable.

    D. The VTY password is missing.

13. What information is displayed by the `show hosts` command? (Choose two.)

    A. Temporary DNS entries

    B. The names of the routers created using the `hostname` command

    C. The IP addresses of workstations allowed to access the router

    D. Permanent name-to-address mappings created using the `ip host` command

    E. The length of time a host has been connected to the router via Telnet

14. Which three commands can be used to check LAN connectivity problems on a router? (Choose three.)

    A. `show interfaces`

    B. `show ip route`

    C. `tracert`

    D. `ping`

    E. `dns lookups`

15. You telnet to a router and make your necessary changes; now you want to end the Telnet session. What command do you type in?

    A. close

    B. disable

    C. disconnect

    D. exit

16. You telnet into a remote device and type `debug ip rip`, but no output from the `debug` command is seen. What could the problem be?

    A. You must type the `show ip rip` command first.

    B. IP addressing on the network is incorrect.

    C. You must use the `terminal monitor` command.

    D. Debug output is sent only to the console.

17. Which command displays the configuration register setting?

    A. show ip route

    B. show boot version

    C. show version

    D. show flash

18. You need to gather the IP address of a remote switch that is located in Hawaii. What can you do to find the address?

    A. Fly to Hawaii, console into the switch, then relax and have a drink with an umbrella in it.

    B. Issue the `show ip route` command on the router connected to the switch.

    C. Issue the `show cdp neighbor` command on the router connected to the switch.

    D. Issue the `show ip arp` command on the router connected to the switch.

    E. Issue the `show cdp neighbors detail` command on the router connected to the switch.

19. You have your laptop directly connected into a router's Ethernet port. Which of the following are among the requirements for the `copy flash tftp` command to be successful? (Choose three.)

    A. TFTP server software must be running on the router.

    B. TFTP server software must be running on your laptop.

    C. The Ethernet cable connecting the laptop directly into the router's Ethernet port must be a straight-through cable.

    D. The laptop must be on the same subnet as the router's Ethernet interface.

    E. The `copy flash tftp` command must be supplied the IP address of the laptop.

    F. There must be enough room in the flash memory of the router to accommodate the file to be copied.

20. The configuration register setting of 0x2102 provides what function to a router?

  A. Tells the router to boot into ROM monitor mode

  B. Provides password recovery

  C. Tells the router to look in NVRAM for the boot sequence

  D. Boots the IOS from a TFTP server

  E. Boots an IOS image stored in ROM

Answers to Review Questions

1. B. The default configuration setting is 0x2102, which tells the router to load the IOS from flash and the configuration from NVRAM. 0x2142 tells the router to bypass the configuration in NVRAM so that you can perform password recovery.

2. E. To copy the IOS to a backup host, which is stored in flash memory by default, use the `copy flash tftp` command.

3. B. The command `traceroute` (`trace` for short), which can be issued from user mode or privileged mode, is used to find the path a packet takes through an internetwork and will also show you where the packet stops because of an error on a router.

4. C. Since the configuration looks correct, you probably didn't screw up the copy job. However, when you perform a copy from a network host to a router, the interfaces are automatically shut down and need to be manually enabled with the `no shutdown` command.

5. B. The `show flash` command will provide you with the current IOS name and size and the size of flash memory.

6. C. Before you start to configure the router, you should erase the NVRAM with the `erase startup-config` command and then reload the router using the `reload` command.

7. D. The command `copy tftp flash` will allow you to copy a new IOS into flash memory on your router.

8. C. The best answer is `show version`, which shows you the IOS file running currently on your router. The `show flash` command shows you the contents of flash memory, not which file is running.

9. C. All Cisco routers have a default configuration register setting of 0x2102, which tells the router to load the IOS from flash memory and the configuration from NVRAM.

10. C. If you save a configuration and reload the router and it comes up either in setup mode or as a blank configuration, chances are you have the configuration register setting incorrect.

11. D. To keep open one or more Telnet sessions, use the Ctrl+Shift+6 and then X keystroke combination.

12. B, D. The best answers, the ones you need to remember, are that either an access control list is filtering the Telnet session or the VTY password is not set on the remote device.

13. A, D. The `show hosts` command provides information on temporary DNS entries and permanent name-to-address mappings created using the `ip host` command.

14. A, B, D. The `tracert` command is a Windows command and will not work on a router! A router uses the `traceroute` command.

15. D. Since the question never mentioned anything about a suspended session, you can assume that the Telnet session is still open, and you would just type **exit** to close the session.

16. C. To see console messages through your Telnet session, you must enter the `terminal monitor` command.

17. C. The `show version` command provides you with the current configuration register setting.

18. E. Although answer A is certainly the "best" answer, unfortunately answer E will work just fine and your boss would probably prefer you to use the `show cdp neighbors detail` command.

19. B, D, E. Before you back up an IOS image to a laptop directly connected to a router's Ethernet port, make sure the TFTP server software is running on your laptop, that the Ethernet cable is a "crossover," and that the laptop is in the same subnet as the router's Ethernet port, and then you can use the `copy flash tftp` command from your laptop.

20. C. The default configuration setting of 0x2102 tells the router to look in NVRAM for the boot sequence.

Answers to Written Lab 5

1. `copy flash tftp`
2. `copy start tftp`
3. `copy start run`
4. `config mem`
5. `show cdp neighbor detail` or `show cdp entry *`
6. `show cdp neighbor`
7. Ctrl+Shift+6, then X
8. `show sessions`
9. `copy tftp flash`
10. Either `copy tftp run` or `copy start run`

Chapter

6

IP Routing

THE CCNA EXAM TOPICS COVERED IN THIS CHAPTER INCLUDE THE FOLLOWING:

✓ **Describe how a network works**

- Determine the path between two hosts across a network

✓ **Configure, verify, and troubleshoot basic router operation and routing on Cisco devices**

- Describe basic routing concepts (including: packet forwarding, router lookup process)

- Configure, verify, and troubleshoot RIPv2

- Access and utilize the router to set basic parameters (including: CLI/SDM)

- Connect, configure, and verify operation status of a device interface

- Verify device configuration and network connectivity using ping, traceroute, telnet, SSH or other utilities

- Perform and verify routing configuration tasks for a static or default route given specific routing requirements

- Compare and contrast methods of routing and routing protocols

- Verify network connectivity (including: using ping, traceroute, and telnet or SSH)

- Troubleshoot routing issues

- Verify router hardware and software operation using SHOW & DEBUG commands

- Implement basic router security

In this chapter, I'm going to discuss the IP routing process. This is an important subject to understand since it pertains to all routers and configurations that use IP. IP routing is the process of moving packets from one network to another network using routers. And as before, by routers I mean Cisco routers, of course!

But before you read this chapter, you must understand the difference between a routing protocol and a routed protocol. A *routing protocol* is used by routers to dynamically find all the networks in the internetwork and to ensure that all routers have the same routing table. Basically, a routing protocol determines the path of a packet through an internetwork. Examples of routing protocols are RIP, RIPv2, EIGRP, and OSPF.

Once all routers know about all networks, a *routed protocol* can be used to send user data (packets) through the established enterprise. Routed protocols are assigned to an interface and determine the method of packet delivery. Examples of routed protocols are IP and IPv6.

I'm pretty sure that I don't have to tell you that this is definitely important stuff to know. You most likely understand that from what I've said so far. IP routing is basically what Cisco routers do, and they do it very well. Again, this chapter is dealing with truly fundamental material—these are things you must know if you want to understand the objectives covered in this book!

In this chapter, I'm going to show you how to configure and verify IP routing with Cisco routers. I'll be covering the following:

- Routing basics

- The IP routing process

- Static routing

- Default routing

- Dynamic routing

In Chapter 7, "Enhanced IGRP (EIGRP) and Open Shortest Path First (OSPF)," I'll be moving into more advanced, dynamic routing with EIGRP and OSPF. But first, you've really got to nail down the basics of how packets actually move through an internetwork, so let's get started!

For up-to-the minute updates for this chapter, please see www.lammle.com and/or www.sybex.com.

Routing Basics

Once you create an internetwork by connecting your WANs and LANs to a router, you'll need to configure logical network addresses, such as IP addresses, to all hosts on the internetwork so that they can communicate across that internetwork.

The term *routing* is used for taking a packet from one device and sending it through the network to another device on a different network. Routers don't really care about hosts—they only care about networks and the best path to each network. The logical network address of the destination host is used to get packets to a network through a routed network, and then the hardware address of the host is used to deliver the packet from a router to the correct destination host.

If your network has no routers, then it should be apparent that you are not routing. Routers route traffic to all the networks in your internetwork. To be able to route packets, a router must know, at a minimum, the following:

- Destination address

- Neighbor routers from which it can learn about remote networks

- Possible routes to all remote networks

- The best route to each remote network

- How to maintain and verify routing information

The router learns about remote networks from neighbor routers or from an administrator. The router then builds a routing table (a map of the internetwork) that describes how to find the remote networks. If a network is directly connected, then the router already knows how to get to it.

If a network isn't directly connected to the router, the router must use one of two ways to learn how to get to the remote network: static routing, meaning that someone must hand-type all network locations into the routing table, or something called dynamic routing.

In *dynamic routing*, a protocol on one router communicates with the same protocol running on neighbor routers. The routers then update each other about all the networks they know about and place this information into the routing table. If a change occurs in the network, the dynamic routing protocols automatically inform all routers about the event. If *static routing* is used, the administrator is responsible for updating all changes by hand into all routers. Typically, in a large network, a combination of both dynamic and static routing is used.

Before we jump into the IP routing process, let's take a look at a simple example that demonstrates how a router uses the routing table to route packets out of an interface. We'll be going into a more detailed study of the process in the next section.

Figure 6.1 shows a simple two-router network. Lab_A has one serial interface and three LAN interfaces.

Looking at Figure 6.1, can you see which interface Lab_A will use to forward an IP datagram to a host with an IP address of 10.10.10.10?

FIGURE 6.1 A simple routing example

By using the command show ip route, we can see the routing table (map of the internetwork) that Lab_A uses to make forwarding decisions:

```
Lab_A#sh ip route
[output cut]
Gateway of last resort is not set
C       10.10.10.0/24 is directly connected, FastEthernet0/0
C       10.10.20.0/24 is directly connected, FastEthernet0/1
C       10.10.30.0/24 is directly connected, FastEthernet0/2
C       10.10.40.0/24 is directly connected, Serial 0/0
```

The C in the routing table output means that the networks listed are "directly connected," and until we add a routing protocol—something like RIP, EIGRP, etc.—to the routers in our internetwork (or use static routes), we'll have only directly connected networks in our routing table.

So let's get back to the original question: By looking at the figure and the output of the routing table, can you tell what IP will do with a received packet that has a destination IP address of 10.10.10.10? The router will packet-switch the packet to interface FastEthernet 0/0, and this interface will frame the packet and then send it out on the network segment.

Because we can, let's do another example: Based on the output of the next routing table, which interface will a packet with a destination address of 10.10.10.14 be forwarded from?

```
Lab_A#sh ip route
[output cut]
Gateway of last resort is not set
C       10.10.10.16/28 is directly connected, FastEthernet0/0
```

```
C     10.10.10.8/29 is directly connected, FastEthernet0/1
C     10.10.10.4/30 is directly connected, FastEthernet0/2
C     10.10.10.0/30 is directly connected, Serial 0/0
```

First, you can see that the network is subnetted and each interface has a different mask. And I have to tell you—you just can't answer this question if you can't subnet! 10.10.10.14 would be a host in the 10.10.10.8/29 subnet connected to the FastEthernet0/1 interface. Don't freak out if you don't get it. Just go back and reread Chapter 3 if you're struggling, and this should make perfect sense to you afterward.

For everyone who's ready to move on, let's get into this process in more detail.

The IP Routing Process

The IP routing process is fairly simple and doesn't change, regardless of the size of your network. For an example, we'll use Figure 6.2 to describe step-by-step what happens when Host_A wants to communicate with Host_B on a different network.

FIGURE 6.2   IP routing example using two hosts and one router

In this example, a user on Host_A pings Host_B's IP address. Routing doesn't get simpler than this, but it still involves a lot of steps. Let's work through them:

1. Internet Control Message Protocol (ICMP) creates an echo request payload (which is just the alphabet in the data field).

2. ICMP hands that payload to Internet Protocol (IP), which then creates a packet. At a minimum, this packet contains an IP source address, an IP destination address, and a Protocol field with 01h. (Remember that Cisco likes to use *0x* in front of hex characters, so this could look like 0x01.) All of that tells the receiving host whom it should hand the payload to when the destination is reached—in this example, ICMP.

3. Once the packet is created, IP determines whether the destination IP address is on the local network or a remote one.

4. Since IP determines that this is a remote request, the packet needs to be sent to the default gateway so the packet can be routed to the remote network. The Registry in Windows is parsed to find the configured default gateway.

5. The default gateway of host 172.16.10.2 (Host_A) is configured to 172.16.10.1. For this packet to be sent to the default gateway, the hardware address of the router's interface

Ethernet 0 (configured with the IP address of 172.16.10.1) must be known. Why? So the packet can be handed down to the Data Link layer, framed, and sent to the router's interface that's connected to the 172.16.10.0 network. Because hosts only communicate via hardware addresses on the local LAN, it's important to recognize that for Host_A to communicate to Host_B, it has to send packets to the Media Access Control (MAC) address of the default gateway on the local network.

 MAC addresses are always local on the LAN and never go through and past a router.

6.   Next, the Address Resolution Protocol (ARP) cache of the host is checked to see if the IP address of the default gateway has already been resolved to a hardware address:

   ▪   If it has, the packet is then free to be handed to the Data Link layer for framing. (The hardware destination address is also handed down with that packet.) To view the ARP cache on your host, use the following command:

```
C:\>arp -a
Interface: 172.16.10.2 --- 0x3
  Internet Address      Physical Address       Type
  172.16.10.1           00-15-05-06-31-b0      dynamic
```

   ▪   If the hardware address isn't already in the ARP cache of the host, an ARP broadcast is sent out onto the local network to search for the hardware address of 172.16.10.1. The router responds to the request and provides the hardware address of Ethernet 0, and the host caches this address.

7.   Once the packet and destination hardware address are handed to the Data Link layer, the LAN driver is used to provide media access via the type of LAN being used (in this example, Ethernet). A frame is then generated, encapsulating the packet with control information. Within that frame are the hardware destination and source addresses plus, in this case, an Ether-Type field that describes the Network layer protocol that handed the packet to the Data Link layer—in this instance, IP. At the end of the frame is something called a Frame Check Sequence (FCS) field that houses the result of the cyclic redundancy check (CRC). The frame would look something like what I've detailed in Figure 6.3. It contains Host_A's hardware (MAC) address and the destination hardware address of the default gateway. It does not include the remote host's MAC address—remember that!

FIGURE 6.3   Frame used from Host_A to the Lab_A router when Host_B is pinged

Destination MAC (routers E0 MAC address)	Source MAC (Host_A MAC address)	Ether-Type field	Packet	FCS (CRC)

8. Once the frame is completed, it's handed down to the Physical layer to be put on the physical medium (in this example, twisted-pair wire) one bit at a time.

9. Every device in the collision domain receives these bits and builds the frame. They each run a CRC and check the answer in the FCS field. If the answers don't match, the frame is discarded.

    - If the CRC matches, then the hardware destination address is checked to see if it matches too (which, in this example, is the router's interface Ethernet 0).

    - If it's a match, then the Ether-Type field is checked to find the protocol used at the Network layer.

10. The packet is pulled from the frame, and what is left of the frame is discarded. The packet is handed to the protocol listed in the Ether-Type field—it's given to IP.

11. IP receives the packet and checks the IP destination address. Since the packet's destination address doesn't match any of the addresses configured on the receiving router itself, the router will look up the destination IP network address in its routing table.

12. The routing table must have an entry for the network 172.16.20.0 or the packet will be discarded immediately and an ICMP message will be sent back to the originating device with a destination network unreachable message.

13. If the router does find an entry for the destination network in its table, the packet is switched to the exit interface—in this example, interface Ethernet 1. The output below displays the Lab_A router's routing table. The C means "directly connected." No routing protocols are needed in this network since all networks (all two of them) are directly connected.

```
Lab_A>sh ip route
Codes:C - connected,S - static,I - IGRP,R - RIP,M - mobile,B -
   BGP, D - EIGRP,EX - EIGRP external,O - OSPF,IA - OSPF inter
   area, N1 - OSPF NSSA external type 1, N2 - OSPF NSSA external
   type 2, E1 - OSPF external type 1, E2 - OSPF external type 2,
   E - EGP,i - IS-IS, L1 - IS-IS level-1, L2 - IS-IS level-2, ia
   - IS-IS intearea * - candidate default, U - per-user static
   route, o - ODR P - periodic downloaded static route

Gateway of last resort is not set

     172.16.0.0/24 is subnetted, 2 subnets
C       172.16.10.0 is directly connected, Ethernet0
C       172.16.20.0 is directly connected, Ethernet1
```

14. The router packet-switches the packet to the Ethernet 1 buffer.

15. The Ethernet 1 buffer needs to know the hardware address of the destination host and first checks the ARP cache.

  ▪ If the hardware address of Host_B has already been resolved and is in the router's ARP cache, then the packet and the hardware address are handed down to the Data Link layer to be framed. Let's take a look at the ARP cache on the Lab_A router by using the show ip arp command:

```
Lab_A#sh ip arp
Protocol  Address       Age(min) Hardware Addr   Type  Interface
Internet  172.16.20.1   -          00d0.58ad.05f4  ARPA  Ethernet0
Internet  172.16.20.2   3          0030.9492.a5dd  ARPA  Ethernet0
Internet  172.16.10.1   -          00d0.58ad.06aa  ARPA  Ethernet0
Internet  172.16.10.2   12         0030.9492.a4ac  ARPA  Ethernet0
```

  The dash (-) means that this is the physical interface on the router. From the output above, we can see that the router knows the 172.16.10.2 (Host_A) and 172.16.20.2 (Host_B) hardware addresses. Cisco routers will keep an entry in the ARP table for 4 hours.

  ▪ If the hardware address has not already been resolved, the router sends an ARP request out E1 looking for the hardware address of 172.16.20.2. Host_B responds with its hardware address, and the packet and destination hardware address are both sent to the Data Link layer for framing.

16. The Data Link layer creates a frame with the destination and source hardware address, Ether-Type field, and FCS field at the end. The frame is handed to the Physical layer to be sent out on the physical medium one bit at a time.

17. Host_B receives the frame and immediately runs a CRC. If the result matches what's in the FCS field, the hardware destination address is then checked. If the host finds a match, the Ether-Type field is then checked to determine the protocol that the packet should be handed to at the Network layer—IP in this example.

18. At the Network layer, IP receives the packet and checks the IP destination address. Since there's finally a match made, the Protocol field is checked to find out whom the payload should be given to.

19. The payload is handed to ICMP, which understands that this is an echo request. ICMP responds to this by immediately discarding the packet and generating a new payload as an echo reply.

20. A packet is then created including the source and destination addresses, Protocol field, and payload. The destination device is now Host_A.

21. IP then checks to see whether the destination IP address is a device on the local LAN or on a remote network. Since the destination device is on a remote network, the packet needs to be sent to the default gateway.

22. The default gateway IP address is found in the Registry of the Windows device, and the ARP cache is checked to see if the hardware address has already been resolved from an IP address.

23. Once the hardware address of the default gateway is found, the packet and destination hardware addresses are handed down to the Data Link layer for framing.

24. The Data Link layer frames the packet of information and includes the following in the header:

- The destination and source hardware addresses
- The Ether-Type field with 0x0800 (IP) in it
- The FCS field with the CRC result in tow

25. The frame is now handed down to the Physical layer to be sent out over the network medium one bit at a time.

26. The router's Ethernet 1 interface receives the bits and builds a frame. The CRC is run, and the FCS field is checked to make sure the answers match.

27. Once the CRC is found to be okay, the hardware destination address is checked. Since the router's interface is a match, the packet is pulled from the frame and the Ether-Type field is checked to see what protocol at the Network layer the packet should be delivered to.

28. The protocol is determined to be IP, so it gets the packet. IP runs a CRC check on the IP header first and then checks the destination IP address.

IP does not run a complete CRC as the Data Link layer does—it only checks the header for errors.

Since the IP destination address doesn't match any of the router's interfaces, the routing table is checked to see whether it has a route to 172.16.10.0. If it doesn't have a route over to the destination network, the packet will be discarded immediately. (This is the source point of confusion for a lot of administrators—when a ping fails, most people think the packet never reached the destination host. But as we see here, that's not *always* the case. All it takes is for just one of the remote routers to be lacking a route back to the originating host's network and—*poof!*—the packet is dropped on the *return trip*, not on its way to the host.)

Just a quick note to mention that when (if) the packet is lost on the way back to the originating host, you will typically see a "request timed out" message because it is an unknown error. If the error occurs because of a known issue, such as if a route is not in the routing table on the way to the destination device, you will see a destination unreachable message. This should help you determine if the problem occurred on the way to the destination or on the way back.

29. In this case, the router does know how to get to network 172.16.10.0—the exit interface is Ethernet 0—so the packet is switched to interface Ethernet 0.

30. The router checks the ARP cache to determine whether the hardware address for 172.16.10.2 has already been resolved.

31. Since the hardware address to 172.16.10.2 is already cached from the originating trip to Host_B, the hardware address and packet are handed to the Data Link layer.

32. The Data Link layer builds a frame with the destination hardware address and source hardware address and then puts IP in the Ether-Type field. A CRC is run on the frame and the result is placed in the FCS field.

33. The frame is then handed to the Physical layer to be sent out onto the local network one bit at a time.

34. The destination host receives the frame, runs a CRC, checks the destination hardware address, and looks in the Ether-Type field to find out whom to hand the packet to.

35. IP is the designated receiver, and after the packet is handed to IP at the Network layer, it checks the protocol field for further direction. IP finds instructions to give the payload to ICMP, and ICMP determines the packet to be an ICMP echo reply.

36. ICMP acknowledges that it has received the reply by sending an exclamation point (!) to the user interface. ICMP then attempts to send four more echo requests to the destination host.

You've just experienced Todd's 36 easy steps to understanding IP routing. The key point to understand here is that if you had a much larger network, the process would be the *same*. In a really big internetwork, the packet just goes through more hops before it finds the destination host.

It's super-important to remember that when Host_A sends a packet to Host_B, the destination hardware address used is the default gateway's Ethernet interface. Why? Because frames can't be placed on remote networks—only local networks. So packets destined for remote networks must go through the default gateway.

Let's take a look at Host_A's ARP cache now:

```
C:\ >arp -a
Interface: 172.16.10.2 --- 0x3
   Internet Address      Physical Address      Type
   172.16.10.1           00-15-05-06-31-b0     dynamic
   172.16.20.1           00-15-05-06-31-b0     dynamic
```

Did you notice that the hardware (MAC) address that Host_A uses to get to Host_B is the Lab_A E0 interface? Hardware addresses are *always* local, and they never pass a router's interface. Understanding this process is as important as air to you, so carve this into your memory!

Testing Your IP Routing Understanding

I really want to make sure you understand IP routing because it's super-important. So I'm going to use this section to test your understanding of the IP routing process by having you look at a couple of figures and answer some very basic IP routing questions.

Figure 6.4 shows a LAN connected to RouterA, which is, in turn, connected via a WAN link to RouterB. RouterB has a LAN connected with an HTTP server attached.

FIGURE 6.4   IP routing example 1

The critical information you need to glean from this figure is exactly how IP routing will occur in this example. Okay—we'll cheat a bit. I'll give you the answer, but then you should go back over the figure and see if you can answer example 2 without looking at my answers.

1. The destination address of a frame, from HostA, will be the MAC address of the F0/0 interface of the RouterA router.

2. The destination address of a packet will be the IP address of the network interface card (NIC) of the HTTP server.

3. The destination port number in the segment header will have a value of 80.

That example was a pretty simple one, and it was also very to the point. One thing to remember is that if multiple hosts are communicating to the server using HTTP, they must all use a different source port number. That is how the server keeps the data separated at the Transport layer.

Let's mix it up a little and add another internetworking device into the network and then see if you can find the answers. Figure 6.5 shows a network with only one router but two switches.

FIGURE 6.5   IP routing example 2

What you want to understand about the IP routing process here is what happens when HostA sends data to the HTTPS server:

1. The destination address of a frame, from HostA, will be the MAC address of the F0/0 interface of the RouterA router.

2. The destination address of a packet will be the IP address of the network interface card (NIC) of the HTTPS server.

3. The destination port number in the segment header will have a value of 443.

Notice that the switches weren't used as either a default gateway or another destination. That's because switches have nothing to do with routing. I wonder how many of you chose the switch as the default gateway (destination) MAC address for HostA? If you did, don't feel bad—just take another look with that fact in mind. It's very important to remember that the destination MAC address will always be the router's interface—if your packets are destined for outside the LAN, as they were in these last two examples.

Before we move into some of the more advanced aspects of IP routing, let's discuss ICMP in more detail, as well as how ICMP is used in an internetwork. Take a look at the network shown in Figure 6.6. Ask yourself what will happen if the LAN interface of Lab_C goes down.

FIGURE 6.6 ICMP error example

Lab_C will use ICMP to inform Host A that Host B can't be reached, and it will do this by sending an ICMP destination unreachable message. Lots of people think that the Lab_A router would be sending this message, but they would be wrong because the router that sends the message is the one with that interface that's down.

Let's look at another problem: Look at the output of a corporate router's routing table:

```
Corp#sh ip route
[output cut]
R    192.168.215.0 [120/2] via 192.168.20.2, 00:00:23, Serial0/0
R    192.168.115.0 [120/1] via 192.168.20.2, 00:00:23, Serial0/0
R    192.168.30.0 [120/1] via 192.168.20.2, 00:00:23, Serial0/0
C    192.168.20.0 is directly connected, Serial0/0
C    192.168.214.0 is directly connected, FastEthernet0/0
```

What do we see here? If I were to tell you that the corporate router received an IP packet with a source IP address of 192.168.214.20 and a destination address of 192.168.22.3, what do you think the Corp router will do with this packet?

If you said, "The packet came in on the FastEthernet 0/0 interface, but since the routing table doesn't show a route to network 192.168.22.0 (or a default route), the router will discard the packet and send an ICMP destination unreachable message back out interface FastEthernet 0/0," you're a genius! The reason it does this is because that's the source LAN where the packet originated from.

Now, let's check out another figure and talk about the frames and packets in detail. Really, we're not exactly chatting about anything new; I'm just making sure that you totally, completely, fully understand basic IP routing. That's because this book, and the exam objectives it's geared toward, are all about IP routing, which means you need to be all over this stuff! We'll use Figure 6.7 for the next few questions.

FIGURE 6.7   Basic IP routing using MAC and IP addresses

Referring to Figure 6.7, here's a list of all the questions you need the answers to emblazoned in your brain:

1. In order to begin communicating with the Sales server, Host 4 sends out an ARP request. How will the devices exhibited in the topology respond to this request?

2. Host 4 has received an ARP reply. Host 4 will now build a packet, then place this packet in the frame. What information will be placed in the header of the packet that leaves Host 4 if Host 4 is going to communicate to the Sales server?

3. At last, the Lab_A router has received the packet and will send it out Fa0/0 onto the LAN toward the server. What will the frame have in the header as the source and destination addresses?

4. Host 4 is displaying two web documents from the Sales server in two browser windows at the same time. How did the data find its way to the correct browser windows?

I probably should write the following in a teensy font and put them upside down in another part of the book so it would be really hard for you to cheat and peek, but since it's actually you who's going to lose out if you peek, here are your answers:

1. In order to begin communicating with the server, Host 4 sends out an ARP request. How will the devices exhibited in the topology respond to this request? Since MAC addresses must stay on the local network, the Lab_B router will respond with the MAC address of

the Fa0/0 interface and Host 4 will send all frames to the MAC address of the Lab_B Fa0/0 interface when sending packets to the Sales server.

2. Host 4 has received an ARP reply. Host 4 will now build a packet, then place this packet in the frame. What information will be placed in the header of the packet that leaves Host 4 if Host 4 is going to communicate to the Sales server? Since we're now talking about packets, not frames, the source address will be the IP address of Host 4 and the destination address will be the IP address of the Sales server.

3. Finally, the Lab_A router has received the packet and will send it out Fa0/0 onto the LAN toward the server. What will the frame have in the header as the source and destination addresses? The source MAC address will be the Lab_A router's Fa0/0 interface, and the destination MAC address will be the Sales server's MAC address. (All MAC addresses must be local on the LAN.)

4. Host 4 is displaying two web documents from the Sales server in two different browser windows at the same time. How did the data find its way to the correct browser windows? TCP port numbers are used to direct the data to the correct application window.

Great! But we're not quite done yet. I've got a few more questions for you before you actually get to configure routing in a real network. Ready? Figure 6.8 shows a basic network, and Host 4 needs to get email. Which address will be placed in the destination address field of the frame when it leaves Host 4?

FIGURE 6.8   Testing basic routing knowledge

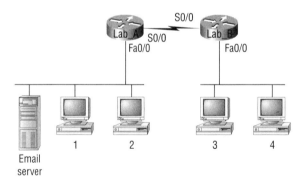

The answer is that Host 4 will use the destination MAC address of the Fa0/0 interface of the Lab_B router—which I'm so sure you knew, right? Look at Figure 6.8 again: Host 4 needs to communicate to Host 1. Which OSI layer 3 source address will be placed in the packet header when it reaches Host 1?

Hopefully you know this: At layer 3, the source IP address will be Host 4 and the destination address in the packet will be the IP address of Host 1. Of course, the destination MAC address from Host 4 will always be the Fa0/0 address of the Lab_B router, right? And since we have more than one router, we'll need a routing protocol that communicates between both of them so that traffic can be forwarded in the right direction to reach the network in which Host 1 is attached.

Okay—one more question and you're on your way to being an IP routing genius! Again, using Figure 6.8., Host 4 is transferring a file to the email server connected to the Lab_A router. What would be the layer 2 destination address leaving Host 4? Yes, I've asked this question more than once. But not this one: What will be the source MAC address when the frame is received at the email server?

Hopefully, you answered that the layer 2 destination address leaving Host 4 will be the MAC address of the Fa0/0 interface of the Lab_B router and that the source layer 2 address that the email server will receive will be the Fa0/0 interface of the Lab_A router.

If you did, you're all set to get the skinny on how IP routing is handled in a larger network.

Configuring IP Routing

It's time to get serious and configure a real network! Figure 6.9 shows five routers: Corp, Remote1, Remote2, Remote3, and the 871W (which is a wireless router). Remember that, by default, these routers only know about networks that are directly connected to them. You also want to keep in mind that the 1242 shown in the figure is an access point—not a wireless router like the 871W. Think of the access point as more of a hub than a router.

FIGURE 6.9 Configuring IP routing

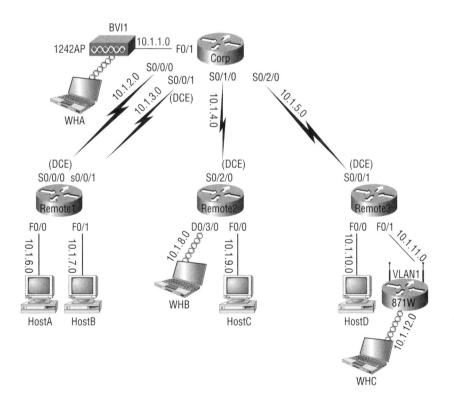

As you might guess, I've got quite a nice collection of routers for us to play with. The Corp router is a 2811 with a Wireless Controller module; something you'll get to see in Chapter 12. Remote routers 1 and 3 are 1841 ISR routers, and Remote2 is a 2801 with a wireless WIC card and a switch module. I'm simply going to call the group of remote routers R1, R2, and R3. (You can still perform most of the commands I use in this book with older routers, but you need at least a new 800 or 1800 series to run the SDM.)

The first step for this project is to correctly configure each router with an IP address on each interface. Table 6.1 shows the IP address scheme I'm going to use to configure the network. After we go over how the network is configured, I'll cover how to configure IP routing. Each network in the following table has a 24-bit subnet mask (255.255.255.0), which makes the interesting (subnet) octet the third one.

TABLE 6.1   Network Addressing for the IP Network

Router	Network Address	Interface	Address
CORP			
Corp	10.1.1.0	F0/1	10.1.1.1
Corp	10.1.2.0	S0/0/0	10.1.2.1
Corp	10.1.3.0	S0/0/1(DCE)	10.1.3.1
Corp	10.1.4.0	s0/1/0	10.1.4.1
Corp	10.1.5.0	s0/2/0	10.1.5.1
R1			
R1	10.1.2.0	S0/0/0 (DCE)	10.1.2.2
R1	10.1.3.0	S0/0/1	10.1.3.2
R1	10.1.6.0	F0/0	10.1.6.1
R1	10.1.7.0	F0/1	10.1.7.1
R2			
R2	10.1.4.0	S0/2/0 (DCE)	10.1.4.2
R2	10.1.8.0	D0/3/0	10.1.8.1
R2	10.1.9.0	F0/0	10.1.9.1

TABLE 6.1   Network Addressing for the IP Network *(continued)*

Router	Network Address	Interface	Address
R3			
R3	10.1.5.0	S0/0/0/ (DCE)	10.1.5.2
R3	10.1.10.0	F0/0	10.1.10.1
R3	10.1.11.0	F0/1	10.1.11.1
871W			
871W	10.1.11.0	Vlan 1	10.1.11.2
871W	10.1.12.0	Dot11radio0	10.1.12.1
1242 AP			
1242 AP	10.1.1.0	BVI 1	10.1.1.2

The router configuration is really a pretty straightforward process since you just need to add IP addresses to your interfaces and then perform a no shutdown on those same interfaces. It gets a tad more complex later on, but for right now, let's configure the IP addresses in the network.

Corp Configuration

We need to configure five interfaces to configure the Corp router. And configuring the hostnames of each router will make identification much easier. While we're at it, why not set the interface descriptions, banner, and router passwords too? It's a really good idea to make a habit of configuring these commands on every router.

To get started, I performed an erase startup-config on the router and reloaded, so we'll start in setup mode. I choose no to entering setup mode, which will get us straight to the username prompt of the console. I'm going to configure all my routers this way except for R3, which I'll configure using the SDM just for fun. You can configure your routers either way.

Here's how I did all that:

```
    --- System Configuration Dialog ---

Would you like to enter the initial configuration dialog? [yes/no]: n
[output cut]
Press RETURN to get started!
Router>en
```

```
Router#config t
Router(config)#hostname Corp
Corp(config)#enable secret todd
Corp(config)#interface fastEthernet 0/1
Corp(config-if)#ip address 10.1.1.1 255.255.255.0
Corp(config-if)#description Connection to 1242 AP
Corp(config-if)#no shutdown
Corp(config-if)#int s0/0/0
Corp(config-if)#ip address 10.1.2.1 255.255.255.0
Corp(config-if)#description 1st Connection to R1
Corp(config-if)#no shut
Corp(config-if)#int s0/0/1
Corp(config-if)#ip address 10.1.3.1 255.255.255.0
Corp(config-if)#description 2nd Connection to R1
Corp(config-if)#no shut
Corp(config-if)#int s0/1/0
Corp(config-if)#ip address 10.1.4.1 255.255.255.0
Corp(config-if)#description Connection to R2
Corp(config-if)#no shut
Corp(config-if)#int s0/2/0
Corp(config-if)#ip address 10.1.5.1 255.255.255.0
Corp(config-if)#description Connection to R3
Corp(config-if)#no shut
Corp(config-if)#line con 0
Corp(config-line)#password console
Corp(config-line)#login
Corp(config-line)#logging synchronous
Corp(config-line)#exec-timeout 0 0
Corp(config-line)#line aux 0
Corp(config-line)#password aux
Corp(config-line)#login
Corp(config-line)#exit
Corp(config)#line vty 0 ?
  <1-1180>  Last Line number
  <cr>
Corp(config)#line vty 0 1180
Corp(config-line)#password telnet
Corp(config-line)#login
Corp(config-line)#exit
Corp(config)#no ip domain-lookup
```

```
Corp(config)#banner motd # This is my Corp 2811 ISR Router #
Corp(config-if)#^Z
Corp#copy running-config startup-config
Destination filename [startup-config]?[enter]
Building configuration...
[OK]
Corp#
```

If you have a hard time understanding this configuration process, refer back to Chapter 4, "Cisco's Internetworking Operating System (IOS) and Security Device Manager (SDM)."

To view the IP routing tables created on a Cisco router, use the command show ip route. The command output is shown as follows:

```
Corp#sh ip route
Codes: C - connected, S - static, R - RIP, M - mobile, B - BGP
       D - EIGRP, EX - EIGRP external, O - OSPF, IA - OSPF inter area
       N1 - OSPF NSSA external type 1, N2 - OSPF NSSA external type 2
       E1 - OSPF external type 1, E2 - OSPF external type 2
       i - IS-IS, su - IS-IS summary, L1 - IS-IS level-1, L2 - IS-IS
   level-2, ia - IS-IS inter area, * - candidate default, U - per-user
   static route, o - ODR, P - periodic downloaded static route

Gateway of last resort is not set

     10.0.0.0/24 is subnetted, 1 subnets
C       10.1.1.0 is directly connected, FastEthernet0/1
Corp#
```

It's important to remember that only configured, directly connected networks are going to show up in the routing table. So why is it that I only see the FastEthernet0/1 interface in the routing table? No worries—that's just because you won't see the serial interfaces come up until the other side of the serial links is operational. As soon as we configure our R1, R2, and R3 routers, all those interfaces should pop right up.

But did you notice the C on the left side of the output of the routing table? When you see that there, it means that the network is directly connected. The codes for each type of connection are listed at the top of the show ip route command, along with their abbreviations.

In the interest of brevity, the codes will be cut in the rest of this chapter.

The Corp serial interface 0/0/1 is a DCE connection, which means that we need to add the clock rate command to the interface. Remember that you don't need to use the clock rate command in production. Even though this is very true, it's still imperative that you know how/ when you can use it and that you understand it really well when studying for your CCNA exam!

We can see our clocking with the show controllers command:

```
Corp#sh controllers s0/0/1
Interface Serial0/0/1
Hardware is GT96K
DCE V.35, clock rate 2000000
```

One last thing before we get into configuring the Remote routers: Did you notice the clock rate is 2000000 under the s0/0/1 interface of the Corp router? That's important because if you think back to when we were configuring the Corp router, you'll recall that I didn't set the clock rate. The reason I didn't is because ISR routers will auto-detect a DCE-type cable and automatically configure the clock rate—a really sweet feature!

R1 Configuration

Now we're ready to configure the next router—R1. To make that happen correctly, keep in mind that we have four interfaces to deal with: serial 0/0/0, serial 0/0/1, FastEthernet 0/0, and FastEthernet 0/1. So let's make sure we don't forget to add the hostname, passwords, interface descriptions, and banner to the router configuration. As I did with the Corp router, I erased the configuration and reloaded.

Here's the configuration I used:

```
R1#erase start
% Incomplete command.
R1#erase startup-config
Erasing the nvram filesystem will remove all configuration files!
   Continue? [confirm][enter]
[OK]
Erase of nvram: complete
R1#reload
Proceed with reload? [confirm][enter]
[output cut]
%Error opening tftp://255.255.255.255/network-confg (Timed out)
%Error opening tftp://255.255.255.255/cisconet.cfg (Timed out)


        --- System Configuration Dialog ---


Would you like to enter the initial configuration dialog? [yes/no]: n
```

Before we move on, I really want to discuss the above output with you. First, notice that the new 12.4 ISR routers will no longer take the command `erase start`. The router has only one command after `erase` that starts with *s*, as shown here:

```
Router#erase s?
startup-config
```

I know, you'd think that the IOS would continue to accept the command, but nope—sorry! The second thing I want to point out is that the output tells us the router is looking for a TFTP host to see if it can download a configuration. When that fails, it goes straight into setup mode. This gives you a great picture of the Cisco router default boot sequence we talked about in Chapter 5.

Okay, let's get back to configuring our router:

```
Press RETURN to get started!
Router>en
Router#config t
Router(config)#hostname R1
R1(config)#enable secret todd
R1(config)#int s0/0/0
R1(config-if)#ip address 10.1.2.2 255.255.255.0
R1(config-if)#Description 1st Connection to Corp Router
R1(config-if)#no shut
R1(config-if)#int s0/0/1
R1(config-if)#ip address 10.1.3.2 255.255.255.0
R1(config-if)#no shut
R1(config-if)#description 2nd connection to Corp Router
R1(config-if)#int f0/0
R1(config-if)#ip address 10.1.6.1 255.255.255.0
R1(config-if)#description Connection to HostA
R1(config-if)#no shut
R1(config-if)#int f0/1
R1(config-if)#ip address 10.1.7.1 255.255.255.0
R1(config-if)#description Connection to HostB
R1(config-if)#no shut
R1(config-if)#line con 0
R1(config-line)#password console
R1(config-line)#login
R1(config-line)#logging synchronous
R1(config-line)#exec-timeout 0 0
R1(config-line)#line aux 0
R1(config-line)#password aux
```

```
R1(config-line)#login
R1(config-line)#exit
R1(config)#line vty 0 ?
  <1-807>  Last Line number
  <cr>
R1(config)#line vty 0 807
R1(config-line)#password telnet
R1(config-line)#login
R1(config-line)#banner motd # This is my R1 ISR Router #
R1(config)#no ip domain-lookup
R1(config)#exit
R1#copy run start
Destination filename [startup-config]?[enter]
Building configuration...
[OK]
R1#
```

Let's take a look at our configuration of the interfaces.

```
R1#sh run | begin interface
interface FastEthernet0/0
 description Connection to HostA
 ip address 10.1.6.1 255.255.255.0
 duplex auto
 speed auto
!
interface FastEthernet0/1
 description Connection to HostB
 ip address 10.1.7.1 255.255.255.0
 duplex auto
 speed auto
!
interface Serial0/0/0
 description 1st Connection to Corp Router
 ip address 10.1.2.2 255.255.255.0
!
interface Serial0/0/1
 description 2nd connection to Corp Router
 ip address 10.1.3.2 255.255.255.0
!
```

The show ip route command displays the following:

```
R1#show ip route
      10.0.0.0/24 is subnetted, 4 subnets
C        10.1.3.0 is directly connected, Serial0/0/1
C        10.1.2.0 is directly connected, Serial0/0/0
C        10.1.7.0 is directly connected, FastEthernet0/1
C        10.1.6.0 is directly connected, FastEthernet0/0
R1#
```

Notice that router R1 knows how to get to networks 10.1.3.0, 10.1.2.0, 10.1.7.0, and 10.1.6.0. We can now ping to the Corp router from R1:

```
R1#ping 10.1.2.1

Type escape sequence to abort.
Sending 5, 100-byte ICMP Echos to 10.1.2.1, timeout is 2 seconds:
!!!!!
Success rate is 100 percent (5/5), round-trip min/avg/max = 1/2/4 ms
R1#
```

Now let's go back to the Corp router and look at the routing table:

```
Corp#sh ip route
[output cut]
      10.0.0.0/24 is subnetted, 4 subnets
C        10.1.3.0 is directly connected, Serial0/0/1
C        10.1.2.0 is directly connected, Serial0/0/0
C        10.1.1.0 is directly connected, FastEthernet0/1
Corp#
```

Since the serial links are up—remember, DCE is now detected automatically with ISR routers and the clock rate is automatically added to the interface configuration—we can now see all three. And once we configure R2 and R3, we'll see two more networks in the routing table of the Corp router. The Corp router can't see either the 10.1.6.0 or 10.1.7.0 networks because we don't have any routing configured yet.

R2 Configuration

To configure R2, we're going to do pretty much the same thing we did with the other two routers. There are three interfaces: serial 0/2/0, FastEthernet 0/0/0, and Dot11radio 0/3/0 to deal with, and again, we'll be sure to add the hostname, passwords, interface descriptions, and a banner to the router configuration:

```
Router>en
Router#config t
Router(config)#hostname R2
```

```
R2(config)#enable secret todd
R2(config)#int s0/2/0
R2(config-if)#ip address 10.1.4.2 255.255.255.0
R2(config-if)#description Connection to Corp ISR Router
R2(config-if)#no shut
R2(config-if)#int f0/0
R2(config-if)#ip address 10.1.9.1 255.255.255.0
R2(config-if)#description Connection to HostC
R2(config-if)#no shut
R2(config-if)#int dot11radio 0/3/0
R2(config-if)#ip address 10.1.8.1 255.255.255.0
R2(config-if)#description Admin WLAN
R2(config-if)#ssid ADMIN
R2(config-if-ssid)#guest-mode
R2(config-if-ssid)#authentication open
R2(config-if-ssid)#infrastructure-ssid
R2(config-if-ssid)#no shut
R2(config-if)#line con 0
R2(config-line)#password console
R2(config-line)#login
R2(config-line)#logging sync
R2(config-line)#exec-timeout 0 0
R2(config-line)#line aux 0
R2(config-line)#password aux
R2(config-line)#login
R2(config-line)#exit
R2(config)#line vty 0 ?
  <1-807>  Last Line number
  <cr>
R2(config)#line vty 0 807
R2(config-line)#password telnet
R2(config-line)#login
R2(config-line)#exit
R2(config)#banner motd # This is my R2 ISR Router #
R2(config)#no ip domain-lookup
R2(config)#^Z
R2#copy run start
Destination filename [startup-config]?[enter]
Building configuration...
[OK]
R2#
```

Nice—everything was pretty straightforward except for that wireless interface. It's true, the wireless interface is really just another interface on a router, and it looks just like that in the routing table as well. But, in order to bring up the wireless interface, more configurations are needed than for a simple FastEthernet interface. So check out the following output, and then I'll tell you about the special configuration needs for this wireless interface:

```
R2(config-if)#int dot11radio0/3/0
R2(config-if)#ip address 10.1.8.1 255.255.255.0
R2(config-if)#description Connection to WLAN
R2(config-if)#no shut
R2(config-if)#ssid ADMIN
R2(config-if-ssid)#guest-mode
R2(config-if-ssid)#authentication open
R2(config-if-ssid)#infrastructure-ssid
R2(config-if-ssid)#no shut
```

So, what we see here is that everything is pretty commonplace until we get to the SSID configuration. This is the Service Set Identifier that creates a wireless network that hosts can connect to. Unlike access points, the interface on the R2 router is actually a routed interface, which is the reason why the IP address is placed under the physical interface—typically the IP address would be placed under the management VLAN or Bridge-Group Virtual Interface (BVI).

That guest-mode line means that the interface will broadcast the SSID so wireless hosts will understand that they can connect to this interface. Authentication open means just that...no authentication. (Even so, you still have to type that command in at minimum to make the wireless interface work.) Last, the infrastructure-ssid indicates that this interface can be used to communicate to other access points, or other devices on the infrastructure—to the actual wired network itself.

But wait, we're not done yet—we still need to configure the DHCP pool for the wireless clients:

```
R2#config t
R2(config)#ip dhcp pool Admin
R2(dhcp-config)#network 10.1.8.0 255.255.255.0
R2(dhcp-config)#default-router 10.1.8.1
R2(dhcp-config)#exit
R2(config)#ip dhcp excluded-address 10.1.8.1
R2(config)#
```

Creating DHCP pools on a router is actually a pretty simple process. To do so, you just create the pool name, add the network/subnet and the default gateway, and exclude any addresses you don't want handed out (like the default gateway address). And you'd usually add a DNS server as well.

The output of the following show ip route command displays the directly connected networks of 10.1.9.0, 8.0, and 4.0, as you can see here:

```
R2#sh ip route
     10.0.0.0/24 is subnetted, 3 subnets
```

```
C       10.1.9.0 is directly connected, FastEthernet0/0
C       10.1.8.0 is directly connected, Dot11Radio0/3/0
C       10.1.4.0 is directly connected, Serial0/2/0
R2#
```

The Corp, R1, and R2 routers now have all their links up. But we still need to configure R3 (the 871W router) and the 1241 AP.

> Wireless networks will be discussed in detail in Chapter 12, "Cisco's Wireless Technologies."

R3 Configuration

Just as I said, I'm going to use the SDM for the R3 router. My first step is to set an IP address on the F0/0 interface. I used a crossover cable to connect my PC directly to the f0/0 port.

Now since I want to set up the router with security, I've got to configure the router back to the factory defaults. I can do this via the CLI just as I showed you back in Chapter 4, but it's actually a whole lot easier to do this using SDM!

Using HTTP, I was able to access the R3 router, go to the Configure page, and choose Additional Tasks. Then, I just clicked on Configuration Management and Reset to Factory Default.

I clicked the Reset Router button in the bottom-right corner and then configured my PC using the directions shown on the screen in the above screen shot.

Again, using HTTPS, I connected back to SDM using the 10.10.10.1 address that was provided in the directions. SDM had me log in twice with the username *cisco* as well as a password of *cisco*. I then had to accept the certificate from the router, and I'm good to go with a secure connection.

The first thing the router had me do after SDM was loaded was change the username and password.

Then I needed to log in again using my new name and password.

After that, I chose Configure and then Interfaces and Connections, which is in the upper-left corner, under Home. Clicking the Serial (PPP, HDLC or Frame Relay) button got me to where I could choose Create New Connection.

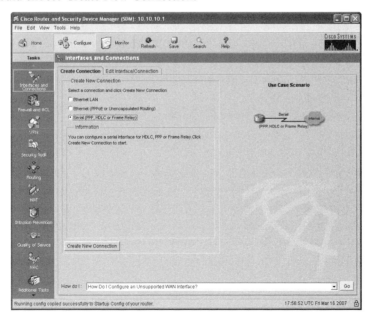

The Create New Connection button took me to the WAN Wizard.

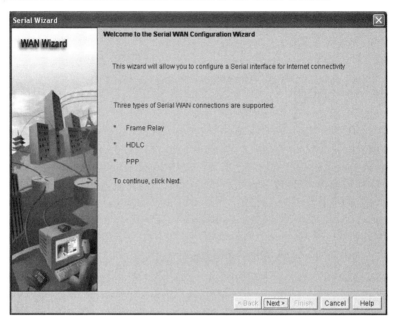

I was then able to choose my interface; then I clicked Next.

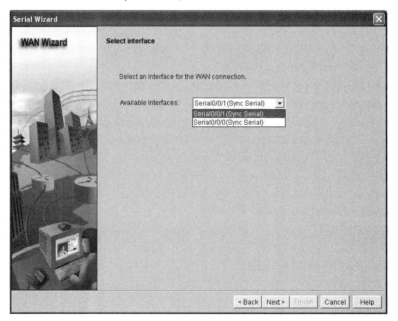

I then chose High-Level Data Link Control and clicked Next. (I'll get into HDLC in Chapter 14.)

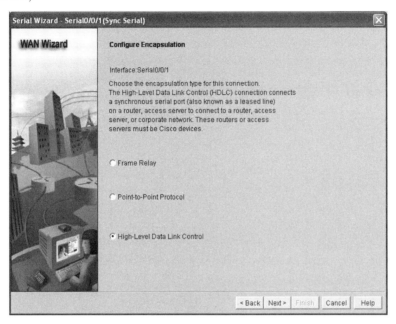

I was then able to add my IP address and mask.

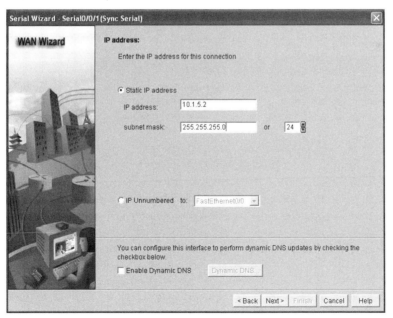

IP Unnumbered is truly an interesting configuration because it lets you set up a network connection without using an IP address. Instead, you "borrow" an IP address from another active interface. This comes in pretty handy if you happen to be a bit short on subnets!

Anyway, the next screen asked if I wanted to set up static routing and NAT. Again, this is something I'll get into more later on, so we're not going to configure it just yet.

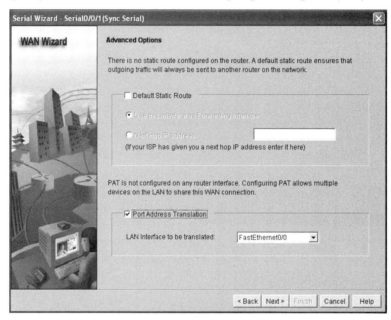

Moving on, I clicked Next and received a summary of my serial 0/0/1 configuration.

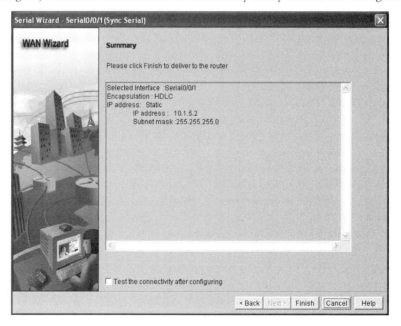

I clicked Finish, and the commands were uploaded to my R3 router. (I'm going to configure both the F0/0 and F0/1 interfaces the same way.)

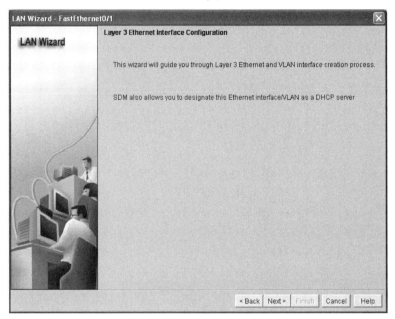

After choosing the FastEthernet 0/1 interface from the same location from where I started to configure the s0/0/1 interface. I chose Create New Connection and was taken to the LAN Wizard.

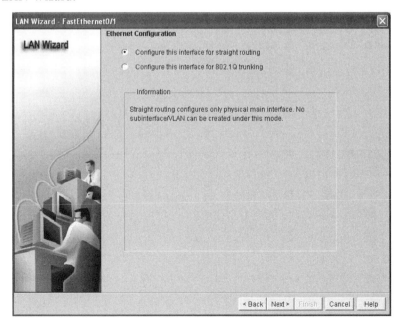

The LAN Wizard allows you to either choose straight routing (which is what we want to do here) or configure 802.1Q trunking, which I'll discuss in detail in Chapter 9, "Virtual LANs." I configured the IP address and mask and then clicked Next.

What's cool about the SDM at this point is that it would build a DHCP server for this LAN if I wanted it too. Man, this is easy.

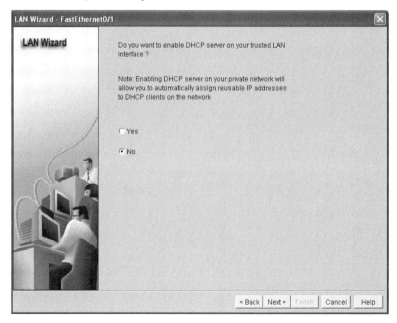

Since I accidentally entered the wrong IP address for F0/1, the only way to change it now is to choose Configure and Edit Interface/Connection in the SDM, or use the CLI.

From here, I can double-click on the FastEthernet 0/1 interface and change the IP address.

After using the LAN Wizard to set up F0/0, I had to save the configuration and then reconfigure my PC into the right network and reconnect to SDM to verify my configuration.

We're good—R3 is now configured! Even though my console and VTY password get configured automatically when I set up the user todd, I still had to choose Configure and then Additional Tasks and then Router Properties to set the hostname and enable secret password.

871W Configuration

Although I can configure the 871 router with SDM, I'll configure it using the CLI. First, I need to erase the default configuration and reload it, as I did with the other routers (except R3).

```
Router>en
Router#config t
Router(config)#hostname 871W
871W(config)#int vlan 1
871W(config-if)#ip address 10.1.11.2 255.255.255.0
```

```
871W(config-if)#no shut
871W(config-if)#int dot11radio 0
871W(config-if)#ip address 10.1.12.1 255.255.255.0
871W(config-if)#no shut
871W(config-if)#ssid R3WLAN
871W(config-if-ssid)#guest-mode
871W(config-if-ssid)#authentication open
871W(config-if-ssid)#infrastructure-ssid
871W(config-if-ssid)#line con 0
871W(config-line)#password console
871W(config-line)#logging sync
871W(config-line)#exec-timeout 0 0
871W(config-line)#exit
871W(config)#line vty 0 ?
  <1-4>  Last Line number
  <cr>
871W(config)#line vty 0 4
871W(config-line)#password telnet
871W(config-line)#login
871W(config-line)#ip dhcp pool R3WLAN
871W(dhcp-config)#network 10.1.12.0 255.255.255.0
871W(dhcp-config)#default-router 10.1.12.1
871W(dhcp-config)#exit
871W(config)#ip dhcp excluded-address 10.1.12.1
871W(config)#exit
871W#copy run start
Destination filename [startup-config]?[enter]
Building configuration...
[OK]
871W#
```

The 871W has a four-port switch, which means that you've got to place the IP address under the management VLAN interface. You just can't get away with simply putting IP addresses on layer 2 switch interfaces.

To be totally honest, I think this was a faster configuration than using SDM. But I guess, in production, the SDM with HTTPS would really be a more secure way to administer the router. And as promised, I'll show you soon (in Chapter 12) why using SDM is the easier way to go when you want to set up wireless security.

Let's take a look at the routing table now:

```
871W#sh ip route
     10.0.0.0/24 is subnetted, 2 subnets
```

```
C       10.1.11.0 is directly connected, Vlan1
C       10.1.12.0 is directly connected, Dot11Radio0
```

We have both our networks showing directly connected. Let's configure our last device, and then we'll start configuring routing.

1242AP Configuration

Configuring the 1242AP is a bit different because it's an access point (again, think hub), not a router. I'll configure this device from the CLI, but you can use an HTTP interface as well. But you can't use SDM. The HTTP interface will be easier to use when we start adding security and when we get into some more complex configurations.

Check out the output:

```
ap>en
Password:
ap#config t
ap(config)#hostname 1242AP
1242AP(config)#enable secret todd
1242AP(config)#int dot11Radio 0
1242AP(config-if)#description CORPWLAN
1242AP(config-if)#no shutdown
1242AP(config-if)#ssid CORPWLAN
1242AP(config-if-ssid)#guest-mode
1242AP(config-if-ssid)#authentication open
1242AP(config-if-ssid)#infrastructure-ssid
1242AP(config-if-ssid)#exit
1242AP(config-if)#exit
1242AP(config)#line con 0
1242AP(config-line)#password console
1242AP(config-line)#login
1242AP(config-line)#logging synchronous
1242AP(config-line)#exec-timeout 0 0
1242AP(config-line)#exit
1242AP(config)#line vty 0 ?
  <1-15>  Last Line number
  <cr>
1242AP(config)#line vty 0 15
1242AP(config-line)#password telnet
1242AP(config-line)#login
1242AP(config-line)#int bvi 1
1242AP(config-if)#ip address 10.1.1.2 255.255.255.0
1242AP(config-if)#no shut
1242AP(config-if)#exit
```

```
1242AP(config)#ip default-gateway 10.1.1.1
1242AP(config)#ip dhcp pool CORPWLAN
1242AP(dhcp-config)#network 10.1.1.0 255.255.255.0
1242AP(dhcp-config)#default-router 10.1.1.1
1242AP(dhcp-config)#exit
1242AP(config)#ip dhcp excluded-address 10.1.1.1
1242AP(config)#ip dhcp excluded-address 10.1.1.2
1242AP(config)#no ip domain-lookup
1242AP(config)#^Z
1242AP#copy run start
Destination filename [startup-config]?[enter]
Building configuration...
[OK]
1242AP#
```

Even though the SSID configuration is the same as it is for the R2 routed radio interface, notice there's no IP address under the Dot11radio 0 interface. Why? Because it's not a routed port, so the IP address is instead placed under the Bridge Virtual Interface (BVI). I also set a default gateway so this device can be managed from outside the LAN.

You need to know that just as with a switch, you don't need to add an IP address to the AP for it to function. I could just as easily have added the DHCP pool to the Corp router for the wireless LAN, not added an IP address or pool to the AP at all, and it still would have worked just the same.

Configuring IP Routing in Our Network

Our network is good to go—right? After all, it's been correctly configured with IP addressing, administrative functions, and even clocking (automatically on the ISR routers). But how does a router send packets to remote networks when the only way it can send them is by looking at the routing table to find out how to get to the remote networks? Our configured routers only have information about directly connected networks in each routing table. And what happens when a router receives a packet for a network that isn't listed in the routing table? It doesn't send a broadcast looking for the remote network—the router just discards it. Period.

So we're not exactly ready to rock after all. But no worries—there are several ways to configure the routing tables to include all the networks in our little internetwork so that packets will be forwarded. And what's best for one network isn't necessarily what's best for another. Understanding the different types of routing will really help you come up with the best solution for your specific environment and business requirements.

You'll learn about the following types of routing in the following sections:

- Static routing
- Default routing
- Dynamic routing

I'm going to start off by describing and implementing static routing on our network because if you can implement static routing *and* make it work, it means you have a solid understanding of the internetwork. So let's get started.

Static Routing

Static routing occurs when you manually add routes in each router's routing table. There are pros and cons to static routing, but that's true for all routing processes.

Static routing has the following benefits:

- There is no overhead on the router CPU, which means you could possibly buy a cheaper router than you would use if you were using dynamic routing.

- There is no bandwidth usage between routers, which means you could possibly save money on WAN links.

- It adds security because the administrator can choose to allow routing access to certain networks only.

Static routing has the following disadvantages:

- The administrator must really understand the internetwork and how each router is connected in order to configure routes correctly.

- If a network is added to the internetwork, the administrator has to add a route to it on all routers—by hand.

- It's not feasible in large networks because maintaining it would be a full-time job in itself.

Okay—that said, here's the command syntax you use to add a static route to a routing table:

```
ip route [destination_network] [mask] [next-hop_address or
  exitinterface] [administrative_distance] [permanent]
```

This list describes each command in the string:

ip route   The command used to create the static route.

destination_network   The network you're placing in the routing table.

mask   The subnet mask being used on the network.

next-hop_address   The address of the next-hop router that will receive the packet and forward it to the remote network. This is a router interface that's on a directly connected network. You must be able to ping the router interface before you add the route. If you type in the wrong next-hop address or the interface to that router is down, the static route will show up in the router's configuration but not in the routing table.

exitinterface   Used in place of the next-hop address if you want, and shows up as a directly connected route.

administrative_distance   By default, static routes have an administrative distance of 1 (or even 0 if you use an exit interface instead of a next-hop address). You can change the default value by adding an administrative weight at the end of the command. I'll talk a lot more about this subject later in the chapter when we get to the section on dynamic routing.

permanent   If the interface is shut down or the router can't communicate to the next-hop router, the route will automatically be discarded from the routing table. Choosing the permanent option keeps the entry in the routing table no matter what happens.

Before we dive into configuring static routes, let's take a look at a sample static route and see what we can find out about it.

```
Router(config)#ip route 172.16.3.0 255.255.255.0 192.168.2.4
```

- The ip route command tells us simply that it is a static route.
- 172.16.3.0 is the remote network we want to send packets to.
- 255.255.255.0 is the mask of the remote network.
- 192.168.2.4 is the next hop, or router, we will send packets to.

However, suppose the static route looked like this:

```
Router(config)#ip route 172.16.3.0 255.255.255.0 192.168.2.4 150
```

The 150 at the end changes the default administrative distance (AD) of 1 to 150. No worries—I'll talk much more about AD when we get into dynamic routing. For now, just remember that the AD is the trustworthiness of a route, where 0 is best and 255 is worst.

One more example, then we'll start configuring:

```
Router(config)#ip route 172.16.3.0 255.255.255.0 s0/0/0
```

Instead of using a next-hop address, we can use an exit interface that will make the route show up as a directly connected network. Functionally, the next hop and exit interface work exactly the same. To help you understand how static routes work, I'll demonstrate the configuration on the internetwork shown previously in Figure 6.9.

Corp

Each routing table automatically includes directly connected networks. To be able to route to all networks within the internetwork, the routing table must include information that describes where these other networks are located and how to get to them.

The Corp router is connected to five networks. For the Corp router to be able to route to all networks, the following networks have to be configured into its routing table:

- 10.1.6.0
- 10.1.7.0
- 10.1.8.0
- 10.1.9.0
- 10.1.10.0
- 10.1.11.0
- 10.1.12.0

The following router output shows the static routes on the Corp router and the routing table after the configuration. For the Corp router to find the remote networks, I had to place an entry into the routing table describing the remote network, the remote mask, and where to send the packets. I am going to add a "150" at the end of each line to raise the administrative distance. (When we get to dynamic routing, you'll see why I did it this way.)

```
Corp(config)#ip route 10.1.6.0 255.255.255.0 10.1.2.2 150
Corp(config)#ip route 10.1.6.0 255.255.255.0 10.1.3.2 151
Corp(config)#ip route 10.1.7.0 255.255.255.0 10.1.3.2 150
Corp(config)#ip route 10.1.7.0 255.255.255.0 10.1.2.2 151
Corp(config)#ip route 10.1.8.0 255.255.255.0 10.1.4.2 150
Corp(config)#ip route 10.1.9.0 255.255.255.0 10.1.4.2 150
Corp(config)#ip route 10.1.10.0 255.255.255.0 10.1.5.2 150
Corp(config)#ip route 10.1.11.0 255.255.255.0 10.1.5.2 150
Corp(config)#ip route 10.1.12.0 255.255.255.0 10.1.5.2 150
Corp(config)#do show run | begin ip route
ip route 10.1.6.0 255.255.255.0 10.1.2.2 150
ip route 10.1.6.0 255.255.255.0 10.1.3.2 151
ip route 10.1.7.0 255.255.255.0 10.1.3.2 150
ip route 10.1.7.0 255.255.255.0 10.1.2.2 151
ip route 10.1.8.0 255.255.255.0 10.1.4.2 150
ip route 10.1.9.0 255.255.255.0 10.1.4.2 150
ip route 10.1.10.0 255.255.255.0 10.1.5.2 150
ip route 10.1.11.0 255.255.255.0 10.1.5.2 150
ip route 10.1.12.0 255.255.255.0 10.1.5.2 150
```

For networks 10.1.6.0 and 10.1.7.0, I put in both paths to each network, but I made one link a higher (151) AD. This will be a backup route in case the other link fails. If I made them both the same AD, we would end up with a routing loop. (Static routing can't handle multiple links to the same destination.) After the router is configured, you can type **show ip route** to see the static routes:

```
Corp(config)#do show ip route
     10.0.0.0/24 is subnetted, 12 subnets
S       10.1.11.0 [150/0] via 10.1.5.2
S       10.1.10.0 [150/0] via 10.1.5.2
S       10.1.9.0 [150/0] via 10.1.4.2
S       10.1.8.0 [150/0] via 10.1.4.2
S       10.1.12.0 [150/0] via 10.1.5.2
C       10.1.3.0 is directly connected, Serial0/0/1
C       10.1.2.0 is directly connected, Serial0/0/0
C       10.1.1.0 is directly connected, FastEthernet0/1
```

```
S      10.1.7.0 [150/0] via 10.1.3.2
S      10.1.6.0 [150/0] via 10.1.2.2
C      10.1.5.0 is directly connected, Serial0/2/0
C      10.1.4.0 is directly connected, Serial0/1/0
```

The Corp router is configured to route and know about all routes to all networks. I configured two routes to each remote network on R1, but the routing table will only show the route with the lower AD. The other link will show up in the routing table only if the link with that lower value it's currently using fails.

I want you to understand that if the routes don't appear in the routing table, it's because the router can't communicate with the next-hop address you've configured. You can use the permanent parameter to keep the route in the routing table even if the next-hop device can't be contacted.

The S in the preceding routing table entries means that the network is a static entry. The [1/0] is the administrative distance and metric (something we'll cover later) to the remote network. Here, the next-hop interface is 0, indicating that it's directly connected.

Okay—we're good. The Corp router now has all the information it needs to communicate with the other remote networks. But keep in mind that if the R1, R2, R3, and 871W routers aren't configured with all the same information, the packets will simply be discarded. We'll need to fix this by configuring static routes.

Don't stress about the 150/151 at the end of the static route configuration. I promise I will discuss the topic really soon in this chapter, not a later one! Be assured that you don't need to worry about it at this point.

R1

The R1 router is directly connected to the networks 10.1.2.0, 10.1.3.0, 10.1.6.0, and 10.1.7.0, so we've got to configure the following static routes on the R1 router:

- 10.1.1.0
- 10.1.4.0
- 10.1.5.0
- 10.1.8.0
- 10.1.9.0
- 10.1.10.0
- 10.1.11.0
- 10.1.12.0

Here's the configuration for the R1 router. Remember, we'll never create a static route to any network we're directly connected to, and we can use the next hop of either 10.1.2.1 or

10.1.3.1 since we have two links between the Corp and R1 routers. I'll change between next hops so all data doesn't go down one link. It really doesn't matter which link I use since I can't load-balance with static routing. We'll be able to load-balance when we use dynamic routing like RIP, EIGRP, and OSPF, but for now, the links will just provide a backup route to each network. Let's check out the output:

```
R1(config)#ip route 10.1.1.0 255.255.255.0 10.1.2.1 150
R1(config)#ip route 10.1.1.0 255.255.255.0 10.1.3.1 151
R1(config)#ip route 10.1.4.0 255.255.255.0 10.1.2.1 150
R1(config)#ip route 10.1.4.0 255.255.255.0 10.1.3.1 151
R1(config)#ip route 10.1.5.0 255.255.255.0 10.1.2.1 150
R1(config)#ip route 10.1.5.0 255.255.255.0 10.1.3.1 151
R1(config)#ip route 10.1.8.0 255.255.255.0 10.1.3.1 150
R1(config)#ip route 10.1.8.0 255.255.255.0 10.1.2.1 151
R1(config)#ip route 10.1.9.0 255.255.255.0 10.1.3.1 150
R1(config)#ip route 10.1.9.0 255.255.255.0 10.1.2.1 151
R1(config)#ip route 10.1.10.0 255.255.255.0 10.1.3.1 150
R1(config)#ip route 10.1.10.0 255.255.255.0 10.1.2.1 151
R1(config)#ip route 10.1.11.0 255.255.255.0 10.1.3.1 150
R1(config)#ip route 10.1.11.0 255.255.255.0 10.1.2.1 151
R1(config)#ip route 10.1.12.0 255.255.255.0 10.1.3.1 150
R1(config)#ip route 10.1.12.0 255.255.255.0 10.1.2.1 151
R1(config)#do show run | begin ip route
ip route 10.1.1.0 255.255.255.0 10.1.2.1 150
ip route 10.1.1.0 255.255.255.0 10.1.3.1 151
ip route 10.1.4.0 255.255.255.0 10.1.2.1 150
ip route 10.1.4.0 255.255.255.0 10.1.3.1 151
ip route 10.1.5.0 255.255.255.0 10.1.2.1 150
ip route 10.1.5.0 255.255.255.0 10.1.3.1 151
ip route 10.1.8.0 255.255.255.0 10.1.3.1 150
ip route 10.1.8.0 255.255.255.0 10.1.2.1 151
ip route 10.1.9.0 255.255.255.0 10.1.3.1 150
ip route 10.1.9.0 255.255.255.0 10.1.2.1 151
ip route 10.1.10.0 255.255.255.0 10.1.3.1 150
ip route 10.1.10.0 255.255.255.0 10.1.2.1 151
ip route 10.1.11.0 255.255.255.0 10.1.3.1 150
ip route 10.1.11.0 255.255.255.0 10.1.2.1 151
ip route 10.1.12.0 255.255.255.0 10.1.3.1 150
ip route 10.1.12.0 255.255.255.0 10.1.2.1 151
```

This was a pretty long configuration because I configured two paths to each network. By looking at the routing table, you can see that the R1 router now understands how to find each network:

```
R1(config)#do show ip route
     10.0.0.0/24 is subnetted, 12 subnets
S       10.1.11.0 [150/0] via 10.1.3.1
S       10.1.10.0 [150/0] via 10.1.3.1
S       10.1.9.0 [150/0] via 10.1.3.1
S       10.1.8.0 [150/0] via 10.1.3.1
S       10.1.12.0 [150/0] via 10.1.3.1
C       10.1.3.0 is directly connected, Serial0/0/1
C       10.1.2.0 is directly connected, Serial0/0/0
S       10.1.1.0 [150/0] via 10.1.2.1
C       10.1.7.0 is directly connected, FastEthernet0/1
C       10.1.6.0 is directly connected, FastEthernet0/0
S       10.1.5.0 [150/0] via 10.1.2.1
S       10.1.4.0 [150/0] via 10.1.2.1
```

The R1 router now has a complete routing table. As soon as the other routers in the internetwork have all the networks in their routing table, R1 will be able to communicate with all remote networks.

Remember, the route with the higher administrative distance will not show up in the routing table unless the route with the lower administrative distance goes away.

R2

The R2 router is directly connected to three networks 10.1.4.0, 10.1.8.0, and 10.1.9.0, so these routes need to be added:

- 10.1.1.0
- 10.1.2.0
- 10.1.3.0
- 10.1.5.0
- 10.1.6.0
- 10.1.7.0
- 10.1.10.0

- 10.1.11.0
- 10.1.12.0

Here's the configuration for the R2 router:

```
R2(config)#ip route 10.1.1.0 255.255.255.0 10.1.4.1 150
R2(config)#ip route 10.1.2.0 255.255.255.0 10.1.4.1 150
R2(config)#ip route 10.1.3.0 255.255.255.0 10.1.4.1 150
R2(config)#ip route 10.1.5.0 255.255.255.0 10.1.4.1 150
R2(config)#ip route 10.1.6.0 255.255.255.0 10.1.4.1 150
R2(config)#ip route 10.1.7.0 255.255.255.0 10.1.4.1 150
R2(config)#ip route 10.1.10.0 255.255.255.0 10.1.4.1 150
R2(config)#ip route 10.1.11.0 255.255.255.0 10.1.4.1 150
R2(config)#ip route 10.1.12.0 255.255.255.0 10.1.4.1 150
R2(config)#do show run | begin ip route
ip route 10.1.1.0 255.255.255.0 10.1.4.1 150
ip route 10.1.2.0 255.255.255.0 10.1.4.1 150
ip route 10.1.3.0 255.255.255.0 10.1.4.1 150
ip route 10.1.5.0 255.255.255.0 10.1.4.1 150
ip route 10.1.6.0 255.255.255.0 10.1.4.1 150
ip route 10.1.7.0 255.255.255.0 10.1.4.1 150
ip route 10.1.10.0 255.255.255.0 10.1.4.1 150
ip route 10.1.11.0 255.255.255.0 10.1.4.1 150
ip route 10.1.12.0 255.255.255.0 10.1.4.1 150
```

The following output shows the routing table on the R2 router:

```
R2(config)#do show ip route
     10.0.0.0/24 is subnetted, 12 subnets
S       10.1.11.0 [150/0] via 10.1.4.1
S       10.1.10.0 [150/0] via 10.1.4.1
C       10.1.9.0 is directly connected, FastEthernet0/0
C       10.1.8.0 is directly connected, Dot11Radio0/3/0
S       10.1.12.0 [150/0] via 10.1.4.1
S       10.1.3.0 [150/0] via 10.1.4.1
S       10.1.2.0 [150/0] via 10.1.4.1
S       10.1.1.0 [150/0] via 10.1.4.1
S       10.1.7.0 [150/0] via 10.1.4.1
S       10.1.6.0 [150/0] via 10.1.4.1
S       10.1.5.0 [150/0] via 10.1.4.1
C       10.1.4.0 is directly connected, Serial0/2/0
```

R2 now shows all 12 networks in the internetwork, so it too can now communicate with all routers and networks (that are configured so far).

R3

The R3 router is directly connected to networks 10.1.5.0, 10.1.10.0, and 10.1.11.0, but we need to add these routes:

- 10.1.1.0
- 10.1.2.0
- 10.1.3.0
- 10.1.4.0
- 10.1.6.0
- 10.1.7.0
- 10.1.8.0
- 10.1.9.0
- 10.1.12.0

As before, I'm going to use SDM to configure the static routing for the R3 router. The configuration is pretty simple, and I can use either the next-hop address or the exit interface. Since I like to type as little as possible, I'm going with the exit interface because it only takes a mouse click.

After all our routes are configured, we can see them in the routing screen.

From this screen, it is easy to edit the static routes.

Let's take a look at the configuration and the routing table uploaded to the router from SDM:

```
R3#show run | begin ip route
ip route 10.1.1.0 255.255.255.0 Serial0/0/1 150 permanent
ip route 10.1.2.0 255.255.255.0 Serial0/0/1 150 permanent
ip route 10.1.3.0 255.255.255.0 Serial0/0/1 150 permanent
ip route 10.1.4.0 255.255.255.0 Serial0/0/1 150 permanent
ip route 10.1.6.0 255.255.255.0 Serial0/0/1 150 permanent
ip route 10.1.7.0 255.255.255.0 Serial0/0/1 150 permanent
ip route 10.1.8.0 255.255.255.0 Serial0/0/1 150 permanent
ip route 10.1.9.0 255.255.255.0 Serial0/0/1 150 permanent
ip route 10.1.12.0 255.255.255.0 FastEthernet0/1 150 permanent
R3#show ip route
     10.0.0.0/24 is subnetted, 12 subnets
C       10.1.11.0 is directly connected, FastEthernet0/1
C       10.1.10.0 is directly connected, FastEthernet0/0
S       10.1.9.0 is directly connected, Serial0/0/1
S       10.1.8.0 is directly connected, Serial0/0/1
```

```
S       10.1.12.0 is directly connected, FastEthernet0/1
S       10.1.3.0 is directly connected, Serial0/0/1
S       10.1.2.0 is directly connected, Serial0/0/1
S       10.1.1.0 is directly connected, Serial0/0/1
S       10.1.7.0 is directly connected, Serial0/0/1
S       10.1.6.0 is directly connected, Serial0/0/1
C       10.1.5.0 is directly connected, Serial0/0/1
S       10.1.4.0 is directly connected, Serial0/0/1
R3#
```

Looking at the show ip route command output, you can see that the static routes are listed as directly connected. Strange? Not really, because I used the exit interface instead of the next-hop address, and functionally, there's no difference. We really don't need the permanent command because all that will do is ensure that the route stays in the routing table even if the link to that route goes down. I configured the permanent command only because it was easy to do with SDM (just another mouse click). We're almost there—just one more router to go: the 871W.

871W

Now for this router, I'm going to configure something called default routing since the 871W is configured as a stub. A stub indicates that the wireless network in this design has only one way out to reach all other networks. I'll show you the configuration, verify the network in the next section, then I'll discuss default routing in detail. Here's the configuration:

```
871W(config)#ip route 0.0.0.0 0.0.0.0 10.1.11.1
871W(config)#ip classless
871W(config)#do show ip route
     10.0.0.0/24 is subnetted, 2 subnets
C       10.1.11.0 is directly connected, Vlan1
C       10.1.12.0 is directly connected, Dot11Radio0
S*   0.0.0.0/0 [1/0] via 10.1.11.1
871W(config)#
```

This seems a lot easier, doesn't it? And it is, but there's a catch—you can't do things like this on all routers, only on stub networks. I could've used default routing in routers R1 and R2 as well, and I didn't add the 150 to this default route even though I easily could have. I didn't do that because it's really simple to just remove the route when we get to dynamic routing later.

So we're there—we've done it! All the routers have the correct routing table, so all routers and hosts should be able to communicate without a hitch—for now. But if you add even one more network or another router to the internetwork, you'll have to update each and every router's routing tables by hand—yikes! This isn't a problem at all if you've got a small network, but it's obviously extremely time-consuming if you're dealing with a large internetwork!

Verifying Your Configuration

We're not done yet—once all the routers' routing tables are configured, they need to be verified. The best way to do this, besides using the show ip route command, is with the Ping program. I'll test and verify by pinging from the 871W router.

Here's the output:

```
871W#ping 10.1.1.2
Type escape sequence to abort.
Sending 5, 100-byte ICMP Echos to 10.1.1.2, timeout is 2 seconds:
!!!!!
Success rate is 100 percent (5/5), round-trip min/avg/max = 1/2/4 ms
```

From router 871W, a ping to HostA, B, C, and D will also test for good IP connectivity. Here's the router output:

```
871W#ping 10.1.6.2
Type escape sequence to abort.
Sending 5, 100-byte ICMP Echos to 10.1.6.2, timeout is 2 seconds:
!!!!!
Success rate is 100 percent (5/5), round-trip min/avg/max = 4/6/12 ms
871W#ping 10.1.7.2
Type escape sequence to abort.
Sending 5, 100-byte ICMP Echos to 10.1.7.2, timeout is 2 seconds:
!!!!!
Success rate is 100 percent (5/5), round-trip min/avg/max = 4/4/4 ms
871W#ping 10.1.9.2
Type escape sequence to abort.
Sending 5, 100-byte ICMP Echos to 10.1.9.2, timeout is 2 seconds:
!!!!!
Success rate is 100 percent (5/5), round-trip min/avg/max = 4/4/4 ms
871W#ping 10.1.10.2
Type escape sequence to abort.
Sending 5, 100-byte ICMP Echos to 10.1.10.2, timeout is 2 seconds:
!!!!!
Success rate is 100 percent (5/5)
```

Also, we can trace from the 871W router to see the hops the packet takes to get to HostA:

```
871W#trace 10.1.6.2
Type escape sequence to abort.
Tracing the route to 10.1.6.2
  1 10.1.11.1 0 msec 0 msec 0 msec
  2 10.1.5.1 4 msec 0 msec 4 msec
```

```
3 10.1.2.2 0 msec 0 msec 4 msec
4 10.1.6.2 4 msec 4 msec *
```

Since we can communicate from end to end and to each host without a problem, our static route configuration has been successful!

Default Routing

We use *default routing* to send packets with a remote destination network not in the routing table to the next-hop router. You should only use default routing on stub networks—those with only one exit path out of the network.

In the internetworking example used in the previous section, the only routers that are considered to be in a stub network are R1, R2, and the 871W. If you tried to put a default route on router R3, packets wouldn't be forwarded to the correct networks because they have more than one interface routing to other routers. You can easily create loops with default routing, so be careful!

To configure a default route, you use wildcards in the network address and mask locations of a static route (as I demonstrated in the 871W configuration). In fact, you can just think of a default route as a static route that uses wildcards instead of network and mask information.

By using a default route, you can just create one static route entry instead. This sure is easier then typing in all those routes!

```
871W(config)#ip route 0.0.0.0 0.0.0.0 10.1.11.1
871W(config)#ip classless
871W(config)#do show ip route
  Gateway of last resort is 10.1.11.1 to network 0.0.0.0
 10.0.0.0/24 is subnetted, 2 subnets
C      10.1.11.0 is directly connected, Vlan1
C      10.1.12.0 is directly connected, Dot11Radio0
S*   0.0.0.0/0 [1/0] via 10.1.11.1
871W(config)#
```

If you look at the routing table, you'll see only the two directly connected networks plus an S*, which indicates that this entry is a candidate for a default route. I could have completed the default route command another way:

```
871W(config)#ip route 0.0.0.0 0.0.0.0 vlan1
```

What this is telling us is that if you don't have an entry for a network in the routing table, just forward it out VLAN1 (which will send it out FastEthernet0/0). You can choose the IP address of the next-hop router or the exit interface—either way, it will work the same. Remember, I used this exit interface configuration with the R3 static route configs.

Notice also in the routing table that the gateway of last resort is now set. Even so, there's one more command you must be aware of when using default routes: the ip classless command.

All Cisco routers are classful routers, meaning they expect a default subnet mask on each interface of the router. When a router receives a packet for a destination subnet that's not in the routing table, it will drop the packet by default. If you're using default routing, you must use the `ip classless` command because it is possible that no remote subnets will be in the routing table.

Since I have version 12.4 of the IOS on my routers, the `ip classless` command is on by default. If you're using default routing and this command isn't in your configuration, you will need to add it if you have subnetted networks on your routers. The command is shown here:

```
871W(config)#ip classless
```

Notice that it's a global configuration mode command. The interesting part of the `ip classless` command is that without it, default routing sometimes works but sometimes doesn't. To be on the safe side, you should always turn on the `ip classless` command when you use default routing.

There's another command you can use to configure a gateway of last resort—the `ip default-network` command. Figure 6.10 shows a network that needs to have a gateway of last resort statement configured.

FIGURE 6.10   Configuring a gateway of last resort

Here are three commands (all providing the same solution) for adding a gateway of last resort on the gateway router to the ISP.

```
Gateway(config)#ip route 0.0.0.0 0.0.0.0 217.124.6.1
```

```
Gateway(config)#ip route 0.0.0.0 0.0.0.0 s0/0
```

```
Gateway(config)#ip default-network 217.124.6.0
```

As I said before, all three of these commands would accomplish the goal of setting the gateway of last resort, but there are some small differences between them. First, the exit interface solution would be used over the other two solutions because it has an AD of 0. Also, the `ip default-network` command would advertise the default network when you configure an IGP (like RIP) on the router. This is so other routers in your internetwork will receive this route as a default route automatically.

But what happens if you misconfigured a default route? Let's take a look at the output of a `show ip route` command and compare that to the network in Figure 6.11 and see if you can find a problem:

```
Router#sh ip route
[output cut]
Gateway of last resort is 172.19.22.2 to network 0.0.0.0

C       172.17.22.0 is directly connected, FastEthernet0/0
C       172.18.22.0  is directly connected, Serial0/0
S*      0.0.0.0/0 [1/0] via 172.19.22.2
```

FIGURE 6.11   Misconfigured default route

172.18.22.0

172.17.22.0   172.31.5.0

Find anything? You can see by looking at the figure and the directly connected routes in the routing table that the WAN link is on network 172.18.22.0 and that the default route is forwarding all packets to the 172.19.22.0 network. This is just bad—it will never work, so the problem is a misconfigured static (default) route.

One last thing before moving on to dynamic routing. If you have the routing table output as shown in the following lines, what happens if the router receives a packet from 10.1.6.100 destined for host 10.1.8.5?

```
Corp#sh ip route
[output cut]
Gateway of last resort is 10.1.5.5 to network 0.0.0.0

R       10.1.3.0 [120/1] via 10.1.2.2, 00:00:00, Serial 0/0
C       10.1.2.0  is directly connected, Serial0/0
C       10.1.5.0  is directly connected, Serial0/1
C       10.1.6.0  is directly connected, Fastethernet0/0
R*      0.0.0.0/0 [120/0] via 10.1.5.5, 00:00:00 Serial 0/1
```

This is a tad different than what I've shown you up until now because the default route is listed as R*, which means it's a RIP-injected route. This is because someone configured the `ip default-network` command on a remote router as well as configuring RIP, causing RIP to advertise this route through the internetwork as a default route. Since the destination address is 10.1.8.5 and there is no route to network 10.1.8.0, the router would use the default route and send the packet out serial 0/1.

Dynamic Routing

Dynamic routing is when protocols are used to find networks and update routing tables on routers. True, this is easier than using static or default routing, but it'll cost you in terms of router CPU processes and bandwidth on the network links. A routing protocol defines the set of rules used by a router when it communicates routing information between neighbor routers.

The routing protocol I'm going to talk about in this chapter is Routing Information Protocol (RIP) versions 1 and 2, with a bit of Interior Gateway Routing Protocol (IGRP) thrown in.

Two types of routing protocols are used in internetworks: interior gateway protocols (IGPs) and exterior gateway protocols (EGPs). IGPs are used to exchange routing information with routers in the same autonomous system (AS). An AS is a collection of networks under a common administrative domain, which basically means that all routers sharing the same routing table information are in the same AS. EGPs are used to communicate between ASes. An example of an EGP is Border Gateway Protocol (BGP), which is beyond the scope of this book.

Since routing protocols are so essential to dynamic routing, I'm going to give you the basic information you need to know about them next. Later on in this chapter, we'll focus on configuration.

Routing Protocol Basics

There are some important things you should know about routing protocols before getting deeper into RIP. Specifically, you need to understand administrative distances, the three different kinds of routing protocols, and routing loops. We will look at each of these in more detail in the following sections.

Administrative Distances

The *administrative distance (AD)* is used to rate the trustworthiness of routing information received on a router from a neighbor router. An administrative distance is an integer from 0 to 255, where 0 is the most trusted and 255 means no traffic will be passed via this route.

If a router receives two updates listing the same remote network, the first thing the router checks is the AD. If one of the advertised routes has a lower AD than the other, then the route with the lowest AD will be placed in the routing table.

If both advertised routes to the same network have the same AD, then routing protocol metrics (such as *hop count* or bandwidth of the lines) will be used to find the best path to the remote network. The advertised route with the lowest metric will be placed in the routing table. But if both advertised routes have the same AD as well as the same metrics, then the routing protocol will load-balance to the remote network (which means that it sends packets down each link).

Table 6.2 shows the default administrative distances that a Cisco router uses to decide which route to take to a remote network.

TABLE 6.2 Default Administrative Distances

Route Source	Default AD
Connected interface	0
Static route	1
EIGRP	90
IGRP	100
OSPF	110
RIP	120
External EIGRP	170
Unknown	255 (this route will never be used)

If a network is directly connected, the router will always use the interface connected to the network. If you configure a static route, the router will then believe that route over any other learned routes. You can change the administrative distance of static routes, but by default, they have an AD of 1. In our static route configuration, the AD of each route is set at 150 or 151. This lets us configure routing protocols without having to remove the static routes. They'll be used as backup routes in case the routing protocol experiences a failure of some type.

For example, if you have a static route, a RIP-advertised route, and an IGRP-advertised route listing the same network, then by default, the router will always use the static route unless you change the AD of the static route—which we did.

Routing Protocols

There are three classes of routing protocols:

Distance vector The *distance-vector protocols* find the best path to a remote network by judging distance. Each time a packet goes through a router, that's called a *hop*. The route with the least number of hops to the network is determined to be the best route. The vector indicates the direction to the remote network. Both RIP and IGRP are distance-vector routing protocols. They send the entire routing table to directly connected neighbors.

Link state In *link-state protocols*, also called *shortest-path-first protocols*, the routers each create three separate tables. One of these tables keeps track of directly attached neighbors, one determines the topology of the entire internetwork, and one is used as the routing table. Link-state routers know more about the internetwork than any distance-vector routing protocol. OSPF is an IP routing protocol that is completely link state. Link-state protocols send updates containing the state of their own links to all other routers on the network.

Hybrid *Hybrid protocols* use aspects of both distance vector and link state—for example, EIGRP.

There's no set way of configuring routing protocols for use with every business. This is something you really have to do on a case-by-case basis. If you understand how the different routing protocols work, you can make good, solid decisions that truly meet the individual needs of any business.

Distance-Vector Routing Protocols

The distance-vector routing algorithm passes complete routing table contents to neighboring routers, which then combine the received routing table entries with their own routing tables to complete the router's routing table. This is called routing by rumor, because a router receiving an update from a neighbor router believes the information about remote networks without actually finding out for itself.

It's possible to have a network that has multiple links to the same remote network, and if that's the case, the administrative distance of each received update is checked first. If the AD is the same, the protocol will have to use other metrics to determine the best path to use to that remote network.

RIP uses only hop count to determine the best path to a network. If RIP finds more than one link with the same hop count to the same remote network, it will automatically perform a round-robin load balancing. RIP can perform load balancing for up to six equal-cost links (four by default).

However, a problem with this type of routing metric arises when the two links to a remote network are different bandwidths but the same hop count. Figure 6.12, for example, shows two links to remote network 172.16.10.0.

FIGURE 6.12   Pinhole congestion

Since network 172.16.30.0 is a T1 link with a bandwidth of 1.544Mbps and network 172.16.20.0 is a 56K link, you'd want the router to choose the T1 over the 56K link, right? But because hop count is the only metric used with RIP routing, the two links would be seen as being of equal cost. This little snag is called *pinhole congestion*.

It's important to understand what a distance-vector routing protocol does when it starts up. In Figure 6.13, the four routers start off with only their directly connected networks in their routing tables. After a distance-vector routing protocol is started on each router, the routing tables are updated with all route information gathered from neighbor routers.

As shown in Figure 6.13, each router has only the directly connected networks in each routing table. Each router sends its complete routing table out to each active interface. The routing table of each router includes the network number, exit interface, and hop count to the network.

FIGURE 6.13   The internetwork with distance-vector routing

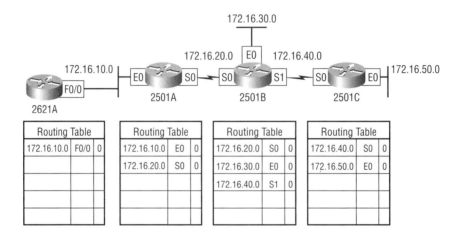

In Figure 6.14, the routing tables are complete because they include information about all the networks in the internetwork. They are considered *converged*. When the routers are converging, it is possible that no data will be passed. That's why fast convergence time is a serious plus. In fact, that's one of the problems with RIP—its slow convergence time.

The routing table in each router keeps information regarding the remote network number, the interface to which the router will send packets to reach that network, and the hop count or metric to the network.

Routing Loops

Distance-vector routing protocols keep track of any changes to the internetwork by broadcasting periodic routing updates out all active interfaces. This broadcast includes the complete routing table. This works just fine, but it's expensive in terms of CPU process and link bandwidth. And if a network outage happens, real problems can occur. Plus, the slow convergence of distance-vector routing protocols can result in inconsistent routing tables and routing loops.

Routing loops can occur because every router isn't updated simultaneously, or even close to it. Here's an example—let's say that the interface to Network 5 in Figure 6.15 fails. All routers know about Network 5 from RouterE. RouterA, in its tables, has a path to Network 5 through RouterB.

FIGURE 6.14   Converged routing tables

FIGURE 6.15   Routing loop example

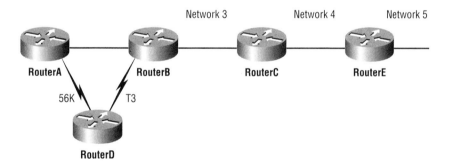

When Network 5 fails, RouterE tells RouterC. This causes RouterC to stop routing to Network 5 through RouterE. But routers A, B, and D don't know about Network 5 yet, so they keep sending out update information. RouterC will eventually send out its update and cause B to stop routing to Network 5, but routers A and D are still not updated. To them, it appears that Network 5 is still available through RouterB with a metric of 3.

The problem occurs when RouterA sends out its regular 30-second "Hello, I'm still here— these are the links I know about" message, which includes the ability to reach Network 5, and now routers B and D receive the wonderful news that Network 5 can be reached from RouterA, so routers B and D then send out the information that Network 5 is available. Any packet destined for Network 5 will go to RouterA, to RouterB, and then back to RouterA. This is a routing loop—how do you stop it?

Maximum Hop Count

The routing loop problem just described is called *counting to infinity*, and it's caused by gossip (broadcasts) and wrong information being communicated and propagated throughout the internetwork. Without some form of intervention, the hop count increases indefinitely each time a packet passes through a router.

One way of solving this problem is to define a *maximum hop count*. RIP permits a hop count of up to 15, so anything that requires 16 hops is deemed unreachable. In other words, after a loop of 15 hops, Network 5 will be considered down. Thus, the maximum hop count will control how long it takes for a routing table entry to become invalid or questionable.

Split Horizon

Another solution to the routing loop problem is called *split horizon*. This reduces incorrect routing information and routing overhead in a distance-vector network by enforcing the rule that routing information cannot be sent back in the direction from which it was received.

In other words, the routing protocol differentiates which interface a network route was learned on, and once this is determined, it won't advertise the route back out that same interface. This would have prevented RouterA from sending the updated information it received from RouterB back to RouterB.

Route Poisoning

Another way to avoid problems caused by inconsistent updates and stop network loops is *route poisoning*. For example, when Network 5 goes down, RouterE initiates route poisoning by advertising Network 5 as 16, or unreachable (sometimes referred to as *infinite*).

This poisoning of the route to Network 5 keeps RouterC from being susceptible to incorrect updates about the route to Network 5. When RouterC receives a route poisoning from RouterE, it sends an update, called a *poison reverse*, back to RouterE. This ensures that all routes on the segment have received the poisoned route information.

Holddowns

A *holddown* prevents regular update messages from reinstating a route that is going up and down (called *flapping*). Typically, this happens on a serial link that's losing connectivity and then coming back up. If there wasn't a way to stabilize this, the network would never converge and that one flapping interface could bring the entire network down!

Holddowns prevent routes from changing too rapidly by allowing time for either the downed route to come back up or the network to stabilize somewhat before changing to the next best route. These also tell routers to restrict, for a specific time period, changes that might affect recently removed routes. This prevents inoperative routes from being prematurely restored to other routers' tables.

Routing Information Protocol (RIP)

Routing Information Protocol (RIP) is a true distance-vector routing protocol. RIP sends the complete routing table out to all active interfaces every 30 seconds. RIP only uses hop count to determine the best way to a remote network, but it has a maximum allowable hop count of 15 by default, meaning that 16 is deemed unreachable. RIP works well in small networks, but it's inefficient on large networks with slow WAN links or on networks with a large number of routers installed.

RIP version 1 uses only *classful routing*, which means that all devices in the network must use the same subnet mask. This is because RIP version 1 doesn't send updates with subnet mask information in tow. RIP version 2 provides something called *prefix routing* and does send subnet mask information with the route updates. This is called *classless routing*.

In the following sections, we will discuss the RIP timers and then RIP configuration.

RIP Timers

RIP uses four different kinds of timers to regulate its performance:

Route update timer   Sets the interval (typically 30 seconds) between periodic routing updates in which the router sends a complete copy of its routing table out to all neighbors.

Route invalid timer   Determines the length of time that must elapse (180 seconds) before a router determines that a route has become invalid. It will come to this conclusion if it hasn't heard any updates about a particular route for that period. When that happens, the router will send out updates to all its neighbors letting them know that the route is invalid.

Holddown timer   This sets the amount of time during which routing information is suppressed. Routes will enter into the holddown state when an update packet is received that indicated the route is unreachable. This continues either until an update packet is received with a better metric or until the holddown timer expires. The default is 180 seconds.

Route flush timer   Sets the time between a route becoming invalid and its removal from the routing table (240 seconds). Before it's removed from the table, the router notifies its neighbors of that route's impending demise. The value of the route invalid timer must be less than that of the route flush timer. This gives the router enough time to tell its neighbors about the invalid route before the local routing table is updated.

Configuring RIP Routing

To configure RIP routing, just turn on the protocol with the `router rip` command and tell the RIP routing protocol which networks to advertise. That's it. Let's configure our five-router internetwork (Figure 6.9) with RIP routing.

Corp

RIP has an administrative distance of 120. Static routes have an administrative distance of 1 by default, and since we currently have static routes configured, the routing tables won't be propagated with RIP information. However, because I added the 150/151 to the end of each static route, we're good to go.

You can add the RIP routing protocol by using the `router rip` command and the `network` command. The `network` command tells the routing protocol which classful network to advertise.

Look at the Corp router configuration and see how easy this is:

```
Corp#config t
Corp(config)#router rip
Corp(config-router)#network 10.0.0.0
```

That's it. Two or three commands and you're done—sure makes your job a lot easier than when using static routes, doesn't it? However, keep in mind the extra router CPU process and bandwidth that you're consuming.

Notice I didn't type in subnets, only the classful network address (all subnet bits and host bits off!). It is the job of the routing protocol to find the subnets and populate the routing tables. Since we have no router buddies running RIP, we won't see any RIP routes in the routing table yet.

Remember that RIP uses the classful address when configuring the network address. Because of this, all subnet masks must be the same on all devices in the network (this is called classful routing). To clarify this, let's say you're using a Class B network address of 172.16.0.0/24 with subnets 172.16.10.0, 172.16.20.0, and 172.16.30.0. You would only type in the classful network address of 172.16.0.0 and let RIP find the subnets and place them in the routing table.

R1

Let's configure our R1 router :

```
R1#config t
R1(config)#router rip
R1(config-router)#network 10.0.0.0
R1(config-router)#do show ip route
     10.0.0.0/24 is subnetted, 12 subnets
S       10.1.11.0 [150/0] via 10.1.3.1
S       10.1.10.0 [150/0] via 10.1.3.1
S       10.1.9.0 [150/0] via 10.1.3.1
S       10.1.8.0 [150/0] via 10.1.3.1
S       10.1.12.0 [150/0] via 10.1.3.1
C       10.1.3.0 is directly connected, Serial0/0/1
C       10.1.2.0 is directly connected, Serial0/0/0
R       10.1.1.0 [120/1] via 10.1.3.1, 00:00:04, Serial0/0/1
```

```
                [120/1] via 10.1.2.1, 00:00:04, Serial0/0/0
C       10.1.7.0 is directly connected, FastEthernet0/1
C       10.1.6.0 is directly connected, FastEthernet0/0
R       10.1.5.0 [120/1] via 10.1.3.1, 00:00:04, Serial0/0/1
                [120/1] via 10.1.2.1, 00:00:04, Serial0/0/0
R       10.1.4.0 [120/1] via 10.1.3.1, 00:00:09, Serial0/0/1
                [120/1] via 10.1.2.1, 00:00:09, Serial0/0/0
R1(config-router)#
```

That was pretty straightforward. Let's talk about this routing table. Since we have one RIP buddy out there that we are exchanging routing tables with, we can see the RIP networks coming from the Corp router. (All the other routes still show up as static.) RIP also found both connections to the Corp router and will load-balance between them.

R2

Let's configure our R2 router with RIP:

```
R2#config t
R2(config)#router rip
R2(config-router)#network 10.0.0.0
R2(config-router)#do show ip route
     10.0.0.0/24 is subnetted, 12 subnets
S       10.1.11.0 [150/0] via 10.1.4.1
S       10.1.10.0 [150/0] via 10.1.4.1
C       10.1.9.0 is directly connected, FastEthernet0/0
C       10.1.8.0 is directly connected, Dot11Radio0/3/0
S       10.1.12.0 [150/0] via 10.1.4.1
R       10.1.3.0 [120/1] via 10.1.4.1, 00:00:03, Serial0/2/0
R       10.1.2.0 [120/1] via 10.1.4.1, 00:00:03, Serial0/2/0
R       10.1.1.0 [120/1] via 10.1.4.1, 00:00:03, Serial0/2/0
R       10.1.7.0 [120/2] via 10.1.4.1, 00:00:03, Serial0/2/0
R       10.1.6.0 [120/2] via 10.1.4.1, 00:00:03, Serial0/2/0
R       10.1.5.0 [120/1] via 10.1.4.1, 00:00:03, Serial0/2/0
```

The routing table is growing Rs as we add RIP buddies! We can still see that all routes are in the routing table; some are still static routes. Two more routers to go.

R3

Let's configure our R3 router with RIP—as usual with R3, we'll use the SDM.

From the routing screen, I clicked the Edit button to the right of Dynamic Routing. I then was able to configure RIP and the network number and then clicked on the interfaces I didn't want RIP to be broadcast out. The interfaces that RIP will broadcast out will be unchecked.

These are called passive interfaces and we'll talk about it more in a minute. No reason to broadcast RIP out an interface where no routers will be.

From the SDM screen, we can see that we're done with R3.

871W

Here is the last router's RIP configuration:

```
871W#config t
871W(config)#no ip route 0.0.0.0 0.0.0.0 10.1.11.1
871W(config)#router rip
871W(config-router)#network 10.0.0.0
871W(config-router)#do sh ip route
      10.0.0.0/24 is subnetted, 12 subnets
C        10.1.11.0 is directly connected, Vlan1
R        10.1.10.0 [120/1] via 10.1.11.1, 00:00:23, Vlan1
R        10.1.9.0 [120/3] via 10.1.11.1, 00:00:23, Vlan1
R        10.1.8.0 [120/3] via 10.1.11.1, 00:00:23, Vlan1
C        10.1.12.0 is directly connected, Dot11Radio0
R        10.1.3.0 [120/2] via 10.1.11.1, 00:00:23, Vlan1
R        10.1.2.0 [120/2] via 10.1.11.1, 00:00:23, Vlan1
R        10.1.1.0 [120/2] via 10.1.11.1, 00:00:23, Vlan1
R        10.1.7.0 [120/3] via 10.1.11.1, 00:00:24, Vlan1
R        10.1.6.0 [120/3] via 10.1.11.1, 00:00:24, Vlan1
R        10.1.5.0 [120/1] via 10.1.11.1, 00:00:24, Vlan1
R        10.1.4.0 [120/2] via 10.1.11.1, 00:00:24, Vlan1
871W#
```

Finally, all routes showing in the routing table are RIP injected routes.

It's important to remember administrative distances and why we needed to either remove the static routes before we added RIP routing or set them higher than 120 as we did.

By default, directly connected routes have an administrative distance of 0, static routes have an administrative distance of 1, and RIP has an administrative distance of 120. I call RIP the "gossip protocol" because it reminds me of junior high school, where if you hear a rumor (advertised route), it just has to be true without exception. And that pretty much sums up how RIP behaves on an internetwork—rumor mill as protocol!

Verifying the RIP Routing Tables

Each routing table should now have all directly connected routes as well as RIP-injected routes received from neighboring routers.

This output shows us the contents of the Corp routing table:

```
      10.0.0.0/24 is subnetted, 12 subnets
R        10.1.11.0 [120/1] via 10.1.5.2, 00:00:28, Serial0/2/0
R        10.1.10.0 [120/1] via 10.1.5.2, 00:00:28, Serial0/2/0
```

```
R       10.1.9.0 [120/1] via 10.1.4.2, 00:00:26, Serial0/1/0
R       10.1.8.0 [120/1] via 10.1.4.2, 00:00:26, Serial0/1/0
R       10.1.12.0 [120/2] via 10.1.5.2, 00:00:28, Serial0/2/0
C       10.1.3.0 is directly connected, Serial0/0/1
C       10.1.2.0 is directly connected, Serial0/0/0
C       10.1.1.0 is directly connected, FastEthernet0/1
R       10.1.7.0 [120/1] via 10.1.3.2, 00:00:07, Serial0/0/1
                 [120/1] via 10.1.2.2, 00:00:10, Serial0/0/0
R       10.1.6.0 [120/1] via 10.1.3.2, 00:00:07, Serial0/0/1
                 [120/1] via 10.1.2.2, 00:00:10, Serial0/0/0
C       10.1.5.0 is directly connected, Serial0/2/0
C       10.1.4.0 is directly connected, Serial0/1/0
```

This output shows us that the routing table has the same entries that it had when we were using static routes—except for that R. The R means that the networks were added dynamically using the RIP routing protocol. The [120/1] is the administrative distance of the route (120) along with the number of hops to that remote network (1). From the Corp router, all networks are one hop away except network 10.1.12.0, which is two hops away.

So while yes, it's true that RIP has worked in our little internetwork, it's not the solution for every enterprise. That's because this technique has a maximum hop count of only 15 (16 is deemed unreachable). Plus, it performs full routing-table updates every 30 seconds, which would bring a larger internetwork to a painful crawl pretty quick!

There's one more thing I want to show you about RIP routing tables and the parameters used to advertise remote networks. Notice, as an example, that the following routing table shows [120/15] in the 10.1.3.0 network metric. This means that the administrative distance is 120, the default for RIP, but the hop count is 15. Remember that each time a router sends out an update to a neighbor router, it increments the hop count by one for each route.

```
R3#sh ip route
     10.0.0.0/24 is subnetted, 12 subnets
C       10.1.11.0 is directly connected, FastEthernet0/1
C       10.1.10.0 is directly connected, FastEthernet0/0
R       10.1.9.0 [120/2] via 10.1.5.1, 00:00:15, Serial0/0/1
R       10.1.8.0 [120/2] via 10.1.5.1, 00:00:15, Serial0/0/1
R       10.1.12.0 [120/1] via 10.1.11.2, 00:00:00, FastEthernet0/1
R       10.1.3.0 [120/15] via 10.1.5.1, 00:00:15, Serial0/0/1
R       10.1.2.0 [120/1] via 10.1.5.1, 00:00:15, Serial0/0/1
R       10.1.1.0 [120/1] via 10.1.5.1, 00:00:15, Serial0/0/1
R       10.1.7.0 [120/2] via 10.1.5.1, 00:00:15, Serial0/0/1
R       10.1.6.0 [120/2] via 10.1.5.1, 00:00:15, Serial0/0/1
C       10.1.5.0 is directly connected, Serial0/0/1
R       10.1.4.0 [120/1] via 10.1.5.1, 00:00:15, Serial0/0/1
R3#
```

So this [120/15] is really bad because the next router that receives the table from router R3 will just discard the route to network 10.1.3.0 since the hop count would then be 16, which is invalid.

> If a router receives a routing update that contains a higher-cost path to a network that's already in its routing table, the update will be ignored.

Configuring RIP Routing Example 2

Before we move onto learning more about RIP configurations, let's take a look at Figure 6.16. In this example, we first will find and implement our subnets and then add the RIP configuration to the router.

FIGURE 6.16   RIP routing example 2

For this configuration, we are going to consider that the Lab_B and Lab_C routers are already configured and we just need to configure the Lab_A router. We will use the network ID of 192.168.164.0/28. The s0/0 interface of Lab_A will use the last available IP address in the eighth subnet and the fa0/0 will use the last available IP address in the second subnet. Do not consider the zero subnet valid.

Before we start, you do know that /28 is a 255.255.255.240 mask, right? And that we have a block size of 16 in the fourth octet? It is very important that you know this, and if you need another review of Chapters 2 and 3, that's okay! Reviewing subnetting will never hurt you.

Since we have a block size of 16, our subnets are 16 (remember we are not starting at zero for this example), 32, 48, 64, 80, 96, 112, 128, 144, etc. The eighth subnet (which we will use for the s0/0 interface) is subnet 128. The valid host range for the 128 subnet is 129 through 142, and 143 is the broadcast address of the 128 subnet. The second subnet (which we will use for the fa0/0 interface) is the 32 subnet. The valid hosts are 33 through 46, and 47 is the broadcast address of the 32 subnet.

So, here is what our configuration on the Lab_A router will look like:

```
Lab_A(config)#interface s0/0
Lab_A(config-if)#ip address 192.168.164.142 255.255.255.240
Lab_A(config-if)#no shutdown
```

```
Lab_A(config-if)#interface fa0/0
Lab_A(config-if)#ip address 192.168.164.46 255.255.255.240
Lab_A(config-if)#no shutdown
Lab_A(config-if)#router rip
Lab_A(config-router)#network 192.168.164.0
Lab_A(config-router)#^Z
Lab_A#
```

Finding the subnets and configuring the last valid host should be pretty straightforward. If not, head back to Chapter 3. However, what I really want you to notice is that although we added two subnets to the Lab_A router, we only had one network statement under RIP. Sometimes it is hard to remember that you configure only the classful network statement, which means you turn all host bits off.

This was the real purpose of this second RIP configuration example—to remind you of classful network addressing. And it never hurts to practice subnetting, right?

Holding Down RIP Propagations

You probably don't want your RIP network advertised everywhere on your LAN and WAN. There's not a whole lot to be gained by advertising your RIP network to the Internet, now, is there?

There's a few different ways to stop unwanted RIP updates from propagating across your LANs and WANs, and the easiest one is through the `passive-interface` command that I showed you during the R3 configuration. This command prevents RIP update broadcasts from being sent out a specified interface, yet that same interface can still receive RIP updates.

Here's an example of how to configure a `passive-interface` on a router using the CLI:

```
Lab_A#config t
Lab_A(config)#router rip
Lab_A(config-router)#network 192.168.10.0
Lab_A(config-router)#passive-interface serial 0/0
```

This command will stop RIP updates from being propagated out serial interface 0/0, but serial interface 0/0 can still receive RIP updates. This is easily done within the SDM configuration as well, as I demonstrated with the R3 router.

RIP Version 2 (RIPv2)

Let's spend a couple of minutes discussing RIPv2 before we move into the distance-vector, Cisco-proprietary routing protocol IGRP.

RIP version 2 is mostly the same as RIP version 1. Both RIPv1 and RIPv2 are distance-vector protocols, which means that each router running RIP sends its complete routing tables out all active interfaces at periodic time intervals. Also, the timers and loop-avoidance schemes are the same in both RIP versions (i.e., holddown timers and split horizon rule). Both RIPv1 and RIPv2 are configured as classful addressing (but RIPv2 is considered classless because subnet information is sent with each route update), and both have the same administrative distance (120).

⊕ Real World Scenario

Should We Really Use RIP in an Internetwork?

You have been hired as a consultant to install a couple of Cisco routers into a growing network. They have a couple of old Unix routers that they want to keep in the network. These routers do not support any routing protocol except RIP. I guess this means you just have to run RIP on the entire network.

Well, yes and no. You can run RIP on a router connecting that old network, but you certainly don't need to run RIP throughout the whole internetwork!

You can do what is called *redistribution*, which is basically translating from one type of routing protocol to another. This means that you can support those old routers using RIP but use Enhanced IGRP, for example, on the rest of your network.

This will stop RIP routes from being sent all over the internetwork and eating up all that precious bandwidth.

But there are some important differences that make RIPv2 more scalable than RIPv1. And I've got to add a word of advice here before we move on; I'm definitely not advocating using RIP of either version in your network. But since RIP is an open standard, you can use RIP with any brand of router. You can also use OSPF (discussed in Chapter 7) since OSPF is an open standard as well. RIP just requires too much bandwidth, making it pretty intensive to use in your network. Why go there when you have other, more elegant options?

Table 6.3 discusses the differences between RIPv1 and RIPv2.

TABLE 6.3   RIPv1 vs. RIPv2

RIPv1	RIPv2
Distance vector	Distance vector
Maximum hop count of 15	Maximum hop count of 15
Classful	Classless
Broadcast based	Uses multicast 224.0.0.9
No support for VLSM	Supports VLSM networks
No authentication	Allows for MD5 authentication
No support for discontiguous networks	Supports discontiguous networks

RIPv2, unlike RIPv1, is a classless routing protocol (even though it is configured as classful, like RIPv1), which means that it sends subnet mask information along with the route updates. By sending the subnet mask information with the updates, RIPv2 can support Variable Length Subnet Masks (VLSMs) as well as the summarization of network boundaries. In addition, RIPv2 can support discontiguous networking, which I'll go over more in Chapter 7.

Configuring RIPv2 is pretty straightforward. Here's an example:

```
Lab_C(config)#router rip
Lab_C(config-router)#network 192.168.40.0
Lab_C(config-router)#network 192.168.50.0
Lab_C(config-router)#version 2
```

That's it; just add the command **version 2** under the (`config-router`)# prompt and you are now running RIPv2.

 RIPv2 is classless and works in VLSM and discontiguous networks.

Interior Gateway Routing Protocol (IGRP)

Interior Gateway Routing Protocol (IGRP) is a Cisco-proprietary distance-vector routing protocol. This means that to use IGRP in your network, all your routers must be Cisco routers. Cisco created this routing protocol to overcome the problems associated with RIP.

IGRP has a maximum hop count of 255 with the default being 100 (same as EIGRP). This is helpful in larger networks and solves the problem of 15 hops being the maximum possible in a RIP network.

IGRP also uses a different metric than RIP. IGRP uses bandwidth and delay of the line by default as a metric for determining the best route to an internetwork. This is called a *composite metric*. Reliability, load, and maximum transmission unit (MTU) can also be used, although they are not used by default.

 The main difference between RIP and IGRP configuration is that when you configure IGRP, you supply the autonomous system number. All routers must use the same number in order to share routing table information.

Table 6.4 shows a list of IGRP characteristics that you won't find in RIP.

TABLE 6.4 IGRP vs. RIP

IGRP	RIP
Can be used in large internetworks	Works best in smaller networks
Uses an autonomous system number for activation	Does not use autonomous system numbers
Gives a full route table update every 90 seconds	Gives a full route table update every 30 seconds
Has an administrative distance of 100	Has an administrative distance of 120
Uses bandwidth and delay of the line as metric (lowest composite metric), with a maximum hop count of 255	Uses only hop count to determine the best path to a remote network, with 15 hops being the maximum

Why is this the end of the IGRP section? Because watch what happens when I try to configure IGRP on my router:

```
R3#config t
Enter configuration commands, one per line.  End with CNTL/Z.
R3(config)#router igrp 10
                   ^
% Invalid input detected at '^' marker.
R3(config)#
```

There's your reason—Cisco no longer supports IGRP. Why should it? All you have to do is put an *E* in front of *IGRP* and you're running a much, much better routing protocol. We'll get to EIGRP in the next chapter, but first, let's go through some verification commands for RIP.

Verifying Your Configurations

It's important to verify your configurations once you've completed them, or at least once you *think* you've completed them. The following list includes the commands you can use to verify the routed and routing protocols configured on your Cisco routers:

- `show ip route`
- `show ip protocols`
- `debug ip rip`

The first command was covered in the previous section—I'll go over the others in the sections that follow.

The *show ip protocols* Command

The show ip protocols command shows you the routing protocols that are configured on your router. Looking at the following output, you can see that RIP is running on the router and the timers that RIP uses:

```
R3#sh ip protocols
Routing Protocol is "rip"
  Outgoing update filter list for all interfaces is not set
  Incoming update filter list for all interfaces is not set
  Sending updates every 30 seconds, next due in 24 seconds
  Invalid after 180 seconds, hold down 180, flushed after 240
  Redistributing: rip
  Default version control: send version 1, receive version 1
    Interface             Send  Recv  Triggered RIP  Key-chain
    FastEthernet0/1       1     1
    Serial0/0/1           1     1
  Automatic network summarization is not in effect
  Maximum path: 4
  Routing for Networks:
    10.0.0.0
  Passive Interface(s):
    FastEthernet0/0
    Serial0/0/0
  Routing Information Sources:
    Gateway         Distance      Last Update
    10.1.11.2            120      00:00:10
    10.1.5.1             120      00:00:22
  Distance: (default is 120)
```

Notice in this output that RIP is sending updates every 30 seconds, which is the default. The timers used in distance vector are also shown.

Notice further down that RIP is routing for directly connected interfaces f0/1 and s0/0/1. The version is listed to the right of the interfaces—RIPv1.

F0/0 and s0/0/0 are listed as passive interfaces (they will not send RIP information out). The neighbors it found are 10.1.11.2 and 10.1.5.1. The last entry is the default AD for RIP (120).

Troubleshooting with the *show ip protocols* Command

Let's use a sample router and use the show ip protocols command to see what we can determine about routing by looking at this output from a router on another network:

```
Router#sh ip protocols
Routing Protocol is "rip"
```

```
Sending updates every 30 seconds, next due in 6 seconds
Invalid after 180 seconds, hold down 180, flushed after240
Outgoing update filter list for all interfaces is
Incoming update filter list for all interfaces is
Redistributing: rip
Default version control: send version 1, receive any version
    Interface        Send  Recv   Key-chain
    Serial0/0          1    1 2
    Serial0/1          1    1 2
Routing for Networks:
    10.0.0.0
Routing Information Sources:
    Gateway          Distance    Last Update
    10.168.11.14        120      00:00:21
Distance: (default is 120)
```

Let's also look at the `show ip interface brief` command from the same router and see what we find out:

```
Router#sh ip interface brief
Interface        IP-Address     OK?    Method Status
FastEthernet0/0  192.168.18.1   YES    manual up
Serial0/0        10.168.11.17   YES    manual up
FastEthernet0/1  unassigned     YES    NRAM   Administratively down
Serial0/1        192.168.11.21  YES    manual up
```

Under the `show ip protocols` output, you can see that we're using RIP routing for network 10.0.0.0, which means our configuration would look like this:

```
Router(config)#router rip
Router(config-router)#network 10.0.0.0
```

Also, only serial 0/0 and serial 0/1 are participating in the RIP network. And last, our neighbor router is 10.168.11.14.

From the output of the `show ip interface brief` command, you can see that only serial 0/0 is in the 10.0.0.0 network. This means that the router will only send and receive routing updates with the 10.0.0.0 network and not advertise the 192.168.0.0 networks out any interface.

The *debug ip rip* Command

The `debug ip rip` command sends routing updates as they are sent and received on the router to the console session. If you are telnetted into the router, you'll need to use the `terminal monitor` command to be able to receive the output from the `debug` commands.

We can see in this output that RIP is both sending and receiving (the metric is the hop count):

```
R3#debug ip rip
RIP protocol debugging is on
R3#terminal monitor
*Mar 17 19:08:34.371: RIP: sending v1 update to 255.255.255.255 via
    Serial0/0/1 (10.1.5.2)
*Mar 17 19:08:34.371: RIP: build update entries
*Mar 17 19:08:34.371:    subnet 10.1.10.0 metric 1
*Mar 17 19:08:34.371:    subnet 10.1.11.0 metric 1
*Mar 17 19:08:34.371:    subnet 10.1.12.0 metric 2
*Mar 17 19:08:40.107: RIP: received v1 update from 10.1.5.1 on
    Serial0/0/1
*Mar 17 19:08:40.107:        10.1.1.0 in 1 hops
*Mar 17 19:08:40.107:        10.1.2.0 in 1 hops
*Mar 17 19:08:40.107:        10.1.3.0 in 1 hops
*Mar 17 19:08:40.107:        10.1.4.0 in 1 hops
*Mar 17 19:08:40.107:        10.1.6.0 in 2 hops
*Mar 17 19:08:40.107:        10.1.7.0 in 2 hops
*Mar 17 19:08:40.107:        10.1.8.0 in 2 hops
*Mar 17 19:08:40.107:        10.1.9.0 in 2 hops
*Mar 17 19:08:47.535: RIP: sending v1 update to 255.255.255.255 via
    FastEthernet0/1 (10.1.11.1)
*Mar 17 19:08:47.535: RIP: build update entries
*Mar 17 19:08:47.535:    subnet 10.1.1.0 metric 2
*Mar 17 19:08:47.535:    subnet 10.1.2.0 metric 2
*Mar 17 19:08:47.535:    subnet 10.1.3.0 metric 2
*Mar 17 19:08:47.535:    subnet 10.1.4.0 metric 2
*Mar 17 19:08:47.535:    subnet 10.1.5.0 metric 1
*Mar 17 19:08:47.535:    subnet 10.1.6.0 metric 3
*Mar 17 19:08:47.535:    subnet 10.1.7.0 metric 3
*Mar 17 19:08:47.535:    subnet 10.1.8.0 metric 3
*Mar 17 19:08:47.535:    subnet 10.1.9.0 metric 3
*Mar 17 19:08:47.535:    subnet 10.1.10.0 metric 1
*Mar 17 19:08:49.331: RIP: received v1 update from 10.1.11.2 on
    FastEthernet0/1
*Mar 17 19:08:49.331:        10.1.12.0 in 1 hops
R3#undeug all
*Mar 17 19:08:47.535:    subnet 10.1.10.0 metric 1
*Mar 17 19:08:49.331: RIP: received v1 update from 10.1.11.2 on
    FastEthernet0/1
```

Let's talk about the parts I highlighted. First, RIP is sending v1 packet to 255.255.255.255—an "all-hands" broadcast—out interface serial0/0/1 via 10.1.5.2. This is where RIPv2 will come in handy. Why? Because RIPv2 doesn't send broadcasts; it used the multicast 224.0.0.9. So even though the RIP packets could be transmitted onto a network with no routers, all hosts would just ignore them, making RIPv2 a bit of an improvement over RIPv1. On our R3, we are using the `passive-interface` so we are not sending broadcasts out to a LAN with no routers connected.

Okay—now check out the fact that it's sending advertisements for all networks except 10.1.11.0 and 10.1.12.0 out FastEthernet0/1, yet the last advertisement out serial0/0/1 is only advertising networks 10.1.10.0, 10.1.11.0, and 10.1.12.0. Why? If you answered split horizon rules, you nailed it! Our R3 router will not advertise all those networks received from the Corp router back to the Corp router.

 If the metric of a route shows 16, this is a route poison, and the route being advertised is unreachable.

Troubleshooting with the *debug ip rip* Command

Now let's use the `debug ip rip` command to both discover a problem and figure out how RIP was configured on a router from a different sample network:

```
07:12:58: RIP: sending v1 update to 255.255.255.255 via
  FastEthernet0/0 (172.16.1.1)
07:12:58:  network 10.0.0.0, metric 1
07:12:58:  network 192.168.1.0, metric 2
07:12:58: RIP: sending v1 update to 255.255.255.255 via
  Serial0/0 (10.0.8.1)
07:12:58:  network 172.16.0.0, metric 1
07:12:58: RIP: Received v1 update from 10.0.15.2 n Serial0/0
07:12:58: 192.168.1.0 in one hop
07:12:58: 192.168.168.0 in 16 hops (inaccessible)
```

You can see from the updates that we're sending out information about networks 10.0.0.0, 192.168.1.0, and 172.16.0.0. But both the 10.0.0.0 network and the 172.16.0.0 network are being advertised with a hop count (metric) of 1, meaning that these networks are directly connected. The 192.168.1.0 is being advertised as a metric of 2, which means that it is not directly connected.

For this to be happening, our configuration would have to look like this:

```
Router(config)#router rip
Router(config-router)#network 10.0.0.0
Router(config-router)#network 172.16.0.0
```

And there's something else you can find out by looking at this: There are at least two routers participating in the RIP network because we're sending out two interfaces but only receiving RIP updates on one interface. Also, notice that the network 192.168.168.0 is being advertised as 16 hops away. RIP has a maximum hop count of 15, so 16 is considered unreachable, making this network inaccessible. So what will happen if you try to ping to a host on network 192.168.168.0? You just will not be successful, that's what! But if you try any pings to network 10.0.0.0, you should be successful.

I have one more output I want to show you—see if you can find the problem. Both a debug ip rip and a show ip route output are shown from our sample router:

```
07:12:56: RIP: received v1 update from 172.16.100.2 on Serial0/0
07:12:56:       172.16.10.0 in 1 hops
07:12:56:       172.16.20.0 in 1 hops
07:12:56:       172.16.30.0 in 1 hops
```

```
Router#sh ip route
[output cut]
Gateway of last resort is not set

   172.16.0.0/24 is subnetted, 8 subnets
C  172.16.150.0 is directly connected, FastEthernet0/0
C  172.16.220.0 is directly connected, Loopback2
R  172.16.210.0 is directly connected, Loopback1
R  172.16.200.0 is directly connected, Loopback0
R  172.16.30.0 [120/2] via 172.16.100.2, 00:00:04, Serial0/0
S  172.16.20.0 [120/2] via 172.16.150.15
R  172.16.10.0 [120/2] via 172.16.100.2, 00:00:04, Serial0/0
R  172.16.100.0 [120/2] is directly connected, Serial0/0
```

Looking at the two outputs, can you tell why users can't access 172.16.20.0?

The debug output shows that network 172.16.20.0 is one hop away and being received on serial0/0 from 172.16.100.2. By checking out the show ip route output, you can see that packets with a destination of 172.16.20.0 are being sent to 172.16.150.15 because of a static route. The output also shows that 172.16.150.0 is directly connected to FastEthernet 0/0 and network 172.16.20.0 is out serial 0/0.

Enabling RIPv2 on Our Internetwork

Before we move on to Chapter 7 and configure EIGRP and OSPF, I want to enable RIPv2 on our routers. It'll only take a second. Here are my configurations:

```
Corp#config t
Corp(config)#router rip
```

```
Corp(config-router)#version 2
Corp(config-router)#^Z

R1#config t
R1(config)#router rip
R1(config-router)#version 2
R1(config-router)#^Z

R2#config t
Enter configuration commands, one per line.  End with CNTL/Z.
R2(config)#router rip
R2(config-router)#version 2
R2(config-router)#^Z
```

For the R3 router, I just clicked the Version2 button and clicked OK. Done.

```
871W#config t
871W#(config)#router rip
871W#(config-router)#version 2
871W#(config-router)#^Z
```

This was probably the easiest configuration we have done in the book so far. Let's see if we can find a difference in our routing tables. Here's the R3 router's routing table now:

```
    10.0.0.0/24 is subnetted, 12 subnets
C       10.1.11.0 is directly connected, FastEthernet0/1
C       10.1.10.0 is directly connected, FastEthernet0/0
R       10.1.9.0 [120/2] via 10.1.5.1, 00:00:23, Serial0/0/1
R       10.1.8.0 [120/2] via 10.1.5.1, 00:00:23, Serial0/0/1
R       10.1.12.0 [120/1] via 10.1.11.2, 00:00:18, FastEthernet0/1
R       10.1.3.0 [120/1] via 10.1.5.1, 00:00:23, Serial0/0/1
R       10.1.2.0 [120/1] via 10.1.5.1, 00:00:23, Serial0/0/1
R       10.1.1.0 [120/1] via 10.1.5.1, 00:00:23, Serial0/0/1
R       10.1.7.0 [120/2] via 10.1.5.1, 00:00:23, Serial0/0/1
R       10.1.6.0 [120/2] via 10.1.5.1, 00:00:23, Serial0/0/1
C       10.1.5.0 is directly connected, Serial0/0/1
R       10.1.4.0 [120/1] via 10.1.5.1, 00:00:23, Serial0/0/1
R3#
```

Well—looks the same to me. I'm going to turn on debugging and see if that shows us anything new:

```
*Mar 17 19:34:00.123: RIP: sending v2 update to 224.0.0.9 via
   Serial0/0/1 (10.1.5.2)
*Mar 17 19:34:00.123: RIP: build update entries
*Mar 17 19:34:00.123:    10.1.10.0/24 via 0.0.0.0, metric 1, tag 0
*Mar 17 19:34:00.123:    10.1.11.0/24 via 0.0.0.0, metric 1, tag 0
*Mar 17 19:34:00.123:    10.1.12.0/24 via 0.0.0.0, metric 2, tag 0col
*Mar 17 19:34:03.795: RIP: received v2 update from 10.1.5.1 on
   Serial0/0/1
[output cut]
```

Bingo! Look at that! The networks are still being advertised every 30 seconds, but they're now sending the advertisements as v2 and as a multicast address of 224.0.0.9. Let's take a look at the show ip protocols output:

```
R3#sh ip protocols
Routing Protocol is "rip"
  Outgoing update filter list for all interfaces is not set
  Incoming update filter list for all interfaces is not set
  Sending updates every 30 seconds, next due in 27 seconds
  Invalid after 180 seconds, hold down 180, flushed after 240
  Redistributing: rip
  Default version control: send version 2, receive version 2
```

```
   Interface            Send  Recv  Triggered RIP  Key-chain
   FastEthernet0/1       2     2
   Serial0/0/1           2     2
Automatic network summarization is not in effect
Maximum path: 4
Routing for Networks:
   10.0.0.0
Passive Interface(s):
   FastEthernet0/0
   Serial0/0/0
Routing Information Sources:
   Gateway        Distance      Last Update
   10.1.11.2           120      00:00:00
   10.1.5.1            120      00:00:02
Distance: (default is 120)
```

We are now sending and receiving RIPv2. Nice when things work out well, huh? You're ready now to move on to the next chapter!

Summary

This chapter covered IP routing in detail. It's extremely important that you really understand the basics we covered in this chapter because everything that's done on a Cisco router typically will have some type of IP routing configured and running.

You learned in this chapter how IP routing uses frames to transport packets between routers and to the destination host. From there, we configured static routing on our routers and discussed the administrative distance used by IP to determine the best route to a destination network. If you have a stub network, you can configure default routing, which sets the gateway of last resort on a router.

We then discussed dynamic routing in detail, specifically RIP and how it works on an internetwork (not well). We finished by verifying RIP and then adding RIPv2 to our little internetwork.

In the next chapter, we'll continue on with dynamic routing by discussing EIGRP and OSPF.

Exam Essentials

Understand the basic IP routing process.   You need to remember that the frame changes at each hop but that the packet is never changed or manipulated in any way until it reaches the destination device.

Understand that MAC addresses are always local. A MAC (hardware) address will only be used on a local LAN. It will never pass a router's interface.

Understand that a frame carries a packet to only two places. A frame uses MAC (hardware) addresses to send a packet on a LAN. The frame will take the packet to either a host on the LAN or a router's interface if the packet is destined for a remote network

Understand how to configure RIP routing. To configure RIP routing, first you must be in global configuration mode and then you type the command **router rip**. Then you add all directly connected networks, making sure to use the classful address.

Remember how to verify RIP routing. The show ip route command will provide you with the contents of the routing table. An R on the left side of the table indicates a RIP-found route. The debug ip rip command will show you RIP updates being sent and received on your router. If you see a route with a metric of 16, that route is considered down.

Remember the differences between RIPv1 and RIPv2. RIPv1 sends broadcasts every 30 seconds and has an AD of 120. RIPv2 sends multicasts (224.0.0.9) every 30 seconds and also has an AD of 120. RIPv2 sends subnet mask information with the route updates, which allows it to support classless networks and discontiguous networks. RIPv2 also supports authentication between routers and RIPv1 does not.

Written Lab 6

Write the answers to the following questions:

1. Create a static route to network 172.16.10.0/24 with a next-hop gateway of 172.16.20.1 and an administrative distance of 150.

2. From the SDM you have just enabled RIP and the passive-interface box for your serial interface is unchecked. What does this mean?

3. What command will you type to create a default route to 172.16.40.1?

4. If you are using default routing, what command must also be used?

5. You would use a default route on which type of network?

6. To see the routing table on your router, what command will you use?

7. When creating a static or default route, you don't have to use the next-hop IP address; you can use the _____.

8. True/False: To reach a destination host, you must know the MAC address of the remote host.

9. True/False: To reach a destination host, you must know the IP address of the remote host.

10. If you have a DCE serial interface, what command must you enter for that interface to work?

11. Write the commands used to turn RIP routing on in a router and advertise network 10.0.0.0.

12. Write the commands to stop a router from propagating RIP information out serial 1.

13. What works with triggered updates to help stop routing loops in distance-vector networks?

14. What stops routing loops in distance-vector networks by sending out a maximum hop count as soon as a link fails?

15. What stops routing loops in distance-vector networks by not resending information learned on an interface out that same interface?

16. What command is used to send RIP routing updates as they are sent and received on the router to the console session?

(The answers to Written Lab 6 can be found following the answers to the review questions for this chapter.)

Hands-on Labs

In the following hands-on labs, you will configure a network with three routers.

> The hands-on labs in this section is included for use with real Cisco routers. If you are using software from RouterSim or Sybex, please use the hands-on labs found in those programs.

This chapter includes:
Lab 6.1: Creating Static Routes
Lab 6.2: Configuring RIP Routing
Figure 6.17 will be used to configure all routers.

FIGURE 6.17   Hands-on lab internetwork

Table 6.5 shows our IP addresses for each router (each interface uses a /24 mask).

TABLE 6.5   Our IP Addresses

Router	Interface	IP Address
Lab_A	F0/0	172.16.10.1
Lab_A	S0/0	172.16.20.1
Lab_B	S0/0	172.16.20.2
Lab_B	S0/1	172.16.30.1
Lab_C	S0/0	172.16.30.2
Lab_C	Fa0/0	172.16.40.1

These labs were written without using the LAN interface on the Lab_B router. You can choose to add that LAN into the labs if necessary.

Hands-on Lab 6.1: Creating Static Routes

In this lab, you will create a static route in all three routers so that the routers see all networks. Verify with the Ping program when complete.

1. The Lab_A router is connected to two networks, 172.16.10.0 and 172.16.20.0. You need to add routes to networks 172.16.30.0 and 172.16.40.0.

   ```
   Lab_A#config t
   Lab_A(config)#ip route 172.16.30.0 255.255.255.0
     172.16.20.2
   Lab_A(config)#ip route 172.16.40.0 255.255.255.0
     172.16.20.2
   ```

2. Save the current configuration for the Lab_A router by going to the privileged mode, typing **copy run start**, and pressing Enter.

3. On the Lab_B router, you have direct connections to networks 172.16.20.0 and 172.16.30.0. You need to add routes to networks 172.16.10.0 and 172.16.40.0.

   ```
   Lab_B#config t
   Lab_B(config)#ip route 172.16.10.0 255.255.255.0
     172.16.20.1
   Lab_B(config)#ip route 172.16.40.0 255.255.255.0
     172.16.30.2
   ```

4. Save the current configuration for router Lab_B by going to the enabled mode, typing **copy run start**, and pressing Enter.

5. On Router Lab_C, create a static route to see networks 172.16.10.0 and 172.16.20.0, which are not directly connected. Create static routes so that Router Lab_C can see all networks, as shown here:

```
Lab_C#config t
Lab_C(config)#ip route 172.16.10.0 255.255.255.0
    172.16.30.1
Lab_C(config)#ip route 172.16.20.0 255.255.255.0
    172.16.30.1
```

6. Save the current configuration for Router Lab_C by going to the enable mode, typing **copy run start**, and pressing Enter.

7. Check your routing tables to make sure all four networks show up.

8. Now ping from each router to your hosts and from each router to each router. If it is set up correctly, it will work.

Hands-on Lab 6.2: Configuring RIP Routing

In this lab, we will use the dynamic routing protocol RIP instead of static routing.

1. Remove any static routes or default routes configured on your routers by using the no ip route command. For example, here is how you would remove the static routes on the Lab_A router:

```
Lab_A#config t
Lab_A(config)#no ip route 172.16.30.0 255.255.255.0
    172.16.20.2
Lab_A(config)#no ip route 172.16.40.0 255.255.255.0
    172.16.20.2
```

Do the same thing for routers Lab_B and Lab_C. Verify that only your directly connected networks are in the routing tables.

2. After your static and default routes are clear, go into configuration mode on Router Lab_A by typing **config t**.

3. Tell your router to use RIP routing by typing **router rip** and pressing Enter, as shown here:

```
config t
router rip
```

4. Add the network number you want to advertise by typing **network 172.16.0.0** and pressing Enter.

5. Press Ctrl+Z to get out of configuration mode.

6.   Go to routers Lab_B and Lab_C and type the same commands, as shown here:

```
Config t
Router rip
network 172.16.0.0
```

7.   Verify that RIP is running at each router by typing the following commands at each router:

```
show ip protocols
show ip route
show running-config or show run
```

8.   Save your configurations by typing **copy run start** or **copy running-config startup-config** and pressing Enter at each router.

9.   Verify the network by pinging all remote networks and hosts.

Review Questions

The following questions are designed to test your understanding of this chapter's material. For more information on how to get additional questions, please see this book's Introduction.

1. Network 206.143.5.0 was assigned to the Acme Company to connect to its ISP. The administrator of Acme would like to configure one router with the commands to access the Internet. Which commands could be configured on the Gateway router to allow Internet access to the entire network? (Choose two.)

   A. Gateway(config)#**ip route 0.0.0.0 0.0.0.0 206.143.5.2**

   B. Gateway(config)#**router rip**

   Gateway(config-router)#**network 206.143.5.0**

   C. Gateway(config)#**router rip**

   Gateway(config-router)#**network 206.143.5.0 default**

   D. Gateway(config)#**ip route 206.143.5.0 255.255.255.0 default**

   E. Gateway(config)#**ip default-network 206.143.5.0**

2. What command is used to stop RIP routing updates from exiting out an interface but still allow the interface to receive RIP route updates?

   A. Router(config-if)#**no routing**

   B. Router(config-if)#**passive-interface**

   C. Router(config-router)#**passive-interface s0**

   D. Router(config-router)#**no routing updates**

3. Which of the following statements are true regarding the command ip route 172.16.4.0 255.255.255.0 192.168.4.2? (Choose two.)

   A. The command is used to establish a static route.

   B. The default administrative distance is used.

   C. The command is used to configure the default route.

   D. The subnet mask for the source address is 255.255.255.0.

   E. The command is used to establish a stub network.

4. What destination addresses will be used by Host_A to send data to the HTTPS server as shown in the following network? (Choose two.)

RouterA

Fa0/1

Fa0/0

HTTPS Server

HostA

A. The IP address of the switch

B. The MAC address of the remote switch

C. The IP address of the HTTPS server

D. The MAC address of the HTTPS server

E. The IP address of RouterA's Fa0/0 interface

F. The MAC address of RouterA's Fa0/0 interface

5. Which of the following is true regarding the following output? (Choose two.)

```
04:06:16: RIP: received v1 update from 192.168.40.2 on Serial0/1
04:06:16:      192.168.50.0 in 16 hops (inaccessible)
04:06:40: RIP: sending v1 update to 255.255.255.255 via
   FastEthernet0/0 (192.168.30.1)
04:06:40: RIP: build update entries
04:06:40:      network 192.168.20.0 metric 1
04:06:40:      network 192.168.40.0 metric 1
04:06:40:      network 192.168.50.0 metric 16
04:06:40: RIP: sending v1 update to 255.255.255.255 via Serial0/1
   (192.168.40.1)
```

A. There are three interfaces on the router participating in this update.

B. A ping to 192.168.50.1 will be successful.

C. There are at least two routers exchanging information.

D. A ping to 192.168.40.2 will be successful.

6. What is split horizon?

A. Information about a route should not be sent back in the direction from which the original update came.

B. It splits the traffic when you have a large bus (horizon) physical network.

C. It holds the regular updates from broadcasting to a downed link.

D. It prevents regular update messages from reinstating a route that has gone down.

7. Which of the following would be true if HostA is trying to communicate to HostB and interface F0/0 of RouterC goes down? (Choose two.)

RouterA   RouterB   RouterC

HostA   HostB

A. RouterC will use an ICMP to inform HostA that HostB cannot be reached.

B. RouterC will use ICMP to inform RouterB that HostB cannot be reached.

C. RouterC will use ICMP to inform HostA, RouterA, and RouterB that HostB cannot be reached.

D. RouterC will send a destination unreachable message type.

E. RouterC will send a router selection message type.

F. RouterC will send a source quench message type.

8. Which statement is true regarding classless routing protocols? (Choose two.)

A. The use of discontiguous networks is not allowed.

B. The use of variable length subnet masks is permitted.

C. RIPv1 is a classless routing protocol.

D. IGRP supports classless routing within the same autonomous system.

E. RIPv2 supports classless routing.

9. Which two of the following are true regarding the distance-vector and link-state routing protocols?

A. Link state sends its complete routing table out all active interfaces on periodic time intervals.

B. Distance vector sends its complete routing table out all active interfaces on periodic time intervals.

C. Link state sends updates containing the state of its own links to all routers in the internetwork.

D. Distance vector sends updates containing the state of its own links to all routers in the internetwork.

10. Which command displays RIP routing updates?

A. `show ip route`

B. `debug ip rip`

C. `show protocols`

D. `debug ip route`

11. What does RIPv2 use to prevent routing loops? (Choose two.)

    A. CIDR

    B. Split horizon

    C. Authentication

    D. Classless masking

    E. Holddown timers

12. A network administrator views the output from the show ip route command. A network that is advertised by both RIP and IGRP appears in the routing table flagged as an IGRP route. Why is the RIP route to this network not used in the routing table?

    A. IGRP has a faster update timer.

    B. IGRP has a lower administrative distance.

    C. RIP has a higher metric value for that route.

    D. The IGRP route has fewer hops.

    E. The RIP path has a routing loop.

13. You type **debug ip rip** on your router console and see that 172.16.10.0 is being advertised to you with a metric of 16. What does this mean?

    A. The route is 16 hops away.

    B. The route has a delay of 16 microseconds.

    C. The route is inaccessible.

    D. The route is queued at 16 messages a second.

14. IGRP uses which of the following as default parameters for finding the best path to a remote network? (Choose two.)

    A. Hop count

    B. MTU

    C. Cumulative interface delay

    D. STP

    E. Path bandwidth value

15. The Corporate router receives an IP packet with a source IP address of 192.168.214.20 and a destination address of 192.168.22.3. Looking at the output from the Corporate router, what will the router do with this packet?

    ```
    Corp#sh ip route
    [output cut]
    R    192.168.215.0 [120/2] via 192.168.20.2, 00:00:23, Serial0/0
    R    192.168.115.0 [120/1] via 192.168.20.2, 00:00:23, Serial0/0
    R    192.168.30.0 [120/1] via 192.168.20.2, 00:00:23, Serial0/0
    C    192.168.20.0 is directly connected, Serial0/0
    C    192.168.214.0 is directly connected, FastEthernet0/0
    ```

   A. The packet will be discarded.

   B. The packet will be routed out the S0/0 interface.

   C. The router will broadcast looking for the destination.

   D. The packet will be routed out the Fa0/0 interface.

16. If your routing table has a static, a RIP, and an IGRP route to the same network, which route will be used to route packets by default?

   A. Any available route

   B. RIP route

   C. Static route

   D. IGRP route

   E. They will all load-balance.

17. You have the following routing table. Which of the following networks will not be placed in the neighbor routing table?

```
R     192.168.30.0/24 [120/1] via 192.168.40.1, 00:00:12, Serial0
C     192.168.40.0/24 is directly connected, Serial0
      172.16.0.0/24 is subnetted, 1 subnets
C        172.16.30.0 is directly connected, Loopback0
R     192.168.20.0/24 [120/1] via 192.168.40.1, 00:00:12, Serial0
R     10.0.0.0/8 [120/15] via 192.168.40.1, 00:00:07, Serial0
C     192.168.50.0/24 is directly connected, Ethernet0
```

   A. 172.16.30.0

   B. 192.168.30.0

   C. 10.0.0.0

   D. All of them will be placed in the neighbor routing table.

18. Two connected routers are configured with RIP routing. What will be the result when a router receives a routing update that contains a higher-cost path to a network already in its routing table?

   A. The updated information will be added to the existing routing table.

   B. The update will be ignored and no further action will occur.

   C. The updated information will replace the existing routing table entry.

   D. The existing routing table entry will be deleted from the routing table and all routers will exchange routing updates to reach convergence.

19. What is route poisoning?

   A. It sends back the protocol received from a router as a poison pill, which stops the regular updates.

   B. It is information received from a router that can't be sent back to the originating router.

   C. It prevents regular update messages from reinstating a route that has just come up.

   D. It describes when a router sets the metric for a downed link to infinity.

20. Which of the following is true regarding RIPv2?

    A. It has a lower administrative distance than RIPv1.

    B. It converges faster than RIPv1.

    C. It has the same timers as RIPv1.

    D. It is harder to configure than RIPv1.

Answers to Review Questions

1. A, E. There are actually three different ways to configure the same default route, but only two are shown in the answer. First, you can set a default route with the 0.0.0.0 0.0.0.0 mask and then specify the next hop, as in answer A. Or you can use 0.0.0.0 0.0.0.0 and use the exit interface instead of the next hop. Finally, you can use answer E with the `ip default-network` command.

2. C. The `(config-router)#`**`passive-interface`** command stops updates from being sent out an interface, but route updates are still received.

3. A, B. Although answer D almost seems right, it is not; the mask is the mask used on the remote network, not the source network. Since there is no number at the end of the static route, it is using the default administrative distance of 1.

4. C, F. The switches are not used as either a default gateway or other destination. Switches have nothing to do with routing. It is very important to remember that the destination MAC address will always be the router's interface. The destination address of a frame, from HostA, will be the MAC address of the F0/0 interface of RouterA. The destination address of a packet will be the IP address of the network interface card (NIC) of the HTTPS server. The destination port number in the segment header will have a value of 443 (HTTPS).

5. C, D. The route to 192.168.50.0 is unreachable and only interfaces s0/1 and FastEthernet 0/0 are participating in the RIP update. Since a route update was received, at least two routers are participating in the RIP routing process. Since a route update for network 192.168.40.0 is being sent out f0/0 and a route was received from 192.168.40.2, we can assume a ping to that address will be successful.

6. A. A split horizon will not advertise a route back to the same router it learned the route from.

7. A, D. RouterC will use ICMP to inform HostA that HostB cannot be reached. It will perform this by sending a destination unreachable ICMP message type.

8. B, E. Classful routing means that all hosts in the internetwork use the same mask. Classless routing means that you can use Variable Length Subnet Masks (VLSMs) and can also support discontiguous networking.

9. B, C. The distance-vector routing protocol sends its complete routing table out all active interfaces at periodic time intervals. Link-state routing protocols send updates containing the state of its own links to all routers in the internetwork.

10. B. `Debug ip rip` is used to show the Internet Protocol (IP) Routing Information Protocol (RIP) updates being sent and received on the router.

11. B, E. RIPv2 uses the same timers and loop-avoidance schemes as RIPv1. Split horizon is used to stop an update from being sent out the same interface it was received on. Holddown timers allow time for a network to become stable in the case of a flapping link.

12. B. RIP has an administrative distance (AD) of 120, while IGRP has an administrative distance of 100, so the router will discard any route with a higher AD than 100.

13. C. You cannot have 16 hops on a RIP network by default. If you receive a route advertised with a metric of 16, this means it is inaccessible.

14. C, E. IGRP uses bandwidth and delay of the line, by default, to determine the best path to a remote network. Delay of the line can sometimes be called the cumulative interface delay.

15. A. Since the routing table shows no route to the 192.168.22.0 network, the router will discard the packet and send an ICMP destination unreachable message out interface FastEthernet 0/0, which is the source LAN where the packet originated from.

16. C. Static routes have an administrative distance of 1 by default. Unless you change this, a static route will always be used over any other found route. IGRP has an administrative distance of 100, and RIP has an administrative distance of 120, by default.

17. C. The network 10.0.0.0 cannot be placed in the next router's routing table because it already is at 15 hops. One more hop would make the route 16 hops, and that is not valid in RIP networking.

18. B. When a routing update is received by a router, the router first checks the administrative distance (AD) and always chooses the route with the lowest AD. However, if two routes are received and they both have the same AD, then the router will choose the one route with the lowest metrics, or in RIP's case, hop count.

19. D. Another way to avoid problems caused by inconsistent updates and to stop network loops is route poisoning. When a network goes down, the distance-vector routing protocol initiates route poisoning by advertising the network with a metric of 16, or unreachable (sometimes referred to as *infinite*).

20. C. RIPv2 is pretty much just like RIPv1. It has the same administrative distance and timers and is configured just like RIPv1.

Answers to Written Lab 6

1. ip route 172.16.10.0 255.255.255.0 172.16.20.1 150
2. If the box next to an interface is unchecked, this means that passive-interface will not be used and RIP will be sent and received on that interface.
3. ip route 0.0.0.0 0.0.0.0 172.16.40.1
4. Router(config)#**ip classless**
5. Stub network
6. Router#**show ip route**
7. Exit interface
8. False. The MAC address would be the router interface, not the remote host.
9. True
10. Router(config-if)#**clock rate** *speed*
11. Router rip, network 10.0.0.0
12. Router rip, passive-interface s1
13. Holddown timers
14. Route poisoning
15. Split horizon
16. debug ip rip

Chapter

7

Enhanced IGRP (EIGRP) and Open Shortest Path First (OSPF)

THE CCNA EXAM TOPICS COVERED IN THIS CHAPTER INCLUDE THE FOLLOWING:

✓ **Configure, verify, and troubleshoot basic router operation and routing on Cisco devices**

- Access and utilize the router to set basic parameters (including: CLI/SDM)
- Connect, configure, and verify operation status of a device interface
- Verify device configuration and network connectivity using ping, traceroute, telnet, SSH or other utilities
- Perform and verify routing configuration tasks for a static or default route given specific routing requirements
- Compare and contrast methods of routing and routing protocols
- Configure, verify, and troubleshoot OSPF
- Configure, verify, and troubleshoot EIGRP
- Verify network connectivity (including: using ping, traceroute, and telnet or SSH)
- Troubleshoot routing issues
- Verify router hardware and software operation using SHOW & DEBUG commands
- Implement basic router security

Enhanced Interior Gateway Routing Protocol (EIGRP) is a proprietary Cisco protocol that runs on Cisco routers. It is important for you to understand EIGRP because it is probably one of the two most popular routing protocols in use today. In this chapter, I'll show you the many features of EIGRP and describe how it works, with particular focus on the unique way it discovers, selects, and advertises routes.

I'm also going to introduce you to the Open Shortest Path First (OSPF) routing protocol, which is the other popular routing protocol in use today. You'll build a solid foundation for understanding OSPF by first becoming familiar with the terminology and internal operation of it and then learning about OSPF's advantages over RIP. Next, we'll explore the issues surrounding implementations of OSPF in broadcast and non-broadcast networks of various types. I'll explain how to implement single-area OSPF in different and specific networking environments and demonstrate how to verify that everything is running smoothly.

For up-to-the minute updates for this chapter, please see www.lammle.com and/or www.sybex.com.

EIGRP Features and Operation

Enhanced IGRP (EIGRP) is a classless, enhanced distance-vector protocol that gives us a real edge over another Cisco proprietary protocol, Interior Gateway Routing Protocol (IGRP). That's basically why it's called Enhanced IGRP. Like IGRP, EIGRP uses the concept of an autonomous system to describe the set of contiguous routers that run the same routing protocol and share routing information. But unlike IGRP, EIGRP includes the subnet mask in its route updates. And as you now know, the advertisement of subnet information allows us to use Variable Length Subnet Masks (VLSMs) and summarization when designing our networks!

EIGRP is sometimes referred to as a *hybrid routing protocol* because it has characteristics of both distance-vector and link-state protocols. For example, EIGRP doesn't send link-state packets as OSPF does; instead, it sends traditional distance-vector updates containing information about networks plus the cost of reaching them from the perspective of the advertising router. And EIGRP has link-state characteristics as well—it synchronizes routing tables between neighbors at startup and then sends specific updates only when topology changes occur. This makes EIGRP suitable for very large networks. EIGRP has a maximum hop count of 255 (the default is set to 100).

There are a number of powerful features that make EIGRP a real standout from IGRP and other protocols. The main ones are listed here:

- Support for IP and IPv6 (and some other useless routed protocols) via protocol-dependent modules

- Considered classless (same as RIPv2 and OSPF)

- Support for VLSM/CIDR

- Support for summaries and discontiguous networks

- Efficient neighbor discovery

- Communication via Reliable Transport Protocol (RTP)

- Best path selection via Diffusing Update Algorithm (DUAL)

 Cisco calls EIGRP a distance-vector routing protocol or sometimes an advanced distance-vector or even a hybrid routing protocol.

Protocol-Dependent Modules

One of the most interesting features of EIGRP is that it provides routing support for multiple Network layer protocols: IP, IPX, AppleTalk, and now IPv6. (Obviously we won't use IPX and AppleTalk, but EIGRP does support them.) The only other routing protocol that comes close and supports multiple network layer protocols is *Intermediate System-to-Intermediate System (IS-IS)*.

EIGRP supports different Network layer protocols through the use of *protocol-dependent modules (PDMs)*. Each EIGRP PDM will maintain a separate series of tables containing the routing information that applies to a specific protocol. What this means to you is that there will be IP/EIGRP tables and IPv6/EIGRP tables, for example.

Neighbor Discovery

Before EIGRP routers are willing to exchange routes with each other, they must become neighbors. There are three conditions that must be met for neighborship establishment:

- Hello or ACK received

- AS numbers match

- Identical metrics (K values)

Link-state protocols tend to use Hello messages to establish neighborship (also called adjacencies) because they normally do not send out periodic route updates and there has to be some mechanism to help neighbors realize when a new peer has moved in or an old one has left or gone down. To maintain the neighborship relationship, EIGRP routers must also continue receiving Hellos from their neighbors.

EIGRP routers that belong to different autonomous systems (ASes) don't automatically share routing information and they don't become neighbors. This behavior can be a real benefit when used in larger networks to reduce the amount of route information propagated through a specific AS. The only catch is that you might have to take care of redistribution between the different ASes manually.

The only time EIGRP advertises its entire routing table is when it discovers a new neighbor and forms an adjacency with it through the exchange of Hello packets. When this happens, both neighbors advertise their entire routing tables to one another. After each has learned its neighbor's routes, only changes to the routing table are propagated from then on.

When EIGRP routers receive their neighbors' updates, they store them in a local topology table. This table contains all known routes from all known neighbors and serves as the raw material from which the best routes are selected and placed into the routing table.

Let's define some terms before we move on:

Feasible distance   This is the best metric along all paths to a remote network, including the metric to the neighbor that is advertising that remote network. This is the route that you will find in the routing table because it is considered the best path. The metric of a feasible distance is the metric reported by the neighbor (called reported or advertised distance) plus the metric to the neighbor reporting the route.

Reported/advertised distance   This is the metric of a remote network, as reported by a neighbor. It is also the routing table metric of the neighbor and is the same as the second number in parentheses as displayed in the topology table, the first number being the feasible distance.

Neighbor table   Each router keeps state information about adjacent neighbors. When a newly discovered neighbor is learned, the address and interface of the neighbor are recorded, and this information is held in the neighbor table, stored in RAM. There is one neighbor table for each protocol-dependent module. Sequence numbers are used to match acknowledgments with update packets. The last sequence number received from the neighbor is recorded so that out-of-order packets can be detected.

Topology table   The topology table is populated by the protocol-dependent modules and acted upon by the Diffusing Update Algorithm (DUAL). It contains all destinations advertised by neighboring routers, holding each destination address and a list of neighbors that have advertised the destination. For each neighbor, the advertised metric, which comes only from the neighbor's routing table, is recorded. If the neighbor is advertising this destination, it must be using the route to forward packets.

 The neighbor and topology tables are stored in RAM and maintained through the use of Hello and update packets. Yes, the routing table is also stored in RAM, but that information is gathered only from the topology table.

Feasible successor   A feasible successor is a path whose reported distance is less than the feasible distance, and it is considered a backup route. EIGRP will keep up to six feasible successors in the topology table. Only the one with the best metric (the successor) is copied and placed in the routing table. The `show ip eigrp topology` command will display all the EIGRP feasible successor routes known to a router.

A feasible successor is a backup route and is stored in the topology table. A successor route is stored in the topology table and is copied and placed in the routing table.

Successor   A successor route (think successful!) is the best route to a remote network. A successor route is used by EIGRP to forward traffic to a destination and is stored in the routing table. It is backed up by a feasible successor route that is stored in the topology table—if one is available.

By using the feasible distance, and having feasible successors in the topology table as backup links, the network can converge instantly, and updates to any neighbor make up the only traffic sent from EIGRP.

Reliable Transport Protocol (RTP)

EIGRP uses a proprietary protocol called *Reliable Transport Protocol (RTP)* to manage the communication of messages between EIGRP-speaking routers. And as the name suggests, reliability is a key concern of this protocol. Cisco has designed a mechanism that leverages multicasts and unicasts to deliver updates quickly and to track the receipt of the data.

When EIGRP sends multicast traffic, it uses the Class D address 224.0.0.10. As I said, each EIGRP router is aware of who its neighbors are, and for each multicast it sends out, it maintains a list of the neighbors who have replied. If EIGRP doesn't get a reply from a neighbor, it will switch to using unicasts to resend the same data. If it still doesn't get a reply after 16 unicast attempts, the neighbor is declared dead. People often refer to this process as *reliable multicast*.

Routers keep track of the information they send by assigning a sequence number to each packet. With this technique, it's possible for them to detect the arrival of old, redundant, or out-of-sequence information.

Being able to do these things is highly important because EIGRP is a quiet protocol. It depends upon its ability to synchronize routing databases at startup time and then maintain the consistency of databases over time by only communicating any changes. So the permanent loss of any packets, or the out-of-order execution of packets, can result in corruption of the routing database.

Diffusing Update Algorithm (DUAL)

EIGRP uses *Diffusing Update Algorithm (DUAL)* for selecting and maintaining the best path to each remote network. This algorithm allows for the following:

- Backup route determination if one is available
- Support of VLSMs
- Dynamic route recoveries
- Queries for an alternate route if no route can be found

DUAL provides EIGRP with possibly the fastest route convergence time among all protocols. The key to EIGRP's speedy convergence is twofold: First, EIGRP routers maintain a copy of all of their neighbors' routes, which they use to calculate their own cost to each remote network. If the best path goes down, it may be as simple as examining the contents of the topology table to select the best replacement route. Second, if there isn't a good alternative in the local topology table, EIGRP routers very quickly ask their neighbors for help finding one—they aren't afraid to ask directions! Relying on other routers and leveraging the information they provide accounts for the "diffusing" character of DUAL.

And as I said, the whole idea of the Hello protocol is to enable the rapid detection of new or dead neighbors. RTP answers this call by providing a reliable mechanism for conveying and sequencing messages. Building upon this solid foundation, DUAL is responsible for selecting and maintaining information about the best paths.

Using EIGRP to Support Large Networks

EIGRP includes a bunch of cool features that make it suitable for use in large networks:

- Support for multiple ASes on a single router
- Support for VLSM and summarization
- Route discovery and maintenance

Each of these capabilities adds one small piece to the complex puzzle of supporting a huge number of routers and multiple networks.

Multiple ASes

EIGRP uses autonomous system numbers to identify the collection of routers that share route information. Only routers that have the same autonomous system numbers share routes. In large networks, you can easily end up with really complicated topology and route tables, and that can markedly slow convergence during diffusing computation operations.

So what's an administrator to do to mitigate the impact of managing really big networks? Well, it's possible to divide the network into multiple distinct EIGRP autonomous systems, or ASes. Each AS is populated by a contiguous series of routers, and route information can be shared among the different ASes via redistribution.

The use of redistribution within EIGRP leads us to another interesting feature. Normally, the administrative distance (AD) of an EIGRP route is 90, but this is true only for what is known as an *internal EIGRP route*. These are routes originated within a specific autonomous system by EIGRP routers that are members of the same autonomous system. The other type of route is called an *external EIGRP route* and has an AD of 170, which is not so good. These routes appear within EIGRP route tables courtesy of either manual or automatic redistribution, and they represent networks that originated outside of the EIGRP autonomous system. And it doesn't matter if the routes originated from another EIGRP autonomous system or from another routing protocol such as OSPF—they're all considered to be external routes when redistributed within EIGRP.

I have some good news regarding EIGRP and redistribution. Let's say you have an existing company that has IGRP running on all the routers. You have just been hired as the network administrator and have decided to run EIGRP on the network because you read my book and know the many benefits of EIGRP over IGRP.

Since you need to migrate slowly over to EIGRP and cannot change all the routers simultaneously, you need to configure redistribution—right? Not with EIGRP! As long as you use the same autonomous system number for EIGRP that you used for IGRP, EIGRP will automatically redistribute the routes from IGRP into EIGRP. Of course, EIGRP will see these as external routes (AD of 170), so this isn't something you want to use forever. You want to migrate as quickly as possible, but because of this automatic redistribution feature, you don't have to migrate in one weekend.

VLSM Support and Summarization

As one of the more sophisticated classless routing protocols, EIGRP supports the use of Variable Length Subnet Masks. This is really important because it allows for the conservation of address space through the use of subnet masks that more closely fit the host requirements, such as using 30-bit subnet masks for point-to-point networks. And because the subnet mask is propagated with every route update, EIGRP also supports the use of discontiguous subnets, something that gives us a lot more flexibility when designing the network's IP address plan.

What's a discontiguous network? It's one that has two or more subnetworks of a classful network connected together by different classful networks. Figure 7.1 displays a typical discontiguous network.

The subnets 172.16.10.0 and 172.16.20.0 are connected together with a 10.3.1.0 network. By default, each router thinks it has the only 172.16.0.0 classful network.

FIGURE 7.1   A discontiguous network

It's important to understand that discontiguous networks just won't work with RIPv1 or IGRP at all. And they don't work by default on RIPv2 or EIGRP either, but discontiguous networks do work on OSPF networks by default because OSPF does not auto-summarize like EIGRP. But no worries about EIGRP—there are ways to make EIGRP work. I'll show you how to do that a bit later in this chapter.

EIGRP also supports the manual creation of summaries at any and all EIGRP routers, which can substantially reduce the size of the route table. However, EIGRP automatically summarizes networks at their classful boundaries, and Figure 7.2 shows how a router running EIGRP would see the network plus the boundaries that it would auto-summarize.

FIGURE 7.2   EIGRP auto-summarization

Obviously, this would never work by default! Make a note to yourself that RIPv1, RIPv2, and IGRP would also auto-summarize these same classful boundaries by default, but OSPF won't.

 RIPv2 and EIGRP support discontiguous networking, but not by default. OSPF does support discontiguous networking by default because it doesn't auto-summarize classful boundaries as RIPv2 and EIGRP do.

Route Discovery and Maintenance

The hybrid nature of EIGRP is fully revealed in its approach to route discovery and maintenance. Like many link-state protocols, EIGRP supports the concept of neighbors that are discovered via a Hello process and whose states are monitored. Like many distance-vector protocols, EIGRP uses the routing-by-rumor mechanism I talked about earlier that implies many routers never hear about a route update firsthand. Instead, they hear about it from another router that may also have heard about it from another one, and so on.

Given the huge amount of information that EIGRP routers have to collect, it makes sense that they have a place to store it, right? Well they do—EIGRP uses a series of tables to store important information about its environment:

Neighborship table   The *neighborship table* (usually referred to as the neighbor table) records information about routers with whom neighborship relationships have been formed.

Topology table   The *topology table* stores the route advertisements about every route in the internetwork received from each neighbor.

Route table   The *route table* stores the routes that are currently used to make routing decisions. There would be separate copies of each of these tables for each protocol that is actively being supported by EIGRP, whether it's IP or IPv6.

I am now going to discuss the EIGRP metrics and then move right into the *easy* configuration of EIGRP.

EIGRP Metrics

Another really sweet thing about EIGRP is that unlike many other protocols that use a single factor to compare routes and select the best possible path, EIGRP can use a combination of four:

- *Bandwidth*
- *Delay*
- *Load*
- *Reliability*

Like IGRP, EIGRP uses only bandwidth and delay of the line to determine the best path to a remote network by default. Cisco sometimes likes to call these *path bandwidth value* and *cumulative line delay*—go figure.

And it's worth noting that there's a fifth element, *maximum transmission unit (MTU)* size. This element has never been used in EIGRP calculations, but it's a required parameter in some EIGRP-related commands, especially those involving redistribution. The value of the MTU element represents the smallest MTU value encountered along the path to the destination network.

Maximum Paths and Hop Count

By default, EIGRP can provide equal-cost load balancing of up to four links (actually, all routing protocols do this). However, you can have EIGRP actually load-balance across up to six links (equal or unequal) by using the following command:

```
Pod1R1(config)#router eigrp 10
Pod1R1(config-router)#maximum-paths ?
  <1-6>  Number of paths
```

In addition, EIGRP has a maximum hop count of 100, but it can be set up to 255. Chances are you wouldn't want to ever change this, but if you did, here is how you would do it:

```
Pod1R1(config)#router eigrp 10
Pod1R1(config-router)#metric maximum-hops ?
  <1-255>  Hop count
```

As you can see from this router output, EIGRP can be set to a maximum of 255 hops, and even though it doesn't use hop count in the path metric calculation, it still uses the maximum hop count to limit the scope of the AS.

By default, all routing protocols can load-balance across four equal-cost links. However, EIGRP allows you to load-balance across six, and through the use of the `variance` command, EIGRP can load-balance up to six unequal-cost links.

Configuring EIGRP

Although EIGRP can be configured for IP, IPv6, IPX, and AppleTalk, as a future Cisco Certified Network Associate, you really only need to focus on the configuration of IP for now. (IPv6 configurations will be shown in Chapter 13.)

There are two modes from which EIGRP commands are entered: router configuration mode and interface configuration mode. Router configuration mode enables the protocol, determines which networks will run EIGRP, and sets global characteristics. Interface configuration mode allows customization of summaries, metrics, timers, and bandwidth.

To start an EIGRP session on a router, use the `router eigrp` command followed by the autonomous system number of your network. You then enter the network numbers connected to the router using the `network` command followed by the network number.

Let's look at an example of enabling EIGRP for autonomous system 20 on a router connected to two networks, with the network numbers being 10.3.1.0/24 and 172.16.10.0/24:

```
Router#config t
Router(config)#router eigrp 20
Router(config-router)#network 172.16.0.0
Router(config-router)#network 10.0.0.0
```

Remember—as with RIP, you use the classful network address, which is all subnet and host bits turned off.

Understand that the AS number is irrelevant—that is, as long as all routers use the same number! You can use any number from 1 to 65,535.

Say you need to stop EIGRP from working on a specific interface, such as a BRI interface or a serial connection to the Internet. To do that, you would flag the interface as passive using the `passive-interface` *interface* command, as discussed in Chapter 6 with RIP. The following command shows you how to make interface serial 0/1 a passive interface:

```
Router(config)#router eigrp 20
Router(config-router)#passive-interface serial 0/1
```

Doing this will prohibit the interface from sending or receiving Hello packets and, as a result, stop it from forming adjacencies. This means that it won't send or receive route information on this interface.

> The impact of the `passive-interface` command depends upon the routing protocol under which the command is issued. For example, on an interface running RIP, the `passive-interface` command will prohibit the sending of route updates but allow their receipt. Thus, a RIP router with a passive interface will still learn about the networks advertised by other routers. This is different from EIGRP, where a `passive-interface` will neither send nor receive updates.

Okay, let's configure the same network that we configured in the last chapter with RIP and RIPv2. It doesn't matter that RIPv2 (as well as our static routes) are already running—unless you're worried about bandwidth consumption and CPU cycles, of course, because EIGRP has an AD of 90. Remember that our static routes were changed to an AD of 150/151, and RIP is 120, so only EIGRP routes will populate the routing tables, even if RIP and static routing are enabled.

Figure 7.3 shows the network that we've been working with—the same one we're going to use to configure with EIGRP.

FIGURE 7.3   Our internetwork

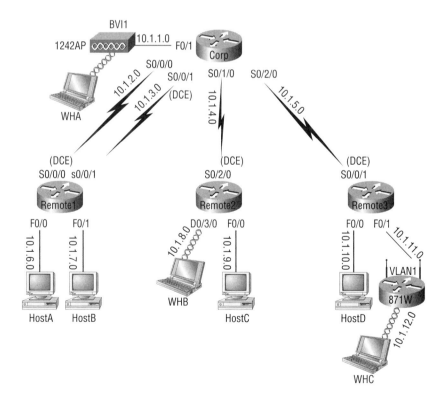

So you can use it as a reminder, Table 7.1 contains the IP addresses we've been using on each interface.

TABLE 7.1   Network Addressing for the IP Network

Router	Network Address	Interface	Address
Corp			
Corp	10.1.1.0	F0/1	10.1.1.1
Corp	10.1.2.0	S0/0/0	10.1.2.1
Corp	10.1.3.0	S0/0/1(DCE)	10.1.3.1
Corp	10.1.4.0	s0/1/0	10.1.4.1
Corp	10.1.5.0	s0/2/0	10.1.5.1
R1			
R1	10.1.2.0	S0/0/0 (DCE)	10.1.2.2
R1	10.1.3.0	S0/0/1	10.1.3.2
R1	10.1.6.0	F0/0	10.1.6.1
R1	10.1.7.0	F0/1	10.1.7.1
R2			
R2	10.1.4.0	S0/2/0 (DCE)	10.1.4.2
R2	10.1.8.0	D0/3/0	10.1.8.1
R2	10.1.9.0	F0/0	10.1.9.1
R3			
R3	10.1.5.0	S0/0/0/ (DCE)	10.1.5.2
R3	10.1.10.0	F0/0	10.1.10.1
R3	10.1.11.0	F0/1	10.1.11.1

TABLE 7.1   Network Addressing for the IP Network *(continued)*

Router	Network Address	Interface	Address
871W			
871W	10.1.11.0	Vlan 1	10.1.11.2
871W	10.1.12.0	Dot11radio0	10.1.12.1
1242 AP			
1242 AP	10.1.1.0	BVI 1	10.1.1.2

It's actually really easy to add EIGRP to our internetwork—this is the beauty of EIGRP.

Corp

The AS number, as shown in the following router output, can be any number from 1 to 65,535. A router can be a member of as many ASes as you want it to be, but for this book's purposes, we're just going to configure a single AS:

```
Corp#config t
Corp(config)#router eigrp ?
  <1-65535>  Autonomous system number

Corp(config)#router eigrp 10
Corp(config-router)#network 10.0.0.0
```

The router eigrp [as] command turns EIGRP routing on in the router. As with RIPv1, you still need to add the classful network numbers you want to advertise. But unlike RIP, EIGRP uses classless routing—but you still configure it as classful. Classless, which I'm sure you remember, means that the subnet mask information is sent along with routing protocol updates (RIPv2 is classless).

R1

To configure the R1 router, all you need to do is turn on EIGRP routing using AS 10 and then add the network number like this:

```
R1#config t
R1(config)#router eigrp 10
R1(config-router)#network 10.0.0.0
*Mar 21 19:18:12.935: %DUAL-5-NBRCHANGE: IP-EIGRP(0) 10: Neighbor
   10.1.2.2 (Serial0/0/0) is up: new adjacency
*Mar 21 19:18:12.935: %DUAL-5-NBRCHANGE: IP-EIGRP(0) 10: Neighbor
   10.1.3.2 (Serial0/0/1) is up: new adjacency
```

The R1 router found the Corp neighbor—the two routers are adjacent! Notice that it found both links connected between the routers. This is a good thing.

R2

To configure the R2 router, all you need to do is again turn on EIGRP using AS 10:

```
R2#config t
R2(config)#router eigrp 10
R2(config-router)#network 10.0.0.0
*Mar 21 19:20:29.023: %DUAL-5-NBRCHANGE: IP-EIGRP(0) 10: Neighbor
   10.1.4.2 (Serial0/1/0) is up: new adjacency
```

That's it—really! Most routing protocols are pretty simple to set up, and EIGRP is no exception. But that's only for the basic configuration, of course.

R3

Let's use the SDM to configure EIGRP just as we've done throughout the last few chapters. The configuration process itself won't take long at all—it's the logging in part that I'm going to do first that's going to really eat up some of my time!

Looking at this first screen shot, we can see that we still have both our static routes and RIPv2 running on our router.:

Let's enable EIGRP by adding AS 10 and also choosing to set our passive interfaces—only because it is so easy to do so!

Last, we can see that EIGRP is now running with AS 10.

That's it, done.

Our configuration seems pretty solid, but remember—only EIGRP routes are going to wind up in the routing table because EIGRP has the lowest AD. So by having RIP running in the background, we're not only using more memory and CPU cycles on the router, we're sucking up precious bandwidth across every one of our links! This is definitely not good, and it's something you'll really want to keep in mind.

Now we're going to configure our last router. Because the IOS image I have for my 871W router doesn't support EIGRP, we'll keep RIPv2 running. I'm going to configure redistribution (translation) from the R3 router to the 871W router—something I think you'll find pretty interesting, so let's get started.

Redistributing to the 871W Router from R3

From the R3 router, we just need to add the redistribution commands under EIGRP and RIP. Understand that the SDM definitely has its limitations, so we'll need to get this done using the CLI:

```
R3#config t
R3(config)#router eigrp 10
R3(config-router)#redistribute rip ?
  metric     Metric for redistributed routes
  route-map  Route map reference
  <cr>
R3(config-router)#redistribute rip metric ?
  <1-4294967295>  Bandwidth metric in Kbits per second
R3(config-router)#redistribute rip metric 10000000 ?
  <0-4294967295>  EIGRP delay metric, in 10 microsecond units
R3(config-router)#redistribute rip metric 10000000 20000 ?
  <0-255>  EIGRP reliability metric where 255 is 100% reliable
R3(config-router)#redistribute rip metric 10000000 20000 255 ?
  <1-255>  EIGRP Effective bandwidth metric (Loading) where 255 is 100% loaded
R3(config-router)#redistribute rip metric 10000000 20000 255 1 ?
  <1-65535>  EIGRP MTU of the path
R3(config-router)#redistribute rip metric 10000000 20000 255 1 1500
R3(config-router)#do show run | begin router eigrp 10
router eigrp 10
 redistribute rip metric 10000000 20000 255 1 1500
 passive-interface FastEthernet0/0
 passive-interface Serial0/0/0
 network 10.0.0.0
 no auto-summary
!
```

We needed to change RIP's metric of hop count to match EIGRP's bandwidth metric, delay, reliability, load, and MTU. Even though EIGRP may only use bandwidth and delay of the line by default, when you configure redistribution, you have to configure all metric values.

Our R3 router is now bilingual and speaks both RIP and EIGRP. It will even serve as a kind of interpreter for the rest of our routers—well, most of them. That means we're not done just yet—we still need to configure redistribution from EIGRP to RIP too (mutual redistribution) so that the 871W will receive the EIGRP routes as RIP routes because the 871W router only "speaks" RIP:

```
R3(config)#router rip
R3(config-router)#redistribute eigrp 10 ?
  metric     Metric for redistributed routes
  route-map  Route map reference
  <cr>
R3(config-router)#redistribute eigrp 10 metric ?
  <0-16>       Default metric
  transparent  Transparently redistribute metric

R3(config-router)#redistribute eigrp 10 metric 1
```

The preceding output shows us that we're redistributing EIGRP into RIP and changing the metric to hop count.

But the only way to find out if this is really and truly working is to disable RIP on all routers except the R3 router—the one that's providing the translation to and from the 871W router. Here's a look at how I did that:

```
Corp#config t
Corp(config)#no router rip
R1#config t
R1(config)#no router rip
R2#config t
R2(config)#no router rip
```

Let's check out the Corp's routing table:

```
Corp#sh ip route
    10.0.0.0/24 is subnetted, 12 subnets
D       10.1.11.0 [90/2172416] via 10.1.5.2, 00:04:57, Serial0/2/0
D       10.1.10.0 [90/2172416] via 10.1.5.2, 00:04:57, Serial0/2/0
D       10.1.9.0 [90/2195456] via 10.1.4.2, 00:04:57, Serial0/1/0
D       10.1.8.0 [90/2195456] via 10.1.4.2, 00:04:57, Serial0/1/0
D       10.1.12.0 [90/2172416] via 10.1.5.2, 00:03:00, Serial0/2/0
C       10.1.3.0 is directly connected, Serial0/0/1
C       10.1.2.0 is directly connected, Serial0/0/0
```

```
C       10.1.1.0 is directly connected, FastEthernet0/1
D       10.1.7.0 [90/2195456] via 10.1.3.2, 00:04:58, Serial0/0/1
                 [90/2195456] via 10.1.2.2, 00:04:58, Serial0/0/0
D       10.1.6.0 [90/2195456] via 10.1.3.2, 00:04:58, Serial0/0/1
                 [90/2195456] via 10.1.2.2, 00:04:58, Serial0/0/0
C       10.1.5.0 is directly connected, Serial0/2/0
C       10.1.4.0 is directly connected, Serial0/1/0
```

Okay, cool—all routes are showing up, including 10.1.12.0, which is the wireless LAN connected to the 871W router. And not only is it there, it's showing up as an EIGRP network because R3 is translating from RIP to EIGRP for us. Here's the 871W router's routing table showing that it's receiving all routes as RIP routes from the R3 router:

```
871W#sh ip route
     10.0.0.0/24 is subnetted, 12 subnets
C       10.1.11.0 is directly connected, Vlan1
R       10.1.10.0 [120/1] via 10.1.11.1, 00:00:19, Vlan1
R       10.1.9.0 [120/2] via 10.1.11.1, 00:00:19, Vlan1
R       10.1.8.0 [120/2] via 10.1.11.1, 00:00:19, Vlan1
C       10.1.12.0 is directly connected, Dot11Radio0
R       10.1.3.0 [120/2] via 10.1.11.1, 00:00:19, Vlan1
R       10.1.2.0 [120/2] via 10.1.11.1, 00:00:19, Vlan1
R       10.1.1.0 [120/2] via 10.1.11.1, 00:00:19, Vlan1
R       10.1.7.0 [120/2] via 10.1.11.1, 00:00:19, Vlan1
R       10.1.6.0 [120/2] via 10.1.11.1, 00:00:19, Vlan1
R       10.1.5.0 [120/1] via 10.1.11.1, 00:00:19, Vlan1
R       10.1.4.0 [120/2] via 10.1.11.1, 00:00:19, Vlan1
```

We can see all the networks in the routing table. And as far as the 871W router is concerned, the whole network is just running RIP. Pretty sweet! This is a great example of a way to configure a network if you happen to have an old router involved that's running RIP and you don't want to install RIP on all your other routers.

Configuring Discontiguous Networks

There's one more configuration that you need to be aware of that has to do with autosummarization. Remember Figure 7.1 and how it demonstrated how EIGRP would autosummarize the boundaries on a discontiguous network? Take a look at that figure again, and then I'll configure both routers with EIGRP.

In the figure, the Lab_A router is connected to a 172.16.10.0/24 network and the 10.3.1.0/24 backbone. The Lab_B router is connected to the 172.16.20.0/24 network and the 10.3.1.0/24 backbone. Both routers, by default, would automatically summarize the classful boundaries and routing would not work. Here's the configuration that would make this network work:

```
Lab_A#config t
Lab_A(config)#router eigrp 100
Lab_A(config-router)#network 172.16.0.0
Lab_A(config-router)#network 10.0.0.0
Lab_A(config-router)#no auto-summary

Lab_B#config t
Lab_B(config)#router eigrp 100
Lab_B(config-router)#network 172.16.0.0
Lab_B(config-router)#network 10.0.0.0
Lab_B(config-router)#no auto-summary
```

Because I used the no auto-summary command, EIGRP will advertise all the subnets between the two routers. If the networks were larger, you could then provide manual summarization on these same boundaries.

When I configured the R3 router using SDM, it automatically added the no auto-summary under EIGRP. It didn't even ask me if I wanted to or not, and I could only verify this, or disable it, from the CLI.

Load Balancing with EIGRP

You might know that by default, EIGRP can load-balance up to four equal-cost links. But did you remember that we can configure EIGRP to load-balance across up to six equal-/unequal-cost links to a remote network? Well, we can, so let's play with both our Corp and R1 routers and do some load balancing. First, let's take a look at the R1 routing table and make sure that EIGRP has already found both links between the routers:

```
R1#sh ip route
     10.0.0.0/24 is subnetted, 12 subnets
D       10.1.11.0 [90/2684416] via 10.1.3.1, 00:50:37, Serial0/0/1
                  [90/2684416] via 10.1.2.1, 00:50:37, Serial0/0/0
D       10.1.10.0 [90/2707456] via 10.1.3.1, 01:04:40, Serial0/0/1
                  [90/2707456] via 10.1.2.1, 01:04:40, Serial0/0/0
D       10.1.9.0 [90/2707456] via 10.1.3.1, 01:24:09, Serial0/0/1
                 [90/2707456] via 10.1.2.1, 01:24:09, Serial0/0/0
D       10.1.8.0 [90/2707456] via 10.1.3.1, 01:24:09, Serial0/0/1
                 [90/2707456] via 10.1.2.1, 01:24:09, Serial0/0/0
```

```
D       10.1.12.0 [90/2684416] via 10.1.3.1, 00:10:10, Serial0/0/1
                  [90/2684416] via 10.1.2.1, 00:10:10, Serial0/0/0
C       10.1.3.0 is directly connected, Serial0/0/1
C       10.1.2.0 is directly connected, Serial0/0/0
D       10.1.1.0 [90/2172416] via 10.1.3.1, 01:24:11, Serial0/0/1
                 [90/2172416] via 10.1.2.1, 01:24:11, Serial0/0/0
C       10.1.7.0 is directly connected, FastEthernet0/1
C       10.1.6.0 is directly connected, FastEthernet0/0
D       10.1.5.0 [90/2681856] via 10.1.3.1, 01:24:11, Serial0/0/1
                 [90/2681856] via 10.1.2.1, 01:24:11, Serial0/0/0
D       10.1.4.0 [90/2681856] via 10.1.3.1, 01:24:11, Serial0/0/1
                 [90/2681856] via 10.1.2.1, 01:24:11, Serial0/0/0
```

Now this is new and different—a very interesting routing table indeed! You can see that we have two links to every route in our internetwork, and again, EIGRP will load balance across the s0/0/0 and s0/0/1 links by default because they're the same metric.

EIGRP really does offer some really cool features, and one of them is automatic load balancing. But how about bundling links? Well, EIGRP can allow us to do this too—even with no extra configuration! Let me show you how this works. I'm going to configure the links between our Corp and R1 routers with the same subnet, meaning both links will have all interfaces within the same subnet. Check out my configuration:

```
Corp#config t
Corp(config)#int s0/0/1
Corp(config-if)#ip address 10.1.2.4 255.255.255.0
```

```
R1#config t
R1(config)#int s0/0/1
R1(config-if)#ip address 10.1.2.3 255.255.255.0
R1(config-if)#do show run | begin interface
interface Serial0/0/0
 description 1st Connection to Corp Router
 ip address 10.1.2.2 255.255.255.0
!
interface Serial0/0/1
 description 2nd connection to Corp Router
 ip address 10.1.2.3 255.255.255.0
```

Now both links have all four interfaces in the same subnet.

```
R1(config-if)#do show ip route
     10.0.0.0/24 is subnetted, 12 subnets
D       10.1.11.0 [90/2684416] via 10.1.2.4, 00:04:44, Serial0/0/1
                  [90/2684416] via 10.1.2.1, 00:04:44, Serial0/0/0
```

```
D       10.1.10.0 [90/2707456] via 10.1.2.4, 00:04:44, Serial0/0/1
                  [90/2707456] via 10.1.2.1, 00:04:44, Serial0/0/0
D       10.1.9.0 [90/2707456] via 10.1.2.4, 00:04:44, Serial0/0/1
                 [90/2707456] via 10.1.2.1, 00:04:44, Serial0/0/0
D       10.1.8.0 [90/2707456] via 10.1.2.4, 00:04:44, Serial0/0/1
                 [90/2707456] via 10.1.2.1, 00:04:44, Serial0/0/0
D       10.1.12.0 [90/2684416] via 10.1.2.4, 00:04:44, Serial0/0/1
                  [90/2684416] via 10.1.2.1, 00:04:44, Serial0/0/0
D       10.1.3.0 [90/3193856] via 10.1.2.4, 00:04:44, Serial0/0/1
                 [90/3193856] via 10.1.2.1, 00:04:44, Serial0/0/0
C       10.1.2.0 is directly connected, Serial0/0/0
                 is directly connected, Serial0/0/1
D       10.1.1.0 [90/2172416] via 10.1.2.4, 00:03:56, Serial0/0/1
                 [90/2172416] via 10.1.2.1, 00:03:56, Serial0/0/0
C       10.1.7.0 is directly connected, FastEthernet0/1
C       10.1.6.0 is directly connected, FastEthernet0/0
D       10.1.5.0 [90/2681856] via 10.1.2.4, 00:04:46, Serial0/0/1
                 [90/2681856] via 10.1.2.1, 00:04:46, Serial0/0/0
D       10.1.4.0 [90/2681856] via 10.1.2.4, 00:04:46, Serial0/0/1
                 [90/2681856] via 10.1.2.1, 00:04:46, Serial0/0/0
```

 To make this fabulous configuration work, EIGRP positively must be enabled first. If not, you'll get an error on your router that the addresses overlap!

Did you notice there's a subtle change or two in the routing table now? Networks 10.1.2.0 and 10.1.3.0 used to show up as individual, directly connected interfaces, but not anymore. Now only the 10.1.2.0 network shows up as two directly connected interfaces, and the router now has a 3MB pipe through that line instead of just two 1.5Mbps T1 links. And just because these changes are subtle doesn't make them any less cool!

But wait a minute here.... Why is 10.1.3.0 still showing up in the routing table, and why is it showing up as a *D*, meaning DUAL for EIGRP, even though subnet 10.1.3.0 is nonexistent? The answer is pretty simple—when we configured our static routes on our R3 router through SDM, I clicked the Permanent route option. The effect of that command is, "If any static network goes down, keep that route in the routing table of R3." Network 10.1.3.0 was unconfigured between the Corp and R1 routers, so the R3 router is advertising 10.1.3.0 as available even though it really isn't, and it's doing that because we deployed our redistribution command.

 This is a really good reason why *not* to use the permanent option with static routes, because if you do, your routing tables could actually show you a subnet that doesn't even exist!

I am going to add subnet 10.1.3.0 back into the network so we can have some more fun with these dual links. I'll go to the Corp and R1 s0/0/1 interfaces and configure 10.1.3.1/24 and 10.1.3.2/24. Now 10.1.3.0 is being advertised again, but this time it's for a network that actually exists! Let's mix things up a bit and change the metric of the 10.1.3.0 link and see what happens:

```
R1#config t
R1(config)#int s0/0/1
R1(config-if)#bandwidth 256000
R1(config-if)#delay 300000
Corp#config t
Corp(config)#int s0/0/1
Corp(config-if)#bandwidth 256000
Corp(config-if)#delay 300000
```

Since by default, EIGRP uses bandwidth and delay of the line to determine the best path to each network, I lowered the bandwidth and raised the delay of the s0/0/1 interfaces of the both the R1 and Corp routers. Now, let's verify EIGRP on our network, plus check out what our dual links are up to now between the R1 and Corp routers.

Verifying EIGRP

There are several commands that can be used on a router to help you troubleshoot and verify the EIGRP configuration. Table 7.2 contains all of the most important commands that are used in conjunction with verifying EIGRP operation and offers a brief description of what each command does.

TABLE 7.2 EIGRP Troubleshooting Commands

Command	Description/Function
show ip route	Shows the entire routing table
show ip route eigrp	Shows only EIGRP entries in the routing table
show ip eigrp neighbors	Shows all EIGRP neighbors
show ip eigrp topology	Shows entries in the EIGRP topology table
debug eigrp packet	Shows Hello packets sent/received between adjacent routers
Debug ip eigrp notification	Shows EIGRP changes and updates as they occur on your network

I'll demonstrate how you would use the commands in Table 7.2 by using them on our internetwork that we just configured—not including the discontiguous network example.

The following router output is from the Corp router in our example:

```
Corp#sh ip route
      10.0.0.0/24 is subnetted, 12 subnets
D        10.1.11.0 [90/2172416] via 10.1.5.2, 00:01:05, Serial0/2/0
D        10.1.10.0 [90/2195456] via 10.1.5.2, 00:01:05, Serial0/2/0
D        10.1.9.0 [90/2195456] via 10.1.4.2, 00:01:05, Serial0/1/0
D        10.1.8.0 [90/2195456] via 10.1.4.2, 00:01:05, Serial0/1/0
D        10.1.12.0 [90/2172416] via 10.1.5.2, 00:01:05, Serial0/2/0
C        10.1.3.0 is directly connected, Serial0/0/1
C        10.1.2.0 is directly connected, Serial0/0/0
C        10.1.1.0 is directly connected, FastEthernet0/1
D        10.1.7.0 [90/2195456] via 10.1.2.2, 00:01:06, Serial0/0/0
D        10.1.6.0 [90/2195456] via 10.1.2.2, 00:01:06, Serial0/0/0
C        10.1.5.0 is directly connected, Serial0/2/0
C        10.1.4.0 is directly connected, Serial0/1/0
```

You can see that all routes are there in the routing table (10.1.3.0 shows that it's directly connected again) and we have only one link to networks 10.1.6.0 and 10.1.7.0! Notice that EIGRP routes are indicated with simply a *D* designation (DUAL) and that the default AD of these routes is 90. This represents internal EIGRP routes. Let's take a look at the R1 router table now that we've changed the metrics:

```
R1#sh ip route
      10.0.0.0/24 is subnetted, 12 subnets
D        10.1.11.0 [90/2684416] via 10.1.2.1, 00:00:09, Serial0/0/0
D        10.1.10.0 [90/2707456] via 10.1.2.1, 00:00:09, Serial0/0/0
D        10.1.9.0 [90/2707456] via 10.1.2.1, 00:00:09, Serial0/0/0
D        10.1.8.0 [90/2707456] via 10.1.2.1, 00:00:09, Serial0/0/0
D        10.1.12.0 [90/2684416] via 10.1.2.1, 00:00:09, Serial0/0/0
C        10.1.3.0 is directly connected, Serial0/0/1
C        10.1.2.0 is directly connected, Serial0/0/0
D        10.1.1.0 [90/2172416] via 10.1.2.1, 00:00:09, Serial0/0/0
C        10.1.7.0 is directly connected, FastEthernet0/1
C        10.1.6.0 is directly connected, FastEthernet0/0
D        10.1.5.0 [90/2681856] via 10.1.2.1, 00:00:09, Serial0/0/0
D        10.1.4.0 [90/2681856] via 10.1.2.1, 00:00:09, Serial0/0/0
```

Now we have only one route to each remote network, and the 10.1.3.0 network is our backup link. Obviously, it would be better if we could use both links at the same time, but in my example, I made the 10.1.3.0 network a backup link.

Let's go back to the Corp router and see what it shows us in the neighbor table:

```
Corp#sh ip eigrp neighbors
IP-EIGRP neighbors for process 10
H   Address     Interface  Hold Uptime   SRTT  RTO Q  Seq
                           (sec)         (ms)     Cnt Num
1   10.1.3.2    Se0/0/1    14 00:35:10    1    200 0  81
3   10.1.5.2    Se0/2/0    10 02:51:22    1    200 0  31
2   10.1.4.2    Se0/1/0    13 03:17:20    1    200 0  20
0   10.1.2.2    Se0/0/0    10 03:19:37    1    200 0  80
```

We read the information in this output like this:

- The H field indicates the order in which the neighbor was discovered.

- The hold time is how long this router will wait for a Hello packet to arrive from a specific neighbor.

- The uptime indicates how long the neighborship has been established.

- The SRTT field is the smooth round-trip timer—an indication of the time it takes for a round-trip from this router to its neighbor and back. This value is used to determine how long to wait after a multicast for a reply from this neighbor. If a reply isn't received in time, the router will switch to using unicasts in an attempt to complete the communication. The time between multicast attempts is specified by…

- The Retransmission Time Out (RTO) field, which is the amount of time EIGRP waits before retransmitting a packet from the retransmission queue to a neighbor.

- The Q value indicates whether there are any outstanding messages in the queue—consistently large values would indicate a problem.

- The Seq field indicates the sequence number of the last update from that neighbor—something that's used to maintain synchronization and avoid duplicate or out-of-sequence processing of messages.

The show ip eigrp neighbors command allows you to check the IP addresses as well as the retransmit interval and queue counts for the neighbors that have established an adjacency.

Now let's see what's in the Corp topology table by using the show ip eigrp topology command—this should be interesting!

```
Corp#sh ip eigrp topology
IP-EIGRP Topology Table for AS(10)/ID(10.1.5.1)
Codes: P - Passive, A - Active, U - Update, Q - Query, R - Reply,
       r - reply Status, s - sia Status
P 10.1.11.0/24, 1 successors, FD is 2172416
        via 10.1.5.2 (2172416/28160), Serial0/2/0
```

```
P 10.1.10.0/24, 1 successors, FD is 2172416
        via 10.1.5.2 (2195456/281600), Serial0/2/0
P 10.1.9.0/24, 1 successors, FD is 2195456
        via 10.1.4.2 (2195456/281600), Serial0/1/0
P 10.1.8.0/24, 1 successors, FD is 2195456
        via 10.1.4.2 (2195456/72960), Serial0/1/0
P 10.1.12.0/24, 1 successors, FD is 2172416
        via 10.1.5.2 (2172416/28160), Serial0/2/0
P 10.1.3.0/24, 1 successors, FD is 76839936
        via Connected, Serial0/0/1
        via 10.1.2.2 (9849856/7719936), Serial0/0/0
P 10.1.2.0/24, 1 successors, FD is 2169856
        via Connected, Serial0/0/0
        via 10.1.2.2 (2681856/551936), Serial0/0/0
P 10.1.1.0/24, 1 successors, FD is 28160
        via Connected, FastEthernet0/1
P 10.1.7.0/24, 1 successors, FD is 793600
        via 10.1.2.2 (2195456/281600), Serial0/0/0
        via 10.1.3.2 (77081600/281600), Serial0/0/1
P 10.1.6.0/24, 1 successors, FD is 793600
        via 10.1.2.2 (2195456/281600), Serial0/0/0
        via 10.1.3.2 (77081600/281600), Serial0/0/1
P 10.1.5.0/24, 1 successors, FD is 2169856
        via Connected, Serial0/2/0
P 10.1.4.0/24, 1 successors, FD is 2169856
        via Connected, Serial0/1/0
```

Notice that every route is preceded by a *P*. This means that the route is in the *passive state*, which is a good thing because routes in the *active state (A)* indicate that the router has lost its path to this network and is searching for a replacement. Each entry also indicates the feasible distance, or FD, to each remote network plus the next-hop neighbor through which packets will travel to their destination. Plus, each entry also has two numbers in parentheses. The first indicates the feasible distance, and the second the advertised distance to a remote network.

Now here's where things get interesting—notice that under the 10.1.7.0 and 10.1.6.0 outputs there are two links to each network and that the feasible distance and advertised distance are different. What this means is that we have one successor to the networks and one feasible successor—a backup route! So very cool! You need to remember that even though both routes to network 10.1.6.0 and 10.1.7.0 are in the topology table, only the successor route (the one with the lowest metrics) will be copied and placed into the routing table.

In order for the route to be a feasible successor, its advertised distance must be less than the feasible distance of the successor route.

EIGRP will load-balance across both links automatically when they are of equal variance (equal cost), but EIGRP can also load-balance across unequal-cost links as well if we use the `variance` command. The variance metric is set to 1 by default, meaning that only equal-cost links will load-balance. You can change the metric anywhere up to 128. Changing a variance value enables EIGRP to install multiple, loop-free routes with unequal cost in a local routing table.

So basically, if the variance is set to 1, only routes with the same metric as the successor will be installed in the local routing table. And, for example, if the variance is set to 2, any EIGRP-learned route with a metric less than two times the successor metric will be installed in the local routing table (if it is already a feasible successor).

Now's a great time for us to check out some debugging outputs. First, let's use the `debug eigrp packet` command that will show our Hello packets being sent between neighbor routers:

```
Corp#debug eigrp packet
EIGRP Packets debugging is on
    (UPDATE, REQUEST, QUERY, REPLY, HELLO, IPXSAP, PROBE, ACK, STUB,
    SIAQUERY, SIAREPLY)
Corp#
*Mar 21 23:17:35.050: EIGRP: Sending HELLO on FastEthernet0/1
*Mar 21 23:17:35.050:   AS 10, Flags 0x0, Seq 0/0 idbQ 0/0 iidbQ un/rely 0/0
*Mar 21 23:17:35.270: EIGRP: Received HELLO on Serial0/1/0 nbr 10.1.4.2
*Mar 21 23:17:35.270:   AS 10, Flags 0x0, Seq 0/0 idbQ 0/0 iidbQ
   un/rely 0/0 peerQ un/rely 0/0
*Mar 21 23:17:35.294: EIGRP: Received HELLO on Serial0/0/0 nbr 10.1.2.2
*Mar 21 23:17:35.294:   AS 10, Flags 0x0, Seq 0/0 idbQ 0/0 iidbQ
   un/rely 0/0 peerQ un/rely 0/0
*Mar 21 23:17:38.014: EIGRP: Received HELLO on Serial0/2/0 nbr 10.1.5.2
*Mar 21 23:17:38.014:   AS 10, Flags 0x0, Seq 0/0 idbQ 0/0 iidbQ
   un/rely 0/0 peerQ un/rely 0/0
```

Since my Corp router is connected to three EIGRP neighbors, and because the 224.0.0.10 multicast is sent out every 5 seconds, I didn't have any problem seeing the updates. The Hello packets are sent out every active interface as well as all the interfaces that we have neighbors connected to. Did you notice that the AS number is provided in the update? This is because if a neighbor doesn't have the same AS number, the Hello update would just be discarded.

I want to show you one more important debugging command—the `debug ip eigrp notification` command (called `debug ip eigrp events` on pre-12.4 routers), plus the resulting output. What's important, and probably surprising to you, is that this command's output shouldn't show you anything at all! That's right—the only time you'll see output from this command is if there's a problem on your network or you've added or deleted a network from a router in your internetwork. So because I so humbly know I have a super-cool, problem-free network, I'm going to shut down an interface on my Corp router in order to see some output:

```
Corp(config)#int f0/1
Corp(config-if)#shut
```

```
*Mar 21 23:25:43.506: IP-EIGRP(Default-IP-Routing-Table:10): Callback:
   route_adjust FastEthernet0/1
*Mar 21 23:25:43.506: IP-EIGRP: Callback: ignored connected AS 0 10.1.1.0/24
*Mar 21 23:25:43.506:              into: eigrp AS 10
*Mar 21 23:25:43.506: IP-EIGRP(Default-IP-Routing-Table:10): Callback:
   callbackup_routes 10.1.1.0/24
Corp(config-if)#n
*Mar 21 23:25:45.506: %LINK-5-CHANGED: Interface FastEthernet0/1,
   changed state to administratively down
*Mar 21 23:25:46.506: %LINEPROTO-5-UPDOWN: Line protocol on Interface
   FastEthernet0/1, changed state to down
Corp(config-if)#no shut
Corp(config-if)#^Z
*Mar 21 23:25:49.570: %LINK-3-UPDOWN: Interface FastEthernet0/1,
   changed state to up
*Mar 21 23:25:49.570: IP-EIGRP(Default-IP-Routing-Table:10): Callback:
   lostroute 10.1.1.0/24
*Mar 21 23:25:49.570: IP-EIGRP(Default-IP-Routing-Table:0): Callback:
   redist connected (config change) FastEthernet0/1
*Mar 21 23:25:49.570: IP-EIGRP(Default-IP-Routing-Table:0): Callback:
   redist connected (config change) Serial0/0/0
*Mar 21 23:25:49.570: IP-EIGRP(Default-IP-Routing-Table:0): Callback:
   redist connected (config change) Serial0/0/1
*Mar 21 23:25:49.570: IP-EIGRP(Default-IP-Routing-Table:0): Callback:
   redist connected (config change) Serial0/1/0
*Mar 21 23:25:49.570: IP-EIGRP(Default-IP-Routing-Table:0): Callback:
   redist connected (config change) Serial0/2/0
*Mar 21 23:25:49.570: IP-EIGRP(Default-IP-Routing-Table:10): Callback:
   route_adjust FastEthernet0/1
*Mar 21 23:25:50.570: %LINEPROTO-5-UPDOWN: Line protocol on Interface
   FastEthernet0/1, changed state to up
```

I'm going to repeat this because it's that important—you don't want to see output from this command on your production network! If you do, odds are you have a problem or two that you'd better find and fix.

I know you've learned a lot about EIGRP so far, but stick around because you're not done with this chapter just yet! It's now time to give you the skinny on OSPF!

Open Shortest Path First (OSPF) Basics

Open Shortest Path First (OSPF) is an open standard routing protocol that's been implemented by a wide variety of network vendors, including Cisco. If you have multiple routers and not all of them are Cisco (what!), then you can't use EIGRP, can you? So your remaining CCNA objective options are basically RIP, RIPv2, and OSPF. If it's a large network, then, really, your only options are OSPF and something called route redistribution—a translation service between routing protocols that we discussed earlier in this chapter.

OSPF works by using the Dijkstra algorithm. First, a shortest path tree is constructed, and then the routing table is populated with the resulting best paths. OSPF converges quickly, although perhaps not as quickly as EIGRP, and it supports multiple, equal-cost routes to the same destination. Like EIGRP, it does support both IP and IPv6 routed protocols.

OSPF provides the following features:

- Consists of areas and autonomous systems
- Minimizes routing update traffic
- Allows scalability
- Supports VLSM/CIDR
- Has unlimited hop count
- Allows multi-vendor deployment (open standard)

OSPF is the first link-state routing protocol that most people are introduced to, so it's useful to see how it compares to more traditional distance-vector protocols such as RIPv2 and RIPv1. Table 7.3 gives you a comparison of these three protocols.

TABLE 7.3 OSPF and RIP comparison

Characteristic	OSPF	RIPv2	RIPv1
Type of protocol	Link state	Distance vector	Distance vector
Classless support	Yes	Yes	No
VLSM support	Yes	Yes	No
Auto-summarization	No	Yes	Yes
Manual summarization	Yes	No	No
Discontiguous support	Yes	Yes	No
Route propagation	Multicast on change	Periodic multicast	Periodic broadcast
Path metric	Bandwidth	Hops	Hops
Hop count limit	None	15	15

TABLE 7.3   OSPF and RIP comparison *(continued)*

Characteristic	OSPF	RIPv2	RIPv1
Convergence	Fast	Slow	Slow
Peer authentication	Yes	Yes	No
Hierarchical network	Yes (using areas)	No (flat only)	No (flat only)
Updates	Event triggered	Route table updates	Route table updates
Route computation	Dijkstra	Bellman-Ford	Bellman-Ford

OSPF has many features beyond the few I've listed in Table 7.3, and all of them contribute to a fast, scalable, and robust protocol that can be actively deployed in thousands of production networks.

OSPF is supposed to be designed in a hierarchical fashion, which basically means that you can separate the larger internetwork into smaller internetworks called areas. This is the best design for OSPF.

The following are reasons for creating OSPF in a hierarchical design:

- To decrease routing overhead
- To speed up convergence
- To confine network instability to single areas of the network

This does not make configuring OSPF easier, but more elaborate and difficult.

Figure 7.4 shows a typical OSPF simple design. Notice how each router connects to the backbone—called area 0, or the backbone area. OSPF must have an area 0, and all other areas should connect to this area. (Areas that do not connect directly to area 0 by using virtual links are beyond the scope of this book.) Routers that connect other areas to the backbone area within an AS are called Area Border Routers (ABRs). Still, at least one interface of the ABR must be in area 0.

FIGURE 7.4   OSPF design example

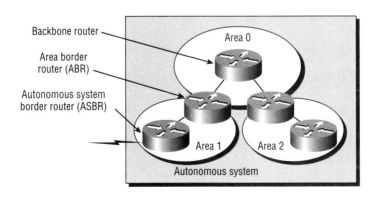

OSPF runs inside an autonomous system, but it can also connect multiple autonomous systems together. The router that connects these ASes is called an Autonomous System Boundary Router (ASBR).

Ideally, you would create other areas of networks to help keep route updates to a minimum and to keep problems from propagating throughout the network. But that's beyond the scope of this chapter. Just make note of it.

As in the section on EIGRP, I'll first cover the essential terminology you need to understand OSPF.

OSPF Terminology

Imagine how challenging it would be if you were given a map and compass but had no knowledge of east or west, north or south, river or mountain, lake or desert. You'd probably not get very far putting your new tools to good use without knowing about this stuff. For this reason, you'll begin your exploration of OSPF with a long list of terms that will prevent you from getting lost in the later sections. The following are important OSPF terms to familiarize yourself with before you proceed:

Link   A *link* is a network or router interface assigned to any given network. When an interface is added to the OSPF process, it's considered by OSPF to be a link. This link, or interface, will have state information associated with it (up or down) as well as one or more IP addresses.

Router ID   The *Router ID (RID)* is an IP address used to identify the router. Cisco chooses the Router ID by using the highest IP address of all configured loopback interfaces. If no loopback interfaces are configured with addresses, OSPF will choose the highest IP address of all active physical interfaces.

Neighbor   *Neighbors* are two or more routers that have an interface on a common network, such as two routers connected on a point-to-point serial link.

Adjacency   An *adjacency* is a relationship between two OSPF routers that permits the direct exchange of route updates. OSPF is really picky about sharing routing information—unlike EIGRP, which directly shares routes with all of its neighbors. Instead, OSPF directly shares routes only with neighbors that have also established adjacencies. And not all neighbors will become adjacent—this depends upon both the type of network and the configuration of the routers.

Hello protocol   The OSPF Hello protocol provides dynamic neighbor discovery and maintains neighbor relationships. Hello packets and Link State Advertisements (LSAs) build and maintain the topological database. Hello packets are addressed to 224.0.0.5.

Neighborship database   The *neighborship database* is a list of all OSPF routers for which Hello packets have been seen. A variety of details, including the Router ID and state, are maintained on each router in the neighborship database.

Topological database   The *topological database* contains information from all of the Link State Advertisement packets that have been received for an area. The router uses the information from the topology database as input into the Dijkstra algorithm that computes the shortest path to every network.

LSA packets are used to update and maintain the topological database.

Link State Advertisement A *Link State Advertisement (LSA)* is an OSPF data packet containing link-state and routing information that's shared among OSPF routers. There are different types of LSA packets, and I'll go into these shortly. An OSPF router will exchange LSA packets only with routers to which it has established adjacencies.

Designated router A *Designated Router (DR)* is elected whenever OSPF routers are connected to the same multi-access network. Cisco likes to call these "broadcast" networks, but really, they are networks that have multiple recipients. Try not to confuse multi-access with multipoint, which can be easy to do sometimes.

A prime example is an Ethernet LAN. To minimize the number of adjacencies formed, a DR is chosen (elected) to disseminate/receive routing information to/from the remaining routers on the broadcast network or link. This ensures that their topology tables are synchronized. All routers on the shared network will establish adjacencies with the DR and backup designated router (BDR)—I'll define this next. The election is won by the router with the highest priority, and the Router ID is used as a tiebreaker if the priority of more than one router turns out to be the same.

Backup designated router A *Backup Designated Router (BDR)* is a hot standby for the DR on multi-access links (remember that Cisco sometimes likes to call these "broadcast" networks). The BDR receives all routing updates from OSPF adjacent routers but doesn't flood LSA updates.

OSPF areas An *OSPF area* is a grouping of contiguous networks and routers. All routers in the same area share a common Area ID. Because a router can be a member of more than one area at a time, the Area ID is associated with specific interfaces on the router. This would allow some interfaces to belong to area 1 while the remaining interfaces can belong to area 0. All of the routers within the same area have the same topology table. When configuring OSPF, you've got to remember that there must be an area 0 and that this is typically configured on the routers that connect to the backbone of the network. Areas also play a role in establishing a hierarchical network organization—something that really enhances the scalability of OSPF!

Broadcast (multi-access) *Broadcast (multi-access) networks* such as Ethernet allow multiple devices to connect to (or access) the same network as well as provide a *broadcast* ability in which a single packet is delivered to all nodes on the network. In OSPF, a DR and a BDR must be elected for each broadcast multi-access network.

Non-broadcast multi-access *Non-broadcast multi-access (NBMA) networks* are types such as Frame Relay, X.25, and Asynchronous Transfer Mode (ATM). These networks allow for multi-access but have no broadcast ability like Ethernet. So, NBMA networks require special OSPF configuration to function properly and neighbor relationships must be defined.

DR and BDR are elected on broadcast and non-broadcast multi-access networks. Elections are covered in detail later in this chapter.

Point-to-point *Point-to-point* refers to a type of network topology consisting of a direct connection between two routers that provides a single communication path. The point-to-point connection can be physical, as in a serial cable directly connecting two routers, or it can be logical, as in two routers that are thousands of miles apart yet connected by a circuit in a Frame Relay network. In either case, this type of configuration eliminates the need for DRs or BDRs—but neighbors are discovered automatically.

Point-to-multipoint *Point-to-multipoint* refers to a type of network topology consisting of a series of connections between a single interface on one router and multiple destination routers. All of the interfaces on all of the routers sharing the point-to-multipoint connection belong to the same network. As with point-to-point, no DRs or BDRs are needed.

All of these terms play an important part in understanding the operation of OSPF, so again, make sure you're familiar with each of them. Reading through the rest of this chapter will help you to place the terms within their proper context.

SPF Tree Calculation

Within an area, each router calculates the best/shortest path to every network in that same area. This calculation is based upon the information collected in the topology database and an algorithm called *shortest path first (SPF)*. Picture each router in an area constructing a tree—much like a family tree—where the router is the root and all other networks are arranged along the branches and leaves. This is the shortest path tree used by the router to insert routes into the routing table.

It's important to understand that this tree contains only networks that exist in the same area as the router itself does. If a router has interfaces in multiple areas, then separate trees will be constructed for each area. One of the key criteria considered during the route selection process of the SPF algorithm is the metric or cost of each potential path to a network. But this SPF calculation doesn't apply to routes from other areas.

OSPF uses a metric referred to as *cost*. A cost is associated with every outgoing interface included in an SPF tree. The cost of the entire path is the sum of the costs of the outgoing interfaces along the path. Because cost is an arbitrary value as defined in RFC 2338, Cisco had to implement its own method of calculating the cost for each OSPF-enabled interface. Cisco uses a simple equation of 10^8/bandwidth. The bandwidth is the configured bandwidth for the interface. Using this rule, a 100Mbps Fast Ethernet interface would have a default OSPF cost of 1 and a 10Mbps Ethernet interface would have a cost of 10.

 An interface set with a bandwidth of 64,000 would have a default cost of 1,563.

This value may be overridden by using the `ip ospf cost` command. The cost is manipulated by changing the value to a number within the range of 1 to 65,535. Because the cost is assigned to each link, the value must be changed on the interface that you want to change the cost.

Cisco bases link cost on bandwidth. Other vendors may use other metrics to calculate a given link's cost. When connecting links between routers from different vendors, you may have to adjust the cost to match another vendor's router. Both routers must assign the same cost to the link for OSPF to work.

Configuring OSPF

Configuring basic OSPF isn't as simple as RIP, IGRP, and EIGRP, and it can get really complex once the many options that are allowed within OSPF are factored in. But that's okay—for your studies, you should be interested in the basic single-area OSPF configuration. The following sections describe how to configure single-area OSPF.

These two elements are the basic elements of OSPF configuration:

- Enabling OSPF
- Configuring OSPF areas

Enabling OSPF

The easiest and also least scalable way to configure OSPF is to just use a single area. Doing this requires a minimum of two commands.

The command you use to activate the OSPF routing process is as follows:

```
Lab_A(config)#router ospf ?
<1-65535>
```

A value in the range 1–65,535 identifies the OSPF Process ID. It's a unique number on this router that groups a series of OSPF configuration commands under a specific running process. Different OSPF routers don't have to use the same Process ID in order to communicate. It's purely a local value that essentially has little meaning, but it cannot start at 0; it has to start at a minimum of 1.

You can have more than one OSPF process running simultaneously on the same router if you want, but this isn't the same as running multi-area OSPF. The second process will maintain an entirely separate copy of its topology table and manage its communications independently of the first process. And because the CCNA objectives only cover single-area OSPF with each router running a single OSPF process, that's what I'm going to focus on in this book.

The OSPF Process ID is needed to identify a unique instance of an OSPF database and is locally significant.

Configuring OSPF Areas

After identifying the OSPF process, you need to identify the interfaces that you want to activate OSPF communications on as well as the area in which each resides. This will also configure the networks you're going to advertise to others. OSPF uses wildcards in the configuration—which are also used in access-list configurations (covered in Chapter 11).

Here's an OSPF basic configuration example for you:

```
Lab_A#config t
Lab_A(config)#router ospf 1
Lab_A(config-router)#network 10.0.0.0 0.255.255.255
 area ?
  <0-4294967295>  OSPF area ID as a decimal value
  A.B.C.D         OSPF area ID in IP address format
Lab_A(config-router)#network 10.0.0.0 0.255.255.255
 area 0
```

 The areas can be any number from 0 to 4.2 billion. Don't get these numbers confused with the Process ID, which is from 1 to 65,535.

Remember, the OSPF Process ID number is irrelevant. It can be the same on every router on the network, or it can be different—doesn't matter. It's locally significant and just enables the OSPF routing on the router.

The arguments of the network command are the network number (10.0.0.0) and the wildcard mask (0.255.255.255). The combination of these two numbers identifies the interfaces that OSPF will operate on and will also be included in its OSPF LSA advertisements. OSPF will use this command to find any interface on the router configured in the 10.0.0.0 network, and it will place any interface it finds into area 0. Notice that you can create about 4.2 billion areas. (I doubt that a router would let you actually create that many, but you can certainly name them using the numbers up to 4.2 billion.) You can also label an area using an IP address format.

A quick review of wildcards: A 0 octet in the wildcard mask indicates that the corresponding octet in the network must match exactly. On the other hand, a 255 indicates that you don't care what the corresponding octet is in the network number. A network and wildcard mask combination of 1.1.1.1 0.0.0.0 would match 1.1.1.1 only, and nothing else. This is really useful if you want to activate OSPF on a specific interface in a very clear and simple way. If you insist on matching a range of networks, the network and wildcard mask combination of 1.1.0.0 0.0.255.255 would match anything in the range 1.1.0.0–1.1.255.255. Because of this, it's simpler and safer to stick to using wildcard masks of 0.0.0.0 and identify each OSPF interface individually.

The final argument is the area number. It indicates the area to which the interfaces identified in the network and wildcard mask portion belong. Remember that OSPF routers will only become neighbors if their interfaces share a network that's configured to belong to the same area number. The format of the area number is either a decimal value from the range 1–4,294,967,295 or a value represented in standard dotted-decimal notation. For example, area 0.0.0.0 is a legitimate area and is identical to area 0.

Wildcard Example

Before getting down to configuring our network, let's take a quick peek at a harder OSPF network configuration to find out what our OSPF network statements would be if we were using subnets and wildcards.

You have a router with these four subnets connected to four different interfaces:

- 192.168.10.64/28
- 192.168.10.80/28
- 192.168.10.96/28
- 192.168.10.8/30

All interfaces need to be in area 0. Seems to me, the easiest configuration would be this:

```
Test#config t
Test(config)#router ospf 1
Test(config-router)#network 192.168.10.0 0.0.0.255 area 0
```

But easy isn't always best, so although this is easier, what fun is that? And worse, it's not likely to cover the CCNA objectives for you! So let's create a separate network statement for each interface using the subnet numbers and wildcards. Doing that would look something like this:

```
Test#config t
Test(config)#router ospf 1
Test(config-router)#network 192.168.10.64 0.0.0.15 area 0
Test(config-router)#network 192.168.10.80 0.0.0.15 area 0
Test(config-router)#network 192.168.10.96 0.0.0.15 area 0
Test(config-router)#network 192.168.10.8 0.0.0.3 area 0
```

Wow, now that's a different looking config! Truthfully, OSPF would work exactly the same way as in the easy configuration I showed you first—but unlike the easy configuration, this one covers the CCNA objectives!

Just remember, when configuring wildcards, they're always one less than the block size. A /28 is a block size of 16, so we'd add our network statement using the subnet number and then add a wildcard of 15 in the interesting octet. For the /30, which is a block size of 4, we'd use a wildcard of 3.

Let's use Figure 7.5 as an example and configure that network with OSPF using wildcards to make sure you have a solid grip on this. Figure 7.5 shows a three-router network with the IP addresses of each interface.

The very first thing you need to be able to do is to look at each interface and determine the subnet that the addresses are in. Hold on, I know what you're thinking: "Why don't I just use the exact IP addresses of the interface with the 0.0.0.0 wildcard?" Well, you can, but we're paying attention to CCNA objectives here, not just what's easiest, remember?

FIGURE 7.5   Sample OSPF wildcard configuration

The IP addresses for each interface are shown in the figure. The Lab_A router has two directly connected subnets: 192.168.10.64/29 and 10.255.255.80/30. Here's the OSPF configuration using wildcards:

```
Lab_A#config t
Lab_A(config)#router ospf 1
Lab_A(config-router)#network 192.168.10.64 0.0.0.7 area 0
Lab_A(config-router)#network 10.255.255.80 0.0.0.3 area 0
```

The Lab_A router is using a /29 or 255.255.255.248 mask on the ethernet0 interface. This is a block size of 8, which is a wildcard of 7. The s0 interface is a mask of 255.255.255.252—block size of 4, with a wildcard of 3. You can't configure OSPF this way if you can't look at the IP address and slash notation and then figure out the subnet, mask, and wildcard, can you?

Here are our other two configurations:

```
Lab_B#config t
Lab_B(config)#router ospf 1
Lab_B(config-router)#network 192.168.10.48 0.0.0.7 area 0
```

```
Lab_B(config-router)#network 10.255.255.80 0.0.0.3 area 0
Lab_B(config-router)#network 10.255.255.8 0.0.0.3 area 0

Lab_C#config t
Lab_C(config)#router ospf 1
Lab_C(config-router)#network 192.168.10.16 0.0.0.7 area 0
Lab_C(config-router)#network 10.255.255.8 0.0.0.3 area 0
```

As I mentioned with the Lab_A configuration, you've got to be able to determine the subnet, mask, and wildcard just by looking at the IP address of an interface. If you can't do that, you won't be able to configure OSPF using wildcards as I just demonstrated. So go over this until you're really comfortable with it!

Configuring Our Network with OSPF

Okay—now we get to have some fun! Let's configure our internetwork with OSPF using just area 0. Before we do that, we've got to remove EIGRP because OSPF has an administrative distance of 110. (EIGRP is 90—but you already knew that, right?) I know we've already removed RIP from our routers, but now we can also remove RIP from the 871W and R3 routers because the 871W supports the OSPF routing protocol.

There's a bunch of different ways to configure OSPF, and as I said, the simplest and easiest is to use the wildcard mask of 0.0.0.0. But I want to demonstrate that we can configure each router differently with OSPF and still come up with the exact same result. This is one reason why OSPF is more fun than other routing protocols—it gives us all a lot more ways to screw things up!

Corp

Here's the Corp router's configuration:

```
Corp#config t
Corp(config)#no router eigrp 10
Corp(config)#router ospf 132
Corp(config-router)#network 10.1.1.1 0.0.0.0 area 0
Corp(config-router)#network 10.1.2.1 0.0.0.0 area 0
Corp(config-router)#network 10.1.3.1 0.0.0.0 area 0
Corp(config-router)#network 10.1.4.1 0.0.0.0 area 0
Corp(config-router)#network 10.1.5.1 0.0.0.0 area 0
```

Hmmmm—it seems we have a few things to discuss here. First, I removed EIGRP, then added OSPF. So why did I use OSPF 132? It really doesn't matter—the number is irrelevant!

The network commands are pretty straightforward. I typed in the IP address of each interface and used the wildcard mask of 0.0.0.0, which means that the IP address must match each octet exactly. But if this is one of those times where easier is better—just do this:

```
Corp(config)#router ospf 132
Corp(config-router)#network 10.1.0.0 0.0.255.255 area 0
```

One line instead of five! I really want you to understand that no matter which way you configure the network statement, OSPF will work the same here. Now, let's move on to R1. To keep things simple, we're going to use our same sample configuration.

R1

The R1 router has four directly connected networks. Instead of typing in each interface, I can use the one network command example and still make it work exactly the same:

```
R1#config t
R1(config)#no router eigrp 10
R1(config)#router ospf 1
R1(config-router)#network 10.1.0.0 0.0.255.255 area0
                                                    ^
% Invalid input detected at '^' marker.

R1(config-router)#network 10.1.0.0 0.0.255.255 area 0
```

Okay—other than my little typo, where I forgot to place a space between the area command and the area number, this is truly a fast and efficient configuration.

All I did was to first disable EIGRP, and then I turned on OSPF routing process 1 and added the network command 10.1.0.0 with a wildcard of 0.0.255.255. What this did is basically say, "Find any interface that starts with 10.1, and place those interfaces into area 0." Quick, easy, and slick!

R2

Let's give the R2 router that's directly connected to three networks some attention:

```
R2#config t
R2(config)#no router eigrp 10
R2(config)#router ospf 45678
R2(config-router)#network 10.0.0.0 0.255.255.255 area 0
```

I can use any process ID I want—as long as it's a value from 1 to 65,535. And notice I used the 10.0.0.0 with wildcard 0.255.255.255. This works well too.

R3

For the R3 router, we need to turn off RIP and EIGRP, although RIP won't bother OSPF since OSPF has a lower AD. But we should turn it off anyway. And, as usual, we'll use the SDM.

Our first screen shot shows RIP disabled.

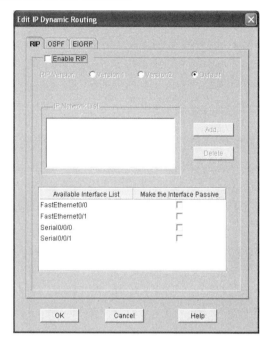

Our next graphic shows EIGRP being disabled. (I just clicked the Delete button.)

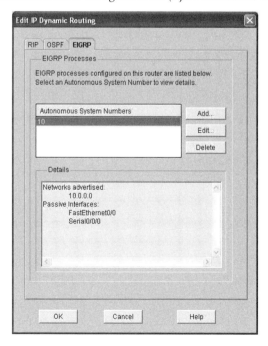

After clicking on the OSPF tab, I clicked Add Network and added my OSPF information.

I then clicked OK, chose my passive interfaces, and clicked OK again.

We're good—you can see that we have only OSPF running on the R3 router.

871W

Finally, our last router! Let's disable RIP and add OSPF:

```
871W#config t
871W(config)#no router rip
871W(config)#router ospf 1
871W(config-router)#network 10.1.11.0 0.0.0.255 area 0
871W(config-router)#network 10.1.12.0 0.0.0.255 area 0
```

Cool! Now that we've configured all the routers with OSPF, what's next? Miller Time? Nope—not yet. It's that verification thing again. We still have to make sure that OSPF is really working. That's exactly what we're going to do next.

Verifying OSPF Configuration

There are several ways to verify proper OSPF configuration and operation, and in the following sections I'll show you the OSPF show commands you need to know in order to do this. We're going to start by taking a quick look at the routing table of the Corp router:

So, let's issue a show ip route command on the Corp router:

```
   10.0.0.0/24 is subnetted, 12 subnets
O     10.1.11.0 [110/65] via 10.1.5.2, 00:01:31, Serial0/2/0
O     10.1.10.0 [110/65] via 10.1.5.2, 00:01:31, Serial0/2/0
O     10.1.9.0 [110/74] via 10.1.4.2, 00:01:31, Serial0/1/0
O     10.1.8.0 [110/65] via 10.1.4.2, 00:01:31, Serial0/1/0
O     10.1.12.0 [110/66] via 10.1.5.2, 00:01:31, Serial0/2/0
C     10.1.3.0 is directly connected, Serial0/0/1
C     10.1.2.0 is directly connected, Serial0/0/0
C     10.1.1.0 is directly connected, FastEthernet0/1
O     10.1.7.0 [110/74] via 10.1.3.2, 00:01:32, Serial0/0/1
                [110/74] via 10.1.2.2, 00:01:32, Serial0/0/0
O     10.1.6.0 [110/74] via 10.1.3.2, 00:01:32, Serial0/0/1
                [110/74] via 10.1.2.2, 00:01:32, Serial0/0/0
C     10.1.5.0 is directly connected, Serial0/2/0
C     10.1.4.0 is directly connected, Serial0/1/0
```

The Corp router shows the found routes for all 12 of our networks, with the O representing OSPF internal routes (the Cs are obviously our directly connected networks). It also found the dual routes to networks 10.1.6.0 and 10.1.7.0. I removed the bandwidth and delay commands from under the interface so the defaults are being used to determine the metric. But remember, OSPF only uses bandwidth to determine the best path to a network.

Important note: OSPF can load-balance only across links of equal costs. It can't load-balance across unequal-cost links as EIGRP can.

It's time to show you all the OSPF verification commands that you need to know.

The *show ip ospf* Command

The show ip ospf command is used to display OSPF information for one or all OSPF processes running on the router. Information contained therein includes the Router ID, area information, SPF statistics, and LSA timer information. Let's check out the output from the Corp router:

```
Corp#sh ip ospf
 Routing Process "ospf 132" with ID 10.1.5.1
 Start time: 04:32:04.116, Time elapsed: 01:27:10.156
 Supports only single TOS(TOS0) routes
 Supports opaque LSA
 Supports Link-local Signaling (LLS)
 Supports area transit capability
 Router is not originating router-LSAs with maximum metric
 Initial SPF schedule delay 5000 msecs
 Minimum hold time between two consecutive SPFs 10000 msecs
 Maximum wait time between two consecutive SPFs 10000 msecs
 Incremental-SPF disabled
 Minimum LSA interval 5 secs
 Minimum LSA arrival 1000 msecs
 LSA group pacing timer 240 secs
 Interface flood pacing timer 33 msecs
 Retransmission pacing timer 66 msecs
 Number of external LSA 0. Checksum Sum 0x000000
 Number of opaque AS LSA 0. Checksum Sum 0x000000
 Number of DCbitless external and opaque AS LSA 0
 Number of DoNotAge external and opaque AS LSA 0
 Number of areas in this router is 1. 1 normal 0 stub 0 nssa
 Number of areas transit capable is 0
 External flood list length 0
    Area BACKBONE(0)
        Number of interfaces in this area is 5
        Area has no authentication
        SPF algorithm last executed 00:14:52.220 ago
```

```
    SPF algorithm executed 14 times
    Area ranges are
    Number of LSA 6. Checksum Sum 0x03C06F
    Number of opaque link LSA 0. Checksum Sum 0x000000
    Number of DCbitless LSA 0
    Number of indication LSA 0
    Number of DoNotAge LSA 0
    Flood list length 0
```

Notice the Router ID (RID) of 10.1.5.1, which is the highest IP address configured on the router.

The *show ip ospf database* Command

Using the `show ip ospf database` command will give you information about the number of routers in the internetwork (AS) plus the neighboring router's ID (this is the topology database I mentioned earlier). Unlike the `show ip eigrp topology` command, this command shows the "OSPF routers," not each and every link in the AS as EIGRP does.

The output is broken down by area. Here's a sample output, again from Corp:

```
Corp#sh ip ospf database

            OSPF Router with ID (10.1.5.1) (Process ID 132)

            Router Link States (Area 0)

Link ID        ADV Router      Age      Seq#        Checksum Link count
10.1.5.1       10.1.5.1        72       0x80000002 0x00F2CA 9
10.1.7.1       10.1.7.1        83       0x80000004 0x009197 6
10.1.9.1       10.1.9.1        73       0x80000001 0x00DA1C 4
10.1.11.1      10.1.11.1       67       0x80000005 0x00666A 4
10.1.12.1      10.1.12.1       67       0x80000004 0x007631 2

            Net Link States (Area 0)

Link ID        ADV Router      Age      Seq#        Checksum
10.1.11.2      10.1.12.1       68       0x80000001 0x00A337
```

You can see all five routers and the RID of each router (the highest IP address on each router). The router output shows the link ID—remember that an interface is also a link—and the RID of the router on that link under the ADV router, or advertising router.

The *show ip ospf interface* Command

The show ip ospf interface command displays all interface-related OSPF information. Data is displayed about OSPF information for all interfaces or for specified interfaces. (I'll bold some of the important things.)

```
Corp#sh ip ospf interface f0/1
FastEthernet0/1 is up, line protocol is up
  Internet Address 10.1.1.1/24, Area 0
  Process ID 132, Router ID 10.1.5.1, Network Type BROADCAST, Cost: 1
  Transmit Delay is 1 sec, State DR, Priority 1
  Designated Router (ID) 10.1.5.1, Interface address 10.1.1.1
  No backup designated router on this network
  Timer intervals configured, Hello 10, Dead 40, Wait 40, Retransmit 5
    oob-resync timeout 40
    Hello due in 00:00:01
  Supports Link-local Signaling (LLS)
  Index 1/1, flood queue length 0
  Next 0x0(0)/0x0(0)
  Last flood scan length is 0, maximum is 0
  Last flood scan time is 0 msec, maximum is 0 msec
  Neighbor Count is 0, Adjacent neighbor count is 0
  Suppress hello for 0 neighbor(s)
```

The following information is displayed by this command:

- Interface IP address
- Area assignment
- Process ID
- Router ID
- Network type
- Cost
- Priority
- DR/BDR election information (if applicable)
- Hello and Dead timer intervals
- Adjacent neighbor information

The reason I used the show ip ospf interface f0/1 command is because I knew that there would be a designated router elected on the FastEthernet broadcast multi-access network. We'll get into DR and DBR elections in detail in a minute.

The *show ip ospf neighbor* Command

The show ip ospf neighbor command is super-useful because it summarizes the pertinent OSPF information regarding neighbors and the adjacency state. If a DR or BDR exists, that information will also be displayed. Here's a sample:

```
Corp#sh ip ospf neighbor
Neighbor ID  Pri  State   Dead Time     Address     Interface
10.1.11.1    0    FULL/  -  00:00:37    10.1.5.2    Serial0/2/0
10.1.9.1     0    FULL/  -  00:00:34    10.1.4.2    Serial0/1/0
10.1.7.1     0    FULL/  -  00:00:38    10.1.3.2    Serial0/0/1
10.1.7.1     0    FULL/  -  00:00:34    10.1.2.2    Serial0/0/0
```

This is a super-important command to understand because it's extremely useful in production networks. Let's take a look at the R3 and 871W routers outputs:

```
R3#sh ip ospf neighbor
Neighbor ID  Pri  State    Dead Time     Address     Interface
10.1.5.1     0    FULL/  -   00:00:39    10.1.5.1    Serial0/0/1
10.1.11.2    1    FULL/BDR   00:00:31    10.1.11.2   FastEthernet0/1
871W#sh ip ospf nei
Neihbor ID   Pri  State    Dead Time     Address     Interface
10.1.11.1    1    FULL/DR    00:00:30    10.1.11.1   Vlan1
```

Since there's an Ethernet link (broadcast multi-access) on the R3 router, there's going to be an election to determine who will be the designated router and who will be the non-designated router. We can see that the 871W became the designated router, and it won because it had the highest IP address on the network. You can change this, but that's the default.

The reason that the Corp connections to R1, R2, and R3 don't have a DR or BDR listed in the output is that by default, elections don't happen on point-to-point links. But we can see that the Corp router is fully adjacent to all three routers (and on both connections to R1) from its output.

The *show ip protocols* Command

The show ip protocols command is also useful, whether you're running OSPF, EIGRP, IGRP, RIP, BGP, IS-IS, or any other routing protocol that can be configured on your router. It provides an excellent overview of the actual operation of all currently running protocols.

Check out the output from the Corp router:

```
Corp#sh ip protocols
Routing Protocol is "ospf 132"
  Outgoing update filter list for all interfaces is not set
  Incoming update filter list for all interfaces is not set
```

```
Router ID 10.1.5.1
Number of areas in this router is 1. 1 normal 0 stub 0 nssa
Maximum path: 4
Routing for Networks:
   10.1.1.1 0.0.0.0 area 0
   10.1.2.1 0.0.0.0 area 0
   10.1.3.1 0.0.0.0 area 0
   10.1.4.1 0.0.0.0 area 0
   10.1.5.1 0.0.0.0 area 0
Reference bandwidth unit is 100 mbps
 Routing Information Sources:
   Gateway         Distance      Last Update
   10.1.11.1          110        00:28:53
   10.1.11.2          110        00:28:53
   10.1.9.1           110        00:28:53
   10.1.7.1           110        00:28:53
Distance: (default is 110)
```

From looking at this output, you can determine the OSPF Process ID, OSPF Router ID, type of OSPF area, networks and areas configured for OSPF, and the OSPF Router IDs of neighbors—that's a lot. Read, efficient! And hold on a second. Did you notice the absence of timers like the ones we were shown before in the RIP outputs from this command? That's because link-state routing protocols don't use timers to keep the network stable like distance-vector routing algorithms do.

Debugging OSPF

Debugging is a great tool for any protocol, so let's take a look in Table 7.4 at a few debugging commands for troubleshooting OSPF.

TABLE 7.4   Debugging Commands for Troubleshooting OSPF

Command	Description/Function
debug ip ospf packet	Shows Hello packets being received on your router
debug ip ospf hello	Shows Hello packets being sent and received on your router. Shows more detail than the debug ip ospf packet output
debug ip ospf adj	Shows DR and DBR elections on a broadcast and non-broadcast multi-access network

I'll start by showing you the output from the Corp router I got using the debug ip ospf packet command:

```
Corp#debug ip ospf packet
OSPF packet debugging is on
*Mar 23 01:20:42.199: OSPF: rcv. v:2 t:1 l:48 rid:172.16.10.3
    aid:0.0.0.0 chk:8075 aut:0 auk: from Serial0/1/0
Corp#
*Mar 23 01:20:45.507: OSPF: rcv. v:2 t:1 l:48 rid:172.16.10.2
    aid:0.0.0.0 chk:8076 aut:0 auk: from Serial0/0/0
*Mar 23 01:20:45.531: OSPF: rcv. v:2 t:1 l:48 rid:172.16.10.2
    aid:0.0.0.0 chk:8076 aut:0 auk: from Serial0/0/1
*Mar 23 01:20:45.531: OSPF: rcv. v:2 t:1 l:48 rid:172.16.10.4
    aid:0.0.0.0 chk:8074 aut:0 auk: from Serial0/2/0
*Mar 23 01:20:52.199: OSPF: rcv. v:2 t:1 l:48 rid:172.16.10.3
    aid:0.0.0.0 chk:8075 aut:0 auk: from Serial0/1/0
*Mar 23 01:20:55.507: OSPF: rcv. v:2 t:1 l:48 rid:172.16.10.2
    aid:0.0.0.0 chk:8076 aut:0 auk: from Serial0/0/0
*Mar 23 01:20:55.527: OSPF: rcv. v:2 t:1 l:48 rid:172.16.10.2
    aid:0.0.0.0 chk:8076 aut:0 auk: from Serial0/0/1
*Mar 23 01:20:55.531: OSPF: rcv. v:2 t:1 l:48 rid:172.16.10.4
    aid:0.0.0.0 chk:8074 aut:0 auk: from Serial0/2/0
```

In the preceding output, we can see that our router is both sending and receiving Hello packets every 10 seconds from neighbor (adjacent) routers. The next command will provide us with the same information, but with more detail. For example, we can see the multicast address used (224.0.0.5) and the area:

```
Corp#debug ip ospf hello
*Mar 23 01:18:41.103: OSPF: Send hello to 224.0.0.5 area 0 on
  Serial0/1/0 from 10.1.4.1
*Mar 23 01:18:41.607: OSPF: Send hello to 224.0.0.5 area 0 on
  FastEthernet0/1 from 10.1.1.1
*Mar 23 01:18:41.607: OSPF: Send hello to 224.0.0.5 area 0 on
  Serial0/0/0 from 10.1.2.1
*Mar 23 01:18:41.611: OSPF: Send hello to 224.0.0.5 area 0 on
  Serial0/2/0 from 10.1.5.1
*Mar 23 01:18:41.611: OSPF: Send hello to 224.0.0.5 area 0 on
  Serial0/0/1 from 10.1.3.1
*Mar 23 01:18:42.199: OSPF: Rcv hello from 172.16.10.3 area 0 from
  Serial0/1/0 10.1.4.2
*Mar 23 01:18:42.199: OSPF: End of hello processing
```

```
*Mar 23 01:18:45.519: OSPF: Rcv hello from 172.16.10.2 area 0 from
   Serial0/0/0 10.1.2.2
*Mar 23 01:18:45.519: OSPF: End of hello processing
*Mar 23 01:18:45.543: OSPF: Rcv hello from 172.16.10.2 area 0 from
   Serial0/0/1 10.1.3.2
*Mar 23 01:18:45.543: OSPF: End of hello processing
*Mar 23 01:18:45.543: OSPF: Rcv hello from 172.16.10.4 area 0 from
   Serial0/2/0 10.1.5.2
*Mar 23 01:18:45.543: OSPF: End of hello processing
```

The last debug command I'm going show you is the debug ip ospf adj command that will show us elections as they occur on broadcast and non-broadcast multi-access networks:

```
Corp#debug ip ospf adj
OSPF adjacency events debugging is on
*Mar 23 01:24:34.823: OSPF: Interface FastEthernet0/1 going Down
*Mar 23 01:24:34.823: OSPF: 172.16.10.1 address 10.1.1.1 on
   FastEthernet0/1 is dead, state DOWN
*Mar 23 01:24:34.823: OSPF: Neighbor change Event on interface
   FastEthernet0/1
*Mar 23 01:24:34.823: OSPF: DR/BDR election on FastEthernet0/1
*Mar 23 01:24:34.823: OSPF: Elect BDR 0.0.0.0
*Mar 23 01:24:34.823: OSPF: Elect DR 0.0.0.0
*Mar 23 01:24:34.823: OSPF: Elect BDR 0.0.0.0
*Mar 23 01:24:34.823: OSPF: Elect DR 0.0.0.0
*Mar 23 01:24:34.823:          DR: none    BDR: none
*Mar 23 01:24:34.823: OSPF: Flush network LSA immediately
*Mar 23 01:24:34.823: OSPF: Remember old DR 172.16.10.1 (id)
*Mar 23 01:24:35.323: OSPF: We are not DR to build Net Lsa for
   interface FastEthernet0/1
*Mar 23 01:24:35.323: OSPF: Build router LSA for area 0, router ID
   172.16.10.1, seq 0x80000006
*Mar 23 01:24:35.347: OSPF: Rcv LS UPD from 172.16.10.2 on Serial0/0/1
   length 148 LSA count 1
*Mar 23 01:24:40.703: OSPF: Interface FastEthernet0/1 going Up
*Mar 23 01:24:41.203: OSPF: Build router LSA for area 0, router ID
   172.16.10.1, seq 0x80000007
*Mar 23 01:24:41.231: OSPF: Rcv LS UPD from 172.16.10.2 on Serial0/0/1
   length 160 LSA count 1
```

All right—let's move on and discover how elections occur in an OSPF network.

OSPF DR and BDR Elections

In this chapter, I have discussed OSPF in detail; however, I need to expand the section on designated routers and backup designated routers that I've only briefly touched on so far. I'm also going to delve deeper into verifying the election process as well as provide you with a hands-on lab at the end of the chapter to help you understand that process even better.

To start with, I need to make sure you fully understand the terms *neighbors* and *adjacencies* again because they're really crucial to the DR and BDR election process. The election process happens when a broadcast or non-broadcast multi-access network is connected to a router and the link comes up. (Think Ethernet or Frame Relay.)

Neighbors

Routers that share a common segment become neighbors on that segment. These neighbors are elected via the Hello protocol. Hello packets are sent periodically out of each interface using IP multicast.

Two routers won't become neighbors unless they agree on the following:

Area ID   The idea here is that the two routers' interfaces have to belong to the same area on a particular segment. And of course, those interfaces have to belong to the same subnet.

Authentication   OSPF allows for the configuration of a password for a specific area. Although authentication between routers isn't required, you have the option to set it if you need to do so. Also, keep in mind that in order for routers to become neighbors, they need to have the same password on a segment if you're using authentication.

Hello and Dead intervals   OSPF exchanges Hello packets on each segment. This is a keepalive system used by routers to acknowledge their existence on a segment and for electing a designated router (DR) on both broadcast and non-broadcast multi-access segments.

The Hello interval specifies the number of seconds between Hello packets. The Dead interval is the number of seconds that a router's Hello packets can go without being seen before its neighbors declare the OSPF router dead (down). OSPF requires these intervals to be exactly the same between two neighbors. If any of these intervals are different, the routers won't become neighbors on that segment. You can see these timers with the `show ip ospf interface` command.

Adjacencies

In the election process, adjacency is the next step after the neighboring process. Adjacent routers are routers that go beyond the simple Hello exchange and proceed into the database exchange process. In order to minimize the amount of information exchanged on a particular segment, OSPF elects one router to be a designated router (DR) and one router to be a backup designated router (BDR) on each multi-access segment.

The BDR is elected as a backup router in case the DR goes down. The idea behind this is that routers have a central point of contact for information exchange. Instead of each router exchanging updates with every other router on the segment, every router exchanges information with the DR and BDR. The DR and BDR then relay the information to everybody else.

DR and BDR Elections

DR and BDR election is accomplished via the Hello protocol. Hello packets are exchanged via IP multicast packets on each segment. However, only segments that are broadcast and non-broadcast multi-access networks (such as Ethernet and Frame Relay) will perform DR and BDR elections. Point-to-point links, like a serial WAN for example, will not have a DR election process.

On a broadcast or non-broadcast multi-access network, the router with the highest OSPF priority on a segment will become the DR for that segment. This priority is shown with the `show ip ospf interface` command, which is set to 1 by default. If all routers have the default priority set, the router with the highest Router ID (RID) will win.

As you know, the RID is determined by the highest IP address on any interface at the moment of OSPF startup. This can be overridden with a loopback (logical) interface, which I'll talk about in the next section.

If you set a router's interface to a priority value of zero, that router won't participate in the DR or BDR election on that interface. The state of the interface with priority zero will then be DROTHER.

Now let's play with the RID on an OSPF router.

OSPF and Loopback Interfaces

Configuring loopback interfaces when using the OSPF routing protocol is important, and Cisco suggests using them whenever you configure OSPF on a router.

Loopback interfaces are logical interfaces, which are virtual, software-only interfaces; they are not real router interfaces. Using loopback interfaces with your OSPF configuration ensures that an interface is always active for OSPF processes.

They can be used for diagnostic purposes as well as OSPF configuration. The reason you want to configure a loopback interface on a router is because if you don't, the highest IP address on a router will become that router's RID. The RID is used to advertise the routes as well as elect the DR and BDR.

By default, OSPF uses the highest IP address on any active interface at the moment of OSPF startup. However, this can be overridden by a logical interface. The highest IP address of any logical interface will always become a router's RID.

In the following sections, you will see how to configure loopback interfaces and how to verify loopback addresses and RIDs.

Configuring Loopback Interfaces

Configuring loopback interfaces rocks mostly because it's the easiest part of OSPF configuration, and we all need a break about now—right? So hang on—we're in the home stretch!

First, let's see what the RID is on the Corp router with the show ip ospf command:

```
Corp#sh ip ospf
 Routing Process "ospf 132" with ID 10.1.5.1
[output cut]
```

We can see that the RID is 10.1.5.1, or the serial 0/2/0 interface of the router. So let's configure a loopback interface using a completely different IP addressing scheme:

```
Corp(config)#int loopback 0
*Mar 22 01:23:14.206: %LINEPROTO-5-UPDOWN: Line protocol on Interface
   Loopback0, changed state to up
Corp(config-if)#ip address 172.16.10.1 255.255.255.255
```

The IP scheme really doesn't matter here, but each router has to be in a separate subnet. By using the /32 mask, we can use any IP address we want as long as the addresses are never the same on any two routers.

Let's configure the other routers:

```
R1#config t
R1(config)#int loopback 0
*Mar 22 01:25:11.206: %LINEPROTO-5-UPDOWN: Line protocol on Interface
   Loopback0, changed state to up
R1(config-if)#ip address 172.16.10.2 255.255.255.255
```

Here's the configuration of the loopback interface on R2:

```
R2#config t
R2(config)#int loopback 0
*Mar 22 02:21:59.686: %LINEPROTO-5-UPDOWN: Line protocol on Interface
   Loopback0, changed state to up
R2(config-if)#ip address 172.16.10.3 255.255.255.255
```

Here's the configuration of the loopback interface on R3:

```
R3#config t
R3(config)#int loopback 0
*Mar 22 02:01:49.686: %LINEPROTO-5-UPDOWN: Line protocol on Interface
   Loopback0, changed state to up
R3(config-if)#ip address 172.16.10.4 255.255.255.255
```

I'm going to hold off on setting a logical interface on the 871W router. You'll find out why in a minute.

I'm pretty sure you're wondering what the IP address mask of 255.255.255.255 (/32) means and why we don't just use 255.255.255.0 instead. Well, either mask works, but the /32 mask is called a host mask and works fine for loopback interfaces, and it allows us to save subnets. Notice how I was able to use 172.16.10.1, .2, .3, and .4? If I didn't use the /32, I'd have to use a separate subnet for each and every router!

Now, before we move on, did we actually change the RIDs of our router by setting the loopback interfaces? Let's check into that by taking a look at the Corp's RID:

```
Corp#sh ip ospf
 Routing Process "ospf 132" with ID 10.1.5.1
```

What happened? You'd think that because we set logical interfaces, the IP addresses under the logical interfaces automatically become the RID of the router, right? Well, sort of—but only if you do one of two things: either reboot the router or delete OSPF and re-create the database on your router. And neither is really that great an option.

I'm going with rebooting the Corp router because it's the easier of the two.

Now let's look and see what our RID is:

```
Corp#sh ip ospf
 Routing Process "ospf 132" with ID 172.16.1.1
```

Okay, that did it. The Corp router now has a new RID! So I guess I'll just go ahead and reboot all my routers (except the 871W) to get their RIDs reset to our logical addresses.

Or not—there is *one* other way. What would you say about adding a new RID for the router right under the router ospf *process-id* command instead? I'd say let's give it a shot! Here's an example of doing that on the 871W router:

```
871W#sh ip ospf
 Routing Process "ospf 1" with ID 10.1.12.1
871W#config t
871W(config)#router ospf 1
871W(config-router)#router-id 172.16.10.5
Reload or use "clear ip ospf process" command, for this to take effect
871W(config-router)#do clear ip ospf process
Reset ALL OSPF processes? [no]: yes
*Mar 23 01:33:00.051: OSPF: Rcv LS UPD from 172.16.10.4 on Serial0/2/0
   length 76 LSA count 1
*Mar 23 01:33:00.071: OSPF: Rcv LS UPD from 172.16.10.2 on Serial0/0/1
   length 76 LSA count 1
871W(config-router)#do sh ip ospf
 Routing Process "ospf 1" with ID 172.16.10.5
```

Take a look at that—it worked! We changed the RID without reloading the router! But wait—remember, we didn't set a loopback (logical interface) yet. So let's try that now—let's set a logical interface IP address, reload the router, and see if the loopback interface overrides the `router-id` command we just used:

```
871W(config-router)#int lo0
871W(config-if)#ip address 172.16.10.6 255.255.255.255
871W(config-if)#^Z
871W#reload
System configuration has been modified. Save? [yes/no]: y
Building configuration...

871W#sh ip ospf
 Routing Process "ospf 1" with ID 172.16.10.5
```

Well, there's our answer. A logical (loopback) interface will *not* override the `router-id` command, and we don't have to reboot the router to make it take effect as the RID.

The only thing left now is to decide whether you want to advertise the loopback interfaces under OSPF. There are pros and cons to using an address that won't be advertised versus using an address that will be. Using an unadvertised address saves on real IP address space, but the address won't appear in the OSPF table, which means you can't ping it.

So basically, what you're faced with here is a choice that equals a trade-off between the ease of debugging the network and conservation of address space—what to do? A really tight strategy is to use a private IP address scheme as I did. Do this, and all will be well!

OSPF Interface Priorities

Another way to configure DRs and BDRs in OSPF is to "fix" elections instead of using loopback interfaces. We can do this by configuring interfaces on our router to gain a better priority over another router when elections occur. In other words, we can use priorities instead of logical addresses to force a certain router to become the DR or BDR in a network.

Let's use Figure 7.6 as an example. Looking at Figure 7.6, what options would you use to ensure that the R2 router will be elected the designated router (DR) for the LAN (broadcast multi-access) segment? The first thing you'd need to do is determine what the RID is of each router and which router is the default DR for the 172.16.1.0 LAN.

At this point, we can see that R3 will be the DR by default because it has the highest RID of 192.168.11.254. That gives us three options to ensure that R2 will be elected the DR for the LAN segment 172.16.1.0/24:

- Configure the priority value of the Fa0/0 interface of the R2 router to a higher value than any other interface on the Ethernet network.
- Configure a loopback interface on the R2 with an IP address higher than any IP address on the other routers.
- Change the priority value of the Fa0/0 interface of R1 and R3 to zero.

FIGURE 7.6 Ensuring your designated router

What options can you configure that will ensure that R2
will be the DR of the LAN segment?

If we set a priority of zero (0) on the R1 and R3 routers, they wouldn't be allowed to participate in the election process. But that may not be the best way to go—we might just be better off choosing options one and two.

Since you already know how to configure a loopback (logical) interface, here's how to set a priority on the Fa0/0 interface on the R2 router:

```
R2#config t
R2(config)#int f0/0
R2(config-if)#ip ospf priority ?
  <0-255>  Priority
R2(config-if)#ip ospf priority 2
```

That's it! All router interfaces default to a priority of 1, so by setting this interface to 2, I've ensured that it will automatically become the DR of the LAN segment. Setting an interface to 255 means that no one can beat your router!

Hold on though. Even if you change the priority of the interface, the router will not become the DR of the LAN segment until both the existing DR and the BDR are shut down. Once an election occurs, that's all she wrote, and the election won't happen again until the DR and BDR are reloaded and/or shut down. Just having a router with a better RID come up on your network doesn't mean your DR or BDR will change!

You can see your priority with the show ip ospf interface command:

```
R2(config-if)#do show ip ospf int f0/0
FastEthernet0/0 is up, line protocol is up
```

```
Internet Address 10.1.13.1/24, Area 0
Process ID 132, Router ID 172.16.30.1, Network Type BROADCAST,Cost:1
Transmit Delay is 1 sec, State UP, Priority 2
```

Remember, you can see the elections occur on a broadcast or non-broadcast multi-access network with the debug ip ospf adj command.

Troubleshooting OSPF

This section will have you verify sample OSPF configurations and configuration outputs in order to troubleshoot, maintain, and fix OSPF-related issues.

If you see a configuration as shown here, you must know that there is no way a router will accept this input because the wildcard is incorrect:

```
Router(config)#router ospf 1
Router(config-router)#network 10.0.0.0 255.0.0.0 area 0
```

This would be correct statement:

```
Router(config)#router ospf 1
Router(config-router)#network 10.0.0.0 0.255.255.255 area 0
```

Next, let's take a look at a figure and see if we can determine which of the routers will become the designated router of the area. Figure 7.7 shows a network with six routers connected by two switches and a WAN link.

Looking at Figure 7.7, which routers are likely to be elected as a designated router (DR)? All the router OSPF priorities are at the default.

Notice the RIDs of each router. The routers with the highest RIDs are routers A and B, since they have the highest IP addresses. RouterB should be the DR and RouterA should be the BDR. Okay, now here's the thing: Since elections do not occur on point-to-point links by default, the top LAN would have its own election. But since you're reading this because you're studying for the CCNA exam objectives, RouterB is the best answer.

Let's use another command to verify an OSPF configuration: the show ip ospf interface command. Look at the following output for routers A and B and see if you can determine why the two directly connected routers cannot establish an adjacency:

```
RouterA#sh ip ospf interface e0/0
Ethernet0/0 is up, line protocol is up
  Internet Address 172.16.1.2/16, Area 0
  Process ID 2, Router ID 172.126.1.1, Network Type BROADCAST, Cost: 10
  Transmit Delay is 1 sec, State DR, Priority 1
  Designated Router (ID) 172.16.1.2, interface address 172.16.1.1
```

```
No backup designated router on this network
Timer intervals configured, Hello 5, Dead 20, Wait 20, Retransmit 5
```

RouterB#**sh ip ospf interface e0/0**
```
Ethernet0/0 is up, line protocol is up
  Internet Address 172.16.1.1/16, Area 0
  Process ID 2, Router ID 172.126.1.1, Network Type BROADCAST, Cost: 10
  Transmit Delay is 1 sec, State DR, Priority 1
  Designated Router (ID) 172.16.1.1, interface address 172.16.1.2
  No backup designated router on this network
  Timer intervals configured, Hello 10, Dead 40, Wait 40, Retransmit 5
```

Everything in the two outputs looks pretty good, except that the Hello and Dead timers are not the same. RouterA has Hello and Dead timers of 5 and 20, and RouterB has Hello and Dead timers of 10 and 40, which are the default timers for OSPF. If two directly connected routers do not have the timers set the same, they will not form an adjacency. Notice also that the show ip ospf interface command will show you who the designated and backup designated routers (DR/BDR) are for your area.

FIGURE 7.7 Designated router example

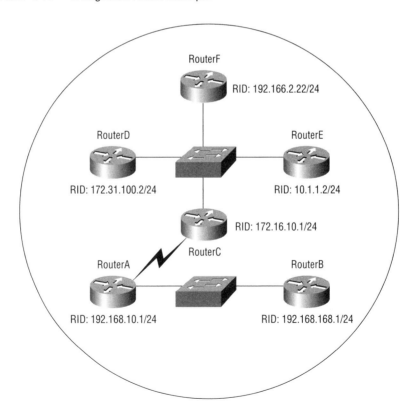

Take a look at the network shown in Figure 7.8 with four routers and two different routing protocols.

If all parameters are set to default and redistribution is not configured, which path do you think RouterA will use to reach RouterD? Since IGRP has an AD of 100 and OSPF has an AD of 110, RouterA will send packets to RouterD through RouterC.

Study Figure 7.9 carefully. You are running OSPF on the routers as shown and an ISDN link provides connectivity to the remote sales office.

What type of route should be configured on the Corporate router to connect to the sales office's remote network while minimizing network overhead on the ISDN link as shown in Figure 7.9?

The best solution to this problem is to dump the ISDN link and connect a broadband link from the remote office to the Internet and then create a VPN from the Corporate office to the remote office through the Internet. Yeah, well, wouldn't that be nice? Anyway, the question asks how we can make this work with the ISDN link and minimize network overhead. The only way we can do that is to create a static route on the Corporate router to connect to the remote network; anything else would be too bandwidth intensive.

FIGURE 7.8   Multiple routing protocols and OSPF

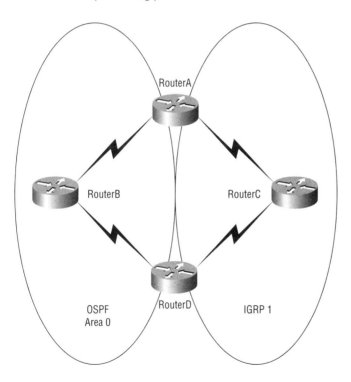

FIGURE 7.9 OSPF and ISDN connectivity

Configuring EIGRP and OSPF Summary Routes

This section will provide you with the commands to summarize both EIGRP and OSPF. Although OSPF can be summarized a few different ways, I'll provide the most common OSPF summary command, which summarizes multiple-area OSPF networks into area 0.

You learned in Chapter 3 how to determine summary routes for a network. This section will have you apply the summary routes to a router's configuration.

Figure 7.10 shows a contiguous network design—yes, contiguous networks do not happen by accident; they have to be planned! Figure 7.10 shows six networks with four block sizes of 4 (WAN links) and two block sizes of 8 (LAN connections). This network design fits nicely into a block size of 32. The network address used is 192.168.10.64 and with a block size of 32, the mask would be 255.255.255.224—because as you know, 224 provides a block size of 32.

On the core (backbone connection) router, for EIGRP we'll place the summary route on Ethernet0, which will advertise our summary route out to the backbone network (10.10.10.0 network). This will stop all six of our networks from being advertised individually and instead advertise them as one route to the other routers in the internetwork. However, it is imperative that no other router outside our contiguous networks have a subnet in this advertised block behind it, which would allow it to advertise conflicting routes.

Here is the complete configuration of EIGRP on the core router:

```
Core#config t
Core(config)#router eigrp 10
Core(config-router)#network 192.168.10.0
Core(config-router)#network 10.0.0.0
Core(config-router)#no auto-summary
Core(config-router)#interface ethernet 0
Core(config-if)#ip summary-address eigrp 10 192.168.10.64 255.255.255.224
```

FIGURE 7.10   Contiguous network design

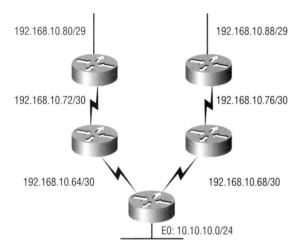

The above EIGRP configuration for autonomous system 10 advertises directly connected networks 192.168.10.0 and 10.0.0.0. Since EIGRP auto-summarizes at classful boundaries, you must use the no auto-summary command as well. The summary route we will advertise to the backbone network is placed on the interface connected to the backbone, not under the routing process. This summary route tells EIGRP to find all networks in the 192.168.10.64 network with a block size of 32 and advertise them as one route out interface E0. This means, basically, that any packet with a destination IP address of 192.168.10.64 through 192.168.10.95 will be forwarded via this summary route.

To summarize the contiguous network with OSPF we used with the EIGRP example we need to configure OSPF into multiple areas, as shown in Figure 7.11.

To summarize area 1 into the area 0 backbone, use the following command under the OSPF Process ID. Here is the complete OSPF configuration for the Core (backbone) router:

```
Core#config t
Core(config)#router ospf 1
Core(config-router)#network 192.168.10.64 0.0.0.3 area 1
Core(config-router)#network 192.168.10.68 0.0.0.3 area 1
```

```
Core(config-router)#network 10.10.10.0 0.0.0.255 area 0
Core(config-router)#area 1 range 192.168.10.64 255.255.255.224
```

The no auto-summary command is not needed since OSPF does not summarize at any boundary by default. The preceding OSPF configuration will summarize all the networks from area 1 to the backbone area as one entry of 192.168.10.64/27.

FIGURE 7.11 OSPF multiple area design

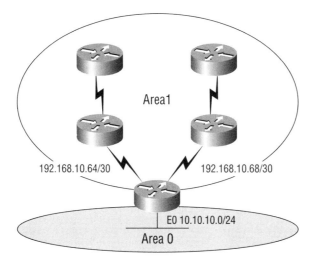

Summary

I know—this chapter has been, you could say, a touch on the extensive side. But it's really important! EIGRP, the main focus of the chapter, is a hybrid of link-state routing and distance-vector protocols. It allows for unequal-cost load balancing, controlled routing updates, and formal neighbor adjacencies.

EIGRP uses the capabilities of the Reliable Transport Protocol (RTP) to communicate between neighbors and utilizes the Diffusing Update Algorithm (DUAL) to compute the best path to each remote network.

EIGRP also supports large networks through features such as support for VLSM, discontiguous networks, and summarization. The ability to configure EIGRP behavior over NBMA networks also makes it a really hot protocol for large networks.

I also went over the configuration of EIGRP and explored a number of troubleshooting commands.

This chapter also provided you with a great deal of information about OSPF. It's really difficult to include everything about OSPF because so much of it falls outside the scope of this chapter and book, but I've given you a few tips here and there, so you're good to go—as long as you make sure you've got what I presented to you dialed in, that is!

I talked about a lot of OSPF topics, including terminology, operations, and configuration as well as verification and monitoring.

Each of these topics encompasses quite a bit of information—the terminology section just scratched the surface of OSPF. But you've got the goods for your studies—things like configuring single-area OSPF, VLSM implementation, and summarizing contiguous boundaries. Finally, I gave you a tight survey of commands useful in observing the operation of OSPF so you can verify that things are moving along as they should. So eat it all up, and you're set!

Exam Essentials

Know EIGRP features.   EIGRP is a classless, advanced distance-vector protocol that supports IP, IPX, AppleTalk, and now IPv6. EIGRP uses a unique algorithm, called DUAL, to maintain route information and uses RTP to communicate with other EIGRP routers reliably.

Know how to configure EIGRP.   Be able to configure basic EIGRP. This is configured the same as IGRP with classful addresses.

Know how to verify EIGRP operation.   Know all of the EIGRP `show` commands and be familiar with their output and the interpretation of the main components of their output.

Compare OSPF and RIPv1.   OSPF is a link-state protocol that supports VLSM and classless routing; RIPv1 is a distance-vector protocol that does not support VLSM and supports only classful routing.

Know how OSPF routers become neighbors and/or adjacent.   OSPF routers become neighbors when each router sees the other's Hello packets.

Know the different OSPF NBMA network types.   There are five different OSPF network types that Cisco routers can be configured to support. Two of these are non-proprietary based (non-broadcast and point-to-multipoint) and three are Cisco proprietary (broadcast, point-to-point, and point-to-multipoint non-broadcast). Each network type is further characterized by how routers become adjacent and whether they require the election of a DR/BDR.

Be able to configure single-area OSPF.   A minimal single-area configuration involves only two commands: `router ospf process-id` and `network x.x.x.x y.y.y.y area Z`.

Be able to verify the operation of OSPF.   There are many `show` commands that provide useful details on OSPF, and it is useful to be completely familiar with the output of each: `show ip ospf`, `show ip ospf database`, `show ip ospf interface`, `show ip ospf neighbor`, and `show ip protocols`.

Written Lab 7

1. What four routed protocols are supported by EIGRP?
2. When is redistribution required for EIGRP?

3.   What command would be used to enable EIGRP with an autonomous system number of 300?

4.   What command will tell EIGRP that it is connected to network 172.10.0.0?

5.   What type of EIGRP interface will neither send nor receive Hello packets?

6.   Write the command that will enable OSPF process 101 on a router.

7.   Write the command that will display details of all OSPF routing processes enabled on a router.

8.   Write the command that will display interface-specific OSPF information.

9.   Write the command that will display all OSPF neighbors.

10. Write the command that will display all different OSPF route types that are currently known by the router.

(The answers to Written Lab 7 can be found following the answers to the Review Questions for this chapter.)

Hands-on Labs

In this section, you will use the following network and add EIGRP and OSPF routing.

The first lab (Lab 7.1) requires you to configure three routers for EIGRP and then view the configuration. In the last four labs, you will be asked to enable OSPF routing on the same network. Note that the labs in this chapter were written to be used with real equipment.

You must remove EIGRP before starting Labs 7.2–7.4 because the routing protocols have a lower administrative distance than OSPF.

The labs in this chapter are as follows:

   Lab 7.1: Configuring and Verifying EIGRP

   Lab 7.2: Enabling the OSPF Process

   Lab 7.3 Configuring OSPF Neighbors

   Lab 7.4: Verifying OSPF Operation

   Lab 7.5: OSPF DR and DBR Elections

Table 7.5 shows our IP addresses for each router (each interface uses a /24 mask).

TABLE 7.5 Our IP Addresses

router	Interface	IP address
2621A	F0/0	172.16.10.1
2501A	E0	172.16.10.2
2501A	S0	172.16.20.1
2501B	E0	172.16.30.1
2501B	S0	172.16.20.2
2501B	S1	172.16.40.1
2501C	S0	172.16.40.2
2501C	E0	172.16.50.1

Hands-on Lab 7.1: Configuring and Verifying EIGRP

1. Implement EIGRP on 2621A:

   ```
   2621A#conf t
   Enter configuration commands, one per line.
     End with CNTL/Z.
   2621A(config)#router eigrp 100
   2621A(config-router)#network 172.16.0.0
   2621A(config-router)#^Z
   2621A#
   ```

2. Implement EIGRP on 2501A:

   ```
   2501A#conf t
   Enter configuration commands, one per line.
     End with CNTL/Z.
   2501A(config)#router eigrp 100
   2501A(config-router)#network 172.16.0.0
   2501A(config-router)#exit
   2501A#
   ```

3. Implement EIGRP on 2501B:

```
2501B#conf t
Enter configuration commands, one per line.
  End with CNTL/Z.
2501B(config)#router eigrp 100
2501B(config-router)#network 172.16.0.0
2501B(config-router)#^Z
2501B#
```

4. Implement EIGRP on 2501C:

```
2501C#conf t
Enter configuration commands, one per line.
  End with CNTL/Z.
2501C(config)#router eigrp 100
2501C(config-router)#network 172.16.0.0
2501C(config-router)#^Z
2501C#
```

5. Display the topology table for 2501B:

```
2501B#show ip eigrp topology
```

6. Display the routing table on the 2501B router:

```
2501B#show ip route
```

7. Display the neighbor table on the 2501B router:

```
2501B#show ip eigrp neighbor
```

Hands-on Lab 7.2: Enabling the OSPF Process

1. Enable OSPF process 100 on 2621A:

```
2621A#conf t
Enter configuration commands, one per line.
  End with CNTL/Z.
2621A(config)#router ospf 100
2621A(config-router)#^Z
```

2. Enable OSPF process 101 on 2501A:

```
2501A#conf t
Enter configuration commands, one per line.
  End with CNTL/Z.
2501A(config)#router ospf 101
2501A(config-router)#^Z
```

3. Enable OSPF process 102 on 2501B:

```
2501B#conf t
Enter configuration commands, one per line.
  End with CNTL/Z.
2501B(config)#router ospf 102
2501B(config-router)#^Z
```

4. Enable OSPF process 103 on 2501C:

```
2501C#conf t
Enter configuration commands, one per line.
  End with CNTL/Z.
Router(config)#router ospf 103
2501C(config-router)#^Z
```

Hands-on Lab 7.3: Configuring OSPF Neighbors

1. Configure the network between 2621A and 2501A. Assign it to area 0:

```
2621A#conf t
Enter configuration commands, one per line.
  End with CNTL/Z.
2621A(config)#router ospf 100
2621A(config-router)#network 172.16.10.1 0.0.0.0 area 0
2621A(config-router)#^Z
2621A#
```

2. Configure the networks on the 2501A router. Assign them to area 0:

```
2501A#conf t
Enter configuration commands, one per line.
  End with CNTL/Z.
2501A(config)#router ospf 101
2501A(config-router)#network 172.16.10.2 0.0.0.0 area 0
2501A(config-router)#network 172.16.20.1 0.0.0.0
  area 0
2501A(config-router)#^Z
2501A#
```

3. Configure the networks on the 2501B router. Assign them to area 0:

```
2501B#conf t
Enter configuration commands, one per line.
  End with CNTL/Z.
2501B(config)#router ospf 102
2501B(config-router)#network 172.16.20.2 0.0.0.0 area 0
```

```
2501B(config-router)#network 172.16.30.1 0.0.0.0 area 0
2501B(config-router)#network 172.16.40.1 0.0.0.0 area 0
2501B(config-router)#^Z
2501B#
```

4. Configure the networks on the 2501C router. Assign them to area 0:

```
2501C#conf t
Enter configuration commands, one per line.
  End with CNTL/Z.
2501C(config)#router ospf 103
2501C(config-router)#network 172.16.40.2 0.0.0.0 area 0
2501C(config-router)#network 172.16.50.1 0.0.0.0 area 0
2501C(config-router)#^Z
2501C#
```

Hands-on Lab 7.4: Verifying OSPF Operation

1. Execute a show ip ospf neighbors command from the 2621 router and view the results:

```
2621A#sho ip ospf neig
```

2. Execute a show ip route command to verify that all other routers are learning all routes:

```
2621A#sho ip route
```

Hands-on Lab 7.5: OSPF DR and BDR Elections

In this lab, you'll watch the DR and BDR elections on your test network by forcing and verifying the election process. You're going to start by using Figure 7.12 to build your network. The more routers you have the better, but you need at least three routers connected via a LAN segment to complete this lab.

FIGURE 7.12 OSPF hands-on lab network diagram

 In this lab, I am using 2500 series routers, but you can use any type of router with any type of LAN interface. Or you can use the Sybex or RouterSim software products instead of real routers.

1. First, connect the network together as shown in Figure 7.12. Create an IP scheme for the network—something simple like 10.1.1.1/24, 10.1.1.2/24, and 10.1.1.3/24 will work great.

2. Now configure OSPF, and place all routers into area 0. Only the Ethernet LAN interface needs to be configured in this lab because, as you know, elections don't take place on serial connections.

3. Next, type **show ip ospf interface e0** on each router to verify Area ID, DR, BDR information, and the Hello and Dead timers of the interface connected to the LAN network

4. By looking at the show ip ospf interface e0 output, determine which router is the DR and which router is the BDR.

5. Now verify the network type of your router. Because the connection is on an Ethernet LAN, the network type is BROADCAST. If you were viewing a serial connection, you'd want a point-to-point network.

6. Here you have to set the priority for the router. The priority of all routers, by default, is 1. If you were to change the priority to 0, the router would never participate in the election process for the LAN. (Remember that elections do not occur on serial point-to-point links.)

7. Now you need to decide which router will be the new DR.

8. Next, enable the debugging process that allows you to see the DR and BDR election take place. Type **debug ip ospf adjacency** on all your routers.

Try to open more than one console connection by telnetting into the other routers. Remember to use the terminal monitor command on the Telnet session or you won't see any debugging output.

9. Here, set the priority of the new DR Ethernet 0 interface to 3 by typing **ip ospf priority 3**.

10. Next, shut down the Ethernet interface of the DR router and bring it back up with the no shutdown command. Obviously, if you're telnetted into that router, you'll lose your session at this point.

11. Here's where the election should take place and the router you picked to be the DR should now actually be the DR.

12. Finally, type **show ip ospf interface e0** to verify the DR and BDR information on each router.

The priority of a router's interface can be set all the way up to 255, which means it will always be the DR of the area. You can then set a router in your test network with a higher priority and see that the priority takes precedence over a high RID on a router, even if you are using a loopback (logical) interface.

Review Questions

1. Your company is running IGRP using an AS of 10. You want to configure EIGRP on the network but want to migrate slowly to EIGRP and don't want to configure redistribution. What command would allow you to migrate over time to EIGRP without configuring redistribution?

    A. router eigrp 11

    B. router eigrp 10

    C. router eigrp 10 redistribute igrp

    D. router igrp combine eigrp 10

2. Which EIGRP information is held in RAM and maintained through the use of Hello and update packets? (Choose two.)

    A. Neighbor table

    B. STP table

    C. Topology table

    D. DUAL table

3. Which of the following describe the process identifier that is used to run OSPF on a router? (Choose two.)

    A. It is locally significant.

    B. It is globally significant.

    C. It is needed to identify a unique instance of an OSPF database.

    D. It is an optional parameter required only if multiple OSPF processes are running on the router.

    E. All routes in the same OSPF area must have the same Process ID if they are to exchange routing information.

4. Where are EIGRP successor routes stored?

    A. In the routing table only

    B. In the neighbor table only

    C. In the topology table only

    D. In the routing table and neighbor table

    E. In the routing table and the topology table

    F. In the topology table and the neighbor table

5. Which command will display all the EIGRP feasible successor routes known to a router?

   A. `show ip routes *`

   B. `show ip eigrp summary`

   C. `show ip eigrp topology`

   D. `show ip eigrp adjacencies`

   E. `show ip eigrp neighbors detail`

6. You get a call from a network administrator who tells you that he typed the following into his router:

```
Router(config)#router ospf 1
Router(config-router)#network 10.0.0.0 255.0.0.0 area 0
```

He tells you he still can't see any routes in the routing table. What configuration error did the administrator make?

   A. The wildcard mask is incorrect.

   B. The OSPF area is wrong.

   C. The OSPF Process ID is incorrect.

   D. The AS configuration is wrong.

7. Which of the following protocols support VLSM, summarization, and discontiguous networking? (Choose three.)

   A. RIPv1

   B. IGRP

   C. EIGRP

   D. OSPF

   E. BGP

   F. RIPv2

8. Which of the following are true regarding OSPF areas? (Choose three.)

   A. You must have separate loopback interfaces configured in each area.

   B. The numbers you can assign an area go up to 65,535.

   C. The backbone area is also called area 0.

   D. If your design is hierarchical, then you don't need multiple areas.

   E. All areas must connect to area 0.

   F. If you have only one area, it must be called area 1.

9. Which of the following network types have a designated router and a backup designated router assigned? (Choose two.)

   A. Broadcast

   B. Point-to-point

   C. NBMA

   D. NBMA point-to-point

   E. NBMA point-to-multipoint

10. A network administrator needs to configure a router with a distance-vector protocol that allows classless routing. Which of the following satisfies those requirements?

    A. IGRP

    B. OSPF

    C. RIPv1

    D. EIGRP

    E. IS-IS

11. You need the IP address of the devices with which the router has established an adjacency. Also, the retransmit interval and the queue counts for the adjacent routers need to be checked. What command will display the required information?

    A. show ip eigrp adjacency

    B. show ip eigrp topology

    C. show ip eigrp interfaces

    D. show ip eigrp neighbors

12. For some reason, you cannot establish an adjacency relationship on a common Ethernet link between two routers. Looking at the output below, what is the cause of the problem?

    ```
    RouterA#
    Ethernet0/0 is up, line protocol is up
      Internet Address 172.16.1.2/16, Area 0
      Process ID 2, Router ID 172.126.1.1, Network Type BROADCAST, Cost: 10
      Transmit Delay is 1 sec, State DR, Priority 1
      Designated Router (ID) 172.16.1.2, interface address 172.16.1.1
      No backup designated router on this network
      Timer intervals configured, Hello 5, Dead 20, Wait 20, Retransmit 5


    RouterB#
    Ethernet0/0 is up, line protocol is up
      Internet Address 172.16.1.1/16, Area 0
      Process ID 2, Router ID 172.126.1.1, Network Type BROADCAST, Cost: 10
      Transmit Delay is 1 sec, State DR, Priority 1
    ```

```
Designated Router (ID) 172.16.1.1, interface address 172.16.1.2
No backup designated router on this network
Timer intervals configured, Hello 10, Dead 40, Wait 40, Retransmit 5
```

- **A.** The OSPF area is not configured properly.
- **B.** The priority on RouterA should be set higher.
- **C.** The cost on RouterA should be set higher.
- **D.** The Hello and Dead timers are not configured properly.
- **E.** A backup designated router needs to be added to the network.
- **F.** The OSPF Process ID numbers must match.

13. Which is true regarding EIGRP successor routes? (Choose two.)
- **A.** A successor route is used by EIGRP to forward traffic to a destination.
- **B.** Successor routes are saved in the topology table to be used if the primary route fails.
- **C.** Successor routes are flagged as "active" in the routing table.
- **D.** A successor route may be backed up by a feasible successor route.
- **E.** Successor routes are stored in the neighbor table following the discovery process.

14. Which type of OSPF network will elect a backup designated router? (Choose two.)
- **A.** Broadcast multi-access
- **B.** Non-broadcast multi-access
- **C.** Point-to-point
- **D.** Broadcast multipoint

15. Which two of the following commands will place network 10.2.3.0/24 into area 0? (Choose two.)
- **A.** `router eigrp 10`
- **B.** `router ospf 10`
- **C.** `router rip`
- **D.** `network 10.0.0.0`
- **E.** `network 10.2.3.0 255.255.255.0 area 0`
- **F.** `network 10.2.3.0 0.0.0.255 area0`
- **G.** `network 10.2.3.0 0.0.0.255 area 0`

16. With which network type will OSPF establish router adjacencies but not perform the DR/BDR election process?
- **A.** Point-to-point
- **B.** Backbone area 0
- **C.** Broadcast multi-access
- **D.** Non-broadcast multi-access

17. What are three reasons for creating OSPF in a hierarchical design? (Choose three.)

   A. To decrease routing overhead

   B. To speed up convergence

   C. To confine network instability to single areas of the network

   D. To make configuring OSPF easier

18. What is the administrative distance of OSPF?

   A. 90

   B. 100

   C. 110

   D. 120

19. You have an internetwork as shown in the following illustration. However, the two networks are not sharing routing table route entries. Which command is needed to fix the problem?

   A. `version 2`

   B. `no auto-summary`

   C. `redistribute eigrp 10`

   D. `default-information originate`

20. If routers in a single area are configured with the same priority value, what value does a router use for the OSPF Router ID in the absence of a loopback interface?

   A. The lowest IP address of any physical interface

   B. The highest IP address of any physical interface

   C. The lowest IP address of any logical interface

   D. The highest IP address of any logical interface

Answers to Review Questions

1. B. If you enable EIGRP on a router with the same autonomous system (AS) number, EIGRP will automatically redistribute IGRP into EIGRP. You will see the IGRP injected routes as external (EX) routes with an EIGRP AD of 170. This is a nice feature that lets you migrate slowly to EIGRP with no extra configuration.

2. A, C. EIGRP holds three tables in RAM: neighbor, topology, and routing. The neighbor and topology tables are built and maintained with the use of Hello packets.

3. A, C. The Process ID for OSPF on a router is only locally significant and you can use the same number on each router, or each router can have a different number—it just doesn't matter. The numbers you can use are from 1 to 65,535. Don't get this confused with area numbers, which can be from 0 to 4.2 billion.

4. E. Successor routes are going to be in the routing table since they are the best path to a remote network. However, the topology table has a link to each and every network, so the best answer is topology table and routing table. Any secondary route to a remote network is considered a feasible successor, and those routes are only found in the topology table and used as backup routes in case of primary route failure.

5. C. Any secondary route to a remote network is considered a feasible successor, and those routes are only found in the topology table and used as backup routes in case of primary route failure. You can see the topology table with the `show ip eigrp topology` command.

6. A. The administrator typed in the wrong wildcard mask configuration. The wildcard should have been 0.0.0.255.

7. C, D, F. RIPv1 and IGRP are true distance-vector routing protocols and can't do much, really—except build and maintain routing tables and use a lot of bandwidth! RIPv2, EIGRP, and OSPF build and maintain routing tables, but they also provide classless routing, which allows for VLSM, summarization, and discontiguous networking.

8. C, D, E. Loopback interfaces are created on a router, and the highest IP address on a loopback (logical) interface becomes the RID of the router but has nothing to do with areas and is optional, so option A is wrong. The numbers you can create an area with are from 0 to 4,294,967,295—option B is wrong. The backbone area is called area 0, so option C is correct. All areas must connect to area 0, so option E is correct. If you have only one area, it must be called area 0, so option F is incorrect. This leaves option D, which must be correct; it doesn't make much sense, but it is the best answer.

9. A, C. No DR is assigned on any type of point-to-point link. No DR/BDR is assigned on the NBMA point-to-multipoint due to the hub/spoke topology. DR and BDR are elected on broadcast and non-broadcast multi-access networks. Frame Relay is a non-Broadcast Multi-Access (NBMA) network by default.

10. D. In this question, we're calling EIGRP just plain old distance vector. EIGRP is an "advanced" distance-vector routing protocol, sometimes called a hybrid routing protocol because it uses the characteristics of both distance-vector and link-state routing protocols.

11. D. The `show ip eigrp neighbors` command allows you to check the IP addresses as well as the retransmit interval and queue counts for the neighbors that have established an adjacency.

12. D. The Hello and Dead timers must be set the same on two routers on the same link or they will not form an adjacency (relationship). The default timers for OSPF are 10 seconds for the Hello timer and 40 seconds for the Dead timer.

13. A, D. Successor routes are the routes picked from the topology table as the best route to a remote network, so these are the routes that IP uses in the routing table to forward traffic to a remote destination. The topology table contains any route that is not as good as the successor route and is considered a feasible successor, or backup route. Remember that all routes are in the topology table, even successor routes.

14. A, B. DR and BDR are elected on broadcast and non-broadcast multi-access networks. Frame Relay is a non-broadcast multi-access (NBMA) network by default. No DR is assigned on any type of point-to-point link. No DR/BDR is assigned on the NBMA point-to-multipoint due to the hub/spoke topology.

15. B, G. To enable OSPF, you must first start OSPF using a Process ID. The number is irrelevant; just choose a number from 1 to 65,535 and you're good to go. After you start the OSPF process, you must configure any network that you want advertised via OSPF using wildcards and the area command. Answer F is wrong because there must be a space after the parameter area and before you list the area number.

16. A. No DR is assigned on any type of point-to-point link. No DR/BDR is assigned on the NBMA point-to-multipoint due to the hub/spoke topology. DR and BDR are elected on broadcast and non-broadcast multi-access networks. Frame Relay is a non-broadcast multi-access (NBMA) network by default.

17. A, B, C. OSPF is created in a hierarchical design, not a flat design like RIP. This decreases routing overhead, speeds up convergence, and confines network instability to a single area of the network.

18. C. The administrative distance (AD) is a very important parameter in a routing protocol. The lower the AD, the more trusted the route. If you have IGRP and OSPF running, by default IGRP routes would be placed in the routing table because IGRP has a lower AD of 100. OSPF has an AD of 110. RIPv1 and RIPv2 both have an AD of 120, and EIGRP is the lowest, at 90.

19. B. The network in the diagram is considered a discontiguous network because you have one classful address subnetted and separated by another classful address. Only RIPv2, OSPF, and EIGRP can work with discontiguous networks, but RIPv2 and EIGRP won't work by default. You must use the `no auto-summary` command under the routing protocol configuration.

20. B. At the moment of OSPF process startup, the highest IP address on any active interface will be the Router ID (RID) of the router. If you have a loopback interface configured (logical interface), then that will override the interface IP address and become the RID of the router automatically.

Answers to Written Lab 7

1. The four routed protocols supported by EIGRP are IP, IPv6, IPX, and AppleTalk.

2. Redistribution is required when more than one EIGRP session or process is running and they are identified with different ASNs. Redistribution shares topology information between EIGRP sessions.

3. `router eigrp 300`

4. `network 172.10.0.0`

5. Passive interface

6. `router ospf 101`

7. `show ip ospf`

8. `show ip ospf interface`

9. `show ip ospf neighbor`

10. `show ip ospf database`

Chapter

8

Layer 2 Switching and Spanning Tree Protocol (STP)

THE CCNA EXAM TOPICS COVERED IN THIS CHAPTER INCLUDE THE FOLLOWING:

✓ **Configure, verify, and troubleshoot a switch with VLANs and interswitch communications**

- Select the appropriate media, cables, ports, and connectors to connect switches to other network devices and hosts

- Explain the technology and media access control method for Ethernet networks

- Explain network segmentation and basic traffic management concepts

- Explain basic switching concepts and the operation of Cisco switches

- Perform and verify initial switch configuration tasks including remote access management

- Verify network status and switch operation using basic utilities (including: ping, traceroute, telnet, SSH, arp, ipconfig), SHOW & DEBUG commands

- Identify, prescribe, and resolve common switched network media issues, configuration issues, auto negotiation, and switch hardware failures

When folks at Cisco discuss switching, they're talking about layer 2 switching unless they say otherwise. Layer 2 switching is the process of using the hardware address of devices on a LAN to segment a network. Since you've got the basic ideas down, I'm now going to focus on the particulars of layer 2 switching and nail down how it works.

You know that switching breaks up large collision domains into smaller ones and that a collision domain is a network segment with two or more devices sharing the same bandwidth. A hub network is a typical example of this type of technology. But since each port on a switch is actually its own collision domain, you can make a much better Ethernet LAN network just by replacing your hubs with switches!

Switches truly have changed the way networks are designed and implemented. If a pure switched design is properly implemented, it absolutely will result in a clean, cost-effective, and resilient internetwork. In this chapter, we'll survey and compare how networks were designed before and after switching technologies were introduced.

Routing protocols (such as RIP, which you learned about in Chapter 6, "IP Routing") have processes for stopping network loops from occurring at the Network layer. However, if you have redundant physical links between your switches, routing protocols won't do a thing to stop loops from occurring at the Data Link layer. That's exactly the reason Spanning Tree Protocol was developed—to put a stop to loops in a layer 2 switched network. The essentials of this vital protocol, as well as how it works within a switched network, are also important subjects that we'll cover thoroughly in this chapter.

I'll be using three switches to start our configuration of a switched network, and we'll actually continue with their configuration in Chapter 9, "Virtual LANs (VLANs)."

For up-to-the minute updates for this chapter, please see www.lammle.com and/or www.sybex.com.

Before Layer 2 Switching

Let's go back in time a bit and take a look at the condition of networks before switches and how switches have helped segment the corporate LAN. Before LAN switching, the typical network design looked like the network in Figure 8.1.

The design in Figure 8.1 was called a collapsed backbone because all hosts would need to go to the corporate backbone to reach any network services—both LAN and mainframe.

FIGURE 8.1   Before switching

Going back even further, before networks like the one shown in Figure 8.1 had physical segmentation devices such as routers and hubs, there was the mainframe network. This network included the mainframe (IBM, Honeywell, Sperry, DEC, etc.), controllers, and dumb terminals that connected into the controller. Any remote sites were connected to the mainframe with bridges.

And then the PC began its rise to stardom and the mainframe was connected to the Ethernet or to a Token Ring LAN where the servers were installed. These servers were usually OS/2 or LAN Manager because this was "pre-NT." Each floor of a building ran either coax or twisted-pair wiring to the corporate backbone and was then connected to a router. PCs ran an emulating software program that allowed them to connect to the mainframe services, giving those PCs the ability to access services from the mainframe and LAN simultaneously. Eventually the PC became robust enough to allow application developers to port applications more effectively than they could ever before—an advance that markedly reduced networking prices and enabled businesses to grow at a much faster rate.

When Novell became more popular in the late 1980s and early 1990s, OS/2 and LAN Manager servers were by and large replaced with NetWare servers. This made the Ethernet network even more popular, because that's what Novell 3.*x* servers used to communicate with client/server software.

So that's the story about how the network in Figure 8.1 came into being. There was only one problem—the corporate backbone grew and grew, and as it grew, network services became slower. A big reason for this was that, at the same time this huge burst in growth was taking place, LAN services needed even faster service and the network was becoming totally saturated. Everyone was dumping the Macs and dumb terminals used for the mainframe service in favor of those slick new PCs so they could more easily connect to the corporate backbone and network services.

All this was taking place before the Internet's momentous popularity, so everyone in the company needed to access the corporate network's services. Why? Because without the Internet, all network services were internal—exclusive to the company network. This created a screaming need to segment that one humongous and plodding corporate network, connected with sluggish old routers. At first, Cisco just created faster routers (no doubt about that), but more segmentation was needed, especially on the Ethernet LANs. The invention of FastEthernet was a very good and helpful thing, too, but it didn't address that network segmentation need at all.

But devices called bridges did, and they were first used in the network to break up collision domains. Bridges were sorely limited by the number of ports and other network services they could provide, and that's when layer 2 switches came to the rescue. These switches saved the day by breaking up collision domains on each and every port—like a bridge—and switches could provide hundreds of ports! This early, switched LAN looked like the network pictured in Figure 8.2.

FIGURE 8.2   The first switched LAN

Each hub was placed into a switch port, an innovation that vastly improved the network. Now, instead of each building being crammed into the same collision domain, each hub became its own separate collision domain. But there was a catch—switch ports were still very new, hence unbelievably expensive. Because of that, simply adding a switch into each floor of the building just wasn't going to happen—at least, not yet. Thanks to whomever you choose to thank for these things, the price has dropped dramatically, so now having every one of your users plugged into a switch port is both good and feasible.

So there it is—if you're going to create a network design and implement it, including switching services is a must. A typical contemporary network design would look something like Figure 8.3, a complete switched network design and implementation.

FIGURE 8.3   The typical switched network design

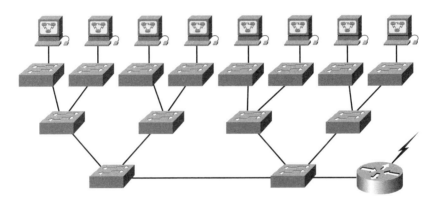

"But I still see a router in there," you say! Yes, it's not a mirage—there *is* a router in there. But its job has changed. Instead of performing physical segmentation, it now creates and handles logical segmentation. Those logical segments are called VLANs, and I promise I'll explain them thoroughly—both in the duration of this chapter and in Chapter 9, where they'll be given a starring role.

Switching Services

Unlike bridges, which use software to create and manage a filter table, switches use application-specific integrated circuits (ASICs) to build and maintain their filter tables. But it's still okay to think of a layer 2 switch as a multiport bridge because their basic reason for being is the same: to break up collision domains.

Layer 2 switches and bridges are faster than routers because they don't take up time looking at the Network layer header information. Instead, they look at the frame's hardware addresses before deciding to either forward, flood or drop the frame.

Switches create private, dedicated collision domains and provide independent bandwidth on each port, unlike hubs. Figure 8.4 shows five hosts connected to a switch—all running 10Mbps half-duplex to the server. Unlike with a hub, each host has 10Mbps dedicated communication to the server.

FIGURE 8.4   Switches create private domains.

10Mbps Half-duplex links

Server

Layer 2 switching provides the following:

- Hardware-based bridging (ASIC)
- Wire speed
- Low latency
- Low cost

What makes layer 2 switching so efficient is that no modification to the data packet takes place. The device only reads the frame encapsulating the packet, which makes the switching process considerably faster and less error-prone than routing processes are.

And if you use layer 2 switching for both workgroup connectivity and network segmentation (breaking up collision domains), you can create a flatter network design with more network segments than you can with traditional routed networks.

Plus, layer 2 switching increases bandwidth for each user because, again, each connection (interface) into the switch is its own collision domain. This feature makes it possible for you to connect multiple devices to each interface.

In the following sections, I will dive deeper into the layer 2 switching technology.

Limitations of Layer 2 Switching

Since we commonly stick layer 2 switching into the same category as bridged networks, we also tend to think it has the same hang-ups and issues that bridged networks do. Keep in mind that bridges are good and helpful things if we design the network correctly, keeping their features as well as their limitations in mind. And to design well with bridges, these are the two most important considerations:

- We absolutely must break up the collision domains correctly.
- The right way to create a functional bridged network is to make sure that its users spend 80 percent of their time on the local segment.

Bridged networks break up collision domains, but remember, that network is still one large broadcast domain. Neither layer 2 switches nor bridges break up broadcast domains by default—something that not only limits your network's size and growth potential, but also can reduce its overall performance.

Broadcasts and multicasts, along with the slow convergence time of spanning trees, can give you some major grief as your network grows. These are the big reasons layer 2 switches and bridges cannot completely replace routers (layer 3 devices) in the internetwork.

Bridging vs. LAN Switching

It's true—layer 2 switches really are pretty much just bridges that give us a lot more ports, but there are some important differences you should always keep in mind:

- Bridges are software based, while switches are hardware based because they use ASIC chips to help make filtering decisions.
- A switch can be viewed as a multiport bridge.
- There can be only one spanning-tree instance per bridge, while switches can have many. (I'm going to tell you all about spanning trees in a bit.)
- Switches have a higher number of ports than most bridges.
- Both bridges and switches forward layer 2 broadcasts.
- Bridges and switches learn MAC addresses by examining the source address of each frame received.
- Both bridges and switches make forwarding decisions based on layer 2 addresses.

Three Switch Functions at Layer 2

There are three distinct functions of layer 2 switching (you need to remember these!): *address learning*, *forward/filter decisions*, and *loop avoidance*.

Address learning   Layer 2 switches and bridges remember the source hardware address of each frame received on an interface, and they enter this information into a MAC database called a forward/filter table.

Forward/filter decisions   When a frame is received on an interface, the switch looks at the destination hardware address and finds the exit interface in the MAC database. The frame is only forwarded out the specified destination port.

Loop avoidance If multiple connections between switches are created for redundancy purposes, network loops can occur. Spanning Tree Protocol (STP) is used to stop network loops while still permitting redundancy.

I'm going to talk about address learning, forward/filtering decisions, and loop avoidance in detail in the next sections.

Address Learning

When a switch is first powered on, the MAC forward/filter table is empty, as shown in Figure 8.5.

FIGURE 8.5 Empty forward/filter table on a switch

When a device transmits and an interface receives a frame, the switch places the frame's source address in the MAC forward/filter table, allowing it to remember which interface the sending device is located on. The switch then has no choice but to flood the network with this frame out of every port except the source port because it has no idea where the destination device is actually located.

If a device answers this flooded frame and sends a frame back, then the switch will take the source address from that frame and place that MAC address in its database as well, associating this address with the interface that received the frame. Since the switch now has both of the relevant MAC addresses in its filtering table, the two devices can now make a point-to-point connection. The switch doesn't need to flood the frame as it did the first time because now the frames can and will be forwarded only between the two devices. This is exactly the thing that makes layer 2 switches better than hubs. In a hub network, all frames are forwarded out all ports every time—no matter what. Figure 8.6 shows the processes involved in building a MAC database.

FIGURE 8.6 How switches learn hosts' locations

In this figure, you can see four hosts attached to a switch. When the switch is powered on, it has nothing in its MAC address forward/filter table, just as in Figure 8.5. But when the hosts start communicating, the switch places the source hardware address of each frame in the table along with the port that the frame's address corresponds to.

Let me give you an example of how a forward/filter table is populated:

1. Host A sends a frame to Host B. Host A's MAC address is 0000.8c01.000A; Host B's MAC address is 0000.8c01.000B.

2. The switch receives the frame on the E0/0 interface and places the source address in the MAC address table.

3. Since the destination address is not in the MAC database, the frame is forwarded out all interfaces—except the source port.

4. Host B receives the frame and responds to Host A. The switch receives this frame on interface E0/1 and places the source hardware address in the MAC database.

5. Host A and Host B can now make a point-to-point connection and only the two devices will receive the frames. Hosts C and D will not see the frames, nor are their MAC addresses found in the database because they haven't yet sent a frame to the switch.

If Host A and Host B don't communicate to the switch again within a certain amount of time, the switch will flush their entries from the database to keep it as current as possible.

Forward/Filter Decisions

When a frame arrives at a switch interface, the destination hardware address is compared to the forward/filter MAC database. If the destination hardware address is known and listed in the database, the frame is only sent out the correct exit interface. The switch doesn't transmit the frame out any interface except for the destination interface. This preserves bandwidth on the other network segments and is called *frame filtering*.

But if the destination hardware address is not listed in the MAC database, then the frame is flooded out all active interfaces except the interface the frame was received on. If a device answers the flooded frame, the MAC database is updated with the device's location (interface).

If a host or server sends a broadcast on the LAN, the switch will flood the frame out all active ports except the source port by default. Remember, the switch creates smaller collision domains, but it's still one large broadcast domain by default.

In Figure 8.7, Host A sends a data frame to Host D. What will the switch do when it receives the frame from Host A?

FIGURE 8.7   Forward/filter table

```
Switch#sh mac address-table
Vlan    Mac Address      Ports
----    -----------      -----
   1    0005.dccb.d74b   Fa0/4
   1    000a.f467.9e80   Fa0/5
   1    000a.f467.9e8b   Fa0/6
```

Since Host A's MAC address is not in the forward/filter table, the switch will add the source address and port to the MAC address table and then forward the frame to Host D. If Host D's MAC address was not in the forward/filter table, the switch would have flooded the frame out all ports except for port Fa0/3.

Now let's take a look at the output of a show mac address-table:

```
Switch#sh mac address-table
Vlan    Mac Address      Type        Ports
----    -----------      --------    -----
   1    0005.dccb.d74b   DYNAMIC     Fa0/1
   1    000a.f467.9e80   DYNAMIC     Fa0/3
   1    000a.f467.9e8b   DYNAMIC     Fa0/4
   1    000a.f467.9e8c   DYNAMIC     Fa0/3
   1    0010.7b7f.c2b0   DYNAMIC     Fa0/3
   1    0030.80dc.460b   DYNAMIC     Fa0/3
   1    0030.9492.a5dd   DYNAMIC     Fa0/1
   1    00d0.58ad.05f4   DYNAMIC     Fa0/1
```

Suppose the preceding switch received a frame with the following MAC addresses:

Source MAC: 0005.dccb.d74b

Destination MAC: 000a.f467.9e8c

How will the switch handle this frame? Answer: The destination MAC address will be found in the MAC address table and the frame will be forwarded out Fa0/3 only. Remember that if the destination MAC address is not found in the forward/filter table, it will forward the frame out all ports of the switch looking for the destination device. Now that we can see the MAC address table and how switches add hosts addresses to the forward filter table, how can we secure it from unauthorized users?

Port Security

So just how do you stop someone from simply plugging a host into one of your switch ports— or worse, adding a hub, switch, or access point into the Ethernet jack in their office? By default, MAC addresses will just dynamically appear in your MAC forward/filter database. You can stop them in their tracks by using port security. Here are your options:

```
Switch#config t
Switch(config)#int f0/1
Switch(config-if)#switchport port-security ?
    aging           Port-security aging commands
    mac-address     Secure mac address
    maximum         Max secure addresses
    violation       Security violation mode
    <cr>
```

You can see clearly in the preceding output that the `switchport port-security` command can be used with four options. Personally, I like the `port-security` command because it allows me to easily control users on my network. You can use the `switchport port-security mac-address` *mac-address* command to assign individual MAC addresses to each switch port, but if you choose to go there, you'd better have a lot of time on your hands!

If you want to set up a switch port to allow only one host per port, and to shut down the port if this rule is violated, use the following commands:

```
Switch#config t
Switch(config)#int f0/1
Switch(config-if)#switchport port-security maximum 1
Switch(config-if)#switchport port-security violation shutdown
```

These commands are probably the most popular because they prevent users from connecting to a switch or access point that's in their office. The `maximum` setting of 1 means only one MAC address can be used on that port; if the user tries to add another host on that segment, the switch port will shut down. If that happens, you'd have to manually go into the switch and enable the port with a `no shutdown` command.

Probably one of my favorite commands is the `sticky` command. Not only does it perform a cool function, it's got a cool name! You can find this command under the `mac-address` command:

```
Switch(config-if)#switchport port-security mac-address sticky
Switch(config-if)#switchport port-security maximum 2
Switch(config-if)#switchport port-security violation shutdown
```

Basically, what this does is provide static MAC address security without having to type in everyone's MAC address on the network. As I said—cool!

In the preceding example, the first two MAC addresses into the port "stick" as static addresses and will stay that way for however long you set the aging command for. Why did I set it to 2? Well, I needed one for the PC/data and one for telephony/phone. I'll cover this type of configuration more in the next chapter, which is about VLANs.

 I'll be going over port security again in the configuration examples later in this chapter.

Loop Avoidance

Redundant links between switches are a good idea because they help prevent complete network failures in the event one link stops working.

Sounds great, but even though redundant links can be extremely helpful, they often cause more problems than they solve. This is because frames can be flooded down all redundant links simultaneously, creating network loops as well as other evils. Here's a list of some of the ugliest problems:

- If no loop avoidance schemes are put in place, the switches will flood broadcasts endlessly throughout the internetwork. This is sometimes referred to as a *broadcast storm*. (But most of the time it's referred to in ways we're not permitted to repeat in print!) Figure 8.8 illustrates how a broadcast can be propagated throughout the network. Observe how a frame is continually being flooded through the internetwork's physical network media.

FIGURE 8.8   Broadcast storm

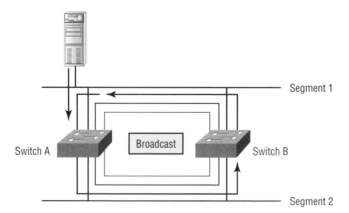

- A device can receive multiple copies of the same frame since that frame can arrive from different segments at the same time. Figure 8.9 demonstrates how a whole bunch of frames can arrive from multiple segments simultaneously. The server in the figure sends a unicast frame to Router C. Since it's a unicast frame, Switch A forwards the frame and Switch B provides the same service—it forwards the broadcast. This is bad because it means that Router C receives that unicast frame twice, causing additional overhead on the network.

FIGURE 8.9   Multiple frame copies

- You may have thought of this one: The MAC address filter table could be totally confused about the device's location because the switch can receive the frame from more than one link. And what's more, the bewildered switch could get so caught up in constantly updating the MAC filter table with source hardware address locations that it will fail to forward a frame! This is called thrashing the MAC table.
- One of the nastiest things that can happen is multiple loops generating throughout a network. This means that loops can occur within other loops, and if a broadcast storm were to also occur, the network wouldn't be able to perform frame switching—period!

All of these problems spell disaster (or at least close to it) and are decidedly evil situations that must be avoided, or at least fixed somehow. That's where the Spanning Tree Protocol comes into the game. It was developed to solve each and every one of the problems I just told you about.

Spanning Tree Protocol (STP)

Once upon a time a company called Digital Equipment Corporation (DEC) was purchased and renamed Compaq. But before that happened, DEC created the original version of *Spanning Tree Protocol*, or *STP*. The IEEE later created its own version of STP called 802.1D. The bad news is that by default, Cisco switches run the IEEE 802.1D version of STP, which isn't compatible with the DEC version. The good news is that Cisco is moving toward another industry standard in its newer switches called 802.1w. I'll cover that STP version in this section as well, but first, let's define some important STP basics.

STP's main task is to stop network loops from occurring on your layer 2 network (bridges or switches). It vigilantly monitors the network to find all links, making sure that no loops occur by shutting down any redundant links. STP uses the spanning-tree algorithm (STA) to first create a topology database and then search out and destroy redundant links. With STP running, frames will be forwarded only on the premium, STP-picked links.

In the following sections, I am going to hit the nitty-gritty of the Spanning Tree Protocol.

 STP is a layer 2 protocol that is used to maintain a loop-free switched network.

The Spanning Tree Protocol is necessary in networks such as the one shown in Figure 8.10.

FIGURE 8.10 A switched network with switching loops

In Figure 8.10, we have a switched network with a redundant topology (switching loops). Without some type of layer 2 mechanism to stop the network loop, we would have the problems we discussed previously: broadcast storms and multiple frame copies.

 Understand that the network in Figure 8.10 would actually sort of work, albeit extremely slowly. This clearly demonstrates the danger of switching loops. And to make matters worse, it can be super hard to find this problem once it starts!

Spanning Tree Terms

Before I get into describing the details of how STP works in the network, you need to understand some basic ideas and terms and how they relate within the layer 2 switched network:

Root bridge The *root bridge* is the bridge with the best bridge ID. With STP, the key is for all the switches in the network to elect a root bridge that becomes the focal point in the network. All other decisions in the network—such as which port is to be blocked and which port is to be put in forwarding mode—are made from the perspective of this root bridge.

BPDU   All the switches exchange information to use in the selection of the root switch as well as in subsequent configuration of the network. Each switch compares the parameters in the *Bridge Protocol Data Unit (BPDU)* that it sends to one neighbor with the one that it receives from another neighbor.

Bridge ID   The bridge ID is how STP keeps track of all the switches in the network. It is determined by a combination of the bridge priority (32,768 by default on all Cisco switches) and the base MAC address. The bridge with the lowest bridge ID becomes the root bridge in the network.

Nonroot bridges   These are all bridges that are not the root bridge. Nonroot bridges exchange BPDUs with all bridges and update the STP topology database on all switches, preventing loops and providing a measure of defense against link failures.

Port cost   Port cost determines the best path when multiple links are used between two switches and none of the links is a root port. The cost of a link is determined by the bandwidth of a link.

Root port   The root port is always the link directly connected to the root bridge, or the shortest path to the root bridge. If more than one link connects to the root bridge, then a port cost is determined by checking the bandwidth of each link. The lowest-cost port becomes the root port. If multiple links have the same cost, the bridge with the lower advertising bridge ID is used. Since multiple links can be from the same device, the lowest port number will be used.

Designated port   A *designated port* is one that has been determined as having the best (lowest) cost. A designated port will be marked as a forwarding port.

Nondesignated port   A *nondesignated port* is one with a higher cost than the designated port. Nondesignated ports are put in blocking mode—they are not forwarding ports.

Forwarding port   A forwarding port forwards frames.

Blocked port   A blocked port is the port that, in order to prevent loops, will not forward frames. However, a blocked port will always listen to frames.

Spanning Tree Operations

As I've said before, STP's job is to find all links in the network and shut down any redundant ones, thereby preventing network loops from occurring.

STP accomplishes this by first electing a root bridge that will forward through all ports and act as a point of reference for all other devices in the STP domain. Once all switches agree on who the root bridge is, every bridge must find its one and only allotted root port. Each and every link between two switches must have one, and only one, designated port—the port on that link that provides the highest bandwidth to the root. It's really important to remember that a bridge can go through many other bridges to get to the root, meaning that it's not always the shortest path but the fastest (highest bandwidth) path that will be the one used.

Obviously, every port on the root switch is a designated port, as you can get no closer to the root than being the root. After the dust settles, any port that is not either a root port or a designated port—which means it is a nonroot, nondesignated port—is placed in the blocking state, thus breaking the switching loop.

Things tend to go a lot more smoothly when you don't have more than one person making a navigational decision, so similarly there can be only one root bridge in any given network. I'll discuss the root bridge election process more completely in the next section.

Selecting the Root Bridge

The bridge ID is used to elect the root bridge in the STP domain and to determine the root port for each of the remaining devices in the STP domain. This ID is 8 bytes long and includes both the priority and the MAC address of the device. The default priority on all devices running the IEEE STP version is 32,768.

To determine the root bridge, you combine the priority of each bridge with its MAC address. If two switches or bridges happen to have the same priority value, the MAC address becomes the tiebreaker for figuring out which one has the lowest (best) ID. It's like this: If two switches—I'll name them A and B—both use the default priority of 32768, then the MAC address will be used instead. If Switch A's MAC address is 0000.0c00.1111 and Switch B's MAC address is 0000.0c00.2222, then Switch A would become the root bridge. Just remember that the lower value is the better one when it comes to electing a root bridge.

By default, BPDUs are sent every two seconds out all active ports on a bridge/switch—again, the bridge with the lowest (best) bridge ID is elected the root bridge. You can change the bridge's ID by lowering its priority so that it will become a root bridge automatically. Being able to do that is important in a large switched network—it ensures that the best paths are chosen. Efficiency is what you're after here!

Figure 8.11 shows a typical switched network with redundant switched paths. First, let's find out which switch is the root; then we can have the nonroot bridge become the root by changing the priority of the switch.

FIGURE 8.11 A switched network with redundant switched paths

By looking at Figure 8.11, you can tell that Switch A is the root bridge because it's the one with the lowest bridge ID. Switch B must shut down one of its ports connected to Switch A to prevent a switching loop from occurring. Remember that even though Switch B won't transmit out the blocked port, it will still receive through it—including BPDUs.

To determine which port STP will shut down on Switch B, it will first check each link's amount of bandwidth and then shut down the link with the lowest bandwidth value. Since both links between Switch A and Switch B are 100Mbps, STP will typically shut down the higher of the port numbers, but not always. In this example, 12 is higher than 11, so port 12 would be put into blocking mode.

Changing the default priority is the best way to choose a root bridge. This is important because you want the core switch (the one closest to the center of your network) to be the root bridge in your network so STP will converge quickly.

Let's have some fun and make Switch B the root in our network. Here's the output from Switch B that shows the default priority. We'll use the show spanning-tree command:

```
Switch B(config)#do show spanning-tree
VLAN0001
  Spanning tree enabled protocol ieee
  Root ID    Priority    32769
             Address     0005.74ae.aa40
             Cost        19
             Port        1 (FastEthernet0/1)
             Hello Time   2 sec  Max Age 20 sec  Forward Delay 15 sec

  Bridge ID  Priority    32769  (priority 32768 sys-id-ext 1)
             Address     0012.7f52.0280
             Hello Time   2 sec  Max Age 20 sec  Forward Delay 15 sec
             Aging Time 300
[output cut]
```

There are two things to notice right off the bat here: Switch B is running the IEEE 801.d protocol, and the first output (Root ID) is the root bridge information for the switched network. But it's not Switch B. Switch B's port (called root port) to the root bridge is port 1. The Bridge ID is the actual spanning tree information for Switch B and for VLAN 1, listed as VLAN0001—each VLAN can have a different root bridge, although this is rare. Switch B's MAC address is listed as well, and you can see that it's different than the root bridge's MAC address.

Switch B's priority is 32,768—the default for every switch. You see it listed as 32769, but the actual VLAN ID is added, so in this case it shows up as 32769 for VLAN 1. VLAN 2 would be 32770, and so on.

As I said, you can change the priority to force a switch to become the root of your STP network, so let's do that now for Switch B. Use the following command to change a bridge priority on a Catalyst switch:

```
Switch B(config)#spanning-tree vlan 1 priority ?
  <0-61440>  bridge priority in increments of 4096
Switch B(config)#spanning-tree vlan 1 priority 4096
```

You can set the priority to any value from 0 through 61440. Setting it to zero (0) means that the switch will always be a root bridge, and the bridge priority is set in increments of 4096. If you want to set a switch to be the root bridge for every VLAN in your network, then you have to change the priority for each VLAN, with 0 being the lowest priority you can use. It would not be advantageous to set all switches to a priority of 0.

Check out the following output—now that we've changed the priority of Switch B for VLAN 1 to 4096, we've successfully forced this switch to become the root:

```
Switch B(config)#do show spanning-tree
VLAN0001
  Spanning tree enabled protocol ieee
  Root ID    Priority    4097
             Address     0012.7f52.0280
             This bridge is the root
             Hello Time   2 sec  Max Age 20 sec  Forward Delay 15 sec

  Bridge ID  Priority    4097    (priority 4096 sys-id-ext 1)
             Address     0012.7f52.0280
             Hello Time   2 sec  Max Age 20 sec  Forward Delay 15 sec
             Aging Time 15
[output cut]
```

Both the root's MAC address and the bridge ID of Switch B are now the same, meaning that Switch B is now the root bridge, and it tells us so. Knowing the show spanning-tree command is a very important thing; we'll use it again toward the end of this chapter.

 Believe it or not, there's yet another command that you can use to set your root bridge, and I promise to tell you all about it when I show you my switch configuration examples later in this chapter.

Spanning-Tree Port States

The ports on a bridge or switch running STP can transition through five different states:

Blocking   A blocked port won't forward frames; it just listens to BPDUs. The purpose of the blocking state is to prevent the use of looped paths. All ports are in blocking state by default when the switch is powered up.

Listening   The port listens to BPDUs to make sure no loops occur on the network before passing data frames. A port in listening state prepares to forward data frames without populating the MAC address table.

Learning   The switch port listens to BPDUs and learns all the paths in the switched network. A port in learning state populates the MAC address table but doesn't forward data frames. Forward delay means the time it takes to transition a port from listening to learning mode, which is set to 15 seconds by default and can be seen in the show spanning-tree output.

Forwarding   The port sends and receives all data frames on the bridged port. If the port is still a designated or root port at the end of the learning state, it enters the forwarding state.

Disabled   A port in the disabled state (administratively) does not participate in the frame forwarding or STP. A port in the disabled state is virtually nonoperational.

Switches populate the MAC address table in learning and forwarding modes only.

Switch ports are most often in either the blocking or forwarding state. A forwarding port is one that has been determined to have the lowest (best) cost to the root bridge. But when and if the network experiences a topology change (because of a failed link or because someone adds in a new switch), you'll find the ports on a switch in listening and learning states.

As I mentioned, blocking ports is a strategy for preventing network loops. Once a switch determines the best path to the root bridge, all other redundant ports will be in blocking mode. Blocked ports can still receive BPDUs—they just don't send out any frames.

If a switch determines that a blocked port should now be the designated or root port because of a topology change, it will go into listening mode and check all BPDUs it receives to make sure it won't create a loop once the port goes to forwarding mode.

Convergence

Convergence occurs when all ports on bridges and switches have transitioned to either forwarding or blocking modes. No data will be forwarded until convergence is complete. And before data can begin being forwarded again, all devices must be updated. Yes—you read that right: When STP is converging, all host data stops transmitting! So if you want to remain on speaking terms with your network's users (or remain employed for any length of time), you positively must make sure that your switched network is physically designed really well so that STP can converge quickly.

Figure 8.12 shows you some really great considerations for designing and implementing your switched network so that STP converges efficiently.

FIGURE 8.12   An optimal hierarchical switch design

Create core switch as STP root for fastest STP convergence

Convergence is truly important because it ensures that all devices have the same database. But as I've drilled into you, it does cost you some time. It usually takes 50 seconds to go from blocking to forwarding mode, and I don't recommend changing the default STP timers. (But you can adjust those timers if necessary.) By creating your physical switch design in a hierarchical manner, as shown in Figure 8.12, you can make your core switch the STP root, which will then make STP convergence time nice and quick.

Because the typical spanning-tree topology's time to convergence from blocking to forwarding on a switch port is 50 seconds, this could create time-out problems on your servers or hosts—for example, when you reboot them. To address this hitch, you can disable spanning tree on individual ports using PortFast.

Spanning Tree PortFast

If you have a server or other devices connected into your switch that you're totally sure won't create a switching loop if STP is disabled, you can use something called `portfast` on these ports. Using it means the port won't spend the usual 50 seconds to come up into forwarding mode while STP is converging.

Here are the commands—they're pretty simple:

```
Switch(config-if)#spanning-tree portfast ?
  disable  Disable portfast for this interface
  trunk    Enable portfast on the interface even in trunk mode
  <cr>
```

We haven't discussed trunk ports yet, but basically, these are used to connect switches together and pass VLAN information between them. You have to specifically tell portfast if you want to enable it on a trunk port. This isn't a typical configuration because ports between switches should usually run STP. So let's take a look at the message I get when I turn on portfast on an interface:

```
Switch(config-if)#spanning-tree portfast
%Warning: portfast should only be enabled on ports connected to a
    single host. Connecting hubs, concentrators, switches, bridges,
    etc... to this interface  when portfast is enabled, can cause
    temporary bridging loops.
 Use with CAUTION
%Portfast has been configured on FastEthernet0/1 but will only
 have effect when the interface is in a non-trunking mode.
Switch(config-if)#
```

Portfast is enabled on port f0/1, but notice that you get a pretty long message telling you to be careful. One last helpful interface command I want to tell you about is the `range` command, which you can use on switches to help you configure multiple ports at the same time. Here's an example:

```
Switch(config)#int range fastEthernet 0/1 - 12
Switch(config-if-range)#spanning-tree portfast
```

The preceding `range` command allows me to set all 12 of my switch ports into `portfast` mode by typing in one command and then simply pressing the Enter key. Sure hope I didn't create any loops! Again, just be super careful with the `portfast` command. I also want you to know that the `interface range` command can be used in conjunction with any command. I just used it with the `portfast` command as an example.

Spanning Tree UplinkFast

UplinkFast is a Cisco-specific feature that improves the convergence time of STP in case of a link failure. And beware, just as with the `portfast` command, you've got to be really careful where you use this command! The UplinkFast feature is designed to run in a switched environment when the switch has at least one alternate/backup root port (a port in blocking state). This is why Cisco recommends that UplinkFast be enabled only for switches with blocked ports and, typically, at the Access layer.

UplinkFast allows a switch to find alternate paths to the root bridge before the primary link fails. This means that if the primary link fails, the secondary link would come up more quickly—the port wouldn't wait for the normal STP convergence time of 50 seconds. So if you're running the 802.1d STP and you have redundant links on your Access layer switches, you definitely want to turn on UplinkFast. But don't use it on switches without the implied topology knowledge of an alternative/backup root link that's typically used for distribution and core switches in Cisco multilayer design.

Spanning Tree BackboneFast

Unlike UplinkFast, which is used to determine and quickly fix link failures on the local switch, another Cisco-proprietary STP extension called BackboneFast is used for speeding up convergence when a link that's not directly connected to the switch fails. If a switch running BackboneFast receives an inferior BPDU from its designated bridge, it knows that a link on the path to the root has failed. Just to make sure you're clear on this, an inferior BPDU is one that lists the same switch for the root bridge and the designated bridge.

And again, unlike UplinkFast, which is only configured on Access layer switches or switches with redundant links and at least one link in blocking mode, BackboneFast should be enabled on all Catalyst switches to allow for detection of indirect link failures. Enabling BackboneFast is also beneficial because it starts the spanning tree reconfiguration more quickly—it can save 20 seconds on the default 50-second STP convergence time.

Rapid Spanning Tree Protocol (RSTP) 802.1w

How would you like to have a good STP configuration running on your switched network (regardless of the brand of switches) and have all the features we just discussed built in and enabled on every switch? Absolutely—yes! Well then, welcome to the world of Rapid Spanning Tree Protocol (RSTP).

Cisco created PortFast, UplinkFast, and BackboneFast to "fix" the holes and liabilities the IEEE 802.1d standard presented. The drawbacks to these enhancements are only that they are Cisco proprietary and need additional configuration. But the new 802.1w standard (RSTP) addresses all these "issues" in one tight package—just turn on RSTP and you're good to go.

It's important that you make sure all the switches in your network are running the 802.1w protocol for 802.1w to work properly!

> It might come as a surprise, but RSTP actually can interoperate with legacy STP protocols. Just know that the inherently fast convergence ability of 802.1w is lost when it interacts with legacy bridges.

I'll show you how to configure RSTP later in this chapter. It's pretty easy, actually.

EtherChannel

Instead of having redundant links and allowing STP to put one of the links in BLK (blocked) mode, we can bundle the links and create a logical aggregation so that our multiple links will then appear as a single one. Since doing this would still provide the same redundancy as STP, why wouldn't we want to bundle our redundant links?

Well, as usual, there's the Cisco version of EtherChannel and the IEEE version to choose from—take your pick. Cisco's version is called Port Aggregation Protocol (PAgP) and the IEEE 802.3ad standard is called Link Aggregation Control Protocol (LACP). Both versions work equally as well, but how you configure each is different. I'm going to bundle some links toward the end of this chapter to demonstrate this just for fun. And no worries—I'm also going to cover all configurations for the STP extensions coming right up in the next section.

Configuring Catalyst Switches

Cisco Catalyst switches come in many flavors—some run 10Mbps, and some jam all the way up to 10Gbps switched ports with a combination of twisted-pair and fiber. These newer switches (specifically the 2960s and 3560s) have more intelligence, so they can give you data fast—video and voice services, too.

It's time to get down to it—I'm going to show you how to start up and configure a Cisco Catalyst switch using the command-line interface (CLI). After you get the basic commands down in this chapter, in the next chapter, I'll show you how to configure virtual LANs (VLANs) plus Inter-Switch Link (ISL), 802.1q routing, and Cisco's Virtual Trunk Protocol (VTP).

Here's a list of the basic tasks we'll be covering in this section:

- Administrative functions
- Configuring the IP address and subnet mask
- Setting the IP default gateway
- Setting port security
- Setting PortFast
- Enabling BPDUGuard and BPDUFilter
- Enabling UplinkFast

- Enabling BackboneFast
- Enabling RSTP (802.1w)
- Enabling EtherChannel
- Configuring an STP root switch
- Using the CNA to configure a switch

> You can learn all about the Cisco family of Catalyst switches at www.cisco
> .com/en/US/products/hw/switches/index.html.

Catalyst Switch Configuration

Just as we did with the routers we configured in Chapters 6 and 7, we'll use a diagram and switch setup to configure in this chapter as well as in Chapter 9, "Virtual LANs (VLANs)." Figure 8.13 shows the switched network we'll be working on.

FIGURE 8.13   Our switched network

I'm going to use a new 3560, a 2960, and a 3550 switch. Keep in mind that the hosts, phones, and router shown in the network will become more important later when we get to Chapter 9.

But before we actually get into configuring one of the Catalyst switches, I've got to fill you in regarding the bootup process of these switches, just as I did with the routers in Chapter 4. Figure 8.14 shows the detail of a typical Cisco Catalyst switch, and I need to tell you about the different interfaces and features of this product.

FIGURE 8.14 A Cisco Catalyst switch

The first thing I want you to know is that the console port for the Catalyst switches are typically located on the back of the switch. But on a smaller switch like the 3560 shown in the figure, the console is right in the front to make it easier to use. (The eight-port 2960 looks exactly the same.) If the POST completes successfully, the system LED turns green; if the POST fails, it will turn amber. And seeing the amber glow is a very bad thing—typically fatal. So you may just want to keep a spare switch around—especially in case it happens to be a production switch that's croaked! The bottom button is used to show you which lights are providing Power over Ethernet (PoE). You can see this by pressing the Mode button. The PoE is a very nice feature of these switches. It allows me to power my access point and phone by just connecting them into the switch with an Ethernet cable! Sweet.

After a switch boots up, you can use the Express Setup HTTP screen. Figure 8.15 shows the screen you'll get when you connect to a new switch and use 10.0.0.1 in the HTTP field of your browser. Oh, and obviously your host needs to be in the same subnet.

FIGURE 8.15 Express Setup HTTP screen

The screen shows us that we can set some basic functions. To me, it's easier to configure the information from the CLI, which I'll show you next, but this is actually just one of your options. You can configure the IP address, mask, and default gateway of the switch, plus the passwords. You can also configure the management VLAN, but I'm going to hold off on that for now and show you how to do that in the next chapter. Moving on, optionally, you can configure the hostname, system contact, and location and set up Telnet access. And last, the Express Setup HTTP screen provides you with some simple help on setting the switch up with SNMP so your Network Management System (NMS) can find it.

Now if we connect our switches to each other, as shown in Figure 8.13, remember that first we'll need a crossover cable between the switches. My 2960 and 3560 switches autodetect the connection type, so I was able to use straight-through cables. But a 2950 or 3550 switch won't autodetect the cable type. Different switches have different needs and abilities, so just keep this in mind when connecting your various switches together.

When you first connect the switch ports to each other, the link lights are orange and then turn green indicating normal operation. This is spanning-tree converging, and as you already know, this process takes around 50 seconds with no extensions enabled. But if you connect into a switch port and the switch port LED is alternating green and amber, this means the port is experiencing errors. If this happens, check the host NIC card or the cabling.

S1

Okay—let's start our configuration by connecting into each switch and setting the administrative functions. We'll also assign an IP address to each switch, but this isn't really necessary to make our network function. The only reason we're going to do that is so we can manage/administer it. Let's use a simple IP scheme like 192.168.10.16/28. This mask should be familiar to you! Check out the following output.

```
Switch>en
Switch#config t
Enter configuration commands, one per line.  End with CNTL/Z.
Switch(config)#hostname S1
S1(config)#enable secret todd
S1(config)#int f0/1
S1(config-if)#description 1st Connection to Core Switch
S1(config-if)#int f0/2
S1(config-if)#description 2nd Connection to Core Switch
S1(config-if)#int f0/3
S1(config-if)#description Connection to HostA
S1(config-if)#int f0/4
S1(config-if)#description Connection to PhoneA
S1(config-if)#int f0/8
S1(config-if)#description Connection to IVR
S1(config-if)#line console 0
S1(config-line)#password console
S1(config-line)#login
S1(config-line)#exit
S1(config)#line vty 0 ?
```

```
  <1-15>  Last Line number
  <cr>
S1(config)#line vty 0 15
S1(config-line)#password telnet
S1(config-line)#login
S1(config-line)#int vlan 1
S1(config-if)#ip address 192.168.10.17 255.255.255.240
S1(config-if)#no shut
S1(config-if)#exit
S1(config)#banner motd # This is the S1 switch #
S1(config)#exit
S1#copy run start
Destination filename [startup-config]? [enter]
Building configuration...
[OK]
S1#
```

The first thing to notice about this is that there's no IP address configured on the switch's interfaces. Since all ports on a switch are enabled by default, there's not so much to configure. The IP address is configured under a logical interface, called a management domain or VLAN. You would typically use the default VLAN 1 to manage a switched network just as we're doing here. The rest of the configuration is basically the same as the process you go through for router configuration. Remember, no IP addresses on switch interfaces, no routing protocols, and so on. We're performing layer 2 switching at this point, not routing! Also, note that there is no aux port on Cisco switches.

S2

Here is the S2 configuration:

```
Switch#config t
Switch(config)#hostname S2
S2(config)#enable secret todd
S2(config)#int fa0/1
2(config-if)#description 1st Connection to Core
S2(config-if)#int fa0/2
S2(config-if)#description 2nd Connection to Core
S2(config-if)#int fa0/3
S2(config-if)#description Connection to HostB
S2(config-if)#int fa0/4
S2(config-if)#description Connection to PhoneB
S2(config-if)#line con 0
S2(config-line)#password console
S2(config-line)#login
```

```
S2(config-line)#exit
S2(config)#line vty 0 ?
  <1-15>  Last Line number
  <cr>
S2(config)#line vty 0 15
S2(config-line)#password telnet
S2(config-line)#login
S2(config-line)#int vlan 1
S2(config-if)#ip address 192.168.10.18 255.255.255.240
S2(config-if)#no shut
S2(config-if)#exit
S2(config)#banner motd # This is my S2 Switch #
S2(config)#exit
S2#copy run start
Destination filename [startup-config]?[enter]
Building configuration...
[OK]
S2#
```

We should now be able to ping from S2 to S1. Let's try it:

```
S2#ping 192.168.10.17

Type escape sequence to abort.
Sending 5, 100-byte ICMP Echos to 192.168.10.17, timeout is 2 seconds:
.!!!!
Success rate is 80 percent (4/5), round-trip min/avg/max = 1/1/1 ms
S2#
```

I have two questions for you: How can I ping through the core switch if I haven't configured it yet, and why did I get only four pings to work instead of five? (The first period [.] is a time-out; the exclamation point [!] is a success.)

Both are good questions. Here's why: First, you don't need the switch configured to make it work. All ports are enabled by default, so by just turning it on you should be able to communicate between hosts. Second, the first ping didn't work because of the time that ARP takes to resolve the IP address to a hardware MAC address.

Core

Here is the Core switch configuration:

```
Switch>en
Switch#config t
Switch(config)#hostname Core
Core(config)#enable secret todd
```

```
Core(config)#int f0/5
Core(config-if)#description 1st Connection to S2
Core(config-if)#int fa0/6
Core(config-if)#description 2nd Connection to S2
Core(config-if)#int f0/7
Core(config-if)#desc 1st Connection to S1
Core(config-if)#int f0/8
Core(config-if)#desc 2nd Connection to S1
Core(config-if)#line con 0
Core(config-line)#password console
Core(config-line)#login
Core(config-line)#line vty 0 15
Core(config-line)#password telnet
Core(config-line)#login
Core(config-line)#int vlan 1
Core(config-if)#ip address 192.168.10.19 255.255.255.240
Core(config-if)#no shut
Core(config-if)#exit
Core(config)#banner motd # This is the Core Switch #
Core(config)#exit
Core#copy run start
Destination filename [startup-config]?[enter]
Building configuration...
[OK]
Core#
```

Now let's ping to S1 and S2 from the Core switch and see what happens:

```
Core#ping 192.168.10.17
Type escape sequence to abort.
Sending 5, 100-byte ICMP Echos to 192.168.10.17, timeout is 2 seconds:
.!!!!
Success rate is 80 percent (4/5), round-trip min/avg/max = 1/1/1 ms
Core#ping 192.168.10.18
Type escape sequence to abort.
Sending 5, 100-byte ICMP Echos to 192.168.10.18, timeout is 2 seconds:
.!!!!
Success rate is 80 percent (4/5), round-trip min/avg/max = 1/1/1 ms
Core#sh ip arp
Protocol  Address          Age (min)  Hardware Addr   Type    Interface
Internet  192.168.10.18            0  001a.e2ce.ff40  ARPA    Vlan1
```

```
Internet   192.168.10.19         -   000d.29bd.4b80   ARPA    Vlan1
Internet   192.168.10.17         0   001b.2b55.7540   ARPA    Vlan1
Core#
```

Now, before we move on to verifying the switch configurations, there's one more command you need to know about, even though we don't need it in our current network because we don't have a router involved. It's the ip default-gateway command. If you want to manage your switches from outside your LAN, you need to set a default gateway on the switches, just as you would with a host. You do this from global config. Here's an example where we introduce our router with an IP address using the last IP address in our subnet range (we'll use the router in our next chapter, on VLANs):

```
Core#config t
Enter configuration commands, one per line.  End with CNTL/Z.
Core(config)#ip default-gateway 192.168.10.30
Core(config)#exit
Core#
```

Now that we have all three switches basically configured, let's have some fun with them.

Port Security

As I said earlier in the chapter, it's usually not a good thing to have your switches available for anyone to just plug into and play around with. I mean, you demand wireless security, so why wouldn't you want switch security just as much?

The answer is, you do, and by using port security, you can limit the number of MAC addresses that can be assigned dynamically to a port, set a static MAC address, and—here's my favorite part—set penalties for users who abuse your policy. Personally, I like to have the port shut down when the security policy is violated and then make the abusers bring me a memo from their boss explaining to me why they violated the security policy before I'll enable their port again. That usually really helps them remember to behave!

A secured switch port can associate anywhere from 1 to 8,192 MAC addresses, but the '50 series can support only 192, which seems like enough to me. You can choose to allow the switch to learn these values dynamically, or you can set a static address for each port using the switchport port-security mac-address *mac-address* command.

So let's set port security on our S1 switch now. Ports fa0/3 and fa0/4 have only one device connected in our lab. By using port security, we can know for certain that no other device can connect once our host in port fa0/3 and the phone in fa0/4 are connected. Here's how we'll do that:

```
S1#config t
Enter configuration commands, one per line.  End with CNTL/Z.
S1(config)#int range fa0/3 - 4
S1(config-if-range)#switchport port-security maximum ?
  <1-8192>  Maximum addresses
S1(config-if-range)#switchport port-security maximum 1
```

```
S1(config-if-range)#switchport port-security mac-address sticky
S1(config-if-range)#switchport port-security violation ?
  protect   Security violation protect mode
  restrict  Security violation restrict mode
  shutdown  Security violation shutdown mode
S1(config-if-range)#switchport port-security violation shutdown
S1(config-if-range)#exit
```

The preceding command set port security on port fa0/3 and fa0/4 to allow a maximum association of one MAC address, and only the first MAC address associated to the port will be able to send frames through the switch. If a second device with a different MAC address were to try and send a frame into the switch, the port would be shut down because of our violation command. I use the sticky command because I am way too lazy to type in all the MAC addresses of each device by hand!

There are two other modes you can use instead of just shutting down the port. The protect mode means that another host can connect but its frames will just be dropped. Restrict mode is also pretty cool—it alerts you via SNMP that a violation has occurred on a port. You can then call the abuser and tell them they're so busted—you can see them, you know what they did, and they're in big-time trouble!

In our connection between switches we have redundant links, so it's best to let STP run on those links (for now). But on our S1 and S2 switches, we also have hosts connected to port fa0/3 and fa0/4 (not the Core). So let's turn STP off on those ports.

> Understand that hosts can directly connect physically to the back of phones since phones typically will have an Ethernet jack. So we really need only one port on the switch for both devices. I'll go over that in depth in the telephony section of Chapter 9.

PortFast

If we use the portfast command on our switches, we prevent the problem of our hosts possibly being unable to receive a DHCP address because STP takes way too long to converge and the host's DHCP request times out. So I'm going to use PortFast on port fa0/3 and fa0/4 on both the S1 and S2 switches:

```
S1#config t
S1(config)#int range f0/3-4
S1(config-if-range)#spanning-tree portfast ?
  disable  Disable portfast for this interface
  trunk    Enable portfast on the interface even in trunk mode
  <cr>
S1(config-if-range)#spanning-tree portfast
%Warning: portfast should only be enabled on ports connected to a
```

```
   single host. Connecting hubs, concentrators, switches, bridges,
   etc... to this interface when portfast is enabled, can cause
   temporary bridging loops.
 Use with CAUTION

%Portfast has been configured on FastEthernet0/2 but will only
 have effect when the interface is in a non-trunking mode.
 S1(config-if-range)#
```

Now that I have configured S1, I won't show you the next output, but I'm going over to S2 to enable PortFast on fa0/3-4 as well. Again, just a reminder to be careful when using PortFast—you definitely do not want to create a network loop! Why? Because if you let this happen, even though the network may still work (well, kind of), data will pass super slowly, and worse, it could take you a really long time to find the source of the problem, making you very unpopular. So proceed carefully.

It would be good to know that there are some safeguard commands you can use when using PortFast in case someone accidentally causes a loop in a port that's configured with PortFast enabled. Here they are.

BPDUGuard

I talked about this a bit earlier: If you turn on PortFast for a switch port, turning on BPDUGuard is a really good idea. If a switch port that has PortFast enabled receives a BPDU on that port, it will place the port into error disabled state. This stops an administrator from accidentally connecting another switch or hub port into a switch port configured with PortFast. Basically, you're preventing (guarding) this from happening and bringing down, or at least severely crippling, your network. You'd only configure this command on your Access layer switches—switches where users are directly connected—so we wouldn't configure this on our Core switch.

BPDUFilter

Another helpful command to use with PortFast is BPDUFilter. Since a switch port that has PortFast enabled will still receive BPDUs by default, you can use BPDUFilter to completely stop BPDUs from coming to or going from that port. BPDUFilter filtering will immediately take a port out of PortFast if it receives a BPDU and force the port to be part of the STP topology again. Unlike BPDUGuard, which places the port into error disabled state, the BPDUFilter will keep a port up, but without PortFast running. There's just no reason to have BPDUs received on an interface configured with PortFast. To be perfectly honest, I have no idea why BPDUGuard or BPDUFilter are not enabled by default when PortFast is enabled.

So let's configure our S1 and S2 interfaces that are already configured with PortFast with both the BPDUGuard and BPDUFilter now—it's easy:

```
S1(config-if-range)#spanning-tree bpduguard ?
  disable  Disable BPDU guard for this interface
  enable   Enable BPDU guard for this interface
S1(config-if-range)#spanning-tree bpduguard enable
```

```
S1(config-if-range)#spanning-tree bpdufilter ?
  disable  Disable BPDU filtering for this interface
  enable   Enable BPDU filtering for this interface
S1(config-if-range)#spanning-tree bpdufilter enable

S2(config-if-range)#spanning-tree bpduguard enable
S2(config-if-range)#spanning-tree bpdufilter enable
```

Understand that you typically would use one command or the other because both bpduguard and bpdufilter accomplish the same thing, so configuring both commands is somewhat overkill. We're also going to configure a couple more STP 802.1d extensions that you can use when configuring STP.

UplinkFast

Here's how to configure UplinkFast on our Access layer switches (S1 and S2):

```
S1#config t
S1(config)#spanning-tree uplinkfast

S2#config t
S2(config)#spanning-tree uplinkfast
S1(config)#do show spanning-tree uplinkfast
UplinkFast is enabled

Station update rate set to 150 packets/sec.

UplinkFast statistics
-----------------------
Number of transitions via uplinkFast (all VLANs)         : 1
Number of proxy multicast addresses transmitted (all VLANs) : 8

Name                Interface List
------------------- ------------------------------------
VLAN0001            Fa0/1(fwd), Fa0/2
S1(config)#
```

The uplinkfast command is a global command and it's enabled on every port.

BackboneFast

Here's how you would configure BackboneFast on a switch:

```
S1(config)#spanning-tree backbonefast
S2(config)#spanning-tree backbonefast
Core(config)#spanning-tree backbonefast
```

```
S2(config)#do show spanning-tree backbonefast
BackboneFast is enabled

BackboneFast statistics
-----------------------
Number of transition via backboneFast (all VLANs)      : 0
Number of inferior BPDUs received (all VLANs)          : 2
Number of RLQ request PDUs received (all VLANs)        : 0
Number of RLQ response PDUs received (all VLANs)       : 1
Number of RLQ request PDUs sent (all VLANs)            : 1
Number of RLQ response PDUs sent (all VLANs)           : 0
S2(config)#
```

Notice that unlike what I did with UplinkFast, I configured BackboneFast on all switches in the network, not just the Access layer switches. Remember, BackboneFast is used to determine link failures on a remote switch, unlike UplinkFast, which is used to both determine and quickly fix link failures on the local switch.

RSTP (802.1w)

Configuring RSTP actually is as easy as configuring any of our other 802.1d extensions. Considering how much better it is than 802.1d, you'd think the configuration would be more complex, but we're in luck—it's not. So let's turn it on in the Core switch now and see what happens:

```
Core#config t
Core(config)#spanning-tree mode ?
  mst        Multiple spanning tree mode
  pvst       Per-Vlan spanning tree mode
  rapid-pvst  Per-Vlan rapid spanning tree mode
Core(config)#spanning-tree mode rapid-pvst
Core(config)#
1d02h: %LINEPROTO-5-UPDOWN: Line protocol on Interface Vlan1,
 changed state to down
1d02h: %LINEPROTO-5-UPDOWN: Line protocol on Interface Vlan1,
 changed state to up
```

Sweet! The Core switch is now running the 802.1w STP. Let's verify that:

```
Core(config)#do show spanning-tree
VLAN0001
  Spanning tree enabled protocol rstp
  Root ID    Priority    32769
             Address     000d.29bd.4b80
```

```
                This bridge is the root
                Hello Time   2 sec  Max Age 20 sec  Forward Delay 15 sec

  Bridge ID  Priority    32769  (priority 32768 sys-id-ext 1)
                Address     000d.29bd.4b80
                Hello Time   2 sec  Max Age 20 sec  Forward Delay 15 sec
                Aging Time 300

Interface         Role Sts Cost      Prio.Nbr Type
---------------- ---- --- --------- -------- ------------
Fa0/5            Desg FWD 19         128.5    P2p Peer(STP)
Fa0/6            Desg FWD 19         128.6    P2p Peer(STP)
Fa0/7            Desg FWD 19         128.7    P2p Peer(STP)
Fa0/8            Desg FWD 19         128.8    P2p Peer(STP)
```

Interesting… it looks like nothing really happened. I can see on my two other switches that all ports have converged. Once everything was up, everything looked the same. 802.1d and 802.1w seem to be cohabiting with no problem.

But, if we were to look under the hood more closely, we'd see that the 802.1w switch has changed from 802.1w BPDUs to 802.1d BPDUs on the ports connecting to the other switches running 802.1d (which is all of them).

The S1 and S2 switches believe that the Core switch is actually running 802.1d because the Core reverted back to 802.1d BPDUs just for them. And even though the S1 and S2 switches receive the 802.1w BPDUs, they don't understand them, so they simply drop them. However, the Core does receive the 802.1d BPDUs and accepts them from the S1 and S2 switches, now knowing which ports to run 802.1d on. In other words, turning 802.1w on for just one switch didn't really help our network at all!

One small annoying issue is that once the Core switch knows to send 802.1d BPDUs out the ports connected to S1 and S2, it won't change this automatically if the S1 and S2 switches were later configured with 802.1w—we'd still need to reboot the Core switch to stop the 802.1d BPDUs.

EtherChannel

The easiest way to configure EtherChannel is through the Cisco Network Assistant, and I'll show you this at the very end of the chapter. For now, I'm going with the CLI because you need to know CLI commands too. Remember, there are two versions of EtherChannel, the Cisco version and the IEEE version. I'm going to use the Cisco version and bundle the links between the S1 switch and the Core.

I'll use the `interface port-channel` global command and the `channel-group` and the `channel-protocol` interface commands on the S1 and Core switches. Here's what that looks like:

```
S1#config t
S1(config)#int port-channel 1
S1(config-if)#int range f0/1-2
```

```
S1(config-if-range)#switchport mode trunk
1d03h: %SPANTREE_FAST-7-PORT_FWD_UPLINK: VLAN0001 FastEthernet0/2
 moved to Forwarding (UplinkFast).
S1(config-if-range)#switchport nonegotiate
S1(config-if-range)#channel-group 1 mode desirable
S1(config-if-range)#do sh int fa0/1 etherchannel
Port state     = Up Sngl-port-Bndl Mstr Not-in-Bndl
Channel group = 1     Mode = Desirable-Sl     Gcchange = 0
Port-channel  = null   GC   = 0x00010001    Pseudo port-channel = Po1
Port index    = 0      Load = 0x00           Protocol =    PAgP
[output cut]


Core#config t
Core(config)#int port-channel 1
Core(config-if)#int range f0/7-8
Core(config-if-range)#switchport trunk encap dot1q
Core(config-if-range)#switchport mode trunk
1d03h: %SPANTREE_FAST-7-PORT_FWD_UPLINK: VLAN0001 FastEthernet0/2
 moved to Forwarding (UplinkFast).
Core(config-if-range)#switchport nonegotiate
Core(config-if-range)#channel-group 1 mode desirable
1d04h: %SPANTREE_FAST-7-PORT_FWD_UPLINK: VLAN0001 FastEthernet0/2
 moved to Forwarding (UplinkFast).
1d04h: %SPANTREE_FAST-7-PORT_FWD_UPLINK: VLAN0001 FastEthernet0/2
 moved to Forwarding (UplinkFast).
1d04h: %LINK-3-UPDOWN: Interface Port-channel1, changed state to up
1d04h: %LINEPROTO-5-UPDOWN: Line protocol on Interface
Port-channel1, changed state to up
Core(config-if-range)#do show int port-channel 1
Port-channel1 is up, line protocol is up (connected)
  Hardware is EtherChannel, address is 001b.2b55.7501 (bia 001b.2b55.7501)
  MTU 1500 bytes, BW 200000 Kbit, DLY 100 usec,
     reliability 255/255, txload 1/255, rxload 1/255
  Encapsulation ARPA, loopback not set
  Full-duplex, 100Mb/s, link type is auto, media type is unknown
[output cut]
```

I added the `switchport nonegotiate` interface command to stop the switches from trying to autodetect the link types and also to automatically set up trunking; instead, I statically configured my trunk links. The two links between the S1 and the Core are now bundled using the Cisco EtherChannel version of PAgP.

Okay—but wait, we still need to verify our switch configurations and play with our root bridge before we can learn about Virtual LANs in the next chapter.

Verifying Cisco Catalyst Switches

The first thing I like to do with any router or switch is to run through the configurations with a show running-config command. Why? Because doing this gives me a really great headshot of each device. However, it's time consuming, and showing you all the configs would take up a whole bunch of pages in this book. Besides, we can run other commands that will still stock us with really good information.

For example, to verify the IP address set on a switch, we can use the show interface command. Here is the output:

```
S1#sh int vlan 1
Vlan1 is up, line protocol is up
  Hardware is EtherSVI, address is 001b.2b55.7540 (bia 001b.2b55.7540)
  Internet address is 192.168.10.17/28
  MTU 1500 bytes, BW 1000000 Kbit, DLY 10 usec,
      reliability 255/255, txload 1/255, rxload 1/255
  Encapsulation ARPA, loopback not set, reliability 255/255, txload 1/255,
rxload 1/255
  [output cut]
```

 Remember that IP addresses aren't needed on a switch. The only reason we would set an IP address, mask, and default gateway is for management purposes.

show mac address-table

I'm sure you remember being shown this command earlier in the chapter. Using it displays the forward filter table, also called a content addressable memory (CAM) table. Here's the output from the S1 switch:

```
S1#sh mac address-table
        Mac Address Table
-------------------------------------------

Vlan    Mac Address       Type        Ports
----    -----------       --------    -----
 All    0100.0ccc.cccc    STATIC      CPU
 All    ffff.ffff.ffff    STATIC      CPU
[output cut]
   1    0002.1762.b235    DYNAMIC     Po1
   1    0009.b79f.c080    DYNAMIC     Po1
```

1	000d.29bd.4b87	DYNAMIC	Po1
1	000d.29bd.4b88	DYNAMIC	Po1
1	0016.4662.52b4	DYNAMIC	Fa0/4
1	0016.4677.5eab	DYNAMIC	Po1
1	001a.2f52.49d8	DYNAMIC	Po1
1	001a.2fe7.4170	DYNAMIC	Fa0/8
1	001a.e2ce.ff40	DYNAMIC	Po1
1	0050.0f02.642a	DYNAMIC	Fa0/3

```
Total Mac Addresses for this criterion: 31
S1#
```

The switches use what are called base MAC addresses that are assigned to the CPU, and the 2960s use 20. From the preceding output, you can see that we have seven MAC addresses dynamically assigned to EtherChannel port 1. Ports Fa0/3, Fa0/8, and Fa0/4 only have one MAC address assigned, and all ports are assigned to VLAN 1.

Let's take a look at the S2 switch CAM and see what we can find. Keep in mind that the S2 switch doesn't have EtherChannel configured as the S1 switch does, so STP will shut down one of the redundant links to the Core switch:

```
S2#sh mac address-table
          Mac Address Table
-------------------------------------------
```

Vlan	Mac Address	Type	Ports
----	-----------	--------	-----
All	0008.205a.85c0	STATIC	CPU
All	0100.0ccc.cccc	STATIC	CPU
All	0100.0ccc.cccd	STATIC	CPU
All	0100.0cdd.dddd	STATIC	CPU
[output cut]			
1	0002.1762.b235	DYNAMIC	Fa0/3
1	000d.29bd.4b80	DYNAMIC	Fa0/1
1	000d.29bd.4b85	DYNAMIC	Fa0/1
1	0016.4662.52b4	DYNAMIC	Fa0/1
1	0016.4677.5eab	DYNAMIC	Fa0/4
1	001b.2b55.7540	DYNAMIC	Fa0/1

```
Total Mac Addresses for this criterion: 26
S2#
```

We can see in the preceding output that we have four MAC addresses assigned to Fa0/1. And of course, we can also see that we have one connection for each host on ports 3 and 4. But where's port 2? Since port 2 is a redundant link, STP placed Fa0/2 into blocking mode. I'll get into more about this again in a minute.

Assigning Static MAC Addresses

You can set a static MAC address in the MAC address table, but like setting static MAC port security, it's a ton of work. But in case you want to do it, here's how it's done:

```
S1#config t
S1(config)#mac-address-table static aaaa.bbbb.cccc vlan 1 int fa0/5
S1(config)#do show mac address-table
          Mac Address Table
-------------------------------------------

Vlan    Mac Address     Type      Ports
----    -----------     --------  -----
 All    0100.0ccc.cccc  STATIC    CPU
[output cut]
  1     0002.1762.b235  DYNAMIC   Po1
  1     0009.b79f.c080  DYNAMIC   Po1
  1     000d.29bd.4b87  DYNAMIC   Po1
  1     000d.29bd.4b88  DYNAMIC   Po1
  1     0016.4662.52b4  DYNAMIC   Fa0/4
  1     0016.4677.5eab  DYNAMIC   Po1
  1     001a.2f52.49d8  DYNAMIC   Po1
  1     001a.2fe7.4170  DYNAMIC   Fa0/8
  1     001a.e2ce.ff40  DYNAMIC   Po1
  1     0050.0f02.642a  DYNAMIC   Fa0/3
  1     aaaa.bbbb.cccc  STATIC    Fa0/5
Total Mac Addresses for this criterion: 31
S1(config)#
```

You can see that a static MAC address is now assigned permanently to interface Fa0/5 and that it's also assigned to VLAN 1 only.

show spanning-tree

By this time you know that the show spanning-tree command is important. With it, you can see who the root bridge is and what our priorities are set to for each VLAN.

Understand that Cisco switches run what is called Per-VLAN Spanning Tree (PVST), which basically means that each VLAN runs its own instance of the STP protocol. If we typed **show spanning-tree**, we'd receive information for each VLAN, starting with VLAN 1. So, say we've got multiple VLANs and we want to see what's up with VLAN 2—we'd use the command **show spanning-tree vlan 2**.

Here is an output from the show spanning-tree command from switch S1. Since we are only using VLAN 1, we don't need to add the VLAN number to the command:

```
S1#sh spanning-tree
VLAN0001
```

```
Spanning tree enabled protocol ieee
Root ID    Priority    32769
           Address     000d.29bd.4b80
           Cost        3012
           Port        56 (Port-channel1)
           Hello Time   2 sec  Max Age 20 sec  Forward Delay 15 sec

Bridge ID  Priority    49153  (priority 49152 sys-id-ext 1)
           Address     001b.2b55.7500
           Hello Time   2 sec  Max Age 20 sec  Forward Delay 15 sec
           Aging Time 15
Uplinkfast enabled


Interface        Role Sts Cost      Prio.Nbr Type
---------------- ---- --- --------- -------- ----------
Fa0/3            Desg FWD 3100      128.3    Edge Shr
Fa0/4            Desg FWD 3019      128.4    Edge P2p
Fa0/8            Desg FWD 3019      128.8    P2p
Po1              Root FWD 3012      128.56   P2p
```

Since we only have VLAN 1 configured, there's no more output for this command, but if we had more, we would get another page for each VLAN configured on the switch. The default priority is 32768, but there's something called the system ID extension (sys-id-ext), which is the VLAN identifier. The Bridge ID priority is incremented by the number of that VLAN. And since we only have VLAN 1, we increment by one to 32769. But understand, by default, Backbone-Fast raises the default priority to 49152 to prevent that bridge from becoming the root.

The top of the output shows us who the root bridge is:

```
VLAN0001
    Root ID  Priority    32769
             Address     000d.29bd.4b80
             Cost        3012
             Port        56 (Port-channel1)
             Hello Time   2 sec  Max Age 20 sec  Forward Delay 15 sec
```

EtherChannel Port 1 is our root port, which means that it's our chosen path to the root bridge, and it has an identifier of 000d.29bd.4b80. That can only be either the Core switch or S2, and we'll find out which one it is in a minute.

The last output from the command displays the ports that are running STP and have a connection to another device. Because we're running EtherChannel, we have no blocked ports. One way to determine if your bridge is the root is to look to see whether there are any Altn BLK ports (meaning blocked ports that are alternates). A root bridge would never have a blocked port on any interface, but all our ports on S1 show forwarding (FWD) because of our EtherChannel configuration.

Determining Our Root Bridge

To determine our root bridge, we would obviously use the show spanning-tree command. Let's take a look at our other two switches and see which switch is the default root bridge. Make a mental note of the Bridge ID MAC address as well as the priority of the S1 switch. Here's the S2 output:

```
S2#sh spanning-tree


VLAN0001
  Spanning tree enabled protocol ieee
  Root ID    Priority    32769
             Address     000d.29bd.4b80
             Cost        3019
             Port        2 (FastEthernet0/1)
             Hello Time   2 sec  Max Age 20 sec  Forward Delay 15 sec


  Bridge ID  Priority    49153  (priority 49152 sys-id-ext 1)
             Address     001a.e2ce.ff00
             Hello Time   2 sec  Max Age 20 sec  Forward Delay 15 sec
             Aging Time 300
  Uplinkfast enabled


Interface        Role Sts Cost      Prio.Nbr Type
---------------- ---- --- --------- -------- ------------
Fa0/1            Root FWD 3019      128.2    P2p
Fa0/2            Altn BLK 3019      128.3    P2p
Fa0/3            Desg FWD 3100      128.4    Edge Shr
Fa0/4            Desg FWD 3019      128.5    Edge P2p
S2#
```

We can see that port Fa0/2 is blocked, so this cannot be our root bridge. A root bridge cannot have blocked ports. Again, pay special attention to the Bridge ID MAC address and the priority. Here's the output from the Core switch:

```
Core#sh spanning-tree
VLAN0001
  Spanning tree enabled protocol rstp
  Root ID    Priority    32769
             Address     000d.29bd.4b80
             This bridge is the root
             Hello Time   2 sec  Max Age 20 sec  Forward Delay 15 sec
```

```
Bridge ID  Priority    32769  (priority 32768 sys-id-ext 1)
           Address     000d.29bd.4b80
           Hello Time   2 sec  Max Age 20 sec  Forward Delay 15 sec
           Aging Time 300

Interface        Role Sts Cost      Prio.Nbr Type
---------------- ---- --- --------- -------- --------------
Fa0/5            Desg FWD 19        128.5    P2p Peer(STP)
Fa0/6            Desg FWD 19        128.6    P2p Peer(STP)
Po1              Desg FWD 12        128.66   P2p Peer(STP)
```

Well there you have it— "This bridge is the root."

But think about this—why does the Core switch just have the default of 32768 and not 49152 like the other switches? Because it's running the 802.1w version of STP, and BackBone-Fast is disabled by default.

Let's take a look at the bridge MAC address of each switch:

- *S1 address:* 001b.2b55.7500
- *S2 address:* 001a.e2ce.ff00
- *Core address:* 000d.29bd.4b80

By checking out the MAC addresses, and if all switches are set to the default priority, which switch do you think will be the root switch? Start reading the MAC addresses from the left, moving toward the right. Core is obviously the lowest MAC address, and by looking at the output of the show spanning-tree command, we can see that it is, indeed, our root bridge (even if all switches had the same priority). It's good practice to figure out the root bridge by comparing the MAC addresses of the switches once in awhile.

Setting Our Root Bridge

It's kind of convenient that the Core switch is our root bridge by default because that's right where I'd typically choose to set the root. But just for fun, let's change it. Here's how we'll do that:

```
S1#config t
S1(config)#spanning-tree vlan 1 priority ?
  <0-61440>  bridge priority in increments of 4096
S1(config)#spanning-tree vlan 1 priority 16384
S1(config)#do show spanning-tree
VLAN0001
Spanning tree enabled protocol ieee
  Root ID    Priority    16385
             Address     001b.2b55.7500
             This bridge is the root
             Hello Time   2 sec  Max Age 20 sec  Forward Delay 15 sec
```

```
Bridge ID  Priority    16385  (priority 16384 sys-id-ext 1)
           Address     001b.2b55.7500
           Hello Time   2 sec  Max Age 20 sec  Forward Delay 15 sec
           Aging Time 300

Interface        Role Sts Cost      Prio.Nbr Type
---------------- ---- --- --------- -------- -----------
Fa0/3            Desg FWD 100       128.3    Edge Shr
Fa0/4            Desg FWD 19        128.4    Edge P2p
Fa0/8            Desg FWD 19        128.8    P2p
Po1              Desg FWD 12        128.56   P2p
```

When you lower the S1 priority to 16384, the S1 switch immediately became the root bridge. You can set your priorities all the way from 0 to 61440. Zero (0) means that the switch will always be the root bridge, and 61440 means the switch will never be a root.

There's one last command I want to tell you about, if you want to skip all this verification and configuration of the root bridge stuff—and no, you don't get to skip all that if you want to pass the Cisco exams! Here's a simple command you can run on a switch to set it as a root bridge:

```
S1(config)#spanning-tree vlan 1 root ?
  primary    Configure this switch as primary root for this spanning tree
  secondary  Configure switch as secondary root
S1(config)#spanning-tree vlan 1 root primary
```

Understand that this does not override a low-priority switch—this command would only work for you if all your switches had the same priority, or higher, set. Oh, and did I mention that you would have to configure this per VLAN, and that you can also set a primary and secondary switch as roots? Yep, you can, and it's certainly a whole lot easier than how we've done it in this chapter! But this is, first and foremost, a guide to prepare you for the CCNA exam—something you definitely want to pass. So make sure you know how to do it like we did even though it really is the hard way!

Cisco Network Assistant

The Cisco Network Assistant (CNA) can make configuring your switches a breeze, which, as with the SDM, is both good and bad. It's good in that it makes it easier for us to create much harder configs, and it's bad because it makes it easier for everyone else to do that as well. But still, it can be a little tricky at first, so download it and get familiar with the CNA as much as possible.

Once we connect to a switch using the CNA, we'll get a screen like this one.

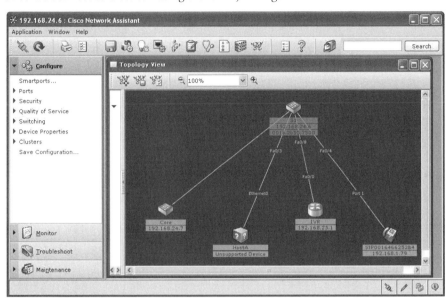

We get a nice topology view of all connected devices. We can see my IP phone, the Core switch, and the inter-VLAN router (IVR), which happens to be the hostname of my 2811 router. But you need to understand that we see only directly connected devices in this output, which means we can't see devices on the other side of the Core.

Probably one of the most helpful menu choices on the left side of the CNA screen is Smartports. Once you click Smartports, you get a close-up view of the switch.

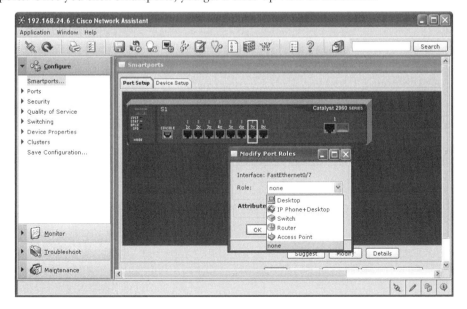

All you need to do is highlight a port, or all of them, and then right-click and choose the type of device that port, or group of ports, will be connecting to. Nice feature! However, an interesting aspect of Smartports is what exactly it configures. For example, I used Smartports to configure port 6 of my S1 switch to be connected to a desktop (meaning a PC). Here are the commands it downloaded to my switch:

```
!
interface FastEthernet0/6
 switchport mode access
 switchport port-security
 switchport port-security aging time 2
 switchport port-security violation restrict
 switchport port-security aging type inactivity
 macro description cisco-desktop
 spanning-tree portfast
 spanning-tree bpduguard enable
!
```

Holy smokes! Check that out—I don't even need to understand any of the features we discussed in this chapter to configure my switch. Instead, I just need to choose the type of device connected to the interface and, wham—the switch is automatically configured with the commands that it "thinks" are the smart choices for that type of port. Wow—this little beauty really rocks!

Now before we move on with the CNA, let's talk a bit about the configuration that was placed under the interface. We've already discussed `port-security`, the `spanning-tree portfast`, and `bpduguard` in this chapter, but what about the `macro` and `port-security aging` commands that it also set? The macros are the default programs that are stored on the new Cisco switches that are run when a Smartport is set. The `port-security aging` command does just that—it sets the aging rate of the port. There are two options you can use with the `aging` command: `absolute` and `inactivity`. The `absolute` option will delete the secure addresses on a port after the specified time—anywhere from 0 to 1440 minutes. The `inactivity` option means that the addresses on the port will be deleted when they are inactive for the specified time. That time is also set in minutes from 0 to 1440. So, when you use the command `switchport port-security aging time 2` with the command `switchport port-security aging type inactivity`, all the MAC addresses associated to the port will be deleted after two minutes. And not only that, the command `switchport port-security violation restrict` means that a trap will be sent to an SNMP server, or Network Management Station (NMS). Even though this seems a little overboard, to me it's still pretty cool.

You can view the port security on an interface with this command:

S1#sh port-security interface f0/6
```
Port Security              : Enabled
```

```
Port Status                 : Secure-down
Violation Mode              : Restrict
Aging Time                  : 2 mins
Aging Type                  : Inactivity
SecureStatic Address Aging  : Disabled
Maximum MAC Addresses       : 1
Total MAC Addresses         : 0
Configured MAC Addresses    : 0
Sticky MAC Addresses        : 0
Last Source Address:Vlan    : 0000.0000.0000:0
Security Violation Count    : 0
```

Wait a minute—what's happening with that macro command in there? Well, no worries. It's just a switch command that lets you create and run macros, and Cisco's new switches have six of those preconfigured. Weirdly, you can't see them in the running configuration; you can only view them with the show parser command. Here's the macro that was run on our port f0/6:

```
S1#sh parser macro
Total number of macros = 6
--------------------------------------------------------------
Macro name : cisco-desktop
Macro type : default interface
# macro keywords $access_vlan
# Basic interface - Enable data VLAN only
# Recommended value for access vlan should not be 1
switchport access vlan $access_vlan
switchport mode access

# Enable port security limiting port to a single
# MAC address -- that of desktop
switchport port-security
switchport port-security maximum 1

# Ensure port-security age is greater than one minute
# and use inactivity timer
switchport port-security violation restrict
switchport port-security aging time 2
switchport port-security aging type inactivity

# Configure port as an edge network port
```

```
spanning-tree portfast
spanning-tree bpduguard enable
[output cut]
```

All right, all's good. At least now we know how all those command were configured on our switch—there's a macro for each of the devices under Smartports, as shown by the show parser macro brief command:

S1#**sh parser macro brief**
```
    default global    : cisco-global
    default interface: cisco-desktop
    default interface: cisco-phone
    default interface: cisco-switch
    default interface: cisco-router
    default interface: cisco-wireless
```

Anyway, getting back to the CNA, under Ports, you'll find Port Settings.

Here's where you'll find all the ports with basic configuration information that you can both view and change. Also under Ports, you'll find EtherChannels.

This may be an easier way to bundle some ports instead of using the CLI. With it, you can bundle up to eight ports between switches. After clicking EtherChannel, just choose your group and indicate the ports you want to bundle and the protocol you're going to use. That's it!

And this is very cool—by clicking Device Properties, you can set many of your switch's features from here: the IP addresses, hostname, users and passwords, and more.

From the Topology View screen, you can right-click a device and click on a variety of options, but the Device Manager is interesting.

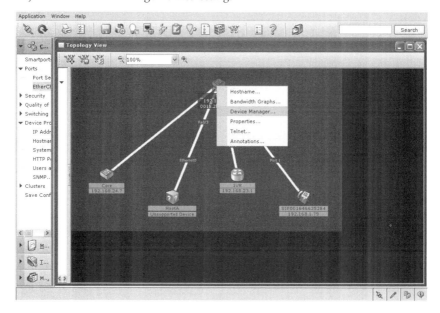

One you choose Device Manager, your default HTTP browser will open, and it's now time to begin configuring and verifying your switch from an HTTP browser—however, it has a slower response time than through the CNA so I don't personally use it.

There's a lot more to the CNA, and I recommend that you take the time to download it and play with it as much as possible.

Now admit it—even though this was a huge chapter, you really did learn a lot, and well, maybe you even had a little fun along the way! You've now configured and verified all switches, set port security, and navigated STP extensions as well as set your root bridge. That means you're now ready to learn all about virtual LANs! I'm going to save all our switch configurations so we'll be able to start right from here in Chapter 9, "Virtual LANs (VLANs)."

Summary

In this chapter, I talked about the differences between switches and bridges and how they both work at layer 2 and create a MAC address forward/filter table in order to make decisions on whether to forward or flood a frame.

I also discussed problems that can occur if you have multiple links between bridges (switches) and how to solve these problems by using the Spanning Tree Protocol (STP).

I also covered detailed configuration of Cisco's Catalyst switches, including verifying the configuration, setting the Cisco STP extensions, and changing the root bridge by setting a bridge priority.

Last, I went through the Cisco Network Assistant, which can help you tremendously with your switch configurations.

Exam Essentials

Remember the three switch functions.   Address learning, forward/filter decisions, and loop avoidance are the functions of a switch.

Remember the command `show mac address-table`.   The command `show mac address-table` will show you the forward/filter table used on the LAN switch

Understand the main purpose of the Spanning Tree Protocol in a switched LAN.   The main purpose of STP is to prevent switching loops in a network with redundant switched paths.

Remember the states of STP.   The purpose of the blocking state is to prevent the use of looped paths. A port in listening state prepares to forward data frames without populating the MAC address table. A port in learning state populates the MAC address table but doesn't forward data frames. A port in forwarding state sends and receives all data frames on the bridged port. Last, a port in the disabled state is virtually nonoperational.

Remember the command `show spanning-tree`.   You must be familiar with the command `show spanning-tree` and how to determine who the root bridge is.

Written Lab 8

Write the answers to the following questions:

1.   What command will show you the forward/filter table?

2.   If a destination MAC address is not in the forward/filter table, what will the switch do with the frame?

3.   What are the three switch functions at layer 2?

4.   If a frame is received on a switch port and the source MAC address is not in the forward/filter table, what will the switch do?

5.   What is used at layer 2 to prevent switching loops?

6.   802.1w is also called what?

7.   When is STP considered to be converged?

8.   Switches break up _____ domains.

9.   What is used to prevent switching loops in a network with redundant switched paths?

10.   Which Cisco 802.1d extension stops BPDU from being transmitted out a port?

   (The answers to Written Lab 8 can be found following the review questions for this chapter.)

Review Questions

The following questions are designed to test your understanding of this chapter's material. For more information on how to get additional questions, please see this book's Introduction.

1. Which of the following is a layer 2 protocol used to maintain a loop-free network?

   A. VTP

   B. STP

   C. RIP

   D. CDP

2. What command will display the forward/filter table?

   A. `show mac filter`

   B. `show run`

   C. `show mac address-table`

   D. `show mac filter-table`

3. What is the result of segmenting a network with a bridge (switch)? (Choose two options.)

   A. It increases the number of collision domains.

   B. It decreases the number of collision domains.

   C. It increases the number of broadcast domains.

   D. It decreases the number of broadcast domains.

   E. It makes smaller collision domains.

   F. It makes larger collision domains.

4. Which statement describes a spanning-tree network that has converged?

   A. All switch and bridge ports are in the forwarding state.

   B. All switch and bridge ports are assigned as either root or designated ports.

   C. All switch and bridge ports are in either the forwarding or blocking state.

   D. All switch and bridge ports are either blocking or looping.

5. What is the purpose of Spanning Tree Protocol in a switched LAN?

   A. To provide a mechanism for network monitoring in switched environments

   B. To prevent routing loops in networks with redundant paths

   C. To prevent switching loops in networks with redundant switched paths

   D. To manage the VLAN database across multiple switches

   E. To create collision domains

6. What are the three distinct functions of layer 2 switching that increase available bandwidth on the network? (Choose three.)

   A. Address learning

   B. Routing

   C. Forwarding and filtering

   D. Creating network loops

   E. Loop avoidance

   F. IP addressing

7. Your switch has a port status LED that is alternating between green and amber. What could this indicate?

   A. The port is experiencing errors.

   B. The port is shut down.

   C. The port is in STP blocking mode.

   D. Nothing; this is normal.

8. Which of the following statements is true?

   A. A switch creates a single collision domain and a single broadcast domain. A router creates a single collision domain.

   B. A switch creates separate collision domains but one broadcast domain. A router provides a separate broadcast domain.

   C. A switch creates a single collision domain and separate broadcast domains. A router provides a separate broadcast domain as well.

   D. A switch creates separate collision domains and separate broadcast domains. A router provides separate collision domains.

9. You need to configure a Catalyst switch so it can be managed remotely. Which of the following would you use to accomplish this task?

   A.
   ```
   Switch(configs)#int fa0/1
   Switch(configs-if)#ip address 192.168.10.252 255.255.255.0
   Switch(configs-if)#no shut
   ```

   B.
   ```
   Switch(configs)#int vlan 1
   Switch(configs-if)#ip address 192.168.10.252 255.255.255.0
   Switch(configs-if)#ip default-gateway 192.168.10.254 255.255.255.0
   ```

   C.
   ```
   Switch(configs)#ip default-gateway 192.168.10.254
   Switch(configs)#int vlan 1
   Switch(configs-if)#ip address 192.168.10.252 255.255.255.0
   Switch(configs-if)#no shut
   ```

   D.
   ```
   Switch(configs)#ip default-network 192.168.10.254
   Switch(configs)#int vlan 1
   Switch(configs-if)#ip address 192.168.10.252 255.255.255.0
   Switch(configs-if)#no shut
   ```

10. What does a switch do when a frame is received on an interface and the destination hardware address is unknown or not in the filter table?

   A. Forwards the switch to the first available link

   B. Drops the frame

   C. Floods the network with the frame looking for the device

   D. Sends back a message to the originating station asking for a name resolution

11. If a switch receives a frame and the source MAC address is not in the MAC address table but the destination address is, what will the switch do with the frame?

   A. Discard it and send an error message back to the originating host

   B. Flood the network with the frame

   C. Add the source address and port to the MAC address table and forward the frame out the destination port

   D. Add the destination to the MAC address table and then forward the frame

12. You want to run the new 802.1w on your switches. Which of the following would enable this protocol?

   A. `Switch(config)#spanning-tree mode rapid-pvst`

   B. `Switch#spanning-tree mode rapid-pvst`

   C. `Switch(config)#spanning-tree mode 802.1w`

   D. `Switch#spanning-tree mode 802.1w`

13. In which circumstance are multiple copies of the same unicast frame likely to be transmitted in a switched LAN?

   A. During high-traffic periods

   B. After broken links are reestablished

   C. When upper-layer protocols require high reliability

   D. In an improperly implemented redundant topology

14. Which command was used to produce the following output:

```
Vlan    Mac Address       Type        Ports
----    -----------       --------    -----
   1    0005.dccb.d74b    DYNAMIC     Fa0/1
   1    000a.f467.9e80    DYNAMIC     Fa0/3
   1    000a.f467.9e8b    DYNAMIC     Fa0/4
   1    000a.f467.9e8c    DYNAMIC     Fa0/3
   1    0010.7b7f.c2b0    DYNAMIC     Fa0/3
   1    0030.80dc.460b    DYNAMIC     Fa0/3
```

   A. `show vlan`

   B. `show ip route`

   C. `show mac address-table`

   D. `show mac address-filter`

15. If you want to disable STP on a port connected to a server, which command would you use?

A. `disable spanning-tree`

B. `spanning-tree off`

C. `spanning-tree security`

D. `spanning-tree portfast`

16. Refer to the Graphic. Why does the switch have two MAC addresses assigned to the Fast-Ethernet 0/1 port in the switch address table?

MAC Address	Type	Ports
0005.dccb.d74b	DYNAMIC	Fa0/1
000a.f467.9e80	DYNAMIC	Fa0/1
000a.f467.9e8b	DYNAMIC	Fa0/4
000a.f467.9e8c	DYNAMIC	Fa0/3

A. Data from HostC and HostD have been received by the switch port FastEthernet 0/1.

B. Data from two of the devices connected to the switch have been forwarded out to HostD.

C. HostC and HostD had their NIC replaced.

D. HostC and HostD are on different VLANs.

17. Layer 2 switching provides which of the following? (Choose four.)

A. Hardware-based bridging (ASIC)

B. Wire speed

C. Low latency

D. Low cost

E. Routing

F. WAN services

18. You type **show mac address-table** and receive the following output:

```
Switch#sh mac address-table
Vlan    Mac Address      Type       Ports
----    -----------      --------   -----
   1    0005.dccb.d74b   DYNAMIC    Fa0/1
   1    000a.f467.9e80   DYNAMIC    Fa0/3
   1    000a.f467.9e8b   DYNAMIC    Fa0/4
   1    000a.f467.9e8c   DYNAMIC    Fa0/3
   1    0010.7b7f.c2b0   DYNAMIC    Fa0/3
   1    0030.80dc.460b   DYNAMIC    Fa0/3
```

Suppose the above switch received a frame with the following MAC addresses:

- Source MAC: 0005.dccb.d74b

- Destination MAC: 000a.f467.9e8c

What will it do?

A. It will discard the frame.

B. It will forward the frame out port Fa0/3 only.

C. It will forward it out Fa0/1 only.

D. It will send it out all ports except Fa0/1.

19. You need to allow one host to be permitted to attach dynamically to each switch interface. Which two commands must you configure on your catalyst switch to meet this policy? (Choose two.)

A. `Switch(config-if)#ip access-group 10`

B. `Switch(config-if)#switchport port-security maximum 1`

C. `Switch(config)#access-list 10 permit ip host 1`

D. `Switch(config-if)#switchport port-security violation shutdown`

E. `Switch(config)#mac-address-table secure`

20. You have two switches connected together with two crossover cables for redundancy, and STP is disabled. Which of the following will happen between the switches?

A. The routing tables on the switches will not update.

B. The MAC forward/filter table will not update on the switch.

C. Broadcast storms will occur on the switched network.

D. The switches will automatically load-balance between the two links.

Answers to Review Questions

1. B. The Spanning Tree Protocol is used to stop switching loops in a switched network with redundant paths.

2. C. The command `show mac address-table` displays the forward/filter table on the switch.

3. A, E. Bridges break up collision domains, which would increase the number of collision domains in a network and also make smaller collision domains.

4. C. Convergence occurs when all ports on bridges and switches have transitioned to either the forwarding or blocking states. No data is forwarded until convergence is complete. Before data can be forwarded again, all devices must be updated.

5. C. The Spanning Tree Protocol (STP) was designed to stop layer 2 loops. All Cisco switches have the STP on by default.

6. A, C, E. Layer 2 features include address learning, forwarding and filtering of the network, and loop avoidance.

7. A. When you connect to a switch port, at first the link lights are orange/amber, and then they turn green, indicating normal operation. If the link light is blinking, you have a problem.

8. B. Switches break up collision domains, and routers break up broadcast domains.

9. C. To manage a switch remotely, you must set an IP address under the management VLAN, which is, by default, interface vlan 1. Then, from global configuration mode, you set the default gateway with the `ip default-gateway` command.

10. C. Switches flood all frames that have an unknown destination address. If a device answers the frame, the switch will update the MAC address table to reflect the location of the device.

11. C. Since the source MAC address is not in the MAC address table, the switch will add the source address and the port it is connected to into the MAC address table and then forward the frame to the outgoing port.

12. A. 802.1w is the also called Rapid Spanning Tree Protocol. It is not enabled by default on Cisco switches, but it is a better STP to run since it has all the fixes that the Cisco extensions provide with 802.1d.

13. D. If the Spanning Tree Protocol is not running on your switches and you connect them together with redundant links, you will have broadcast storms and multiple frame copies.

14. C. The command `show mac address-table` will display the forward/filter table, also called a CAM table on a switch.

15. D. If you have a server or other devices connected into your switch that you're totally sure won't create a switching loop if STP is disabled, you can use something called `portfast` on these ports. Using it means the port won't spend the usual 50 seconds to come up while STP is converging.

16. A. A switch can have multiple MAC addresses associated with a port. In the Graphic, a hub is connected to port Fa0/1, which has two hosts connected.

17. A, B, C, D. Switches, unlike bridges, are hardware based. Cisco says its switches are wire speed and provide low latency, and I guess they are low cost compared to their prices in the 1990s.

18. B. Since the destination MAC address is in the MAC address table (forward/filter table), it will send it out port Fa0/3 only.

19. B, D. `switchport port-security` is an important command, and it's super easy with the CNA; however, from the CLI, you can set the maximum number of MAC addresses allowed into the port, and then set the penalty if this maximum has been passed.

20. C. If spanning tree is disabled on a switch and you have redundant links to another switch, broadcast storms will occur, among other possible problems.

Answers to Written Lab 8.1

1. `show mac address-table`
2. Flood the frame out all ports except the port it was received on.
3. Address learning, forward/filter decisions, and loop avoidance
4. It will add the source MAC address in the forward/filter table and associate it with the port the frame was received on.
5. Spanning Tree Protocol (STP)
6. Rapid Spanning Tree Protocol (RSTP)
7. When all ports are in either the blocking or forwarding mode
8. Collision
9. Spanning Tree Protocol (STP)
10. PortFast

Chapter

9

Virtual LANs (VLANs)

THE CCNA EXAM TOPICS COVERED IN THIS CHAPTER INCLUDE THE FOLLOWING:

✓ **Describe how a network works**

- Describe the impact of applications (Voice Over IP and Video Over IP) on a network

✓ **Configure, verify and troubleshoot a switch with VLANs and interswitch communications**

- Verify network status and switch operation using basic utilities (including: ping, traceroute, telnet, SSH, arp, ipconfig), SHOW & DEBUG commands

- Identify, prescribe, and resolve common switched network media issues, configuration issues, auto negotiation, and switch hardware failures

- Describe enhanced switching technologies (including: VTP, RSTP, VLAN, PVSTP, 802.1q)

- Describe how VLANs create logically separate networks and the need for routing between them

- Configure, verify, and troubleshoot VLANs

- Configure, verify, and troubleshoot trunking on Cisco switches

- Configure, verify, and troubleshoot interVLAN routing

- Configure, verify, and troubleshoot VTP

- Configure, verify, and troubleshoot RSTP operation

- Interpret the output of various show and debug commands to verify the operational status of a Cisco switched network

- Implement basic switch security (including: port security, trunk access, management vlan other than vlan1, etc.)

I know I keep telling you this, but I've got to be sure you never forget it, so here I go, one last time: By default, switches break up collision domains and routers break up broadcast domains. Okay, I feel better! Now we can move on.

In contrast to the networks of yesterday that were based on collapsed backbones, today's network design is characterized by a flatter architecture—thanks to switches. So now what? How do we break up broadcast domains in a pure switched internetwork? By creating a virtual local area network (VLAN). A VLAN is a logical grouping of network users and resources connected to administratively defined ports on a switch. When you create VLANs, you're given the ability to create smaller broadcast domains within a layer 2 switched internetwork by assigning different ports on the switch to different subnetworks. A VLAN is treated like its own subnet or broadcast domain, meaning that frames broadcast onto the network are only switched between the ports logically grouped within the same VLAN.

So, does this mean we no longer need routers? Maybe yes; maybe no. It really depends on what you want or what your needs are. By default, hosts in a specific VLAN cannot communicate with hosts that are members of another VLAN, so if you want inter-VLAN communication, the answer is that you still need a router.

In this chapter, you're going to learn, in detail, exactly what a VLAN is and how VLAN memberships are used in a switched network. Also, I'm going to tell you all about how VLAN Trunk Protocol (VTP) is used to update switch databases with VLAN information and how trunking is used to send information from all VLANs across a single link. I'll wrap things up by demonstrating how you can make inter-VLAN communication happen by introducing a router into a switched network.

Of course, we'll configure our switched network with VLANs and inter-VLAN routing, and we'll finish the chapter by using the Cisco Network Assistant (CNA) to configure VLANs on our switches.

For up-to-the-minute updates to this chapter, please see www.lammle.com and/or www.sybex.com.

VLAN Basics

Figure 9.1 shows how layer 2 switched networks are typically designed—as flat networks. With this configuration, every broadcast packet transmitted is seen by every device on the network regardless of whether the device needs to receive that data or not.

By default, routers allow broadcasts to occur only within the originating network, while switches forward broadcasts to all segments. Oh, and by the way, the reason it's called a *flat network* is because it's one *broadcast domain*, not because the actual design is physically flat. In Figure 9.1 we see Host A sending out a broadcast and all ports on all switches forwarding it—all except the port that originally received it.

FIGURE 9.1   Flat network structure

Now check out Figure 9.2. It pictures a switched network and shows Host A sending a frame with Host D as its destination. What's important is that, as you can see, that frame is only forwarded out the port where Host D is located. This is a huge improvement over the old hub networks, unless having one *collision domain* by default is what you really want. (Probably not!)

Now you already know that the largest benefit you gain by having a layer 2 switched network is that it creates individual collision domain segments for each device plugged into each port on the switch. This scenario frees us from the Ethernet distance constraints, so now larger networks can be built. But often, each new advance comes with new issues. For instance, the larger the number of users and devices, the more broadcasts and packets each switch must handle.

FIGURE 9.2   The benefit of a switched network

And here's another issue: security! This one's real trouble because within the typical layer 2 switched internetwork, all users can see all devices by default. And you can't stop devices from broadcasting, plus you can't stop users from trying to respond to broadcasts. This means your security options are dismally limited to placing passwords on your servers and other devices.

But wait—there's hope! That is, if you create a *virtual LAN (VLAN)*. You can solve many of the problems associated with layer 2 switching with VLANs, as you'll soon see.

Here's a short list of ways VLANs simplify network management:

- Network adds, moves, and changes are achieved with ease by just configuring a port into the appropriate VLAN.

- A group of users that need an unusually high level of security can be put into its own VLAN so that users outside of the VLAN can't communicate with them.

- As a logical grouping of users by function, VLANs can be considered independent from their physical or geographic locations.

- VLANs greatly enhance network security.

- VLANs increase the number of broadcast domains while decreasing their size.

Coming up, I'm going to tell you all about switching characteristics and thoroughly describe how switches provide us with better network services than hubs can in our networks today.

Broadcast Control

Broadcasts occur in every protocol, but how often they occur depends upon three things:

- The type of protocol
- The application(s) running on the internetwork
- How these services are used

Some older applications have been rewritten to reduce their bandwidth appetites, but there's a new generation of applications that are incredibly bandwidth greedy that will consume any and all they can find. These bandwidth gluttons are multimedia applications that use both broadcasts and multicasts extensively. And faulty equipment, inadequate segmentation, and poorly designed firewalls seriously compound the problems that these broadcast-intensive applications create. All of this has added a major new dimension to network design and presents a bunch of new challenges for an administrator. Positively making sure your network is properly segmented so you can quickly isolate a single segment's problems to prevent them from propagating throughout your entire internetwork is imperative! And the most effective way to do that is through strategic switching and routing.

Since switches have become more affordable lately, a lot of companies are replacing their flat hub networks with pure switched network and VLAN environments. All devices within a VLAN are members of the same broadcast domain and receive all broadcasts. By default, these broadcasts are filtered from all ports on a switch that aren't members of the same VLAN. This is great because you get all the benefits you would with a switched design without getting hit with all the problems you'd have if all your users were in the same broadcast domain—sweet!

Security

Okay, I know. There's always a catch, though, right? Time to get back to those security issues. A flat internetwork's security used to be tackled by connecting hubs and switches together with routers. So it was basically the router's job to maintain security. This arrangement was pretty ineffective for several reasons. First, anyone connecting to the physical network could access the network resources located on that particular physical LAN. Second, all anyone had to do to observe any and all traffic happening in that network was to simply plug a network analyzer into the hub. And similar to that last ugly fact, users could join a workgroup by just plugging their workstations into the existing hub. That's about as secure as an open barrel of honey in a bear enclosure!

But that's exactly what makes VLANs so cool. If you build them and create multiple broadcast groups, you have total control over each port and user! So the days when anyone could just plug their workstations into any switch port and gain access to network resources are history because now you get to control each port, plus whatever resources that port can access. What's more, with the new 2960/3560 switches, this actually happens automatically!

And it doesn't end there my friends, because VLANs can be created in accordance with the network resources a given user requires, plus switches can be configured to inform a network management station of any unauthorized access to network resources. And if you need inter-VLAN communication, you can implement restrictions on a router to make that happen. You can also place restrictions on hardware addresses, protocols, and applications. *Now* we're talking security—the honey barrel is now sealed, shrouded in razor wire, and made of solid titanium!

Flexibility and Scalability

If you were paying attention to what you've read so far, you know that layer 2 switches only read frames for filtering—they don't look at the Network layer protocol. And by default, switches forward all broadcasts. But if you create and implement VLANs, you're essentially creating smaller broadcast domains at layer 2.

What this means is that broadcasts sent out from a node in one VLAN won't be forwarded to ports configured to belong to a different VLAN. So by assigning switch ports or users to VLAN groups on a switch or group of connected switches, you gain the flexibility to add only the users you want into that broadcast domain regardless of their physical location. This setup can also work to block broadcast storms caused by a faulty network interface card (NIC) as well as prevent an intermediate device from propagating broadcast storms throughout the entire internetwork. Those evils can still happen on the VLAN where the problem originated, but the disease will instead be quarantined to that one ailing VLAN.

Another advantage is that when a VLAN gets too big, you can create more VLANs to keep the broadcasts from consuming too much bandwidth—the fewer users in a VLAN, the fewer users affected by broadcasts. This is all well and good, but you seriously need to keep network services in mind and understand how the users connect to these services when you create your VLAN. It's a good move to try to keep all services, except for the email and Internet access that everyone needs, local to all users whenever possible.

To understand how a VLAN looks to a switch, it's helpful to begin by first looking at a traditional network. Figure 9.3 shows how a network was created by using hubs to connect physical LANs to a router.

FIGURE 9.3   Physical LANs connected to a router

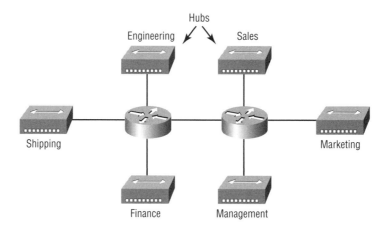

Here you can see that each network is attached with a hub port to the router (each segment also has its own logical network number even though this isn't obvious looking at the figure). Each node attached to a particular physical network has to match that network's number in order to be able to communicate on the internetwork. Notice that each department has its own LAN, so if you needed to add new users to, let's say, Sales, you would just plug them into the Sales LAN and they would automatically be part of the Sales collision and broadcast domain. This design really did work well for many years.

But there was one major flaw: What happens if the hub for Sales is full and we need to add another user to the Sales LAN? Or, what do we do if there's no more physical space where the Sales team is located for this new employee? Well, let's say there just happens to be plenty of room in the Finance section of the building. That new Sales team member will just have to sit on the same side of the building as the Finance people, and we'll just plug the poor soul into the hub for Finance.

Doing this obviously makes the new user part of the Finance LAN, which is very bad for many reasons. First and foremost, we now have a major security issue. Because the new Sales employee is a member of the Finance broadcast domain, the newbie can see all the same servers and access all network services that the Finance folks can. Second, for this user to access the Sales network services they need to get their job done, they would have to go through the router to log in to the Sales server—not exactly efficient!

Now let's look at what a switch accomplishes for us. Figure 9.4 demonstrates how switches come to the rescue by removing the physical boundary to solve our problem. It also shows how six VLANs (numbered 2 through 7) are used to create a broadcast domain for each department. Each switch port is then administratively assigned a VLAN membership, depending on the host and which broadcast domain it's placed in.

FIGURE 9.4   Switches removing the physical boundary

Marketing	VLAN2	172.16.20.0/24
Shipping	VLAN3	172.16.30.0/24
Engineering	VLAN4	172.16.40.0/24
Finance	VLAN5	172.16.50.0/24
Management	VLAN6	172.16.60.0/24
Sales	VLAN7	172.16.70.0/24

So now, if we needed to add another user to the Sales VLAN (VLAN 7), we could just assign the port to VLAN 7 regardless of where the new Sales team member is physically located—nice! This illustrates one of the sweetest advantages to designing your network with VLANs over the old collapsed backbone design. Now, cleanly and simply, each host that needs to be in the Sales VLAN is merely assigned to VLAN 7. And by using the new switches with the predefined macros, we can just use CNA and Smartports to configure the port to be a Desktop connection and voilà! The port configuration is simply completed for us.

Notice that I started assigning VLANs with VLAN number 2. The number is irrelevant, but you might be wondering what happened to VLAN 1? Well that VLAN is an administrative VLAN, and even though it can be used for a workgroup, Cisco recommends that you use it for administrative purposes only. You can't delete or change the name of VLAN 1, and by default, all ports on a switch are members of VLAN 1 until you change them.

Since each VLAN is considered a broadcast domain, it's got to also have its own subnet number (refer again to Figure 9.4). And if you're also using IPv6, then each VLAN must also be assigned its own IPv6 network number. So you don't get confused, just keep thinking of VLANs as separate subnets or networks.

Now let's get back to that "because of switches, we don't need routers anymore" misconception. Looking at Figure 9.4, notice that there are seven VLANs, or broadcast domains, counting VLAN 1. The nodes within each VLAN can communicate with each other but not with anything in a different VLAN because the nodes in any given VLAN "think" that they're actually in a collapsed backbone, as illustrated in Figure 9.3.

So what handy little tool do we need to enable the hosts in Figure 9.4 to communicate to a node or host on a different VLAN? You guessed it—a router! Those nodes positively need to go through a router, or some other layer 3 device, just as when they're configured for inter-network communication (as shown in Figure 9.3). It works the same way it would if we were trying to connect different physical networks. Communication between VLANs must go through a layer 3 device. So don't expect mass router extinction any time soon!

> We'll use both a router and the 3560 switch to provide inter-VLAN routing on our switched network toward the end of this chapter. We can actually employ the 3560 to be a layer 3 switch, just like a router.

VLAN Memberships

Most of the time, VLANs are created by a sys admin who proceeds to assign switch ports to each VLAN. VLANs of this type are known as *static VLANs*. If you don't mind doing a little more work when you begin this process, assign all the host devices' hardware addresses into a database so your switches can be configured to assign VLANs dynamically any time you plug a host into a switch. I hate saying things like "obviously," but obviously, this type of VLAN is known as a *dynamic VLAN*. I'll be covering both static and dynamic VLANs in the next couple of sections.

Static VLANs

Creating static VLANs is the most common way to create a VLAN, and one of the reasons for that is because static VLANs are the most secure. This security stems from the fact that any switch port you've assigned a VLAN association to will always maintain it unless you change the port assignment manually.

Static VLAN configuration is pretty easy to set up and supervise, and it works really well in a networking environment where any user movement within the network needs to be controlled. It can be helpful to use network management software to configure the ports, but you don't have to use it if you don't want to.

In Figure 9.4, each switch port was configured manually with a VLAN membership based upon which VLAN the host needed to be a member of—remember, the device's actual physical location doesn't matter a bit. Which broadcast domain your hosts become members of is purely up to you. And again, remember that each host also has to have the correct IP address information. For instance, you must configure each host in VLAN 2 into the 172.16.20.0/24 network for them to become members of that VLAN. It's also a good idea to keep in mind that if you plug a host into a switch, you have to verify the VLAN membership of that port. If the membership is different than what's needed for that host, the host won't be able to gain access to the network services that it needs, such as a workgroup server.

Static access ports are either manually assigned to a VLAN or are assigned through a RADIUS server for use with IEEE 802.1x.

Dynamic VLANs

On the other hand, a dynamic VLAN determines a node's VLAN assignment automatically. Using intelligent management software, you can base VLAN assignments on hardware (MAC) addresses, protocols, or even applications that create dynamic VLANs.

For example, let's say MAC addresses have been entered into a centralized VLAN management application and you hook up a new node. If you attached it to an unassigned switch port, the VLAN management database can look up the hardware address and both assign and configure the switch port into the correct VLAN. Needless to say, this makes management and configuration much easier because if a user moves, the switch will simply assign them to the correct VLAN automatically. But here again, there's a catch: You've got to do a lot more work initially setting up the database. It can be very worthwhile though!

And here's some good news: You can use the VLAN Management Policy Server (VMPS) service to set up a database of MAC addresses to be used for the dynamic addressing of your VLANs. The VMPS database automatically maps MAC addresses to VLANs.

A dynamic-access port can belong to one VLAN (VLAN ID 1 all the way up to 4094) and, as I said, is dynamically assigned by the VMPS. The Catalyst 2960 switch can be a VMPS client only. You can have dynamic-access ports and trunk ports on the same switch, but you have to connect the dynamic-access port to an end station or hub—*not* to another switch!

Identifying VLANs

Know that switch ports are layer 2–only interfaces that are associated with a physical port. A switch port can belong to only one VLAN if it is an access port or all VLANs if it is a trunk port. You can manually configure a port as an access or trunk port, or you can let the Dynamic Trunking Protocol (DTP) operate on a per-port basis to set the switchport mode. DTP does this by negotiating with the port on the other end of the link.

Switches are definitely pretty busy devices. As frames are switched throughout the network, they've got to be able to keep track of all the different types plus understand what to do with them depending on the hardware address. And remember—frames are handled differently according to the type of link they're traversing.

There are two different types of links in a switched environment:

Access ports   An access port belongs to and carries the traffic of only one VLAN. Traffic is both received and sent in native formats with no VLAN tagging whatsoever. Anything arriving on an access port is simply assumed to belong to the VLAN assigned to the port. So, what do you think will happen if an access port receives a tagged packet, like IEEE 802.1Q tagged? Right—

that packet would simply be dropped. But why? Well, because an access port doesn't look at the source address, so tagged traffic can be forwarded and received only on trunk ports.

With an access link, this can be referred to as the *configured VLAN* of the port. Any device attached to an *access link* is unaware of a VLAN membership—the device just assumes it's part of the same broadcast domain, but it doesn't have the big picture, so it doesn't understand the physical network topology at all.

Another good bit of information to know is that switches remove any VLAN information from the frame before it's forwarded out to an access-link device. Remember that access-link devices can't communicate with devices outside their VLAN unless the packet is routed. And you can only create a switch port to be either an access port or a trunk port—not both. So you've got to choose one or the other and know that if you make it an access port, that port can be assigned to one VLAN only.

> **Voice access ports**   Not to confuse you, but all that I just said about the fact that an access port can be assigned to only one VLAN is really only sort of true. Nowadays, most switches will allow you to add a second VLAN to an access port on a switch port for your voice traffic; it's called the voice VLAN. The voice VLAN used to be called the auxiliary VLAN, which allowed it to be overlaid on top of the data VLAN, enabling both types of traffic through the same port. Even though this is technically considered to be a different type of link, it's still just an access port that can be configured for both data and voice VLANs. This allows you to connect both a phone and a PC device to one switch port but still have each device in a separate VLAN. I'll go into voice VLANs in detail and clear all this up for you in the section "Telephony: Configuring Voice VLANs" later in this chapter.

Trunk Ports   Believe it or not, the term *trunk port* was inspired by the telephone system trunks that carry multiple telephone conversations at a time. So it follows that trunk ports can similarly carry multiple VLANs at a time.

A *trunk link* is a 100- or 1000Mbps point-to-point link between two switches, between a switch and router, or even between a switch and server, and it carries the traffic of multiple VLANs—from 1 to 4,094 at a time (though it's really only up to 1,005 unless you're going with extended VLANs).

Trunking can be a real advantage because with it, you get to make a single port part of a whole bunch of different VLANs at the same time. This is a great feature because you can actually set ports up to have a server in two separate broadcast domains simultaneously so your users won't have to cross a layer 3 device (router) to log in and access it. Another benefit to trunking comes into play when you're connecting switches. Trunk links can carry various amounts of VLAN information across the link, but by default, if the links between your switches aren't trunked, only information from the configured VLAN will be switched across that link.

It's good to know that all VLANs send information on a trunked link unless you clear each VLAN by hand, and no worries, I'll show you how to clear individual VLANs from a trunk in a bit.

Check out Figure 9.5. It shows how the different links are used in a switched network. All hosts connected to the switches can communicate to all ports in their VLAN because of the trunk link between them. Remember, if we used an access link between the switches, this would allow only one VLAN to communicate between switches. As you can see, these hosts are using access links to connect to the switch, so they're communicating in one VLAN only. That means that without a router, no host can communicate outside its own VLAN, but they can send data over trunked links to hosts on another switch configured in their same VLAN.

FIGURE 9.5   Access and trunk links in a switched network

Okay—it's finally time to tell you about frame tagging and the VLAN identification methods used in it.

Frame Tagging

As you now know, you can set up your VLANs to span more than one connected switch. You can see that going on in Figure 9.4, which depicts hosts from various VLANs spread across a bunch of switches. This flexible, power-packed capability is probably the main advantage to implementing VLANs.

But it can get kind of complicated—even for a switch—so there needs to be a way for each one to keep track of all the users and frames as they travel the switch fabric and VLANs. When I say "switch fabric," I'm just referring to a group of switches that share the same VLAN information. And this just happens to be where *frame tagging* enters the scene. This frame identification method uniquely assigns a user-defined ID to each frame. Sometimes people refer to it as a "VLAN ID" or even "color."

Here's how it works: Each switch that the frame reaches must first identify the VLAN ID from the frame tag. It then finds out what to do with the frame by looking at the information in what's known as the filter table. If the frame reaches a switch that has another trunked link, the frame will be forwarded out the trunk-link port.

Once the frame reaches an exit that's determined by the forward/filter table to be an access link matching the frame's VLAN ID, the switch will remove the VLAN identifier. This is so the destination device can receive the frames without being required to understand their VLAN identification.

Another thing about trunk ports is that they will support tagged and untagged traffic simultaneously (if you are using 802.1Q trunking, which we will talk about in the next section). The trunk port is assigned a default port VLAN ID (PVID) for a VLAN that all untagged traffic will travel on. This VLAN is also called the native VLAN and is always VLAN 1 by default (but can be changed to any VLAN number).

Similarly, any untagged or tagged traffic with a NULL (unassigned) VLAN ID is assumed to belong to the VLAN with the port default PVID (again, VLAN 1 by default). A packet with a VLAN ID equal to the outgoing port default PVID is sent untagged and can only communicate to hosts or devices in VLAN 1. All other VLAN traffic has to be sent with a VLAN tag to communicate in a particular VLAN that corresponds with that tag.

VLAN Identification Methods

VLAN identification is what switches use to keep track of all those frames as they're traversing a switch fabric. It's how switches identify which frames belong to which VLANs, and there's more than one trunking method.

Inter-Switch Link (ISL)

Inter-Switch Link (ISL) is a way of explicitly tagging VLAN information onto an Ethernet frame. This tagging information allows VLANs to be multiplexed over a trunk link through an external encapsulation method (ISL), which allows the switch to identify the VLAN membership of a frame over the trunked link.

By running ISL, you can interconnect multiple switches and still maintain VLAN information as traffic travels between switches on trunk links. ISL functions at layer 2 by encapsulating a data frame with a new header and cyclic redundancy check (CRC).

Of note is that this is proprietary to Cisco switches, and it's used for Fast Ethernet and Gigabit Ethernet links only. *ISL routing* is pretty versatile and can be used on a switch port, router interfaces, and server interface cards to trunk a server.

IEEE 802.1Q

Created by the IEEE as a standard method of frame tagging, IEEE 802.1Q actually inserts a field into the frame to identify the VLAN. If you're trunking between a Cisco switched link and a different brand of switch, you've got to use 802.1Q for the trunk to work.

It works like this: You first designate each port that is going to be a trunk with 802.1Q encapsulation. The ports must be assigned a specific VLAN ID, which makes them the native VLAN, in order for them to communicate. The ports that populate the same trunk create a group with this native VLAN, and each port gets tagged with an identification number reflecting that, again the default being VLAN 1. The native VLAN allows the trunks to carry information that was received without any VLAN identification or frame tag.

The 2960s support only the IEEE 802.1Q trunking protocol, but the 3560s will support both the ISL and IEEE methods.

 The basic purpose of ISL and 802.1Q frame-tagging methods is to provide inter-switch VLAN communication. Also, remember that any ISL or 802.1Q frame tagging is removed if a frame is forwarded out an access link—tagging is used across trunk links only!

VLAN Trunking Protocol (VTP)

Cisco created this one too. The basic goals of *VLAN Trunking Protocol (VTP)* are to manage all configured VLANs across a switched internetwork and to maintain consistency throughout that network VTP allows you to add, delete, and rename VLANs—information that is then propagated to all other switches in the VTP domain.

Here's a list of some of the cool features VTP has to offer:

- Consistent VLAN configuration across all switches in the network
- VLAN trunking over mixed networks, such as Ethernet to ATM LANE or even FDDI
- Accurate tracking and monitoring of VLANs
- Dynamic reporting of added VLANs to all switches in the VTP domain
- Plug and Play VLAN adding

Very nice, but before you can get VTP to manage your VLANs across the network, you have to create a VTP server. All servers that need to share VLAN information must use the same domain name, and a switch can be in only one domain at a time. So basically, this means that a switch can only share VTP domain information with other switches if they're configured into the same VTP domain. You can use a VTP domain if you have more than one switch connected in a network, but if you've got all your switches in only one VLAN, you just don't need to use VTP. Do keep in mind that VTP information is sent between switches only via a trunk port.

Switches advertise VTP management domain information as well as a configuration revision number and all known VLANs with any specific parameters. But there's also something called *VTP transparent mode*. In it, you can configure switches to forward VTP information through trunk ports but not to accept information updates or update their VTP databases.

If you've got sneaky users adding switches to your VTP domain behind your back, you can include passwords, but don't forget—every switch must be set up with the same password. And as you can imagine, this little snag can be a real hassle administratively!

Switches detect any added VLANs within a VTP advertisement, then prepare to send information on their trunk ports with the newly defined VLAN in tow. Updates are sent out as revision numbers that consist of the notification plus 1. Any time a switch sees a higher revision number, it knows the information it's getting is more current, so it will overwrite the existing database with the latest information.

You should know these three requirements for VTP to communicate VLAN information between switches:

- The VTP management domain name of both switches must be set the same.

- One of the switches has to be configured as a VTP server.

- No router is necessary.

Now that you've got that down, we're going to delve deeper in the world of VTP with VTP modes and VTP pruning.

VTP Modes of Operation

Figure 9.6 shows you all three different modes of operation within a VTP domain:

Server   This is the default mode for all Catalyst switches. You need at least one server in your VTP domain to propagate VLAN information throughout that domain. Also important: The switch must be in server mode to be able to create, add, and delete VLANs in a VTP domain. VTP information has to be changed in server mode, and any change made to a switch in server mode will be advertised to the entire VTP domain. In VTP server mode, VLAN configurations are saved in NVRAM.

Client   In client mode, switches receive information from VTP servers, but they also send and receive updates, so in this way, they behave like VTP servers. The difference is that they can't create, change, or delete VLANs. Plus, none of the ports on a client switch can be added to a new VLAN before the VTP server notifies the client switch of the new VLAN. Also good to know is that VLAN information sent from a VTP server isn't stored in NVRAM, which is important because it means that if the switch is reset or reloaded, the VLAN information will be deleted. Here's a hint: If you want a switch to become a server, first make it a client so it receives all the correct VLAN information, then change it to a server—so much easier!

So basically, a switch in VTP client mode will forward VTP summary advertisements and process them. This switch will learn about but won't save the VTP configuration in the running configuration, and it won't save it in NVRAM. Switches that are in VTP client mode will only learn about and pass along VTP information—that's it!

FIGURE 9.6   VTP modes

Server configuration: Saved in NVRAM

Client configuration: Not saved in NVRAM   Transparent configuration: Saved in NVRAM

So, When Do I Need to Consider Using VTP?

Here's a scenario for you. Bob, a senior network administrator at Acme Corporation in San Francisco, has about 25 switches all connected together, and he wants to configure VLANs to break up broadcast domains. When do you think he should start to consider using VTP?

If you answered that he should have used VTP the moment he had more than one switch and multiple VLANs, you're right. If you have only one switch, then VTP is irrelevant. It also isn't a player if you're not configuring VLANs in your network. But if you do have multiple switches that use multiple VLANs, you'd better configure your VTP server and clients, and you better do it right!

When you first bring up your switched network, verify that your main switch is a VTP server and that all the other ones are VTP clients. When you create VLANs on the main VTP server, all switches will receive the VLAN database.

If you have an existing switched network and you want to add a new switch, make sure to configure it as a VTP client before you install it. If you don't, it's possible—okay, highly probable— that your new little beauty will send out a new VTP database to all your other switches, effectively wiping out all your existing VLANs like a nuclear blast. No one needs that!

Transparent Switches in transparent mode don't participate in the VTP domain or share its VLAN database, but they'll still forward VTP advertisements through any configured trunk links. They can create, modify, and delete VLANs because they keep their own database—one they keep secret from the other switches. Despite being kept in NVRAM, the VLAN database in transparent mode is actually only locally significant. The whole purpose of transparent mode is to allow remote switches to receive the VLAN database from a VTP server-configured switch through a switch that is not participating in the same VLAN assignments.

VTP only learns about normal-range VLANs, with VLAN IDs 1 to 1005; VLANs with IDs greater than 1005 are called extended-range VLANs and they're not stored in the VLAN database. The switch must be in VTP transparent mode when you create VLAN IDs from 1006 to 4094, so it would be pretty rare that you'd ever use these VLANs. One other thing: VLAN IDs 1 and 1002 to 1005 are automatically created on all switches and can't be removed.

VTP Pruning

VTP gives you a way to preserve bandwidth by configuring it to reduce the amount of broadcasts, multicasts, and unicast packets. This is called *pruning*. VTP pruning enabled switches sends broadcasts only to trunk links that actually must have the information.

Here's what this means: If Switch A doesn't have any ports configured for VLAN 5 and a broadcast is sent throughout VLAN 5, that broadcast wouldn't traverse the trunk link to Switch A. By default, VTP pruning is disabled on all switches. Seems to me this would be a good default parameter.

When you enable pruning on a VTP server, you enable it for the entire domain. By default, VLANs 2 through 1001 are pruning eligible, but VLAN 1 can never prune because it's an administrative VLAN. VTP pruning is supported with both VTP version 1 and version 2.

By using the show interface trunk command, we can see that all VLANs are allowed across a trunked link by default:

```
S1#sh int trunk

Port       Mode        Encapsulation  Status       Native vlan
Fa0/1      auto        802.1q         trunking     1
Fa0/2      auto        802.1q         trunking     1

Port       Vlans allowed on trunk
Fa0/1      1-4094
Fa0/2      1-4094

Port       Vlans allowed and active in management domain
Fa0/1      1
Fa0/2      1

Port       Vlans in spanning tree forwarding state and not pruned
Fa0/1      1
Fa0/2      none
S1#
```

Looking at the preceding output, you can see that VTP pruning is disabled by default. I'm going to go ahead and enable pruning. It only takes one command and it is enabled on your entire switched network for the listed VLANs. Let's see what happens:

```
S1#config t
S1(config)#int f0/1
S1(config-if)#switchport trunk ?
  allowed  Set allowed VLAN characteristics when interface is
  in trunking mode
  native   Set trunking native characteristics when interface
  is in trunking mode
  pruning  Set pruning VLAN characteristics when interface is
  in trunking mode
S1(config-if)#switchport trunk pruning ?
  vlan  Set VLANs enabled for pruning when interface is in
  trunking mode
S1(config-if)#switchport trunk pruning vlan 3-4
```

The valid VLANs that can be pruned are 2 to 1001. Extended-range VLANs (VLAN IDs 1006 to 4094) can't be pruned, and these pruning-ineligible VLANs can receive a flood of traffic.

Routing between VLANs

Hosts in a VLAN live in their own broadcast domain and can communicate freely. VLANs create network partitioning and traffic separation at layer 2 of the OSI, and as I said when I told you why we still need routers, if you want hosts or any other IP-addressable device to communicate between VLANs, you just have to have a layer 3 device—period.

For this, you can use a router that has an interface for each VLAN or a router that supports ISL or 802.1Q routing. The least expensive router that supports ISL or 802.1Q routing is the 2600 series router. (You'd have to buy that from a used-equipment reseller, because they are end of life, or EOL.) The 1600, 1700, and 2500 series don't support ISL or 802.1Q routing. I'd recommend at least a 2800 as a bare minimum, and that only supports 802.1Q—Cisco is really moving away from ISL, so you probably should only be using 802.1Q anyway. (Some IOSs on the 2800 may support both ISL and 802.1Q—I just have never seen it supported.)

As shown in Figure 9.7, if you had only a few VLANs (two or three), you could get by with a router equipped with two or three Fast Ethernet connections. And 10BaseT is okay for home use, and I mean only for home use, but for anything else I'd honestly recommend Fast Ethernet or Gigabit interfaces for something serious under the hood.

FIGURE 9.7   Router with individual VLAN associations

Router connecting three VLANs
together for inter-VLAN communication,
one interface for each VLAN.

What we see in Figure 9.7 is that each router interface is plugged into an access link. This means that each of the routers' interface IP addresses would then become the default gateway address for each host in each VLAN.

If you have more VLANs available than router interfaces, you can configure trunking on one Fast Ethernet interface or buy a layer 3 switch, like the Cisco 3560 or a higher-end switch like a 6500.

Instead of using a router interface for each VLAN, you can use one Fast Ethernet interface and run ISL or 802.1Q trunking. Figure 9.8 shows how a Fast Ethernet interface on a router will look when configured with ISL or 802.1Q trunking. This allows all VLANs to communicate through one interface. Cisco calls this a "router on a stick."

FIGURE 9.8   "Router on a stick"

Router connecting all VLANs together
allowing for inter-VLAN communication,
using only one router interface
(router on a stick).

I need to point out that this creates a bottleneck, as well as a single point of failure, so your host/VLAN count is limited. How many? That depends on your traffic level. To really make things really right, you'd be better off using a higher-end switch and routing on the backplane, but if you just happen to have a router sitting around, configuring this method is free, right?

Configuring VLANs

It may come as a surprise to you, but configuring VLANs is actually pretty easy. Figuring out which users you want in each VLAN is not; it's extremely time consuming. But once you've decided on the number of VLANs you want to create and established which users you want to belong to each one, it's time to bring your first VLAN into the world.

To configure VLANs on a Cisco Catalyst switch, use the global config vlan command. In the following example, I'm going to demonstrate how to configure VLANs on the S1 switch by creating three VLANs for three different departments—again, remember that VLAN 1 is the native and administrative VLAN by default:

```
S1#config t
S1(config)#vlan ?
  WORD      ISL VLAN IDs 1-4094
  internal  internal VLAN
S1(config)#vlan 2
S1(config-vlan)#name Sales
S1(config-vlan)#vlan 3
S1(config-vlan)#name Marketing
```

```
S1(config-vlan)#vlan 4
S1(config-vlan)#name Accounting
S1(config-vlan)#^Z
S1#
```

From the preceding above, you can see that you can create VLANs from 2 to 4094. This is only mostly true. As I said, VLANs can really only be created up to 1005, and you can't use, change, rename, or delete VLANs 1 and 1002 through 1005 because they're reserved. The VLAN numbers above that are called extended VLANs and won't be saved in the database unless your switch is set to VTP transparent mode. You won't see these VLAN numbers used too often in production. Here's an example of setting my S1 switch to VLAN 4000 when my switch is set to VTP server mode (the default VTP mode):

```
S1#config t
S1(config)#vlan 4000
S1(config-vlan)#^Z
% Failed to create VLANs 4000
Extended VLAN(s) not allowed in current VTP mode.
%Failed to commit extended VLAN(s) changes.
```

After you create the VLANs that you want, you can use the show vlan command to check them out. But notice that, by default, all ports on the switch are in VLAN 1. To change the VLAN associated with a port, you need to go to each interface and tell it which VLAN to be a part of.

 Remember that a created VLAN is unused until it is assigned to a switch port or ports and that all ports are always assigned in VLAN 1 unless set otherwise.

Once the VLANs are created, verify your configuration with the show vlan command (sh vlan for short):

```
S1#sh vlan
```

VLAN	Name	Status	Ports
1	default	active	Fa0/3, Fa0/4, Fa0/5, Fa0/6
			Fa0/7, Fa0/8, Gi0/1
2	Sales	active	
3	Marketing	active	
4	Accounting	active	

```
 [output cut]
```

This may seem repetitive, but it's important, and I want you to remember it: You can't change, delete, or rename VLAN 1 because it's the default VLAN and you just can't change that—period. It's the native VLAN of all switches by default, and Cisco recommends that you use it as your administrative VLAN. Basically, any packets that aren't specifically assigned to a different VLAN will be sent down to the native VLAN.

In the preceding S1 output, you can see that ports Fa0/3 through Fa0/8 and the Gi0/1 uplink are all in VLAN 1, but where are ports 1 and 2? Remember that in the previous chapter I trunked and created an EtherChannel bundle. Any port that is a trunk port won't show up in the VLAN database. You have to use the `show interface trunk` command to see your trunked ports.

Now that we can see the VLANs created, we can assign switch ports to specific ones. Each port can be part of only one VLAN, with the exception of our voice access ports. With the trunking we went over earlier, you can make a port available to traffic from all VLANs. I'll cover that next.

Assigning Switch Ports to VLANs

You configure a port to belong to a VLAN by assigning a membership mode that specifies the kind of traffic the port carries, plus the number of VLANs to which it can belong. You can configure each port on a switch to be in a specific VLAN (access port) by using the interface `switchport` command. You can also configure multiple ports at the same time with the `interface range` command we talked about in Chapter 8.

Remember that you can configure either static memberships or dynamic memberships on a port. For this book's purpose, I'm only going to cover the static flavor. In the following example, I'll configure interface fa0/3 to VLAN 3. This is the connection from the S1 switch to the HostA device:

```
S1#config t
S1(config)#int fa0/3
S1(config-if)#switchport ?
  access        Set access mode characteristics of the interface
  backup        Set backup for the interface
  block         Disable forwarding of unknown uni/multi cast addresses
  host          Set port host
  mode          Set trunking mode of the interface
  nonegotiate   Device will not engage in negotiation protocol on this
                interface
  port-security Security related command
  priority      Set appliance 802.1p priority
  protected     Configure an interface to be a protected port
  trunk         Set trunking characteristics of the interface
  voice         Voice appliance attributes
```

Well now, what do we have here? There's some new stuff showing up in the preceding output. We can see various commands—some that I've already covered, but no worries; I'm going to cover the access, mode, nonegotiate, trunk, and voice commands very soon in this chapter. Let's start with setting an access port on S1, which is probably the most widely used type of port on production switches that has VLANs configured:

```
S1(config-if)#switchport mode ?
  access   Set trunking mode to ACCESS unconditionally
  dynamic  Set trunking mode to dynamically negotiate access or
  trunk mode
  trunk    Set trunking mode to TRUNK unconditionally

S1(config-if)#switchport mode access
S1(config-if)#switchport access vlan 3
```

By starting with the switchport mode access command, you're telling the switch that this is a layer 2 port. You can then assign a VLAN to the port with the switchport access command. Remember, you can choose many ports to configure at the same time if you use the interface range command. The dynamic and trunk commands are used for trunk ports exclusively.

That's it. Well, sort of. If you plugged devices into each VLAN port, they can only talk to other devices in the same VLAN. We want to enable inter-VLAN communication and we're going to do that, but first you need to learn a bit more about trunking.

Configuring Trunk Ports

The 2960 switch only runs the IEEE 802.1Q encapsulation method. To configure trunking on a Fast Ethernet port, use the interface command trunk [*parameter*]. It's a tad different on the 3560 switch, and I'll show you that in the next section.

The following switch output shows the trunk configuration on interface fa0/8 as set to trunk on:

```
S1#config t
S1(config)#int fa0/8
S1(config-if)#switchport mode trunk
```

The following list describes the different options available when configuring a switch interface:

switchport mode access   I discussed this in the previous section, but this puts the interface (access port) into permanent nontrunking mode and negotiates to convert the link into a nontrunk link. The interface becomes a nontrunk interface regardless of whether the neighboring interface is a trunk interface. The port would be a dedicated layer 2 port.

switchport mode dynamic auto   This mode makes the interface able to convert the link to a trunk link. The interface becomes a trunk interface if the neighboring interface is set to trunk or desirable mode. This is now the default switchport mode for all Ethernet interfaces on all new Cisco switches.

switchport mode dynamic desirable   This one makes the interface actively attempt to convert the link to a trunk link. The interface becomes a trunk interface if the neighboring interface is set to trunk, desirable, or auto mode. I used to see this mode as the default on some older switches, but not any longer. The default is dynamic auto now.

switchport mode trunk   Puts the interface into permanent trunking mode and negotiates to convert the neighboring link into a trunk link. The interface becomes a trunk interface even if the neighboring interface isn't a trunk interface.

switchport nonegotiate   Prevents the interface from generating DTP frames. You can use this command only when the interface switchport mode is access or trunk. You must manually configure the neighboring interface as a trunk interface to establish a trunk link.

> Dynamic Trunking Protocol (DTP) is used for negotiating trunking on a link between two devices, as well as negotiating the encapsulation type of either 802.1Q or ISL. I use the nonegotiate command when I want dedicated trunk ports no questions asked.

To disable trunking on an interface, use the switchport mode access command, which sets the port back to a dedicated layer 2 switch port.

Trunking with the Cisco Catalyst 3560 switch

Okay, let's take a look at one more switch—the Cisco Catalyst 3560. The configuration is pretty much the same as it is for a 2960, with the exception that the 3560 can provide layer 3 services and the 2960 can't. Plus, the 3560 can run both the ISL and the IEEE 802.1Q trunking encapsulation methods—the 2960 can only run 802.1Q. With all this in mind, let's take a quick look at the VLAN encapsulation difference regarding the 3560 switch.

The 3560 has the encapsulation command, which the 2960 switch doesn't:

```
Core(config-if)#switchport trunk encapsulation ?
  dot1q      Interface uses only 802.1q trunking encapsulation
 when trunking
  isl        Interface uses only ISL trunking encapsulation
 when trunking
  negotiate  Device will negotiate trunking encapsulation with peer on
             interface
Core(config-if)#switchport trunk encapsulation dot1q
Core(config-if)#switchport mode trunk
```

As you can see, we've got the option to add either the IEEE 802.1Q (dot1q) encapsulation or the ISL encapsulation to the 3560 switch. After you set the encapsulation, you still have to set the interface mode to trunk. Honestly, it's pretty rare that you'd continue to use the ISL encapsulation method. Cisco is moving away from ISL—its new routers don't even support it.

Defining the Allowed VLANs on a Trunk

As I've mentioned, trunk ports send and receive information from all VLANs by default, and if a frame is untagged, it's sent to the management VLAN. This applies to the extended range VLANs as well.

But we can remove VLANs from the allowed list to prevent traffic from certain VLANs from traversing a trunked link. Here's how you'd do that:

```
S1#config t
S1(config)#int f0/1
S1(config-if)#switchport trunk allowed vlan ?
  WORD    VLAN IDs of the allowed VLANs when this port is in
  trunking mode
  add     add VLANs to the current list
  all     all VLANs
  except  all VLANs except the following
  none    no VLANs
  remove  remove VLANs from the current list
S1(config-if)#switchport trunk allowed vlan remove ?
  WORD  VLAN IDs of disallowed VLANS when this port is in trunking mode
S1(config-if)#switchport trunk allowed vlan remove 4
```

The preceding command stopped the trunk link configured on S1 port f0/1, causing it to drop all traffic sent and received for VLAN 4. You can try to remove VLAN 1 on a trunk link, but it will still send and receive management like CDP, PAgP, LACP, DTP, and VTP, so what's the point?

To remove a range of VLANs, just use the hyphen:

```
S1(config-if)#switchport trunk allowed vlan remove 4-8
```

If by chance someone has removed some VLANs from a trunk link and you want to set the trunk back to default, just use this command:

```
S1(config-if)#switchport trunk allowed vlan all
```

Or this command to accomplish the same thing:

```
S1(config-if)#no switchport trunk allowed vlan
```

Next, I want to show you how to configure pruning for VLANs before we start routing between VLANs.

Changing or Modifying the Trunk Native VLAN

You really don't want to change the trunk port native VLAN from VLAN 1, but you can, and some people do it for security reasons. To change the native VLAN, use the following command:

```
S1#config t
S1(config)#int f0/1
```

```
S1(config-if)#switchport trunk ?
  allowed  Set allowed VLAN characteristics when interface is
  in trunking mode
  native   Set trunking native characteristics when interface
  is in trunking mode
  pruning  Set pruning VLAN characteristics when interface is
  in trunking mode
S1(config-if)#switchport trunk native ?
  vlan  Set native VLAN when interface is in trunking mode
S1(config-if)#switchport trunk native vlan ?
  <1-4094>  VLAN ID of the native VLAN when this port is in
  trunking mode
S1(config-if)#switchport trunk native vlan 40
S1(config-if)#^Z
```

So we've changed our native VLAN on our trunk link to 40, and by using the show running-config command, I can see the configuration under the trunk link:

```
!
interface FastEthernet0/1
 switchport trunk native vlan 40
 switchport trunk allowed vlan 1-3,9-4094
 switchport trunk pruning vlan 3,4
!
```

Hold on there partner! You didn't think it would be this easy and would just start working, did you? Sure you didn't. Here's the rub: If all switches don't have the same native VLAN configured on the trunk links, then we'll start to receive this error:

```
19:23:29: %CDP-4-NATIVE_VLAN_MISMATCH: Native VLAN mismatch
discovered on FastEthernet0/1 (40), with Core FastEthernet0/7 (1).
19:24:29: %CDP-4-NATIVE_VLAN_MISMATCH: Native VLAN mismatch
discovered on FastEthernet0/1 (40), with Core FastEthernet0/7 (1).
```

Actually, this is a good, noncryptic error, so either we go to the other end of our trunk link(s) and change the native VLAN or we set the native VLAN back to the default. Here's how we'd do that:

```
S1(config-if)#no switchport trunk native vlan
```

Now our trunk link is using the default VLAN 1 as the native VLAN. Just remember that all switches must use the same native VLAN or you'll have some serious problems. Now, let's mix it up by connecting a router into our switched network and configuring inter-VLAN communication.

Configuring Inter-VLAN Routing

By default, only hosts that are members of the same VLAN can communicate. To change this and allow inter-VLAN communication, you need a router or a layer 3 switch. I'm going to start with the router approach.

To support ISL or 802.1Q routing on a Fast Ethernet interface, the router's interface is divided into logical interfaces—one for each VLAN. These are called *subinterfaces*. From a Fast Ethernet or Gigabit interface, you can set the interface to trunk with the encapsulation command:

```
ISR#config t
ISR(config)#int f0/0.1
ISR(config-subif)#encapsulation ?
  dot1Q  IEEE 802.1Q Virtual LAN
ISR(config-subif)#encapsulation dot1Q ?
  <1-4094>  IEEE 802.1Q VLAN ID
```

Notice that my 2811 router (named ISR) only supports 802.1Q. We'd need an older-model router to run the ISL encapsulation, but why bother?

The subinterface number is only locally significant, so it doesn't matter which subinterface numbers are configured on the router. Most of the time, I'll configure a subinterface with the same number as the VLAN I want to route. It's easy to remember that way since the subinterface number is used only for administrative purposes.

It's really important that you understand that each VLAN is a separate subnet. True, I know—they don't *have* to be. But it really is a good idea to configure your VLANs as separate subnets, so just do that.

Now, I need to make sure you're fully prepared to configure inter-VLAN routing, as well as determine the port IP addresses of hosts connected in a switched VLAN environment. And as always, it's also a good idea to be able to fix any problems that may arise. To set you up for success, let me give you few examples.

First, start by looking at Figure 9.9, and read the router and switch configuration within it. By this point in the book, you should be able to determine the IP address, masks, and default gateways of each of the hosts in the VLANs.

The next step after that is to figure out which subnets are being used. By looking at the router configuration in the figure, you can see that we're using 192.168.1.64/26 with VLAN 1 and 192.168.1.128/27 with VLAN 10. And by looking at the switch configuration, you can see that ports 2 and 3 are in VLAN 1 and port 4 is in VLAN 10. This means that HostA and HostB are in VLAN 1 and HostC is in VLAN 10.

Here's what the hosts' IP addresses should be:

HostA: 192.168.1.66, 255.255.255.192, default gateway 192.168.1.65

HostB: 192.168.1.67, 255.255.255.192, default gateway 192.168.1.65

HostC: 192.168.1.130, 255.255.255.224, default gateway 192.168.1.129

The hosts could be any address in the range—I just choose the first available IP address after the default gateway address. That wasn't so hard, was it?

FIGURE 9.9 Configuring Inter-VLAN example 1

```
interface fastethernet 0/1.1
   encapsulation dot1q 1
   ip address 192.168.1.65 255.255.255.192
interface fastethernet 0/1.10
   encapsulation dot1q 10
   ip address 192.168.1.129 255.255.255.224
```

Port 1: dot1q trunk
Ports 2, 3: VLAN 1
Port 4: VLAN 10

fa0/1

HostA   HostB   HostC

Now, again using Figure 9.9, let's go through the commands necessary to configure switch port 1 to establish a link with the router and provide inter-VLAN communication using the IEEE version for encapsulation. Keep in mind that the commands can vary slightly depending on what type of switch you're dealing with.

For a 2960 switch, use the following:

```
2960#config t
2960(config)#interface fa0/1
2960(config-if)#switchport mode trunk
```

As you already know, the 2960 switch can only run the 802.1Q encapsulation so there's no need to specify it. You can't anyway! For a 3560, it's basically the same, but since it can run ISL and 802.1Q, you have to specify the trunking protocol you're going to use.

Remember that when you create a trunked link, all VLANs are allowed to pass data by default.

Let's take a look at Figure 9.10 and see what we can learn from it. This figure shows three VLANs, with two hosts in each of them.

The router in Figure 9.10 is connected to the fa0/1 switch port, and VLAN 2 is configured on port f0/6. Looking at the diagram, these are the things that Cisco expects you to know:

- The router is connected to the switch using subinterfaces.
- The switch port connecting to the router is a trunk port.
- The switch ports connecting to the clients and the hub are access ports, not trunk ports.

FIGURE 9.10   Inter-VLAN example 2

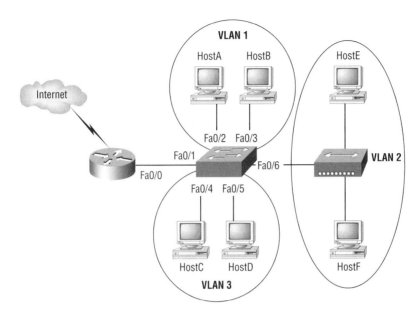

The configuration of the switch would look something like this:

```
2960#config t
2960(config)#int f0/1
2960(config-if)#switchport mode trunk
2960(config-if)#int f0/2
2960(config-if)#switchport access vlan 1
2960(config-if)#int f0/3
2960(config-if)#switchport access vlan 1
2960(config-if)#int f0/4
2960(config-if)#switchport access vlan 3
2960(config-if)#int f0/5
2960(config-if)#switchport access vlan 3
2960(config-if)#int f0/6
2960(config-if)#switchport access vlan 2
```

Before we configure the router, we need to design our logical network:

VLAN 1: 192.168.10.16/28

VLAN 2: 192.168.10.32/28

VLAN 3: 192.168.10.48/28

The configuration of the router would then look like this:

```
ISR#config t
ISR(config)#int f0/0
```

```
ISR(config-if)#no ip address
ISR(config-if)#no shutdown
ISR(config-if)#int f0/0.1
ISR(config-subif)#encapsulation dot1q 1
ISR(config-subif)#ip address 192.168.10.17 255.255.255.240
ISR(config-subif)#int f0/0.2
ISR(config-subif)#encapsulation dot1q 2
ISR(config-subif)#ip address 192.168.10.33 255.255.255.240
ISR(config-subif)#int f0/0.3
ISR(config-subif)#encapsulation dot1q 3
ISR(config-subif)#ip address 192.168.10.49 255.255.255.240
```

The hosts in each VLAN would be assigned an address from their subnet range, and the default gateway would be the IP address assigned to the router's subinterface in that VLAN.

Now, let's take a look at another figure and see if you can determine the switch and router configurations without looking at the answer—no cheating! Figure 9.11 shows a router connected to a 2960 switch with two VLANs. One host in each VLAN is assigned an IP address. What are your router and switch configurations based on these IP addresses?

Since the hosts don't list a subnet mask, you have to look for the number of hosts used in each VLAN to figure out the block size. VLAN 1 has 85 hosts and VLAN 2 has 115 hosts. Each of these will fit in a block size of 128, which is a /25 mask, or 255.255.255.128.

FIGURE 9.11 Inter-VLAN example 3

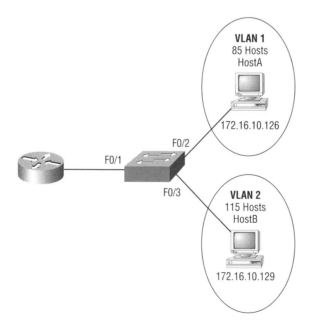

You should know by now that the subnets are 0 and 128; the 0 subnet (VLAN 1) has a host range of 1–126, and the 128 subnet (VLAN 2) has a range of 129–254. You can almost be fooled since HostA has an IP address of 126, which makes it *almost* seem that HostA and B are in the same subnet. But they're not, and you're way too smart by now to be fooled by this one!

Here is the switch configuration:

```
2960#config t
2960(config)#int f0/1
2960(config-if)#switchport mode trunk
2960(config-if)#int f0/2
2960(config-if)#switchport access vlan 1
2960(config-if)#int f0/3
2960(config-if)#switchport access vlan 2
```

Here is the router configuration:

```
ISR#config t
ISR(config)#int f0/0
ISR(config-if)#no ip address
ISR(config-if)#no shutdown
ISR(config-if)#int f0/0.1
ISR(config-subif)#encapsulation dot1q 1
ISR(config-subif)#ip address 172.16.10.1 255.255.255.128
ISR(config-subif)#int f0/0.2
ISR(config-subif)#encapsulation dot1q 2
ISR(config-subif)#ip address 172.16.10.254 255.255.255.128
```

I used the first address in the host range for VLAN 1 and the last address in the range for VLAN 2, but any address in the range would work. You just have to configure the host's default gateway to whatever you make the router's address.

Now, before we go on to the next example, I need to make sure you know how to set the IP address on the switch. Since VLAN 1 is typically the administrative VLAN, we'll use an IP address from that pool of addresses. Here's how to set the IP address of the switch (I'm not nagging, but you really should already know this!):

```
2960#config t
2960(config)#int vlan 1
2960(config-if)#ip address 172.16.10.2 255.255.255.128
2960(config-if)#no shutdown
```

Yes, you have to do a no shutdown on the VLAN interface.

One more example, and then we'll move on to VTP—another important subject that you definitely don't want to miss! In Figure 9.12 there are two VLANs. By looking at the router configuration, what's the IP address, mask, and default gateway of HostA? Use the last IP address in the range for HostA's address:

FIGURE 9.12   Inter-VLAN example 4

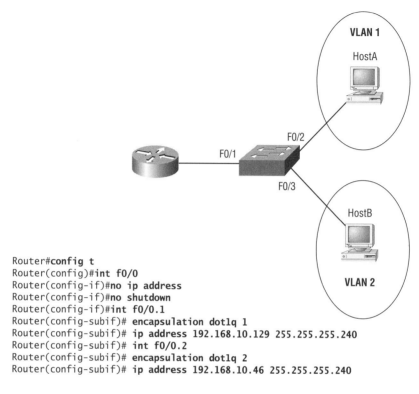

```
Router#config t
Router(config)#int f0/0
Router(config-if)#no ip address
Router(config-if)#no shutdown
Router(config-if)#int f0/0.1
Router(config-subif)# encapsulation dot1q 1
Router(config-subif)# ip address 192.168.10.129 255.255.255.240
Router(config-subif)# int f0/0.2
Router(config-subif)# encapsulation dot1q 2
Router(config-subif)# ip address 192.168.10.46 255.255.255.240
```

If you really look carefully at the router configuration (the hostname in this figure is just Router), there is a simple and quick answer. Both subnets are using a /28, or 255.255.255.240 mask, which is a block size of 16. The router's address for VLAN 1 is in subnet 128. The next subnet is 144, so the broadcast address of VLAN 1 is 143 and the valid host range is 129–142. So the host address would be this:

IP Address: 192.168.10.142

Mask: 255.255.255.240

Default Gateway: 192.168.10.129

Configuring VTP

All Cisco switches are configured to be VTP servers by default. To configure VTP, first you have to configure the domain name you want to use. And of course, once you configure the VTP information on a switch, you need to verify it.

When you create the VTP domain, you have a bunch of options, including setting the domain name, password, operating mode, and pruning capabilities of the switch. Use the vtp global configuration mode command to set all this information. In the following example, I'll set the S1 switch to vtp server, the VTP domain to Lammle, and the VTP password to todd:

```
S1#config t
S1#(config)#vtp mode server
Device mode already VTP SERVER.
S1(config)#vtp domain Lammle
Changing VTP domain name from null to Lammle
S1(config)#vtp password todd
Setting device VLAN database password to todd
S1(config)#do show vtp password
VTP Password: todd
S1(config)#do show vtp status
VTP Version                    : 2
Configuration Revision         : 0
Maximum VLANs supported locally : 255
Number of existing VLANs       : 8
VTP Operating Mode             : Server
VTP Domain Name                : Lammle
VTP Pruning Mode               : Disabled
VTP V2 Mode                    : Disabled
VTP Traps Generation           : Disabled
MD5 digest                     : 0x15 0x54 0x88 0xF2 0x50 0xD9 0x03 0x07
Configuration last modified by 192.168.24.6 at 3-14-93 15:47:32
Local updater ID is 192.168.24.6 on interface Vl1 (lowest numbered VLAN
interface found)
```

Please make sure you remember that all switches are set to VTP server mode by default, and if you want to change any VLAN information on a switch, you absolutely must be in VTP server mode. After you configure the VTP information, you can verify it with the show vtp command as shown in the preceding output. The preceding switch output shows the VTP domain, the VTP password, and the switch's mode.

Before we move onward to configuring the Core and the S2 switch with VTP information, take a minute to reflect on the fact that the show vtp status output shows that the maximum number of VLANs supported locally is only 255. Since you can create over 1,000 VLANs on a switch, this seems like it would definitely be a problem if you have more then 255 switches and you're using VTP. And, well, yes, it is problem—if you are trying to configure the 256th VLAN on a switch, you'll get a nice little error message stating that there are not enough hardware resources available, and then it will shut down the VLAN and the 256th VLAN will show up in suspended state in the output of the show vlan command. Not so good!

Let's go to the Core and S2 switches and set them into the Lammle VTP domain. It is very important to remember that the VTP domain name is case sensitive! VTP is not forgiving—one teeny small mistake and it just won't work.

```
Core#config t
Core(config)#vtp mode client
Setting device to VTP CLIENT mode.
Core(config)#vtp domain Lammle
Changing VTP domain name from null to Lammle
Core(config)#vtp password todd
Setting device VLAN database password to todd
Core(config)#do show vtp status
VTP Version                   : 2
Configuration Revision        : 0
Maximum VLANs supported locally : 1005
Number of existing VLANs      : 5
VTP Operating Mode            : Server
VTP Domain Name               : Lammle
VTP Pruning Mode              : Disabled
VTP V2 Mode                   : Disabled
VTP Traps Generation          : Disabled
MD5 digest                    : 0x2A 0x6B 0x22 0x17 0x04 0x4F 0xB8 0xC2
Configuration last modified by 192.168.10.19 at 3-1-93 03:13:16
Local updater ID is 192.168.24.7 on interface Vl1 (first interface found)
S2#config t
S2(config)#vtp mode client
Setting device to VTP CLIENT mode.
S2(config)#vtp domain Lammle
Changing VTP domain name from null to Lammle
S2(config)#vtp password todd
Setting device VLAN database password to todd
S2(config)#do show vtp status
VTP Version                   : 2
Configuration Revision        : 0
Maximum VLANs supported locally : 1005
Number of existing VLANs      : 5
VTP Operating Mode            : Client
VTP Domain Name               : Lammle
VTP Pruning Mode              : Disabled
VTP V2 Mode                   : Disabled
VTP Traps Generation          : Disabled
MD5 digest                    : 0x02 0x11 0x18 0x4B 0x36 0xC5 0xF4 0x1F
Configuration last modified by 0.0.0.0 at 0-0-00 00:00:00
```

Nice—now that all our switches are set to the same VTP domain and password, the VLANs I created earlier on the S1 switch should be advertised to the Core and S2 VTP client switches. Let's take a look using the show vlan brief command on the Core and S2 switch:

```
Core#sh vlan brief
VLAN Name                 Status    Ports
---- ------------------  --------- ---------------------
1    default             active    Fa0/1,Fa0/2,Fa0/3,Fa0/4
                                   Fa0/9,Fa0/10,Fa0/11,Fa0/12
                                   Fa0/13,Fa0/14,Fa0/15,
                                   Fa0/16,Fa0/17, Fa0/18, Fa0/19,
                                   Fa0/20,Fa0/21, Fa0/22, Fa0/23,
                                   Fa0/24, Gi0/1, Gi0/2
2    Sales               active
3    Marketing           active
4    Accounting          active
[output cut]


S2#sh vlan bri
VLAN Name                  Status    Ports
---- --------------------  --------- ---------------------
1    default              active    Fa0/3, Fa0/4, Fa0/5, Fa0/6
                                    Fa0/7, Fa0/8, Gi0/1
2    Sales                active
3    Marketing            active
4    Accounting           active
[output cut]
```

The VLAN database that I created on the S1 (2960) switch earlier in this chapter was uploaded to the Core and S2 switch via VTP advertisements. VTP is a great way to keep VLAN naming consistent across the switched network. We can now assign VLANs to the ports on the Core and S1 switches and they'll communicate with the hosts in the same VLANs on the S1 switch across the trunked ports between switches.

 It's imperative that you can assign a VTP domain name, set the switch to VTP server mode, and create a VLAN!

Troubleshooting VTP

You connect your switches with crossover cables, the lights go green on both ends, and you're up and running! Yeah—in a perfect world, right? Don't you wish it was that easy? Well, actually, it pretty much is—without VLANs, of course. But if you're using VLANs—and you definitely should be—then you need to use VTP if you have multiple VLANs configured in your switched network.

But here there be monsters: If VTP is not configured correctly, it (surprise!) will not work, so you absolutely must be capable of troubleshooting VTP. Let's take a look at a couple of configurations and solve the problems. Study the output from the two following switches:

```
SwitchA#sh vtp status
VTP Version                   : 2
Configuration Revision        : 0
Maximum VLANs supported locally : 64
Number of existing VLANs      : 7
VTP Operating Mode            : Server
VTP Domain Name               : RouterSim
VTP Pruning Mode              : Disabled
VTP V2 Mode                   : Disabled
VTP Traps Generation          : Disabled

SwitchB#sh vtp status
VTP Version                   : 2
Configuration Revision        : 1
Maximum VLANs supported locally : 64
Number of existing VLANs      : 7
VTP Operating Mode            : Server
VTP Domain Name               : GlobalNet
VTP Pruning Mode              : Disabled
VTP V2 Mode                   : Disabled
VTP Traps Generation          : Disabled
```

So what's happening with these two switches? Why won't they share VLAN information? At first glance, it seems that both servers are in VTP server mode, but that's not the problem. Servers in VTP server mode will share VLAN information using VTP. The problem is that they're in two different VTP *domains*. SwitchA is in VTP domain RouterSim and SwitchB is in VTP domain GlobalNet. They will never share VTP information because the VTP domain names are configured differently.

Now that you know how to look for common VTP domain configuration errors in your switches, let's take a look at another switch configuration:

```
SwitchC#sh vtp status
VTP Version                   : 2
Configuration Revision        : 1
Maximum VLANs supported locally : 64
Number of existing VLANs      : 7
VTP Operating Mode            : Client
VTP Domain Name               : Todd
VTP Pruning Mode              : Disabled
```

```
VTP V2 Mode                    : Disabled
VTP Traps Generation           : Disabled
```

There you are just trying to create a new VLAN on SwitchC and what do you get for your trouble? A loathsome error! Why can't you create a VLAN on SwitchC? Well, the VTP domain name isn't the important thing in this example. What is critical here is the VTP *mode*. The VTP mode is client, and a VTP client cannot create, delete, add, or change VLANs, remember? VTP clients only keep the VTP database in RAM, and that's not saved to NVRAM. So, in order to create a VLAN on this switch, you've got to make the switch a VTP server first.

Here's what will happen when you have the preceding VTP configuration:

```
SwitchC(config)#vlan 50
VTP VLAN configuration not allowed when device is in CLIENT mode.
```

So to fix this problem, here's what you need to do:

```
SwitchC(config)#vtp mode server
Setting device to VTP SERVER mode
SwitchC(config)#vlan 50
SwitchC(config-vlan)#
```

Wait, we're not done. Now take a look at the output from these two switches and determine why SwitchB is not receiving VLAN information from SwitchA:

```
SwitchA#sh vtp status
VTP Version                    : 2
Configuration Revision         : 4
Maximum VLANs supported locally : 64
Number of existing VLANs       : 7
VTP Operating Mode             : Server
VTP Domain Name                : GlobalNet
VTP Pruning Mode               : Disabled
VTP V2 Mode                    : Disabled
VTP Traps Generation           : Disabled


SwitchB#sh vtp status
VTP Version                    : 2
Configuration Revision         : 14
Maximum VLANs supported locally : 64
Number of existing VLANs       : 7
VTP Operating Mode             : Server
VTP Domain Name                : GlobalNet
VTP Pruning Mode               : Disabled
VTP V2 Mode                    : Disabled
VTP Traps Generation           : Disabled
```

You may be tempted to say it's because they're both VTP servers, but that is not the problem. All your switches can be servers and they can still share VLAN information. As a matter of fact, Cisco actually suggests that all switches stay VTP servers and that you just make sure the switch you want to advertise VTP VLAN information has the highest revision number. If all switches are VTP servers, then all of the switches will save the VLAN database. But SwitchB isn't receiving VLAN information from SwitchA because SwitchB has a higher revision number than SwitchA. It's very important that you can recognize this problem.

There are a couple ways to go about resolving this issue. The first thing you could do is to change the VTP domain name on SwitchB to another name, then set it back to GlobalNet, which will reset the revision number to zero (0) on SwitchB. The second approach would be to create or delete VLANs on SwitchA until the revision number passes the revision number on SwitchB. I didn't say the second way was better; I just said it's another way to fix it!

Telephony: Configuring Voice VLANs

If you do yoga, meditate, chain smoke, or consume mass quantities of comfort food when stressed, take a little break and do that now because, and I'm going to be honest, this isn't the easiest part of the chapter—or even the book, for that matter. But I promise that I'll do my best to make this as painless for you as possible.

The voice VLAN feature enables access ports to carry IP voice traffic from an IP phone. When a switch is connected to a Cisco IP phone, the IP phone sends voice traffic with layer 3 IP precedence and layer 2 class of service (CoS) values, which are both set to 5 for voice traffic; all other traffic defaults to 0.

Because the sound quality of an IP phone call can deteriorate if the data is unevenly sent, the switch supports quality of service (QoS) based on IEEE 802.1p CoS. (802.1p provides a mechanism for implementing QoS at the MAC level.) The 802.1p field is carried in the 802.1Q trunk header. If you look at the fields in an 802.1Q tag, you will see a field called the priority field; this is where the 802.1p information goes. QoS uses classification and scheduling to send network traffic from the switch in an organized, predictable manner.

The Cisco IP phone is a configurable device, and you can configure it to forward traffic with an IEEE 802.1p priority. You can also configure the switch to either trust or override the traffic priority assigned by an IP phone—which is exactly what we're going to do. The Cisco phone basically has a three-port switch: one to connect to the Cisco switch, one to a PC device, and one to the actual phone, which is internal.

You can also configure an access port with an attached Cisco IP phone to use one VLAN for voice traffic and another VLAN for data traffic from a device attached to the phone—like a PC. You can configure access ports on the switch to send Cisco Discovery Protocol (CDP) packets that instruct an attached Cisco IP phone to send voice traffic to the switch in any of these ways:

- In the voice VLAN tagged with a layer 2 CoS priority value
- In the access VLAN tagged with a layer 2 CoS priority value
- In the access VLAN, untagged (no layer 2 CoS priority value)

The switch can also process tagged data traffic (traffic in IEEE 802.1Q or IEEE 802.1p frame types) from the device attached to the access port on the Cisco IP phone. You can configure layer 2 access ports on the switch to send CDP packets that instruct the attached Cisco IP phone to configure the IP phone access port in one of these modes:

- In trusted mode, all traffic received through the access port on the Cisco IP phone passes through the IP phone unchanged.

- In untrusted mode, all traffic in IEEE 802.1Q or IEEE 802.1p frames received through the access port on the IP phone receive a configured layer 2 CoS value. The default layer 2 CoS value is 0. Untrusted mode is the default.

Configuring the Voice VLAN

By default, the voice VLAN feature is disabled; you enable it by using the interface command `switchport voice vlan`. When the voice VLAN feature is enabled, all untagged traffic is sent according to the default CoS priority of the port. The CoS value is not trusted for IEEE 802.1p or IEEE 802.1Q tagged traffic.

These are the voice VLAN configuration guidelines:

- You should configure voice VLAN on switch access ports; voice VLAN isn't supported on trunk ports, even though you can actually configure it!

- The voice VLAN should be present and active on the switch for the IP phone to correctly communicate on it. Use the `show vlan` privileged EXEC command to see if the VLAN is present—if it is, it'll be listed in the display.

- Before you enable the voice VLAN, it's recommend that you enable QoS on the switch by entering the `mls qos` global configuration command and set the port trust state to trust by entering the `mls qos trust cos` interface configuration command.

- You must make sure that CDP is enabled on the switch port connected to the Cisco IP phone to send the configuration. This is on by default, so unless you disabled it, you shouldn't have a problem.

- The PortFast feature is automatically enabled when the voice VLAN is configured, but when you disable the voice VLAN, the PortFast feature isn't automatically disabled.

- To return the port to its default setting, use the `no switchport voice vlan` interface configuration command.

Configuring IP Phone Voice Traffic

You can configure a port connected to the Cisco IP phone to send CDP packets to the phone to configure the way in which the phone sends voice traffic. The phone can carry voice traffic in IEEE 802.1Q frames for a specified voice VLAN with a layer 2 CoS value. It can use IEEE 802.1p priority tagging to give voice traffic a higher priority as well as forward all voice traffic through the native (access) VLAN. The IP phone can also send untagged voice traffic, or use its own configuration to send voice traffic in the access VLAN. In all configurations, the voice traffic carries a layer 3 IP precedence value—again, for voice the setting is usually 5.

I think it's about time to give you some actual examples to make this clear to you. This example shows you how to configure four things:

1. How to configure a port connected to an IP phone to use the CoS value for classifying incoming traffic

2. How to configure the port to use IEEE 802.1p priority tagging for voice traffic

3. How to configure it to use the Voice VLAN (10) to carry all voice traffic

4. And last, how to configure VLAN 3 to carry PC data

```
Switch#configure t
Switch(config)#mls qos
Switch(config)#interface f0/1
Switch(config-if)#switchport priority extend ?
  cos    Override 802.1p priority of devices on appliance
  trust  Trust 802.1p priorities of devices on appliance
Switch(config-if)#switchport priority extend trust
Switch(config-if)#mls qos trust cos
Switch(config-if)#switchport voice vlan dot1p
Switch(config-if)#switchport mode access
Switch(config-if)#switchport access vlan 3
Switch(config-if)#switchport voice vlan 10
```

The command mls qos trust cos will configure the interface to classify incoming traffic packets by using the packet CoS value. For untagged packets, the port's default CoS value will be used. But before configuring the port trust state, you must first globally enable QoS by using the mls qos global configuration command.

Notice how I added two access VLANs to the same port? I can only do this if I have one for a data VLAN and another one for a voice VLAN.

This section was probably the hardest part of this entire book, and I honestly created the simplest configuration you should use to get you through it! So you can relax a bit because using the CNA with the preconfigured macros makes configuring phones connected to your switch a day at the beach. You just really should know how to do it both ways. I'll demonstrate configuration using the CNA in the next section.

Using the CNA to Configure VLANs and Inter-VLAN Routing

This chapter has focused pretty heavily on enabling routing between VLANs through the use of an actual router, but increasingly, you'll find that you'll use a switch backplane for routing most often in a large corporate environment. But this time, instead of using the command-line interface (CLI), I'm going to use the CNA to show you both how to configure VLANs on a 2960 and how to perform inter-VLAN routing on a 3560 switch. After that, I'm going to configure our switch ports with our phone ports using the CNA Smartports to show you how easy it is to do that using the new CNA instead of grinding through all the work we did in the previous section. And trust me, even though it probably seems like we did a lot, we really just scratched the surface of telephony in this chapter.

I'm going to get started by connecting to my 2960 switch (S1) that already has the three new VLANs configured from earlier in this chapter and taking a look at them. Then I'm going to add a new voice VLAN. At the first screen, I clicked Configure, Switching, and VLANs and received a new screen that shows the status of my ports.

Now we can see that ports 1 and 2 are trunked dynamically, and since they're set to `dynamic auto` by default, they'll automatically became trunk links with the connections to the Core switch. In order to make this happen before, I erased the configuration of the switch and reloaded, which of course deleted my EtherChannel configuration. But the VLAN database that's stored in flash memory is still there. You can also see that port 3 is a member of VLAN 3—the VLAN access port I set earlier in the chapter.

A nice feature of this screen is the Modify button you find toward the bottom right. I high-lighted port 1, clicked Modify, and that took me to this new screen.

Moving right along, from this screen, I can change the different administrative modes and encapsulations plus set the VLANs allowed on the trunk port as well as set my VTP pruning. But what I'm most interested in is the Configure VLANs tab on the VLANs screen.

From here, I can see my configured VLANs, and I can also modify, add, and delete them. (Remember, you have to be a VTP server, not just a client, in order to do this.) I clicked the Create button and received this screen.

I then clicked Create, added a new VLAN named Todd (how creative), and clicked OK.

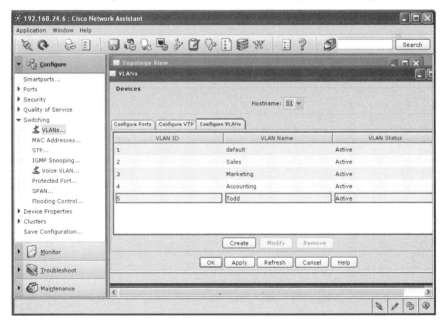

Now, let's have some fun and create a voice VLAN. I clicked Voice VLAN under Configure and received this screen.

I then highlighted port 4 where my phone is connected and clicked Modify. I created a new voice VLAN (Voice VLAN 10) and clicked OK.

All good—now I want to go to the 3560 switch and configure inter-VLAN routing using the switch instead of using a router as we've done so far.

So now I'm connected to my Core switch (3560). Under Configure I clicked Routing and Enable/Disable. From the screen that appeared, I clicked Enable IP Routing, and it automatically added my configured default gateway—way cool!

After I clicked OK, I clicked Inter-VLAN Routing Wizard and this screen appeared.

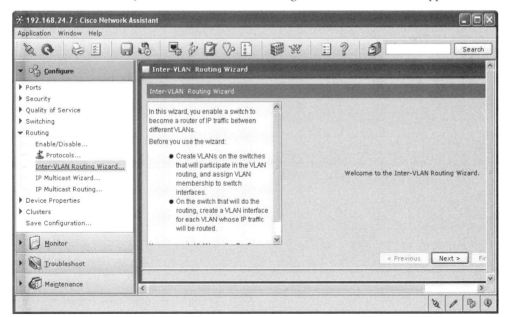

Well, the party is kind of over—we've reached the point where it really isn't much easier than configuring from a command-line interface. When you see the finished configuration in RAM, you'll know what I mean. So, after clicking Next, I got this screen.

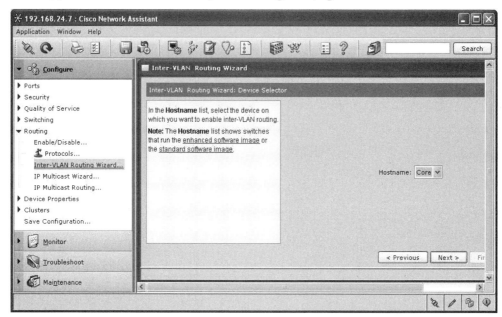

Not much to do here but click Next to go to the next screen.

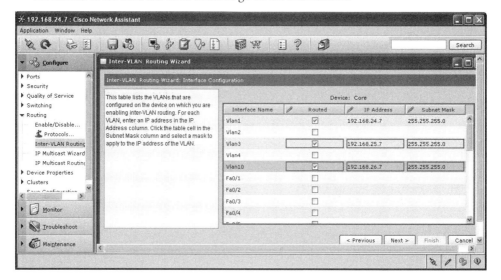

Now this screen is where things happen—you get to do the inter-VLAN routing configuration. I clicked on the VLANs that I wanted to provide inter-VLAN communication between, added new subnets and subnet masks for each separate VLAN, and then clicked Next to get to this screen.

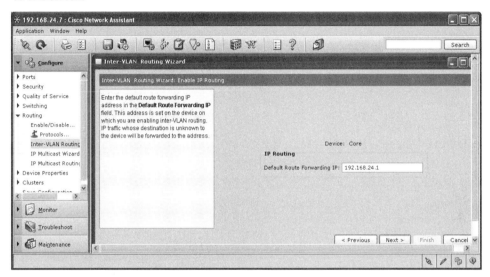

This screen already had the IP default gateway set as the default route of the switch, which is fine, so I again clicked Next.

Here's where the party starts again—I just sat back and watched the router auto-configure itself. You can see that there's a separate logical interface for each VLAN with the IP address I specified for each. IP routing becomes enabled, and then the default route is set. To be honest, I could have typed this in faster using the CLI, but now, by looking at the commands, you know both ways to configure inter-VLAN routing on a switch. To finish, I again clicked Next, and the configuration was then uploaded to the running-config.

And here's the running-config's output:

```
!
interface Vlan1
 ip address 192.168.24.7 255.255.255.0
!
interface Vlan3
 ip address 192.168.25.7 255.255.255.0
!
interface Vlan10
 ip address 192.168.26.7 255.255.255.0
!
```

Pretty simple, straightforward, and looking good—all of our hosts/phones should now be able to communicate freely between VLANs. However, I do want you to understand that I'm not saying that you should actually route between all your VLANs—but for demonstration purposes, this configuration works great!

Before I finish the chapter, I want to connect to the 2960 and use a Smartport macro to configure the port my phone is plugged into. Now, in contrast to what I said about the routing configuration on the 3560 and how it is just as easy to use the CLI, the phone configuration via the CLI, as you already know, is Godzilla, so let's do it the easy way.

I opened the CNA for the 2960 (S1) and clicked Smartports. Then I highlighted port 4, right-clicked, and chose IP Phone+Desktop.

I then chose the access VLAN—VLAN 3, which my PC is using—and the voice VLAN I created earlier (10). Once I clicked OK, the macro was run and the configuration was loaded into the running-config. Here's the output of the running-config after the cisco-phone macro ran on port 4:

```
!
interface FastEthernet0/4
 switchport access vlan 3
 switchport mode access
 switchport voice vlan 10
 switchport port-security maximum 2
 switchport port-security
 switchport port-security aging time 2
 switchport port-security violation restrict
 switchport port-security aging type inactivity
 srr-queue bandwidth share 10 10 60 20
 srr-queue bandwidth shape  10  0  0  0
 mls qos trust device cisco-phone
 mls qos trust cos
 macro description cisco-phone
 auto qos voip cisco-phone
 spanning-tree portfast
 spanning-tree bpduguard enable
!
```

Wow, and I thought the Desktop macro added a lot of configuration lines to the router interface! And this does not count the 44—that's right, 44—lines of queuing it added to the running-config as well. If someone looks at your configurations and doesn't know you used the CNA, you're going to look like a genius for sure!

Now I can connect both a PC-type device and a phone to the same port and they will run in separate VLANs.

Now this was quite a chapter! I can't stress enough that you have to get hands-on experience with at least 2960 switches, and you must be able to configure the switches using both the CLI and the CNA.

Summary

This chapter introduced you to the world of virtual LANs and described how Cisco switches can use them. We talked about how VLANs break up broadcast domains in a switched inter-network—a very important, necessary thing because layer 2 switches only break up collision domains and, by default, all switches make up one large broadcast domain. I also described access links to you and we went over how trunked VLANs work across a Fast Ethernet link.

Trunking is a crucial technology to understand well when you're dealing with a network populated by multiple switches that are running several VLANs. I also talked at length about VLAN Trunk Protocol (VTP), which, in reality, has nothing to do with trunking. You learned that it does send VLAN information down a trunked link but that the trunk configuration in and of itself isn't part of VTP.

And then there was the telephony gauntlet—something you may want to forget, but if you want to succeed, you'll make sure you've got it down even if it means going through it all again!

I finished the chapter off by providing troubleshooting and configuration examples of VTP, trunking, and VLAN configurations as well as how to configure 2960 and 3560 switches using the CNA.

Exam Essentials

Understand the term *frame tagging*. *Frame tagging* refers to VLAN identification; this is what switches use to keep track of all those frames as they're traversing a switch fabric. It's how switches identify which frames belong to which VLANs.

Understand the ISL VLAN identification method. Inter-Switch Link (ISL) is a way of explicitly tagging VLAN information onto an Ethernet frame. This tagging information allows VLANs to be multiplexed over a trunk link through an external encapsulation method, which allows the switch to identify the VLAN membership of a frame over the link. ISL is a Cisco-proprietary frame-tagging method that can only be used with Cisco switches and routers.

Understand the 802.1Q VLAN identification method. This is a nonproprietary IEEE method of frame tagging. If you're trunking between a Cisco switched link and a different brand of switch, you have to use 802.1Q for the trunk to work.

Remember how to set a trunk port on a 2960 switch. To set a port to trunking on a 2960, use the `switchport mode trunk` command.

Remember to check a switch port's VLAN assignment when plugging in a new host. If you plug a new host into a switch, then you must verify the VLAN membership of that port. If the membership is different than what is needed for that host, the host will not be able to reach the needed network services, such as a workgroup server.

Understand the purpose and configuration of VTP VTP provides propagation of the VLAN database throughout your switched network. All switches must be in the same VTP domain.

Remember how to create a Cisco "router on a stick" to provide inter-VLAN communication. You can use a Cisco Fast Ethernet or Gigabit Ethernet interface to provide inter-VLAN routing. The switch port connected to the router must be a trunk port; then you must create virtual interfaces (subinterfaces) on the router port for each VLAN connecting. The hosts in each VLAN will use this subinterface address as their default gateway address.

Written Lab 9

In this section, write the answers to the following questions:

1. What VTP mode can only accept VLAN information and not change it?

2. What VLAN identification method is proprietary to Cisco routers?

3. VLANs break up _____ domains.

4. Switches, by default, only break up _____ domains.

5. What is the default VTP mode?

6. What does trunking provide?

7. What is frame tagging?

8. True/False: The ISL encapsulation is removed from the frame if the frame is forwarded out an access link.

9. What type of link is only part of one VLAN and is referred to as the "native VLAN" of the port?

10. What type of Cisco tagging information allows VLANs to be multiplexed over a trunk link through an external encapsulation method?

(The answers to Written Lab 9 can be found following the answers to the review questions for this chapter.)

Review Questions

The following questions are designed to test your understanding of this chapter's material. For more information on how to get additional questions, please see this book's Introduction.

1. Which of the following is true regarding VLANs?

   A. You must have at least two VLANs defined in every Cisco switched network.

   B. All VLANs are configured at the fastest switch and, by default, propagate this information to all other switches.

   C. You should not have more than 10 switches in the same VTP domain.

   D. VTP is used to send VLAN information to switches in a configured VTP domain.

2. According to the following diagram, which of the following describes the router port configuration and the switch port configuration as shown in the topology? (Choose three.)

   A. The router WAN port is configured as a trunk port.

   B. The router port connected to the switch is configured using subinterfaces.

   C. The router port connected to the switch is configured at 10Mbps.

   D. The switch port connected to the hub is configured as full duplex.

   E. The switch port connected to the router is configured as a trunking port.

   F. The switch ports connected to the hosts are configured as access ports.

3. A switch has been configured for three different VLANs: VLAN2, VLAN3, and VLAN4. A router has been added to provide communication between the VLANs. What type of interface is necessary on the router if only one connection is to be made between the router and the switch?

A. 10Mbps Ethernet

B. 56Kbps Serial

C. 100Mbps Ethernet

D. 1Gbps Ethernet

4. You want to improve network performance by increasing the bandwidth available to hosts and limit the size of the broadcast domains. Which of the following options will achieve this goal?

A. Managed hubs

B. Bridges

C. Switches

D. Switches configured with VLANs

5. Which of the following protocols are used to configure trunking on a switch? (Choose two.)

A. VLAN Trunk Protocol

B. VLAN

C. 802.1Q

D. ISL

6. When a new trunk link is configured on an IOS-based switch, which VLANs are allowed over the link?

A. By default, all VLANs are allowed on the trunk.

B. No VLAN's are allowed, you must configure each VLAN by hand.

C. Only configured VLAN's are allowed on the link.

D. Only extended VLAN's are allowed by default.

7. Which switching technology reduces the size of a broadcast domain?

A. ISL

B. 802.1Q

C. VLANs

D. STP

8. What VTP mode allows you to change VLAN information on the switch?

A. Client

B. STP

C. Server

D. Transparent

9. Which command will configure a switch port to use the IEEE standard method of inserting VLAN membership information into Ethernet frames?

A. `Switch(config)#switchport trunk encapsulation isl`

B. `Switch(config)#switchport trunk encapsulation ietf`

C. `Switch(config)#switchport trunk encapsulation dot1q`

D. `Switch(config-if)#switchport trunk encapsulation isl`

E. `Switch(config-if)#switchport trunk encapsulation ietf`

F. `Switch(config-if)#switchport trunk encapsulation dot1q`

10. Which of the following is true regarding VTP?

A. All switches are VTP servers by default.

B. All switches are VTP transparent by default.

C. VTP is on by default with a domain name of Cisco on all Cisco switches.

D. All switches are VTP clients by default.

11. Which protocol reduces administrative overhead in a switched network by allowing the configuration of a new VLAN to be distributed to all the switches in a domain?

A. STP

B. VTP

C. DHCP

D. ISL

12. Which of the following commands sets a trunk port on a 2960 switch?

A. `trunk on`

B. `trunk all`

C. `switchport trunk on`

D. `switchport mode trunk`

13. Which of the following is an IEEE standard for frame tagging?

A. ISL

B. 802.3Z

C. 802.1Q

D. 802.3U

14. You connect a host to a switch port, but the new host cannot log into the server that is plugged into the same switch. What could the problem be? (Choose the most likely answer.)

A. The router is not configured for the new host.

B. The VTP configuration on the switch is not updated for the new host.

C. The host has an invalid MAC address.

D. The switch port the host is connected to is not configured to the correct VLAN membership.

15. According to the diagram, which three commands can be used to establish a link with the router's Fast Ethernet interface using the IEEE version of frame tagging? (Choose three.)

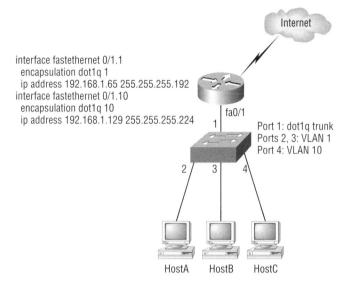

```
interface fastethernet 0/1.1
  encapsulation dot1q 1
  ip address 192.168.1.65 255.255.255.192
interface fastethernet 0/1.10
  encapsulation dot1q 10
  ip address 192.168.1.129 255.255.255.224
```

Port 1: dot1q trunk
Ports 2, 3: VLAN 1
Port 4: VLAN 10

A. `Switch(config)#interface fastethernet 0/1`

B. `Switch(config-if)#switchport mode access`

C. `Switch(config-if)#switchport mode trunk`

D. `Switch(config-if)#switchport access vlan 1`

E. `Switch(config-if)#switchport trunk encapsulation isl`

F. `Switch(config-if)#switchport trunk encapsulation dot1q`

16. These two switches are not sharing VLAN information. From the following output, what is the reason these switches are not sharing VTP messages?

```
SwitchA#sh vtp status
VTP Version                      : 2
Configuration Revision           : 0
Maximum VLANs supported locally  : 64
Number of existing VLANs         : 7
VTP Operating Mode               : Server
VTP Domain Name                  : RouterSim
VTP Pruning Mode                 : Disabled

SwitchB#sh vtp status
VTP Version                      : 2
Configuration Revision           : 1
Maximum VLANs supported locally  : 64
```

```
Number of existing VLANs      : 7
VTP Operating Mode            : Server
VTP Domain Name               : GlobalNet
VTP Pruning Mode              : Disabled
```

A. One of the switches needs to be set to VTP version 1.

B. Both switches are set to VTP server and one must be set to client.

C. The VTP domain names are not configured correctly.

D. VTP pruning is disabled.

17. Which of the following provide inter-switch VLAN communication? (Choose two.)

A. ISL

B. VTP

C. 802.1Q

D. 802.3Z

18. To configure the VLAN trunking protocol to communicate VLAN information between two switches, what two requirements must be met? (Choose two.)

A. Each end of the trunk link must be set to the IEEE 802.1e encapsulation.

B. The VTP management domain name of both switches must be set the same.

C. All ports on both the switches must be set as access ports.

D. One of the two switches must be configured as a VTP server.

E. A rollover cable is required to connect the two switches together.

F. A router must be used to forward VTP traffic between VLANs.

19. Which of the following are benefits of VLANs? (Choose three.)

A. They increase the size of collision domains.

B. They allow logical grouping of users by function.

C. They can enhance network security.

D. They increase the size of broadcast domains while decreasing the number of collision domains.

E. They simplify switch administration.

F. They increase the number of broadcast domains while decreasing the size of the broadcast domains.

20. Which of the following modes are valid when a switch port is used as a VLAN trunk? (Choose three.)

A. Blocking

B. Dynamic auto

C. Dynamic desirable

D. Nonegotiate

E. Access

F. Learning

Answers to Review Questions

1. D. Switches do not propagate VLAN information by default; you must configure the VTP domain. VLAN Trunk Protocol (VTP) is used to propagate VLAN information across a trunked link.

2. B, E, F. A router connected to a switch that provides inter-VLAN communication is configured using subinterfaces. The switch port connected to the router must be using either ISL or 802.1Q trunking protocol, and the hosts are all connected as access ports, which is the default on all switch ports.

3. C. Although you can use either 100Mbps or 1Gbps Ethernet, the 100Mbps is necessary at a minimum and is the best answer to this question. You need to trunk the link from the switch to the router to make this connection work with inter-VLAN communication.

4. D. By creating and implementing VLANs in your switched network, you can break up broadcast domains at layer 2. For hosts on different VLANs to communicate, you must have a router or layer 3 switch.

5. C, D. Cisco has a proprietary trunking protocol called ISL. The IEEE version is 802.1Q.

6. A. By default, all VLANs are allowed on the trunk link and you must remove by hand each VLAN that you don't want traversing the trunked link.

7. C. Virtual LANs break up broadcast domains in layer 2 switched internetworks.

8. C. Only in server mode can you change VTP information on a switch.

9. F. If you are on a 2950 switch, then the interface command is just `switchport mode trunk`, since the 2950 can only run the IEEE 802.1Q version. However, a 3550 can run both ISL and 802.1Q, so you must use the `encapsulation` command. The argument to choose 802.1Q for a trunking protocol is `dot1q`.

10. A. All Cisco switches are VTP servers by default. No other VTP information is configured on a Cisco switch by default. You must set the VTP domain name on all switches to be the same domain name or they will not share the VTP database.

11. B. Virtual Trunk Protocol (VTP) is used to pass a VLAN database to any or all switches in the switched network. The three VTP modes are server, client, and transparent.

12. D. To set a switch port to trunk mode, which allows all VLAN information to pass down the link, use the `switchport mode trunk` command.

13. C. 802.1Q was created to allow trunked links between disparate switches.

14. D. This question is a little vague, but the best answer is that the VLAN membership for the port is not configured.

15. A, C, F. To create a trunked link on a switch port, you first need to go to the interface—in this question, interface FastEthernet 0/1. Then you choose your trunking command, either `switchport mode trunk` for the 2950 (IEEE 802.1Q is the only version the 2960 switch runs) or `switchport trunk encapsulation dot1q` for a 3560 switch.

16. C. Although one of the switches can be set to client, that would not stop them from sharing VLAN information through VTP. However, they will not share VLAN information through VTP if the domain names are not set the same.

17. A, C. ISL is a Cisco-proprietary frame-tagging method. IEEE 802.1Q is the nonproprietary version of frame tagging.

18. B, D. You must have the same VTP domain name on all switches in order to share VLAN information between the switches. At least one of the switches must be a VTP server; the other switches should be set to VTP client.

19. B, C, F. VLANs break up broadcast domains in a switched layer 2 network, which means smaller broadcast domains. They allow configuration by logical function instead of physical location and can create some security if configured correctly.

20. B, C, D. The valid modes of a VLAN trunk on a switch are dynamic auto, dynamic desirable, trunk (on), and nonegotiate.

Answers to Written Lab 9.1

1. Client

2. Inter-Switch Link (ISL)

3. Broadcast

4. Collision

5. Server

6. Trunking allows you to make a single port part of multiple VLANs at the same time.

7. Frame identification (frame tagging) uniquely assigns a user-defined ID to each frame. This is sometimes referred to as a VLAN ID or color.

8. True

9. Access link

10. Inter-Switch Link (ISL)

Chapter

10

Security

THE CCNA EXAM TOPICS COVERED IN THIS CHAPTER INCLUDE THE FOLLOWING:

✓ **Identify security threats to a network and describe general methods to mitigate those threats**

- Describe today's increasing network security threats and explain the need to implement a comprehensive security policy to mitigate the threats

- Explain general methods to mitigate common security threats to network devices, hosts, and applications

- Describe the functions of common security appliances and applications

- Describe security recommended practices including initial steps to secure network devices

✓ **Configure, verify, and troubleshoot basic router operation and routing on Cisco devices**

- Implement basic router security

✓ **Implement, verify, and troubleshoot NAT and ACLs in a medium-size Enterprise branch office network**

- Describe the purpose and types of ACLs

- Configure and apply ACLs based on network filtering requirements (including: CLI/SDM)

- Configure and apply an ACLs to limit telnet and SSH access to the router using (including: SDM/CLI)

- Verify and monitor ACLs in a network environment

- Troubleshoot ACL issues

If you're a sys admin, it's my guess that shielding sensitive, critical data, as well as your network's resources, from every possible evil exploit is a top priority of yours. Right? Good to know you're on the right page—Cisco has some really effective security solutions that will arm you with the tools you need to make this happen.

Basically, covering you and your network's posterior is going to be the focus of this chapter. You'll learn a lot about deterring the most common threats to your network's security with Cisco routers and IOS firewalls that, together, offer quite a powerful, integrated detection package against many types of invasions. I'm going to give you the lowdown on how the Cisco IOS Firewall provides actual security and policy enforcement for both your internal and external networking needs. And I'll also show you how to create secure connections to any remote locations you may have living on the fringes, too.

Access control lists (ACLs)are an integral part of Cisco's security solution, and I'll show you the keys of both simple and advanced access lists that will equip you with the ability to ensure internetwork security as well as how to mitigate most security-oriented network threats.

The proper use and configuration of access lists is a vital part of router configuration because access lists are such versatile networking accessories. Contributing mightily to the efficiency and operation of your network, access lists give network managers a huge amount of control over traffic flow throughout the enterprise. With access lists, managers can gather basic statistics on packet flow and security policies can be implemented. Sensitive devices can also be protected from unauthorized access.

In this chapter, we'll discuss access lists for TCP/IP and MAC access lists on a layer 2 switch as well as cover some of the tools available to test and monitor the functionality of applied access lists.

After we cover the Cisco IOS Firewall and configuring access lists using the CLI, I'll show how easy it is to do using Cisco's Security Device Manager (SDM).

Although virtual private networks (VPNs) can be an important part of your corporate security, I'll cover VPNs in Chapter 14, "Wide Area Networks."

For up-to-the minute updates for this chapter, please see www.lammle.com and/or www.sybex.com.

Perimeter, Firewall, and Internal Routers

You see this a lot—typically, in medium to large enterprise networks, the various strategies for security are based on a some recipe of internal and perimeter routers plus firewall devices.

Internal routers provide additional security to the network by screening traffic to various parts of the protected corporate network, and they do this using access lists. You can see where each of these types of devices are found in Figure 10.1.

FIGURE 10.1   A typical secured network

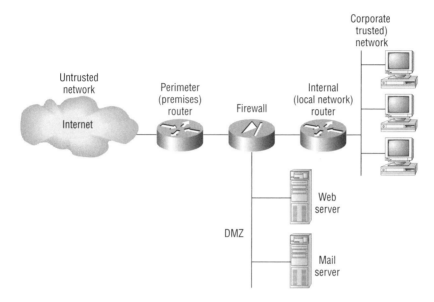

I'll use the terms *trusted network* and *untrusted network* throughout this chapter and in Chapter 11, "Network Address Translation (NAT)," so it's important that you can see where they are found in a typical secured network. The demilitarized zone (DMZ) can be global (real) Internet addresses or private addresses, depending on how you configure your firewall, but this is typically where you'll find the HTTP, DNS, email, and other Internet-type corporate servers.

Instead of having routers, we can (as you already know) use virtual local area networks (VLANs) with switches on the inside trusted network. Multilayer switches containing their own security features can sometimes replace internal (LAN) routers to provide higher performance in VLAN architectures.

Let's discuss the security threats a typical secured internetwork faces; then I'll provide some ways of protecting the internetwork using the Cisco IOS Firewall feature set and access lists.

Recognizing Security Threats

Yes, it's true: Security attacks vary considerably in their complexity and threat level, and some even happen because of WUI, or witless user ignorance. (This term isn't an exam objective, but it does occur more than you'd think!)

You see, it all comes down to planning, or rather, lack thereof. Basically, the vital tool that the Internet has become today was absolutely unforeseen by those who brought it into being. This is a big reason why security is now such an issue—most IP implementations are innately insecure. No worries though, because Cisco has a few tricks up its sleeve to help us with this. But first, let's examine some common attack profiles:

Application-layer attacks   These attacks commonly zero in on well-known holes in the software that's typically found running on servers. Favorite targets include FTP, sendmail, and HTTP. Because the permissions level granted to these accounts is most often "privileged," bad guys simply access and exploit the machine that's running one of the applications I just mentioned.

Autorooters   You can think of these as a kind of hacker automaton. Bad guys use something called a rootkit to probe, scan, and then capture data on a strategically positioned computer that's poised to give them "eyes" into entire systems—automatically!

Backdoors   These are simply paths leading into a computer or network. Through simple invasions, or via more elaborate "Trojan horse" code, bad guys can use their implanted inroads into a specific host or even a network whenever they want to—until you detect and stop them, that is!

Denial of service (DoS) and distributed denial of service (DDoS) attacks   These are bad— pretty tough to get rid of too! But even hackers don't respect other hackers that execute them because, though nasty, they're really easy to accomplish. (This means that some 10-year-old could actually bring you to your knees, and that is just wrong!) Basically, a service is made unavailable by overwhelming the system that normally provides it. And there are several different flavors:

> **TCP SYN flood**   Begins when a client initiates a seemingly run-of-the-mill TCP connection and sends a SYN message to a server. The server predictably responds by sending a SYN-ACK message back to the client machine, which then establishes the connection by returning an ACK message. Sounds fine, but it's actually during this process—when the connection is only halfway open—that the victim machine is literally flooded with a deluge of half-open connections and pretty much becomes paralyzed.

> **"Ping of death" attacks**   You probably know that TCP/IP's maximum packet size is 65,536 octets. It's okay if you didn't know that—just understand that this attack is executed by simply pinging with oversized packets, causing a device to keep rebooting incessantly, freeze up, or just totally crash.

> **Tribe Flood Network (TFN) and Tribe Flood Network 2000 (TFN2K)**   These nasty little numbers are more complex in that they initiate synchronized DoS attacks from multiple sources and can target multiple devices. This is achieved, in part, by something known as "IP spoofing," which I'll be describing soon.

> **Stacheldraht**   This attack is actually a mélange of methods, and it translates from the German term for barbed wire. It basically incorporates TFN and adds a dash of encryption. It all begins with a huge invasion at the root level, followed up with a DoS attack finale.

IP spoofing   This is pretty much what it sounds like it is—a bad guy from within or outside of your network masquerades as a trusted host machine by doing one of two things: presenting with an IP address that's inside your network's scope of trusted addresses or using an approved, trusted external IP address. Because the hacker's true identity is veiled behind the spoofed address, this is often just the beginning of your problems.

Man-in-the-middle attacks   Interception! But it's not a football, it's a bunch of your network's packets—your precious data! A common guilty party could be someone working for your very own ISP using a tool known as a sniffer (discussed later) and augmenting it with routing and transport protocols.

Network reconnaissance   Before breaking into a network, hackers often gather all the information they can about it, because the more they know about the network, the better they can compromise it. They accomplish their objectives through methods like port scans, DNS queries, and ping sweeps.

Packet sniffers   This is the tool I mentioned earlier, but I didn't tell you what it is, and it may come as a surprise that it's actually software. Here's how it works—a network adapter card is set to promiscuous mode so it will send all packets snagged from the network's physical layer through to a special application to be viewed and sorted out. A packet sniffer can nick some highly valuable, sensitive data including, but not limited to, passwords and usernames, making them prized among identity thieves.

Password attacks   These come in many flavors, and even though they can be achieved via more sophisticated types of attacks like IP spoofing, packet sniffing, and Trojan horses, their sole purpose is to—surprise—discover user passwords so the thief can pretend they're a valid user and then access that user's privileges and resources.

Brute force attack   Another software-oriented attack that employs a program running on a targeted network that tries to log in to some type of shared network resource like a server. For the hacker, it's ideal if the accessed accounts have a lot of privileges because then the bad guys can form back doors to use for gaining access later and bypass the need for passwords entirely.

Port redirection attacks   This approach requires a host machine the hacker has broken into and uses to get wonky traffic (that normally wouldn't be allowed passage) through a firewall.

Trojan horse attacks and viruses   These two are actually pretty similar—both Trojan horses and viruses infect user machines with malicious code and mess it up with varying degrees of paralysis, destruction, even death! But they do have their differences—viruses are really just nasty programs attached to command.com, which just happens to be the main interpreter for all Windows systems. Viruses then run amok, deleting files and infecting any flavor of command.com it finds on the now diseased machine. The difference between a virus and a Trojan horse is that Trojans are actually complete applications encased inside code that makes them appear to be a completely different entity—say, a simple, innocent game—than the ugly implements of destruction they truly are!

Trust exploitation attacks   These happen when someone exploits a trust relationship inside your network. For example, a company's perimeter network connection usually shelters important things like SMTP, DNS, and HTTP servers, making the servers really vulnerable because they're all on the same segment.

To be honest, I'm not going to go into detail on how to mitigate each and every one of the security threats I just talked about, not only because that would be outside the scope of this book, but also because the methods I am going to teach you will truly protect you from being attacked in general. You will learn enough tricks to make all but the most determined bad guys give up on you and search for easier prey. So basically, think of this as a chapter on how to practice "safe networking."

Mitigating Security Threats

Hmm…what solution should we use to mitigate security threats? Something from Juniper, McAfee, or some other firewall product? Nah—we probably should use something from Cisco. Cisco has a very cool product called the Adaptive Security Appliance, or ASA. But there's a catch or two—it's a pretty pricey little beauty that scales in cost depending on the modules you choose (for example, intrusion prevention). Plus, the ASA is actually above the objectives of this book. I just personally think is the best product on the market—it truly rocks!

Cisco IOS software runs on upwards of 80 percent of the Internet backbone routers out there; it's probably the most critical part of network infrastructure. So let's just keep it real and use the Cisco IOS's software-based security, known as the Cisco IOS Firewall feature set, for our end-to-end Internet, intranet, and remote-access network security solutions. It's a good idea to go with this because Cisco ACLs really are quite efficient tools for mitigating many of the most common threats around—and if you just happen to be studying for your CCNA exam, you need to solidly understand how ACLs work more than anything else in this chapter!

Cisco's IOS Firewall

Here's where we're going to find out how to mitigate some of the more common security threats on the list I gave you earlier by using these Cisco IOS Firewall features:

Stateful IOS Firewall inspection engine   This is your perimeter protection feature because it gives your internal users secure access control on a per-application basis. People often call it Context-Based Access Control (CBAC).

Intrusion detection   A deep packet inspection tool that lets you monitor, intercept, and respond to abuse in real time by referencing 102 of the most common attack and intrusion detection signatures.

Firewall voice traversal   An application-level feature based on the protocol's understanding of call flow as well as the relevant open channels. It supports both the H.323v2 and Session Initiation Protocol (SIP) voice protocols.

ICMP inspection   Basically permits responses to ICMP packets like ping and traceroute that come from inside your firewall while denying other ICMP traffic.

Authentication proxy   A feature that makes users authenticate any time they want to access the network's resources through HTTP, HTTPS, FTP, and Telnet. It keeps personal network access profiles for users and automatically gets them for you from a RADIUS or TACACS+ server and applies them as well.

Destination URL policy management   A buffet of features that's commonly referred to as URL Filtering.

Per-user firewalls   These are basically personalized, user-specific, downloadable firewalls obtained through service providers. You can also get personalized ACLs and other settings via AAA server profile storage.

Cisco IOS router and firewall provisioning   Allows for no-touch router provisioning, version updates, and security policies.

Denial of service (DoS) detection and prevention   A feature that checks packet headers and drops any packets it finds suspicious.

Dynamic port mapping   A sort of adapter that permits applications supported by firewalls on nonstandard ports.

Java applet blocking   Protects you from any strange, unrecognized Java applets.

Basic and Advanced Traffic Filtering

You can use standard, extended, even dynamic ACLs like Lock-and-Key traffic filtering with Cisco's IOS Firewall. And you get to apply access controls to any network segment you want. Plus, you can specify the exact kind of traffic you want to allow to pass through any segment.

Policy-based, multi-interface support   Allows you to control user access by IP address and interface depending on your security policy.

Network Address Translation (NAT)   Conceals the internal network from the outside, increasing security. (I'll talk a lot about NAT in Chapter 11.)

Time-based access lists   Determine security policies based upon the exact time of day and the particular day of the week.

Peer router authentication   Guarantees that routers are getting dependable routing information from actual, trusted sources. (For this to work, you need a routing protocol that supports authentication, like RIPv2, EIGRP, or OSPF.)

Now that you've been briefed on security threats, relevant features of the Cisco IOS Firewall, and how to use that software to your advantage, let's dive deep into the world of access lists and learn how to use ACLs to mitigate security threats. They really are powerful tools, so pay attention!

Introduction to Access Lists

An *access list* is essentially a list of conditions that categorize packets. They can be really helpful when you need to exercise control over network traffic. An access list would be your tool of choice for decision making in these situations.

One of the most common and easiest to understand uses of access lists is filtering unwanted packets when implementing security policies. For example, you can set them up to make very specific decisions about regulating traffic patterns so that they'll allow only certain hosts to access web resources on the Internet while restricting others. With the right combination of access lists, network managers arm themselves with the power to enforce nearly any security policy they can invent.

Access lists can even be used in situations that don't necessarily involve blocking packets. For example, you can use them to control which networks will or won't be advertised by dynamic routing protocols. How you configure the access list is the same. The difference here is simply how you apply it—to a routing protocol instead of an interface. When you apply an access list in this way, it's called a distribute list, and it doesn't stop routing advertisements, it just controls their content. You can also use access lists to categorize packets for queuing or QoS-type services and for controlling which types of traffic can activate a pricey ISDN link.

Creating access lists is really a lot like programming a series of `if-then` statements—if a given condition is met, then a given action is taken. If the specific condition isn't met, nothing happens and the next statement is evaluated. Access-list statements are basically packet filters that packets are compared against, categorized by, and acted upon accordingly. Once the lists are built, they can be applied to either inbound or outbound traffic on any interface. Applying an access list causes the router to analyze every packet crossing that interface in the specified direction and take the appropriate action.

There are a few important rules that a packet follows when it's being compared with an access list:

- It's always compared with each line of the access list in sequential order—that is, it'll always start with the first line of the access list, then go to line 2, then line 3, and so on.

- It's compared with lines of the access list only until a match is made. Once the packet matches the condition on a line of the access list, the packet is acted upon and no further comparisons take place.

- There is an implicit "deny" at the end of each access list—this means that if a packet doesn't match the condition on any of the lines in the access list, the packet will be discarded.

Each of these rules has some powerful implications when filtering IP packets with access lists, so keep in mind that creating effective access lists truly takes some practice.

There are two main types of access lists:

Standard access lists   These use only the source IP address in an IP packet as the condition test. All decisions are made based on the source IP address. This means that standard access lists basically permit or deny an entire suite of protocols. They don't distinguish between any of the many types of IP traffic such as web, Telnet, UDP, and so on.

Extended access lists   Extended access lists can evaluate many of the other fields in the layer 3 and layer 4 headers of an IP packet. They can evaluate source and destination IP addresses, the protocol field in the Network layer header, and the port number at the Transport layer header. This gives extended access lists the ability to make much more granular decisions when controlling traffic.

Named access lists   Hey, wait a minute—I said there were two types of access lists but listed three! Well, technically there really are only two since *named access lists* are either standard or extended and not actually a new type. I'm just distinguishing them because they're created and referred to differently than standard and extended access lists, but they're functionally the same.

We will look at these types of access lists in more depth later in the chapter.

Once you create an access list, it's not really going to do anything until you apply it. Yes, they're there on the router, but they're inactive until you tell that router what to do with them. To use an access list as a packet filter, you need to apply it to an interface on the router where you want the traffic filtered. And you've got to specify which direction of traffic you want the access list applied to. There's a good reason for this—you may want different controls in place for traffic leaving your enterprise destined for the Internet than you'd want for traffic coming into your enterprise from the Internet. So, by specifying the direction of traffic, you can—and frequently you'll need to—use different access lists for inbound and outbound traffic on a single interface:

Inbound access lists   When an access list is applied to inbound packets on an interface, those packets are processed through the access list before being routed to the outbound interface. Any packets that are denied won't be routed because they're discarded before the routing process is invoked.

Outbound access lists   When an access list is applied to outbound packets on an interface, those packets are routed to the outbound interface and then processed through the access list before being queued.

There are some general access-list guidelines that should be followed when you're creating and implementing access lists on a router:

- You can assign only one access list per interface per protocol per direction. This means that when creating IP access lists, you can have only one inbound access list and one outbound access list per interface.

When you consider the implications of the implicit deny at the end of any access list, it makes sense that you can't have multiple access lists applied on the same interface in the same direction for the same protocol. That's because any packets that don't match some condition in the first access list would be denied and there wouldn't be any packets left over to compare against a second access list.

- Organize your access lists so that the more specific tests are at the top of the access list.

- Any time a new entry is added to the access list, it will be placed at the bottom of the list. Using a text editor for access lists is highly suggested.

- You cannot remove one line from an access list. If you try to do this, you will remove the entire list. It is best to copy the access list to a text editor before trying to edit the list. The only exception is when using named access lists.

You can delete a single line from a named access list. I'll show this to you shortly.

- Unless your access list ends with a `permit any` command, all packets will be discarded if they do not meet any of the list's tests. Every list should have at least one `permit` statement or it will deny all traffic.

- Create access lists and then apply them to an interface. Any access list applied to an interface without an access list present will not filter traffic.

- Access lists are designed to filter traffic going through the router. They will not filter traffic that has originated from the router.

- Place IP standard access lists as close to the destination as possible. This is the reason we don't really want to use standard access lists in our networks. You cannot put a standard access list close to the source host or network because you can only filter based on source address and nothing would be forwarded.

- Place IP extended access lists as close to the source as possible. Since extended access lists can filter on very specific addresses and protocols, you don't want your traffic to traverse the entire network and then be denied. By placing this list as close to the source address as possible, you can filter traffic before it uses up your precious bandwidth.

Before I move on to how to configure basic and advanced access lists, let's discuss how ACLs can be used to mitigate the security threats I discussed earlier in this chapter.

Mitigating Security Issues with ACLs

Here's a list of the many security threats you can mitigate with ACLs:

- IP address spoofing, inbound

- IP address spoofing, outbound

- Denial of service (DoS) TCP SYN attacks, blocking external attacks

- DoS TCP SYN attacks, using TCP Intercept

- DoS smurf attacks

- Filtering ICMP messages, inbound

- Filtering ICMP messages, outbound

- Filtering traceroute

It's generally wise not to allow into a private network any IP packets that contain the source address of any internal hosts or networks—just don't do it!

Here's a list of rules to live by when configuring ACLs from the Internet to your production network to mitigate security problems:

- Deny any addresses from your internal networks.

- Deny any local host addresses (127.0.0.0/8).

- Deny any reserved private addresses.

- Deny any addresses in the IP multicast address range (224.0.0.0/4).

None of the above addresses should be allowed to enter your internetwork. Okay, finally, let's get to work on configuring some basic and advanced access lists.

Standard Access Lists

Standard IP access lists filter network traffic by examining the source IP address in a packet. You create a *standard IP access list* by using the access-list numbers 1–99 or 1300–1999 (expanded range). Access-list types are generally differentiated using a number. Based on the number used when the access list is created, the router knows which type of syntax to expect as the list is entered. By using numbers 1–99 or 1300–1999, you're telling the router that you want to create a standard IP access list, so the router will expect syntax specifying only the source IP address in the test lines.

The following is an example of the many access-list number ranges that you can use to filter traffic on your network (the protocols for which you can specify access lists depend on your IOS version):

```
Corp(config)#access-list ?
  <1-99>            IP standard access list
  <100-199>         IP extended access list
  <1100-1199>       Extended 48-bit MAC address access list
  <1300-1999>       IP standard access list (expanded range)
  <200-299>         Protocol type-code access list
  <2000-2699>       IP extended access list (expanded range)
  <700-799>         48-bit MAC address access list
  compiled          Enable IP access-list compilation
  dynamic-extended  Extend the dynamic ACL absolute timer
  rate-limit        Simple rate-limit specific access list
```

Let's take a look at the syntax used when creating a standard access list:

```
Corp(config)#access-list 10 ?
  deny    Specify packets to reject
  permit  Specify packets to forward
  remark  Access list entry comment
```

As I said, by using the access-list numbers 1–99 or 1300–1999, you're telling the router that you want to create a standard IP access list.

After you choose the access-list number, you need to decide whether you're creating a permit or deny statement. For this example, you will create a deny statement:

```
Corp(config)#access-list 10 deny ?
  Hostname or A.B.C.D  Address to match
  any                  Any source host
  host                 A single host address
```

The next step requires a more detailed explanation. There are three options available. You can use the any parameter to permit or deny any host or network, you can use an IP address to specify either a single host or a range of them, or you can use the host command to specify a specific host only. The any command is pretty obvious—any source address matches the statement, so every packet compared against this line will match. The host command is relatively simple. Here's an example using it:

```
Corp(config)#access-list 10 deny host ?
  Hostname or A.B.C.D  Host address
Corp(config)#access-list 10 deny host 172.16.30.2
```

This tells the list to deny any packets from host 172.16.30.2. The default parameter is host. In other words, if you type **access-list 10 deny 172.16.30.2**, the router assumes you mean host 172.16.30.2.

But there's another way to specify either a particular host or a range of hosts—you can use wildcard masking. In fact, to specify any range of hosts, you have to use wildcard masking in the access list.

What's wildcard masking? You'll learn all about it using a standard access list example, as well as how to control access to a virtual terminal, in the following sections.

Wildcard Masking

Wildcards are used with access lists to specify an individual host, a network, or a certain range of a network or networks. To understand a *wildcard*, you need to understand what a *block size* is; it's used to specify a range of addresses. Some of the different block sizes available are 64, 32, 16, 8, and 4.

When you need to specify a range of addresses, you choose the next-largest block size for your needs. For example, if you need to specify 34 networks, you need a block size of 64. If you want to specify 18 hosts, you need a block size of 32. If you only specify 2 networks, then a block size of 4 would work.

Wildcards are used with the host or network address to tell the router a range of available addresses to filter. To specify a host, the address would look like this:

```
172.16.30.5 0.0.0.0
```

The four zeros represent each octet of the address. Whenever a zero is present, it means that octet in the address must match exactly. To specify that an octet can be any value, the value of 255 is used. As an example, here's how a /24 subnet is specified with a wildcard:

```
172.16.30.0 0.0.0.255
```

This tells the router to match up the first three octets exactly, but the fourth octet can be any value.

Now, that was the easy part. What if you want to specify only a small range of subnets? This is where the block sizes come in. You have to specify the range of values in a block size. In other words, you can't choose to specify 20 networks. You can only specify the exact amount as the block size value. For example, the range would have to be either 16 or 32, but not 20.

Let's say that you want to block access to part of the network that is in the range from 172.16.8.0 through 172.16.15.0. That is a block size of 8. Your network number would be

172.16.8.0, and the wildcard would be 0.0.7.255. Whoa! What is that? The 7.255 is what the router uses to determine the block size. The network and wildcard tell the router to start at 172.16.8.0 and go up a block size of eight addresses to network 172.16.15.0.

Seriously—it really is easier than it looks—really! I could certainly go through the binary math for you, but no one needs that. Actually, all you have to do is remember that the wildcard is always one number less than the block size. So, in our example, the wildcard would be 7 since our block size is 8. If you used a block size of 16, the wildcard would be 15. Easy, huh?

But just in case, we'll go through some examples to help you nail it. The following example tells the router to match the first three octets exactly but that the fourth octet can be anything:

```
Corp(config)#access-list 10 deny 172.16.10.0 0.0.0.255
```

The next example tells the router to match the first two octets and that the last two octets can be any value:

```
Corp(config)#access-list 10 deny 172.16.0.0
  0.0.255.255
```

Try to figure out this next line:

```
Corp(config)#access-list 10 deny 172.16.16.0 0.0.3.255
```

This configuration tells the router to start at network 172.16.16.0 and use a block size of 4. The range would then be 172.16.16.0 through 172.16.19.0.

The following example shows an access list starting at 172.16.16.0 and going up a block size of 8 to 172.16.23.0:

```
Corp(config)#access-list 10 deny 172.16.16.0 0.0.7.255
```

The next example starts at network 172.16.32.0 and goes up a block size of 16 to 172.16.47.0:

```
Corp(config)#access-list 10 deny 172.16.32.0 0.0.15.255
```

The next example starts at network 172.16.64.0 and goes up a block size of 64 to 172.16.127.0:

```
Corp(config)#access-list 10 deny 172.16.64.0 0.0.63.255
```

The last example starts at network 192.168.160.0 and goes up a block size of 32 to 192.168.191.255:

```
Corp(config)#access-list 10 deny 192.168.160.0 0.0.31.255
```

Here are two more things to keep in mind when working with block sizes and wildcards:

- Each block size must start at 0 or a multiple of the block size. For example, you can't say that you want a block size of 8 and then start at 12. You must use 0–7, 8–15, 16–23, etc. For a block size of 32, the ranges are 0–31, 32–63, 64–95, etc.
- The command any is the same thing as writing out the wildcard 0.0.0.0 255.255.255.255.

Wildcard masking is a crucial skill to master when creating IP access lists. It's used identically when creating standard and extended IP access lists.

Standard Access List Example

In this section, you'll learn how to use a standard access list to stop specific users from gaining access to the Finance department LAN.

In Figure 10.2, a router has three LAN connections and one WAN connection to the Internet. Users on the Sales LAN should not have access to the Finance LAN, but they should be able to access the Internet and the marketing department. The Marketing LAN needs to access the Finance LAN for application services.

FIGURE 10.2 IP access list example with three LANs and a WAN connection

On the router in the figure, the following standard IP access list is configured:

```
Lab_A#config t
Lab_A(config)#access-list 10 deny 172.16.40.0 0.0.0.255
Lab_A(config)#access-list 10 permit any
```

It's very important to know that the any command is the same thing as saying the following using wildcard masking:

```
Lab_A(config)#access-list 10 permit 0.0.0.0
  255.255.255.255
```

Since the wildcard mask says that none of the octets are to be evaluated, every address matches the test condition. So this is functionally the same as using the any keyword.

At this point, the access list is configured to deny source addresses from the Sales LAN access to the Finance LAN and allow everyone else. But remember, no action will be taken until the access list is applied on an interface in a specific direction. But where should this access list be placed? If you place it as an incoming access list on E0, you might as well shut down the Ethernet interface because all of the Sales LAN devices will be denied access to all networks attached to the router. The best place to apply this access list is on the E1 interface as an outbound list:

```
Lab_A(config)#int e1
Lab_A(config-if)#ip access-group 10 out
```

This completely stops traffic from 172.16.40.0 from getting out Ethernet 1. It has no effect on the hosts from the Sales LAN accessing the Marketing LAN and the Internet since traffic to those destinations doesn't go through interface E1. Any packet trying to exit out E1 will have to go through the access list first. If there were an inbound list placed on E0, then any packet trying to enter interface E0 would have to go through the access list before being routed to an exit interface.

Let's take a look at another example of a standard access list. Figure 10.3 shows an internetwork of two routers with three LANs and one serial WAN connection.

FIGURE 10.3   IP standard access list example 2

You want to stop the Accounting users from accessing the Human Resources server attached to the Lab_B router but allow all other users access to that LAN. What standard access list would you create and where would you place it?

The real answer is that you should use an extended access list and place it closest to the source, but the question specifies that you should use a standard access list. Standard access lists, by rule of thumb, are placed closest to the destination—in this example, Ethernet 0 outbound on the Lab_B router. Here is the access list that should be placed on the Lab_B router:

```
Lab_B#config t
Lab_B(config)#access-list 10 deny 192.168.10.128 0.0.0.31
Lab_B(config)#access-list 10 permit any
Lab_B(config)#interface Ethernet 0
Lab_B(config-if)#ip access-group 10 out
```

Before we move on to restricting Telnet access on a router, let's take a look at one more standard access list example, but it will require some thought. In Figure 10.4 you have a router with four LAN connections and one WAN connection to the Internet.

You need to write an access list that will stop access from each of the four LANs shown in the diagram to the Internet. Each of the LANs shows a single host's IP address, and from that you need to determine the subnet and use wildcards to configure the access list.

FIGURE 10.4 IP standard access list example 3

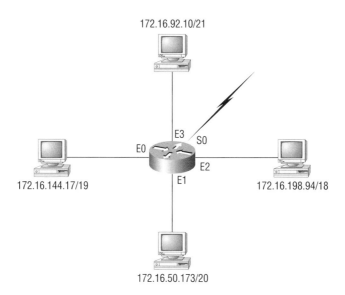

Here is an example of what your answer should look like (starting with the network on E0 and working through to E3):

```
Router(config)#access-list 1 deny 172.16.128.0 0.0.31.255
Router(config)#access-list 1 deny 172.16.48.0 0.0.15.255
Router(config)#access-list 1 deny 172.16.192.0 0.0.63.255
Router(config)#access-list 1 deny 172.16.88.0 0.0.7.255
Router(config)#access-list 1 permit any
Router(config)#interface serial 0
Router(config-if)#ip access-group 1 out
```

Okay, what would be the purpose of creating this list? If you actually applied this access list on the router, you'd effectively shut down access to the Internet, so what's the purpose of even having an Internet connection? I wrote this exercise so you can practice how to use block sizes with access lists—which is critical for your success when studying the CCNA objectives.

Controlling VTY (Telnet) Access

You'll probably have a difficult time trying to stop users from telnetting to a large router because any active interface on a router is fair game for VTY access. You could try to create an extended IP access list that limits Telnet access to every IP address on the router. But if you did that, you'd have to apply it inbound on every interface, and that really wouldn't scale well to a large router with dozens, even hundreds, of interfaces, would it? Here's a much better solution: Use a standard IP access list to control access to the VTY lines themselves.

Why does this work? Because when you apply an access list to the VTY lines, you don't need to specify the Telnet protocol since access to the VTY implies terminal access. You also don't need to specify a destination address since it really doesn't matter which interface address the user used as a target for the Telnet session. You really only need to control where the user is coming from—their source IP address.

To perform this function, follow these steps:

1. Create a standard IP access list that permits only the host or hosts you want to be able to telnet into the routers.

2. Apply the access list to the VTY line with the `access-class` command.

   Here is an example of allowing only host 172.16.10.3 to telnet into a router:

```
Lab_A(config)#access-list 50 permit 172.16.10.3
Lab_A(config)#line vty 0 4
Lab_A(config-line)#access-class 50 in
```

 Real World Scenario

Should You Secure Your Telnet Lines on a Router?

You're monitoring your network and notice that someone has telnetted into your core router by using the show users command. You use the disconnect command and they are disconnected from the router, but you notice they are back into the router a few minutes later. You are thinking about putting an access list on the router interfaces, but you don't want to add a lot of latency on each interface since your router is already pushing a lot of packets. You are considering putting an access list on the VTY lines themselves, but not having done this before, you are not sure if this is a safe alternative to putting an access list on each interface. Is putting an access list on the VTY lines a good idea for this network?

Yes, absolutely, and the access-class command illustrated in this section is the best way to do this. Why? Because it doesn't use an access list that just sits on an interface looking at every packet that is coming and going. This can cause overhead on the packets trying to be routed.

When you put the access-class command on the VTY lines, only packets trying to telnet into the router will be looked at and compared. This provides nice, easy-to-configure security for your router.

Because of the implied deny any at the end of the list, the access list stops any host from telnetting into the router except the host 172.16.10.3, regardless of which individual IP address on the router is used as a target.

 Cisco recommends that you use Secure Shell (SSH) instead of Telnet on the VTY lines of a router. See Chapter 4 for more information on SSH and how to configure SSH on your routers and switches.

Extended Access Lists

In the standard IP access list example earlier, notice how you had to block all access from the Sales LAN to the finance department. What if you needed Sales to gain access to a certain server on the Finance LAN but not to other network services, for security reasons? With a standard IP access list, you can't allow users to get to one network service and not another. Said another way, when you need to make decisions based on both source and destination addresses, a standard access list won't allow you to do that since it only makes decisions based on source address.

But an *extended access list* will hook you up. That's because extended access lists allow you to specify source and destination address as well as the protocol and port number that identify the upper-layer protocol or application. By using extended access lists, you can effectively allow users access to a physical LAN and stop them from accessing specific hosts—or even specific services on those hosts.

Here's an example of an extended IP access list:

```
Corp(config)#access-list ?
  <1-99>             IP standard access list
  <100-199>          IP extended access list
  <1100-1199>        Extended 48-bit MAC address access list
  <1300-1999>        IP standard access list (expanded range)
  <200-299>          Protocol type-code access list
  <2000-2699>        IP extended access list (expanded range)
  <700-799>          48-bit MAC address access list
  compiled           Enable IP access-list compilation
  dynamic-extended   Extend the dynamic ACL absolute timer
  rate-limit         Simple rate-limit specific access list
```

The first command shows the access-list numbers available. You'll use the extended access-list range from 100 to 199. Be sure to notice that the range 2000–2699 is also available for extended IP access lists.

At this point, you need to decide what type of list entry you are making. For this example, you'll choose a deny list entry.

```
Corp(config)#access-list 110 ?
  deny     Specify packets to reject
  dynamic  Specify a DYNAMIC list of PERMITs or DENYs
  permit   Specify packets to forward
  remark   Access list entry comment
```

Once you choose the access-list type, you then need to select a protocol field entry.

```
Corp(config)#access-list 110 deny ?
  <0-255>  An IP protocol number
  ahp      Authentication Header Protocol
  eigrp    Cisco's EIGRP routing protocol
  esp      Encapsulation Security Payload
  gre      Cisco's GRE tunneling
  icmp     Internet Control Message Protocol
  igmp     Internet Gateway Message Protocol
  ip       Any Internet Protocol
  ipinip   IP in IP tunneling
  nos      KA9Q NOS compatible IP over IP tunneling
  ospf     OSPF routing protocol
  pcp      Payload Compression Protocol
  pim      Protocol Independent Multicast
  tcp      Transmission Control Protocol
  udp      User Datagram Protocol
```

 If you want to filter by Application layer protocol, you have to choose the appropriate layer 4 transport protocol after the permit or deny statement. For example, to filter Telnet or FTP, you choose TCP since both Telnet and FTP use TCP at the Transport layer. If you were to choose IP, you wouldn't be allowed to specify a specific application protocol later.

Here, you'll choose to filter an Application layer protocol that uses TCP by selecting TCP as the protocol. You'll specify the specific TCP port later. Next, you will be prompted for the source IP address of the host or network (you can choose the any command to allow any source address):

```
Corp(config)#access-list 110 deny tcp ?
  A.B.C.D  Source address
  any      Any source host
  host     A single source host
```

After the source address is selected, the destination address is chosen:

```
Corp(config)#access-list 110 deny tcp any ?
  A.B.C.D  Destination address
  any      Any destination host
  eq       Match only packets on a given port number
  gt       Match only packets with a greater port number
  host     A single destination host
  lt       Match only packets with a lower port number
  neq      Match only packets not on a given port number
  range    Match only packets in the range of port numbers
```

In the following example, any source IP address that has a destination IP address of 172.16.30.2 has been denied.

```
Corp(config)#access-list 110 deny tcp any host 172.16.30.2 ?
  ack          Match on the ACK bit
  dscp         Match packets with given dscp value
  eq           Match only packets on a given port number
  established  Match established connections
  fin          Match on the FIN bit
  fragments    Check non-initial fragments
  gt           Match only packets with a greater port number
  log          Log matches against this entry
  log-input    Log matches against this entry, including input interface
  lt           Match only packets with a lower port number
  neq          Match only packets not on a given port number
  precedence   Match packets with given precedence value
  psh          Match on the PSH bit
  range        Match only packets in the range of port numbers
  rst          Match on the RST bit
  syn          Match on the SYN bit
  time-range   Specify a time-range
  tos          Match packets with given TOS value
  urg          Match on the URG bit
  <cr>
```

You can press Enter here and leave the access list as is. But if you do that, all TCP traffic to host 172.16.30.2 will be denied, regardless of destination port. You can be even more specific: once you have the host addresses in place, just specify the type of service you are denying.

The following help screen shows you the available options. You can choose a port number or use the application or protocol name:

```
Corp(config)#access-list 110 deny tcp any host 172.16.30.2 eq ?
  <0-65535>    Port number
  bgp          Border Gateway Protocol (179)
  chargen      Character generator (19)
  cmd          Remote commands (rcmd, 514)
  daytime      Daytime (13)
  discard      Discard (9)
  domain       Domain Name Service (53)
  drip         Dynamic Routing Information Protocol (3949)
  echo         Echo (7)
  exec         Exec (rsh, 512)
  finger       Finger (79)
  ftp          File Transfer Protocol (21)
  ftp-data     FTP data connections (20)
  gopher       Gopher (70)
  hostname     NIC hostname server (101)
  ident        Ident Protocol (113)
  irc          Internet Relay Chat (194)
  klogin       Kerberos login (543)
  kshell       Kerberos shell (544)
  login        Login (rlogin, 513)
  lpd          Printer service (515)
  nntp         Network News Transport Protocol (119)
  pim-auto-rp  PIM Auto-RP (496)
  pop2         Post Office Protocol v2 (109)
  pop3         Post Office Protocol v3 (110)
  smtp         Simple Mail Transport Protocol (25)
  sunrpc       Sun Remote Procedure Call (111)
  syslog       Syslog (514)
  tacacs       TAC Access Control System (49)
  talk         Talk (517)
  telnet       Telnet (23)
  time         Time (37)
  uucp         Unix-to-Unix Copy Program (540)
  whois        Nicname (43)
  www          World Wide Web (HTTP, 80)
```

At this point, let's block Telnet (port 23) to host 172.16.30.2 only. If the users want to FTP, fine—that's allowed. The `log` command is used to log messages every time the access list is hit. This can be an extremely cool way to monitor inappropriate access attempts. Here is how to do this:

```
Corp(config)#access-list 110 deny tcp any host 172.16.30.2 eq 23 log
```

You need to keep in mind that the next line is an implicit deny any by default. If you apply this access list to an interface, you might as well just shut the interface down since by default there is an implicit deny all at the end of every access list. You've got to follow up the access list with the following command:

```
Corp(config)#access-list 110 permit ip any any
```

Remember, the 0.0.0.0 255.255.255.255 is the same command as any, so the command could look like this:

```
Corp(config)#access-list 110 permit ip 0.0.0.0 255.255.255.255
0.0.0.0 255.255.255.255
```

Once the access list is created, you need to apply it to an interface (it's the same command as the IP standard list):

```
Corp(config-if)#ip access-group 110 in
```

Or this:

```
Corp(config-if)#ip access-group 110 out
```

In the following section, we'll look at an example of how to use an extended access list.

Extended Access List Example 1

Using Figure 10.2 from the IP standard access list example earlier, let's use the same network and deny access to a host at 172.16.30.5 on the Finance department LAN for both Telnet and FTP services. All other services on this and all other hosts are acceptable for the sales and marketing departments to access.

The following access list should be created:

```
Lab_A#config t
Lab_A(config)#access-list 110 deny tcp any host
  172.16.30.5 eq 21
Lab_A(config)#access-list 110 deny tcp any host
  172.16.30.5 eq 23
Lab_A(config)#access-list 110 permit ip any any
```

The `access-list` 110 tells the router you are creating an extended IP access list. The `tcp` is the protocol field in the Network layer header. If the list doesn't say `tcp` here, you cannot filter by port numbers 21 and 23 as shown in the example. (These are FTP and Telnet, and they both use TCP for connection-oriented services.) The `any` command is the source, which means any IP address, and the `host` is the destination IP address.

> Remember that instead of the host `172.16.30.5` command when we created the extended access list, we could have entered `172.16.30.5 0.0.0.0` instead and there would be no difference in the result—other than the router would change the command to host `172.16.30.5` in the running-config.

After the list is created, it needs to be applied to the Ethernet 1 interface outbound. This applies the policy we created to all hosts and effectively blocks all FTP and Telnet access to 172.16.30.5 from outside the local LAN. If this list were created to only block access from the Sales LAN, then we'd have put this list closer to the source, or on Ethernet interface 0. So, in this situation, we'd apply the list to inbound traffic.

Let's go ahead and apply the list to interface E1 and block all outside FTP and Telnet access to the host:

```
Lab_A(config-if)#ip access-group 110 out
```

Extended Access List Example 2

In this example, we'll again use Figure 10.4, which has four LANs and a serial connection. What we need to do is stop Telnet access to the networks attached to the Ethernet 1 and Ethernet 2 interfaces. If we only used one access list, it would not be a very effective one because of the latency that will be caused on the Ethernet 1 and 2 interfaces (since every packet going out these interfaces must be looked at), but if we used two lists, the latency could be less on each interface if configured correctly. However, since we're studying the CCNA objectives, we're going to look at this with only one access list.

The configuration on the router would look something like this, although the answer can vary:

```
Router(config)#access-list 110 deny tcp any 172.16.48.0 0.0.15.255
eq 23
Router(config)#access-list 110 deny tcp any 172.16.192.0 0.0.63.255
eq 23
Router(config)#access-list 110 permit ip any any
Router(config)#interface Ethernet 1
Router(config-if)#ip access-group 110 out
Router(config-if)#interface Ethernet 2
Router(config-if)#ip access-group 110 out
```

The important information that you need to understand from this list is as follows: First, you need to verify that the number range is correct for the type of access list you are creating—in this example it's extended, so the range must be 100–199. Second, you need to verify that the protocol field matches the upper-layer process or application—in this example, port 23 (Telnet).

The protocol parameter must be TCP since Telnet uses TCP. If the question stated to use TFTP, for example, then the protocol parameter would have to be UDP since TFTP uses UDP. Third, verify that the destination port number matches the application you are filtering for—in this case, port 23 matches Telnet, which is correct. Finally, the test statement `permit ip any any` is important to have at the end of the list to enable all packets other than Telnet packets destined for the LANs connected to Ethernet 1 and Ethernet 2.

Advanced Access Lists

In this section, I am going to show you some more advanced ways to use access lists. Most of the advanced access-list topics are beyond the objectives of this book, so I'll just discuss them briefly and you can find more information on the Cisco website if you are interested.

However, with that said, there are some important access-list options that you need to know, and the first one is named access lists.

Named ACLs

As I said earlier, named access lists are just another way to create standard and extended access lists. In medium to large enterprises, management of access lists can become, well, a real hassle over time. For example, when you need to make a change to an access list, a frequent practice is to copy the access list to a text editor, change the number, edit the list, then paste the new list back into the router. With this done, you can simply change the access-list number on the interface from the old one to the new one and there will never be a time on the network where an access list isn't in place.

This would work pretty well if it weren't for what I call "packrat" mentality. The question becomes, What do I do with the old access list? Delete it? Or should I save it in case I find a problem with the new list and need to back out of the change? What happens is that over time—through this and countless other scenarios—you can end up with a whole bunch of unapplied access lists building up on a router. What were they for? Are they important? Do I need them? All good questions, and named access lists could be your answer.

This can also apply to access lists that are up and running. Let's say you come into an existing network and are looking at access lists on a router. Suppose you find an access list 177 (which is an extended access list) that is 33 lines long. This could cause you much needless existential questioning—What is it for? Why is it here? Instead, wouldn't an access list called, say, finance LAN be more descriptive than one that's named 177?

Named access lists allow you to use names to both create and apply either standard or extended access lists. There is nothing new or different about these access lists aside from being able to refer to them in a way that makes sense to humans. But there are some subtle changes to the syntax, so let's re-create the standard access list we created earlier for our test network in Figure 10.2 using a named access list:

```
Lab_A#config t
Enter configuration commands, one per line.  End with CNTL/Z.
Lab_A(config)#ip access-list ?
  extended  Extended Acc
  logging   Control access list logging
  standard  Standard Access List
```

Notice that I started by typing **ip access-list**, not **access-list**. This allows me to enter a named access list. Next, I'll need to specify that it's to be a standard access list:

```
Lab_A(config)#ip access-list standard ?
  <1-99>  Standard IP access-list number
  WORD    Access-list name
```

```
Lab_A(config)#ip access-list standard BlockSales
Lab_A(config-std-nacl)#
```

I've specified a standard access list, then added a name: BlockSales. Notice that I could've used a number for a standard access list, but instead, I chose to use a descriptive name. Also, notice that after entering the name, I hit Enter and the router prompt changed. I'm now in named access list configuration mode and entering the named access list:

```
Lab_A(config-std-nacl)#?
Standard Access List configuration commands:
  default  Set a command to its defaults
  deny     Specify packets to reject
  exit     Exit from access-list configuration mode
  no       Negate a command or set its defaults
  permit   Specify packets to forward
```

```
Lab_A(config-std-nacl)#deny 172.16.40.0 0.0.0.255
Lab_A(config-std-nacl)#permit any
Lab_A(config-std-nacl)#exit
Lab_A(config)#^Z
Lab_A#
```

I enter the access list, and then exit out of configuration mode. Next, I'll take a look at the running configuration to verify that the access list is indeed in the router:

```
Lab_A#show running-config
```

```
!
ip access-list standard BlockSales
 deny    172.16.40.0 0.0.0.255
 permit any
!
```

The BlockSales access list has truly been created and is in the running-config of the router. Next, I'll need to apply the access list to an interface:

```
Lab_A#config t
Enter configuration commands, one per line.  End with CNTL/Z.
Lab_A(config)#int e1
Lab_A(config-if)#ip access-group BlockSales out
Lab_A(config-if)#^Z
Lab_A#
```

All right! At this point, we've re-created the work done earlier using a named access list.

Switch Port ACLs

Okay, now remember this: You can only apply port ACLs to layer 2 interfaces on your switches. Why? Because they're only supported on physical layer 2 interfaces. Another good thing to keep in mind is that you can apply them as only inbound lists on your interfaces, and you can use only named lists as well.

Here's a short list of supported access lists:

- As I mentioned, standard IP access lists use only source addresses to filter traffic.

- On the other hand, extended IP access lists use both source and destination addresses as well as optional protocol information and port numbers.

- There are also MAC extended access lists that use source and destination MAC addresses and optional protocol type information.

Switches scrutinize all inbound ACLs applied to a certain interface and decide to allow traffic through depending on whether the traffic is a good match to the ACL or not. So I'm sure you can see how important ACLs are to security—they're gatekeepers with the power to permit or deny access to a special segment of your network, or all of it—period!

ACLs can also be used to control traffic on VLANs. To make this happen, you just need to apply a port ACL to a trunk port. But do beware—if you do this on a port that has a voice VLAN, that ACL will actually filter your data VLANs too. So tread carefully here!

Port ACLs control IP traffic via IP access lists. Any non-IP traffic is filtered through the use of MAC addresses. And even though you can apply both types of filter to a single interface, you only get to apply one of each. If you try to put an additional ACL of either type on an interface that's already got them in place, the new one will override the one you had there before. So it's a good idea to be careful here—look before you leap.

Let's check out the access list:

```
S1#config t
S1(config)#mac access-list ?
  extended  Extended Access List
S1(config)#mac access-list extended ?
  WORD  access-list name
S1(config)#mac access-list extended Todd_MAC_List
S1(config-ext-macl)#deny ?
  H.H.H  48-bit source MAC address
  any    any source MAC address
  host   A single source host
S1(config-ext-macl)#deny any ?
  H.H.H  48-bit destination MAC address
  any    any destination MAC address
  host   A single destination host
S1(config-ext-macl)#deny any host ?
  H.H.H  48-bit destination MAC address
S1(config-ext-macl)#deny any host 000d.29bd.4b85
S1(config-ext-macl)#permit ?
  H.H.H  48-bit source MAC address
  any    any source MAC address
  host   A single source host
S1(config-ext-macl)#permit any any
S1(config-ext-macl)#do show access-list
Extended MAC access list Todd_MAC_List
    deny   any host 000d.29bd.4b85
    permit any any
S1(config-ext-macl)#
```

All right—you can see that you can only create an extended named access list. You have no other options. And don't forget to add the permit any any at the end!

Here is how you would apply the list to a switch port:

```
S1(config-ext-macl)#int f0/6
S1(config-if)#mac access-group Todd_MAC_List in
```

This is pretty much the same as it is with an IP list, except that you start with the command mac.

But do you really want to deny MAC addresses? Doesn't this sound like a bad hangover before you even start? While it's true there are special circumstances where you would, there is another option, and I think it's usually the better one: Just deny access based on the ether-type field in the Ethernet frame header instead. Take a look:

```
S1(config-ext-macl)#deny any any ?
  <0-65535>      An arbitrary EtherType in decimal, hex, or octal
  aarp           EtherType: AppleTalk ARP
  amber          EtherType: DEC-Amber
  appletalk      EtherType: AppleTalk/EtherTalk
  cos            CoS value
  dec-spanning   EtherType: DEC-Spanning-Tree
  decnet-iv      EtherType: DECnet Phase IV
  diagnostic     EtherType: DEC-Diagnostic
  dsm            EtherType: DEC-DSM
  etype-6000     EtherType: 0x6000
  etype-8042     EtherType: 0x8042
  lat            EtherType: DEC-LAT
  lavc-sca       EtherType: DEC-LAVC-SCA
  lsap           LSAP value
  mop-console    EtherType: DEC-MOP Remote Console
  mop-dump       EtherType: DEC-MOP Dump
  msdos          EtherType: DEC-MSDOS
  mumps          EtherType: DEC-MUMPS
  netbios        EtherType: DEC-NETBIOS
  vines-echo     EtherType: VINES Echo
  vines-ip       EtherType: VINES IP
  xns-idp        EtherType: XNS IDP
  <cr>
```

It's cool—I know. But don't go nuts here and start denying all ether-type numbers available or you'll end up with some issues that will make you regret it. But who actually uses DecNet and AppleTalk? They definitely deserve to be denied access to your beautiful, well-oiled network, don't they?

If you read Chapter 1, you would know that if you blocked 0x800, you'd block all of IP, right? This could come in handy in the future if you decided you wanted to force everyone to run IPv6. But for now, just don't go there!

Lock and Key (Dynamic ACLs)

This flavor of ACL depends on either remote or local Telnet authentication in combination with extended ACLs.

Before you can configure a dynamic ACL, you need to apply an extended ACL on your router to stop the flow of traffic through it. The only way anyone can get through the blockade is if they telnet to the router and gain authentication. It works like this: The Telnet connection the user initiated gets dropped and is replaced with a single-entry dynamic ACL that's appended to the extended ACL already in place. This causes traffic to be allowed through for a specific amount of time, and as you may have guessed, time-outs can and do happen.

Reflexive ACLs

These ACLs filter IP packets depending upon upper-layer session information, and they often permit outbound traffic to pass but place limitations on inbound traffic. You can't define reflexive ACLs with numbered or standard IP ACLs, or any other protocol ACLs for that matter. They can be used along with other standard or static extended ACLs, but they're only defined with extended named IP ACLs—that's it.

Time-Based ACLs

Time-based ACLs work a lot like extended ACLs do, but their type of access control is totally time oriented. Basically, you specify a certain time of day and week and then identify that particular period by giving it a name referenced by a task. So, by necessity, the reference function will fall under whatever time constraints you've dictated. The time period is based upon the router's clock, but I highly recommend using it in conjunction with Network Time Protocol (NTP) synchronization.

Here's an example:

```
Corp#config t
Corp(config)#time-range no-http
Corp(config-time-range)#periodic we?
Wednesday  weekdays  weekend
Corp(config-time-range)#periodic weekend ?
  hh:mm  Starting time
Corp(config-time-range)#periodic weekend 06:00 to 12:00
Corp(config-time-range)#exit
Corp(config)#time-range tcp-yes
Corp(config-time-range)#periodic weekend 06:00 to 12:00
Corp(config-time-range)#exit
Corp(config)#ip access-list extended Time
Corp(config-ext-nacl)#deny tcp any any eq www time-range no-http
Corp(config-ext-nacl)#permit tcp any any time-range tcp-yes
Corp(config-ext-nacl)#interface f0/0
Corp(config-if)#ip access-group Time in
Corp(config-if)#do show time-range
time-range entry: no-http (inactive)
   periodic weekdays 8:00 to 15:00
   used in: IP ACL entry
```

```
time-range entry: tcp-yes (inactive)
   periodic weekend 8:00 to 13:00
   used in: IP ACL entry
Corp(config-if)#
```

The `time-range` command is pretty flexible and will drive users crazy if you deny them basic network access or access to the Internet during off-hours. Be careful with the preceding commands—make sure you test your list on a nonproduction network before you implement the lists on your production network.

Remarks

This is the tool you grab to use the `remark` keyword, and it's really important because it arms you with the ability to include comments, or rather remarks, regarding the entries you've made in both your IP standard and extended ACLs. Remarks are very cool because they efficiently increase your ability to examine and understand your ACLs to the super-hero level. Without them, you'd be caught in a quagmire of meaningless numbers without anything to help you recall what those numbers mean.

Even though you have the option of placing your remarks either before or after a `permit` or `deny` statement, I totally recommend that you chose to position them consistently so you don't get confused about which remark is relevant to which one of your `permit` or `deny` statements.

To get this going for both standard and extended ACLs, just use the `access-list` *access-list number* `remark` *remark* `global configuration` command. And if you want to get rid of a remark, just use the command's no form.

Let's take a look at an example of how to use the `remark` command:

```
R2#config t
R2(config)#access-list 110 remark Permit Bob from Sales Only To Finance
R2(config)#access-list 110 permit ip host 172.16.10.1 172.16.20.0 0.0.0.255
R2(config)#access-list 110 deny ip 172.16.10.0 0.0.0.255
172.16.20.0 0.0.0.255
R2(config)#ip access-list extended No_Telnet
R2(config-ext-nacl)#remark Deny all of Sales from Telnetting
to Marketing
R2(config-ext-nacl)#deny tcp 172.16.30.0 0.0.0.255
172.16.40.0 0.0.0.255 eq 23
R2(config-ext-nacl)#permit ip any any
R2(config-ext-nacl)#do show run
[output cut]
!
ip access-list extended No_Telnet
 remark Stop all of Sales from Telnetting to Marketing
 deny   tcp 172.16.30.0 0.0.0.255 172.16.40.0 0.0.0.255 eq telnet
 permit ip any any
```

```
!
access-list 110 remark Permit Bob from Sales Only To Finance
access-list 110 permit ip host 172.16.10.1 172.16.20.0 0.0.0.255
access-list 110 deny   ip 172.16.10.0 0.0.0.255 172.16.20.0 0.0.0.255
!
```

I was able to add a `remark` to both an extended list and a named access list. However, you cannot see these remarks in the output of the `show access-list` command, only in the running-config. I'll show you this command again when we configure ACLs using the SDM.

Context-Based Access Control (Cisco IOS Firewall)

You've got to have the Cisco IOS Firewall set in the IOS to make use of Context-Based Access Control (CBAC), and the funny thing is, it's rare to hear someone—even Cisco—differentiate between the two. People usually just refer to the Cisco IOS Firewall and leave it at that. But what is it? Well, the CBAC's job is to scrutinize any and all traffic that's attempting to come through the firewall so it can find out about and control the state information for TCP and UDP sessions. And it uses that very information it's gathered to determine whether to create a temporary pathway into the firewall's access lists.

To make this happen, just configure `ip inspect` lists in the same direction the traffic is flowing. If you don't do this, any return traffic won't be able to get back through, which will negatively impact any session connections originating from inside the internal network in a big way.

Take a look at Figure 10.5, which illustrates in a very simple way how the Cisco IOS Firewall (CBAC) works.

FIGURE 10.5   Cisco IOS Firewall (CBACe) example

A router that's configured with the Cisco IOS Firewall will process traffic in the following manner:

1. First, if the inside ACL approves, the router will get all inside packets sent to it.

2. Next, the approved traffic is subjected to the firewall's ip inspect process, which adds the approved connection's state information into the state table.

3. Finally, the traffic passes through the IP inspect process, which then creates a dynamic ACL entry and puts it into the outside ACL so that the return traffic will be allowed to pass back through the router.

4. I'll demonstrate this in a bit when I create a firewall using the SDM.

Authentication Proxy

I have this set on all of my routers, but to be able to do that you must also have the Cisco IOS Firewall feature set up. I have the configuration set up this way because the authentication proxy is a good thing to have on your side. This is true because it authenticates inbound users, outbound users, or both. Those who would normally be blocked by an ACL can just bring up a browser to get through the firewall and then authenticate on a TACACS+ or RADIUS server.

Monitoring Access Lists

Again, it's always good to be able to verify a router's configuration. Table 10.1 lists the commands that can be used to verify the configuration.

TABLE 10.1   Commands Used to Verify Access List Configuration

Command	Effect
show access-list	Displays all access lists and their parameters configured on the router. This command does not show you which interface the list is set on.
show access-list 110	Shows only the parameters for the access list 110. This command does not show you the interface the list is set on.
show ip access-list	Shows only the IP access lists configured on the router.
show ip interface	Shows which interfaces have access lists set.
show running-config	Shows the access lists and which interfaces have access lists set.
Show mac access-group	Displays MAC access lists applied to all layer 2 interfaces or the specified layer 2 interface (used on layer 2 switches only).

We've already used the show running-config command to verify that a named access list was in the router as well as a MAC access list on a layer 2 switch. So now let's take a look at the output from some of the other commands.

The show access-list command will list all access lists on the router, whether they're applied to an interface or not:

```
Lab_A#show access-list
Standard IP access list 10
    deny   172.16.40.0, wildcard bits 0.0.0.255
    permit any
Standard IP access list BlockSales
    deny   172.16.40.0, wildcard bits 0.0.0.255
    permit any
Extended IP access list 110
    deny tcp any host 172.16.30.5 eq ftp
    deny tcp any host 172.16.30.5 eq telnet
    permit ip any any
Lab_A#
```

First, notice that both access list 10 and our named access list appear on this list. Second, notice that even though I entered actual numbers for TCP ports in access list 110, the show command gives us the protocol names rather than TCP ports for readability. (Hey, not everyone has them all memorized!)

Here's the output of the show ip interface command:

```
Lab_A#show ip interface e1
Ethernet1 is up, line protocol is up
  Internet address is 172.16.30.1/24
  Broadcast address is 255.255.255.255
  Address determined by non-volatile memory
  MTU is 1500 bytes
  Helper address is not set
  Directed broadcast forwarding is disabled
  Outgoing access list is BlockSales
  Inbound  access list is not set
  Proxy ARP is enabled
  Security level is default
  Split horizon is enabled
  ICMP redirects are always sent
  ICMP unreachables are always sent
  ICMP mask replies are never sent
  IP fast switching is disabled
```

```
    IP fast switching on the same interface is disabled
    IP Null turbo vector
    IP multicast fast switching is disabled
    IP multicast distributed fast switching is disabled
    Router Discovery is disabled
    IP output packet accounting is disabled
    IP access violation accounting is disabled
    TCP/IP header compression is disabled
    RTP/IP header compression is disabled
    Probe proxy name replies are disabled
    Policy routing is disabled
    Network address translation is disabled
    Web Cache Redirect is disabled
    BGP Policy Mapping is disabled
Lab_A#
```

Be sure to notice the bold line indicating that the outgoing list on this interface is BlockSales but the inbound access list isn't set. One more verification command and then we'll move on to using the SDM to configure firewall security.

As I've already mentioned, you can use the show running-config command to see any and all access lists. However, on a layer 2 switch, you can verify your interface configurations with the show mac access-group command:

```
S1#sh mac access-group
Interface FastEthernet0/1:
    Inbound access-list is not set
    Outbound access-list is not set
Interface FastEthernet0/2:
    Inbound access-list is not set
    Outbound access-list is not set
S1#
```

Depending on how many interfaces you set your MAC access lists on, you can use the interface command to view individual interfaces:

```
S1#sh mac access-group interface f0/6
Interface FastEthernet0/6:
    Inbound access-list is Todd_MAC_List
    Outbound access-list is not set
```

Let's discuss how SDM can provide security on our networks.

Configuring Access Lists Using SDM

I'll start this section by showing you how to create an access list using the SDM, and then I'll use the firewall wizards to add the Cisco IOS Firewall, which creates ACLs (which access lists are huge part of, as you'll see). It's much easier to just use the wizards. I'll show you both ways, but by using the wizards, you really don't need to do much at all but click a few Next buttons to make a good secure router.

Creating ACLs with SDM

Let's begin by simply creating an ACL using the SDM. You can only create named access lists. Let's take a look.

Obviously, your first step in using SDM is to open it. Next, just click Configure ➤ Firewall and ACL and you'll get the Create Firewall screen.

Next, click on the Edit Firewall Policy/ACL tab.

On the top, choose the From and To interfaces from the drop-down menus. I already have chosen s0/0/0 as my From interface and s0/2/0 as my To interface. Then in the middle of the page, click +Add, which provides a pull-down menu. Choose Add New and the following screen appears.

I've already configured the list that's denying telnet (23) to Wireless Host C (WHC) from any host coming in the s0/0/0 interface, and I've also chosen to log matches. I'm going to click OK and then create a permit statement so I don't shut my router's interface down.

A very cool thing about creating lists through the SDM is that the +Add menu asks if you want to create a new test statement and place it before or after the line you've already got in the list. This is great because by using the SDM, you can quickly and efficiently edit your ACLs!

Next, I'm going to create a simple `permit ip any` statement.

After clicking OK, I received the main screen again, which shows me my list. I can easily add, delete, and manage my ACL form here. Very sweet indeed!

Let's see what the router has in the running-config now:

```
!
ip access-list extended sdm_serial0/0/0_in
 remark SDM_ACL Category=1
 remark Deny Telnet to WHC
 deny    tcp any host 10.1.12.2 eq telnet log
 permit ip any any log
!
!
interface Serial0/0/0
 description 1st Connection to R1$FW_INSIDE$
 ip address 10.1.2.1 255.255.255.0
 ip access-group sdm_serial0/0/0_in in
```

Looks good—let's try to telnet to host 10.1.12.2 and see what shows up on the Corp console:

```
Corp#
*May 14 17:34:36.503: %SEC-6-IPACCESSLOGP: list sdm_serial0/0/0_in denied tcp
 10.1.2.2(30491) -> 10.1.12.2(23), 1 packet
```

Okay—now I'm going to telnet to host 10.1.12.1:

```
*May 14 17:34:53.023: %SEC-6-IPACCESSLOGP: list sdm_serial0/0/0_in permitted
 tcp 10.1.2.2(16774) -> 10.1.12.1(23), 1 packet
Corp#
```

Nice! Packets entering s0/0/0 with a destination IP address of host 10.1.12.2 and with a destination of port 23 are being denied, but notice that when I telnetted to host 10.1.12.1, it was allowed.

With all that behind us, I'm going to show you how easy all of this is using the SDM, and make my router even more secure in the process.

Creating Firewalls with SDM

This section will show you how to use both the Basic and Advanced Firewall Wizards to set up the Cisco IOS Firewall software. It really is your best option when configuring security on your routers.

Click Configure ➢ Firewall and ACL, and you'll get a wizard to lead you along the way to creating a Firewall rule. But as I mentioned, there are two wizards to choose from:

Basic Firewall   If your goal is to connect your network that's composed only of host machines, no servers, or servers that you don't want to communicate with the outside world (e.g., the Internet), this is your wizard. To illustrate this fact further, after you've chosen Basic Firewall, a little diagram will come into view at the right. Next, just click Launch and voilà!

Advanced Firewall   This is your go-to wizard for connecting a network that's populated with both host machines and servers in which your servers need to access outside hosts like those found on the Internet. Again, after you've chosen this wizard, you'll see the little diagram at the right depicting your network. So basically, with any network that includes web, email, or other servers that need to communicate via the Internet, choose Advanced Firewall, then just click Launch.

The first screen is the Create Firewall screen.

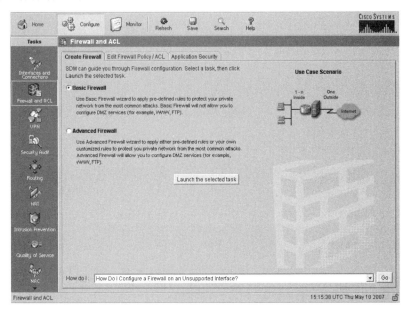

From here, I'm choosing to connect up and create a basic firewall. Then I clicked the Launch the Selected Task button. The next screen tells me what the Basic Firewall Configuration Wizard is going to do.

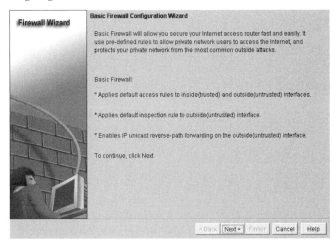

Wow—it looks like it is going to do a whole lot, and you know what? It will! I then just click Next, and from this next screen I am able to choose my inside and outside addresses—trusted and untrusted interfaces.

Once I finish choosing my inside and outside interfaces, I click Next and a ton of access-list test statements are applied to my router—nice!

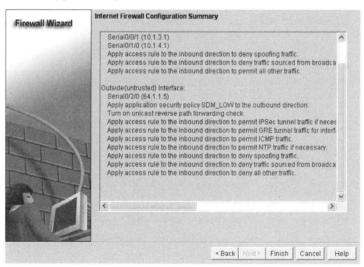

Then I click Finish, and it asks me if I want my configured routing protocol through the outside interface.

I click OK. (Trust me, you may not want to do this in a production network.) I then receive a "You've successfully configured firewall on your router" screen. Am I dreaming or did this really work? Well, let's see. After clicking OK, I get this screen.

Wow, looks that way. It took just a few clicks to set up a firewall on my router! But I really want to see what it put in my running-config. Let's check it out:

```
Corp#sh run
Building configuration...
[output cut]
!
```

```
ip inspect name SDM_LOW cuseeme
ip inspect name SDM_LOW dns
ip inspect name SDM_LOW ftp
ip inspect name SDM_LOW h323
ip inspect name SDM_LOW https
ip inspect name SDM_LOW icmp
ip inspect name SDM_LOW imap
ip inspect name SDM_LOW pop3
ip inspect name SDM_LOW netshow
ip inspect name SDM_LOW rcmd
ip inspect name SDM_LOW realaudio
ip inspect name SDM_LOW rtsp
ip inspect name SDM_LOW esmtp
ip inspect name SDM_LOW sqlnet
ip inspect name SDM_LOW streamworks
ip inspect name SDM_LOW tftp
ip inspect name SDM_LOW tcp
ip inspect name SDM_LOW udp
ip inspect name SDM_LOW vdolive
!
```
[output cut]

So what the Basic Firewall Configuration Wizard added was the IOS firewall that's also called CBAC, or Context-Based Access Control. Cisco just calls it the IOS Firewall now—something I told you earlier.

The `ip inspect` command turned on basic application inspection for mitigating attacks to each individual application.

Notice that each of these `inspect` statements adds a separate protocol to the list. Without the wizard, you get to manually pick the protocols you want to deal with, but using the SDM wizard makes it so much easier, it's still the better way to go. The Basic Firewall Configuration Wizard limits you to two interfaces. Check out the interface it was applied to:

```
!
interface Serial0/2/0
 description Connection to R3$FW_OUTSIDE$
 ip address 64.1.1.5 255.255.255.252
 ip access-group 103 in
 ip verify unicast reverse-path
 ip nat outside
 ip inspect SDM_LOW out
 ip virtual-reassembly
 clock rate 2000000
!
```

The `ip inspect SDM_LOW out` is where the inspect process was applied. Let's take a look at rest of the configuration that SDM threw into the mix:

```
!
access-list 100 remark auto generated by SDM firewall configuration
access-list 100 remark SDM_ACL Category=1
access-list 100 deny    ip 10.1.3.0 0.0.0.255 any
access-list 100 deny    ip 64.1.1.4 0.0.0.3 any
access-list 100 deny    ip 10.1.4.0 0.0.0.255 any
access-list 100 deny    ip host 255.255.255.255 any
access-list 100 deny    ip 127.0.0.0 0.255.255.255 any
access-list 100 permit ip any any
access-list 101 remark auto generated by SDM firewall configuration
access-list 101 remark SDM_ACL Category=1
access-list 101 deny    ip 10.1.2.0 0.0.0.255 any
access-list 101 deny    ip 64.1.1.4 0.0.0.3 any
access-list 101 deny    ip 10.1.4.0 0.0.0.255 any
access-list 101 deny    ip host 255.255.255.255 any
access-list 101 deny    ip 127.0.0.0 0.255.255.255 any
access-list 101 permit ip any any
access-list 102 remark auto generated by SDM firewall configuration
access-list 102 remark SDM_ACL Category=1
access-list 102 deny    ip 10.1.3.0 0.0.0.255 any
access-list 102 deny    ip 10.1.2.0 0.0.0.255 any
access-list 102 deny    ip 64.1.1.4 0.0.0.3 any
access-list 102 deny    ip host 255.255.255.255 any
access-list 102 deny    ip 127.0.0.0 0.255.255.255 any
access-list 102 permit ip any any
```

Notice that ACLs 100–102 are inbound on an inside interface. These ACLs define the traffic that's allowed out and also what's allowed to pass through the inspect firewall. Each ACL denies all the networks that the router knows about as well as the loopback address, leaving only the network that's attached to this interface with permission to be a source address coming into the interface. Let's take a look at the last list the SDM created:

```
access-list 103 remark auto generated by SDM firewall configuration
access-list 103 remark SDM_ACL Category=1
access-list 103 deny    ip 10.1.3.0 0.0.0.255 any
access-list 103 deny    ip 10.1.2.0 0.0.0.255 any
access-list 103 deny    ip 10.1.4.0 0.0.0.255 any
access-list 103 permit icmp any host 64.1.1.5 echo-reply
access-list 103 permit icmp any host 64.1.1.5 time-exceeded
```

```
access-list 103 permit icmp any host 64.1.1.5 unreachable
access-list 103 permit ospf any any
access-list 103 deny    ip 10.0.0.0 0.255.255.255 any
access-list 103 deny    ip 172.16.0.0 0.15.255.255 any
access-list 103 deny    ip 192.168.0.0 0.0.255.255 any
access-list 103 deny    ip 127.0.0.0 0.255.255.255 any
access-list 103 deny    ip host 255.255.255.255 any
access-list 103 deny    ip host 0.0.0.0 any
access-list 103 deny    ip any any log
!
```

You can see that test statement 103 is denying a bit more stuff. First, notice this is your outside and that every network located on the inside, plus all the private ranges, are denied from entering. List 103 is allowing some ICMP and the OSPF traffic but that's it. Right now, even if traffic from the trusted interface went out, the return traffic would be denied. But this is what the firewall process is for—when trusted traffic goes out, the state info is put in the table and a dynamic ACL entry is written for this ACL so that the return traffic gets allowed back in instead of locked out!

Well, it appears that sometimes dreams really do come true—all I did was click a couple of little buttons, and Shazam! Kind of seems like I could have skipped this chapter, huh. Sorry, but you really need to understand the concepts of access lists, and this chapter gave you some major goods on that stuff!

But we still need to take a quick look at the Advanced Firewall Configuration Wizard. After going back to the Firewall and ACL configure button and clicking Advanced Firewall, I received this screen.

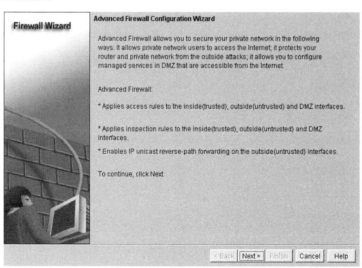

There are a couple differences between the Advanced Firewall Wizard and the Basic Firewall Wizard. The advanced wizard applies the access rules to the inside, outside, and DMZ interfaces, but the Basic Firewall Wizard applies the access rules only to the inside and outside interfaces—DMZ interfaces are not configured using the basic wizard. Another difference is that the advanced wizard applies inspection rules to all inside, outside, and DMZ interfaces, whereas the basic one applies the inspection rules only to the outside interfaces.

The next screen tells me to pick my inside, outside, and DMZ interfaces.

Once you do this, you don't get to access SDM using any of the router's outside interfaces. The rest of the wizard works pretty much the same way as the basic one does, only you end up with a more advanced configuration on your router—one that's beyond the objectives of this book. I highly recommend downloading a copy of the SDM (discussed in Chapter 4). Play around with and familiarize yourself with this GUI as much as possible!

As I've mentioned, the SDM is useful for advanced configurations like ACLs, NAT, and VPNs, and the previous output shows that by just understanding which interfaces are inside your network and which interfaces are outside of it, you can configure ACLs and firewall security like a seasoned pro.

Summary

In this chapter I covered how to configure standard access lists to properly filter IP traffic. You learned what a standard access list is and how to apply it to a Cisco router to add security to your network. You also learned how to configure extended access lists to further filter IP traffic. I also discussed the differences between standard and extended access lists, as well as how to apply them to Cisco routers.

I then moved on to show you how to configure named access lists and apply them to interfaces on the router. Named access lists offer the advantage of being readily identifiable and, therefore, a whole lot easier to manage than access lists that are simply referred to by obscure numbers.

We then covered how to monitor and verify selected access-list operations on both the router and a switch. And we went over some basic monitoring commands to verify both IP and MAC access lists.

Last, I showed you how easy it really is to create both ACLs and firewall policies for a router using the SDM. And my friends, I tell you no lie when I say that this is where SDM truly shines!

Exam Essentials

Remember the standard and extended IP access-list number ranges.   The number ranges you can use to configure a standard IP access list are 1–99 and 1300–1999. The number ranges for an extended IP access list are 100–199 and 2000–2699.

Understand the term *implicit deny*.   At the end of every access list is an implicit deny. What this means is that if a packet does not match any of the lines in the access list, then it will be discarded. Also, if you have nothing but deny statements in your list, the list will not permit any packets.

Understand the standard IP access-list configuration command.   To configure a standard IP access list, use the access-list numbers 1–99 or 1300–1999 in global configuration mode. Choose permit or deny, then choose the source IP address you want to filter on using one of the three techniques covered in this chapter.

Understand the extended IP access-list configuration command.   To configure an extended IP access list, use the access-list numbers 100–199 or 2000–2699 in global configuration mode. Choose permit or deny, the Network layer protocol field, the source IP address you want to filter on, the destination address you want to filter on, and finally the Transport layer port number (if selected).

Remember the command to verify an access list on a router interface.   To see whether an access list is set on an interface and in which direction it is filtering, use the show ip interface command. This command will not show you the contents of the access list, merely which access lists are applied on the interface.

Remember the command to verify the access-list configuration.   To see the configured access lists on your router, use the show access-list command. This command will not show you which interfaces have an access list set.

Written Lab 10.1

In this section, write the answers to the following questions:

1. What command would you use to configure a standard IP access list to prevent all machines on network 172.16.0.0 from accessing your Ethernet network?

2. What command would you use to apply the access list you created in question 1 to an Ethernet interface?

3. What command would you use to create an access list that denies host 192.168.15.5 access to an Ethernet network?

4. Which command verifies that you've entered the access list correctly?

5. Which two commands verify that the access list was properly applied to the Ethernet interface?

6. What command would you use to create an extended access list that stops host 172.16.10.1 from telnetting to host 172.16.30.5?

7. What command would you use to set an access list on a VTY line?

8. From question 1, write the same standard IP access list as a named access list.

9. From question 2, write the command to apply the named access list you created to an interface.

10. Which command verifies the placement and direction of an access list?

(The answers to Written Lab 10 can be found following the answers to the review questions for this chapter.)

Hands-on Labs

In this section, you will complete two labs. To complete these labs, you will need at least three routers. If you are using the RouterSim or Sybex software programs, please use the labs found in those programs.

Lab 10.1: Standard IP Access Lists

Lab 10.2: Extended IP Access Lists

All of the labs will use the following diagram for configuring the routers.

Hands-on Lab 10.1: Standard IP Access Lists

In this lab, you will allow only packets from Host_B from network 172.16.30.0 to enter network 172.16.10.0.

1. Go to Lab_A and enter global configuration mode by typing **config t**.

2. From global configuration mode, type **access-list ?** to get a list of all the different access lists available.

3. Choose an access-list number that will allow you to create an IP standard access list. This is a number between 1 and 99 or 1300 and 1399.

4. Choose to permit host 172.16.30.2, which is Host_B's address:

    ```
    Lab_A(config)#access-list 10 permit 172.16.30.2 ?
      A.B.C.D  Wildcard bits
      <cr>
    ```

    To specify only host 172.16.30.2, use the wildcards 0.0.0.0:

    ```
    Lab_A(config)#access-list 10 permit 172.16.30.2
      0.0.0.0
    ```

5. Now that the access list is created, you must apply it to an interface to make it work:

    ```
    Lab_A(config)#int f0/0
    Lab_A(config-if)#ip access-group 10 out
    ```

6. Verify your access list with the following commands:

    ```
    Lab_A#sh access-list
    Standard IP access list 10
        permit 172.16.30.2
    Lab_A#sh run
    [output cut]
    interface FastEthernet0/0
     ip address 172.16.10.1 255.255.255.0
     ip access-group 10 out
    ```

7. Test your access list by pinging from Host_B (172.16.30.2) to Host_A (172.16.10.2).

8. Ping from Lab_B and Lab_C to Host_A (172.16.10.2); this should fail if your access list is correct.

Hands-on Lab 10.2: Extended IP Access Lists

In this lab, you will use an extended IP access list to stop host 172.16.10.2 from creating a Telnet session to router Lab_B (172.16.20.2). However, the host still should be able to ping the

Lab_B router. IP extended lists should be placed close to the source, so add the extended list on router Lab_A.

1. Remove any access lists on Lab_A and add an extended list to Lab_A.

2. Choose a number to create an extended IP list. The IP extended lists use 100–199 or 2000–2699.

3. Use a deny statement. (You'll add a `permit` statement in step 7 to allow other traffic to still work.)

    ```
    Lab_A(config)#access-list 110 deny ?
      <0-255>  An IP protocol number
      ahp      Authentication Header Protocol
      eigrp    Cisco's EIGRP routing protocol
      esp      Encapsulation Security Payload
      gre      Cisco's GRE tunneling
      icmp     Internet Control Message Protocol
      igmp     Internet Gateway Message Protocol
      igrp     Cisco's IGRP routing protocol
      ip       Any Internet Protocol
      ipinip   IP in IP tunneling
      nos      KA9Q NOS compatible IP over IP tunneling
      ospf     OSPF routing protocol
      pcp      Payload Compression Protocol
      tcp      Transmission Control Protocol
      udp      User Datagram Protocol
    ```

4. Since you are going to deny Telnet, you must choose TCP as a Transport layer protocol:

    ```
    Lab_A(config)#access-list 110 deny tcp ?
      A.B.C.D  Source address
      any      Any source host
      host     A single source host
    ```

5. Add the source IP address you want to filter on, then add the destination host IP address. Use the `host` command instead of wildcard bits.

    ```
    Lab_A(config)#access-list 110 deny tcp host
    172.16.10.2 host 172.16.20.2 ?
      ack          Match on the ACK bit
      eq           Match only packets on a given port
                   number
      established  Match established connections
      fin          Match on the FIN bit
    ```

fragments	Check fragments
gt	Match only packets with a greater port number
log	Log matches against this entry
log-input	Log matches against this entry, including input interface
lt	Match only packets with a lower port number
neq	Match only packets not on a given port number
precedence	Match packets with given precedence value
psh	Match on the PSH bit
range	Match only packets in the range of port numbers
rst	Match on the RST bit
syn	Match on the SYN bit
tos	Match packets with given TOS value
urg	Match on the URG bit
\<cr\>	

6. At this point, you can add the eq telnet command to filter host 172.16.10.2 from telnetting to 172.16.20.2. The log command can also be used at the end of the command so that whenever the access-list line is hit, a log will be generated on the console.

   Lab_A(config)#**access-list 110 deny tcp host**
   172.16.10.2 host 172.16.20.2 eq telnet log

7. It is important to add this line next to create a permit statement. (Remember that 0.0.0.0 255.255.255.255 is the same as the any command.)

   Lab_A(config)#**access-list 110 permit ip any 0.0.0.0**
   255.255.255.255

   You must create a permit statement; if you just add a deny statement, nothing will be permitted at all. Please see the sections earlier in this chapter for more detailed information on the permit command.

8. Apply the access list to the FastEthernet0/0 on Lab_A to stop the Telnet traffic as soon as it hits the first router interface.

   Lab_A(config)#**int f0/0**
   Lab_A(config-if)#**ip access-group 110 in**
   Lab_A(config-if)#**^Z**

9. Try telnetting from host 172.16.10.2 to Lab_A using the destination IP address of 172.16.20.2. The following messages should be generated on Lab_A's console; however, the ping command should work:

```
From host 172.16.10.2: C:\>telnet 172.16.20.2
```

On Lab_A's console, this should appear as follows:

```
01:11:48: %SEC-6-IPACCESSLOGP: list 110 denied tcp
  172.16.10.2(1030) -> 172.16.20.2(23), 1 packet
01:13:04: %SEC-6-IPACCESSLOGP: list 110 denied tcp
  172.16.10.2(1030) -> 172.16.20.2(23), 3 packets
```

Review Questions

 The following questions are designed to test your understanding of this chapter's material. For more information on how to get additional questions, please see this book's Introduction.

1. Which of the following is an example of a standard IP access list?

   A. access-list 110 permit host 1.1.1.1

   B. access-list 1 deny 172.16.10.1 0.0.0.0

   C. access-list 1 permit 172.16.10.1 255.255.0.0

   D. access-list standard 1.1.1.1

2. You need to create an access list that will prevent hosts in the network range of 192.168.160.0 to 192.168.191.0. Which of the following lists will you use?

   A. access-list 10 deny 192.168.160.0 255.255.224.0

   B. access-list 10 deny 192.168.160.0 0.0.191.255

   C. access-list 10 deny 192.168.160.0 0.0.31.255

   D. access-list 10 deny 192.168.0.0 0.0.31.255

3. You have created a named access list called Blocksales. Which of the following is a valid command for applying this to packets trying to enter interface s0 of your router?

   A. (config)#ip access-group 110 in

   B. (config-if)#ip access-group 110 in

   C. (config-if)#ip access-group Blocksales in

   D. (config-if)#blocksales ip access-list in

4. Which of the following are valid ways to refer only to host 172.16.30.55 in an IP access list? (Choose two.)

   A. 172.16.30.55 0.0.0.255

   B. 172.16.30.55 0.0.0.0

   C. any 172.16.30.55

   D. host 172.16.30.55

   E. 0.0.0.0 172.16.30.55

   F. ip any 172.16.30.55

5. Which of the following access lists will allow only HTTP traffic into network 196.15.7.0?

A. `access-list 100 permit tcp any 196.15.7.0 0.0.0.255 eq www`

B. `access-list 10 deny tcp any 196.15.7.0 eq www`

C. `access-list 100 permit 196.15.7.0 0.0.0.255 eq www`

D. `access-list 110 permit ip any 196.15.7.0 0.0.0.255`

E. `access-list 110 permit www 196.15.7.0 0.0.0.255`

6. What router command allows you to determine whether an IP access list is enabled on a particular interface?

A. `show ip port`

B. `show access-lists`

C. `show ip interface`

D. `show access-lists interface`

7. Which router command allows you to view the entire contents of all access lists?

A. Router#**show interface**

B. Router>**show ip interface**

C. Router#**show access-lists**

D. Router>**show all access-lists**

8. If you wanted to deny all Telnet connections to only network 192.168.10.0, which command could you use?

A. `access-list 100 deny tcp 192.168.10.0 255.255.255.0 eq telnet`

B. `access-list 100 deny tcp 192.168.10.0 0.255.255.255 eq telnet`

C. `access-list 100 deny tcp any 192.168.10.0 0.0.0.255 eq 23`

D. `access-list 100 deny 192.168.10.0 0.0.0.255 any eq 23`

9. If you wanted to deny FTP access from network 200.200.10.0 to network 200.199.11.0 but allow everything else, which of the following command strings is valid?

A. `access-list 110 deny 200.200.10.0 to network 200.199.11.0 eq ftp`
   `access-list 111 permit ip any 0.0.0.0 255.255.255.255`

B. `access-list 1 deny ftp 200.200.10.0 200.199.11.0 any any`

C. `access-list 100 deny tcp 200.200.10.0 0.0.0.255 200.199.11.0 0.0.0.255 eq ftp`

D. `access-list 198 deny tcp 200.200.10.0 0.0.0.255 200.199.11.0 0.0.0.255 eq ftp`
   `access-list 198 permit ip any 0.0.0.0 255.255.255.255`

10. You want to create a standard access list that denies the subnet of the following host: 172.16.50.172/20. Which of the following would you start your list with?

A. `access-list 10 deny 172.16.48.0 255.255.240.0`

B. `access-list 10 deny 172.16.0.0 0.0.255.255`

C. `access-list 10 deny 172.16.64.0 0.0.31.255`

D. `access-list 10 deny 172.16.48.0 0.0.15.255`

11. Which command would you use to apply an access list to a router interface?

    A. `ip access-list 101 out`

    B. `access-list ip 101 in`

    C. `ip access-group 101 in`

    D. `access-group ip 101 in`

12. You want to create a standard access list that denies the subnet of the following host: 172.16.198.94/19. Which of the following would you start your list with?

    A. `access-list 10 deny 172.16.192.0 0.0.31.255`

    B. `access-list 10 deny 172.16.0.0 0.0.255.255`

    C. `access-list 10 deny 172.16.172.0 0.0.31.255`

    D. `access-list 10 deny 172.16.188.0 0.0.15.255`

13. You want to create a standard access list that denies the subnet of the following host: 172.16.144.17/21. Which of the following would you start your list with?

    A. `access-list 10 deny 172.16.48.0 255.255.240.0`

    B. `access-list 10 deny 172.16.144.0 0.0.7.255`

    C. `access-list 10 deny 172.16.64.0 0.0.31.255`

    D. `access-list 10 deny 172.16.136.0 0.0.15.255`

14. Which of the following commands connect access list 110 inbound to interface ethernet0?

    A. `Router(config)#`**`ip access-group 110 in`**

    B. `Router(config)#`**`ip access-list 110 in`**

    C. `Router(config-if)#`**`ip access-group 110 in`**

    D. `Router(config-if)#`**`ip access-list 110 in`**

15. What command will permit SMTP mail to only host 1.1.1.1?

    A. `access-list 10 permit smtp host 1.1.1.1`

    B. `access-list 110 permit ip smtp host 1.1.1.1`

    C. `access-list 10 permit tcp any host 1.1.1.1 eq smtp`

    D. `access-list 110 permit tcp any host 1.1.1.1 eq smtp`

16. You configure the following access list:

    ```
    access-list 110 deny tcp 10.1.1.128 0.0.0.63 any eq smtp
    access-list 110 deny tcp any eq 23
    int ethernet 0
    ip access-group 110 out
    ```

    What will the result of this access list be?

    A. Email and Telnet will be allowed out E0.

    B. Email and Telnet will be allowed in E0.

    C. Everything but email and Telnet will be allowed out E0.

    D. No IP traffic will be allowed out E0.

17. Which of the following series of commands will restrict Telnet access to the router?

    A. Lab_A(config)#**access-list 10 permit 172.16.1.1**
        Lab_A(config)#**line con 0**
        Lab_A(config-line)#**ip access-group 10 in**

    B. Lab_A(config)#**access-list 10 permit 172.16.1.1**
        Lab_A(config)#**line vty 0 4**
        Lab_A(config-line)#**access-class 10 out**

    C. Lab_A(config)#**access-list 10 permit 172.16.1.1**
        Lab_A(config)#**line vty 0 4**
        Lab_A(config-line)#**access-class 10 in**

    D. Lab_A(config)#**access-list 10 permit 172.16.1.1**
        Lab_A(config)#**line vty 0 4**
        Lab_A(config-line)#**ip access-group 10 in**

18. Which of the following is true regarding access lists applied to an interface?

    A. You can place as many access lists as you want on any interface until you run out of memory.

    B. You can apply only one access list on any interface.

    C. One access list may be configured, per direction, for each layer 3 protocol configured on an interface.

    D. You can apply two access lists to any interface.

19. You are working on a router that has established privilege levels that restrict access to certain functions. You discover that you are not able to execute the command show running-configuration. How can you view and confirm the access lists that have been applied to the Ethernet 0 interface on your router?

    A. show access-lists

    B. show interface Ethernet 0

    C. show ip access-lists

    D. show ip interface Ethernet 0

20. You want users from the accounting LAN to not have access to the Human Resources server. The following access list has been created:

```
Access-list 10 deny 192.168.10.128 0.0.0.31
Access-list 10 permit any
```

According to the following diagram, which interface of which router, and in which direction, should the access list be placed to prevent accounting users from accessing the network attached to the E0 interface of Lab_B?

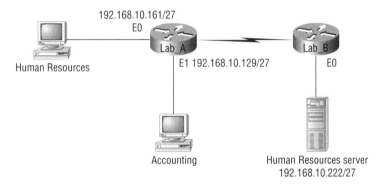

A. Lab_A, S0 out

B. Lab_A, E1 in

C. Lab_A, E1 out

D. Lab_B, S1 in

E. Lab_B, E0 out

F. Lab_B, E0 in

Answers to Review Questions

1. B. Standard IP access lists use the numbers 1–99 and 1300–1999 and filter based on source IP address only. Option C is incorrect because the mask must be in wildcard format.

2. C. The range of 192.168.160.0 to 192.168.191.0 is a block size of 32. The network address is 192.168.160.0 and the mask would be 255.255.224.0, which for an access list must be a wildcard format of 0.0.31.255. The 31 is used for a block size of 32. The wildcard is always one less than the block size.

3. C. Using a named access list just replaces the number used when applying the list to the router's interface. ip access-group Blocksales in is correct.

4. B, D. The wildcard 0.0.0.0 tells the router to match all four octets. This wildcard format alone can be replaced with the host command.

5. A. The first thing to check in a question like this is the access-list number. Right away, you can see that the second option is wrong because it is using a standard IP access-list number. The second thing to check is the protocol. If you are filtering by upper-layer protocol, then you must be using either UDP or TCP; this eliminates the fourth option. The third and last answers have the wrong syntax.

6. C. Only the show ip interface command will tell you which interfaces have access lists applied. show access-lists will not show you which interfaces have an access list applied.

7. C. The show access-lists command will allow you to view the entire contents of all access lists, but it will not show you the interfaces to which the access lists are applied.

8. C. The extended access list ranges are 100–199 and 2000–2699, so the access-list number of 100 is valid. Telnet uses TCP, so the protocol TCP is valid. Now you just need to look for the source and destination address. Only the third option has the correct sequence of parameters. Answer B may work, but the question specifically states "only" to network 192.168.10.0, and the wildcard in answer B is too broad.

9. D. Extended IP access lists use numbers 100–199 and 2000–2699 and filter based on source and destination IP address, protocol number, and port number. The last option is correct because of the second line that specifies permit ip any any. (I used 0.0.0.0 255.255.255.255, which is the same as the any option.) The third option does not have this, so it would deny access but not allow everything else.

10. D. First, you must know that a /20 is 255.255.240.0, which is a block size of 16 in the third octet. Counting by 16s, this makes our subnet 48 in the third octet, and the wildcard for the third octet would be 15 since the wildcard is always one less than the block size.

11. C. To apply an access list, the proper command is ip access-group 101 in.

12. A. First, you must know that a /19 is 255.255.224.0, which is a block size of 32 in the third octet. Counting by 32, this makes our subnet 192 in the third octet, and the wildcard for the third octet would be 31 since the wildcard is always one less than the block size.

13. B. First, you must know that a /21 is 255.255.248.0, which is a block size of 8 in the third octet. Counting by eight, this makes our subnet 144 in the third octet, and the wildcard for the third octet would be 7 since the wildcard is always one less than the block size.

14. C. To place an access list on an interface, use the `ip access-group` command in interface configuration mode.

15. D. When trying to find the best answer to an access-list question, always check the access-list number and then the protocol. When filtering to an upper-layer protocol, you must use an extended list, numbers 100–199 and 2000–2699. Also, when you filter to an upper-layer protocol, you must use either `tcp` or `udp` in the protocol field. If it says `ip` in the protocol field, you cannot filter to an upper-layer protocol. SMTP uses TCP.

16. D. If you add an access list to an interface and you do not have at least one `permit` statement, then you will effectively shut down the interface because of the implicit `deny any` at the end of every list.

17. C. Telnet access to the router is restricted by using either a standard or extended IP access list inbound on the VTY lines of the router. The command `access-class` is used to apply the access list to the VTY lines.

18. C. A Cisco router has rules regarding the placement of access lists on a router interface. You can place one access list per direction for each layer 3 protocol configured on an interface.

19. D. The only command that shows which access lists have been applied to an interface is `show ip interface Ethernet 0`. The command `show access-lists` displays all configured access lists, and `show ip access-lists` displays all configured IP access lists, but neither command indicates whether the displayed access lists have been applied to an interface.

20. E. On a standard access list, you should place the access list as close to the destination as possible. In this example, that is "out, Ethernet 0" of the Lab_B router.

Answers to Written Lab 10.1

1. access-list 10 deny 172.16.0.0 0.0.255.255

   access-list 10 permit any

2. ip access-group 10 out

3. access-list 10 deny host 192.168.15.5

   access-list 10 permit any

4. show access-lists

5. show running-config

   sh ip interface

6. access-list 110 deny tcp host

   172.16.10.1 host   172.16.30.5 eq 23

   access-list 110 permit ip any any

7. line vty 0 4

   access-class 110 in

8. ip access-list standard No172Net

   deny 172.16.0.0 0.0.255.255

   permit any

9. ip access-group No172Net out

10. show ip interfaces

Chapter

11

Network Address Translation (NAT)

THE CCNA EXAM TOPICS COVERED IN THIS CHAPTER INCLUDE THE FOLLOWING:

✓ **Implement, verify, and troubleshoot NAT and ACLs in a medium-size Enterprise branch office network**

- Explain the basic operation of NAT

- Configure NAT for given network requirements using (including: CLI/SDM)

- Troubleshoot NAT issues

In this chapter, I am going to give you the skinny on Network Address Translation (NAT), Dynamic NAT, and Port Address Translation (PAT), also known as NAT Overload. Of course, I'll demonstrate NAT on the internetwork I've been using throughout the book, and then I'm going to finish this chapter by using SDM so you can see how NAT can be configured the easy way.

It will be helpful for you to read Chapter 10 before reading this chapter since we need to use access lists in our NAT configurations.

For up-to-the minute updates for this chapter, please see www.lammle.com and/or www.sybex.com.

When Do We Use NAT?

Similar to Classless Inter-Domain Routing (CIDR), the original intention for NAT was to slow the depletion of available IP address space by allowing many private IP addresses to be represented by some smaller number of public IP addresses.

Since then, it's been discovered that NAT is also a useful tool for network migrations and mergers, server load sharing, and creating "virtual servers." So in this chapter, I'm going to describe the basics of NAT functionality and the terminology common to NAT.

At times, NAT really decreases the overwhelming amount of public IP addresses required in your networking environment. And NAT comes in really handy when two companies that have duplicate internal addressing schemes merge. NAT is also great to have around when an organization changes its Internet service provider (ISP) and the networking manager doesn't want the hassle of changing the internal address scheme.

Here's a list of situations when it's best to have NAT on your side:

- You need to connect to the Internet and your hosts don't have globally unique IP addresses.

- You change to a new ISP that requires you to renumber your network.

- You need to merge two intranets with duplicate addresses.

You typically use NAT on a border router. For an illustration of this, see Figure 11.1.

Now you may be thinking, "NAT's totally cool. It's the grooviest greatest network gadget and I just gotta have it." Well, hang on a minute. There are truly some serious snags related to NAT use. Oh—don't get me wrong: It really can save you sometimes, but there's a dark side you need to know about, too. For a visual of the pros and cons linked to using NAT, check out Table 11.1.

FIGURE 11.1   Where to configure NAT

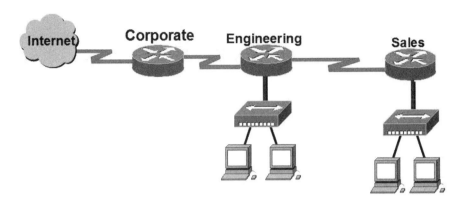

TABLE 11.1   Advantages and Disadvantages of Implementing NAT

Advantages	Disadvantages
Conserves legally registered addresses.	Translation introduces switching path delays.
Reduces address overlap occurrence.	Loss of end-to-end IP traceability.
Increases flexibility when connecting to Internet.	Certain applications will not function with NAT enabled.
Eliminates address renumbering as network changes.	

 The most obvious advantage associated with NAT is that it allows you to conserve your legally registered address scheme. This is why we haven't run out of IPv4 addresses—think about it.

Types of Network Address Translation

In this section, I'm going to go over the three types of NAT with you:

Static NAT   This type of NAT is designed to allow one-to-one mapping between local and global addresses. Keep in mind that the static version requires you to have one real Internet IP address for every host on your network.

Dynamic NAT   This version gives you the ability to map an unregistered IP address to a registered IP address from out of a pool of registered IP addresses. You don't have to statically configure your router to map an inside to an outside address as you would using static NAT, but you do have to have enough real, bona-fide IP addresses for everyone who's going to be sending packets to and receiving them from the Internet.

Overloading   This is the most popular type of NAT configuration. Understand that overloading really is a form of dynamic NAT that maps multiple unregistered IP addresses to a single registered IP address—many-to-one—by using different ports. Now, why is this so special? Well, because it's also known as *Port Address Translation (PAT)*. And by using PAT (NAT Overload), you get to have thousands of users connect to the Internet using only one real global IP address— pretty slick, yeah? Seriously, NAT Overload is the real reason we haven't run out of valid IP address on the Internet. Really—I'm not joking.

Don't worry, I'll show you how to configure all three types of NAT toward the end of this chapter.

NAT Names

The names we use to describe the addresses used with NAT are pretty simple. Addresses used after NAT translations are called *global* addresses. These are usually the public addresses used on the Internet, but remember, you don't need public addresses if you aren't going on the Internet.

Local addresses are the ones we use before NAT translation. So, the inside local address is actually the private address of the sending host that's trying to get to the Internet, while the outside local address is the address of the destination host. The latter is usually a public address (web address, mail server, etc.) and is how the packet begins its journey.

After translation, the inside local address is then called the *inside global address* and the outside global address then becomes the name of the destination host. Check out Table 11.2, which lists all this terminology, for a clear picture of the various names used with NAT.

TABLE 11.2   NAT Terms

Names	Meaning
Inside local	Name of inside source address before translation
Outside local	Name of destination host before translation
Inside global	Name of inside host after translation
Outside global	Name of outside destination host after translation

How NAT Works

Okay, now it's time to look at how this whole NAT thing works. I'm going to start by using Figure 11.2 to describe the basic translation of NAT.

FIGURE 11.2   Basic NAT translation

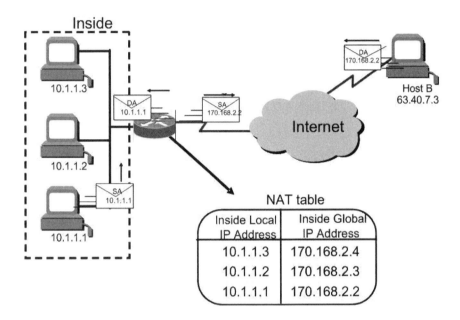

In the example shown in Figure 11.2, host 10.1.1.1 sends an outbound packet to the border router configured with NAT. The router identifies the IP address as an inside local IP address destined for an outside network, translates the address, and documents the translation in the NAT table.

The packet is sent to the outside interface with the new translated source address. The external host returns the packet to the destination host and the NAT router translates the inside global IP address back to the inside local IP address using the NAT table. This is as simple as it gets.

Let's take a look at a more complex configuration using overloading, or what is also referred to as Port Address Translation (PAT). I'll use Figure 11.3 to demonstrate how PAT works.

With overloading, all inside hosts get translated to one single IP address, hence the term *overloading*. Again, the reason we have not run out of available IP addresses on the Internet is because of overloading (PAT).

Take a look at the NAT table in Figure 11.3 again. In addition to the inside local IP address and outside global IP address, we now have port numbers. These port numbers help the router identify which host should receive the return traffic.

FIGURE 11.3   NAT overloading example (PAT)

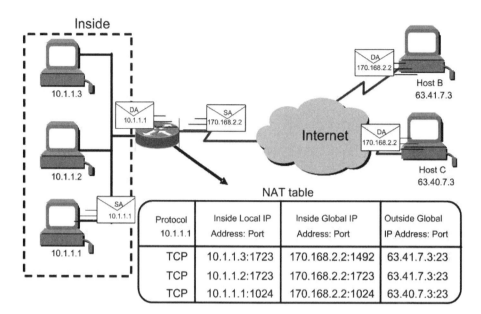

Protocol 10.1.1.1	Inside Local IP Address: Port	Inside Global IP Address: Port	Outside Global IP Address: Port
TCP	10.1.1.3:1723	170.168.2.2:1492	63.41.7.3:23
TCP	10.1.1.2:1723	170.168.2.2:1723	63.41.7.3:23
TCP	10.1.1.1:1024	170.168.2.2:1024	63.40.7.3:23

Port numbers are used at the Transport layer to identify the local host in this example. If we had to use IP addresses to identify the source hosts, that would be called *static NAT* and we would run out of addresses. PAT allows us to use the Transport layer to identify the hosts, which in turn allows us to use (theoretically) up to 65,000 hosts with one real IP address.

Static NAT Configuration

Let's take a look at a simple basic static NAT configuration:

```
ip nat inside source static 10.1.1.1 170.46.2.2
!
interface Ethernet0
 ip address 10.1.1.10 255.255.255.0
 ip nat inside
!
interface Serial0
 ip address 170.46.2.1 255.255.255.0
 ip nat outside
!
```

In the preceding router output, the `ip nat inside source` command identifies which IP addresses will be translated. In this configuration example, the `ip nat inside source` command configures a static translation between the inside local IP address 10.1.1.1 to the outside global IP address 170.46.2.2.

If we look farther down in the configuration, we see that we have an `ip nat` command under each interface. The `ip nat inside` command identifies that interface as the inside interface. The `ip nat outside` command identifies that interface as the outside interface. When you look back at the ip nat inside source command, you see that the command is referencing the inside interface as the source or starting point of the translation. The command could also be used like this—`ip nat outside source`—which is referencing the interface you designated as the outside interface to be the source or starting point for the translation.

Dynamic NAT Configuration

Dynamic NAT means that we have a pool of addresses that we will use to provide real IP addresses to a group of users on the inside. We do not use port numbers, so we have to have real IP addresses for every user trying to get outside the local network.

Here is a sample output of a dynamic NAT configuration:

```
ip nat pool todd 170.168.2.2 170.168.2.254
    netmask 255.255.255.0
ip nat inside source list 1 pool todd
!
interface Ethernet0
 ip address 10.1.1.10 255.255.255.0
 ip nat inside
!
interface Serial0
 ip address 170.168.2.1 255.255.255.0
 ip nat outside
!
access-list 1 permit 10.1.1.0 0.0.0.255
!
```

The `ip nat inside source list 1 pool todd` command tells the router to translate IP addresses that match `access-list 1` to an address found in the IP NAT pool named `todd`. The access list in this case is not being used to permit or deny traffic as we would use it for security reasons to filter traffic. It is being used in this case to select or designate what we often call interesting traffic. When interesting traffic has been matched with the access list, it is pulled into the NAT process to be translated. This is a common use for access lists; they don't always have the dull job of just blocking traffic at an interface.

The `ip nat pool todd 170.168.2.2 170.168.2.254` command creates a pool of addresses that will be distributed to those hosts that require NAT.

PAT (Overloading) Configuration

This last example shows how to configure inside global address overloading. This is the typical NAT that we would use today. It is rare that we would use static or dynamic NAT unless we were statically mapping a server, for example.

Here is a sample output of a PAT configuration:

```
ip nat pool globalnet 170.168.2.1 170.168.2.1
  netmask 255.255.255.0
ip nat inside source list 1 pool globalnet overload
!
interface Ethernet0/0
 ip address 10.1.1.10 255.255.255.0
 ip nat inside
!
interface Serial0/0
 ip address 170.168.2.1 255.255.255.0
 ip nat outside
!
access-list 1 permit 10.1.1.0 0.0.0.255
```

The nice thing about PAT is that the only differences between this configuration and the previous dynamic NAT configuration is that our pool of addresses has shrunk to only one IP address and at the end of our `ip nat inside source` command we included the `overload` command.

Notice in the example that the one IP address that is in the pool for us to use is the IP address of the outside interface. This is perfect if you are configuring NAT Overload for yourself at home or for a small office that only has one IP from your ISP. You could, however, use an additional address such as 170.168.2.2 if you had the address available to you. This could be helpful in a very large implementation where you may have so many internal users that you have to have more than one overloaded IP address on the outside.

Simple Verification of NAT

Once you have configured the type of NAT you are going to use, typically overload (PAT), you need to be able to verify the configuration.

To see basic IP address translation information, use the following command:

Router#**show ip nat translation**

When looking at the IP NAT translations, you may see many translations from the same host to the same host at the destination. This is typical of many connections to the Web.

In addition, you can verify your NAT configuration with the **debug ip nat** command. This output will show the sending address, the translation, and the destination address on each debug line:

Router#**debug ip nat**

How do you clear your NAT entries from the translation table? Use the `clear ip nat translation` command. To clear all entries from the NAT table, use an asterisk (*) at the end of the command.

Testing and Troubleshooting NAT

Cisco's NAT gives you some serious power—and without too much effort, because the configurations are really pretty simple. But we all know nothing's perfect, so in case something goes wrong, you can figure out some of the more common causes by going through this list of possible snags:

- Check the dynamic pools—are they composed of the right scope of addresses?

- Check to see if any dynamic pools overlap.

- Check to see if the addresses used for static mapping and those in the dynamic pools overlap.

- Ensure that your access lists specify the correct addresses for translation.

- Make sure there aren't any addresses left out that need to be there, and ensure none are included that shouldn't be.

- Check to make sure that you've got both the inside and outside interfaces delimited properly.

One thing to keep in mind is that one of the most common problems with a new NAT configuration isn't specific to NAT at all—it usually involves a routing blooper. So, make sure that because you're changing a source or destination address in a packet, your router knows what to do with the new address after the translation!

Supposedly the sky's the limit regarding the number of mappings the NAT table can hold. In reality, however, it comes down to things like memory and CPU or the boundaries set in place by the scope of available addresses or ports that do, in fact, cause there to be limitations placed on the number of entries possible. You see, each NAT mapping devours about 160 bytes of memory. And sometimes—but not very often—the amount of entries has to be limited for the sake of performance or because of policy restrictions. In situations like these, just use the `ip nat translation max-entries` command for help.

Another handy command for troubleshooting is `show ip nat statistics`. Deploying this gives you a summary of the NAT configuration, and it will count the number of active translation types. Also counted are hits to an existing mapping, as well any misses—the latter will result in an attempt to create a mapping. This command will also reveal expired translations. If you want to check into dynamic pools, their types, the total available addresses, how many addresses have been allocated and how many failed, plus the number of translations that have occurred, just use the `pool (refcount)` command.

And did you know you can manually clear dynamic NAT entries from the NAT table? Doing this can come in pretty handy if you need to get rid of a specific rotten entry without sitting around waiting for the time-out to expire. A manual clear also is really useful when you want to clear the whole NAT table to reconfigure a pool of addresses.

You also need to know that the Cisco IOS software just won't allow you to change or delete address pools if any of that pool's addresses are mapped in the NAT table. The `clear ip nat translations` command clears entries—you can indicate a single entry via the global and local address and through TCP and UDP translations (including ports), or you can just type in an asterisk (*) to wipe out the entire table. But know that if you do that, only dynamic entries will be cleared because this command does not remove static entries.

Oh, and there's more—any outside device's packet destination address that happens to be responding to any inside device is known as the IG address. This means that the initial mapping has to be held in the NAT table so that all packets arriving from a specific connection get translated consistently. Holding entries in the NAT table also cuts down on repeated lookups happening each time the same machine sends packets to the same outside destinations on a regular basis.

Here's what I mean: When an entry is placed into the NAT table the first time, a timer begins ticking; the duration of that timer is known as the `translation timeout`. Each time a packet for a given entry translates through the router, the timer gets reset. If the timer expires, the entry will be unceremoniously removed from the NAT table and the dynamically assigned address will then be returned to the pool. Cisco's default translation timeout is 86,400 seconds (24 hours), but you can change that with the command `ip nat translation timeout`.

Before we move on to the configuration section and actually use the commands I just talked about, let's go through a couple of NAT examples and see if you can figure out the configuration that needs to be used. To start, look at Figure 11.4 and ask yourself two things: Where would you implement NAT in this design, and what type of NAT would you configure?

FIGURE 11.4   NAT example

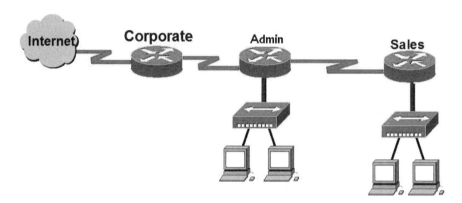

In Figure 11.4, the NAT configuration would be placed on the corporate router and the configuration would be dynamic NAT with overload (PAT). In this NAT example, what type of NAT is being used?

```
ip nat pool todd-nat 170.168.10.10 170.168.10.20 netmask 255.255.255.0
```

The above command uses dynamic NAT. The `pool` in the command gives the answer away, plus there is more than one address in the pool, which means we probably are not using PAT. In the next NAT example, we'll use Figure 11.5 to see if we can figure out the configuration needed.

The example in Figure 11.5 shows a border router that needs to be configured with NAT and will allow the use of six public IP addresses, 192.1.2.109 through 114. However, on the inside network, you have 63 hosts that use the private addresses of 192.168.10.65 through 126. What would your NAT configuration be on the border router?

FIGURE 11.5   Another NAT example

Two different answers would work here, but the following would be my first choice:

```
ip nat pool Todd 192.1.2.109 192.1.2.109 netmask 255.255.255.248
access-list 1 permit 192.168.10.64 0.0.0.63
ip nat inside source list 1 pool Todd overload
```

The command `ip nat pool Todd 192.1.2.109 192.1.2.109 netmask 255.255.255.248` sets the pool name as Todd and creates a dynamic pool of addresses for the NAT to use address 192.1.2.109. Instead of the `netmask` command, you can use the `prefix-length` 29 statement. (And I know what you're thinking, but no, you cannot do this on router interfaces as well.) The second answer would end up with the exact same result of having only 192.1.2.109 as your inside global, but you can type this in and have it work too: `ip nat pool Todd 192.1.2.105 192.1.2.110 netmask 255.255.255.248`. This is a waste because the second through sixth addresses would only be used if there was a conflict with a TCP port number.

If you do not understand the second line where the `access-list` is set, please see Chapter 10, "Security."

The command `ip nat inside source list 1 pool Todd overload` sets the dynamic pool to use Port Address Translation (PAT) by using the `overload` command.

Be sure to add the `ip nat inside` and `ip nat outside` statements on the appropriate interfaces.

Configuring NAT on Our Internetwork

Okay, now I'm going to go ahead and connect the link between our Corp router and the R3 router using a 64.1.1.4/30 network and the LAN F0/0 link on the R3 router using the 64.1.1.8/30 network. After NAT is working, I'll then walk you through the verification commands I've been talking about throughout this chapter.

Our internetwork is shown in Figure 11.6, and the inside local addresses that I've been using throughout this book are shown in Table 11.3.

FIGURE 11.6 Our internetwork with new addressing

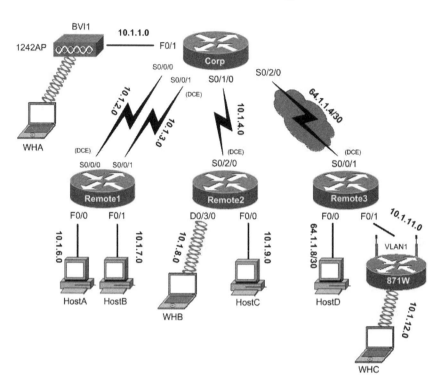

I know—Figure 11.6 shows the same network we've been using, but there's a difference here. The connection between the Corp router and the R3 router is now using global PAT addresses. They can't talk because the other Corp connections have private IP addresses. (In the real world, the ISP would block these, right? So let's make this work!) Remember, we call them "inside locals" when using NAT, meaning before translation, and our ISP is blocking the private IP address ranges. What do we do? Well first we need to configure NAT on the Corp router, so let's get to work!

TABLE 11.3 Network Addressing for the IP Network

Router	Network Address	Interface	Address
Corp			
Corp	10.1.1.0	F0/1	10.1.1.1
Corp	10.1.2.0	S0/0/0	10.1.2.1

TABLE 11.3   Network Addressing for the IP Network *(continued)*

Router	Network Address	Interface	Address
Corp	10.1.3.0	S0/0/1(DCE)	10.1.3.1
Corp	10.1.4.0	S0/1/0	10.1.4.1
Corp	64.1.1.4/30	S0/2/0	64.1.1.5/30
R1			
R1	10.1.2.0	S0/0/0 (DCE)	10.1.2.2
R1	10.1.3.0	S0/0/1	10.1.3.2
R1	10.1.6.0	F0/0	10.1.6.1
R1	10.1.7.0	F0/1	10.1.7.1
R2			
R2	10.1.4.0	S0/2/0 (DCE)	10.1.4.2
R2	10.1.8.0	D0/3/0	10.1.8.1
R2	10.1.9.0	F0/0	10.1.9.1
R3			
R3	64.1.1.4/30	S0/0/1 (DCE)	64.1.1.6/30
R3	64.1.1.8/30	F0/0	64.1.1.9/30
R3	10.1.11.0	F0/1	10.1.11.1
871W			
871W	10.1.11.0	Vlan 1	10.1.11.2
871W	10.1.12.0	Dot11radio0	10.1.12.1
1242 AP			
1242 AP	10.1.1.0	BVI 1	10.1.1.2

Now we all know we need to be able to communicate from all the networks connected to the Corp router out to all the networks connected to the R3 router using the new global address of 64.1.1.5/30. Right? You're nodding your head yes—good! Here we go:

```
Corp#config t
Corp(config)#ip nat pool Todd 64.1.1.5 64.1.1.5 net 255.255.255.252
Corp(config)#access-list 1 permit 10.1.0.0 0.0.255.255
Corp(config)#ip nat inside source list 1 pool Todd overload
```

Before I add the interface configurations, notice I used the IP address of the Corp's outside interface 64.1.1.5 as both a start and finish address of the pool. I did that because it works just fine when using PAT.

Anyway, it's important not to forget to configure NAT on all interfaces:

```
Corp(config)#int s0/2/0
Corp(config-if)#ip nat outside
Corp(config-if)#int f0/1
Corp(config-if)#ip nat inside
Corp(config-if)#int s0/0/0
Corp(config-if)#ip nat inside
Corp(config-if)#int s0/0/1
Corp(config-if)#ip nat inside
Corp(config-if)#int s0/1/0
Corp(config-if)#ip nat inside
Corp(config-if)#
```

Now that PAT is configured and our interfaces are all set, let's telnet from HostC to HostD—wait, first I'll ping from host to host, then I'll telnet:

```
Corp#sh ip nat trans
Pro Inside global      Inside local       Outside local      Outside global
icmp 64.1.1.5:271      10.1.9.2:271       64.1.1.10:271      64.1.1.10:271
tcp 64.1.1.5:11000     10.1.9.2:11000     64.1.1.10:23       64.1.1.10:23
Corp#
```

Now I'm going to turn on debug ip nat on the Corp router, then telnet from HostB to HostD. Let's take a look at the output on the Corp router:

```
Corp#debug ip nat
*May  9 22:57:47.679: NAT*: TCP s=11000->1024, d=23
*May  9 22:57:47.679: NAT*: s=10.1.6.2->64.1.1.5, d=64.1.1.10 [0]
*May  9 22:57:47.683: NAT*: TCP s=23, d=1024->11000
```

```
*May   9 22:57:47.683: NAT*: s=64.1.1.10, d=64.1.1.5->10.1.6.2 [0]
*May   9 22:57:47.699: NAT*: TCP s=11000->1024, d=23
*May   9 22:57:47.699: NAT*: s=10.1.6.2->64.1.1.5, d=64.1.1.10 [1]
*May   9 22:57:47.703: NAT*: TCP s=23, d=1024->11000
*May   9 22:57:47.703: NAT*: s=64.1.1.10, d=64.1.1.5->10.1.6.2 [1]
*May   9 22:57:47.707: NAT*: TCP s=11000->1024, d=23
*May   9 22:57:47.707: NAT*: s=10.1.6.2->64.1.1.5, d=64.1.1.10 [2]
*May   9 22:57:47.711: NAT*: TCP s=11000->1024, d=23
*May   9 22:57:47.711: NAT*: s=10.1.6.2->64.1.1.5, d=64.1.1.10 [3]
*May   9 22:57:47.719: NAT*: TCP s=23, d=1024->11000
*May   9 22:57:47.719: NAT*: s=64.1.1.10, d=64.1.1.5->10.1.6.2 [2]
*May   9 22:57:47.723: NAT*: TCP s=23, d=1024->11000
*May   9 22:57:47.723: NAT*: s=64.1.1.10, d=64.1.1.5->10.1.6.2 [3]
*May   9 22:57:47.723: NAT*: TCP s=11000->1024, d=23
*May   9 22:57:47.723: NAT*: s=10.1.6.2->64.1.1.5, d=64.1.1.10 [4]
*May   9 22:57:47.731: NAT*: TCP s=11000->1024, d=23
*May   9 22:57:47.731: NAT*: s=10.1.6.2->64.1.1.5, d=64.1.1.10 [5]
*May   9 22:57:47.735: NAT*: TCP s=23, d=1024->11000
*May   9 22:57:47.735: NAT*: s=64.1.1.10, d=64.1.1.5->10.1.6.2 [4]
*May   9 22:57:47.735: NAT*: TCP s=11000->1024, d=23
*May   9 22:57:47.735: NAT*: s=10.1.6.2->64.1.1.5, d=64.1.1.10 [6]
*May   9 22:57:47.747: NAT*: TCP s=11000->1024, d=23
*May   9 22:57:47.747: NAT*: s=10.1.6.2->64.1.1.5, d=64.1.1.10 [7]
*May   9 22:57:47.951: NAT*: TCP s=11000->1024, d=23
*May   9 22:57:47.951: NAT*: s=10.1.6.2->64.1.1.5, d=64.1.1.10 [8]
*May   9 22:57:48.103: NAT*: TCP s=23, d=1024->11000
*May   9 22:57:48.103: NAT*: s=64.1.1.10, d=64.1.1.5->10.1.6.2 [5]
Corp#
```

Well, well—this is some pretty interesting output to say the least! You can see that the first line shows our source and destination port numbers that are being used on HostB. The second line shows our inside source being translated to our inside global with the outside local/global address listed last—and then, from the outside host back to our HostB. Let's verify all this with the show ip nat translation command:

```
Corp#sh ip nat trans
Pro Inside global      Inside local      Outside local      Outside global
tcp 64.1.1.5:11000     10.1.9.2:11000    64.1.1.10:23       64.1.1.10:23
Corp#
```

Now, let's use the command show ip nat statistics on the Corp router:

```
Corp#sh ip nat stat
Total active translations: 2 (0 static, 2 dynamic; 2 extended)
Outside interfaces:
  Serial0/2/0
Inside interfaces:
  FastEthernet0/1, Serial0/0/0, Serial0/0/1, Serial0/1/0
Hits: 269  Misses: 13
CEF Translated packets: 227, CEF Punted packets: 0
Expired translations: 27
Dynamic mappings:
-- Inside Source
[Id: 1] access-list 1 pool Todd refcount 2
 pool Todd: netmask 255.255.255.252
        start 64.1.1.5 end 64.1.1.5
        type generic, total addresses 1, allocated 1 (100%), misses 0
Queued Packets: 0
Corp#
```

What we can see here is a summary of our configuration, our two active translations, as well as the inside and outside interfaces that are being used. The pool is listed right there toward the bottom of the output. And it all looks good, so it's time to move on to configure NAT using SDM.

Configuring NAT Using SDM

Configuring NAT using the SDM is really much easier that anyone would think—except for you of course, because you've already been through Chapter 10! Anyway, all you have to do is click Configure ➢ NAT and you get a handy wizard that does a lot more that just hold your hand to create a NAT rule. It's a lot like the one we used to create our firewall in Chapter 10, and also just like in Chapter 10, there's more than one wizard. Again you get to pick between basic and advanced:

Basic NAT Use this wizard if you have some basic PCs/hosts on your trusted network that need access to the Internet. This wizard will guide you through the process of creating a basic NAT configuration.

Advanced NAT If you have a DMZ, or servers on your inside network that users from the outside need to access, you definitely want to opt for the Advanced NAT configuration.

The first screen is the Create NAT Configuration screen.

From here, I'm just going to simply connect up and create a basic NAT. After that, I click Launch the Selected Task, and get the next screen, which tells me what the Basic NAT Wizard is going to do.

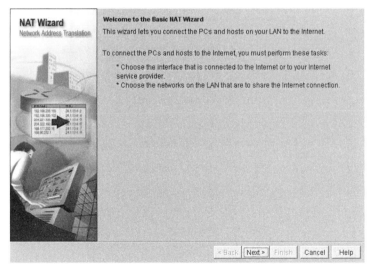

As you might guess, it rocks—all I have to do is to click Next to get to a screen from which I'm able to select all my inside and outside addresses. Seem familiar? Good—that means you've been paying attention!

After choosing my inside and outside interfaces, I click Next. A NAT pool is created and all my interfaces are assigned inside or outside configurations, just like that!

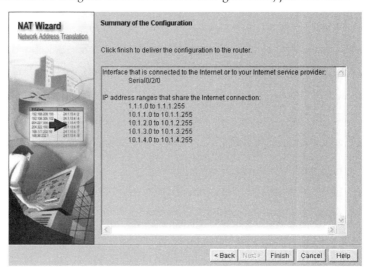

Finally, I click Finish. Let's see what doing that did to my router. Here are the interfaces it configured:

```
!
interface FastEthernet0/0
 ip address 1.1.1.1 255.255.255.0
 ip nat inside
```

```
 ip virtual-reassembly
 duplex auto
 speed auto
!
interface FastEthernet0/1
 description Connection to 1242 AP
 ip address 10.1.1.1 255.255.255.0
 ip nat inside
 ip virtual-reassembly
 duplex auto
 speed auto
!
[output cut]
!
interface Serial0/2/0
 description Connection to R3$FW_OUTSIDE$
 ip address 64.1.1.5 255.255.255.252
 ip access-group 103 in
 ip verify unicast reverse-path
 ip nat outside
 ip inspect SDM_LOW out
 ip virtual-reassembly
 clock rate 2000000
!
[output cut]
```

Here is the `ip nat inside source list` it created:

```
ip nat inside source list 2 interface Serial0/2/0 overload
!
[output cut]
```

And last, here is the access list created for each interface I chose as in inside network:

```
access-list 2 remark SDM_ACL Category=2
access-list 2 permit 1.1.1.0 0.0.0.255
access-list 2 permit 10.1.4.0 0.0.0.255
access-list 2 permit 10.1.1.0 0.0.0.255
access-list 2 permit 10.1.2.0 0.0.0.255
access-list 2 permit 10.1.3.0 0.0.0.255
```

I know I've said this over and over in the book, but I like to repeat this because I want to assure you that SDM really is an incredibly useful tool for creating advanced configurations like ACLs, VPNs, and NAT. This is one thing I think I've nailed down for you, and the last two chapters have really proven that!

Summary

Now this really was a fun chapter. Come on—admit it! You learned a lot about Network Address Translation (NAT) and how it's configured with static, dynamic, and Port Address Translation (PAT)—also called NAT Overload.

I also described how each flavor of NAT is used in a network, as well as how each type is configured on a network. Plus, for your ease and comfort, I used the same intranetwork we've been configuring throughout the book and simply added NAT Overload (PAT) to it.

I also went through some verification and troubleshooting commands and then finished the chapter up by showing you how to use SDM to configure NAT quickly and easily.

Exam Essentials

Understand the term *NAT*.　This may come as news to you, because I didn't—okay, failed to—mention it earlier, but NAT has a few nicknames. In the industry, it's referred to as network masquerading, IP-masquerading, and for those who are besieged with OCD and compelled to spell everything out, Native Address Translation. Whatever you want to dub it, basically, they all refer to the process of rewriting the source/destination addresses of IP packets when they go through a router or firewall. Just focus on the process that's occurring and your understanding of it (i.e., the important part), and you're on it for sure!

Remember the three methods of NAT.　The three methods are static, dynamic, and overloading, which is also called Port Address Translation (PAT).

Understand static NAT.　This type of NAT is designed to allow one-to-one mapping between local and global addresses.

Understand dynamic NAT.　This version gives you the ability to map an unregistered IP address to a registered IP address from out of a pool of registered IP addresses.

Understand overloading.　Overloading really is a form of dynamic NAT that maps multiple unregistered IP addresses to a single registered IP address—many-to-one—by using different ports. It's also known as *Port Address Translation (PAT)*.

Written Lab 11

In this section, write the answers to the following questions:

1. What type of address translation can use only one address to allow thousands of hosts to be translated globally?

2. What command can you use to show the NAT translations as they occur on your router?

3. What command will show you the translation table?

4. What command will clear all your NAT entries from the translation table?

5. How much memory does each NAT mapping use (approximately)?

6. Why would you use the `ip nat translation max-entries` command?

7. Which command can be used for troubleshooting and displays a summary of the NAT configuration as well as counts of active translation types and hits to an existing mapping.

8. What commands must be used on your router interfaces before NAT will translate addresses?

9. In the following output, what type of NAT is being used?

   `ip nat pool todd-nat 170.168.10.10 170.168.10.20 netmask 255.255.255.0`

10. Instead of the `netmask` command, you can use the _____ statement.

Hands-on Labs

I am going to use some basic routers for this lab, but really, almost any Cisco router will work. Here is a list of the labs in this chapter:

   Lab 11.1: Preparing for NAT

   Lab 11.2: Configuring Dynamic NAT

   Lab 11.3: Configuring PAT

I am going to use the network shown in Figure 11.7 for our hands-on lab. I highly recommend you connect up some routers and run through this lab. In this lab, you will configure NAT on router Lab_A to translate the private IP address of 192.168.10.0 to a public address of 171.16.10.0.

Table 11.4 shows the commands we will use and the purpose of each command.

TABLE 11.4   Command Summary for NAT/PAT Hands-on Lab

Command	Purpose
`ip nat inside source list acl pool name`	Translates IPs that match the ACL from the pool
`ip nat inside source static inside_addr outside_addr`	Statically maps an inside address to an outside address
`iP nat pool name`	Creates an address pool

TABLE 11.4   Command Summary for NAT/PAT Hands-on Lab   *(continued)*

Command	Purpose
iP nat inside	Sets an interface to be an inside interface
iP nat outside	Sets an interface to be an outside interface
show ip nat translations	Shows current NAT translations

FIGURE 11.7   Chapter 11 hands-on lab network

Lab 11.1: Preparing for NAT

In this lab, you'll set up your routers with IP addresses and RIP routing.

1. Configure the routers with the IP addresses listed in Table 11.5.

TABLE 11.5   Router IP Address Scheme

Router	Interface	IP Address
ISP	S0	171.16.10.1/24
Lab_A	S0/2	171.16.10.2/24
Lab_A	S0/0	192.168.20.1/24
Lab_B	S0	192.168.20.2/24
Lab_B	E0	192.168.30.1/24
Lab_C	E0	192.168.30.2/24

After you configure the routers, you should be able to ping from router to router, but since we do not have a routing protocol running until the next step, you can only verify from one router to another but not through the network until RIP is set up. You can use any routing protocol you wish; I am just using RIP for simplicity's sake to get this up and running.

2. On Lab_A, configure RIP routing, set a passive interface, and configure the default network:

```
Lab_A#config t
Lab_A(config-router)#network 192.168.20.0
Lab_A(config-router)#network 171.16.0.0
Lab_A(config-router)#passive-interface s0/2
Lab_A(config-router)#exit
Lab_A(config)#ip default-network 171.16.10.1
```

The passive-interface command stops RIP updates from being sent to the ISP and the ip default-network command advertises a default network to the other routers so they know how to get the Internet.

3. On Lab_B, configure RIP routing:

```
Lab_B#config t
Lab_B(config)#router rip
Lab_B(config-router)#network 192.168.30.0
Lab_B(config-router)#network 192.168.20.0
```

4. On Lab_C, configure RIP routing, but also use the `passive-interface` command since there is no reason to send our routing table to the ISP:

```
Lab_C#config t
Lab_C(config)#router rip
Lab_C(config-router)#network 192.168.30.0
```

5. On the ISP router, configure a default route to the corporate network:

```
ISP#config t
ISP(config)#ip route 0.0.0.0 0.0.0.0 s0
```

6. Configure the ISP router so you can telnet into the router without being prompted for a password:

```
ISP#config t
ISP(config)#line vty 0 4
ISP(config-line)#no login
```

7. Verify that you can ping from the ISP router to the Lab_C router and from the Lab_C router to the ISP router. If you cannot, troubleshoot your network.

Lab 11.2: Configuring Dynamic NAT

In this lab, you'll configure dynamic NAT on the Lab_A router.

1. Create a pool of addresses called GlobalNet on the Lab_A router. The pool should contain a range of addresses of 171.16.10.50 through 171.16.10.55.

```
Lab_A(config)#ip nat pool GlobalNet 171.16.10.50 171.16.10.55
net 255.255.255.0
```

2. Create access-list 1. This list permits traffic from the 192.168.20.0 and 192.168.30.0 network to be translated.

```
Lab_A(config)#access-list 1 permit 192.168.20.0 0.0.0.255
Lab_A(config)#access-list 1 permit 192.168.30.0 0.0.0.255
```

3. Map the access list to the pool that was created.

```
Lab_A(config)#ip nat inside source list 1 pool GlobalNet
```

4. Configure serial 0/0 as an inside NAT interface.

```
Lab_A(config)#int s0/0
Lab_A(config-if)#ip nat inside
```

5. Configure serial 0/2 as an outside NAT interface.

```
Lab_A(config-if)#int s0/2
Lab_A(config-if)#ip nat outside
```

6. Log in to the Lab_C router. Telnet from the Lab_C router to the ISP router.

Lab_C#**telnet 171.16.10.1**

7. Log in to the Lab_B router. Telnet from the Lab_B router to the ISP router.

Lab_B#**telnet 171.16.10.1**

8. Execute the command **show users** from the ISP router. (This shows who is accessing the VTY lines.)

ISP#**show users**

a. What does it show as your source IP address?_____

b. What is your real source IP address?_____

The show users output should look something like this:

```
ISP>sh users
      Line        User      Host(s)           Idle        Location
     0 con 0                idle              00:03:32
     2 vty 0                idle              00:01:33 171.16.10.50
*    3 vty 1                idle              00:00:09 171.16.10.51
     Interface  User      Mode                  Idle Peer Address
ISP>
```

Notice that there is a one-to-one translation. This means you must have a real IP address for every host that wants to get to the Internet, which is not always possible.

9. Leave the session open on the ISP and connect to Lab_A. (Use Ctrl+Shift+6, let go, and then press X.)

10. Log in to your Lab_A router and view your current translations by entering the show ip nat translation command. You should see something like this:

```
Lab_A#sh ip nat translations
Pro Inside global    Inside local    Outside local    Outside global
--- 171.16.10.50     192.168.30.2    ---              ---
--- 171.16.10.51     192.168.20.2    ---              ---
Lab_A#
```

11. If you turn on debug ip nat on the Lab_A router and then ping through the router, you will see the actual NAT process take place, which will look something like this:

```
00:32:47: NAT*: s=192.168.30.2->171.16.10.50, d=171.16.10.1 [5]
00:32:47: NAT*: s=171.16.10.1, d=171.16.10.50->192.168.30.2
```

Lab 11.3: Configuring PAT

In this lab, you'll configure Port Address Translation (PAT) on the Lab_A router. We will use PAT because we don't want a one-to-one translation, which uses just one IP address for every user on the network.

1. On the Lab_A router, delete the translation table and remove the dynamic NAT pool:

   ```
   Lab_A#clear ip nat translation *
   Lab_A#config t
   Lab_A(config)#no ip nat pool GlobalNet 171.16.10.50
   171.16.10.55 netmask 255.255.255.0
   Lab_A(config)#no ip nat inside source list 1 pool GlobalNet
   ```

2. On the Lab_A router, create a NAT pool with one address called Lammle. The pool should contain a single address 171.16.10.100. Enter the following command:

   ```
   Lab_A#config t
   Lab_A(config)#ip nat pool Lammle 171.16.10.100 171.16.10.100
   net 255.255.255.0
   ```

3. Create access-list 2. It should permit networks 192.168.20.0 and 192.168.30.0 to be translated.

   ```
   Lab_A(config)#access-list 2 permit 192.168.20.0 0.0.0.255
   Lab_A(config)#access-list 2 permit 192.168.30.0 0.0.0.255
   ```

4. Map the access-list 2 to the new pool, allowing PAT to occur by using the overload command.

   ```
   Lab_A(config)#ip nat inside source list 2 pool Lammle overload
   ```

5. Log in to the Lab_C router and telnet to the ISP router; also, log in to the Lab_B router and telnet to the ISP router.

6. From the ISP router, use the show users command. The output should look like this:

   ```
   ISP>sh users
       Line      User      Host(s)        Idle      Location
   *   0 con 0             idle           00:00:00
       2 vty 0             idle           00:00:39 171.16.10.100
       4 vty 2             idle           00:00:37 171.16.10.100

     Interface  User      Mode           Idle Peer Address

   ISP>
   ```

7. From the Lab_A router, use the show `ip nat translations` command.

```
Lab_A#sh ip nat translations
Pro Inside global   Inside local   Outside local Outside global
tcp 171.16.10.100:11001 192.168.20.2:11001 171.16.10.1:23   171.16.10.1:23
tcp 171.16.10.100:11002 192.168.30.2:11002 171.16.10.1:23   171.16.10.1:23
tcp 171.16.10.100:1024  192.168.20.2:11002 171.16.10.1:23   171.16.10.1:23
```

8. Also make sure that the `debug ip nat` command is on the Lab_A router. If you ping from the Lab_C router to the ISP router, the output will look like this:

```
01:12:36: NAT: s=192.168.30.2->171.16.10.100, d=171.16.10.1 [35]
01:12:36: NAT*: s=171.16.10.1, d=171.16.10.100->192.168.30.2 [35]
01:12:36: NAT*: s=192.168.30.2->171.16.10.100, d=171.16.10.1 [36]
01:12:36: NAT*: s=171.16.10.1, d=171.16.10.100->192.168.30.2 [36]
01:12:36: NAT*: s=192.168.30.2->171.16.10.100, d=171.16.10.1 [37]
01:12:36: NAT*: s=171.16.10.1, d=171.16.10.100->192.168.30.2 [37]
01:12:36: NAT*: s=192.168.30.2->171.16.10.100, d=171.16.10.1 [38]
01:12:36: NAT*: s=171.16.10.1, d=171.16.10.100->192.168.30.2 [38]
01:12:37: NAT*: s=192.168.30.2->171.16.10.100, d=171.16.10.1 [39]
01:12:37: NAT*: s=171.16.10.1, d=171.16.10.100->192.168.30.2 [39]
```

Review Questions

The following questions are designed to test your understanding of this chapter's material. For more information on how to get additional questions, please see this book's Introduction.

1. Which of the following are disadvantages of using NAT? (Choose three.)
   A. Translation introduces switching path delays.
   B. Conserves legally registered addresses.
   C. Causes loss of end-to-end IP traceability.
   D. Increases flexibility when connecting to the Internet.
   E. Certain applications will not function with NAT enabled.
   F. Reduces address overlap occurrence.

2. Which of the following are advantages of using NAT? (Choose three.)
   A. Translation introduces switching path delays.
   B. Conserves legally registered addresses.
   C. Causes loss of end-to-end IP traceability.
   D. Increases flexibility when connecting to the Internet.
   E. Certain applications will not function with NAT enabled.
   F. Reduces address overlap occurrence.

3. Which command will allow you to see real-time translations on your router?
   A. `show ip nat translations`
   B. `show ip nat statistics`
   C. `debug ip nat`
   D. `clear ip nat translations *`

4. Which command will show you all the translations active on your router?
   A. `show ip nat translations`
   B. `show ip nat statistics`
   C. `debug ip nat`
   D. `clear ip nat translations *`

5. Which command will clear all the translations active on your router?
   A. `show ip nat translations`
   B. `show ip nat statistics`
   C. `debug ip nat`
   D. `clear ip nat translations *`

6. Which command will show you the summary of the NAT configuration?

A. show ip nat translations

B. show ip nat statistics

C. debug ip nat

D. clear ip nat translations *

7. Which command will create a dynamic pool named Todd that will provide you with 30 global addresses?

A. ip nat pool Todd 171.16.10.65 171.16.10.94 net 255.255.255.240

B. ip nat pool Todd 171.16.10.65 171.16.10.94 net 255.255.255.224

C. ip nat pool todd 171.16.10.65 171.16.10.94 net 255.255.255.224

D. ip nat pool Todd 171.16.10.1 171.16.10.254 net 255.255.255.0

8. Which are considered the three methods of NAT?

A. Static

B. IP NAT pool

C. Dynamic

D. NAT double-translation

E. Overload

9. When creating a pool of global addresses, which of the following can be used instead of the netmask command?

A. / (slash notation)

B. prefix-length

C. no mask

D. block-size

10. Which of the following would be a good starting point for troubleshooting if your router is not translating?

A. Reboot.

B. Call Cisco.

C. Check your interfaces for the correct configuration.

D. Run the debug all command.

11. Which of the following would be good reasons to run NAT? (Choose three.)

A. You need to connect to the Internet and your hosts don't have globally unique IP addresses.

B. You change to a new ISP that requires you to renumber your network.

C. You don't want any hosts connecting to the Internet.

D. You require two intranets with duplicate addresses to merge.

12. Which of the following is considered to be the address after translation?

   A. Inside local

   B. Outside local

   C. Inside global

   D. Outside global

13. Which of the following is considered to be the address before translation?

   A. Inside local

   B. Outside local

   C. Inside global

   D. Outside global

14. Which of the following is considered to be the destination host before translation?

   A. Inside local

   B. Outside local

   C. Inside global

   D. Outside global

15. Which of the following is considered to be the outside destination host after translation?

   A. Inside local

   B. Outside local

   C. Inside global

   D. Outside global

16. Which command would you place on interface on a private network?

   A. `ip nat inside`

   B. `ip nat outside`

   C. `ip outside global`

   D. `ip inside local`

17. Which command would you place on interface connected to the Internet?

   A. `ip nat inside`

   B. `ip nat outside`

   C. `ip outside global`

   D. `ip inside local`

18. Pat Address Translation is also termed what?

   A. NAT Fast

   B. NAT Static

   C. NAT Overload

   D. Overloading Static

Answers to Review Questions

1. A, C, E. NAT is not perfect and can cause some issues in some networks, but most networks work just fine. NAT can cause delays and troubleshooting problems, and some applications just won't work.

2. B, D, F. NAT is not perfect, but there are some advantages. It conserves global addresses, which allow us to add millions of hosts to the Internet without "real" IP addresses. This provides flexibility in our corporate networks. NAT can also allow you to use the same subnet more than once in the same network without overlapping networks.

3. C. The command `debug ip nat` will show you in real time the translations occurring on your router.

4. A. The command `show ip nat translations` will show you the translation table containing all the active NAT entries.

5. D. The command `clear ip nat translations *` will clear all the active NAT entries in your translation table.

6. B. The `show ip nat statistics` command displays a summary of the NAT configuration as well as counts of active translation types, hits to an existing mapping, misses (causing an attempt to create a mapping), and expired translations.

7. B. The command `ip nat pool` *name* creates the pool that hosts can use to get onto the global Internet. What makes answer B correct is that the range 171.16.10.65 through 171.16.10.94 includes 30 hosts, but the mask has to match 30 hosts as well, and that mask is 255.255.255.224. Answer C is wrong because the pool name has a lower case "T" in the pool name. Pool name's are case sensitive.

8. A, C, E. You can configure NAT three ways on a Cisco router: static, dynamic, and NAT Overload (PAT).

9. B. Instead of the `netmask` command, you can use the `prefix-length` *length* statement.

10. C. In order for NAT to provide translation services, you must have `ip nat inside` and `ip nat outside` configured on your router's interfaces.

11. A, B, D. The most popular use of NAT is if you want to connect to the Internet and you don't want hosts to have global (real) IP addresses, but answers B and D are correct as well.

12. C. The host on the private network after translation is considered to be an inside global host.

13. A. The host on the private network before translation is considered to be an inside local host.

14. B. The host on the global network before translation is considered to be an outside local host.

15. D. The host on the global network after translation is considered to be an outside global host.

16. A. As in access-lists, you must configure your interfaces before NAT will provide any translations. On the inside networks you would use the command `ip nat inside`. On the outside interface, you will use the command `ip nat outside`.

17. B. As in access-lists, you must configure your interfaces before NAT will provide any translations. On the inside networks you would use the command `ip nat inside`. On the outside interface, you will use the command `ip nat outside`.

18. C. Another term for port address translation is NAT Overload because that is the command used to enable port address translation.

Answers to Written Lab 11

1. Port Address Translation (PAT), also called NAT Overload.

2. debug ip nat

3. show ip nat translations

4. clear ip nat translations *

5. 160 bytes of memory

6. In the rare case where the entries must be limited for either performance or policy reasons

7. show ip nat statistics

8. The ip nat inside and ip nat outside commands

9. Dynamic NAT

10. prefix-length

Chapter

12

Cisco's Wireless Technologies

THE CCNA EXAM TOPICS COVERED IN THIS CHAPTER INCLUDE THE FOLLOWING:

✓ **Explain and select the appropriate administrative tasks required for a WLAN**

- Describe standards associated with wireless media (including: IEEE WI-FI Alliance, ITU/FCC)

- Identify and describe the purpose of the components in a small wireless network (including: SSID, BSS, ESS)

- Identify the basic parameters to configure on a wireless network to ensure that devices connect to the correct access point

- Compare and contrast wireless security features and capabilities of WPA security (including: open, WEP, WPA-1/2)

- Identify common issues with implementing wireless networks (including: Interface, Miss configuration)

If you want to understand the basic wireless LANs, or WLANs, that are the most commonly used today, just think 10BaseT Ethernet with hubs. What this means is that our WLANs typically run half-duplex communication—everyone is sharing the same bandwidth and only one user is communicating at a time. This isn't necessarily bad—it's just not good enough. Because most people rely upon wireless networks today, it's critical that they evolve faster than greased lightning to keep up with our rapidly escalating needs. The good news is that this is actually happening—Cisco has reacted by coming up with an answer called the Cisco Unified Wireless Solution that works with all types of wireless connections. And it works securely too!

My goal in this chapter isn't so much to introduce you to wireless technologies in general, it's to familiarize you with Cisco's wireless technologies because as you'd probably guess, there are differences—however subtle. Yes, I will cover basic wireless LAN technologies and committees, but the main objective here is to ensure that you understand wireless through Cisco's eyes and solidly grasp the solutions that Cisco provides.

Cisco's Unified Wireless Solution includes mobility and mesh, so these are the topics I'm going to focus upon. I'm also going to give you the skinny on the all-important topic of wireless security.

This chapter could easily be an extension of Chapter 14, "Wide Area Networks," as wireless cellular networks and other last-mile high-speed wireless technologies are emerging. But I've exalted this chapter's topics by giving them their own chapter because I want you to realize just how important wireless is as an alternative to wide area networks. And in case you were wondering, yes, Cisco Unified Wireless Solution includes Wireless Metropolitan Area Networks (WMANs).

For up-to-the-minute updates on the topics covered in this chapter, please see www.lammle.com and/or www.sybex.com.

Introduction to Wireless Technology

Transmitting a signal using the typical 802.11 specifications works a lot like it does with a basic Ethernet hub: They're both two-way forms of communication, and they both use the same frequency to both transmit and receive, often referred to as half-duplex and mentioned earlier in the chapter. Wireless LANs (WLANs) use radio frequencies (RFs) that are radiated into the air from an antenna that creates radio waves. These waves can be absorbed, refracted, or reflected by walls, water, and metal surfaces, resulting in low signal strength. So because of this innate vulnerability to surrounding environmental factors, it's pretty apparent that wireless will never offer us the same robustness as a wired network can, but that still doesn't mean we're not going to run wireless. Believe me, we definitely will!

We can increase the transmitting power and gain a greater transmitting distance, but doing so can create some nasty distortion, so it has to be done carefully. By using higher frequencies, we can attain higher data rates, but this is, unfortunately, at the cost of decreased transmitting distances. And if we use lower frequencies, we get to transmit greater distances but at lower data rates. This should make it pretty clear to you that understanding all the various types of WLANs you can implement is imperative to creating the LAN solution that best meets the specific requirements of the unique situation you're dealing with.

Also important to note is the fact that the 802.11 specifications were developed so that there would be no licensing required in most countries—to ensure the user the freedom to install and operate without any licensing or operating fees. This means that any manufacturer can create products and sell them at a local computer store or wherever. It also means that all our computers should be able to communicate wirelessly without configuring much, if anything at all.

Various agencies have been around for a very long time to help govern the use of wireless devices, frequencies, standards, and how the frequency spectrums are used. Table 12.1 shows the current agencies that help create, maintain, and even enforce wireless standards worldwide.

TABLE 12.1 Wireless Agencies and Standards

Agency	Purpose	Web Site
Institute of Electrical and Electronics Engineers (IEEE)	Creates and maintains operational standards	www.ieee.org
Federal Communications Commission (FCC)	Regulates the use of wireless devices in the U.S.	www.fcc.gov
European Telecommunications Standards Institute (ETSi)	Chartered to produce common standards in Europe	www.etsi.org
Wi-Fi Alliance	Promotes and tests for WLAN interoperability	www.wi-fi.com
WLAN Association (WLANA)	Educates and raises consumer awareness regarding WLANs	www.wlana.org

Because WLANs transmit over radio frequencies, they're regulated by the same types of laws used to govern things like AM/FM radios. It's the Federal Communications Commission (FCC) that regulates the use of wireless LAN devices, and the Institute of Electrical and Electronics Engineers (IEEE) takes it from there and creates standards based on what frequencies the FCC releases for public use.

The FCC has released three unlicensed bands for public use: 900MHz, 2.4GHz, and 5.7GHz. The 900MHz and 2.4GHz bands are referred to as the Industrial, Scientific, and Medical (ISM) bands, and the 5-GHz band is known as the Unlicensed National Information Infrastructure (UNII) band. Figure 12.1 shows where the unlicensed bands sit within the RF spectrum.

FIGURE 12.1   Unlicensed frequencies

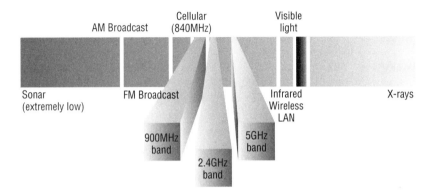

So it follows that if you opt to deploy wireless in a range outside of the three public bands shown in Figure 12.1, you need to get a specific license from the FCC to do so. Once the FCC opened the three frequency ranges for public use, many manufacturers were able to start offering myriad products that flooded the market, with 802.11b/g being the most widely used wireless network found today.

The Wi-Fi Alliance grants certification for interoperability among 802.11 products offered by various vendors. This certification provides a sort of comfort zone for the users purchasing the many types of products, although in my personal experience, it's just a whole lot easier if you buy all your access points from the same manufacturer!

In the current U.S. wireless LAN market, there are several accepted operational standards and drafts created and maintained by the Institute of Electrical and Electronics Engineers (IEEE). Let's take a look at these standards and then talk about how the most commonly used standards work.

The 802.11 Standards

Taking off from what you learned in Chapter 1, "Internetworking," wireless networking has its own 802 standards group—remember, Ethernet's committee is 802.3. Wireless starts with 802.11, and there are various other up-and-coming standard groups as well, like 802.16 and 802.20. And there's no doubt that cellular networks will become huge players in our wireless future. But for now, we're going to concentrate on the 802.11 standards committee and subcommittees.

IEEE 802.11 was the first, original standardized WLAN at 1 and 2Mbps. It runs in the 2.4GHz radio frequency and was ratified in 1997 even though we didn't see many products pop up until around 1999 when 802.11b was introduced. All the committees listed in Table 12.2 are amendments to the original 802.11 standard except for 802.11F and 802.11T, which are both stand-alone documents.

TABLE 12.2   802.11 Committees and Subcommittees

Committee	Purpose
IEEE 802.11a	54Mbps, 5GHz standard
IEEE 802.11b	Enhancements to 802.11 to support 5.5 and 11Mbps
IEEE 802.11c	Bridge operation procedures; included in the IEEE 802.1D standard
IEEE 802.11d	International roaming extensions
IEEE 802.11e	Quality of service
IEEE 802.11F	Inter-Access Point Protocol
IEEE 802.11g	54Mbps, 2.4GHz standard (backward compatible with 802.11b)
IEEE 802.11h	Dynamic Frequency Selection (DFS) and Transmit Power Control (TPC) at 5Ghz
IEEE 802.11i	Enhanced security
IEEE 802.11j	Extensions for Japan and U.S. public safety
IEEE 802.11k	Radio resource measurement enhancements
IEEE 802.11m	Maintenance of the standard; odds and ends
IEEE 802.11n	Higher throughput improvements using MIMO (multiple input, multiple output antennas)
IEEE 802.11p	Wireless Access for the Vehicular Environment (WAVE)
IEEE 802.11r	Fast roaming
IEEE 802.11s	Extended Service Set (ESS) Mesh Networking
IEEE 802.11T	Wireless Performance Prediction (WPP)
IEEE 802.11u	Internetworking with non-802 networks (cellular, for example)
IEEE 802.11v	Wireless network management
IEEE 802.11w	Protected management frames
IEEE 802.11y	3650–3700 operation in the U.S.

Okay, now let's discuss some important specifics of the most popular 802.11 WLANs.

2.4GHz (802.11b)

First on the menu is the 802.11b standard. It was the most widely deployed wireless standard, and it operates in the 2.4GHz unlicensed radio band that delivers a maximum data rate of 11Mbps. The 802.11b standard has been widely adopted by both vendors and customers who found that its 11Mbps data rate worked pretty well for most applications. But now that 802.11b has a big brother (802.11g), no one goes out and just buys an 802.11b card or access point anymore because why would you buy a 10Mbps Ethernet card when you can score a 10/100 Ethernet card for the same price?

An interesting thing about all Cisco 802.11 WLAN products is that they have the ability to data-rate-shift while moving. This allows the person operating at 11Mbps to shift to 5.5Mbps, 2Mbps, and finally still communicate farthest from the access point at 1Mbps. And further-more, this rate shifting happens without losing connection and with no interaction from the user. Rate shifting also occurs on a transmission-by-transmission basis. This is important because it means that the access point can support multiple clients at varying speeds depending upon the location of each client.

The problem with 802.11b lies in how the Data Link layer is dealt with. In order to solve prob-lems in the RF spectrum, a type of Ethernet collision detection was created called CSMA/CA, or Carrier Sense Multiple Access with Collision Avoidance. Check this out in Figure 12.2.

CSMA/CA is also called a Request To Send, Clear To Send (RTS/CTS) because of the way that hosts must communicate to the access point (AP). For every packet sent, an RTS/CTS and acknowledgment must be received, and because of this rather cumbersome process, it's kind of hard to believe it all actually works!

2.4GHz (802.11g)

The 802.11g standard was ratified in June 2003 and is backward compatible with 802.11b. The 802.11g standard delivers the same 54Mbps maximum data rate as 802.11a but runs in the 2.4GHz range—the same as 802.11b.

FIGURE 12.2   802.11b CSMA/CA

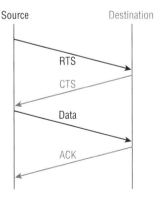

Because 802.11b/g operates in the same 2.4GHz unlicensed band, migrating to 802.11g is an affordable choice for organizations with existing 802.11b wireless infrastructures. Just keep in mind that 802.11b products can't be "software upgraded" to 802.11g. This limitation is because 802.11g radios use a different chipset in order to deliver the higher data rate.

But still, much like Ethernet and Fast Ethernet, 802.11g products can be commingled with 802.11b products in the same network. Yet, for example, completely unlike Ethernet, if you have four users running 802.11g cards and one user starts using an 802.11b card, everyone connected to the same access point is then forced to run the 802.11b CSMA/CA method—an ugly fact that really makes throughput suffer. So to optimize performance, it's recommended that you disable the 802.11b-only modes on all your access points.

To explain this further, 802.11b uses a modulation technique called Direct Sequence Spread Spectrum (DSSS) that's just not as robust as the Orthogonal Frequency Division Multiplexing (OFDM) modulation used by both 802.11g and 802.11a. 802.11g clients using OFDM enjoy much better performance at the same ranges as 802.11b clients do, but—and remember this—when 802.11g clients are operating at the 802.11b rates (11, 5.5, 2, and 1Mbps), they're actually using the same modulation 802.11b does.

Figure 12.3 shows the 14 different channels (each 22Mhz wide) that the FCC released in the 2.4GHz range.

In the U.S., only 11 channels are configurable, with channels 1, 6, and 11 being non-overlapping. This allows you to have three access points in the same area without experiencing interference.

5GHz (802.11a)

The IEEE ratified the 802.11a standard in 1999, but the first 802.11a products didn't begin appearing on the market until late 2001—and boy were they pricey! The 802.11a standard delivers a maximum data rate of 54Mbps with 12 non-overlapping frequency channels. Figure 12.4 shows the UNII bands.

FIGURE 12.3   ISM 2.4GHz channels

FIGURE 12.4   UNII 5GHz band has 12 non-overlapping channels (U.S.).

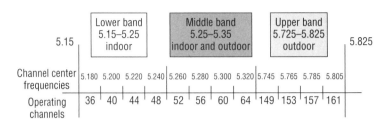

Operating in the 5GHz radio band, 802.11a is also immune to interference from devices that operate in the 2.4GHz band, like microwave ovens, cordless phones, and Bluetooth devices. 802.11a isn't backward compatible with 802.11b because they are different frequencies, so you don't get to just "upgrade" part of your network and expect everything to work together in perfect harmony. But no worries—there are plenty of dual-radio devices that will work in both types of networks. A definite plus for 802.11a is that it can work in the same physical environment without interference from 802.11b users.

Similar to the 802.11b radios, all 802.11a products also have the ability to data-rate-shift while moving. The 802.11a products allow the person operating at 54Mbps to shift to 48Mbps, 36Mbps, 24Mbps, 18Mbps, 12Mbps, 9Mbps, and finally still communicate farthest from the AP at 6Mbps.

There's also an extension of the 802.11a specifications called 802.11h.

5GHz (802.11h)

The FCC added 11 new channels in February 2004, and in 2008, we finally get to begin using these channels based on manufacturers' releases of more 802.11a 5GHz products. This means that soon, we'll gain access to up to 23 non-overlapping channels! And there are two new features of the 5GHz radio that are part of the 802.11h specification: Transmit Power Control (TPC) and Dynamic Frequency Selection (DFS).

DFS   This cool feature continuously monitors a device's operating range for any radar signals that are allowed to operate in portions of the 5GHz band as well as 802.11a before transmitting. If DFS discovers any radar signals, it'll either abandon the occupied channel or mark it as unavailable to prevent interference from occurring on the WLAN.

TPC   Even though it's been used by the mobile phone industry for a long time, this technology has some handy new uses. You can set the client machine's adapter and the access point's transmit power to cover various size ranges—a feature that's useful for many reasons. For one, setting the access point's transmit power to 5mW reduces cell range, which works great if you've got a compact area with high-density usage.

Further advantages include the fact that TPC enables the client and the access point to communicate. This means the client machine can fine-tune its transmit power dynamically so it uses just enough energy to preserve its connection to the access point, conserve its battery power, plus reduce interference on the neighboring WLAN cells—sweet!

Comparing 802.11

Before I move on to Cisco-specific products, take at look at Table 12.3, which lists the pros and cons of 802.11a, b, and g.

TABLE 12.3 802.11 Comparison

802.11b	802.11g	802.11a (h)
2.4GHz	2.4GHz	5GHz
Most common	Higher throughput	Highest throughput
Up to 11Mpbs	Up to 54Mbps*	Up to 54Mbps
DSSS	DSSS/OFDM	OFDM
3 non-overlapping channels	3 non-overlapping channels	up to 23 non-overlapping channels
**About 25 users per cell	About 20 users per cell	About 15 users per cell
Distance limited by multipath	Throughput degraded by 802.11b clients	Lower market penetrations

*Runs Direct Sequence Spread Spectrum when also running the 802.11b at speeds of 11Mbps and below.

**This happens to be Cisco's rule of thumb. Know that the actual number of users per cell varies based on many factors.

Now let's take a look at Figure 12.5, which delimits the range comparisons of each 802.11 standard and shows us the different ranges using an indoor open-office environment as a factor. We'll be using default power settings.

You can see that to get the full 54Mbps benefit of both 802.11a and 802.11g, you need to be between 50 feet and 100 feet (at the farthest) away, and maybe even less if there are any obstructions between the client and the access point.

All good, but there's one more IEEE 802.11 standard I want to cover that we'll use to get even higher speeds at greater distances.

2.4GHz/5GHz (802.11n)

802.11n builds upon previous 802.11 standards by adding Multiple-Input Multiple-Output (MIMO), which employs multiple transmitters and receiver antennas to increase data throughput. 802.11n can have up to eight antennas, but most of today's access points use four. These are sometimes referred to as smart antennas, and if you do have four of them, two would be used for transmitting simultaneously with the other two receiving simultaneously. This setup would allow for much higher data rates than 802.11a/b/g. In fact, the marketing people claim it will provide about 250Mbps, but personally, I'm not buying it. I just don't believe that's what our actual throughput levels can be, and even if what they're saying is true, exactly how would that help if all you've got is a 1 or 2Mbps cable or DSL connection to the Internet?

FIGURE 12.5 Range comparisons of 802.11 standards

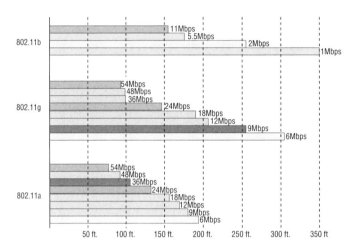

Keep in mind that the 802.11n standard hasn't yet been ratified and isn't expected to be until sometime in 2008—maybe later. This means that the products on the shelf today are proprietary, and they are called "pre-N" products.

With all this in mind, let's move on and take a look at Cisco's solution to the growing wireless market.

Cisco's Unified Wireless Solution

To be honest, if you're brain is already full and you're just cramming for your CCNA Composite exam, you can probably skip this section. But before you do, be sure and check www.lammle.com for the latest dirt on what the Cisco CCNA Composite 640-802 exam objectives are.

With a range of products that support IEEE 802.11a/b/g and soon "n" technologies, Cisco really does offer a pretty complete and impressive line of in-building and outdoor wireless LAN solutions. These products include access points, wireless controllers, wireless LAN client adapters, security and management servers, wireless management devices, wireless integrated switches and routers—even antennas and accessories. Did I say impressive or what?

Since about the year 2000, a lot of corporations have relied upon basic access points as their main wireless networks and connected them into an infrastructure, which allowed users to roam within their network. Figure 12.6 shows a typical infrastructure network, either with one access point or as an extended service set wherein you would have multiple access points—all using the same Service Set Identifier (SSID) for roaming purposes.

FIGURE 12.6   Typical infrastructure network

- Infrastructure mode

- Basic Service Set (BSS)
  - Mobile clients use a single AP
    for connectivity to each other or
    wired network resources.

- Extended Service Set (ESS)
  - Two or more BSSs connected by
    a common distribution system (DS

So what we see here is that each of the APs, in either configuration, is configured as a root AP. If you were to look back in Chapter 4 at the configuration of my two wireless routers (R2 and 871W) and the 1242AP, all three were configured as roots. Basically, this means that each router is essentially saying, "Yo, wireless client, connect to me and get your goods (wired resources)." If the APs weren't root, they could only connect to a root device as a repeater. Nonroot devices include clients, bridges, repeater access points, and work group bridges.

But wait a minute—that was like the IT Cretaceous period or something. Definitely not now when it's almost 2008 and we have on the horizon the Cisco Unified Wireless Solution that provides a comprehensive, integrated WLAN solution! This new, tricked-out technology includes intelligent Cisco APs and Cisco WLAN controllers specifically designed to support APs. The solution is managed either through the controller web interface, from the controller itself, or from Cisco's Wireless Control System (WCS).

But the really sweet thing about this type of network is that after initial installation, it requires zero configuration. This means that you can connect an AP in an outdoor or indoor environment and the AP will automatically configure itself based on the controller's information. It will even check for channel overlap and interference and assign itself a non-overlapping channel—how cool is that? And as I briefly mentioned earlier, if it happens to detect an overlapping channel within its area, it'll lower its transmitting level to limit interference. Cisco calls this "auto RF controls."

The news isn't all sunshine—this product line isn't necessarily for the poor because it can require that you to get your hands on quite a stash of goods. Yep—you'll need more than just an AP for sure. Your minimum shopping list is a Cisco 1020 AP and a controller for an indoor solution, and for outdoors, a Cisco 1520 AP and a controller. And remember, these are minimum requirements. Reality will probably require more stuff—I use both the 1020 and 1520 APs in my classes, and I'm using them to write my book along with two types of controllers—the absolute minimum number of devices I can use to still make this functional. The APs are reasonably priced, and as is usual for Cisco, their cost pretty much follows the product model number. It's the controllers that'll make your coinage disappear—they cost thousands! Hopefully, by the time you read this book, they'll have come down in price to somewhere below the stratosphere. There's always hope!

But for fun, let's pretend you have a decent sized network with unlimited funds to spend on it. First, get a hold of at least two controllers (the good ones run about $20,000 a piece.) Why two? Because every packet from every AP must go to the controller in order to then be placed either on the wired network or back out to the wireless network. The controller decides the packet's destiny based on the Lightweight Access Point Protocol (LWAPP) information that's encapsulated on it. (I'll tell you more about LWAPP in a minute.) Anyway, the reason you need at least two of these beauties is in the unfortunate event that one of them goes down. You'd be full-on nuts to create a design that has only a single point of failure, so, being completely sane, you'll get two and create the redundancy you'll need for this type of network.

Okay, now that you've got the single point of failure thing covered, you need to be able to manage your controllers as well. Cisco has the GUI Wireless Control System (WCS) to manage the entire WLAN from a single interface that also happens to provide you with some seriously detailed insight into the network coverage, the trending of network statistics, and the details on device location. (Remember—money is no object!)

The thing is, you really don't need to have the WCS because the Cisco WLAN controller analyzes the data collected by the APs, which can be managed either at the individual controller or by the comprehensive tools within WCS. But since you're rolling in it, you are definitely going to hook yourself up with that WCS.

You can actually download a 30-day demo of WCS from Cisco's website.

Oh, lest I forget, to make things just a little tougher on you, the controllers only come with gigabit interfaces. This means you need a switch that has both 10/100 ports for your AP connections and a gigabit port to connect your controllers with. It's probably best to get a minimum switch of 3560 (or better) with both types of ports so you can provide inter-VLAN routing as well.

Split-MAC Architecture

Okay—yes. It sounds weird, but this odd-sounding name is actually a pretty cool feature. We're basically splitting the processing of the 802.11 protocol between two devices, the AP and a centralized Cisco WLAN controller. Figure 12.7 shows how the "splitting" of processing occurs at each location

FIGURE 12.7   Split-MAC architecture

Although the 1520 AP and the 1020 AP appear to be directly connected to the controller in Figure 12.7, they can't be—first, because they've go to connect with a switch to provide 10/100 to gigabit conversion, and second, because the controller only forwards LWAPP packets coming from an LWAPP-enabled port. This means you need a router if you want to take an LWAPP packet and forward it out as IP data to a non-LWAPP network. A high-end switch can handle the routing.

The AP handles the portions of the protocol that have real-time requirements:

- The frame exchange handshake between a client and AP when transferring a frame over the air

- Transmitting beacon frames

- Buffering and transmitting frames for clients in power save operations

- Responding to probe request frames from clients

- Forwarding notification of received probe requests to the controller

- Providing real-time signal quality information to the controller with every received frame

- Monitoring each of the radio channels for noise, interference, and other WLANs

- Monitoring for the presence of other APs

- Encryption and decryption except in the case of VPN/IPSec clients

All remaining functionality is handled in the Cisco WLAN controller, so time sensitivity isn't a concern but controller-wide visibility is certainly required. The following are some of the MAC-layer functions provided in the WLAN controller:

- 802.11 authentication

- 802.11 association and reassociation (mobility)

- 802.11 frame translation and bridging

And if a Cisco Wireless Controller in Appliance mode fails, its dropped Cisco APs will poll the network for another Cisco Wireless Controller. When an online Cisco Wireless Controller has any remaining AP ports, the management interface listens to the network for Cisco AP polling messages to auto-discover, associate, and communicate with as many Cisco APs as it can.

Basically, the split-MAC architecture allows the splitting of 802.11 protocol packets between the Cisco LWAPP-based AP that handles real-time portions of the protocol and the WLAN controller that handles any items that are not time sensitive.

MESH and LWAPP

As more vendors migrate to a mesh hierarchical design, and as larger networks are built using lightweight access points, we really need a standardized protocol that governs how lightweight access points communicate with WLAN systems. This is exactly the role filled by one of the Internet Engineering Task Force's (IETF's) latest draft specification, Lightweight Access Point Protocol (LWAPP).

With LWAPP, large multi-vendor wireless networks can be deployed with maximum capabilities and increased flexibility. Well...okay, this is mostly true. No one, and I do mean no one, has actually deployed a Cisco and Motorola network within the same company and is sitting back smugly saying, "Dude, this is really cool!" They're saying something loud for sure, but it isn't that! Cisco is Cisco and Motorola is well, not Cisco, and even though they supposedly run the same IETF protocols, they just don't seem to see the standards exactly the same way. Basically, they don't play well with each other.

So, let's say we're using only Cisco. (Hey, we already have an unlimited budget here, so why not put in all Cisco too, I mean, this is a "Cisco" book, right?)

Okay—so Cisco's mesh networking infrastructure is decentralized and comparably inexpensive for all the nice things it provides because each node only needs to transmit as far as the next node. Nodes act as repeaters to transmit data from nearby nodes to peers that are too far away for a manageable cabled connection, resulting in a network that can span a really large distance, especially over rough or difficult terrain. Figure 12.8 shows a large meshed environment using Cisco 1520 APs to "umbrella" an area with wireless connectivity:

Plus, mesh networks also happen to be extremely reliable—since each node can potentially be connected to several other nodes, if one of them drops out of the network because of hardware failure or something, its neighbors simply find another route. So you get extra capacity and fault tolerance by simply adding more nodes.

FIGURE 12.8   Typical Large meshed outdoor environment

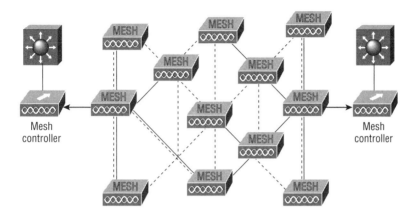

Mesh is a network topology in which devices are
connected with many redundant connections
between nodes.

Wireless mesh connections between AP nodes are formed with a radio, providing many possible paths from a single node to other nodes. Paths through the mesh network can change in response to traffic loads, radio conditions, or traffic prioritization.

Cisco LWAPP-enabled mesh access points are configured, monitored, and operated from and through any Cisco Wireless LAN Controller deployed in the Cisco Mesh Networking Solution—and they must go through a controller, which is why having redundant controllers is an absolute necessary.

Let's define a couple terms used in mesh networks:

Root Access Points (RAPs)   This access point is connected to the wired network and serves as the "root" or "gateway" to the wired network. RAPs have a wired connection back to a Cisco Wireless LAN Controller. They use the backhaul wireless interface to communicate with neighboring Mesh APs.

Mesh Access Points (MAPs)   The Mesh APs are remote APs that are typically located on rooftops or towers and can connect up to 32 MAPs over a 5GHz backhaul. During bootup, an access point will try to become a RAP if it's connected to the wired network. Conversely, if a RAP loses its wired network connection, it will attempt to become a MAP and will search for a RAP.

A typical mesh network would include the devices shown in Figure 12.9.

In Figure 12.9, you can see that there's one RAP connected to the infrastructure, and the MAPs connect to each other as well to the controller through the RAP.

But we're not quite done with this yet—I want to explain one more mesh term before we get into wireless security: AWPP.

FIGURE 12.9 Typical devices found in a Cisco mesh network

AWPP

Each AP runs the Adaptive Wireless Path Protocol (AWPP)—a new protocol designed from the ground up by Cisco specifically for the wireless environment. This protocol allows RAPs to communicate with each other to determine the best path back to the wired network via the RAP. Once the optimal path is established, AWPP continues to run in the background to establish alternative routes back to the RAP just in case the topology changes or conditions cause the link strength to weaken.

This protocol takes into consideration things like interference and characteristics of the specific radio so that the mesh can be self-configuring and self-healing. AWPP actually has the ability to consider all relevant elements of the wireless environment so that the mesh network's functionality isn't disrupted and can provide consistent coverage.

This is pretty powerful considering how truly dynamic a wireless environment is. When there's interference or if APs are added or removed, the Adaptive Wireless Path Protocol reconfigures the path back to the rooftop AP (RAP). Again, in response to the highly dynamic wireless environment, AWPP uses a "stickiness" factor to mitigate routes that ensure that an event, such as a large truck passing through the mesh causing a temporary disruption, doesn't cause the mesh to change unnecessarily.

 For hands-on training with the Cisco Mesh and Mobility (1500/3200 Integration) product line, see www.globalnettraining.com.

Wireless Security

By default, wireless security is nonexistent on access points and clients. The original 802.11 committee just didn't imagine that wireless hosts would one day outnumber bounded media hosts, but that's truly where we're headed. Also, and unfortunately, just like with the IPv4 routed protocol, engineers and scientists didn't add security standards that are robust enough to work in a corporate environment. So we're left with proprietary solution add-ons to aid us in our quest to create a secure wireless network. And no—I'm not just sitting here bashing the standards committees because the security problems we're experiencing were also created by the U.S. government because of export issues with its own security standards. Our world is a complicated place, so it follows that our security solutions are going to be as well.

A good place to start is by discussing the standard basic security that was added into the original 802.11 standards and why those standards are way too flimsy and incomplete to enable us to create a secure wireless network relevant to today's challenges.

Open Access

All Wi-Fi Certified wireless LAN products are shipped in "open-access" mode, with their security features turned off. While open access or no security may be appropriate and acceptable for public hot spots such as coffee shops, college campuses, and maybe airports, it's definitely not an option for an enterprise organization, and likely not even adequate for your private home network.

Security needs to be enabled on wireless devices during their installation in enterprise environments. It may come as quite a shock, but some companies actually don't enable any WLAN security features. Obviously, the companies that do this are exposing their networks to tremendous risk!

The reason that the products are shipped with open access is so that any person who knows absolutely nothing about computers can just buy an access point, plug it into their cable or DSL modem, and voilà—they're up and running. It's marketing, plain and simple, and simplicity sells.

SSIDs, WEP, and MAC Address Authentication

What the original designers of 802.11 did to create basic security was include the use of Service Set Identifiers (SSIDs), open or shared-key authentication, static Wired Equivalency Protocol (WEP), and optional Media Access Control (MAC) authentication. Sounds like a lot, but none of these really offer any type of serious security solution—all they may be close to adequate for is use on a common home network. But we'll go over them anyway...

SSID is a common network name for the devices in a WLAN system that create the wireless LAN. An SSID prevents access by any client device that doesn't have the SSID. The thing is, by default, an access point broadcasts its SSID in its beacon many times a second. And even if SSID broadcasting is turned off, a bad guy can discover the SSID by monitoring the network and just waiting for a client response to the access point. Why? Because, believe it or not, that information, as regulated in the original 802.11 specifications, must be sent in the clear—how secure!

Two types of authentication were specified by the IEEE 802.11 committee: open and shared-key authentication. Open authentication involves little more than supplying the correct SSID—but it's the most common method in use today. With shared-key authentication, the access point sends the client device a challenge-text packet that the client must then encrypt with the correct Wired Equivalency Protocol (WEP) key and return to the access point. Without the correct key, authentication will fail and the client won't be allowed to associate with the access point. But shared-key authentication is still not considered secure because all an intruder has to do to get around this is detect both the clear-text challenge and the same challenge encrypted with a WEP key and then decipher the WEP key. Surprise—shared key isn't used in today's WLANs because of clear-text challenge.

With open authentication, even if a client can complete authentication and associate with an access point, the use of WEP prevents the client from sending and receiving data from the access point unless the client has the correct WEP key. A WEP key is composed of either 40 or 128 bits and, in its basic form, is usually statically defined by the network administrator on the access point and all clients that communicate with that access point. When static WEP keys are used, a network administrator must perform the time-consuming task of entering the same keys on every device in the WLAN. Obviously, we now have fixes for this because this would be administratively impossible in today's huge corporate wireless networks!

Last, client MAC addresses can be statically typed into each access point, and any of them that show up without that MAC addresses in the filter table would be denied access. Sounds good, but of course all MAC layer information must be sent in the clear—anyone equipped with a free wireless sniffer can just read the client packets sent to the access point and spoof their MAC address.

WEP can actually work if administered correctly. But basic static WEP keys are no longer a viable option in today's corporate networks without some of the proprietary fixes that run on top of it. So let's talk about some of these now.

WPA or WPA 2 Pre-Shared Key

Okay, now we're getting somewhere. Although this is another form of basic security that's really just an add-on to the specifications, WPA or WPA2 Pre-Shared Key (PSK) is a better form of wireless security than any other basic wireless security method mentioned so far. I did say basic.

The PSK verifies users via a password or identifying code (also called a passphrase) on both the client machine and the access point. A client only gains access to the network if its password matches the access point's password. The PSK also provides keying material that TKIP or AES uses to generate an encryption key for each packet of transmitted data. While more secure than static WEP, PSK still has a lot in common with static WEP in that the PSK is stored on the client station and can be compromised if the client station is lost or stolen even though finding this key isn't all that easy to do. It's a definite recommendation to use a strong PSK passphrase that includes a mixture of letters, numbers, and nonalphanumeric characters.

Wi-Fi Protected Access (WPA) is a standard developed in 2003 by the Wi-Fi Alliance, formerly known as WECA. WPA provides a standard for authentication and encryption of WLANs that's intended to solve known security problems existing up to and including the year 2003. This takes into account the well-publicized AirSnort and man-in-the-middle WLAN attacks.

WPA is a step toward the IEEE 802.11i standard and uses many of the same components, with the exception of encryption—802.11i uses AES-CCMP encryption. WPA's mechanisms are designed to be implementable by current hardware vendors, meaning that users should be able to implement WPA on their systems with only a firmware/software modification.

 The IEEE 802.11i standard has been sanctioned by WPA and is termed WPA version 2.

Cisco Unified Wireless Network Security

The Cisco Unified Wireless Network delivers many innovative Cisco enhancements and supports Wi-Fi Protected Access (WPA) and Wi-Fi Protected Access 2 (WPA2), which provide access control per user, per session via mutual authentication and data privacy and through strong dynamic encryption. Quality of service (QoS) and mobility are integrated into this solution to enable a rich set of enterprise applications.

The Cisco Unified Wireless Network provides the following:

Secure Connectivity for WLANs   Strong dynamic encryption keys that automatically change on a configurable basis to protect the privacy of transmitted data.

- WPA-TKIP includes encryption enhancements like MIC, per-packet keys via initialization vector hashing, and broadcast key rotation.
- WPA2-AES is the "gold standard" for data encryption.

Trust and Identity for WLANs   A robust WLAN access control that helps to ensure that legitimate clients associate only with trusted access points rather than rogue, or unauthorized access points. It's provided per user, per session via mutual authentication using IEEE 802.1X, a variety of Extensible Authentication Protocol (EAP) types, a Remote Authentication Dial-In User Service (RADIUS), and a Authentication, Authorization, and Accounting (AAA) server. It supports the following:

- The broadest range of 802.1X authentication types, client devices, and client operating systems on the market
- RADIUS accounting records for all authentication attempts

Threat Defense for WLANs   Detection of unauthorized access, network attacks, and rogue access points via an Intrusion Prevention System (IPS), WLAN NAC, and advanced location services. Cisco's IPS allows IT managers to continually scan the RF environment, detect rogue access points and unauthorized events, simultaneously track thousands of devices, and mitigate network attacks. NAC has been specifically designed to help ensure that all wired and wireless endpoint devices like PCs, laptops, servers, and PDAs that are trying to access network resources are adequately protected from security threats. NAC allows organizations to analyze and control all devices coming into the network.

Okay—let's configure some wireless devices now!

Configuring Our Wireless Internetwork

Configuring through the SDM is definitely the easiest way to go for wireless configurations, that is, if you're using any type of security. And of course you should be! Basically, all you need to do to bring up an access point is to just turn it on. But if you do have a wireless card in your router, you'll need to configure it just as I showed you back in Chapter 4.

Here's a screen shot of my R2 router showing that I can configure the wireless card I have installed in slot 3.

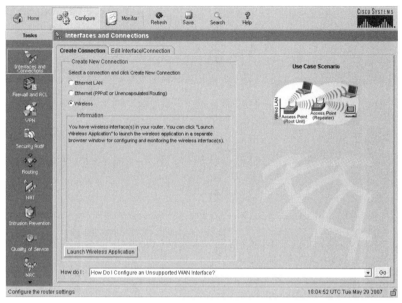

There really isn't too much you can do from within SDM itself, but if I were to click on the Edit Interface/Connection tab and then click Summary, I could enable and disable the interface, as well as click the Edit button, which would allow me to add NAT, access lists, and so on to the interface.

From either the Create Connection screen shown in the first screen of this section, or from the screen that appears when you click the Edit button of the second screen, you can click Launch Wireless Application. This will open up a new HTTP screen that your wireless device is configured from called Express Set-up.

This is the same screen you would see if you just typed HTTP into an access point—one like our 1242AP. The SDM will be used with wireless interfaces for monitoring, to provide statistics, and for gaining access into the wireless configuration mode on a router that has wireless interfaces. This is so we don't have to use the CLI for the hard configurations.

Again, you can only configure some basic information from here. But from the next screen, Wireless Express Security, we can configure the wireless AP in either bridging mode or routing mode—a really cool feature!

The next screen shows the wireless interfaces and the basic settings.

The following screen shot is the second part of the Wireless Interfaces screen.

Under the Wireless Security heading is really where HTTP management shines! You can configure encryption, add SSIDs and configure your Radius sever settings.

Now, if we just HTTP in to the 1242AG AP, we'll see this screen.

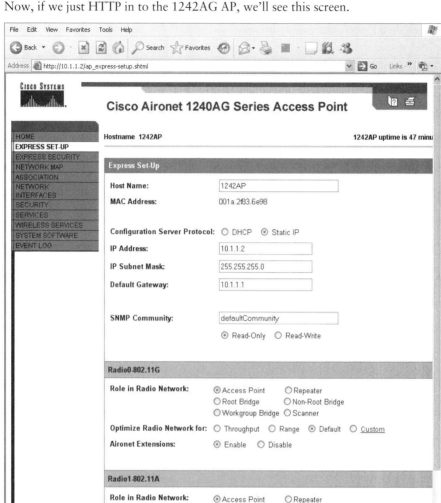

This looks amazingly like the APs we'll find in our ISR routers, and we can configure the same devices and security too.

Summary

Like rock 'n' roll, wireless technologies are here to stay, and for those of us who have come to depend on wireless technologies, it's actually pretty hard to imagine a world without wireless networks—what did we do before cell phones?

So we began this chapter by exploring the essentials and fundamentals of how wireless networks function.

Springing off that foundation, I then introduced you to the basics of wireless RF and the IEEE standards. We discussed 802.11 from its inception through its evolution to current and near future standards and talked about the subcommittees who create them.

All of this lead into a discussion of wireless security—or rather, non-security for the most part, which logically directed us to Cisco's proprietary answer to this dilemma: the Cisco Unified Wireless Solution, which we went over in detail.

We finished the chapter by actually using the SDM to configure our wireless network and its associated devices.

Exam Essentials

Understand the IEEE 802.11a specification.   802.11a runs in the 5 GHz spectrum, and if you use the 802.11h extensions, you have 23 non-overlapping channels. 802.11a can run up to 54 Mbps, but only if you are less than 50 feet from an access point.

Understand the IEEE 802.11b specification.   IEEE 802.11b runs in the 2.4 GHz range and has three non-overlapping channels. It can handle long distances, but with a maximum data rate of up to 11 Mpbs.

Understand the IEEE 802.11g specification.   IEEE 802.11g is 802.11b's big brother and runs in the same 2.4 GHz range, but it has a higher data rate of 54 Mbps if you are less than 100 feet from an access point.

Written Lab 12

In this section, write the answers to the following wireless questions:

1. What is the maximum data rate of IEEE 802.11b?

2. What is the maximum data rate of IEEE 802.11g?

3. What is the maximum data rate of IEEE 802.11a?

4. What is the frequency range of IEEE 802.11b?

5. What is the frequency range of IEEE 802.11g?

6. What is the frequency range of IEEE 802.11a?

7. In Cisco's Unified Wireless Solution, what is the split-MAC architecture?

8. The IEEE 802.11h specification adds what two extensions to IEEE 802.11a?

9. Which IEEE committee has been sanctioned by WPA and is called WPA 2?

10. The IEEE 802.11a basic standard has how many non-overlapping channels?

   (The answers to Written Lab 12 can be found following the answers to the review questions for this chapter.)

Review Questions

 The following questions are designed to test your understanding of this chapter's material. For more information on how to get additional questions, please see this book's Introduction.

1. In Cisco's Unified Wireless Solution, what is the split-MAC architecture?

   A. The split-MAC architecture uses MAC addresses to create a forward/filter table and break up collision domains.

   B. The split-MAC architecture allows the splitting of 802.11 protocol packets between the AP and the controller to allow processing by both devices.

   C. The split-MAC architecture uses MAC addresses on the wireless network and IP addresses on the wired network.

   D. The split-MAC architecture uses MAC addresses to create a forward/filter table and break up broadcast domains.

2. What is the frequency range of the IEEE 802.11b standard?

   A. 2.4Gbps

   B. 5Gbps

   C. 2.4GHz

   D. 5GHz

3. What is the frequency range of the IEEE 802.11a standard?

   A. 2.4Gbps

   B. 5Gbps

   C. 2.4GHz

   D. 5GHz

4. What is the frequency range of the IEEE 802.11g standard?

   A. 2.4Gbps

   B. 5Gbps

   C. 2.4GHz

   D. 5GHz

5. How many non-overlapping channels are available with 802.11h?

   A. 3

   B. 12

   C. 23

   D. 40

6. How many non-overlapping channels are available with 802.11g?

    A. 3

    B. 12

    C. 23

    D. 40

7. How many non-overlapping channels are available with 802.11b?

    A. 3

    B. 12

    C. 23

    D. 40

8. How many non-overlapping channels are available with 802.11a?

    A. 3

    B. 12

    C. 23

    D. 40

9. What is the maximum data rate for the 802.11a standard?

    A. 6Mbps

    B. 11Mbps

    C. 22Mbps

    D. 54Mbps

10. What is the maximum data rate for the 802.11g standard?

    A. 6Mbps

    B. 11Mbps

    C. 22Mbps

    D. 54Mbps

11. What is the maximum data rate for the 802.11b standard?

    A. 6Mbps

    B. 11Mbps

    C. 22Mbps

    D. 54Mbps

12. What is the maximum distance with maximum data rate for 802.11a?

    A. About 65–75 feet

    B. About 90–100 feet

    C. About 150 feet

    D. Over 200 feet

13. What is the maximum distance with maximum data rate for 802.11g?

   A. About 65–75 feet

   B. About 90–100 feet

   C. About 150 feet

   D. Over 200 feet

14. What is the maximum distance with maximum data rate for 802.11b?

   A. About 65–75 feet

   B. About 90–100 feet

   C. About 150 feet

   D. Over 200 feet

15. What is the maximum distance running the lowest data rate for 802.11b?

   A. About 100 feet

   B. About 175 feet

   C. About 300 feet

   D. About 350 feet

16. What is the maximum distance running the lowest data rate for 802.11a?

   A. About 100 feet

   B. About 175 feet

   C. About 300 feet

   D. About 350 feet

17. What is the maximum distance running the lowest data rate for 802.11g?

   A. About 100 feet

   B. About 175 feet

   C. About 300 feet

   D. About 350 feet

18. Cisco's Unified Wireless Solution provides a mesh solution. What devices do you absolutely need to purchase to run a Cisco solution? (Choose two.)

   A. WCS

   B. Controller

   C. Access point

   D. Bridge

19. You are connecting your access point and it is set to root. What does Extended Service Set ID mean?

   A. That you have more than one access point and they are in the same SSID connected by a distribution system

   B. That you have more than one access point and they are in separate SSIDs connected by a distribution system

   C. That you have multiple access points, but they are placed physically in different buildings

   D. That you have multiple access points, but one is a repeater access point

20. You have a Cisco mesh network. What protocol allows multiple APs to connect with many redundant connections between nodes?

   A. LWAPP

   B. AWPP

   C. STP

   D. IEEE

Answers to Review Questions

1. B. The split-MAC architecture allows the splitting of 802.11 protocol packets between the Cisco LWAPP-based AP, which handles real-time portions of the protocol, and the WLAN controller, which handles those items that are not time sensitive.

2. C. The IEEE 802.11b and IEEE 802.11b standards both run in the 2.4GHz RF range.

3. D. The IEEE 802.11a standard runs in the 5GHz RF range.

4. C. The IEEE 802.11b and IEEE 802.11b standards both run in the 2.4GHz RF range.

5. C. The IEEE 802.11h standard provides an addition 11 channels to the 802.11a standard's 12 non-overlapping channel for a total of 23 non-overlapping channels.

6. A. The IEEE 802.11g standard provides three non-overlapping channels.

7. A. The IEEE 802.11b standard provides three non-overlapping channels.

8. B. The IEEE 802.11a standard provides up to 12 non-overlapping channels.

9. D. The IEEE 802.11a standard provides a maximum data rate of up to 54Mbps.

10. D. The IEEE 802.11g standard provides a maximum data rate of up to 54Mbps.

11. B. The IEEE 802.11b standard provides a maximum data rate of up to 11Mbps.

12. A. The IEEE 802.11a standard provides a maximum data rate of up to 54Mbps, but you need to be close to the access point, somewhere around 65 to 75 feet.

13. B. The IEEE 802.11g standard provides a maximum data rate of up to 54Mbps, but you need to be close to the access point, somewhere around 90 to 100 feet.

14. C. The IEEE 802.11b standard provides a maximum data rate of up to only 11Mbps, and you can be around 150 feet, maybe farther, depending on conditions.

15. D. The IEEE 802.11b standard provides the lowest data rate at 1Mbps, but it also has the longest distance, which is about 350 feet.

16. B. The IEEE 802.11a standard's lowest data rate is 6Mbps, but it can run from a distance of about 175 feet.

17. C. The IEEE 802.11g standard's lowest data rate is 6Mbps, but it can run from a distance of about 300 feet.

18. B, C. The Cisco Unified Wireless Solution is a great product, but you must purchase specialized devices. Cisco managed access points and a controller are the devices you need to purchase to run the Unified Wireless Solution.

19. A. Extended Service Set ID means that you have more than one access point and they all are set to the same SSID and all are connected together in the same VLAN or distribution system so users can roam.

20. B. Each AP in a mesh network runs the Adaptive Wireless Path Protocol (AWPP). This protocol allows RAPs to communicate with each other to determine the best path back to the wired network via the RAP.

Answers to Written Lab 12

1. 11Mbps

2. 54Mbps

3. 54Mbps

4. 2.4GHz

5. 2.4GHz

6. 5GHz

7. The split-MAC architecture allows the splitting of 802.11 protocol packets between the Cisco LWAPP-based AP, which handles real-time portions of the protocol, and the WLAN controller, which handles those items that are not time sensitive.

8. There are two new features to the 5GHz radio that are part of the 802.11h specification: Transmit Power Control (TPC) and Dynamic Frequency Selection (DFS).

9. The IEEE 802.11i standard has been sanctioned by WPA and is termed WPA version 2.

10. 12

Chapter

13

Internet Protocol Version 6 (IPv6)

THE CCNA EXAM TOPICS COVERED IN THIS CHAPTER INCLUDE THE FOLLOWING:

✓ **Implement an IP addressing scheme and IP Services to meet network requirements in a medium-size Enterprise branch office network**

- Describe the technological requirements for running IPv6 in conjunction with IPv4 (including: protocols, dual stack, tunneling, etc)
- Describe IPv6 addresses

I hope you're ready to learn about the nuts and bolts of Internet Protocol version 6 (IPv6), because you're going to get the rub on it in this chapter!

You should have a solid hold on IPv4 by now, but if you think you could use a refresher, just page back to Chapter 3, "Subnetting, Variable Length Subnet Masks (VLSMs), and Troubleshooting TCP/IP." And if you're not crystal clear on the address problems inherent to IPv4, you really should review Chapter 11, "Network Address Translation (NAT)."

People refer to IPv6 as "the next-generation Internet protocol," and it was originally created as the answer to IPv4's inevitable, looming address-exhaustion crisis. Though you've probably heard a thing or two about IPv6 already, it has been improved even further in the quest to bring us the flexibility, efficiency, capability, and optimized functionality that can truly meet our ever-increasing needs. The capacity of its predecessor, IPv4, pales in comparison—and that's the reason it will eventually fade into history completely.

The IPv6 header and address structure has been completely overhauled, and many of the features that were basically just afterthoughts and addendums in IPv4 are now included as full-blown standards in IPv6. It's seriously well equipped, poised, and ready to manage the mind-blowing demands of the Internet to come.

I promise—really—to make this chapter pretty painless. In fact, you might even find yourself actually enjoying it—I definitely did! Because IPv6 is so complex yet elegant, innovative and chock-full of features, it fascinates me like some weird combination of a brand-new Lamborghini and a riveting futuristic novel. Hopefully you'll experience this chapter as the cool ride that I did writing it!

For up-to-the-minute updates for this chapter, please see www.lammle.com and/or www.sybex.com.

Why Do We Need IPv6?

Well, the short answer is, because we need to communicate, and our current system isn't really cutting it anymore—kind of like how the Pony Express can't compete with airmail. Just look at how much time and effort we've invested in coming up with slick new ways to conserve bandwidth and IP addresses. We've even come up with Variable Length Subnet Masks (VLSMs) in our struggle to overcome the worsening address drought.

It's reality—the number of people and devices that connect to networks increases each and every day. That's not a bad thing at all—we're finding new and exciting ways to communicate to more people all the time, and that's a good thing. In fact, it's a basic human need. But the forecast isn't exactly blue skies and sunshine because, as I alluded to in this chapter's introduction, IPv4, upon which our ability to communicate is presently dependent, is going to run out of addresses for us to use. IPv4 has only about 4.3 billion addresses available—in theory, and we know that we don't even get to use all of those. There really are only about 250 million addresses that can be assigned to devices. Sure, the use of Classless Inter-Domain Routing (CIDR) and Network Address Translation (NAT) has helped to extend the inevitable dearth of addresses, but we will run out of them, and it's going to happen within a few years. China is barely online, and we know there's a huge population of people and corporations there that surely want to be. There are a lot of reports that give us all kinds of numbers, but all you really need to think about to convince yourself that I'm not just being an alarmist is the fact that there are about 6.5 billion people in the world today, and it's estimated that just over 10 percent of that population is connected to the Internet—wow!

That statistic is basically screaming at us the ugly truth that based on IPv4's capacity, every person can't even have a computer—let alone all the other devices we use with them. I have more than one computer, and it's pretty likely you do too. And I'm not even including in the mix phones, laptops, game consoles, fax machines, routers, switches, and a mother lode of other devices we use every day! So I think I've made it pretty clear that we've got to do something before we run out of addresses and lose the ability to connect with each other as we know it. And that "something" just happens to be implementing IPv6.

The Benefits and Uses of IPv6

So what's so fabulous about IPv6? Is it really the answer to our coming dilemma? Is it really worth it to upgrade from IPv4? All good questions—you may even think of a few more. Of course, there's going to be that group of people with the time-tested and well-known "resistance to change syndrome," but don't listen to them. If we had done that years ago, we'd still be waiting weeks, even months for our mail to arrive via horseback. Instead, just know that the answer is a resounding YES! Not only does IPv6 give us lots of addresses (3.4×10^{38} = definitely enough), but there are many other features built into this version that make it well worth the cost, time, and effort required to migrate to it. Later in the chapter I'll talk about all that effort in the section called "Migrating to IPv6." In it, I'll cover some of the transition types required to move from version 4 to version 6, and I promise you'll discover that the huge benefits of migrating will vastly outweigh any associated cons.

Today's networks, as well as the Internet, have a ton of unforeseen requirements that simply were not considerations when IPv4 was created. We've tried to compensate with a collection of add-ons that can actually make implementing them more difficult than they would be if they were required by a standard. By default, IPv6 has improved upon and included many of those features as standard and mandatory. One of these sweet new standards is IPSec—a feature that provides end-to-end security that I'll cover in Chapter 14, "Wide Area Networks." Another little beauty is known as mobility, and as its name suggests, it allows a device to roam from one network to another without dropping connections.

But it's the efficiency features that are really going to rock the house! For starters, the header in an IPv6 packet have half the fields, and they are aligned to 64 bits, which gives us some seriously souped-up processing speed—compared to IPv4, lookups happen at light speed! Most of the information that used to be bound into the IPv4 header was taken out, and now you can choose to put it, or parts of it, back into the header in the form of optional extension headers that follow the basic header fields.

And of course there's that whole new universe of addresses (3.4 x 10^38) we talked about already. But where did we get them? Did that Criss Angel–Mindfreak dude just show up and, Blammo? I mean, that huge proliferation of addresses had to come from somewhere! Well it just so happens that IPv6 gives us a substantially larger address space, meaning the address is a whole lot bigger—four times bigger as a matter of fact! An IPv6 address is actually 128 bits in length, and no worries—I'm going to break down the address piece by piece and show you exactly what it looks like coming up in the section "IPv6 Addressing and Expressions." For now, let me just say that all that additional room permits more levels of hierarchy inside the address space and a more flexible address architecture. It also makes routing much more efficient and scalable because the addresses can be aggregated a lot more effectively. And IPv6 also allows multiple addresses for hosts and networks. This is especially important for enterprises jonesing for availability. Plus, the new version of IP now includes an expanded use of multicast communication (one device sending to many hosts or to a select group), which will also join in to boost efficiency on networks because communications will be more specific.

IPv4 uses broadcasts very prolifically, causing a bunch of problems, the worst of which is of course the dreaded broadcast storm—an uncontrolled deluge of forwarded broadcast traffic that can bring an entire network to its knees and devour every last bit of bandwidth. Another nasty thing about broadcast traffic is that it interrupts each and every device on the network. When a broadcast is sent out, every machine has to stop what it's doing and respond to the traffic whether the broadcast is meant for it or not.

But smile everyone: There is no such thing as a broadcast in IPv6 because it uses multicast traffic instead. And there are two other types of communication as well: unicast, which is the same as it is in IPv4, and a new type called anycast. Anycast communication allows the same address to be placed on more than one device so that when traffic is sent to one device addressed in this way, it is routed to the nearest host that shares the same address. This is just the beginning—we'll get more into the various types of communication in the section called "Address Types."

IPv6 Addressing and Expressions

Just as understanding how IP addresses are structured and used is critical with IPv4 addressing, it's also vital when it comes to IPv6. You've already read about the fact that at 128 bits, an IPv6 address is much larger than an IPv4 address. Because of this, as well as the new ways the addresses can be used, you've probably guessed that IPv6 will be more complicated to manage. But no worries! As I said, I'll break down the basics and show you what the address looks like, how you can write it, and what many of its common uses are. It's going to be a little weird at first, but before you know it, you'll have it nailed!

So let's take a look at Figure 13.1, which has a sample IPv6 address broken down into sections.

FIGURE 13.1   IPv6 address example

```
2001:0db8:3c4d:0012:0000:0000:1234:56ab
_____|____|_____
Global prefix   Subnet        Interface ID
```

 Remember where you can find this subnet ID because we'll use it in the section "Configuring IPv6 on Our internetwork" later in the chapter when we configure our routers.

So as you can now see, the address is truly much larger—but what else is different? Well, first, notice that it has eight groups of numbers instead of four and also that those groups are separated by colons instead of periods. And hey wait a second... there are letters in that address! Yep, the address is expressed in hexadecimal just like a MAC address is, so you could say this address has eight 16-bit hexadecimal colon-delimited blocks. That's already quite a mouthful, and you probably haven't even tried to say the address out loud yet!

One other thing I want to point out is for when you set up your test network to play with IPv6, because I know you're going to want to do that. When you use a web browser to make an HTTP connection to an IPv6 device, you have to type the address into the browser with brackets around the literal address. Why? Well, a colon is already being used by the browser for specifying a port number. So basically, if you don't enclose the address in brackets, the browser will have no way to identify the information.

Here's an example of how this looks:

```
http://[2001:0db8:3c4d:0012:0000:0000:1234:56ab]/default.html
```

Now obviously if you can, you would rather use names to specify a destination (like www.lammle.com), but even though it's definitely going to be a pain in the rear, we just have to accept the fact that sometimes we have to bite the bullet and type in the address number. So it should be pretty clear that DNS is going to become extremely important when implementing IPv6.

Shortened Expression

The good news is there are a few tricks to help rescue us when writing these monster addresses. For one thing, you can actually leave out parts of the address to abbreviate it, but to get away with doing that you have to follow a couple of rules. First, you can drop any leading zeros in each of the individual blocks. After you do that, the sample address from earlier would then look like this:

```
2001:db8:3c4d:12:0:0:1234:56ab
```

Okay, that's a definite improvement—at least we don't have to write all of those extra zeros! But what about whole blocks that don't have anything in them except zeros? Well, we can kind of lose those too—at least some of them. Again referring to our sample address, we can remove the two blocks of zeros by replacing them with double colons, like this:

`2001:db8:3c4d:12::1234:56ab`

Cool—we replaced the blocks of all zeros with double colons. The rule you have to follow to get away with this is that you can only replace one contiguous block of zeros in an address. So if my address has four blocks of zeros and each of them were separated, I just don't get to replace them all; remember the rule is that you can only replace one contiguous block with a double colon. Check out this example:

`2001:0000:0000:0012:0000:0000:1234:56ab`

And just know that you *can't* do this:

`2001::12::1234:56ab`

Instead, this is the best that you can do:

`2001::12:0:0:1234:56ab`

The reason why the above example is our best shot is that if we remove two sets of zeros, the device looking at the address will have no way of knowing where the zeros go back in. Basically, the router would look at the incorrect address and say, "Well, do I place two blocks into the first set of double colons and two into the second set, or do I place three blocks into the first set and one block into the second set?" And on and on it would go because the information the router needs just isn't there.

Address Types

We're all familiar with IPv4's unicast, broadcast, and multicast addresses that basically define who or at least how many other devices we're talking to. But as I mentioned, IPv6 adds to that trio and introduces the anycast. Broadcasts, as we know them, have been eliminated in IPv6 because of their cumbersome inefficiency.

So let's find out what each of these types of IPv6 addressing and communication methods do for us.

Unicast   Packets addressed to a unicast address are delivered to a single interface. For load balancing, multiple interfaces can use the same address. There are a few different types of unicast addresses, but we don't need to get into that here.

Global unicast addresses   These are your typical publicly routable addresses, and they're the same as they are in IPv4.

Link-local addresses   These are like the private addresses in IPv4 in that they're not meant to be routed. Think of them as a handy tool that gives you the ability to throw a temporary LAN together for meetings or for creating a small LAN that's not going to be routed but still needs to share and access files and services locally.

Unique local addresses   These addresses are also intended for non-routing purposes, but they are nearly globally unique, so it's unlikely you'll ever have one of them overlap. Unique local addresses were designed to replace site-local addresses, so they basically do almost exactly what IPv4 private addresses do—allow communication throughout a site while being routable to multiple local networks. Site-local addresses were denounced as of September 2004.

Multicast   Again, same as in IPv4, packets addressed to a multicast address are delivered to all interfaces identified by the multicast address. Sometimes people call them one-to-many addresses. It's really easy to spot a multicast address in IPv6 because they always start with *FF*. I'll get into greater detail about multicast operation in the section "How IPv6 Works in an Internetwork."

Anycast   Like multicast addresses, an anycast address identifies multiple interfaces, but there's a big difference: the anycast packet is only delivered to one address—actually, to the first one it finds defined in terms of routing distance. And again, this address is special because you can apply a single address to more than one interface. You could call them one-to-one-of-many addresses, but just saying "anycast" is a lot easier.

You're probably wondering if there are any special, reserved addresses in IPv6 because you know they're there in IPv4. Well there are—plenty of them! Let's go over them now.

Special Addresses

I'm going to list some of the addresses and address ranges that you should definitely make a point to remember because you'll eventually use them. They're all special or reserved for specific use, but unlike IPv4, IPv6 gives us a galaxy of addresses, so reserving a few here and there doesn't hurt a thing!

0:0:0:0:0:0:0:0   Equals ::. This is the equivalent of IPv4's 0.0.0.0, and is typically the source address of a host when you're using stateful configuration.

0:0:0:0:0:0:0:1   Equals ::1. The equivalent of 127.0.0.1 in IPv4.

0:0:0:0:0:0:192.168.100.1   This is how an IPv4 address would be written in a mixed IPv6/IPv4 network environment.

2000::/3   The global unicast address range.

FC00::/7   The unique local unicast range.

FE80::/10   The link-local unicast range.

FF00::/8   The multicast range.

3FFF:FFFF::/32   Reserved for examples and documentation.

2001:0DB8::/32   Also reserved for examples and documentation.

2002::/16   Used with 6to4, which is the transition system—the structure that allows IPv6 packets to be transmitted over an IPv4 network without the need to configure explicit tunnels.

We'll get more into this later in "Migrating to IPv6," but for now let me show you how IPv6 actually works in an internetwork. We all know how IPv4 works, so let's see what's new.

How IPv6 Works in an Internetwork

It's time to explore the finer points of IPv6. A great place to start is by showing you how to address a host and what gives it the ability to find other hosts and resources on a network.

I'll also demonstrate a device's ability to automatically address itself—something called stateless autoconfiguration, plus another type of autoconfiguration known as stateful. Keep in mind that stateful autoconfiguration uses a DHCP server in a very similar way to how it's used in an IPv4 configuration. I'll also show you how Internet Control Message Protocol (ICMP) and multicast works for us on an IPv6 network.

Autoconfiguration

Autoconfiguration is an incredibly useful solution because it allows devices on a network to address themselves with a link-local unicast address. This process happens through first learning the prefix information from the router and then appending the device's own interface address as the interface ID. But where does it get that interface ID? Well, you know every device on an Ethernet network has a physical MAC address, and that's exactly what's used for the interface ID. But since the interface ID in an IPv6 address is 64 bits in length and a MAC address is only 48 bits, where do the extra 16 bits come from? The MAC address is padded in the middle with the extra bits—it's padded with FFFE.

For example, let's say I have a device with a MAC address that looks like this: 0060.d673.1987.

After it's been padded, it would look like this: 0260.d6FF.FE73.1987.

So where did that 2 in the beginning of the address come from? Another good question. You see, part of the process of padding (called modified eui-64 format) changes a bit to specify if the address is locally unique or globally unique. And the bit that gets changed is the seventh bit in the address. A bit value of 1 means globally unique, and a bit value of 0 means locally unique, so looking at this example, would you say that this address is globally or locally unique? If you answered that it's a globally unique address, you're right! Trust me, this is going to save you time in addressing your host machines because they communicate with the router to make this happen.

To perform autoconfiguration, a host goes through a basic two-step process:

1. First, the host needs the prefix information (similar to the network portion of an IPv4 address) to configure its interface, so it sends a router solicitation (RS) request for it. This RS is then sent out as a multicast to each router's multicast address. The actual information being sent is a type of ICMP message, and like everything in networking, this ICMP message has a number that identifies it. The RS message is ICMP type 133.

2. The router answers back with the required prefix information via a router advertisement (RA). An RA message also happens to be a multicast packet that's sent to each node's multicast address and is ICMP type 134. RA messages are sent on a periodic basis, but the host sends the RS for an immediate response so it doesn't have to wait until the next scheduled RA to get what it needs.

These two steps are shown in Figure 13.2.

FIGURE 13.2   Two steps to IPv6 autoconfiguration

By the way, this type of autoconfiguration is also known as stateless autoconfiguration because it doesn't contact or connect and receive any further information from the other device. We'll get to stateful configuration when we talk about DHCPv6 in a minute.

Now let's take a look at how to configure Cisco routers with IPv6.

Configuring Cisco Routers with IPv6

In order to enable IPv6 on a router, you have to use the `ipv6 unicast-routing` global configuration command:

```
Corp(config)#ipv6 unicast-routing
```

By default, IPv6 traffic forwarding is disabled, so using this command enables it. Also, as you've probably guessed, IPv6 isn't enabled by default on any interfaces either, so we have to go to each interface individually and enable it.

There are a few different ways to do this, but a really easy way is to just add an address to the interface. You use the interface configuration command `ipv6 address <ipv6prefix>/ <prefix-length> [eui-64]`to get this done.

Here's an example:

```
Corp(config-if)#ipv6 address 2001:db8:3c4d:1:0260.d6FF.FE73.1987/64
```

You can specify the entire 128-bit global IPv6 address or you can use the eui-64 option. Remember, the eui-64 format allows the device to use its MAC address and pad it to make the interface ID. Check it out:

```
Corp(config-if)#ipv6 address 2001:db8:3c4d:1::/64 eui-64
```

As an alternative to typing in an IPv6 address on a router, you can enable the interface instead to permit the application of an automatic link-local address.

Remember, if you only have a link-local address, you will only be able to communicate on that local subnet.

To configure a router so that it only uses link-local addresses, use the `ipv6 enable` interface configuration command:

```
Corp(config-if)#ipv6 enable
```

Okay, now let's dive into stateful IPv6 by configuring a DHCP server for IPv6 use.

DHCPv6

DHCPv6 works pretty much the same way DHCP does in v4, with the obvious difference that it supports the new addressing scheme for IPv6. And it might come as a surprise, but there are a couple of other options that DHCP still provides for us that autoconfiguration doesn't. I'm serious—there's absolutely no mention of DNS servers, domain names, or many of the other options that DHCP has always provided for us via IPv4 with autoconfiguration. This is a big reason why it's likely we'll still be using DHCP in IPv6 most of the time.

Upon booting up in IPv4, a client sent out a DHCP discover message looking for a server to give it the information it needs. But remember, in IPv6, the RS and RA process happens first. If there's a DHCPv6 server on the network, the RA that comes back to the client will tell it if DHCP is available for use. If a router isn't found, the client will respond by sending out a DHCP solicit message—a solicit message that's actually a multicast message addressed with a source of ff02::1:2, meaning all DHCP agents, both servers and relays.

It's good to know that there's some support for DHCPv6 in the Cisco IOS. But it's limited to a stateless DHCP server, meaning it doesn't offer any address management of the pool, plus the options available for configuring that address pool are limited to the DNS, domain name, and SIP servers only.

This means that you're definitely going to need some other server around that can supply and dispense all the additional, required information, as well as manage the address assignment.

Anyway, here's how the configuration looks for the stateless DHCP server in the router IOS—it's really close to what we'd configure with IPv4:

```
Router1(config)#ipv6 dhcp pool ?
WORD  DHCP pool name
Router1(config)#ipv6 dhcp pool test
Router1(config-dhcp)#?
IPv6 DHCP configuration commands:
  default       Set a command to its defaults
  dns-server    DNS servers
  domain-name   Domain name to complete unqualified host names
  exit          Exit from DHCPv6 configuration mode
```

```
  no                 Negate a command or set its defaults
  prefix-delegation  IPv6 prefix delegation
  sip                SIP Servers options
Router1(config-dhcp)#dns-server ?
  Hostname or X:X:X:X::X  Server's name or IPv6 address
Router1(config-dhcp)#domain-name lammle.com
Router1(config-dhcp)#prefix-delegation ?
  X:X:X:X::X/<0-128>  IPv6  x:x::y/<z>
  aaa                Acquire prefix from AAA
  pool               IPv6 prefix pool
Router1(config-dhcp)#prefix-delegation pool ?
  WORD  IPv6 prefix pool
Router1(config-dhcp)#prefix-delegation pool test ?
  lifetime  Configure prefix lifetimes
  <cr>
Router1(config-dhcp)#prefix-delegation pool test lifetime ?
  <60-4294967295>  Valid lifetime (seconds)
  at               Expire prefix at a specific time/date
  infinite         Infinite valid lifetime
Router1(config-dhcp)#prefix-delegation pool test lifetime 3600 ?
  <60-4294967295>  Preferred lifetime (seconds)
  infinite         Infinite preferred lifetime
Router1(config-dhcp)#prefix-delegation pool test lifetime 3600 3600 ?
  <cr>
Router1(config-dhcp)#prefix-delegation pool test lifetime 3600 3600
```

Notice that just like in DHCP with IPv4, you don't need to set a lifetime.

Okay—now that I've got the pool configured, I just have to assign it to an interface, a departure from IPv4:

```
Router1(config)#int fa 0/0
Router1(config-if)#ipv6 dhcp server ?
  WORD  Name of IPv6 DHCP pool
Router1(config-if)#ipv6 dhcp server test
```

Sweet—we now have a fully configured DHCPv6 server applied to our interface fa0/0!

ICMPv6

IPv4 used ICMP for many things, such as error messages like destination unreachable, and troubleshooting functions like Ping and Traceroute. ICMPv6 still does those things for us, but unlike its predecessor, the v6 flavor isn't implemented as a separate layer 4 protocol. It's an integrated part of IPv6 and is carried after the basic IPv6 header information as an extension header. And ICMPv6 adds another cool feature—it prevents IPv6 from doing any fragmentation through an ICMPv6 process called path MTU discovery.

This is how it works: The source node of a connection will send a packet that's equal to the MTU size of its local link's MTU. As this packet traverses the path toward its destination, any link that has an MTU smaller than the size of the current packet will force the intermediate router to send a "packet too big" message back to the source machine. This message tells the source node what the maximum size is that the restrictive link will allow and asks the source to send a new scaled-down packet that can pass through. This process will continue until the destination is finally reached, with the source node now sporting the new path's MTU. So now, when the rest of the data packets are transmitted, they'll be protected from fragmentation.

ICMPv6 now takes over the task of finding the address of other devices on the local link. Address Resolution Protocol used to perform this function for IPv4, but that's been renamed Neighbor Discovery in ICMPv6. This process is accomplished by using a multicast address called the solicited node address, and all hosts join this multicast group when they connect to the network. Part of their IPv6 address (the 24 bits farthest to the right) is added to the end of the multicast address FF02:0:0:0:0:1:FF/104. When this address is queried, the corresponding host will send back its layer 2 address. Devices can find and keep track of other neighbor devices on the network in pretty much the same way. When I talked about RA and RS messages earlier and told you that they use multicast traffic to request and send address information, that too was a function of ICMPv6—specifically, neighbor discovery.

In IPv4, the protocol IGMP was used to allow a host device to tell its local router that it was joining a multicast group and would like to receive the traffic for that group. This IGMP function has been replaced by ICMPv6, and the process has been renamed multicast listener discovery.

IPv6 Routing Protocols

Most of the routing protocols we've already discussed have been upgraded for use in IPv6 networks. Also, many of the functions and configurations that we've already learned will be used in almost the same way as they're used now. Knowing that broadcasts have been eliminated in IPv6, it follows that any protocols that use entirely broadcast traffic will go the way of the dodo—but unlike the dodo, it'll be good to say goodbye to these bandwidth-hogging, performance-annihilating little gremlins!

The routing protocols that we'll still use in v6 got a new name and a facelift. Let's talk about a few of them now.

First on the list is RIPng (next generation). Those of you who have been in IT for awhile know that RIP has worked very well for us on smaller networks, which happens to be the very reason it didn't get whacked and will still be around in IPv6. And we still have EIGRPv6 because it already had protocol-dependent modules and all we had to do was add a new one to it for the IPv6 protocol. Rounding out our group of protocol survivors is OSPFv3—that's not a typo, it really is v3. OSPF for IPv4 was actually v2, so when it got its upgrade to IPv6, it became OSPFv3.

RIPng

To be honest, the primary features of RIPng are the same as they were with RIPv2. It is still a distance-vector protocol, has a max hop count of 15, and uses split horizon, poison reverse, and other loop avoidance mechanisms, but it now uses UDP port 521.

And it still uses multicast to send its updates too, but in IPv6, it uses FF02::9 for the transport address. This is actually kind of cool since in RIPv2, the multicast address was 224.0.0.9, so the address still has a 9 at the end in the new IPv6 multicast range. In fact, most routing protocols got to keep a little bit of their IPv4 identities like that.

But of course there are differences in the new version or it wouldn't be a new version, would it? We know that routers keep the next-hop addresses of their neighbor routers for every destination network in their routing table. The difference is that with RIPng, the router keeps track of this next-hop address using the link-local address, not a global address.

Probably one of the biggest changes with RIPng (and all of the IPv6 routing protocols for that matter) is the fact that you configure or enable the advertisement of a network from interface configuration mode instead of with a network command in router configuration mode. So in RIPng's case, if you enable it directly on an interface without going into router configuration mode and starting a RIPng process, a new RIPng process will simply be started for you. It will look something like this:

```
Router1(config-if)#ipv6 rip 1 enable
```

That 1 you see in this command is a tag that identifies the process of RIPng that's running, and as I said, this will start a process of RIPng so you don't have to go into router configuration mode.

But if you need to go to router configuration mode to configure something else like redistribution, you still can. If you do that, it will look like this on your router:

```
Router1(config)#ipv6 router rip 1
Router1(config-rtr)#
```

So just remember that RIPng will pretty much work the same way as with IPv4, with the biggest difference being that it uses the network itself instead of using the network command you used to use to enable the interface to route the connected network.

EIGRPv6

As with RIPng, EIGRPv6 works much the same as its IPv4 predecessor does—most of the features that EIGRP provided before EIGRPv6 will still be available.

EIGRPv6 is still an advanced distance-vector protocol that has some link-state features. The neighbor discovery process using hellos still happens, and it still provides reliable communication with reliable transport protocol that gives us loop-free fast convergence using the Diffusing Update Algorithm (DUAL).

Hello packets and updates are sent using multicast transmission, and as with RIPng, EIGRPv6's multicast address stayed almost the same. In IPv4 it was 224.0.0.10; in IPv6, it's FF02::A (A = 10 in hexadecimal notation).

But obviously, there are differences between the two versions. Most notably, and just as with RIPng, the use of the network command is gone, and the network and interface to be advertised must be enabled from interface configuration mode. But you still have to use the router configuration mode to enable the routing protocol in EIGRPv6 because the routing process must be literally turned on like an interface with the no shutdown command—interesting!

The configuration for EIGRPv6 is going to look like this:

```
Router1(config)#ipv6 router eigrp 10
```

The 10 in this case is still the autonomous system (AS) number. The prompt changes to (config-rtr), and from here you must perform a no shutdown:

```
Router1(config-rtr)#no shutdown
```

Other options also can be configured in this mode, like redistribution.

So now, let's go to the interface and enable IPv6:

```
Router1(config-if)#ipv6 eigrp 10
```

The 10 in the interface command again references the AS number that was enabled in the configuration mode.

Last to check out in our group is what OSPF looks like in the IPv6 routing protocol.

OSPFv3

The new version of OSPF continues the trend of the routing protocols having many similarities with their IPv4 versions.

The foundation of OSPF remains the same—it is still a link-state routing protocol that divides an entire internetwork or autonomous system into areas, making a hierarchy. And just trust me—be really thankful that multi-area OSPF is out of scope for the CCNA objectives—at least, for now! But a few of the options we discussed in Chapter 7, "Enhanced IGRP (EIGRP) and Open Shortest Path First (OSPF)," are going to be a bit different.

In OSPF version 2, the router ID (RID) is determined by the highest IP addresses assigned to the router (or you could assign it). In version 3, you assign the RID, area ID, and link-state ID, which are all still 32-bit values but are not found using the IP address anymore because an IPv6 address is 128 bits. Changes regarding how these values are assigned, along with the removal of the IP address information from OSPF packet headers, makes the new version of OSPF capable of being routed over almost any Network layer protocol—cool!

Adjacencies and next-hop attributes now use link-local addresses, and OSPFv3 still uses multicast traffic to send its updates and acknowledgments, with the addresses FF02::5 for OSPF routers and FF02::6 for OSPF-designated routers. These new addresses are the replacements for 224.0.0.5 and 224.0.0.6, respectively.

Other, less flexible IPv4 protocols don't give us the ability that OSPFv2 does to assign specific networks and interfaces into the OSPF process—however, this is something that is still configured under the router configuration process. And with OSPFv3, just as with the other IPv6 routing protocols we've talked about, the interfaces and therefore the networks attached to them are configured directly on the interface in interface configuration mode.

The configuration of OSPFv3 is going to look like this:

```
Router1(config)#ipv6 router osfp 10
Router1(config-rtr)#router-id 1.1.1.1
```

You get to perform some configurations from router configuration mode like summarization and redistribution, but we don't even need to configure OSPFv3 from this prompt if we configure OSPFv3 from the interface.

When the interface configuration is completed, the router configuration process is added automatically and the interface configuration looks like this:

```
Router1(config-if)#ipv6 ospf 10 area 0.0.0.0
```

So, if we just go to each interface and assign a process ID and area—poof, we're done!

With all that behind you, it's now time to move on and learn about how to migrate to IPv6 from IPv4.

Migrating to IPv6

We certainly have talked a lot about how IPv6 works and how we can configure it to work on our networks, but what is doing that going to cost us? And how much work is it really going to take? Good questions for sure, but the answers to them won't be the same for everyone. This is because how much you are going to end up having to pony up is highly dependent upon what you've got going on already in terms of your infrastructure. Obviously, if you've been making your really old routers and switches "last" and therefore have to upgrade every one of them so that they're IPv6 compliant, that could very well turn out to be a good-sized chunk of change! Oh, and that sum doesn't even include server and computer operating systems (OSs) and the blood, sweat, and maybe even tears spent on making all your applications compliant. So, my friend, it could cost you quite a bit! The good news is that unless you've really let things go, many OSs and network devices have been IPv6 compliant for a few years—we just haven't been using all their features until now.

Then there's that other question about the amount of work and time. Straight up—this one could still be pretty intense. No matter what, it's going to take you some time to get all of your systems moved over and make sure that things are working correctly. And if you're talking about a huge network with tons of devices, well, it could take a really long time! But don't panic—that's why migration strategies have been created to allow for a slower integration. I'm going to show you three of the primary transition strategies available to us. The first is called dual stacking, which allows a device to have both the IPv4 and IPv6 protocol stack running so it's capable of continuing on with its existing communications and simultaneously run newer IPv6 communications as they're implemented. The next strategy is the 6to4 tunneling approach; this is your choice if you have an all IPv6 network that must communicate over an IPv4 network to reach another IPv6 network. I'll surprise you with the third one just for fun!

Dual Stacking

This is the most common type of migration strategy because, well, it's the easiest on us—it allows our devices to communicate using either IPv4 or IPv6. Dual stacking lets you upgrade your devices and applications on the network one at a time. As more and more hosts and devices on the network are upgraded, more of your communication will happen over IPv6, and after you've arrived—everything's running on IPv6, and you get to remove all the old IPv4 protocol stacks you no longer need.

Plus, configuring dual stacking on a Cisco router is amazingly easy—all you have to do is enable IPv6 forwarding and apply an address to the interfaces already configured with IPv4. It'll look something like this:

```
Corp(config)#ipv6 unicast-routing
Corp(config)#interface fastethernet 0/0
Corp(config-if)#ipv6 address 2001:db8:3c4d:1::/64 eui-64
Corp(config-if)#ip address 192.168.255.1 255.255.255.0
```

But to be honest, it's really a good idea to understand the various tunneling techniques because it'll probably be awhile before we all start running IPv6 as a solo routed protocol.

6to4 Tunneling

6to4 tunneling is really useful for carrying IPv6 data over a network that's still IPv4. It's quite possible that you'll have IPv6 subnets or other portions of your network that are all IPv6, and those networks will have to communicate with each other. Not so complicated, but when you consider that you might find this happening over a WAN or some other network that you don't control, well, that could be a bit ugly. So what do we do about this if we don't control the whole tamale? Create a tunnel that will carry the IPv6 traffic for us across the IPv4 network, that's what.

The whole idea of tunneling isn't a difficult concept, and creating tunnels really isn't as hard as you might think. All it really comes down to is snatching the IPv6 packet that's happily traveling across the network and sticking an IPv4 header onto the front of it. Kind of like catch and release fishing, except for the fish doesn't get something plastered on its face before being thrown back into the stream.

To get a picture of this, take a look at Figure 13.3.

Nice—but to make this happen we're going to need a couple of dual-stacked routers, which I just demonstrated for you, so you should be good to go. Now we have to add a little configuration to place a tunnel between those routers. Tunnels are pretty simple—we just have to tell each router where the tunnel begins and where we want it to end up. Referring again to Figure 13.3, we'll configure the tunnel on each router:

```
Router1(config)#int tunnel 0
Router1(config-if)#ipv6 address 2001:db8:1:1::1/64
Router1(config-if)#tunnel source 192.168.30.1
```

```
Router1(config-if)#tunnel destination 192.168.40.1
Router1(config-if)#tunnel mode ipv6ip

Router2(config)#int tunnel 0
Router2(config-if)#ipv6 address 2001:db8:2:2::1/64
Router2(config-if)#tunnel source 192.168.40.1
Router2(config-if)#tunnel destination 192.168.30.1
Router2(config-if)#tunnel mode ipv6ip
```

FIGURE 13.3   Creating a 6to4 tunnel

IPv6 packet encapsulated in an IPv4 packet

With this in place, our IPv6 networks can now communicate over the IPv4 network. Now, I've got to tell you that this is not meant to be a permanent configuration; your end goal should still be to run a total, complete IPv6 network end to end.

One important note here—if the IPv4 network that you're traversing in this situation has a NAT translation point, it would absolutely break the tunnel encapsulation we've just created! Over the years, NAT has been upgraded a lot so that it can handle specific protocols and dynamic connections, and without one of these upgrades, NAT likes to demolish most connections. And since this transition strategy isn't present in most NAT implementations, that means trouble.

But there is a way around this little problem and it's called Teredo, which allows all your tunnel traffic to be placed in UDP packets. NAT doesn't blast away at UDP packets, so they won't get broken as other protocols packets do. So with Teredo in place and your packets disguised under their UDP cloak, the packets will easily slip by NAT alive and well!

NAT-PT

You've probably heard that IPv6 doesn't have any NAT in it, and you've heard correctly—sort of. By itself, IPv6 doesn't have a NAT implementation. But that's only a technicality because there is a transition strategy known as NAT protocol translation (NAT-PT). Just know that you really only use this approach as a last resort because it's not that great of a solution. With it, your IPv4 hosts can only communicate with other IPv4 hosts, and those that are native IPv6, with other IPv6 hosts. What do I mean by that? Well, with a tunneling approach we took IPv6 packets and disguised them as IPv4 packets. With NAT-PT there is no encapsulation—the data of the source packet is removed from one IP type and repackaged as the new destination IP type. Even though being able to configure NAT-PT is beyond the scope of the CCNA objectives, I still want to explain it to you. And just as it is with NAT for IPv4, there are a couple of ways to implement it.

Static NAT-PT provides a one-to-one mapping of a single IPv4 address to a single IPv6 address (sounds like static NAT). There is also Dynamic NAT-PT, which uses a pool of IPv4 addresses to provide a one-to-one mapping with an IPv6 address (sounding kind of familiar). Finally, there is Network Address Port Translation (NAPT-PT), which provides a many-to-one mapping of multiple IPv6 addresses to one IPv4 address and a port number (well, glad we have that cleared up from NAT).

As you can see, we are not using NAT to translate a public and private IPv6 address as we did with IPv4, but rather between IPv4 and IPv6. Again, this should be used as an absolute last resort. In most cases a tunneling approach will work much better and without the headache of this configuration and system overhead.

Configuring IPv6 on Our Internetwork

In this section, I'll configure the internetwork I've been using throughout this book—five routers connected together—but I'm not going to add IPv6 on the 871W router or to the LAN and WLAN networks connected to the R1, R2, and R3 routers, to keep things simple and easier to understand. So let's get started by adding IPv6 to the Corp, R1, R2, and R3 routers. I'll then add both the RIP and OSPF routing protocols and finish the chapter by running through some verification commands.

As usual, I'll start with the Corp router:

```
Corp#config t
Corp(config)#ipv6 unicast-routing
Corp(config)#int f0/1
Corp(config-if)#ipv6 address 2001:db8:3c4d:11::/64 eui-64
Corp(config-if)#int s0/0/0
Corp(config-if)#ipv6 address 2001:db8:3c4d:12::/64 eui-64
Corp(config-if)#int s0/0/1
Corp(config-if)#ipv6 address 2001:db8:3c4d:13::/64 eui-64
Corp(config-if)#int s0/1/0
Corp(config-if)#ipv6 address 2001:db8:3c4d:14::/64 eui-64
Corp(config-if)#int s0/2/0
Corp(config-if)#ipv6 address 2001:db8:3c4d:15::/64 eui-64
Corp(config-if)#^Z
```

```
Corp#copy run start
Destination filename [startup-config]?[enter]
Building configuration...
[OK]
Corp#
```

In the preceding configuration, I changed the subnet address for each interface only slightly. Let's take a look at the routing table:

```
Corp#sh ipv6 route
IPv6 Routing Table - 12 entries
Codes: C - Connected, L - Local, S - Static, R - RIP, B - BGP
       U - Per-user Static route I1 - ISIS L1, I2 - ISIS L2, IA - ISIS
       interarea, IS - ISIS summary O - OSPF intra, OI - OSPF inter,
       OE1 - OSPF ext 1, OE2 - OSPF ext 2
       ON1 - OSPF NSSA ext 1, ON2 - OSPF NSSA ext 2
C   2001:DB8:3C4D:11::/64 [0/0]
     via ::, FastEthernet0/1
L   2001:DB8:3C4D:11:21A:2FFF:FE55:C9E9/128 [0/0]
     via ::, FastEthernet0/1
C   2001:DB8:3C4D:12::/64 [0/0]
     via ::, Serial0/0/0
L   2001:DB8:3C4D:12:21A:2FFF:FE55:C9E8/128 [0/0]
     via ::, Serial0/0/0
C   2001:DB8:3C4D:13::/64 [0/0]
     via ::, Serial0/0/1
L   2001:DB8:3C4D:13:21A:2FFF:FE55:C9E8/128 [0/0]
     via ::, Serial0/0/1
C   2001:DB8:3C4D:14::/64 [0/0]
     via ::, Serial0/1/0
L   2001:DB8:3C4D:14:21A:2FFF:FE55:C9E8/128 [0/0]
     via ::, Serial0/1/0
C   2001:DB8:3C4D:15::/64 [0/0]
     via ::, Serial0/2/0
L   2001:DB8:3C4D:15:21A:2FFF:FE55:C9E8/128 [0/0]
     via ::, Serial0/2/0
L   FE80::/10 [0/0]
     via ::, Null0
L   FF00::/8 [0/0]
     via ::, Null0
Corp#
```

So what's up with the two addresses for each interface? One shows C connected, and one shows L? Well, the connected address is the IPv6 address I configured on each interface, and the L is the automatically assigned link-local. Notice in the link-local address that the FF:FE is inserted into the address to create the eui-64 address.

One more thing before we move on to the R1 router. Notice that when addressing the interfaces, I added a different number to the subnet number for each one. Also note that they closely match my IPv4 private addresses. I did it this way to make administration easier. Okay—let's configure the R1 router now:

```
R1#config t
R1(config)#ipv6 unicast-routing
R1(config)#int s0/0/0
R1(config-if)#ipv6 address 2001:db8:3c4d:12::/64 eui-64
R1(config-if)#int s0/0/1
R1(config-if)#ipv6 address 2001:db8:3c4d:13::/64 eui-64
R1(config-if)#^Z
R1#show ipv6 route
IPv6 Routing Table - 6 entries
[codes cut]
C    2001:DB8:3C4D:12::/64 [0/0]
      via ::, Serial0/0/0
L    2001:DB8:3C4D:12:21A:6DFF:FE64:9B2/128 [0/0]
      via ::, Serial0/0/0
C    2001:DB8:3C4D:13::/64 [0/0]
      via ::, Serial0/0/1
L    2001:DB8:3C4D:13:21A:6DFF:FE64:9B2/128 [0/0]
      via ::, Serial0/0/1
L    FE80::/10 [0/0]
      via ::, Null0
L    FF00::/8 [0/0]
      via ::, Null0
R1#
```

Notice that I used the exact same IPv6 subnet addresses on each side of the link. Let's configure the R2 and R3 routers, and then add RIPv6:

```
R2#config t
R2(config)#ipv6 unicast-routing
R2(config)#int s0/2/0
R2(config-if)#ipv6 address 2001:db8:3c4d:14::/64 eui-64
R2(config-if)#do show ipv6 route
IPv6 Routing Table - 4 entries
```

```
C   2001:DB8:3C4D:14::/64 [0/0]
      via ::, Serial0/2/0
L   2001:DB8:3C4D:14:213:60FF:FE20:4E4C/128 [0/0]
      via ::, Serial0/2/0
L   FE80::/10 [0/0]
      via ::, Null0
L   FF00::/8 [0/0]
      via ::, Null0
R2(config-if)#
```

Looking good! Let's go to R3:

```
R3#config t
R3(config)#ipv6 unicast-routing
R3(config)#int s0/0/1
R3(config-if)#ipv6 address 2001:db8:3c4d:15::/64 eui-64
R3(config-if)#do show ipv6 route
IPv6 Routing Table - 4 entries

C   2001:DB8:3C4D:15::/64 [0/0]
      via ::, Serial0/0/1
L   2001:DB8:3C4D:15:21A:6DFF:FE37:A44E/128 [0/0]
      via ::, Serial0/0/1
L   FE80::/10 [0/0]
      via ::, Null0
L   FF00::/8 [0/0]
      via ::, Null0
R3(config-if)#
```

Again, notice that I used the exact same IPv6 subnet addresses on each side of the links from the Corp router to the R1, R2, and R3 routers. Now let's start adding routing protocols!

Configuring RIPng

This is really the easy part—all I need to do is to go to each interface on each of our routers and type in one command. Here we go:

```
Corp#config t
Corp(config)#int f0/1
Corp(config-if)#ipv6 rip ?
  WORD  User selected string identifying this RIP process
Corp(config-if)#ipv6 rip 1 enable
Corp(config-if)#int s0/0/0
```

```
Corp(config-if)#ipv6 rip 1 enable
Corp(config-if)#int s0/0/1
Corp(config-if)#ipv6 rip 1 enable
Corp(config-if)#int s0/1/0
Corp(config-if)#ipv6 rip 1 enable
Corp(config-if)#int s0/2/0
Corp(config-if)#ipv6 rip 1 enable
```

Let's configure the R1 router:

```
R1#config t
R1(config)#int s0/0/0
R1(config-if)#ipv6 rip 1 enable
R1(config-if)#int s0/0/1
R1(config-if)#ipv6 rip 1 enable
```

R2 config:

```
R2#config t
R2(config)#int s0/2/0
R2(config-if)#ipv6 rip 1 enable
```

R3 config:

```
R3#config t
R3(config)#int s0/0/1
R3(config-if)#ipv6 rip 1 enable
```

Okay, time to verify my IPv6 routing tables and configurations.

Verifying RIPng

I'm going to start with the usual show ip route command. Here's the output from the R3 router:

```
R3#sh ipv6 route
R    2001:DB8:3C4D:11::/64 [120/2]
       via FE80::21A:2FFF:FE55:C9E8, Serial0/0/1
R    2001:DB8:3C4D:12::/64 [120/2]
       via FE80::21A:2FFF:FE55:C9E8, Serial0/0/1
R    2001:DB8:3C4D:13::/64 [120/2]
       via FE80::21A:2FFF:FE55:C9E8, Serial0/0/1
R    2001:DB8:3C4D:14::/64 [120/2]
       via FE80::21A:2FFF:FE55:C9E8, Serial0/0/1
C    2001:DB8:3C4D:15::/64 [0/0]
       via ::, Serial0/0/1
L    2001:DB8:3C4D:15:21A:6DFF:FE37:A44E/128 [0/0]
```

```
     via ::, Serial0/0/1
L   FE80::/10 [0/0]
     via ::, Null0
L   FF00::/8 [0/0]
     via ::, Null0
R3#
```

Wow, looks just like the regular IPv4 RIP table, including the administrative distance and hop count. I can see subnets 11, 12, 13, 14, and 15.

Let's take a look at a few more verification commands:

```
R3#sh ipv6 protocols
IPv6 Routing Protocol is "connected"
IPv6 Routing Protocol is "static"
IPv6 Routing Protocol is "rip 1"
  Interfaces:
    Serial0/0/1
  Redistribution:
    None
R3#
```

Not too much information provided with the show ipv6 protocols command. Let's try the show ipv6 rip command:

```
R3#sh ipv6 rip
RIP process "1", port 521, multicast-group FF02::9, pid 60
     Administrative distance is 120. Maximum paths is 16
     Updates every 30 seconds, expire after 180
     Holddown lasts 0 seconds, garbage collect after 120
     Split horizon is on; poison reverse is off
     Default routes are not generated
     Periodic updates 44, trigger updates 19
  Interfaces:
    Serial0/0/1
  Redistribution:
    None
```

Okay—now we're talking! We can see that the administrative distance is still 120, plus the multicast group, maximum paths, and timers. So let's go ahead and try two more verification commands, beginning with the show ipv6 interface s0/0/1 command:

```
R3#sh ipv6 interface serial 0/0/1
Serial0/0/1 is up, line protocol is up
  IPv6 is enabled, link-local address is FE80::21A:6DFF:FE37:A44E
```

```
Global unicast address(es):
  2001:DB8:3C4D:1:21A:6DFF:FE37:A44E, subnet is 2001:DB8:3C4D:1::/64 [EUI]
Joined group address(es):
  FF02::1
  FF02::2
  FF02::9
  FF02::1:FF37:A44E
MTU is 1500 bytes
ICMP error messages limited to one every 100 milliseconds
ICMP redirects are enabled
ND DAD is enabled, number of DAD attempts: 1
ND reachable time is 30000 milliseconds
Hosts use stateless autoconfig for addresses.
```

This got us some pretty good information too. But wait, the best is yet to come: the debug ipv6 rip command—this should be good:

```
R3#debug ipv6 rip
*May 24 18:31:11.959: RIPng: Sending multicast update on Serial0/0/1 for 1
*May 24 18:31:11.959:        src=FE80::21A:6DFF:FE37:A44E
*May 24 18:31:11.959:        dst=FF02::9 (Serial0/0/1)
*May 24 18:31:11.959:        sport=521, dport=521, length=32
*May 24 18:31:11.959:        command=2, version=1, mbz=0, #rte=1
*May 24 18:31:11.959:        tag=0, metric=1, prefix=2001:DB8:3C4D:1::/64
*May 24 18:40:44.079: %LINEPROTO-5-UPDOWN: Line protocol on Interface
  Serial0/0/0, changed state to down
*May 24 18:31:24.959: RIPng: response received from
  FE80::21A:2FFF:FE55:C9E8 on Serial0/0/1 for 1
*May 24 18:31:24.959:        src=FE80::21A:2FFF:FE55:C9E8 (Serial0/0/1)
*May 24 18:31:24.959:        dst=FF02::9
*May 24 18:31:24.959:        sport=521, dport=521, length=32
*May 24 18:31:24.959:        command=2, version=1, mbz=0, #rte=1
*May 24 18:31:24.959:        tag=0, metric=16,
  prefix=2001:DB8:3C4D:12::/64
*May 24 18:31:24.959: RIPng: 2001:DB8:3C4D:12::/64, path
  FE80::21A:2FFF:FE55:C9E8/Serial0/0/1 unreachable
*May 24 18:31:24.959: RIPng: 2001:DB8:3C4D:12::/64, expired, ttg is 120
*May 24 18:31:24.959: RIPng: Triggered update requested
*May 24 18:31:25.959: RIPng: generating triggered update for 1
*May 24 18:31:25.959: RIPng: Suppressed null multicast update on
  Serial0/0/1 for 1
```

Now this is interesting. We can see that the source and destination ports used are 521 (yes, we are still using UDP) and that network/subnet 12 is unreachable. This is because the s0/0/0 interface of my Corp router has just decided to go bad. (I swear, writing this book is just like being at work!) Either way, we can see that RIPng still has some basic IPv4 RIP characteristics. Let's go ahead and add OSPFv3 to our routers.

Configuring OSPFv3

Just as with the RIPng configuration, all we have to do to enable OSPF on the internetwork is to go to each interface that we want to run it.

Here is the Corp configuration:

```
Corp#config t
Corp(config)#int f0/1
Corp(config-if)#ipv6 ospf 1 ?
  area  Set the OSPF area ID
Corp(config-if)#ipv6 ospf 1 area 0
Corp(config-if)#int s0/0/1
Corp(config-if)#ipv6 ospf 1 area 0
Corp(config-if)#int s0/1/0
Corp(config-if)#ipv6 ospf 1 area 0
Corp(config-if)#int s0/2/0
Corp(config-if)#ipv6 ospf 1 area 0
Corp(config-if)#^Z
Corp#
```

That wasn't so bad—actually somewhat easier than with IPv4. Let's configure the other three routers:

```
R1#config t
R1(config)#int s0/0/1
R1(config-if)#ipv6 ospf 1 area 0
R1(config-if)#
*May 24 19:24:55.279: %OSPFv3-5-ADJCHG: Process 1, Nbr 172.16.10.2 on
   Serial0/0/1 from LOADING to FULL, Loading Done
```

Sweet! R1 has become adjacent to the Corp router. One interesting output line is that the IPv4 RID is being used in the OSPFv3 adjacent change.

```
R2#config t
R2(config)#int s0/2/0
R2(config-if)#ipv6 ospf 1 area 0
R2(config-if)#
*May 24 19:27:31.399: %OSPFv3-5-ADJCHG: Process 1, Nbr 172.16.10.3 on
   Serial0/1/0 from LOADING to FULL, Loading Done
```

Again, our adjacency popped up—this is great. One more router, then we'll do some verification:

```
R3#config t
R3(config)#int s0/0/1
R3(config-if)#ipv6 ospf 1 area 0
R3(config-if)#
*May 24 19:29:07.231: %OSPFv3-5-ADJCHG: Process 1, Nbr 172.16.10.4 on
   Serial0/2/0 from LOADING to FULL, Loading Done
```

Without even verifying our network, it seems to me that it's up and running. But, we've still got to verify!

Verifying OSPFv3

I'll start as usual with the show ipv6 route command:

```
R3#sh ipv6 route
IPv6 Routing Table - 7 entries
O   2001:DB8:3C4D:11::/64 [110/65]
     via FE80::21A:2FFF:FE55:C9E8, Serial0/0/1
O   2001:DB8:3C4D:13::/64 [110/128]
     via FE80::21A:2FFF:FE55:C9E8, Serial0/0/1
O   2001:DB8:3C4D:14::/64 [110/128]
     via FE80::21A:2FFF:FE55:C9E8, Serial0/0/1
C   2001:DB8:3C4D:15::/64 [0/0]
     via ::, Serial0/0/1
L   2001:DB8:3C4D:15:21A:6DFF:FE37:A44E/128 [0/0]
     via ::, Serial0/0/1
L   FE80::/10 [0/0]
     via ::, Null0
L   FF00::/8 [0/0]
     via ::, Null0
R3#
```

Perfect. I see all the subnets (except 12, which is down because of that bad interface). Let's take a look at the show ipv6 protocols command:

```
R3#sh ipv6 protocols
IPv6 Routing Protocol is "connected"
IPv6 Routing Protocol is "static"
IPv6 Routing Protocol is "rip 1"
  Interfaces:
    Serial0/0/1
```

```
Redistribution:
  None
IPv6 Routing Protocol is "ospf 1"
  Interfaces (Area 0):
    Serial0/0/1
  Redistribution:
    None
```

For the next command, I want to go back to the Corp router so can I see more connections: show ipv6 ospf neighbor.

```
Corp#sh ipv6 ospf neighbor
Neighbor ID    Pri   State     Dead Time   Interface ID  Interface
172.16.10.4      1   FULL/ -  00:00:36    6             Serial0/2/0
172.16.10.3      1   FULL/ -  00:00:33    16            Serial0/1/0
172.16.10.2      1   FULL/ -  00:00:30    6             Serial0/0/1
Corp#
```

Wait! We need to do our debugging commands. I'll use two of them: debug ipv6 ospf packet and debug ipv6 ospf hello (almost the same commands I used with IPv4):

```
Corp#debug ipv6 ospf packet
  OSPFv3 packet debugging is on
Corp#
*May 24 19:38:12.283: OSPFv3: rcv. v:3 t:1 l:40 rid:172.16.10.3
      aid:0.0.0.0 chk:E1D2 inst:0 from Serial0/1/0
Corp#
*May 24 19:38:15.103: OSPFv3: rcv. v:3 t:1 l:40 rid:172.16.10.4
      aid:0.0.0.0 chk:7EBB inst:0 from Serial0/2/0
Corp#
*May 24 19:38:18.875: OSPFv3: rcv. v:3 t:1 l:40 rid:172.16.10.2
      aid:0.0.0.0 chk:192D inst:0 from Serial0/0/1
Corp#
*May 24 19:38:22.283: OSPFv3: rcv. v:3 t:1 l:40 rid:172.16.10.3
      aid:0.0.0.0 chk:E1D2 inst:0 from Serial0/1/0
Corp#un all
All possible debugging has been turned off
Corp#debug ipv6 ospf hello
  OSPFv3 hello events debugging is on
Corp#
*May 24 19:38:32.283: OSPFv3: Rcv hello from 172.16.10.3 area 0 from
  Serial0/1/0 FE80::213:60FF:FE20:4E4C interface ID 16
```

```
*May 24 19:38:32.283: OSPFv3: End of hello processing
Corp#
*May 24 19:38:35.103: OSPFv3: Rcv hello from 172.16.10.4 area 0 from
  Serial0/2/0 FE80::21A:6DFF:FE37:A44E interface ID 6
*May 24 19:38:35.103: OSPFv3: End of hello processing
Corp#
*May 24 19:38:38.875: OSPFv3: Rcv hello from 172.16.10.2 area 0 from
  Serial0/0/1 FE80::21A:6DFF:FE64:9B2 interface ID 6
*May 24 19:38:38.875: OSPFv3: End of hello processing
Corp#un all
All possible debugging has been turned off
Corp#
```

Holy output! Now that is what I call a fun chapter. We even had an interface go bad, just like in the real world. I really hope you found this chapter as rewarding and interesting as I did. The best thing you can do to learn IPv6 is to nick some routers and just have a go at it!

Summary

In this chapter, I covered the very basics of IPv6 and how to make IPv6 work within a Cisco internetwork. As you now know by reading this chapter, even when discussing and configuring the basics, there is a lot to understand—and we just scratched the surface. But trust me when I say this—you now know more than you'll need to meet the CCNA objectives.

I began by talking about why we need IPv6 and the benefits associated with it. I followed that up by covering addressing with IPv6 as well as how to use the shortened expressions. And during the talk on addressing with IPv6, I showed you the different address types, plus the special addresses reserved in IPv6.

IPv6 will mostly be deployed automatically, meaning hosts will use autoconfiguration, so I discussed how IPv6 uses autoconfiguration and how it comes into play when configuring a Cisco router. After that, I showed you how to add a DHCP server to the router so it can provide options to hosts—not addresses, but options like a DNS server address.

ICMP is extremely important with IPv6, and I discussed in detail how ICMP works with IPv6, followed by how to configure RIP, EIGRP, and OSPF with IPv6.

Migrating to IPv6 is no small matter either, and I went over the pros and cons of doing this, and I told you about three migration strategies—dual stacking, tunneling using both IPv4 and IPv6, and a third approach, NAT-PT, to be used only as a last resort.

Last, I showed you how to configure IPv6 on the internetwork that I've been using throughout this book and then demonstrated how to verify the configuration with the various show commands available with IPv6.

Exam Essentials

Understand why we need IPv6.   Without IPv6, the world would be depleted of IP addresses.

Understand link-local.   Link-local is like an IPv4 private IP address, but it can't be routed at all, not even in your organization.

Understand unique local.   This, like link-local, is like private IP addresses in IPv4 and cannot be routed to the Internet. However, the difference between link-local and unique local is that unique local can be routed within your organization or company.

Remember IPv6 addressing.   IPv6 addressing is not like IPv4 addressing. IPv6 addressing has much more address space and is 128 bits long, represented in hexadecimal, unlike IPv4, which is only 32 bits long and represented in decimal.

Written Lab 13

In this section, write the answers to the following IPv6 questions:

1. Which type of packet is addressed and delivered to only a single interface?
2. Which type of address is used just like a regular public routable address in IPv4?
3. Which type of address is not meant to be routed?
4. Which type of address is not meant to be routed to the Internet but is still globally unique?
5. Which type of address is meant to be delivered to multiple interfaces?
6. Which type of address identifies multiple interfaces, but packets are delivered only to the first address it finds?
7. Which routing protocol uses multicast address FF02::5?
8. IPv4 had a loopback address of 127.0.0.1. What is the IPv6 loopback address?
9. What does a link-local address always start with?
10. What does a unique local unicast range start with?

(The answers to Written Lab 13 can be found following the answers to the review questions for this chapter.)

Review Questions

The following questions are designed to test your understanding of this chapter's material. For more information on how to get additional questions, please see this book's Introduction.

1. Which of the following is true when describing a global unicast address?

   A. Packets addressed to a unicast address are delivered to a single interface.

   B. These are your typical publicly routable addresses, just like a regular publicly routable address in IPv4.

   C. These are like private addresses in IPv4 in that they are not meant to be routed.

   D. These addresses are meant for nonrouting purposes, but they are almost globally unique so it is unlikely they will have an address overlap.

2. Which of the following is true when describing a unicast address?

   A. Packets addressed to a unicast address are delivered to a single interface.

   B. These are your typical publicly routable addresses, just like a regular publicly routable address in IPv4.

   C. These are like private addresses in IPv4 in that they are not meant to be routed.

   D. These addresses are meant for nonrouting purposes, but they are almost globally unique so it is unlikely they will have an address overlap.

3. Which of the following is true when describing a link-local address?

   A. Packets addressed to a unicast address are delivered to a single interface.

   B. These are your typical publicly routable addresses, just like a regular publicly routable address in IPv4.

   C. These are like private addresses in IPv4 in that they are not meant to be routed.

   D. These addresses are meant for nonrouting purposes, but they are almost globally unique so it is unlikely they will have an address overlap.

4. Which of the following is true when describing a unique local address?

   A. Packets addressed to a unicast address are delivered to a single interface.

   B. These are your typical publicly routable addresses, just like a regular publicly routable address in IPv4.

   C. These are like private addresses in IPv4 in that they are not meant to be routed.

   D. These addresses are meant for nonrouting purposes, but they are almost globally unique so it is unlikely they will have an address overlap.

5. Which of the following is true when describing a multicast address?

   A. Packets addressed to a unicast address are delivered to a single interface.

   B. Packets are delivered to all interfaces identified by the address. This is also called a one-to-many address.

   C. Identifies multiple interfaces and is only delivered to one address. This address can also be called one-to-one-of-many.

   D. These addresses are meant for nonrouting purposes, but they are almost globally unique so it is unlikely they will have an address overlap.

6. Which of the following is true when describing an anycast address?

   A. Packets addressed to a unicast address are delivered to a single interface.

   B. Packets are delivered to all interfaces identified by the address. This is also called one-to-many addresses.

   C. This address identifies multiple interfaces and the anycast packet is only delivered to one address. This address can also be called one-to-one-of-many.

   D. These addresses are meant for nonrouting purposes, but they are almost globally unique so it is unlikely they will have an address overlap.

7. You want to ping the loopback address of your local host. What will you type?

   A. `ping 127.0.0.1`

   B. `ping 0.0.0.0`

   C. `ping ::1`

   D. `trace 0.0.::1`

8. What two multicast addresses does OSPFv3 use?

   A. FF02::A

   B. FF02::9

   C. FF02::5

   D. FF02::6

9. What multicast addresses does RIPng use?

   A. FF02::A

   B. FF02::9

   C. FF02::5

   D. FF02::6

10. What multicast addresses does EIGRPv6 use?

   A. FF02::A

   B. FF02::9

   C. FF02::5

   D. FF02::6

11. To enable RIPng, which of the following would you use?

    A. `Router1(config-if)# ipv6 ospf 10 area 0.0.0.0`

    B. `Router1(config-if)#ipv6 rip 1 enable`

    C. `Router1(config)# ipv6 router eigrp 10`

    D. `Router1(config-rtr)#no shutdown`

    E. `Router1(config-if)#ipv6 eigrp 10`

12. To enable EIGRP, which three of the following would you use?

    A. `Router1(config-if)# ipv6 ospf 10 area 0.0.0.0`

    B. `Router1(config-if)#ipv6 router rip 1`

    C. `Router1(config)# ipv6 router eigrp 10`

    D. `Router1(config-rtr)#no shutdown`

    E. `Router1(config-if)#ipv6 eigrp 10`

13. To enable OSPFv3, which of the following would you use?

    A. `Router1(config-if)# ipv6 ospf 10 area 0.0.0.0`

    B. `Router1(config-if)#ipv6 router rip 1`

    C. `Router1(config)# ipv6 router eigrp 10`

    D. `Router1(config-rtr)#no shutdown`

    E. `Router1(config-if)#ospf ipv6 10 area 0`

14. What two statements about IPv6 addresses are true? (Choose two.)

    A. Leading zeros are required.

    B. Two colons (::) are used to represent successive hexadecimal fields of zeros.

    C. Two colons (::) are used to separate fields.

    D. A single interface will have multiple IPv6 addresses of different types.

15. What two statements about IPv4 and IPv6 addresses are true?

    A. An IPv6 address is 32 bits long, represented in hexidecimal.

    B. An IPv6 address is 128 bits long, represented in decimal.

    C. An IPv4 address is 32 bits long, represented in decimal.

    D. An IPv6 address is 128 bits long, represented in hexidecimal.

Answers to Review Questions

1. B. Unlike unicast addresses, global unicast addresses are meant to be routed.

2. A. Explanation:Packets addressed to a unicast address are delivered to a single interface. For load balancing, multiple interfaces can use the same address.

3. C. Link-local addresses are meant for throwing together a temporary LAN for meetings or a small LAN that is not going to be routed but needs to share and access files and services locally.

4. D. These addresses are meant for nonrouting purposes like link-local, but they are almost globally unique so it is unlikely they will have an address overlap. Unique local addresses were designed as a replacement for site-local addresses.

5. B. Packets addressed to a multicast address are delivered to all interfaces identified by the multicast address, the same as in IPv4. It is also called a one-to-many address. You can always tell a multicast address in IPv6 because multicast addresses always start with FF.

6. C. Anycast addresses identify multiple interfaces, which is the same as multicast; however, the big difference is that the anycast packet is only delivered to one address, the first one it finds defined in the terms of routing distance. This address can also be called one-to-one-of-many.

7. C. The loopback address with IPv4 is 127.0.0.1. With IPv6, that address is ::1.

8. C, D. Adjacencies and next-hop attributes now use link-local addresses, and OSPFv3 still uses multicast traffic to send its updates and acknowledgments with the addresses FF02::5 for OSPF routers and FF02::6 for OSPF designated routers. These are the replacements for 224.0.0.5 and 224.0.0.6, respectively.

9. B. RIPng uses the multicast IPv6 address of FF02::9. If you remember the multicast addresses for IPv4, the numbers at the end of each IPv6 address are the same.

10. A. EIGRPv6's multicast address stayed very near the same. In IPv4 it was 224.0.0.10; now it is FF02::A (A=10 in hexadecimal notation).

11. B. It's pretty simple to enable RIPng for IPv6. You configure it right on the interface where you want RIP to run with the ipv6 router rip number command.

12. C, D, E. Unlike RIPng and OSPFv3, you need to configure EIGRP both from global configuration mode and from interface mode, and you have to enable the command with the no shutdown command.

13. A. To enable OSPFv3, you enable the protocol as with RIPng. The command string is ipv6 ospf *process-id* area *area-id*.

14. B, D. In order to shorten the written length of an IPv6 address, successive fields of zeros may be replaced by double colons. In trying to shorten the address further, leading zeros may also be removed. Just as with IPv4, a single device's interface can have more than one address; with IPv6 there are more types of addresses and the same rule applies. There can be link-local, global unicast, and multicast addresses all assigned to the same interface.

15. C, D. IPv4 addresses are 32 bits long and are represented in decimal format. IPv6 addresses are 128 bits long and represented in hexadecimal format.

Answers to Written Lab 13.1

1. Unicast
2. Global unicast
3. Link-local
4. Unique local (used to be called site-local)
5. Multicast
6. Anycast
7. OSPF
8. ::1
9. FE80::
10. FC00::

Chapter
14

Wide Area Networks

THE CCNA EXAM TOPICS COVERED IN THIS CHAPTER INCLUDE THE FOLLOWING:

✓ **Implement and verify WAN links**

  ▪ Describe different methods for connecting to a WAN

  ▪ Configure and verify a basic WAN serial connection

  ▪ Configure and verify Frame Relay on Cisco routers

  ▪ Troubleshoot WAN implementation issues

  ▪ Describe VPN technology (including: importance, benefits, role, impact, components)

  ▪ Configure and verify a PPP connection between Cisco routers

✓ **Describe how a network works**

  ▪ Differentiate between LAN/WAN operation and features

The Cisco IOS supports a ton of different wide area network (WAN) protocols that help you extend your local LANs to other LANs at remote sites. And I don't think I have to tell you how positively essential information exchange between disparate sites is these days—it's vital! But even so, it wouldn't exactly be cost effective or efficient to install your own cable and connect all of your company's remote locations yourself, now would it? A much better way to go about doing this is to simply lease the existing installations that service providers already have in place, and save big time.

So it follows that I'm going to discuss the various types of connections, technologies, and devices used in accordance with WANs in this chapter. We'll also get into how to implement and configure High-Level Data-Link Control (HDLC), Point-to-Point Protocol (PPP), Point-to-Point Protocol over Ethernet (PPPoE), cable, DSL, and Frame Relay. I'll also introduce you to WAN security concepts, tunneling, and virtual private network basics.

Even though I could include discussion of wireless networks in this chapter as WAN solutions, I'm instead going to refer you to Chapter 12, which is chock full of detailed information about Cisco's wireless solutions and how they can be used both inside the corporate network and in the outside metropolitan areas.

Just so you know, I'm not going to cover every type of Cisco WAN support here—again, the focus of this book is to equip you with everything you need to successfully meet the CCNA objectives. Because of that, I'm going to focus on cable, DSL, HDLC, PPP, PPPoE, and Frame Relay. Then I'm going to wrap the chapter up with a solid introduction to VPNs.

But first things first—let's begin with an exploration into WAN basics.

For up-to-the-minute updates for this chapter, check out www.lammle.com and/ or www.sybex.com.

Introduction to Wide Area Networks

So what, exactly, is it that makes something a *wide area network (WAN)* instead of a local area network (LAN)? Well, there's obviously the distance thing, but these days, wireless

LANs can cover some serious turf. What about bandwidth? Well, here again, some really big pipes can be had for a price in many places, so that's not it either. So what the heck is it then?

One of the main ways a WAN differs from a LAN is that while you generally own a LAN infrastructure, you usually lease WAN infrastructure from a service provider. To be honest, modern technologies even blur this definition, but it still fits neatly into the context of Cisco's exam objectives.

Anyway, I've already talked about the data link that you usually own (Ethernet), but now we're going to find out about the kind you usually don't own—the type most often leased from a service provider.

The key to understanding WAN technologies is to be familiar with the different WAN terms and connection types commonly used by service providers to join your networks together.

Defining WAN Terms

Before you run out and order a WAN service type from a provider, it would be a really good idea to understand the following terms that service providers typically use:

Customer premises equipment (CPE)   *Customer premises equipment (CPE)* is equipment that's owned by the subscriber and located on the subscriber's premises.

Demarcation point   The *demarcation point* is the precise spot where the service provider's responsibility ends and the CPE begins. It's generally a device in a telecommunications closet owned and installed by the telecommunications company (telco). It's your responsibility to cable (extended demarc) from this box to the CPE, which is usually a connection to a CSU/DSU or ISDN interface.

Local loop   The *local loop* connects the demarc to the closest switching office, which is called a central office.

Central office (CO)   This point connects the customer's network to the provider's switching network. Good to know is that a *central office (CO)* is sometimes referred to as a *point of presence (POP)*.

Toll network   The *toll network* is a trunk line inside a WAN provider's network. This network is a collection of switches and facilities owned by the ISP.

Definitely familiarize yourself with these terms because they're crucial to understanding WAN technologies.

WAN Connection Types

As you're probably aware, a WAN can use a number of different connection types, and I'm going to introduce you to each of the various types of WAN connections you'll find on the market today. Figure 14.1 shows the different WAN connection types that can be used to connect your LANs together (DTE) over a DCE network.

FIGURE 14.1   WAN connection types

Here's a list explaining the different WAN connection types:

Leased lines   These are usually referred to as a *point-to-point* or dedicated connection. A *leased line* is a pre-established WAN communications path that goes from the CPE through the DCE switch, then over to the CPE of the remote site. The CPE enables DTE networks to communicate at any time with no cumbersome setup procedures to muddle through before transmitting data. When you've got plenty of cash, this is really the way to go because it uses synchronous serial lines up to 45Mbps. HDLC and PPP encapsulations are frequently used on leased lines; I'll go over them with you in detail in a bit.

Circuit switching   When you hear the term *circuit switching*, think phone call. The big advantage is cost—you only pay for the time you actually use. No data can transfer before an end-to-end connection is established. Circuit switching uses dial-up modems or ISDN and is used for low-bandwidth data transfers. Okay—I know what you're thinking: "Modems? Did he say modems? Aren't those only in museums by now?" After all, with all the wireless technologies available, who would use a modem these days? Well, some people do have ISDN and it still is viable (and I do suppose someone does use a modem now and then), but circuit switching can be used in some of the newer WAN technologies as well.

Packet switching   This is a WAN switching method that allows you to share bandwidth with other companies to save money. *Packet switching* can be thought of as a network that's designed to look like a leased line yet charges you more like circuit switching. But less cost isn't always better—there's definitely a downside: If you need to transfer data constantly, just forget about this option. Instead, get yourself a leased line. Packet switching will only work for you if your data transfers are the bursty type—not continuous. Frame Relay and X.25 are packet-switching technologies with speeds that can range from 56Kbps up to T3 (45Mbps).

MultiProtocol Label Switching (MPLS) uses a combination of both circuit switching and packet switching, but it's out of this book's range. Even so, after you pass your CCNA exam, it would be well worth your time to look into MPLS, so I'll talk about MPLS briefly in a minute.

WAN Support

Basically, Cisco just supports HDLC, PPP, and Frame Relay on its serial interfaces, and you can see this with the `encapsulation ?` command from any serial interface (your output may vary depending on the IOS version you are running):

```
Corp#config t
Corp(config)#int s0/0/0
Corp(config-if)#encapsulation ?
  atm-dxi      ATM-DXI encapsulation
  frame-relay  Frame Relay networks
  hdlc         Serial HDLC synchronous
  lapb         LAPB (X.25 Level 2)
  ppp          Point-to-Point protocol
  smds         Switched Megabit Data Service (SMDS)
  x25          X.25
```

Understand that if I had other types of interfaces on my router, I would have other encapsulation options, like ISDN or ADSL. And remember, you can't configure Ethernet or Token Ring encapsulation on a serial interface.

Next, I'm going to define the most prominently known WAN protocols used today: Frame Relay, ISDN, LAPB, LAPD, HDLC, PPP, PPPoE, Cable, DSL, MPLS, and ATM. Just so you know, the only WAN protocols you'll usually find configured on a serial interface are HDLC, PPP, and Frame Relay, but who said we're stuck with using only serial interfaces for wide area connections?

The rest of the chapter is going to be dedicated to explaining, in depth, how cable, DSL, and basic WAN protocols work, plus how to configure them with Cisco routers. But since they're important in the world beyond the latest CCNA exam objectives, I'm still going to briefly talk about ISDN, LAPB, LAPD, MPLS, and ATM in this next section. If any of them happen to pop up in the exam objectives, no worries, I promise you'll immediately find an update regarding the information at www.lammle.com.

Frame Relay A packet-switched technology that made its debut in the early 1990s, *Frame Relay* is a high-performance Data Link and Physical layer specification. It's pretty much a successor to X.25, except that much of the technology in X.25 used to compensate for physical errors (noisy lines) has been eliminated. An upside to Frame Relay is that it can be more cost effective than point-to-point links, plus it typically runs at speeds of 64Kbps up to 45Mbps (T3). Another Frame Relay benefit is that it provides features for dynamic bandwidth allocation and congestion control.

ISDN *Integrated Services Digital Network (ISDN)* is a set of digital services that transmit voice and data over existing phone lines. ISDN offers a cost-effective solution for remote users who need a higher-speed connection than analog dial-up links can give them, and it's also a good choice to use as a backup link for other types of links like Frame Relay or T1 connections.

LAPB *Link Access Procedure, Balanced (LAPB)* was created to be a connection-oriented protocol at the Data Link layer for use with X.25, but it can also be used as a simple data link transport. A not-so-good characteristic of LAPB is that it tends to create a tremendous amount of overhead due to its strict time-out and windowing techniques.

LAPD *Link Access Procedure, D-Channel (LAPD)* is used with ISDN at the Data Link layer (layer 2) as a protocol for the D (signaling) channel. LAPD was derived from the Link Access Procedure, Balanced (LAPB) protocol and is designed primarily to satisfy the signaling requirements of ISDN basic access.

HDLC *High-Level Data-Link Control (HDLC)* was derived from Synchronous Data Link Control (SDLC), which was created by IBM as a Data Link connection protocol. HDLC works at the Data Link layer and creates very little overhead compared to LAPB.

It wasn't intended to encapsulate multiple Network layer protocols across the same link—the HDLC header doesn't contain any identification about the type of protocol being carried inside the HDLC encapsulation. Because of this, each vendor that uses HDLC has its own way of identifying the Network layer protocol, meaning each vendor's HDLC is proprietary with regard to its specific equipment.

PPP *Point-to-Point Protocol (PPP)* is a pretty famous, industry-standard protocol. Because all multiprotocol versions of HDLC are proprietary, PPP can be used to create point-to-point links between different vendors' equipment. It uses a Network Control Protocol field in the Data Link header to identify the Network layer protocol and allows authentication and multilink connections to be run over asynchronous and synchronous links.

PPPoE Point-to-Point Protocol over Ethernet encapsulates PPP frames in Ethernet frames and is usually used in conjunction with ADSL services. It gives you a lot of the familiar PPP features like authentication, encryption, and compression, but there's a downside—it has a lower maximum transmission unit (MTU) than standard Ethernet does, and if your firewall isn't solidly configured, this little attribute can really give you some grief!

Still somewhat popular in the United States, PPPoE on Ethernet's main feature is that it adds a direct connection to Ethernet interfaces while providing DSL support as well. It's often used by many hosts on a shared Ethernet interface for opening PPP sessions to various destinations via at least one bridging modem.

Cable   In a modern HFC network, typically 500 to 2,000 active data subscribers are connected to a certain cable network segment, all sharing the upstream and downstream bandwidth. (*Hybrid fibre-coaxial*, or HFC, is a telecommunications industry term for a network that incorporates both optical fiber and coaxial cable to create a broadband network.) The actual bandwidth for Internet service over a cable TV (CATV) line can be up to about 27Mbps on the download path to the subscriber, with about 2.5Mbps of bandwidth on the upload path. Typically users get an access speed from 256Kbps to 6Mbps. This data rate varies greatly throughout the U.S.

DSL   Digital subscriber line is a technology used by traditional telephone companies to deliver advanced services (high-speed data and sometimes video) over twisted-pair copper telephone wires. It typically has lower data carrying capacity than HFC networks, and data speeds can be range limited by line lengths and quality. Digital subscriber line is not a complete end-to-end solution but rather a Physical layer transmission technology like dial-up, cable, or wireless. DSL connections are deployed in the last mile of a local telephone network—the local loop. The connection is set up between a pair of modems on either end of a copper wire that is between the customer premises equipment (CPE) and the Digital Subscriber Line Access Multiplexer (DSLAM). A DSLAM is the device located at the provider's central office (CO) and concentrates connections from multiple DSL subscribers.

MPLS   *MultiProtocol Label Switching (MPLS)* is a data-carrying mechanism that emulates some properties of a circuit-switched network over a packet-switched network. MPLS is a switching mechanism that imposes labels (numbers) to packets and then uses those labels to forward packets. The labels are assigned on the edge of the MPLS of the network, and forwarding inside the MPLS network is done solely based on labels. Labels usually correspond to a path to layer 3 destination addresses (equal to IP destination-based routing). MPLS was designed to support forwarding of protocols other than TCP/IP. Because of this, label switching within the network is performed the same regardless of the layer 3 protocol. In larger networks, the result of MPLS labeling is that only the edge routers perform a routing lookup. All the core routers forward packets based on the labels, which makes forwarding the packets through the service provider network faster. (Most companies are replacing their Frame Relay networks with MPLS today).

ATM   Asynchronous Transfer Mode (ATM) was created for time-sensitive traffic, providing simultaneous transmission of voice, video, and data. ATM uses cells that are a fixed 53 bytes long instead of packets. It also can use isochronous clocking (external clocking) to help the data move faster. Typically, if you are running Frame Relay today, you will be running Frame Relay over ATM.

Cable and DSL

Okay, before I talk about the serial encapsulation connections used on Cisco routers (HDLC, PPP, and Frame Relay), I'm going to discuss cable modems and DSL (including ADSL and PPPoE) as solutions for connections to wide area networks because I think it will really help you understand the practical differences between DSL and cable modem networking.

DSL and cable Internet services truly do have a lot in common, but they still have some basic, essential differences that are important for you to understand:

Speed   Most would say that cable is faster than DSL Internet, but cable doesn't always win the race in real-world use.

Security   DSL and cable are based on different network security models, and until recently, cable has been the reputed loser in this contest. But now, it's pretty much a toss-up, and both offer adequate security that meets the needs of most users. And when I say adequate, I mean that there are still some very real security issues relating to both alternatives, no matter what your ISP says!

Popularity   Cable Internet is definitely "best in show" in the U.S., but DSL is beginning to catch up.

Customer Satisfaction   Here, the reverse is true—in the U.S., DSL is top dog. But still, do you know anyone that's really totally satisfied with their ISP?

Figure 14.2 shows how a connection can terminate from modems to either a PC directly or a router. Typically, your router would run DHCP on that interface, as well as PPPoE. Both DSL and cable high-speed Internet services are available to millions of residential and business consumers worldwide, but in some areas, only one (sometimes neither) service is available.

Surprisingly, some of the differences between DSL and cable modem have nothing to do with the actual technologies—it comes down to the individual ISP. All other things being equal, issues like cost, reliability, and quality of customer support for both installation and maintenance issues vary significantly from one provider to the next.

Cable

Cable is a great cost-effective connection for a small office or home office, or SOHO—yes, there is an acronym for everything! And even in larger organizations, cable (or DSL for that matter) can be great to have as a backup link.

FIGURE 14.2   Broadband access using cable or DSL

Always-on Voice, Video, and Data Services

Here are a few cable network terms:

Headend   This is where all cable signals are received, processed, and formatted. The signals are then transmitted over the distribution network from the headend.

Distribution network   These are relatively small service areas that usually range in size from 100 to 2,000 customers. They're typically composed of a mixed, fiber-coaxial, or HFC architecture, with optical fiber substituting for the distribution network's trunk portion. The fiber forms both the connection from the headend and an optical node that changes light to radio frequency (RF) signals that are then distributed through a coaxial cable throughout the specific area being serviced.

DOCSIS (data over cable service interface specification)   All cable modems and like devices have to measure up to this standard.

Figure 14.3 shows where you would find the various types of networks and how the terms I just listed would be used in a network diagram.

FIGURE 14.3   Cable network and terms

The problem is that ISPs often use a fiber-optic network that extends from the cable operator's master headend, sometimes even to regional headends, out to a neighborhood's hubsite that then arrives at a fiber-optic node, which serves anywhere from 25 to 2,000 or more homes. (Don't get me wrong, all links have problems—I'm not picking on cable—really!)

And here's another issue: If you have cable, open your PC's command prompt, and type `ipconfig` and check out your subnet mask. It's probably a /20 or /21 class B address. Oh my. You already know that's either 4,094 or 2,046 hosts per cable network connection. Not good!

When we say "cable," we really mean using coax (coaxial) cable for transmission. And CATV, or community antenna television, is now used as a means to offer cost-effective broadcasting to subscribers. Cable is able to provide voice and data, plus analog and digital video, without requiring you to pony up your whole paycheck.

Your average cable connection gives you a maximum download speed of 2Mbps. And remember—you have to share that bandwidth with all the other subscribers. As if that weren't enough, there are other things like overloaded web servers and plain old Net congestion that factor in as well. But your email-checking neighbors really aren't making that much of a difference. So who or what is? Well, if you're an online gamer, you would likely notice a bit more lag during peak periods (which could be a matter of virtual life and death!). And if somebody in your neighborhood is uploading a large amount of data—like, well, an entire collection of pirated *Star Wars* movies—that could definitely max out the entire connection and bring everyone's browser to a crawl.

Cable modem access may or may not be faster or easier to install than DSL, and your mileage will vary, depending on where you live plus a variety of other factors. But it's usually more available and a tad less pricey, making it a winner by a nose. But no worries, if cable access isn't available in your neighborhood, DSL is okay—anything is better than dial-up!

Digital Subscriber Line (DSL)

Coming in second in our subscriber-based popularity contest is DSL (digital subscriber line), a technology that uses your garden-variety copper phone wires to give you high-speed data transmission. DSL requires a phone line, a DSL modem (often included with service), either an Ethernet card or a router that has an Ethernet connection, and someone that can provide service wherever you happen to be located.

The acronym *DSL* originally meant digital subscriber loop, but now its meaning has morphed to digital subscriber line. DSL group types fall into two categories based upon the upstream or downstream speed connections:

Symmetrical DSL   The speed for both downstream and upstream connections are equal, or symmetrical.

Asymmetrical DSL   Different transmission speeds occur between two ends of a network—downstream speed is usually faster.

Figure 14.4 shows an average home user with xDSL, which is a transmission technology that moves data over copper pairs.

The term *xDSL* covers a number of DSL variations, such as ADSL, high-bit-rate DSL (HDSL), Rate Adaptive DSL (RADSL), Synchronous DSL (SDSL), ISDN DSL (IDSL), and very-high-data-rate DSL (VDSL).

FIGURE 14.4   xDSL connection from home user to central office

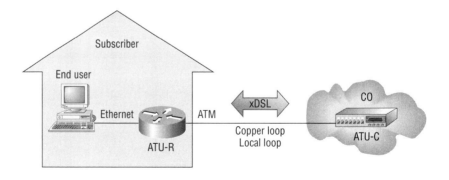

All types of DSL are layer 1 technologies.
ATU-R = ADSL Transmission Unit - Remote
ATU-C = ADSL Transmission Unit - Central

DSL flavors that don't use the voice frequencies band, like ADSL and VDSL, allow DSL lines to carry both data and voice signals simultaneously. Others, like SDSL and IDSL, that occupy the complete frequency range, can only carry data. And by the way, the data service that the DSL connection gives you is always on.

The speed that DSL service can offer depends on how far you are from the CO—the closer the better. In fact, you can blaze at rates up to around 6.1Mbps if you're physically close enough!

ADSL

ADSL supports both voice and data at the same time, but it was created to allot more bandwidth downstream than upstream because it's best for residential subscribers that usually need more downstream bandwidth for doing things like downloading video, movies, and music; online gaming; surfing; and getting emails—some that include sizeable attachments. ADSL will give you a downstream rate from 256Kbps to 8Mbps, but anything going upstream is only going to reach around 1Mbps.

POTS provides a channel for analog voice transmission and can transmit without a problem with ADSL over the same twisted-pair telephone line. Actually, depending on the type of ADSL, not just two, but three information channels commonly utilize the same wiring at the same time. This is why people can use a phone line and an ADSL connection at the same time and not affect either service.

ATM is the Data Link layer protocol typically used over the DSL layer 1 connection from the CPE that's terminated at what's known as the DSLAM—an ATM switch that contains DSL interface cards, or ATU-Cs. After ADSL connections meet their end at the DSLAM, it switches the data over an ATM network to something called an aggregation router—a layer 3 device where the subscriber's IP connection then expires.

You know by now how important encapsulation is, so as you've probably guessed, any IP packets over an ATM and DSL connection must have this done. This happens in one of three ways, depending on your interface type and the service provider's switch:

PPPoE   This will be discussed in more detail in the next section.

RFC1483 Routing   RFC1483 describes two different methods for carrying connectionless network traffic over an ATM network: routed protocols and bridged protocols.

PPPoA   Point-to-Point Protocol (PPP) over ATM is used to encapsulate PPP frames in ATM AAL5 (ATM Adaptation Layer 5). It is typically used with cable modems, DSL, and ADSL services and offers the usual PPP features of authentication, encryption, and compression and actually has less overhead in comparison to PPPoE.

PPPoE

Used with ADSL services, PPPoE (Point-to-Point Protocol over Ethernet) encapsulates PPP frames in Ethernet frames and uses common PPP features like authentication, encryption, and compression. But as I said earlier, it's trouble if you've got a badly configured firewall. This is a tunneling protocol that layers IP and other protocols that run over PPP with the attributes of a PPP link so they can then be used to contact other Ethernet devices and initiate a point-to-point connection to transport IP packets.

Figure 14.5 displays typical usage of PPPoE over ADSL. As you can see, a PPP session is connected from the PC of the end user to the router and the subscriber PC IP address is assigned by the router via IPCP.

FIGURE 14.5   PPPoE with ADSL

PPPoE is used to equip custom PPP-based software with the ability to deal with a connection that's not using a serial line and to be at home in a packet-oriented network environment like Ethernet and to allow for a custom connection with login and password for Internet connection accounting. Another factor is that the opposite side of the link's IP address is only given to it and available for the specific period that the PPPoE connection is open, so reusing IP addresses dynamically is permitted.

PPPoE has a discovery stage and a PPP session stage (see RFC 2516) that works like this: First, a host begins a PPPoE session, during which it has to execute a discovery process so it can determine the best server to meet the needs of the client machine's request. After that, it has to discover the Ethernet MAC address of the peer device and create a PPPoE session ID. So even though PPP delimits a peer-to-peer relationship, the discovery part is innately a client-server relationship.

Okay, before getting into serial connections, there's one last thing I want to cover—Cisco LRE.

Cisco Long Range Ethernet (LRE)

The Cisco Long Range Ethernet solution employs something called VDSL (Very High Data Rate Digital Subscriber Line) technology to significantly expand Ethernet service capacity. And LRE can achieve these impressive results: speeds from 5 to 15Mbps (full duplex) at distances up to 5,000 feet traveling over existing twisted-pair wiring!

So basically, Cisco LRE technology can give us broadband service on POTS, digital telephone, and ISDN traffic lines, and it also can operate in modes that are compatible with ADSL technologies. This flexibility is important because it makes it possible for service providers to make LRE available in structures and/or buildings that have broadband services already in place but need it enhanced—very cool indeed.

Cabling the Serial Wide Area Network

As you can imagine, there are a few things that you need to know before connecting your WAN in order to make sure everything goes well. For starters, you have to understand the kind of WAN Physical layer implementation that Cisco provides as well as ensure that you're familiar with the various types of WAN serial connectors involved.

The good news is that Cisco serial connections support almost any type of WAN service. Your typical WAN connection is a dedicated leased line using HDLC, PPP, and Frame Relay with speeds that can kick it up to 45Mbps (T3).

HDLC, PPP, and Frame Relay can use the same Physical layer specifications, and I'll go over the various types of connections and then move on to telling you all about the WAN protocols specified in the CCNA objectives.

Serial Transmission

WAN serial connectors use *serial transmission*, something that takes place 1 bit at a time over a single channel.

Parallel transmission can pass at least 8 bits at a time, but all WANs use serial transmission.

Cisco routers use a proprietary 60-pin serial connector that you have to get from Cisco or a provider of Cisco equipment. Cisco also has a new, smaller proprietary serial connection that's about one-tenth the size of the 60-pin basic serial cable called the "smart-serial"—I'm not sure why. But I do know that you have to make sure you have the right type of interface in your router before using this cable connector.

The type of connector you have on the other end of the cable depends on your service provider and their particular end-device requirements. There are several different types of ends you'll run into:

- EIA/TIA-232
- EIA/TIA-449
- V.35 (used to connect to a CSU/DSU)
- EIA-530

Make sure you're clear on these things: Serial links are described in frequency or cycles per second (hertz). The amount of data that can be carried within these frequencies is called *bandwidth*. Bandwidth is the amount of data in bits per second that the serial channel can carry.

Data Terminal Equipment and Data Communication Equipment

By default, router interfaces are *data terminal equipment (DTE)*, and they connect into *data communication equipment (DCE)* like a *channel service unit/data service unit (CSU/DSU)*. The CSU/DSU then plugs into a demarcation location (demarc) and is the service provider's last responsibility. Most of the time, the demarc is a jack that has an RJ-45 (8-pin modular) female connector located in a telecommunications closet.

Actually, you may already have heard of demarcs. If you've ever had the glorious experience of reporting a problem to your service provider, they'll usually tell you everything tests out fine up to the demarc, so the problem must be the CPE, or customer premises equipment. In other words, it's your problem not theirs.

Figure 14.6 shows a typical DTE-DCE-DTE connection and the devices used in the network.

The idea behind a WAN is to be able to connect two DTE networks through a DCE network. The DCE network includes the CSU/DSU, through the provider's wiring and switches, all the way to the CSU/DSU at the other end. The network's DCE device (CSU/DSU) provides clocking to the DTE-connected interface (the router's serial interface).

As mentioned, the DCE network provides clocking to the router; this is the CSU/DSU. If you have a nonproduction network and you're using a WAN crossover type of cable and do not have a CSU/DSU, then you need to provide clocking on the DCE end of the cable by using the clock rate command that I showed you in Chapter 4.

Terms such as *EIA/TIA-232, V.35, X.21*, and *HSSI (High-Speed Serial Interface)* describe the Physical layer between the DTE (router) and DCE device (CSU/DSU).

FIGURE 14.6   DTE-DCE-DTE WAN connection

Clocking typically provided by DCE network to routers.

In non-production environments, a DCE network is not always present.

High-Level Data-Link Control (HDLC) Protocol

The High-Level Data-Link Control (HDLC) protocol is a popular ISO-standard, bit-oriented, Data Link layer protocol. It specifies an encapsulation method for data on synchronous serial data links using frame characters and checksums. HDLC is a point-to-point protocol used on leased lines. No authentication can be used with HDLC.

In byte-oriented protocols, control information is encoded using entire bytes. On the other hand, bit-oriented protocols use single bits to represent the control information. Some common bit-oriented protocols include SDLC, LLC, HDLC, TCP, and IP.

HDLC is the default encapsulation used by Cisco routers over synchronous serial links. And Cisco's HDLC is proprietary—it won't communicate with any other vendor's HDLC implementation. But don't give Cisco grief for it—*everyone's* HDLC implementation is proprietary. Figure 14.7 shows the Cisco HDLC format.

FIGURE 14.7   Cisco HDLC frame format

Cisco HDLC

Flag	Address	Control	Proprietary	Data	FCS	Flag

• Each vendor's HDLC has a proprietary data field to support multiprotocol environments.

HDLC

Flag	Address	Control	Data	FCS	Flag

• Supports only single-protocol environments.

As shown in the figure, the reason that every vendor has a proprietary HDLC encapsulation method is that each vendor has a different way for the HDLC protocol to encapsulate multiple Network layer protocols. If the vendors didn't have a way for HDLC to communicate the different layer 3 protocols, then HDLC would only be able to carry one protocol. This proprietary header is placed in the data field of the HDLC encapsulation.

So let's say you only have one Cisco router, and you need to connect to a non-Cisco router because your other Cisco router is on order. What would you do? You couldn't use the default HDLC serial encapsulation because it wouldn't work. Instead, you would use something like PPP, an ISO-standard way of identifying the upper-layer protocols. You can check out RFC 1661 for more information on the origins and standards of PPP. Let's discuss PPP in more detail and how to connect to routers using the PPP encapsulation.

Point-to-Point Protocol (PPP)

Let's spend a little time on Point-to-Point Protocol (PPP). Remember that it's a Data Link layer protocol that can be used over either asynchronous serial (dial-up) or synchronous serial (ISDN) media. It uses Link Control Protocol (LCP) to build and maintain data-link connections. Network Control Protocol (NCP) is used to allow multiple Network layer protocols (routed protocols) to be used on a point-to-point connection.

Since HDLC is the default serial encapsulation on Cisco serial links and it works great, why and when would you choose to use PPP? Well, the basic purpose of PPP is to transport layer 3 packets across a Data Link layer point-to-point link, and it's nonproprietary. So unless you have all Cisco routers, you need PPP on your serial interfaces—the HDLC encapsulation is Cisco proprietary, remember? Plus, since PPP can encapsulate several layer 3 routed protocols and provide authentication, dynamic addressing, and callback, PPP could be the best encapsulation solution for you instead of HDLC.

Figure 14.8 shows the protocol stack compared to the OSI reference model.

FIGURE 14.8   Point-to-Point Protocol stack

PPP contains four main components:

EIA/TIA-232-C, V.24, V.35, and ISDN   A Physical layer international standard for serial communication.

HDLC   A method for encapsulating datagrams over serial links.

LCP   A method of establishing, configuring, maintaining, and terminating the point-to-point connection.

NCP   A method of establishing and configuring different Network layer protocols. NCP is designed to allow the simultaneous use of multiple Network layer protocols. Some examples of protocols here are IPCP (Internet Protocol Control Protocol) and IPXCP (Internetwork Packet Exchange Control Protocol).

Burn it into your mind that the PPP protocol stack is specified at the Physical and Data Link layers only. NCP is used to allow communication of multiple Network layer protocols by encapsulating the protocols across a PPP data link.

Remember that if you have a Cisco router and a non-Cisco router connected with a serial connection, you must configure PPP or another encapsulation method, such as Frame Relay, because the HDLC default just won't work!

Next, I'll cover the options for LCP and PPP session establishment.

Link Control Protocol (LCP) Configuration Options

Link Control Protocol (LCP) offers different PPP encapsulation options, including the following:

Authentication   This option tells the calling side of the link to send information that can identify the user. The two methods are PAP and CHAP.

Compression   This is used to increase the throughput of PPP connections by compressing the data or payload prior to transmission. PPP decompresses the data frame on the receiving end.

Error detection   PPP uses Quality and Magic Number options to ensure a reliable, loop-free data link.

Multilink   Starting with IOS version 11.1, multilink is supported on PPP links with Cisco routers. This option makes several separate physical paths appear to be one logical path at layer 3. For example, two T1s running multilink PPP would show up as a single 3Mbps path to a layer 3 routing protocol.

PPP callback   PPP can be configured to call back after successful authentication. *PPP callback* can be a good thing for you because you can keep track of usage based upon access charges, for accounting records, and a bunch of other reasons. With callback enabled, a calling router (client) will contact a remote router (server) and authenticate as I described earlier. (Know that both routers have to be configured for the callback feature for this to work.) Once authentication is completed, the remote router will terminate the connection and then re-initiate a connection to the calling router from the remote router.

If you have Microsoft devices in your PPP callback, be aware that Microsoft uses a proprietary callback known as Microsoft Callback Control Protocol (CBCP), which is supported in IOS release 11.3(2)T and later.

PPP Session Establishment

When PPP connections are started, the links go through three phases of session establishment, as shown in Figure 14.9.

FIGURE 14.9 PPP session establishment

PPP Session Establishment
1. Link establishment phase
2. Authentication phase (optional)
3. Network layer protocol phase

Link-establishment phase LCP packets are sent by each PPP device to configure and test the link. These packets contain a field called the Configuration Option that allows each device to see the size of the data, compression, and authentication. If no Configuration Option field is present, then the default configurations will be used.

Authentication phase If required, either CHAP or PAP can be used to authenticate a link. Authentication takes place before Network layer protocol information is read. And it's possible that link-quality determination will occur simultaneously.

Network layer protocol phase PPP uses the *Network Control Protocol (NCP)* to allow multiple Network layer protocols to be encapsulated and sent over a PPP data link. Each Network layer protocol (e.g., IP, IPX, AppleTalk, which are routed protocols) establishes a service with NCP.

PPP Authentication Methods

There are two methods of authentication that can be used with PPP links:

Password Authentication Protocol (PAP) The *Password Authentication Protocol (PAP)* is the less secure of the two methods. Passwords are sent in clear text, and PAP is only performed upon the initial link establishment. When the PPP link is first established, the remote node sends the username and password back to the originating router until authentication is acknowledged. Not exactly Fort Knox!

Challenge Handshake Authentication Protocol (CHAP) The *Challenge Handshake Authentication Protocol (CHAP)* is used at the initial startup of a link and at periodic checkups on the link to make sure the router is still communicating with the same host.

After PPP finishes its initial link-establishment phase, the local router sends a challenge request to the remote device. The remote device sends a value calculated using a one-way hash function called MD5. The local router checks this hash value to make sure it matches. If the values don't match, the link is immediately terminated.

Configuring PPP on Cisco Routers

Configuring PPP encapsulation on an interface is really pretty straightforward. To configure it from the CLI, follow these simple router commands:

```
Router#config t
Enter configuration commands, one per line. End with CNTL/Z.
Router(config)#int s0
Router(config-if)#encapsulation ppp
Router(config-if)#^Z
Router#
```

Of course, PPP encapsulation has to be enabled on both interfaces connected to a serial line in order to work, and there are several additional configuration options available to you via the `help` command.

Configuring PPP Authentication

After you configure your serial interface to support PPP encapsulation, you can configure authentication using PPP between routers. First, you need to set the hostname of the router, if it's not already. Then you set the username and password for the remote router that will be connecting to your router:

Here's an example:

```
Router#config t
Enter configuration commands, one per line. End with CNTL/Z.
Router(config)#hostname RouterA
RouterA(config)#username RouterB password cisco
```

When using the `hostname` command, remember that the username is the hostname of the remote router that's connecting to your router. And it's case sensitive too. Also, the password on both routers must be the same. It's a plain-text password that you can see with a `show run` command; you can encrypt the password by using the command `service password-encryption`. You must have a username and password configured for each remote system you plan to connect to. The remote routers must also be configured with usernames and passwords.

Now, after you've set the hostname, usernames, and passwords, choose the authentication type, either CHAP or PAP:

```
RouterA#config t
Enter configuration commands, one per line. End with CNTL/Z.
RouterA(config)#int s0
RouterA(config-if)#ppp authentication chap pap
RouterA(config-if)#^Z
RouterA#
```

If both methods are configured on the same line, as shown here, then only the first method will be used during link negotiation—the second acts as a backup just in case the first method fails.

I'll configure PPP with authentication using SDM later in this chapter, but honestly, the CLI way is easier.

Verifying PPP Encapsulation

Okay—now that PPP encapsulation is enabled, let me show you how to verify that it's up and running. First, let's take a look at a figure of a sample network. Figure 14.10 shows two routers connected with either a point-to-point serial or ISDN connection.

FIGURE 14.10   PPP authentication example

```
hostname Pod1R1
username Pod1R2 password cisco
  interface serial 0
   ip address 10.0.1.1 255.255.255.0
   encapsulation ppp
   ppp authentication chap
```

```
hostname Pod1R2
username Pod1R1 password cisco
  interface serial 0
   ip address 10.0.1.2 255.255.255.0
   encapsulation ppp
   ppp authentication chap
```

You can start verifying the configuration with the show interface command:

```
Pod1R1#sh int s0/0
Serial0/0 is up, line protocol is up
  Hardware is PowerQUICC Serial
  Internet address is 10.0.1.1/24
  MTU 1500 bytes, BW 1544 Kbit, DLY 20000 usec,
     reliability 239/255, txload 1/255, rxload 1/255
  Encapsulation PPP
  loopback not set
  Keepalive set (10 sec)
  LCP Open
  Open: IPCP, CDPCP
[output cut]
```

Notice that the sixth line lists encapsulation as PPP and the eighth line shows that the LCP is open. This means that it has negotiated the session establishment and all is good! The ninth line tells us that NCP is listening for the protocols IP and CDP.

But what will you see if everything isn't perfect? I'm going to type in the configuration shown in Figure 14.11 and find out.

FIGURE 14.11   Failed PPP authentication

```
hostname Pod1R1                      hostname Pod1R2
username Pod1R2 password Cisco       username Pod1R1 password cisco
  interface serial 0                   interface serial 0
  ip address 10.0.1.1 255.255.255.0    ip address 10.0.1.2 255.255.255.0
  encapsulation ppp                    encapsulation ppp
  ppp authentication chap              ppp authentication chap
```

Okay—what's wrong here? Take a look at the usernames and passwords. Do you see the problem now? That's right, the C is capitalized on the Pod1R2 username command found in the configuration of router Pod1R1. This is wrong because the usernames and passwords are case sensitive, remember? Let's take a look at the show interface command and see what happens:

```
Pod1R1#sh int s0/0
Serial0/0 is up, line protocol is down
  Hardware is PowerQUICC Serial
  Internet address is 10.0.1.1/24
  MTU 1500 bytes, BW 1544 Kbit, DLY 20000 usec,
     reliability 243/255, txload 1/255, rxload 1/255
  Encapsulation PPP, loopback not set
  Keepalive set (10 sec)
  LCP Closed
  Closed: IPCP, CDPCP
```

First, notice in the first line of output that Serial0/0 is up, line protocol is down. This is because there are no keepalives coming from the remote router. Next, notice that the LCP is closed because the authentication failed.

Debugging PPP Authentication

To display the CHAP authentication process as it occurs between two routers in the network, just use the command debug ppp authentication.

If your PPP encapsulation and authentication are set up correctly on both routers, and your usernames and passwords are all good, then the debug ppp authentication command will display an output that looks like this:

```
d16h: Se0/0 PPP: Using default call direction
1d16h: Se0/0 PPP: Treating connection as a dedicated line
```

```
1d16h: Se0/0 CHAP: O CHALLENGE id 219 len 27 from "Pod1R1"
1d16h: Se0/0 CHAP: I CHALLENGE id 208 len 27 from "Pod1R2"
1d16h: Se0/0 CHAP: O RESPONSE id 208 len 27 from "Pod1R1"
1d16h: Se0/0 CHAP: I RESPONSE id 219 len 27 from "Pod1R2"
1d16h: Se0/0 CHAP: O SUCCESS id 219 len 4
1d16h: Se0/0 CHAP: I SUCCESS id 208 len 4
```

But if you have the username wrong, as we did previously in the PPP authentication failure example back in Figure 14.11, the output would look something like this:

```
1d16h: Se0/0 PPP: Using default call direction
1d16h: Se0/0 PPP: Treating connection as a dedicated line
1d16h: %SYS-5-CONFIG_I: Configured from console by console
1d16h: Se0/0 CHAP: O CHALLENGE id 220 len 27 from "Pod1R1"
1d16h: Se0/0 CHAP: I CHALLENGE id 209 len 27 from "Pod1R2"
1d16h: Se0/0 CHAP: O RESPONSE id 209 len 27 from "Pod1R1"
1d16h: Se0/0 CHAP: I RESPONSE id 220 len 27 from "Pod1R2"
1d16h: Se0/0 CHAP: O FAILURE id 220 len 25 msg is "MD/DES compare failed"
```

PPP with CHAP authentication is a three-way authentication, and if the username and passwords are not configured exactly the way they should be, then the authentication will fail and the link will be down.

Mismatched WAN Encapsulations

If you have a point-to-point link but the encapsulations aren't the same, the link will never come up. Figure 14.12 shows one link with PPP and one with HDLC.

FIGURE 14.12 Mismatched WAN encapsulations

```
hostname Pod1R1                       hostname Pod1R2
username Pod1R2 password Cisco        username Pod1R1 password cisco
 interface serial 0                    interface serial 0
  ip address 10.0.1.1 255.255.255.0    ip address 10.0.1.2 255.255.255.0
  encapsulation ppp                    encapsulation HDLC
```

Look at router Pod1R1 in this output:

```
Pod1R1#sh int s0/0
Serial0/0 is up, line protocol is down
  Hardware is PowerQUICC Serial
  Internet address is 10.0.1.1/24
  MTU 1500 bytes, BW 1544 Kbit, DLY 20000 usec,
```

```
    reliability 254/255, txload 1/255, rxload 1/255
  Encapsulation PPP, loopback not set
  Keepalive set (10 sec)
  LCP REQsent
Closed: IPCP, CDPCP
```

The serial interface is down and LCP is sending requests but will never receive any responses because router Pod1R2 is using the HDLC encapsulation. To fix this problem, you would have to go to router Pod1R2 and configure the PPP encapsulation on the serial interface. One more thing—even though the usernames are configured and they're wrong, it doesn't matter because the command ppp authentication chap isn't used under the serial interface configuration and the username command isn't relevant in this example.

Always remember that you just can't have PPP on one side and HDLC on the other—they don't get along!

Mismatched IP Addresses

A tricky problem to spot is if you have HDLC or PPP configured on your serial interface but your IP addresses are wrong. Things seem to be just fine because the interfaces will show that they are up. Take a look at Figure 14.13 and see if you can see what I mean—the two routers are connected with different subnets—router Pod1R1 with 10.0.1.1/24 and router Pod1R2 with 10.2.1.2/24.

FIGURE 14.13   Mismatched IP addresses

```
hostname Pod1R1                      hostname Pod1R2
username Pod1R2 password cisco       username Pod1R1 password cisco
  interface serial 0                   interface serial 0
    ip address 10.0.1.1 255.255.255.0    ip address 10.2.1.2 255.255.255.0
    encapsulation ppp                    encapsulation ppp
    ppp authentication chap              ppp authentication chap
```

This will never work. But as I said, take a look at the output:

```
Pod1R1#sh int s0/0
Serial0/0 is up, line protocol is up
  Hardware is PowerQUICC Serial
  Internet address is 10.0.1.1/24
  MTU 1500 bytes, BW 1544 Kbit, DLY 20000 usec,
     reliability 255/255, txload 1/255, rxload 1/255
```

```
Encapsulation PPP, loopback not set
Keepalive set (10 sec)
LCP Open
Open: IPCP, CDPCP
```

See that? The IP addresses between the routers are wrong but the link looks like it's working fine. This is because PPP, like HDLC and Frame Relay, is a layer 2 WAN encapsulation and doesn't care about IP addresses at all. So yes, the link is up, but you can't use IP across this link since it's misconfigured.

To find and fix this problem, you can use the show running-config or the show interfaces command on each router, or you can use what you learned in Chapter 5—the show cdp neighbors detail command:

```
Pod1R1#sh cdp neighbors detail
-------------------------
Device ID: Pod1R2
Entry address(es):
  IP address: 10.2.1.2
```

You can view and verify the directly connected neighbor's IP address and then solve your problem.

Okay—before we move onto Frame Relay, let's take a look at PPPoE.

PPPoE Configuration

If you have a router with an interface that supports PPPoE and the router is connected to a DSL modem, you can configure the router to be a PPPoE client—well, assuming your ISP has provided you with the authentication information, that is.

Let's take a look at configuring a PPPoE client on a router. Here's what it looks like under the physical interface:

```
R1(config)#int f0/0
R1(config-if)#p?
pppoe  pppoe-client  priority-group
R1(config-if)#pppoe ?
  enable        Enable pppoe
  max-sessions  Maximum PPPOE sessions
R1(config-if)#pppoe enable ?
  group  attach a BBA group
  <cr>
R1(config-if)#pppoe enable group ?
  WORD    BBA Group name
  global  Attach global PPPoE group
```

```
R1(config-if)#pppoe enable group global
R1(config-if)#pppoe-client dial-pool-number ?
  <1-255>  Dialer pool number
R1(config-if)#pppoe-client dial-pool-number 1

!
interface FastEthernet4
 description $ETH-WAN$
 no ip address
 duplex auto
 speed auto
 pppoe enable group global
 pppoe-client dial-pool-number 1
!
```

After all that, there really are only two commands needed under the physical interface—the pppoe enable command and the pppoe-client command. And both of them reference the logical interface we haven't created yet.

In order to add a PPPoE connection to your router, you need to also create a dialer interface. This is a logical interface, and under it, I'm going to add the ip address negotiated command so a DHCP address can be received and configured on the interface. And by the way, if you're using private IP addresses between the DSL modem and your router, you can easily add a static IP address on this interface. Take a look:

```
!
interface Dialer0
 ip address negotiated
 ip mtu 1452
 encapsulation ppp
 dialer pool 1
 dialer-group 1
 ppp authentication chap callin
 ppp chap hostname Todd
 ppp chap password 0 lammle
!
```

Take special notice of how the logical interface associates itself to the physical interface with both the dial pool 1 command and the dialer-group 1 command.

Last, under the dialer interface, the PPP authentication is set using the ppp authentication and ppp chap commands. Using the CLI, I provided these commands at global configuration mode, but in this setup, I'll configure the command directly under the logical interface instead.

Although this is a pretty simple configuration, it works really well! Still, I'll show you how to configure PPPoE using the SDM in a bit.

Frame Relay

Frame Relay is still one of the most popular WAN services deployed over the past decade, and there's a good reason for this—cost. And it's a rare network design or designer that has the privilege to ignore that all-important cost factor!

By default, Frame Relay is classified as a non-broadcast multi-access (NBMA) network, meaning it doesn't send any broadcasts like RIP updates across the network. No worries—I'm not going leave you hanging. We'll get into this more soon.

Frame Relay has at its roots a technology called X.25, and it essentially incorporates the components of X.25 that are still relevant to today's reliable and relatively "clean" telecommunications networks while leaving out the no-longer-needed error-correction components. It's substantially more complex than the simple leased-line networks you learned about when I discussed the HDLC and PPP protocols. The leased-line networks are easy to conceptualize—but not so much when it comes to Frame Relay. It can be significantly more complex and versatile, which is why it's often represented as a "cloud" in networking graphics. I'll get to that in a minute—for right now, I'm going to introduce Frame Relay in concept and show you how it differs from simpler leased-line technologies.

Along with your introduction to this technology, you'll get a virtual dictionary of all the new terminology you'll need to solidly grasp the basics of Frame Relay. After that, I'll guide you through some simple Frame Relay implementations.

Introduction to Frame Relay Technology

As a CCNA, you'll need to understand the basics of the Frame Relay technology and be able to configure it in simple scenarios. First, understand that Frame Relay is a packet-switched technology. From everything you've learned so far, just telling you this should make you immediately realize several things about it:

- You won't be using the `encapsulation hdlc` or `encapsulation ppp` command to configure it.

- Frame Relay doesn't work like a point-to-point leased line (although it can be made to look and act like one).

- Frame Relay is usually less expensive than leased lines are, but there are some sacrifices to make to get that savings.

So, why would you even consider using Frame Relay? Take a look at Figure 14.14 to get an idea of what a network looked like before Frame Relay. Now check out Figure 14.15. You can see that there's now only one connection between the Corporate router and the Frame Relay switch. That saves some major cash!

If, for example, you had to add seven remote sites to the corporate office and had only one free serial port on your router—it's Frame Relay to the rescue! Of course, I should probably mention that you now also have one single point of failure, which is not so good. But Frame Relay is used to save money, not to make a network more resilient.

FIGURE 14.14 Before Frame Relay

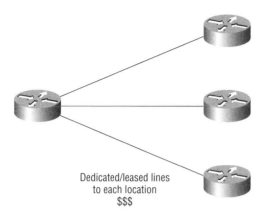

Dedicated/leased lines
to each location
$$$

FIGURE 14.15 After Frame Relay

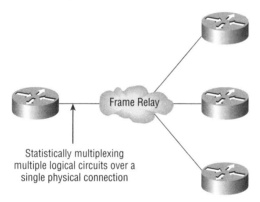

Frame Relay creates a cost-effective mesh network.

Frame Relay

Statistically multiplexing
multiple logical circuits over a
single physical connection

Coming up, I'm going to cover the Frame Relay technology information you need to know about when studying the CCNA objectives.

Committed Information Rate (CIR)

Frame Relay provides a packet-switched network to many different customers at the same time. This is a really good thing because it spreads the cost of the switches among many customers. But remember, Frame Relay is based on the assumption that all customers won't ever need to transmit data constantly, and all at the same time.

Frame Relay works by providing a portion of dedicated bandwidth to each user, and it also allows the user to exceed their guaranteed bandwidth if resources on the telco network happen to be available. So basically, Frame Relay providers allow customers to buy a lower amount of bandwidth than what they really use. There are two separate bandwidth specifications with Frame Relay:

Access rate   The maximum speed at which the Frame Relay interface can transmit.

CIR   The maximum bandwidth of data guaranteed to be delivered. In reality, it's the average amount that the service provider will allow you to transmit.

If these two values are the same, the Frame Relay connection is pretty much just like a leased line. But they can also be set to different values. Here's an example: Let's say that you buy an access rate of T1 (1.544Mbps) and a CIR of 256Kbps. By doing this, the first 256Kbps of traffic you send is guaranteed to be delivered. Anything beyond that is called a "burst"— a transmission that exceeds your guaranteed 256Kbps rate, and can be any amount up to the T1 access rate (if that amount is in your contract). If your combined committed burst (the basis for your CIR) and excess burst sizes, known as the MBR or maximum burst rate when combined, exceed the access rate, you can pretty much say goodbye to your additional traffic. It will most likely be dropped, although this really depends on the subscription level of a particular service provider.

In a perfect world, this always works beautifully—but remember that little word *guarantee*? As in guaranteed rate—of 256Kbps, to be exact? This means that any burst of data you send that exceeds your guaranteed 256Kbps rate will be delivered on something called a "best effort" basis of delivery. Or maybe not—if your telco's equipment doesn't have the capacity to deliver it at the time you transmitted, then your frames will be discarded, and the DTE will be notified. Timing is everything—you can scream data out at six times your guaranteed rate of 256Kbps (T1) *only if* your telco has the capacity available on its equipment at that moment. Remember that "oversubscription" we talked about? Well, here it is in action!

 The CIR is the rate, in bits per second, at which the Frame Relay switch agrees to transfer data.

Frame Relay Encapsulation Types

When configuring Frame Relay on Cisco routers, you need to specify it as an encapsulation on serial interfaces. As I said earlier, you can't use HDLC or PPP with Frame Relay. When you configure Frame Relay, you specify an encapsulation of Frame Relay (as shown in the following output).But unlike HDLC or PPP, with Frame Relay, there are two encapsulation types: Cisco and IETF (Internet Engineering Task Force). The following router output shows these two different encapsulation methods when Frame Relay is chosen on your Cisco router:

```
RouterA(config)#int s0
RouterA(config-if)#encapsulation frame-relay ?
  ietf  Use RFC1490 encapsulation
  <cr>
```

The default encapsulation is Cisco unless you manually type in **ietf**, and Cisco is the type to use when connecting two Cisco devices. You'd opt for the IETF-type encapsulation if you needed to connect a Cisco device to a non-Cisco device with Frame Relay. Whichever you choose, make sure that the Frame Relay encapsulation is the same on both ends.

Virtual Circuits

Frame Relay operates using *virtual circuits* as opposed to the actual circuits that leased lines use. These virtual circuits are what link together the thousands of devices connected to the provider's "cloud." Frame Relay provides a virtual circuit between your two DTE devices, making them appear to be connected via a circuit when in reality, they're dumping their frames into a large, shared infrastructure. You never see the complexity of what's actually happening inside the cloud because you only have a virtual circuit.

And on top of all that, there are two types of virtual circuits—permanent and switched. Permanent virtual circuits (PVCs) are by far the most common type in use today. What "permanent" means here is that the telco creates the mappings inside their gear and as long as you pay the bill, they'll remain in place.

Switched virtual circuits (SVCs) are more like a phone call. The virtual circuit is established when data needs to be transmitted, then it's taken down when the data transfer is complete.

 I have never seen a Frame Relay service using SVCs actually offered by a telco in North America. It's used mainly in private FR networks.

Data Link Connection Identifiers (DLCIs)

Frame Relay PVCs are identified to DTE end devices by *Data Link Connection Identifiers (DLCIs)*. A Frame Relay service provider typically assigns DLCI values, which are used on Frame Relay interfaces to distinguish between different virtual circuits. Because many virtual circuits can be terminated on one multipoint Frame Relay interface, many DLCIs are often affiliated with it.

Let me explain—suppose you have a central HQ with three branch offices. If you were to connect each branch office to HQ using a T1, you would need three serial interfaces on your router at HQ, one for each T1. Simple, right? Well, suppose you use Frame Relay PVCs instead. You could have a T1 at each branch connected to a service provider and only a *single* T1 at HQ. There would be three PVCs on the single T1 at HQ, one going to each branch. And even though there's only a single interface and a single CSU/DSU, the three PVCs function as three separate circuits. Remember what I said about saving money? How much for two additional T1 interfaces and a pair of CSU/DSUs? Answer: A lot! So, why not just go ahead and ask for a percentage of the savings in your bonus?

Okay, before we go on, I want to define Inverse ARP (IARP) and discuss how it's used with DLCIs in a Frame Relay network. Yes, it is somewhat similar to ARP in the fact that it maps a DLCI to an IP address—kind of like ARP does with MAC addresses to IP addresses. And even though you can't configure IARP, you can disable it. It runs on a Frame Relay router and maps the DLCI to an IP address for Frame Relay so it knows how to get to the Frame Relay switch. You can see IP-to-DLCI mappings with the `show frame-relay map` command.

But if you have a non-Cisco router living in your network and it doesn't support IARP, then you're stuck with having to statically provide IP-to-DLCI mappings with the `frame-relay map` command—something I'll demonstrate in a bit.

Inverse ARP (IARP) is used to map a known DLCI to an IP address.

Let's talk about DLCIs a bit more. They're locally significant—global significance requires the entire network to use the LMI extensions that offer global significance. This is why you'll mostly find global DLCIs only in private networks.

But the DLCI doesn't have to be globally significant for it to be functional in getting a frame across the network. Let me explain: When RouterA wants to send a frame to RouterB, it looks up the IARP or manual mapping of the DLCI to the IP address it's trying to get to. Equipped with the DLCI, it then sends the frame out with the DLCI value it found in the DLCI field of the FR header. The provider's ingress switch gets this frame and does a lookup on the DLCI/physical-port combination it observes. Associated with that combination, it finds a new "locally significant" (meaning, between itself and the next-hop switch) DLCI to use in the header, and in the same entry in its table, it finds an outgoing physical port. This happens all the way to RouterB. So basically, you actually could say that the DLCI RouterA identifies the entire virtual circuit to RouterB, even though every DLCI between every pair of devices could be completely different. The big point here is that RouterA is unaware of these differences. That's what makes the DLCI locally significant. So make a mental note that DLCIs really are used by the telco to "find" the other end of your PVC.

To discover why DLCIs are considered locally significant, take a look at Figure 14.16. In the figure, DLCI 100 is considered locally significant to RouterA and identifies the circuit between RouterA and its ingress Frame Relay switch. DLCI 200 would identify the circuit between RouterB and its ingress Frame Relay switch.

FIGURE 14.16   DLCIs are local to your router

DLCI numbers that are used to identify a PVC are typically assigned by the provider and start at 16.

You configure a DLCI number to be applied to an interface like this:

```
RouterA(config-if)#frame-relay interface-dlci ?
  <16-1007> Define a DLCI as part of the current
            subinterface
RouterA(config-if)#frame-relay interface-dlci 16
```

DLCIs identify the logical circuit between the local router and a Frame Relay switch.

Local Management Interface (LMI)

Local Management Interface (LMI) is a signaling standard used between your router and the first Frame Relay switch it's connected to. It allows for passing information about the operation and status of the virtual circuit between the provider's network and the DTE (your router). It communicates information about the following:

Keepalives   These verify that data is flowing.

Multicasting   This is an optional extension of the LMI specification that allows, for example, the efficient distribution of routing information and ARP requests over a Frame Relay network. Multicasting uses the reserved DLCIs from 1019 through 1022.

Global addressing   This provides global significance to DLCIs, allowing the Frame Relay cloud to work exactly like a LAN.

Status of virtual circuits   This provides DLCI status. The status inquiries and messages are used as keepalives when there is no regular LMI traffic to send.

But remember, LMI is not communication between your routers; it's communication between your router and the nearest Frame Relay switch. So it's entirely possible that the router on one end of a PVC is actively receiving LMI while the router on the other end of the PVC is not. And of course, PVCs won't work with one end down. (I say this to clarify the local nature of LMI communications.)

There are three different types of LMI message formats: Cisco, ANSI, and Q.933A. The different kinds in use depend on both the type and configuration of the telco's switching gear, so it's imperative that you configure your router for the correct format, which should be provided by the telco.

Beginning with IOS version 11.2, the LMI type is autosensed. This enables the interface to determine the LMI type supported by the switch. If you're not going to use the autosense feature, you'll need to check with your Frame Relay provider to find out which type to use instead.

On Cisco equipment, the default type is, surprise, Cisco, but you still might have to change to ANSI or Q.933A depending on what your service provider tells you. The three different LMI types are shown in the following router output:

```
RouterA(config-if)#frame-relay lmi-type ?
  cisco
  ansi
  q933a
```

As seen in the output, all three standard LMI signaling formats are supported. Here's a description of each:

Cisco   LMI defined by the Gang of Four (default). The Local Management Interface (LMI) was developed in 1990 by Cisco Systems, StrataCom, Northern Telecom, and Digital Equipment Corporation and became known as the Gang-of-Four LMI, or Cisco LMI.

ANSI   Annex D included with ANSI standard T1.617.

ITU-T (Q.933A)   Annex A included in the ITU-T standard and defined by using the Q.933a command keyword.

Routers receive LMI information from the service provider's Frame Relay switch on a frame-encapsulated interface and update the virtual circuit status to one of three different states:

Active state   Everything is up, and routers can exchange information.

Inactive state   The router's interface is up and working with a connection to the switching office, but the remote router isn't up.

Deleted state   No LMI information is being received on the interface from the switch, which could be due to a mapping problem or a line failure.

Frame Relay Congestion Control

Remember back to our talk about CIR? From that, it should be obvious that the lower your CIR is set, the greater the risk is that your data will become toast. This can be easily avoided if you have just one key piece of information—when and when not to transmit that huge burst! This begs the question, Is there any way for us to find out when our telco's shared infrastructure is free and clear and when it's crammed and jammed? Also, if there is a way to spy this out, how do you do it? Well, that's exactly what I'm going to talk about next—how the Frame Relay switch notifies the DTE of congestion problems—and address those very important questions.

Here are the three congestion bits and their meanings:

Discard Eligibility (DE)   As you know, when you burst (transmit packets beyond the CIR of a PVC), any packets exceeding the CIR are eligible to be discarded if the provider's network is congested at the time. Because of this, the excessive bits are marked with a *Discard Eligibility (DE)* bit in the Frame Relay header. And if the provider's network happens to be congested, the Frame Relay switch will discard the packets with the first DE bit set. So if your bandwidth is configured with a CIR of zero, the DE will always be on.

Forward Explicit Congestion Notification (FECN)   When the Frame Relay network recognizes congestion in the cloud, the switch will set the *Forward Explicit Congestion Notification (FECN)* bit to 1 in a Frame Relay packet header. This will indicate to the destination DTE that the path the frame just traversed is congested.

Backward Explicit Congestion Notification (BECN)   When the switch detects congestion in the Frame Relay network, it'll set the *Backward Explicit Congestion Notification (BECN)* bit in a Frame Relay frame that's destined for the source router. This notifies the router that congestion is ahead. But Cisco routers won't take action on this congestion information unless you tell them to.

To check into this further, search using "Frame Relay Traffic Shaping" on Cisco's website.

Troubleshooting Using Frame Relay Congestion Control

Now let's say all your users are whining about the fact that their Frame Relay connection to the corporate site is super slow. Because you strongly suspect that the link is overloaded, you verify the Frame Relay congestion control information with the show frame-relay pvc command and get this:

```
RouterA#sh frame-relay pvc

PVC Statistics for interface Serial0/0 (Frame Relay DTE)

            Active    Inactive    Deleted      Static
  Local       1          0          0            0
  Switched    0          0          0            0
  Unused      0          0          0            0

DLCI = 100, DLCI USAGE = LOCAL, PVC STATUS = ACTIVE, INTERFACE = Serial0/0
  input pkts 1300        output pkts 1270       in bytes 21212000
  out bytes 21802000     dropped pkts 4         in pkts dropped 147
  out pkts dropped 0     out bytes dropped 0     in FECN pkts 147
   in BECN pkts 192      out FECN pkts 147
  out BECN pkts 259      in DE pkts 0            out DE pkts 214
  out bcast pkts 0       out bcast bytes 0
  pvc create time 00:00:06, last time pvc status changed 00:00:06
Pod1R1#
```

What you want to look for is the in BECN pkts 192 output because this is what's telling the local router that traffic sent to the corporate site is experiencing congestion. BECN means that the path that a frame took to "return" to you is congested.

Frame Relay Implementation and Monitoring

As I've said, there are a ton of Frame Relay commands and configuration options, but I'm going to zero in on the ones you really need to know when studying for the CCNA exam objectives. I'm going to start with one of the simplest configuration options—two routers with a single PVC between them. Next, I'll show you a more complex configuration using subinterfaces, and demonstrate some of the monitoring commands available to verify the configuration.

Single Interface

Let's get started by looking at a simple example. Say that we just want to connect two routers with a single PVC. Here's how that configuration would look:

```
RouterA#config t
Enter configuration commands, one per line.  End with CNTL/Z.
RouterA(config)#int s0/0
RouterA(config-if)#encapsulation frame-relay
RouterA(config-if)#ip address 172.16.20.1 255.255.255.0
RouterA(config-if)#frame-relay lmi-type ansi
RouterA(config-if)#frame-relay interface-dlci 101
RouterA(config-if)#^Z
RouterA#
```

The first step is to specify the encapsulation as Frame Relay. Notice that since I didn't specify a particular encapsulation type—either Cisco or IETF—the Cisco default type was used. If the other router were non-Cisco, I would've specified IETF. Next, I assigned an IP address to the interface, then specified the LMI type of ANSI (the default being Cisco) based on information provided by the telecommunications provider. Finally, I added the DLCI of 101, which indicates the PVC we want to use (again, given to me by my ISP) and assumes there's only one PVC on this physical interface.

That's all there is to it—if both sides are configured correctly, the circuit will come up.

Check out Hands-on Lab 14.3 for a complete example of this type of configuration, including instructions on creating your own Frame Relay switch from a router.

Subinterfaces

You probably know by now that we can have multiple virtual circuits on a single serial interface and yet treat each as a separate interface—I did mention this earlier. We can make this happen by creating *subinterfaces*. Think of a subinterface as a logical interface defined by the IOS software. Several subinterfaces will share a single hardware interface, yet for configuration purposes they operate as if they were separate physical interfaces, something known as multiplexing.

To configure a router in a Frame Relay network so it will avoid split horizon issues by not permitting routing updates, just configure a separate subinterface for each PVC, with a unique DLCI and subnet assigned to the subinterface.

You define subinterfaces using a command like int s0.*subinterface number*. First, you have to set the encapsulation on the physical serial interface, and then you can define the subinterfaces—generally one subinterface per PVC. Here's an example:

```
RouterA(config)#int s0
RouterA(config-if)#encapsulation frame-relay
```

```
RouterA(config-if)#int s0.?
  <0-4294967295>  Serial interface number
RouterA(config-if)#int s0.16 ?
  multipoint       Treat as a multipoint link
  point-to-point  Treat as a point-to-point link
RouterA(config-if)#int s0.16 point-to-point
```

Make sure that you don't have an IP address under the physical interface if you have configured subinterfaces!

You can define a serious amount of subinterfaces on any given physical interface, but keep in mind that there are only about a thousand available DLCIs. In the preceding example, I chose to use subinterface 16 because that represents the DLCI number assigned to that PVC by the carrier. There are two types of subinterfaces:

Point-to-point   Used when a single virtual circuit connects one router to another. Each point-to-point subinterface requires its own subnet.

A point-to-point subinterface maps a single IP subnet per DLCI and addresses and resolves NBMA split horizon issues.

Multipoint   This is when the router is the center of a star of virtual circuits that are using a single subnet for all routers' serial interfaces connected to the frame switch. You'll usually find this implemented with the hub router in this mode and the spoke routers in physical interface (always point-to-point) or point-to-point subinterface mode.

Next, I'll show you an example of a production router running multiple subinterfaces. In the following output, notice that the subinterface number matches the DLCI number—not a requirement, but it majorly helps you administer the interfaces:

```
interface Serial0
 no ip address (notice there is no IP address on the physical interface!)
 no ip directed-broadcast
 encapsulation frame-relay
!
interface Serial0.102 point-to-point
 ip address 10.1.12.1 255.255.255.0
 no ip directed-broadcast
frame-relay interface-dlci 102
!
interface Serial0.103 point-to-point
```

```
 ip address 10.1.13.1 255.255.255.0
 no ip directed-broadcast
frame-relay interface-dlci 103
!
interface Serial0.104 point-to-point
 ip address 10.1.14.1 255.255.255.0
 no ip directed-broadcast
frame-relay interface-dlci 104
!
interface Serial0.105 point-to-point
 ip address 10.1.15.1 255.255.255.0
 no ip directed-broadcast
frame-relay interface-dlci 105
!
```

Notice that there's no LMI type defined. This means that the routers are either running the Cisco default or they're using autodetect (if running Cisco IOS version 11.2 or newer). I also want to point out that each interface maps to a single DLCI and is defined as a separate subnet. Remember—point-to-point subinterfaces solve split horizon issues as well.

Monitoring Frame Relay

Several commands are used frequently to check the status of your interfaces and PVCs once you have Frame Relay encapsulation set up and running. To list them, use the show frame ? command, as seen here:

```
RouterA>sho frame ?
end-to-end     Frame-relay end-to-end VC information
fragment       show frame relay fragmentation information
ip             show frame relay IP statistics
lapf           show frame relay lapf status/statistics
lmi            show frame relay lmi statistics
map            Frame-Relay map table
pvc            show frame relay pvc statistics
qos-autosense  show frame relay qos-autosense information
route          show frame relay route
svc            show frame relay SVC stuff
traffic        Frame-Relay protocol statistics
vofr           Show frame-relay VoFR statistics
```

The most common parameters that you view with the show frame-relay command are lmi, pvc, and map.

Now, let's take a look at the most frequently used commands and the information they provide.

The *show frame-relay lmi* Command

The show frame-relay lmi command will give you the LMI traffic statistics exchanged between the local router and the Frame Relay switch. Here's an example:

```
Router#sh frame lmi

LMI Statistics for interface Serial0 (Frame Relay DTE)
LMI TYPE = CISCO
  Invalid Unnumbered info 0      Invalid Prot Disc 0
  Invalid dummy Call Ref 0       Invalid Msg Type 0
  Invalid Status Message 0       Invalid Lock Shift 0
  Invalid Information ID 0        Invalid Report IE Len 0
  Invalid Report Request 0       Invalid Keep IE Len 0
  Num Status Enq. Sent 0         Num Status msgs Rcvd 0
  Num Update Status Rcvd 0       Num Status Timeouts 0
Router#
```

The router output from the show frame-relay lmi command shows you any LMI errors, plus the LMI type.

The *show frame pvc* Command

The show frame pvc command will present you with a list of all configured PVCs and DLCI numbers. It provides the status of each PVC connection and traffic statistics too. It will also give you the number of BECN and FECN packets received on the router per PVC.

Here is an example:

```
RouterA#sho frame pvc

PVC Statistics for interface Serial0 (Frame Relay DTE)

DLCI = 16,DLCI USAGE = LOCAL,PVC STATUS =ACTIVE,
INTERFACE = Serial0.1
 input pkts 50977876     output pkts 41822892
  in bytes 3137403144
 out bytes 3408047602    dropped pkts 5
  in FECN pkts 0
 in BECN pkts 0       out FECN pkts 0       out BECN pkts 0
 in DE pkts 9393      out DE pkts 0
 pvc create time 7w3d, last time pvc status changed 7w3d

DLCI = 18,DLCI USAGE =LOCAL,PVC STATUS =ACTIVE,
INTERFACE = Serial0.3
```

```
input pkts 30572401    output pkts 31139837
 in bytes 1797291100
out bytes 3227181474    dropped pkts 5
 in FECN pkts 0
in BECN pkts 0       out FECN pkts 0      out BECN pkts 0
in DE pkts 28        out DE pkts 0
pvc create time 7w3d, last time pvc status changed 7w3d
```

If you only want to see information about PVC 16, you can type the command **show frame-relay pvc 16**.

The *show interface* Command

You can use the show interface command to check for LMI traffic. The show interface command displays information about the encapsulation, as well as layer 2 and layer 3 information. It also displays line, protocol, DLCI, and LMI information. Check it out:

```
RouterA#sho int s0
Serial0 is up, line protocol is up
 Hardware is HD64570
 MTU 1500 bytes, BW 1544 Kbit, DLY 20000 usec, rely
  255/255, load 2/255
 Encapsulation FRAME-RELAY, loopback not set, keepalive
  set (10 sec)
 LMI enq sent 451751,LMI stat recvd 451750,LMI upd recvd
  164,DTE LMI up
 LMI enq recvd 0, LMI stat sent 0, LMI upd sent 0
 LMI DLCI 1023 LMI type is CISCO frame relay DTE
 Broadcast queue 0/64, broadcasts sent/dropped 0/0,
  interface broadcasts 839294
```

The LMI DLCI above is used to define the type of LMI being used. If it happens to be 1023, it's the default LMI type of Cisco. If LMI DLCI is zero, then it's the ANSI LMI type (Q.933A uses 0 as well). If LMI DLCI is anything other than 0 or 1023, it's a 911—call your provider; they've got major issues!

The *show frame map* Command

The show frame map command displays the Network layer–to–DLCI mappings. Here's how that looks:

```
RouterB#show frame map
Serial0 (up): ipx 20.0007.7842.3575 dlci 16(0x10,0x400),
          dynamic, broadcast,, status defined, active
Serial0 (up): ip 172.16.20.1 dlci 16(0x10,0x400),
          dynamic, broadcast,, status defined, active
```

```
Serial1 (up): ipx 40.0007.7842.153a dlci 17(0x11,0x410),
             dynamic, broadcast,, status defined, active
Serial1 (up): ip 172.16.40.2 dlci 17(0x11,0x410),
             dynamic, broadcast,, status defined, active
```

Notice that the serial interfaces have two mappings—one for IP and one for IPX. Also important is that the Network layer addresses were resolved with the dynamic protocol Inverse ARP (IARP). After the DLCI number is listed, you can see some numbers in parentheses. The first one is 0x10, which is the hex equivalent for the DLCI number 16, used on serial 0. And the 0x11 is the hex for DLCI 17 used on serial 1. The second numbers, 0x400 and 0x410, are the DLCI numbers configured in the Frame Relay frame. They're different because of the way the bits are spread out in the frame.

The *debug frame lmi* Command

The debug frame lmi command will show output on the router consoles by default (as with any debug command). The information this command gives you will enable you to verify and troubleshoot the Frame Relay connection by helping you determine whether the router and switch are exchanging the correct LMI information. Here's an example:

```
Router#debug frame-relay lmi
Serial3/1(in): Status, myseq 214
RT IE 1, length 1, type 0
KA IE 3, length 2, yourseq 214, myseq 214
PVC IE 0x7 , length 0x6 , dlci 130, status 0x2 , bw 0
Serial3/1(out): StEnq, myseq 215, yourseen 214, DTE up
datagramstart = 0x1959DF4, datagramsize = 13
FR encap = 0xFCF10309
00 75 01 01 01 03 02 D7 D6

Serial3/1(in): Status, myseq 215
RT IE 1, length 1, type 1
KA IE 3, length 2, yourseq 215, myseq 215
Serial3/1(out): StEnq, myseq 216, yourseen 215, DTE up
datagramstart = 0x1959DF4, datagramsize = 13
FR encap = 0xFCF10309
00 75 01 01 01 03 02 D8 D7
```

Troubleshooting Frame Relay Networks

Troubleshooting Frame Relay networks isn't any harder than troubleshooting any other type of network as long as you know what to look for, which is what I'm going to cover now. We'll go over some basic problems that commonly occur in Frame Relay configuration and how to solve them.

First on the list are serial encapsulation problems. As you learned recently, there are two Frame Relay encapsulations: Cisco and IETF. Cisco is the default, and it means that you have a Cisco router on each end of the Frame Relay network. If you don't have a Cisco router on the remote end of your Frame Relay network, then you need to run the IETF encapsulation as shown here:

```
RouterA(config)#int s0
RouterA(config-if)#encapsulation frame-relay ?
  ietf  Use RFC1490 encapsulation
  <cr>
RouterA(config-if)#encapsulation frame-relay ietf
```

Once you verify that you're using the correct encapsulation, you then need to check out your Frame Relay mappings. For example, take a look at Figure 14.17.

FIGURE 14.17   Frame Relay mappings

```
RouterA#show running-config
interface s0/0
ip address 172.16.100.2 255.255.0.0
encapsulation frame-relay
frame-relay map ip 172.16.100.1 200 broadcast
```

So why can't RouterA talk to RouterB across the Frame Relay network? To find that out, take a close look at the `frame-relay map` statement. See the problem now? You cannot use a remote DLCI to communicate to the Frame Relay switch; you must use *your* DLCI number! The mapping should have included DLCI 100 instead of DLCI 200.

Now that you know how to ensure that you have the correct Frame Relay encapsulation, and that DLCIs are only locally significant, let's look into some routing protocol problems typically associated with Frame Relay. See if you can find a problem with the two configurations in Figure 14.18.

FIGURE 14.18   Frame Relay routing problems

```
RouterA#show running-config
interface s0/0
ip address 172.16.100.2 255.255.0.0
encapsulation frame-relay
frame-relay map ip 172.16.100.1 100
router rip
     network 172.16.0.0
```

```
RouterB#show running-config
interface s0/0
ip address 172.16.100.1 255.255.0.0
encapsulation frame-relay
frame-relay map ip 172.16.100.2 200
router rip
     network 172.16.0.0
```

Hmmmm, well, the configs look pretty good. Actually, they look great, so what's the problem? Well, remember that Frame Relay is a non-broadcast multi-access (NBMA) network by default, meaning that it doesn't send any broadcasts across the PVC. So, because the mapping statements do not have the `broadcast` argument at the end of the line, broadcasts, like RIP updates, won't be sent across the PVC.

Okay, now let's use the SDM to configure our serial WAN connections—should be pretty simple!

Using SDM for WAN Connections

I'm going to show you how to set up serial WAN connections using the SDM. My only options are HDLC (the default), PPP, and Frame Relay. Your router may have different options depending on the interfaces installed on it.

Since HDLC is already running, and there's not much to configure or show you with HDLC, I am going to configure PPP between two routers, use authentication, and then show you how to configure Frame Relay on a router interface with SDM.

Configuring PPP with Authentication Using SDM

First, I'm going to configure the serial WAN link between the Corp router and the R3 router using PPP with Authentication. The first thing I need to do is delete the interface from Interfaces and Connections Tasks, then click on the Edit Interface Connection tab, and then click Delete. If I don't do this, the interface won't show up as available to configure through SDM. I could easily do it from the CLI instead, but that's not where we're going here.

Okay—once I deleted the interface configuration, I clicked Create New Connection on the Create Connection tab.

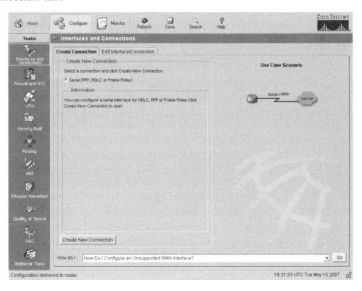

Once I clicked Create New Connection, I received the first screen of the Serial WAN Configuration Wizard.

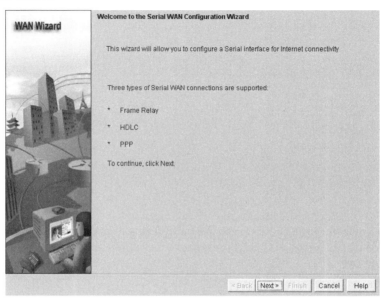

Then, I just clicked Next, and the screen I got showed that HDLC is ready to rock. I would just have to click Next again to make it happen.

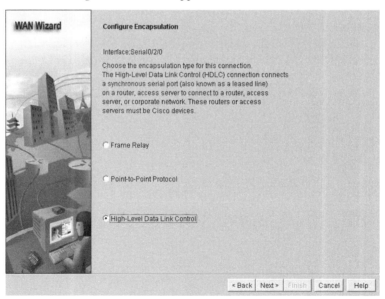

But instead, I clicked Point-to-Point Protocol, and then clicked Next, which brought me to the IP Address screen.

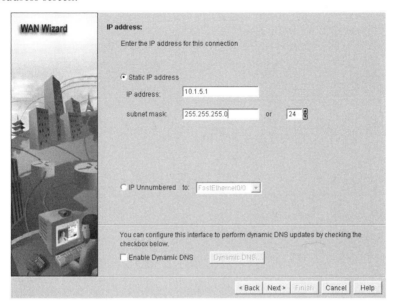

I added the static IP address I wanted to add, and then I clicked Next and got the Authentication screen.

You don't have to enter any authentication information here, but I went ahead and entered the information anyway. The Username field is for the name of the remote router (R3), or whatever information your ISP provided you with—same with the password. (Think back to the PPP configuration I showed you with the CLI earlier.) I then clicked Next. A screen appeared showing a summary of the configuration. I just clicked Finish.

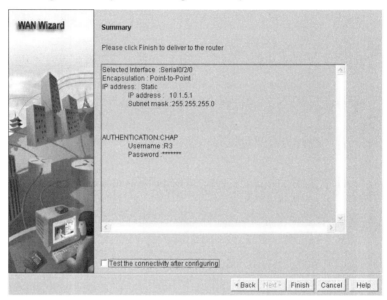

From the Interfaces and Connections task, on the Edit Interface/Connection tab, we can now see that my Serial0/2/0 is configured on the Corp router with PPP and CHAP authentication.

So now I'm going to go to the R3 router and implement the same configuration I just demonstrated on the Corp router. I'll use Corp as the username and assign the same password (just as I showed you in the PPP CLI configuration earlier).

Here's the CLI output from the Corp router after both routers have been configured:

```
!
interface Serial0/2/0
 description Connection to R3$FW_OUTSIDE$
 ip address 10.1.5.1 255.255.255.0
 ip verify unicast reverse-path
 ip virtual-reassembly
 encapsulation ppp
 clock rate 2000000
 ppp authentication chap callin
 ppp chap hostname R3
 ppp chap password 0 cisco
!
```

You'd think I'd be done, right? After all, the links are configured and we're up and running. But we're not. We would be if we were connected to an ISP and don't actually have a point-to-point connection like a T1 (which is what I am simulating). So in reality, the ISP would then provide the authentication commands. The thing is, we have a dedicated point-to-point serial connection, and the SDM PPP with authentication doesn't work without some help from the CLI. Go figure. (I told you it was easier with the CLI!)

Here's how I know things aren't working even though both routers were very easily configured:

```
Corp#sh int s0/2/0
Serial0/2/0 is up, line protocol is down
  Hardware is GT96K Serial
  Description: Connection to R3$FW_OUTSIDE$
  Internet address is 10.1.5.1/24
  MTU 1500 bytes, BW 1544 Kbit, DLY 20000 usec,
     reliability 255/255, txload 1/255, rxload 1/255
  Encapsulation PPP, LCP Listen
[output cut]
```

The first item listed (as you hopefully know) is carrier detect at the Physical layer, but the "line protocol is down" at the Data Link layer. This means we're not getting keepalives from the R3 router. But why? I'm pretty sure I configured it correctly and it definitely wasn't all that difficult! Let's take a look at the authentication in action and see what we can find out:

```
Corp#debug ppp auth
*May 15 18:46:12.039: Se0/2/0 PPP: Authorization required
*May 15 18:46:12.039: Se0/2/0 CHAP: O CHALLENGE id 33 len 23 from "R3"
*May 15 18:46:12.039: Se0/2/0 CHAP: I CHALLENGE id 33 len 25 from "Corp"
*May 15 18:46:12.043: Se0/2/0 CHAP: I RESPONSE id 33 len 25 from "Corp"
```

```
*May 15 18:46:12.043: Se0/2/0 CHAP: Using hostname from interface CHAP
*May 15 18:46:12.043: Se0/2/0 CHAP: Using password from interface CHAP
*May 15 18:46:12.043: Se0/2/0 CHAP: O RESPONSE id 33 len 23 from "R3"
*May 15 18:46:12.043: Se0/2/0 PPP: Sent CHAP LOGIN Request
*May 15 18:46:12.043: Se0/2/0 PPP: Received LOGIN Response FAIL
*May 15 18:46:12.043: Se0/2/0 CHAP: O FAILURE id 33 len 25 msg is
"Authentication failed"
Corp#un all
```

Actually, the authentication commands look like they are trying to work, but things fail at the end. This is where the CLI comes in *if* you are not connecting to a service provider that is configuring your authentication. I now need to go to each router and add the username command. This is pretty simple, but I am surprised that the SDM didn't at least prompt me for this. Okay, here it is:

```
Corp(config)#username R3 password cisco
```

And now for the R3 router:

```
R3(config)#username Corp password cisco
```

Now, finally, we should be up and running. Let's check it out:

```
Corp#debug ppp auth
PPP authentication debugging is on
*May 15 16:53:34.479: Se0/2/0 PPP: Authorization required
*May 15 16:53:34.479: Se0/2/0 CHAP: O CHALLENGE id 1 len 25 from "Corp"
*May 15 16:53:34.483: Se0/2/0 CHAP: I RESPONSE id 1 len 23 from "R3"
*May 15 16:53:34.483: Se0/2/0 PPP: Sent CHAP LOGIN Request
*May 15 16:53:34.483: Se0/2/0 PPP: Received LOGIN Response PASS
*May 15 16:53:34.487: Se0/2/0 PPP: Sent LCP AUTHOR Request
*May 15 16:53:34.487: Se0/2/0 PPP: Sent IPCP AUTHOR Request
*May 15 16:53:34.487: Se0/2/0 LCP: Received AAA AUTHOR Response PASS
*May 15 16:53:34.487: Se0/2/0 IPCP: Received AAA AUTHOR Response PASS
*May 15 16:53:34.487: Se0/2/0 CHAP: O SUCCESS id 1 len 4
*May 15 16:53:34.487: Se0/2/0 PPP: Sent CDPCP AUTHOR Request
*May 15 16:53:34.491: Se0/2/0 PPP: Sent IPCP AUTHOR Request
*May 15 16:53:34.491: Se0/2/0 CDPCP: Received AAA AUTHOR Response PASS
```

Understand that the SDM assumes that you are connecting to an ISP, and that the ISP will provide you with the authentication username and password. Ridiculous, yes, but absolutely true nonetheless!

Configuring PPPoE with SDM

To configure PPPoE with SDM, we'll first need a router connecting to a DSL modem, and then we'll need to configure the interface as a client just as we did earlier. I'll make it painless by using SDM on my 871W router.

After connecting to the router with SDM, I deleted the FastEthernet interface from SDM. Then, under Interfaces and Connections in the Tasks menu, I chose Create Connection.

From here, I clicked Ethernet (PPPoE or Unencapsulated Routing), then clicked Create New Connection, and got the welcome screen of the Ethernet WAN Configuration Wizard.

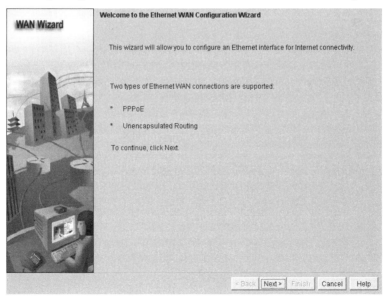

From here, I just clicked Next. From the Encapsulation screen, I checked Enable PPPoE Encapsulation and clicked Next.

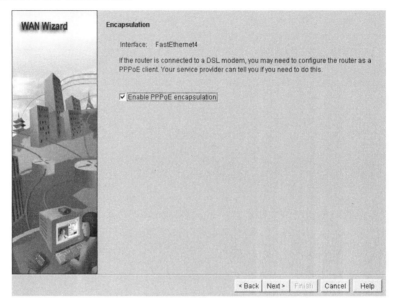

I was then asked for my IP information. I just selected Easy IP (IP Negotiated, meaning DHCP), and clicked Next.

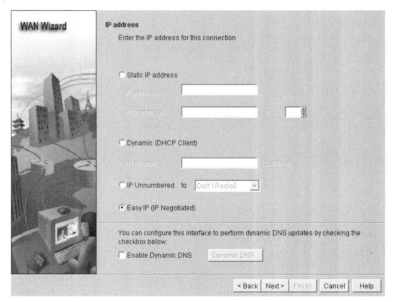

The next screen asked for my authentication information.

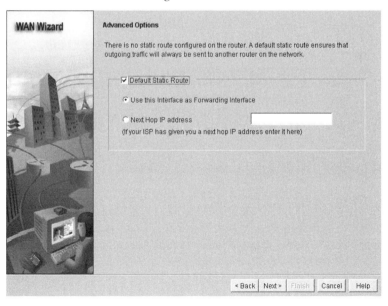

Normally, I would have to be provided with this information from my ISP to make this work. Here, I filled in some basic information and clicked Next.

The next screen asked me for routing information.

I choose to make this my gateway of last resort by checking Default Static Route and selecting Use this Interface as Forwarding Interface. I could have added the next-hop address, but it's possible it could change since I'm using DHCP. After clicking Next, I received a summary of my configuration.

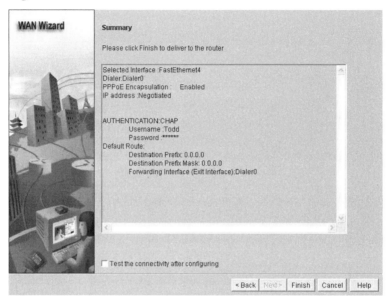

I clicked Next to have the configuration uploaded to my router.
Now, let's move on to configure Frame Relay with SDM.

For more information on configuring PPPoE with SDM, please use the SDM demo. You can install SDM on your computer and run a full demo program as described in Chapter 4, Hands-on Lab 4.6.

Configuring Frame Relay with SDM

Now that our serial connection between the Corp and R3 routers is up and running with PPP and you know how to configure PPPoE, I want to show you how easy it is to set up Frame Relay using SDM. After deleting the interface configuration through the SDM (by the way, I'm starting to get annoyed at this deleting the interface thing before I can reconfigure them!), I get to create a new serial connection.

I'll open the Interface Wizard and choose Frame Relay for the Serial0/2/0 interface of the Corp router.

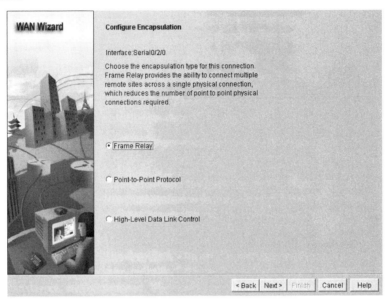

I then got the same screen I got when I configured the PPP interface. I set the static IP address and clicked Next.

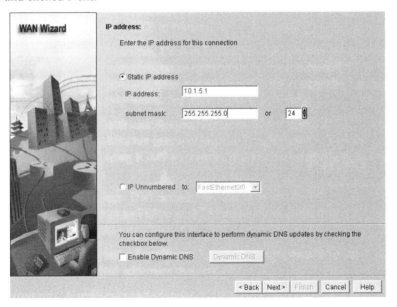

In the real world, this is where I would add the LMI and DLCI information given to me from my provider.

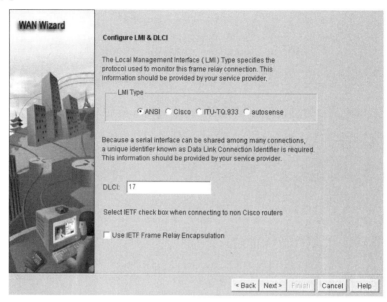

Notice that check box at the bottom left that asks if you want to use IETF encapsulation? Remember, that means you don't have a Cisco router on the other side of the Frame Relay cloud. After clicking Next, I got the Summary screen.

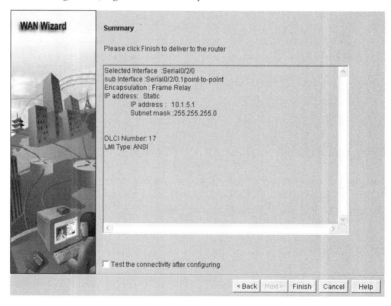

This one shows a summary of my configuration. I clicked Finish to upload it to my router. Let's take a look at the CLI to find out what, exactly, was uploaded to my router. Notice in the following output how the IP address from the physical interface has been moved to the subinterface the SDM created—nice!

```
!
interface Serial0/2/0
 description Connection to R3$FW_OUTSIDE$
 no ip address
 ip verify unicast reverse-path
 ip virtual-reassembly
 encapsulation frame-relay
 clock rate 2000000
 frame-relay lmi-type ansi
!
interface Serial0/2/0.1 point-to-point
 ip address 10.1.5.1 255.255.255.0
 frame-relay interface-dlci 17 CISCO
!
```

If I had this router connected to an ISP and the ISP were correctly configured (that can truly be a big *if*), then my PVC should have come up. Just remember—I used the LMI type Cisco, meaning that my ISP would have a Cisco Frame Relay switch. This is extremely unlikely. Most of the time you would use ANSI LMI.

All right, so now let's create a virtual private network between our Corp router and the R3 router.

Virtual Private Networks

I'd be pretty willing to bet you've heard the term *VPN* more than once before. Maybe you even know what one is, but just in case, a *virtual private network (VPN)* allows the creation of private networks across the Internet, enabling privacy and tunneling of non-TCP/IP protocols. VPNs are used daily to give remote users and disjointed networks connectivity over a public medium like the Internet instead of using more expensive permanent means.

Types of VPNs are named based upon the role they play in a business. There are three different categories of VPNs:

Remote access VPNs   *Remote access VPNs* allow remote users like telecommuters to securely access the corporate network wherever and whenever they need to.

Site-to-site VPNs   *Site-to-site VPNs*, or intranet VPNs, allow a company to connect its remote sites to the corporate backbone securely over a public medium like the Internet instead of requiring more expensive WAN connections like Frame Relay.

Extranet VPNs *Extranet VPNs* allow an organization's suppliers, partners, and customers to be connected to the corporate network in a limited way for business-to-business (B2B) communications.

Now you're interested, huh! And since VPNs are inexpensive and secure, I'm guessing you're really jonesing to find out how VPNs are created right?. Well, there's more than one way to bring a VPN into being. The first approach uses IPSec to create authentication and encryption services between endpoints on an IP network. The second way is via tunneling protocols, allowing you to establish a tunnel between endpoints on a network. And understand that the tunnel itself is a means for data or protocols to be encapsulated inside another protocol—pretty clean!

I'm going to go over the first, IPSec way in a minute, but first, I really want to describe four of the most common tunneling protocols in use:

Layer 2 Forwarding (L2F) *Layer 2 Forwarding (L2F)* is a Cisco-proprietary tunneling protocol, and it was their first tunneling protocol created for virtual private dial-up networks (VPDNs). VPDN allows a device to use a dial-up connection to create a secure connection to a corporate network. L2F was later replaced by L2TP, which is backward compatible with L2F.

Point-to-Point Tunneling Protocol (PPTP) *Point-to-Point Tunneling Protocol (PPTP)* was created by Microsoft to allow the secure transfer of data from remote networks to the corporate network.

Layer 2 Tunneling Protocol (L2TP) *Layer 2 Tunneling Protocol (L2TP)* was created by Cisco and Microsoft to replace L2F and PPTP. L2TP merged the capabilities of both L2F and PPTP into one tunneling protocol.

Generic Routing Encapsulation (GRE) *Generic Routing Encapsulation (GRE)* is another Cisco-proprietary tunneling protocol. It forms virtual point-to-point links, allowing for a variety of protocols to be encapsulated in IP tunnels.

Okay—now that you're clear on both exactly what a VPN is and the various types of VPNs available, it's time to dive into IPSec.

Introduction to Cisco IOS IPSec

Simply put, IPSec is an industry-wide standard suite of protocols and algorithms that allows for secure data transmission over an IP-based network that functions at the layer 3 network layer of the OSI model.

Did you notice I said "IP-based network"? That's really important because by itself, IPSec can't be used to encrypt non-IP traffic. This means that if you run into a situation where you have to encrypt non-IP traffic, you'll need to create a GRE tunnel for it and then use IPSec to encrypt that tunnel!

IPSec Transforms

An *IPSec transform* specifies a single security protocol with its corresponding security algorithm; without these transforms, IPSec wouldn't be able to give us its glory. It's important to be familiar with these technologies, so let me take a second to define the security protocols and briefly introduce the supporting encryption and hashing algorithms that IPSec relies upon.

Security Protocols

The two primary security protocols used by IPSec are *Authentication Header (AH)* and *Encapsulating Security Payload (ESP)*.

Authentication Header (AH)

The AH protocol provides authentication for the data and the IP header of a packet using a one-way hash for packet authentication. It works like this: The sender generates a one-way hash; then the receiver generates the same one-way hash. If the packet has changed in any way, it won't be authenticated and will be dropped. So basically, IPSec relies upon AH to guarantee authenticity. AH checks the entire packet, but it doesn't offer any encryption services.

This is unlike ESP, which only provides an integrity check on the data of a packet.

Encapsulating Security Payload (ESP)

It won't tell you when or how the NASDAQ's gonna bounce up and down like a superball, but ESP will provide confidentiality, data origin authentication, connectionless integrity, anti-replay service, and limited traffic-flow confidentiality by defeating traffic flow analysis. Which is almost as good! Anyway, there are four components of ESP:

Confidentiality   Confidentiality is provided through the use of symmetric encryption algorithms like DES or 3DES. Confidentiality can be selected separately from all other services, but the confidentiality selected must be the same on all endpoints of your VPN.

Data origin authentication and connectionless integrity   Data origin authentication and connectionless integrity are joint services offered as an option in conjunction with the likewise optional confidentiality.

Anti-replay service   You can only use the anti-replay service if data origin authentication is selected. Anti-replay election is based upon the receiver, meaning the service is effective only if the receiver checks the sequence number. In case you were wondering, a replay attack is when a hacker nicks a copy of an authenticated packet and later transmits it to the intended destination. When the duplicate, authenticated IP packet gets to the destination, it can disrupt services and other ugly stuff. The *Sequence Number* field is designed to foil this type of attack.

Traffic flow   For traffic flow confidentiality to work, you have to have tunnel mode selected. And it's most effective if it's implemented at a security gateway where tons of traffic amasses—a situation that can mask the true source-destination patterns of bad guys trying to breach your network's security.

For more detailed information above and beyond the scope of the CCNA objectives, please see www.lammle.com.

Configuring VPNs/IPSec Using the SDM

There are a lot of different ways to configure VPNs on your router. What I am going to do here is add a straight VPN connection between the Corp and R3 routers.

After clicking on VPN in the Tasks bar, I clicked Site-to-Site VPN and received the Create Site to Site VPN tab.

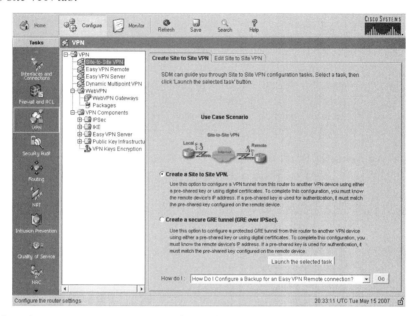

I selected Create a Site to Site VPN and then clicked Launch the Selected Task to get the Site to Site VPN screen.

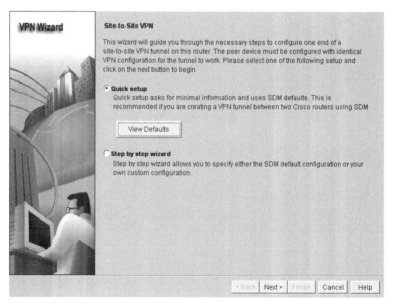

I clicked View Defaults and took a peek at what the router was going to configure:

After clicking Close, I clicked Next to receive the VPN Connection Information screen:

I added the static IP address of my peer router (R3), added a pre-shared key, chose my source address of the Corp router, and the destination address, which happens to be the same address as my peer router (R3). I then clicked Next.

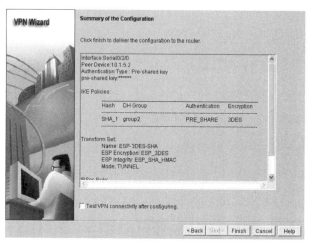

I received a summary of the VPN configuration running IPSec. Whew...man, before SDM, I always had to configure VPNs with IPSec by default. This is so easy! I clicked Finish.

OK, the best part is coming up! I received this next screen from the SDM.

It's asking if it's OK to test the VPN connection. I clicked Yes, of course. SDM then returned another screen asking me for the source and destination addresses and also asking if I wanted to generate traffic or let SDM generate it. I chose to let SDM.

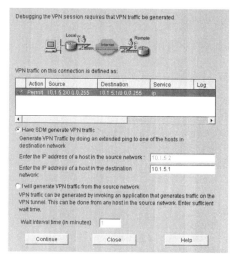

I receive a response from SDM telling me there was a problem with the link and asked if SDM could fix it for me....umm...okay, sure! Once I did that I received this screen.

So, it found a problem and fixed it for me. It's like having my very own advanced tech support elf—sweet! Man, SDM would be worth the money just for this feature alone! Let's take a look at the Corp router's running-config and see what was uploaded to the router's config:

```
!
crypto isakmp policy 1
 encr 3des
 authentication pre-share
 group 2
crypto isakmp key cisco address 10.1.5.2
!
!
crypto ipsec transform-set ESP-3DES-SHA esp-3des esp-sha-hmac
!
crypto map SDM_CMAP_1 1 ipsec-isakmp
 description Tunnel to10.1.5.2
 set peer 10.1.5.2
 set transform-set ESP-3DES-SHA
 match address 104
!
interface Serial0/2/0
[output cut]
 crypto map SDM_CMAP_1
!
access-list 104 remark SDM_ACL Category=4
access-list 104 remark IPSec Rule
access-list 104 permit ip 10.1.5.0 0.0.0.255 10.1.5.0 0.0.0.255
!
```

Yikes! Is this something you think you'd want to try and get working on your own without the help of our tech support elf-genius? The answer is a resounding no! I've done it for years, and it is no day at the beach.

Since we can now do the hardest of hardest configurations easily using SDM elves, why stop now? Let's add some QoS!

Configuring Quality of Service (QoS) across Our VPN Tunnel

Now we all get that the reason we have customer networks is to meet the needs of both applications and users effectively—well, hopefully effectively! And we also know that the blend of the Internet's huge growth, corporate intranets that multiply like rabbits, legions of new applications that voraciously devour bandwidth, and the combined load of voice, data, plus video traffic traveling over our IP infrastructures is totally maxing them out. We basically experience all this when our networks fail to perform well—as poor performance and unprecedented unreliability.

This leads us to QoS. Believe it or not, deploying QoS is actually more secure, cost effective, even faster in today's networking environment! This is why I'm going to show you how to configure QoS on our VPN serial link—a great place to configure QoS in a production network, by the way.

This time, I'm going to start on the R3 router. After connecting with SDM, I'll click the Configure button and then click Quality of Service under the Tasks bar.

From here, I'll click Launch QoS Wizard to get to the first screen of the wizard.

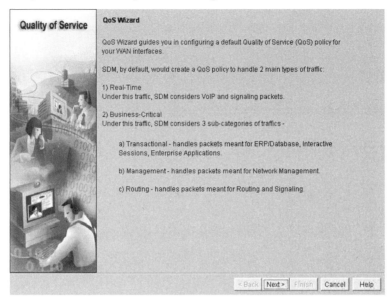

After clicking Next, I'll choose the interface that I want to use as my source or outgoing port and then click Next.

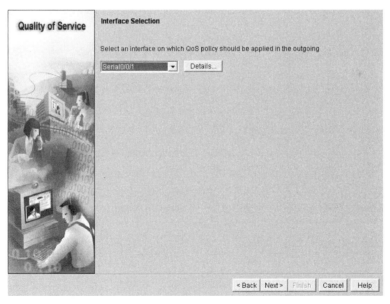

From the QoS Policy Generation screen, I can create bandwidth allocation for various types of data. By default, SDM creates three QoS classes for a typical environment. You can click View Details to get more information. I clicked Next.

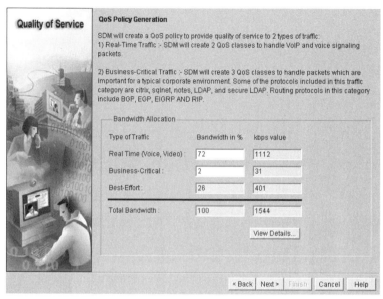

If the SDM gets its way, it will go ahead and enable the NBAR protocol discovery feature for this interface.

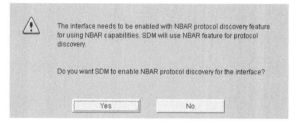

Network Based Application Recognition (NBAR) is very cool because it allows you to both accurately identify and classify your mission-critical and optimization applications—for example, ERP. And after you've got these applications classified, you then get to guarantee them a minimum bandwidth to use. Basically they're policy routed, and if these mission-critical applications are classified, they can be guaranteed a minimum amount of bandwidth, policy routed, and tagged to receive special treatment.

I clicked Yes, and from the next screen, both the QoS class and value of real-time traffic and business-critical traffic are displayed.

Click Close—the configuration's summary is shown, but it's super long, so I'm only showing you the top of the page.

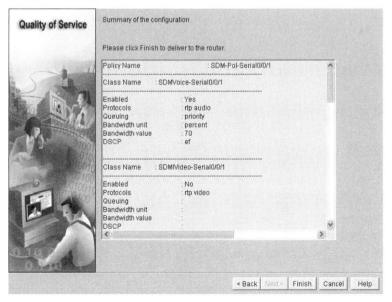

Once I clicked Finish, it uploaded the configuration to the router. In fact, it uploaded a lot—way too much for me to copy into this book! SDM is a powerful tool, and as I've demonstrated, it can be used really effectively for some seriously tough configurations.

Summary

In this chapter, you learned the difference between the following WAN services: cable, DSL, HDLC, PPP, PPPoE, and Frame Relay. You also learned that you can use a VPN once any of those services are up and running.

I have to tell you—you must understand High-Level Data-Link Control (HDLC) and how to verify with the `show interface` command that HDLC is enabled! You've been provided with some really important HDLC information, as well as how the Point-to-Point Protocol (PPP) is used if you need more features than HDLC offers or if you're using two different brands of routers. You now know that this is because HDLC is proprietary and won't work between two different vendors' routers.

When we went through the section on PPP, I discussed the various LCP options as well as the two types of authentication that can be used: PAP and CHAP.

And we talked about Frame Relay and the two different encapsulation methods used with it in detail. We also discussed LMI options, Frame Relay maps, and subinterface configurations. In addition to the Frame Relay terms and features we covered, I demonstrated Frame Relay configuration and verification in depth.

We finished up the chapter with how to use the SDM to configure a WAN link and then discussed VPNs and configured a VPN link with IPSec. We also touched upon using QoS on our WANs.

Exam Essentials

Remember the default serial encapsulation on Cisco routers.   Cisco routers use a proprietary High-Level Data-Link Control (HDLC) encapsulation on all its serial links by default.

Understand the different Frame Relay encapsulations.   Cisco uses two different Frame Relay encapsulation methods on its routers. Cisco is the default and means that the router is connected to a Cisco Frame Relay switch; Internet Engineering Task Force (IETF) means that your router is connecting to anything but a Cisco Frame Relay switch.

Remember what the CIR is in Frame Relay.   The CIR is the average rate, in bits per second, at which the Frame Relay switch agrees to transfer data.

Remember the commands for verifying Frame Relay.   The `show frame-relay lmi` command will give you the LMI traffic statistics exchanged between the local router and the Frame Relay switch. The `show frame pvc` command will list all configured PVCs and DLCI numbers.

Remember the PPP Data Link layer protocols.   The three Data Link layer protocols are Network Control Protocol (NCP), which defines the Network layer protocols; Link Control

Protocol (LCP), a method of establishing, configuring, maintaining, and terminating the point-to-point connection; and High-Level Data-Link Control (HDLC), the MAC layer protocol that encapsulates the packets.

Remember the various type of serial WAN connections.   The serial WAN connections that are most widely used are HDLC, PPP, and Frame Relay

Understand the term *virtual private network*.   You need to understand why and how to use a VPN between two sites.

Written Lab 14

Write the answers to the following WAN questions:

1. Write the command to see the encapsulation method on serial 0 of a Cisco router.
2. Write the commands to configure s0 to PPP encapsulation.
3. Write the commands to configure a username of *todd* and password of *cisco* that is used on a Cisco router for PPP authentication.
4. Write the commands to enable CHAP authentication on a Cisco serial interface. (Assume PPP is the encapsulation type.)
5. Write the commands to configure the DLCI numbers for two serial interfaces, 0 and 1. Use 16 for s0 and 17 for s1.
6. Write the commands to configure a remote office using a point-to-point subinterface. Use DLCI 16 and IP address 172.16.60.1/24.
7. What protocol would you use if you were running xDSL and needed authentication?
8. What are the three protocols specified in PPP?
9. To provide security in your VPN tunnel, what protocol suite would you use?
10. What are the typical three different categories of VPNs?

(The answers to Written Lab 14 can be found following the answers to the review questions for this chapter.)

Hands-on Labs

In this section, you will configure Cisco routers in three different WAN labs using the figure supplied in each lab. (These labs are included for use with real Cisco routers.)

Lab 14.1: Configuring PPP Encapsulation and Authentication

Lab 14.2: Configuring and Monitoring HDLC

Lab 14.3: Configuring Frame Relay and Subinterfaces

Hands-on Lab 14.1: Configuring PPP Encapsulation and Authentication

By default, Cisco routers use High-Level Data-Link Control (HDLC) as a point-to-point encapsulation method on serial links. If you are connecting to non-Cisco equipment, then you can use the PPP encapsulation method to communicate.

The lab you will configure is shown in the following diagram.

RouterA   RouterB

1. Type **sh int s0** on Routers A and B to see the encapsulation method.

2. Make sure that each router has the hostname assigned:

   RouterA#**config t**

   RouterA(config)#**hostname RouterA**

   RouterB#**config t**

   RouterB(config)#**hostname RouterB**

3. To change the default HDLC encapsulation method to PPP on both routers, use the encapsulation command at interface configuration. Both ends of the link must run the same encapsulation method.

   RouterA#**Config t**

   RouterA(config)#**int s0**

   RouterA(config-if)#**Encap ppp**

4. Now go to Router B and set serial 0 to PPP encapsulation.

   RouterB#**config t**

   RouterB(config)#**int s0**

   RouterB(config-if)#**encap ppp**

5. Verify the configuration by typing **sh int s0** on both routers.

6. Notice the IPCP, IPXCP, and CDPCP. This is the information used to transmit the upper-layer (Network layer) information across the HDLC at the MAC sublayer.

7. Define a username and password on each router. Notice that the username is the name of the remote router. Also, the password must be the same.

   RouterA#**config t**

   RouterA(config)#**username RouterB password todd**

   RouterB#**config t**

   RouterB(config)#**username RouterA password todd**

8. Enable CHAP or PAP authentication on each interface.

    RouterA(config)#**int s0**
    RouterA(config-if)#**ppp authentication chap**

    RouterB(config)#**int s0**
    RouterB(config-if)#**ppp authentication chap**

9. Verify the PPP configuration on each router by using these two commands:

    sh int s0
    debug ppp authentication

Hands-on Lab 14.2: Configuring and Monitoring HDLC

There really is no configuration for HDLC, but if you completed Lab 14.1, then the PPP encapsulation would be set on both routers. This is why I put the PPP lab first. This lab allows you to actually configure HDLC encapsulation on a router.

 This second lab will use the same configuration as Lab 14.1 used.

1. Set the encapsulation for each serial interface by using the encapsulation hdlc command.

    RouterA#**config t**
    RouterA(config)#**int s0**
    RouterA(config-if)#**encapsulation hdlc**

    RouterB#**config t**
    RouterB(config)#**int s0**
    RouterB(config-if)#**encapsulation hdlc**

2. Verify the HDLC encapsulation by using the show interface s0 command on each router.

Hands-on Lab 14.3: Configuring Frame Relay and Subinterfaces

In this lab, you will use the following diagram to configure Frame Relay.

In this lab, you will configure the Lab _B router to be a Frame Relay switch. You will then configure the Lab_A and Lab_C routers to use the switch to bring up the PVC.

1. Set the hostname, `frame-relay switching` command, and the encapsulation of each serial interface on the Frame Relay switch.

    Router#**config t**
    Router(config)#**hostname Lab_B**
    Lab_B(config)#**frame-relay switching** *[makes the router an*
    FR switch]
    Lab_B(config)#**int s0/0**
    Lab_B(config-if)#**encapsulation frame-relay**
    Lab_B(config-if)#**int s0/1**
    Lab_B(config-if)#**encapsulation frame-relay**

2. Configure the Frame Relay mappings on each interface. You do not have to have IP addresses on these interfaces because they are only switching one interface to another with Frame Relay frames.

    Lab_B(config-if)#**int s0/0**
    Lab_B(config-if)#**frame intf-type dce**
    [The above command makes this an FR DCE interface, which
    is different than a router's interface being DCE]
    Lab_B(config-if)#**frame-relay route 102 interface**
      Serial0/1 201
    Lab_B(config-if)#**clock rate 64000**
    [The above command is used if you have this as DCE, which
    is different than an FR DCE]

```
Lab_B(config-if)#int s0/1
Lab_B(config-if)#frame intf-type dce
Lab_B(config-if)#frame-relay route 201 interface
  Serial0/0 102
Lab_B(config-if)#clock rate 64000 [if you have this as DCE]
```

This is not as hard as it looks. The route command just says that if you receive frames from PVC 102, send them out int s0/1 using PVC 201. The second mapping on serial 0/1 is just the opposite. Anything that comes in int s0/1 is routed out serial0/ 0 using PVC 102.

3. Configure Lab_A with a point-to-point subinterface.

```
Router#config t
Router(config)#hostname Lab_A
Lab_A(config)#int s0/0
Lab_A(config-if)#encapsulation frame-relay
Lab_A(config-if)#int s0.102 point-to-point
Lab_A(config-if)#ip address 172.16.10.1
  255.255.255.0
Lab_A(config-if)#frame-relay interface-dlci 102
```

4. Configure Lab_C with a point-to-point subinterface.

```
Router#config t
Router(config)#hostname Lab_C
Lab_C(config)#int s0/0
Lab_C(config-if)#encapsulation frame-relay
Lab_C(config-if)#int s0.201 point-to-point
Lab_C(config-if)#ip address 172.16.10.2
  255.255.255.0
Lab_C(config-if)#frame-relay interface-dlci 201
```

5. Verify your configurations with the following commands:

```
Lab_A>sho frame ?
  ip       show frame relay IP statistics
  lmi      show frame relay lmi statistics
  map      Frame-Relay map table
  pvc      show frame relay pvc statistics
  route    show frame relay route
  traffic  Frame-Relay protocol statistics
```

6. Also, use Ping and Telnet to verify connectivity.

Review Questions

The following questions are designed to test your understanding of this chapter's material. For more information on how to get additional questions, please see this book's Introduction.

1. Which command will display the CHAP authentication process as it occurs between two routers in the network?

   A. show chap authentication

   B. show interface serial 0

   C. debug ppp authentication

   D. debug chap authentication

2. Which command is required for connectivity in a Frame Relay network if Inverse ARP is not operational?

   A. frame-relay arp

   B. frame-relay map

   C. frame-relay interface-dci

   D. frame-relay lmi-type

3. Suppose that you have a customer who has a central HQ and six branch offices. They anticipate adding six more branches in the near future. They wish to implement a WAN technology that will allow the branches to economically connect to HQ and you have no free ports on the HQ router. Which of the following would you recommend?

   A. PPP

   B. HDLC

   C. Frame Relay

   D. ISDN

4. Which of the following command options are displayed when you use the Router#**show frame-relay ?** command? (Choose three.)

   A. dlci

   B. neighbors

   C. lmi

   D. pvc

   E. map

5. How should a router that is being used in a Frame Relay network be configured to keep split horizon issues from preventing routing updates?

   A. Configure a separate subinterface for each PVC with a unique DLCI and subnet assigned to the subinterface.

   B. Configure each Frame Relay circuit as a point-to-point line to support multicast and broadcast traffic.

   C. Configure many subinterfaces in the same subnet.

   D. Configure a single subinterface to establish multiple PVC connections to multiple remote router interfaces.

6. Which encapsulations can be configured on a serial interface? (Choose three.)

   A. Ethernet

   B. Token Ring

   C. HDLC

   D. Frame Relay

   E. PPP

7. When setting up Frame Relay for point-to-point subinterfaces, which of the following must not be configured?

   A. The Frame Relay encapsulation on the physical interface

   B. The local DLCI on each subinterface

   C. An IP address on the physical interface

   D. The subinterface type as point-to-point

8. When a router is connected to a Frame Relay WAN link using a serial DTE interface, how is the clock rate determined?

   A. Supplied by the CSU/DSU

   B. By the far end router

   C. By the `clock rate` command

   D. By the Physical layer bit stream timing

9. A default Frame Relay WAN is classified as what type of physical network?

   A. Point-to-point

   B. Broadcast multi-access

   C. Non-broadcast multi-access

   D. Non-broadcast multipoint

10. Which of the following encapsulates PPP frames in Ethernet frames and uses common PPP features like authentication, encryption, and compression?

   A. PPP

   B. PPPoA

   C. PPPoE

   D. Token Ring

11. You need to configure a router for a Frame Relay connection to a non-Cisco router. Which of the following commands will prepare the WAN interface of the router for this connection?

A. Router(config-if)#**encapsulation frame-relay q933a**

B. Router(config-if)#**encapsulation frame-relay ansi**

C. Router(config-if)#**encapsulation frame-relay ietf**

D. Router(config-if)#**encapsulation frame-relay cisco**

12. The Acme Corporation is implementing dial-up services to enable remote-office employees to connect to the local network. The company uses multiple routed protocols, needs authentication of users connecting to the network, and since some calls will be long distance, needs callback support. Which of the following protocols is the best choice for these remote services?

A. 802.1

B. Frame Relay

C. HDLC

D. PPP

E. PAP

13. Which WAN encapsulations can be configured on an asynchronous serial connection? (Choose two.)

A. PPP

B. ATM

C. HDLC

D. SDLC

E. Frame Relay

14. Which of the following uses ATM as the Data Link layer protocol that's terminated at what's known as the DSLAM?

A. DSL

B. PPPoE

C. Frame Relay

D. Dedicated T1

E. Wireless

F. POTS

15. Why won't the serial link between the Corp router and the Remote router come up?

```
Corp#sh int s0/0
Serial0/0 is up, line protocol is down
  Hardware is PowerQUICC Serial
  Internet address is 10.0.1.1/24
  MTU 1500 bytes, BW 1544 Kbit, DLY 20000 usec,
    reliability 254/255, txload 1/255, rxload 1/255
```

```
Encapsulation PPP, loopback not set
```

```
Remote#sh int s0/0
Serial0/0 is up, line protocol is down
  Hardware is PowerQUICC Serial
  Internet address is 10.0.1.2/24
  MTU 1500 bytes, BW 1544 Kbit, DLY 20000 usec,
      reliability 254/255, txload 1/255, rxload 1/255
  Encapsulation HDLC, loopback not set
```

    A. The serial cable is faulty.

    B. The IP addresses are not in the same subnet.

    C. The subnet masks are not correct.

    D. The keepalive settings are not correct.

    E. The layer 2 frame types are not compatible.

16. In which of the following technologies is the term *HFC* used?

    A. DSL

    B. PPPoE

    C. Frame Relay

    D. Cable

    E. Wireless

    F. POTS

17. A remote site has just been connected to the central office. However, remote users cannot access applications at the central office. The remote router can be pinged from the central office router. After reviewing the command output shown below, which do you think is the most likely reason for the problem?

```
Central#show running-config
!
interface Serial0
 ip address 10.0.8.1 255.255.248.0
 encapsulation frame-relay
 frame-relay map ip 10.0.15.2 200
!
Router rip
Network 10.0.0.0

Remote#show running-config
!
interface Serial0
```

```
 ip address 10.0.15.2 255.255.248.0
 encapsulation frame-relay
 frame-relay map ip 10.0.8.1 100
 !
Router rip
Network 10.0.0.0
```

A. The Frame Relay PVC is down.

B. The IP addressing on the Central/Remote router link is incorrect.

C. RIP routing information is not being forwarded.

D. Frame Relay Inverse ARP is not properly configured.

18. Which of the following describes an industry-wide standard suite of protocols and algorithms that allows for secure data transmission over an IP-based network that functions at the layer 3 Network layer of the OSI model?

A. HDLC

B. Cable

C. VPN

D. IPSec

E. xDSL

19. Which of the following describes the creation of private networks across the Internet, enabling privacy and tunneling of non-TCP/IP protocols?

A. HDLC

B. Cable

C. VPN

D. IPSec

E. xDSL

20. Referring to the following diagram, what functions does the Frame Relay DLCI provide with respect to RouterA?

A. Identifies the signaling standard between RouterA and the frame switch

B. Identifies the circuit between RouterB and the frame switch

C. Identifies the encapsulation used between RouterA and RouterB

D. Defines the signaling standard between RouterB and the frame switch.

Answers to Review Questions

1. C. The command `debug ppp authentication` will show you the authentication process that PPP uses between point-to-point connections.

2. B. If you have a router in your Frame Relay network that does not support IARP, you must create Frame Relay maps on your router, which provide known DLCI-to-IP address mappings.

3. C. The key is "there are no free ports" on your router. Only Frame Relay can provide a connection to multiple locations with one interface, and in an economical manner no less.

4. C, D, E. The `show frame-relay ?` command provides many options, but the options available in this question are `lmi`, `pvc`, and `map`.

5. A. If you have a serial port configured with multiple DLCIs connected to multiple remote sites, split horizon rules (discussed in Chapter 5) stop route updates received on an interface from being sent out the same interface. By creating subinterfaces for each PVC, you can avoid the split horizon issues when using Frame Relay.

6. C, D, E. Ethernet and Token Ring are LAN technologies and cannot be configured on a serial interface. PPP, HDLC, and Frame Relay are layer 2 WAN technologies that are typically configured on a serial interface.

7. C. It is very important to remember when studying the CCNA exam objectives, and when configuring Frame Relay with point-to-point subinterfaces, that you do not put an IP address on the physical interface.

8. A. Clocking on a serial interface is always provided by the CSU/DSU (DCE device). However, if you do not have a CSU/DSU in your nonproduction test environment, then you need to supply clocking with the `clock rate` command on the serial interface of the router with the DCE cable attached.

9. C. Frame Relay, by default, is a non-broadcast multi-access (NBMA) network, which means that broadcasts, such as RIP updates, will not be forwarded across the link by default.

10. C. PPPoE encapsulates PPP frames in Ethernet frames and uses common PPP features like authentication, encryption, and compression. PPPoA is used for ATM.

11. C. If you have a Cisco router on one side of a Frame Relay network and a non-Cisco router on the other side, you would need to use the Frame Relay encapsulation type of IETF. The default is Cisco encapsulation, which means that a Cisco router must be on both sides of the Frame Relay network.

12. D. PPP is your only option, as HDLC and Frame Relay do not support these types of business requirements. PPP provides dynamic addressing, authentication using PAP or CHAP, and callback services.

13. A, B. Please do not freak out because ATM is an answer to this question. ATM is not covered in depth on the CCNA exam. PPP is mostly used for dial-up (async) services, but ATM could be used as well, though it typically is not used anymore since PPP is so efficient.

14. A. ATM is the Data-Link layer protocol that's typically used over the DSL layer 1 connection from the CPE and terminated at what's known as the DSLAM—an ATM switch that contains DSL interface cards, or ATU-Cs.

15. E. This is an easy question because the Remote router is using the default HDLC serial encapsulation and the Corp router is using the PPP serial encapsulation. You should go to the Remote router and set that encapsulation to PPP or change the Corp router back to the default of HDLC.

16. D. In a modern network, *hybrid fibre-coaxial (HFC)* is a telecommunications industry term for a network that incorporates both optical fiber and coaxial cable to create a broadband network.

17. C. Even though the IP addresses don't look correct, they are in the same subnet, so answer B is not correct. The question states that you can ping the other side, so the PVC must be up—answer A can't be correct. You cannot configure IARP, so only answer C can be correct. Since a Frame Relay network is a non-broadcast multi-access network by default, broadcasts such as RIP updates cannot be sent across the PVC unless you use the broadcast statement at the end of the `frame-relay map` command.

18. D. IPSec is an industry-wide standard suite of protocols and algorithms that allows for secure data transmission over an IP-based network that functions at the layer 3 Network layer of the OSI model.

19. C. A allows the creation of private networks across the Internet, enabling privacy and tunneling of non-TCP/IP protocols. A VPN can be set up across any type of link.

20. A. As I mentioned many times in this chapter, and you need to remember this: DLCIs are locally significant only and define the circuit from the router to the switch only. They do not reference a remote router or DLCI. RouterA would use DLCI 100 to get to the RouterB networks. RouterB would use DLCI 200 to get to the RouterA networks.

Answers to Written Lab 14.1

1. `sh int s0`

2. `config t`

   `int s0`

   `encap ppp`

3. `config t`

   `username todd password cisco`

4. `config t`

   `int serial 0`

   `ppp authentication chap`

5. `config t`

   `int s0`

   `frame interface-dlci 16`

   `int s1`

   `frame interface-dlci 17`

6. `config t`

   `int s0`

   `encap frame`

   `int s0.16 point-to-point`

   `ip address 172.16.60.1 255.255.255.0`

   `frame interface-dlci 16`

7. PPPoE

8. HDLC, LCP, and NCP

9. IPSec

10. Remote access VPNs, site-to-site VPNs, and extranet VPNs

Glossary

10BaseT   Part of the original IEEE 802.3 standard, 10BaseT is the Ethernet specification of 10Mbps baseband that uses two pairs of twisted-pair, Category 3, 4, or 5 cabling—using one pair to send data and the other to receive. 10BaseT has a distance limit of about 100 meters per segment. *See also: Ethernet* and *IEEE 802.3.*

100BaseT   Based on the IEEE 802.3u standard, 100BaseT is the Fast Ethernet specification of 100Mbps baseband that uses UTP wiring. 100BaseT sends link pulses (containing more information than those used in 10BaseT) over the network when no traffic is present. *See also: 10BaseT, Fast Ethernet,* and *IEEE 802.3.*

100BaseTX   Based on the IEEE 802.3u standard, 100BaseTX is the 100Mbps baseband Fast Ethernet specification that uses two pairs of UTP or STP wiring. The first pair of wires receives data; the second pair sends data. To ensure correct signal timing, a 100BaseTX segment cannot be longer than 100 meters.

A&B bit signaling   Used in T1 transmission facilities and sometimes called "24th channel signaling." Each of the 24 T1 subchannels in this procedure uses one bit of every sixth frame to send supervisory signaling information.

AAA   Authentication, Authorization, and Accounting: A system developed by Cisco to provide network security. *See also: authentication, authorization,* and *accounting.*

AAL   ATM Adaptation Layer: A service-dependent sublayer of the Data Link layer, which accepts data from other applications and brings it to the ATM layer in 48-byte ATM payload segments. CS and SAR are the two sublayers that form AALs. Currently, the four types of AAL recommended by the ITU-T are AAL1, AAL2, AAL3/4, and AAL5. AALs are differentiated by the source-destination timing they use, whether they are CBR or VBR, and whether they are used for connection-oriented or connectionless mode data transmission. *See also: AAL1, AAL2, AAL3/4, AAL5, ATM,* and *ATM layer.*

AAL1   ATM Adaptation Layer 1: One of four AALs recommended by the ITU-T, it is used for connection-oriented, time-sensitive services that need constant bit rates, such as isochronous traffic and uncompressed video. *See also: AAL.*

AAL2   ATM Adaptation Layer 2: One of four AALs recommended by the ITU-T, it is used for connection-oriented services that support a variable bit rate, such as compressed voice traffic. *See also: AAL.*

AAL3/4   ATM Adaptation Layer 3/4: One of four AALs (a product of two initially distinct layers) recommended by the ITU-T, supporting both connectionless and connection-oriented links. Its primary use is in sending SMDS packets over ATM networks. *See also: AAL.*

AAL5   ATM Adaptation Layer 5: One of four AALs recommended by the ITU-T, it is used to support connection-oriented VBR services primarily to transfer classical IP over ATM and LANE traffic. This least complex of the AAL recommendations uses SEAL, offering lower bandwidth costs and simpler processing requirements but also providing reduced bandwidth and error-recovery capacities. *See also: AAL.*

AARP   AppleTalk Address Resolution Protocol: The protocol in an AppleTalk stack that maps data-link addresses to network addresses.

AARP probe packets   Packets sent by the AARP to determine whether a given node ID is being used by another node in a nonextended AppleTalk network. If the node ID is not in use, the sending node appropriates that node's ID. If the node ID is in use, the sending node will select a different ID and then send out more AARP probe packets. *See also: AARP.*

ABM   Asynchronous Balanced Mode: When two stations can initiate a transmission, ABM is an HDLC (or one of its derived protocols) communication technology that supports peer-oriented, point-to-point communications between both stations.

ABR   Area Border Router: An OSPF router that is located on the border of one or more OSPF areas. ABRs are used to connect OSPF areas to the OSPF backbone area.

access layer   One of the layers in Cisco's three-layer hierarchical model. The access layer provides users with access to the internetwork.

access link   A link used with switches that is part of only one virtual LAN (VLAN). Trunk links carry information from multiple VLANs.

access list   A set of test conditions kept by routers that determines "interesting traffic" to and from the router for various services on the network.

access method   The manner in which network devices approach gaining access to the network itself.

access rate   Defines the bandwidth rate of the circuit. For example, the access rate of a T1 circuit is 1.544Mbps. In Frame Relay and other technologies, there may be a fractional T1 connection—256Kbps, for example—however, the access rate and clock rate are still 1.544Mbps.

access server   Also known as a "network access server," it is a communications process connecting asynchronous devices to a LAN or WAN through network and terminal emulation software, providing synchronous or asynchronous routing of supported protocols.

accounting   One of the three components in AAA. Accounting provides auditing and logging functionalities to the security model.

acknowledgment   Verification sent from one network device to another signifying that an event has occurred. May be abbreviated as ACK. *Contrast with: NAK.*

ACR   Allowed cell rate: A designation defined by the ATM Forum for managing ATM traffic. Dynamically controlled using congestion control measures, the ACR varies between the minimum cell rate (MCR) and the peak cell rate (PCR). *See also: MCR and PCR.*

active monitor   The mechanism used to manage a token ring. The network node with the highest MAC address on the ring becomes the active monitor and is responsible for management tasks such as preventing loops and ensuring that tokens are not lost.

active state   In regard to an EIGRP routing table, a route will be in active state when a router is undergoing a route convergence.

address learning   Used with transparent bridges to learn the hardware addresses of all devices on a network. The switch then filters the network with the known hardware (MAC) addresses.

address mapping   By translating network addresses from one format to another, this methodology permits different protocols to operate interchangeably.

address mask   A bit combination descriptor identifying which portion of an address refers to the network or subnet and which part refers to the host. Sometimes simply called the mask. *See also: subnet mask.*

address resolution   The process used for resolving differences between computer addressing schemes. Address resolution typically defines a method for tracing Network layer (layer 3) addresses to Data Link layer (layer 2) addresses. *See also: address mapping.*

adjacency   The relationship made to exchange routing information between defined neighboring routers and end nodes using a common media segment.

administrative distance (AD)   A number between 0 and 255 that expresses the level of trustworthiness of a routing information source. The lower the number, the higher the integrity rating.

administrative weight   A value designated by a network administrator to rate the preference given to a network link. It is one of four link metrics exchanged by PTSPs to test ATM network resource availability.

ADSU   ATM Data Service Unit: The terminal adapter used to connect to an ATM network through an HSSI-compatible mechanism. *See also: DSU.*

advertising   The process whereby routing or service updates are transmitted at given intervals, allowing other routers on the network to maintain a record of viable routes.

AEP   AppleTalk Echo Protocol: A test for connectivity between two AppleTalk nodes where one node sends a packet to another and receives an echo, or copy, in response.

AFI   Authority and Format Identifier: The part of an NSAP ATM address that delineates the type and format of the IDI section of an ATM address.

AFP   AppleTalk Filing Protocol: A Presentation layer protocol, supporting AppleShare and Mac OS File Sharing, that permits users to share files and applications on a server.

AIP   ATM Interface Processor: Supporting AAL3/4 and AAL5, this interface for Cisco 7000 series routers minimizes performance bottlenecks at the UNI. *See also: AAL3/4 and AAL5.*

algorithm   A set of rules or processes used to solve a problem. In networking, algorithms are typically used for finding the best route for traffic from a source to its destination.

alignment error   An error occurring in Ethernet networks, in which a received frame has extra bits—that is, a number not divisible by eight. Alignment errors are generally the result of frame damage caused by collisions.

all-routes explorer packet   An explorer packet that can move across an entire SRB network, tracing all possible paths to a given destination. Also known as an all-rings explorer packet. *See also: explorer packet, local explorer packet,* and *spanning explorer packet.*

AM   Amplitude modulation: A modulation method that represents information by varying the amplitude of the carrier signal. *See also: modulation.*

AMI   Alternate Mark Inversion: A line-code type on T1 and E1 circuits that shows zeros as 01 during each bit cell and ones as 11 or 00, alternately, during each bit cell. The sending device must maintain ones density in AMI but not independently of the data stream. Also known as binary-coded, alternate mark inversion. *Contrast with: B8ZS. See also: ones density.*

amplitude   An analog or digital waveform's highest value.

analog transmission   Signal messaging whereby information is represented by various combinations of signal amplitude, frequency, and phase.

ANSI   American National Standards Institute: The organization of corporate, government, and volunteer members that coordinates standards-related activities, approves U.S. national standards, and develops U.S. positions in international standards organizations. ANSI assists in the creation of international and U.S. standards in disciplines such as communications, networking, and a variety of technical fields. It publishes over 13,000 standards for engineered products and technologies ranging from screw threads to networking protocols. ANSI is a member of the International Electrotechnical Commission (IEC) and International Organization for Standardization (ISO).

anycast   An ATM address that can be shared by more than one end system, allowing requests to be routed to a node that provides a particular service.

AppleTalk   Currently in two versions, the group of communication protocols designed by Apple Computer for use in Macintosh environments. The earlier Phase 1 protocols support one physical network with only one network number that resides in one zone. The later Phase 2 protocols support more than one logical network on a single physical network, allowing networks to exist in more than one zone. *See also: zone.*

Application layer   Layer 7 of the OSI reference network model, supplying services to application procedures (such as electronic mail and file transfer) that are outside the OSI model. This layer chooses and determines the availability of communicating partners along with the resources necessary to make the connection, coordinates partnering applications, and forms a consensus on procedures for controlling data integrity and error recovery. *See also: Data Link layer, Network layer, Physical layer, Presentation layer, Session layer,* and *Transport layer.*

ARA   AppleTalk Remote Access: A protocol for Macintosh users establishing their access to resources and data from a remote AppleTalk location.

area   A logical, rather than physical, set of segments (based on CLNS, DECnet, or OSPF) along with their attached devices. Areas are commonly connected to others using routers to create a single autonomous system. *See also: autonomous system.*

ARM   Asynchronous Response Mode: An HDLC communication mode using one primary station and at least one additional station, in which transmission can be initiated from either the primary or one of the secondary units.

ARP   Address Resolution Protocol: Defined in RFC 826, the protocol that traces IP addresses to MAC addresses. *See also: RARP.*

AS   autonomous system: A group of networks under mutual administration that share the same routing methodology. Autonomous systems are subdivided by areas and must be assigned an individual 16-bit number by the IANA. *See also: area.*

AS path prepending   The use of route maps in BGP to lengthen the autonomous system path by adding false ASNs.

ASBR   Autonomous System Boundary Router: An Area Border Router placed between an OSPF autonomous system and a non-OSPF network that operates both OSPF and an additional routing protocol, such as RIP. ASBRs must be located in a non-stub OSPF area. *See also: ABR, non-stub area,* and *OSPF.*

ASCII   American Standard Code for Information Interchange: An 8-bit code for representing characters, consisting of 7 data bits plus 1 parity bit.

ASICs   Application-specific integrated circuits: Used in layer 2 switches to make filtering decisions. The ASIC looks in the filter table of MAC addresses and determines which port the destination hardware address of a received hardware address is destined for. The frame will be allowed to traverse only that one segment. If the hardware address is unknown, the frame is forwarded out all ports.

ASN.1   Abstract Syntax Notation One: An OSI language used to describe types of data that are independent of computer structures and depicting methods. Described by ISO International Standard 8824.

ASP   AppleTalk Session Protocol: A protocol employing ATP to establish, maintain, and tear down sessions as well as sequence requests. *See also: ATP.*

AST   Automatic Spanning Tree: A function that supplies one path for spanning explorer frames traveling from one node in the network to another, supporting the automatic resolution of spanning trees in SRB networks. AST is based on the IEEE 802.1d standard. *See also: IEEE 802.1* and *SRB.*

asynchronous transmission   Digital signals sent without precise timing, usually with different frequencies and phase relationships. Asynchronous transmissions generally enclose individual characters in control bits (called start and stop bits) that show the beginning and end of each character. *Contrast with: isochronous transmission* and *synchronous transmission.*

ATCP   AppleTalk Control Program: The protocol for establishing and configuring AppleTalk over PPP, defined in RFC 1378. *See also: PPP.*

ATDM   Asynchronous Time-Division Multiplexing: A technique for sending information, it differs from normal TDM in that the time slots are assigned when necessary rather than pre-assigned to certain transmitters. *Contrast with: FDM, statistical multiplexing,* and *TDM.*

ATG   Address Translation Gateway: The mechanism within Cisco DECnet routing software that enables routers to route multiple, independent DECnet networks and to establish a user-designated address translation for chosen nodes between networks.

ATM   Asynchronous Transfer Mode: The international standard, identified by fixed-length 53-byte cells, for transmitting cells in multiple service systems, such as voice, video, or data. Transit delays are reduced because the fixed-length cells permit processing to occur in the hardware. ATM is designed to maximize the benefits of high-speed transmission media, such as SONET, E3, and T3.

ATM ARP server   A device that supplies logical subnets running classical IP over ATM with address-resolution services.

ATM endpoint   The initiating or terminating connection in an ATM network. ATM endpoints include servers, workstations, ATM-to-LAN switches, and ATM routers.

ATM Forum   The international organization founded jointly by Northern Telecom, Sprint, Cisco Systems, and NET/ADAPTIVE in 1991 to develop and promote standards-based implementation agreements for ATM technology. The ATM Forum broadens official standards developed by ANSI and ITU-T and creates implementation agreements before official standards are published.

ATM layer   A sublayer of the Data Link layer in an ATM network that is service independent. To create standard 53-byte ATM cells, the ATM layer receives 48-byte segments from the AAL and attaches a 5-byte header to each. These cells are then sent to the physical layer for transmission across the physical medium. *See also: AAL.*

ATMM   ATM Management: A procedure that runs on ATM switches, managing rate enforcement and VCI translation. *See also: ATM.*

ATM user-user connection   A connection made by the ATM layer to supply communication between at least two ATM service users, such as ATMM processes. These communications can be uni- or bidirectional, using one or two VCs, respectively. *See also: ATM layer and ATMM.*

ATP   AppleTalk Transaction Protocol: A transport-level protocol that enables reliable transactions between two sockets; one requests the other to perform a given task and to report the results. ATP fastens the request and response together, assuring a loss-free exchange of request-response pairs.

attenuation   In communication, weakening or loss of signal energy, typically caused by distance.

AURP   AppleTalk Update-based Routing Protocol: A technique for encapsulating AppleTalk traffic in the header of a foreign protocol that allows the connection of at least two noncontiguous AppleTalk internetworks through a foreign network (such as TCP/IP) to create an AppleTalk WAN. The connection made is called an AURP tunnel. By exchanging routing information between exterior routers, the AURP maintains routing tables for the complete AppleTalk WAN. *See also: AURP tunnel.*

AURP tunnel   A connection made in an AURP WAN that acts as a single, virtual link between AppleTalk internetworks separated physically by a foreign network such as a TCP/IP network. *See also: AURP.*

authentication   The first component in the AAA model. Users are typically authenticated via a username and password, which are used to uniquely identify them.

authority zone   A portion of the domain-name tree associated with DNS for which one name server is the authority. *See also: DNS.*

authorization   The act of permitting access to a resource based on authentication information in the AAA model.

auto-detect mechanism   Used in Ethernet switch, hub, and interface cards to determine the duplex and speed that can be used.

auto duplex   A setting on layer 1 and layer 2 devices that sets the duplex of a switch or hub port automatically.

automatic call reconnect   A function that enables automatic call rerouting away from a failed trunk line.

autonomous confederation   A collection of self-governed systems that depend more on their own network accessibility and routing information than on information received from other systems or groups.

autonomous switching   The ability of Cisco routers to process packets more quickly by using the ciscoBus to switch packets independently of the system processor.

autonomous system   *See: AS.*

autoreconfiguration   A procedure executed by nodes within the failure domain of a token ring wherein nodes automatically perform diagnostics, trying to reconfigure the network around failed areas.

auxiliary port   The console port on the back of Cisco routers that allows you to connect a modem and dial the router and make console configuration settings.

B8ZS   Binary 8-Zero Substitution: A line-code type, interpreted at the remote end of the connection, that uses a special code substitution whenever eight consecutive zeros are transmitted over the link on T1 and E1 circuits. This technique assures ones density independent of the data stream. Also known as bipolar 8-zero substitution. *Contrast with: AMI. See also: ones density.*

backbone   The basic portion of the network that provides the primary path for traffic sent to and initiated from other networks.

back end   A node or software program supplying services to a front end. *See also: server.*

bandwidth   The gap between the highest and lowest frequencies employed by network signals. More commonly, it refers to the rated throughput capacity of a network protocol or medium.

bandwidth on demand (BoD)   This function allows an additional B channel to be used to increase the amount of bandwidth available for a particular connection.

baseband   A feature of a network technology that uses only one carrier frequency. Ethernet is an example. Also named "narrowband." *Compare with: broadband.*

baseline   Baseline information includes historical data about the network and routine utilization information. This information can be used to determine whether there were recent changes made to the network that may contribute to the problem at hand.

Basic Management Setup   Used with Cisco routers when in setup mode. Only provides enough management and configuration to get the router working so someone can telnet into the router and configure it.

baud   Synonymous with bits per second (bps), if each signal element represents 1 bit. It is a unit of signaling speed equivalent to the number of separate signal elements transmitted per second.

B channel   Bearer channel: A full-duplex, 64Kbps channel in ISDN that transmits user data. *Compare with: D channel, E channel,* and *H channel.*

BDR   Backup designated router: This is used in an OSPF network to back up the designated router in case of failure.

beacon   An FDDI frame or Token Ring frame that points to a serious problem with the ring, such as a broken cable. The beacon frame carries the address of the station thought to be down. *See also: failure domain.*

BECN   Backward Explicit Congestion Notification: BECN is the bit set by a Frame Relay network in frames moving away from frames headed into a congested path. A DTE that receives frames with the BECN may ask higher-level protocols to take necessary flow control measures. *Compare with: FECN.*

BGP4   BGP version 4: Version 4 of the interdomain routing protocol most commonly used on the Internet. BGP4 supports CIDR and uses route-counting mechanisms to decrease the size of routing tables. *See also: CIDR.*

BGP Identifier   This field contains a value that identifies the BGP speaker. This is a random value chosen by the BGP router when sending an OPEN message.

BGP neighbors   Two routers running BGP that begin a communication process to exchange dynamic routing information; they use a TCP port at layer 4 of the OSI reference model. Specifically, TCP port 179 is used. Also known as "BGP peers."

BGP peers   *See: BGP neighbors.*

BGP speaker   A router that advertises its prefixes or routes.

bidirectional shared tree   A method of shared tree multicast forwarding. This method allows group members to receive data from the source or the RP, whichever is closer. *See also: RP (rendezvous point).*

binary   A two-character numbering method that uses ones and zeros. The binary numbering system underlies all digital representation of information.

binding   Configuring a Network layer protocol to use a certain frame type on a LAN.

BIP   Bit Interleaved Parity: A method used in ATM to monitor errors on a link, sending a check bit or word in the link overhead for the previous block or frame. This allows bit errors in transmissions to be found and delivered as maintenance information.

BISDN   Broadband ISDN: ITU-T standards created to manage high-bandwidth technologies such as video. BISDN presently employs ATM technology along SONET-based transmission circuits, supplying data rates typically between 155Mbps and 622Mbps and now even into the gigabyte range (if you have the big bucks). *See also: BRI, ISDN, and PRI.*

bit   One binary digit; either a 1 or a 0. Eight bits make a byte.

bit-oriented protocol   Regardless of frame content, the class of Data Link layer communication protocols that transmits frames. Bit-oriented protocols, as compared with byte-oriented, supply more efficient and trustworthy full-duplex operation. *Compare with: byte-oriented protocol.*

block size   Number of hosts that can be used in a subnet. Block sizes typically can be used in increments of 4, 8, 16, 32, 64, and 128.

Boot ROM   Used in routers to put the router into bootstrap mode. Bootstrap mode then boots the device with an operating system. The ROM can also hold a small Cisco IOS.

boot sequence   Defines how a router boots. The configuration register tells the router where to boot the IOS from as well as how to load the configuration.

bootstrap protocol   A protocol used to dynamically assign IP addresses and gateways to requesting clients.

border gateway   A router that facilitates communication with routers in different autonomous systems.

border peer   The device in charge of a peer group; it exists at the edge of a hierarchical design. When any member of the peer group wants to locate a resource, it sends a single explorer to the border peer. The border peer then forwards this request on behalf of the requesting router, thus eliminating duplicate traffic.

border router   Typically defined within Open Shortest Path First (OSPF) as a router that connected an area to the backbone area. However, a border router can be a router that connects a company to the Internet as well. *See also: OSPF.*

BPDU   Bridge Protocol Data Unit: A Spanning Tree Protocol initializing packet that is sent at definable intervals for the purpose of exchanging information among bridges in networks.

BRI   Basic Rate Interface: The ISDN interface that facilitates circuit-switched communication between video, data, and voice; it is made up of two B channels (64Kbps each) and one D channel (16Kbps). *Compare with: PRI. See also: BISDN.*

bridge   A device for connecting two segments of a network and transmitting packets between them. Both segments must use identical protocols to communicate. Bridges function at the Data Link layer, layer 2 of the OSI reference model. The purpose of a bridge is to filter, send, or flood any incoming frame, based on the MAC address of that particular frame.

bridge group   Used in the router configuration of bridging, bridge groups are defined by a unique number. Network traffic is bridged between all interfaces that are members of the same bridge group.

bridge identifier   Used to elect the root bridge in a layer 2 switched internetwork. The bridge ID is a combination of the bridge priority and base MAC address.

bridge priority   Sets the STP priority of the bridge. All bridge priorities are set to 32768 by default.

bridging loop   Loops occur in a bridged network if more than one link to a network exists and the STP protocol is not turned on.

broadband   A transmission methodology for multiplexing several independent signals onto one cable. In telecommunications, broadband is classified as any channel with bandwidth greater than 4kHz (typical voice grade). In LAN terminology, it is classified as a coaxial cable on which analog signaling is employed. Also known as "wideband."

broadcast   A data frame or packet that is transmitted to every node on the local network segment (as defined by the broadcast domain). Broadcasts are known by their broadcast address, which is a destination network and host address with all the bits turned on. Also called "local broadcast." *Compare with: directed broadcast.*

broadcast address   Used in both logical addressing and hardware addressing. In logical addressing, the host addresses will be all ones. With hardware addressing, the hardware address will be all ones in binary (all Fs in hex).

broadcast domain   A group of devices receiving broadcast frames initiating from any device within the group. Because routers do not forward broadcast frames, broadcast domains are not forwarded from one broadcast to another.

broadcast (multi-access) networks   Broadcast (multi-access) networks such as Ethernet allow multiple devices to connect to (or access) the same network, as well as provide a broadcast ability in which a single packet is delivered to all nodes on the network.

broadcast storm   An undesired event on the network caused by the simultaneous transmission of any number of broadcasts across the network segment. Such an occurrence can overwhelm network bandwidth, resulting in time-outs.

buffer   A storage area dedicated to handling data while in transit. Buffers are used to receive/ store sporadic deliveries of data bursts, usually received from faster devices, compensating for the variations in processing speed. Incoming information is stored until everything is received prior to sending data on. Also known as an "information buffer."

bursting   Some technologies, including ATM and Frame Relay, are considered burstable. This means that user data can exceed the bandwidth normally reserved for the connection; however, it cannot exceed the port speed. An example of this would be a 128Kbps Frame Relay CIR on a T1—depending on the vendor, it may be possible to send more than 128Kbps for a short time.

bus   Any common physical path, typically wires or copper, through which a digital signal can be used to send data from one part of a computer to another.

BUS   Broadcast and unknown servers: In LAN emulation, the hardware or software responsible for resolving all broadcasts and packets with unknown (unregistered) addresses into the point-to-point virtual circuits required by ATM. *See also: LANE, LEC, LECS,* and *LES.*

bus topology   A linear LAN architecture in which transmissions from various stations on the network are reproduced over the length of the medium and are accepted by all other stations. *Compare with: ring topology* and *star topology.*

BX.25   AT&T's use of X.25. *See also: X.25.*

bypass mode   An FDDI and Token Ring network operation that deletes an interface.

bypass relay   A device that enables a particular interface in the token ring to be closed down and effectively taken off the ring.

byte   Eight bits. *See also: octet.*

byte-oriented protocol   Any type of data-link communication protocol that, in order to mark the boundaries of frames, uses a specific character from the user character set. These protocols have generally been superseded by bit-oriented protocols. *Compare with: bit-oriented protocol.*

cable range   In an extended AppleTalk network, the range of numbers allotted for use by existing nodes on the network. The value of the cable range can be anywhere from a single network number to a sequence of several touching network numbers. Node addresses are determined by their cable range value.

CAC   Connection Admission Control: The sequence of actions executed by every ATM switch while connection setup is performed in order to determine if a request for connection is violating the guarantees of QoS for established connections. Also, CAC is used to route a connection request through an ATM network.

call admission control   A device for managing traffic in ATM networks, determining the possibility of a path containing adequate bandwidth for a requested VCC.

call establishment   Used to reference an ISDN call setup scheme when the call is working.

call priority   In circuit-switched systems, the defining priority given to each originating port; it specifies in which order calls will be reconnected. Additionally, call priority identifies which calls are allowed during a bandwidth reservation.

call setup   Handshaking scheme that defines how a source and destination device will establish a call to each other.

call setup time   The length of time necessary to effect a switched call between DTE devices.

CBR   Constant bit rate: An ATM Forum QoS class created for use in ATM networks. CBR is used for connections that rely on precision clocking to guarantee trustworthy delivery. *Compare with: ABR* and *VBR*.

CD   Carrier detect: A signal indicating that an interface is active or that a connection generated by a modem has been established.

CDP   Cisco Discovery Protocol: Cisco's proprietary protocol that is used to tell a neighbor Cisco device about the type of hardware, software version, and active interfaces the Cisco device is using. It uses a SNAP frame between devices and is not routable.

CDP holdtime   The amount of time a router will hold Cisco Discovery Protocol information received from a neighbor router before discarding it if the information is not updated by the neighbor. This timer is set to 180 seconds by default.

CDP timer   The amount of time between Cisco Discovery Protocol advertisements transmitted out of all router interfaces, by default. The CDP timer is 90 seconds by default.

CDVT   Cell Delay Variation Tolerance: A QoS parameter for traffic management in ATM networks specified when a connection is established. The allowable fluctuation levels for data samples taken by the PCR in CBR transmissions are determined by the CDVT. *See also: CBR* and *PCR*.

cell   In ATM networking, the basic unit of data for switching and multiplexing. Cells have a defined length of 53 bytes, including a 5-byte header that identifies the cell's data stream and 48 bytes of payload. *See also: cell relay*.

cell payload scrambling   The method by which an ATM switch maintains framing on some medium-speed edge and trunk interfaces (T3 or E3 circuits). Cell payload scrambling rearranges the data portion of a cell to maintain the line synchronization with certain common bit patterns.

cell relay   A technology that uses small packets of fixed size, known as cells. Their fixed length enables cells to be processed and switched in hardware at high speeds, making this technology the foundation for ATM and other high-speed network protocols. *See also: cell*.

Centrex   A local exchange carrier service providing local switching that resembles that of an on-site PBX. Centrex has no on-site switching capability. Therefore, all customer connections return to the central office (CO). *See also: CO*.

CER   Cell error ratio: In ATM, the ratio of transmitted cells having errors to the total number of cells transmitted within a certain span of time.

CGMP   Cisco Group Management Protocol: A proprietary protocol developed by Cisco. The router uses CGMP to send multicast membership commands to Catalyst switches.

channelized E1   Operating at 2.048Mpbs, an access link that is sectioned into 29 B channels and one D channel, supporting DDR, Frame Relay, and X.25. *Compare with: channelized T1*.

channelized T1 Operating at 1.544Mbps, an access link that is sectioned into 23 B channels and one D channel of 64Kbps each, where individual channels or groups of channels connect to various destinations, supporting DDR, Frame Relay, and X.25. *Compare with: channelized E1.*

CHAP Challenge Handshake Authentication Protocol: Supported on lines using PPP encapsulation, it is a security feature that identifies the remote end, helping keep out unauthorized users. After CHAP is performed, the router or access server determines whether a given user is permitted access. It is a newer, more secure protocol than PAP. *Compare with: PAP.*

checksum A test for ensuring the integrity of sent data. It is a number calculated from a series of values taken through a sequence of mathematical functions, typically placed at the end of the data from which it is calculated, and then recalculated at the receiving end for verification. *Compare with: CRC.*

choke packet When congestion exists, it is a packet sent to inform a transmitter that it should decrease its sending rate.

CIDR Classless Inter-Domain Routing: It allows a group of IP networks to appear to other networks as a unified, larger entity. In CIDR, IP addresses and their subnet masks are written as four dotted octets, followed by a forward slash and the number of masking bits (a form of subnet notation shorthand). *See also: BGP4.*

CIP Channel Interface Processor: A channel attachment interface for use in Cisco 7000 series routers that connects a host mainframe to a control unit. This device eliminates the need for an FBP to attach channels.

CIR Committed information rate: Averaged over a minimum span of time and measured in bps, a Frame Relay network's agreed-upon minimum rate of transferring information.

circuit switching Used with dial-up networks such as PPP and ISDN. Passes data, but needs to set up the connection first—just like making a phone call.

Cisco FRAD Cisco Frame Relay Access Device: A Cisco product that supports Cisco IPS Frame Relay SNA services, connecting SDLC devices to Frame Relay without requiring an existing LAN. May be upgraded to a fully functioning multiprotocol router. Can activate conversion from SDLC to Ethernet and Token Ring, but does not support attached LANs. *See also: FRAD.*

CiscoFusion Cisco's name for the internetworking architecture under which its Cisco IOS operates. It is designed to "fuse" together the capabilities of its disparate collection of acquired routers and switches.

Cisco IOS Cisco Internet Operating System software. The kernel of the Cisco line of routers and switches that supplies shared functionality, scalability, and security for all products under its CiscoFusion architecture. *See also: CiscoFusion.*

CiscoView GUI-based management software for Cisco networking devices, enabling dynamic status, statistics, and comprehensive configuration information. Displays a physical view of the Cisco device chassis and provides device-monitoring functions and fundamental troubleshooting capabilities. May be integrated with a number of SNMP-based network management platforms.

Class A network   Part of the Internet Protocol hierarchical addressing scheme. Class A networks have only 8 bits for defining networks and 24 bits for defining hosts and subnets on each network.

Class B network   Part of the Internet Protocol hierarchical addressing scheme. Class B networks have 16 bits for defining networks and 16 bits for defining hosts and subnets on each network.

Class C network   Part of the Internet Protocol hierarchical addressing scheme. Class C networks have 24 bits for defining networks and only 8 bits for defining hosts and subnets on each network.

classful routing   Routing protocols that do not send subnet mask information when a route update is sent out.

classical IP over ATM   Defined in RFC 1577, the specification for running IP over ATM that maximizes ATM features. Also known as "CIA."

classless routing   Routing that sends subnet mask information in the routing updates. Classless routing allows Variable-Length Subnet Masking (VLSM) and supernetting. Routing protocols that support classless routing are RIP version 2, EIGRP, and OSPF.

CLI   Command-line interface: Allows you to configure Cisco routers and switches with maximum flexibility.

CLP   Cell Loss Priority: The area in the ATM cell header that determines the likelihood of a cell being dropped during network congestion. Cells with CLP = 0 are considered insured traffic and are not apt to be dropped. Cells with CLP = 1 are considered best-effort traffic that may be dropped during congested episodes, delivering more resources to handle insured traffic.

CLR   Cell Loss Ratio: The ratio of discarded cells to successfully delivered cells in ATM. CLR can be designated a QoS parameter when establishing a connection.

CO   Central office: The local telephone company office where all loops in a certain area connect and where circuit switching of subscriber lines occurs.

collapsed backbone   A nondistributed backbone where all network segments are connected to each other through an internetworking device. A collapsed backbone can be a virtual network segment at work in a device such as a router, hub, or switch.

collision   The effect of two nodes sending transmissions simultaneously in Ethernet. When they meet on the physical media, the frames from each node collide and are damaged. *See also: collision domain.*

collision domain   The network area in Ethernet over which frames that have collided will be detected. Collisions are propagated by hubs and repeaters, but not by LAN switches, routers, or bridges. *See also: collision.*

composite metric   Used with routing protocols, such as IGRP and EIGRP, that use more than one metric to find the best path to a remote network. IGRP and EIGRP both use bandwidth and delay of the line by default. However, maximum transmission unit (MTU), load, and reliability of a link can be used as well.

compression   A technique to send more data across a link than would be normally permitted by representing repetitious strings of data with a single marker.

configuration register   A 16-bit configurable value stored in hardware or software that determines how Cisco routers function during initialization. In hardware, the bit position is set using a jumper. In software, it is set by specifying specific bit patterns used to set startup options, configured using a hexadecimal value with configuration commands.

congestion   Traffic that exceeds the network's ability to handle it.

congestion avoidance   To minimize delays, the method a network uses to control traffic entering the system. Lower-priority traffic is discarded at the edge of the network when indicators signal it cannot be delivered, thus using resources efficiently.

congestion collapse   The situation that results from the retransmission of packets in ATM networks where little or no traffic successfully arrives at destination points. It usually happens in networks made of switches with ineffective or inadequate buffering capabilities combined with poor packet discard or ABR congestion feedback mechanisms.

connection ID   Identifications given to each Telnet session into a router. The show sessions command will give you the connections a local router will have to a remote router. The show users command will show the connection IDs of users telnetted into your local router.

connectionless   Data transfer that occurs without the creation of a virtual circuit. It has low overhead, uses best-effort delivery, and is not reliable. *Contrast with: connection-oriented. See also: virtual circuit.*

Connectionless Network Service (CLNS)   See *connectionless.*

connection-oriented   Data transfer method that sets up a virtual circuit before any data is transferred. Uses acknowledgments and flow control for reliable data transfer. *Contrast with: connectionless. See also: virtual circuit.*

console port   Typically an RJ-45 (8-pin modular) port on a Cisco router and switch that allows command-line interface capability.

control direct VCC   One of two control connections defined by Phase I LAN emulation; a bidirectional virtual control connection (VCC) established in ATM by an LEC to an LES. *See also: control distribute VCC.*

control distribute VCC   One of two control connections defined by Phase 1 LAN emulation; a unidirectional virtual control connection (VCC) set up in ATM from an LES to an LEC. Usually, the VCC is a point-to-multipoint connection. *See also: control direct VCC.*

convergence   The process required for all routers in an internetwork to update their routing tables and create a consistent view of the network using the best possible paths. No user data is passed during an STP convergence time.

core layer   Top layer in the Cisco three-layer hierarchical model, which helps you design, build, and maintain Cisco hierarchical networks. The core layer passes packets quickly to distribution layer devices only. No packet filtering should take place at this layer.

cost   Also known as path cost, an arbitrary value, based on hop count, bandwidth, or another calculation, that is typically assigned by a network administrator and used by the routing protocol to compare different routes through an internetwork. Routing protocols use cost values to select the best path to a certain destination: the lowest cost identifies the best path. Also known as "path cost." *See also: routing metric.*

count to infinity   A problem occurring in routing algorithms that are slow to converge where routers keep increasing the hop count to particular networks. To avoid this problem, various solutions have been implemented into each of the different routing protocols. Some of those solutions include defining a maximum hop count (defining infinity), route poising, poison reverse, and split horizon.

CPCS   Common Part Convergence Sublayer: One of two AAL sublayers that is service dependent, it is further segmented into the CS and SAR sublayers. The CPCS prepares data for transmission across the ATM network; it creates the 48-byte payload cells that are sent to the ATM layer. *See also: AAL* and *ATM layer.*

CPE   Customer premises equipment: Items such as telephones, modems, and terminals installed at customer locations and connected to the service provider network.

crankback   In ATM, a correction technique used when a node somewhere on a chosen path cannot accept a connection setup request, blocking the request. The path is rolled back to an intermediate node, which then uses GCAC to attempt to find an alternate path to the final destination.

CRC   Cyclic redundancy check: A methodology that detects errors, whereby the frame recipient makes a calculation by dividing frame contents with a prime binary divisor and compares the remainder to a value stored in the frame by the sending node. *Contrast with: checksum.*

crossover cable   Type of Ethernet cable that connects a switch to switch, host to host, hub to hub, or switch to hub.

CSMA/CD   Carrier Sense Multiple Access with Collision Detection: A technology defined by the Ethernet IEEE 802.3 committee. Each device senses the cable for a digital signal before transmitting. Also, CSMA/CD allows all devices on the network to share the same cable, but one at a time. If two devices transmit at the same time, a frame collision will occur and a jamming pattern will be sent; the devices will stop transmitting, wait a predetermined as well as a self-imposed random amount of time, and then try to transmit again.

CSU   Channel service unit: A digital mechanism that connects end-user equipment to the local digital telephone loop. Frequently referred to along with the data service unit as CSU/DSU. *See also: DSU.*

CSU/DSU   Channel service unit/data service unit: Physical layer device used in wide area networks to convert the CPE digital signals to what is understood by the provider's switch. A CSU/DSU is typically one device that plugs into a RJ-45 (8-pin modular) jack, known as the demarcation point.

CTD   Cell Transfer Delay: For a given connection in ATM, the time period between a cell exit event at the source user-network interface (UNI) and the corresponding cell entry event at the destination. The CTD between these points is the sum of the total inter-ATM transmission delay and the total ATM processing delay.

cumulative interface delay   This is a Cisco term for delay of the line. The composite metric in IGRP and EIGRP is calculated by using the bandwidth and delay of the line by default.

cut-through frame switching   A frame-switching technique that flows data through a switch so that the leading edge exits the switch at the output port before the packet finishes entering the input port. Frames will be read, processed, and forwarded by devices that use cut-through switching as soon as the destination address of the frame is confirmed and the outgoing port is identified.

data circuit-terminating equipment   DCE is used to provide clocking to DTE equipment.

data compression   *See: compression.*

data direct VCC   A bidirectional point-to-point virtual control connection (VCC) set up between two LECs in ATM and one of three data connections defined by Phase 1 LAN emulation. Because data direct VCCs do not guarantee QoS, they are generally reserved for UBR and ABR connections. *Compare with: control distribute VCC and control direct VCC.*

data encapsulation   The process in which the information in a protocol is wrapped, or contained, in the data section of another protocol. In the OSI reference model, each layer encapsulates the layer immediately above it as the data flows down the protocol stack.

data frame   Protocol Data Unit encapsulation at the Data Link layer of the OSI reference model. Encapsulates packets from the Network layer and prepares the data for transmission on a network medium.

datagram   A logical collection of information transmitted as a Network layer unit over a medium without a previously established virtual circuit. IP datagrams have become the primary information unit of the Internet. At various layers of the OSI reference model, the terms *cell, frame, message, packet,* and *segment* also define these logical information groupings.

Data Link Control layer   Layer 2 of the SNA architectural model, it is responsible for the transmission of data over a given physical link and compares somewhat to the Data Link layer of the OSI model.

Data Link layer   Layer 2 of the OSI reference model, it ensures the trustworthy transmission of data across a physical link and is primarily concerned with physical addressing, line discipline, network topology, error notification, ordered delivery of frames, and flow control. The IEEE has further segmented this layer into the MAC sublayer and the LLC sublayer. Also known as the link layer. Can be compared somewhat to the data link control layer of the SNA model. *See also: Application layer, LLC, MAC, Network layer, Physical layer, Presentation layer, Session layer,* and *Transport layer.*

data terminal equipment   *See: DTE.*

DCC   Data Country Code: Developed by the ATM Forum, one of two ATM address formats designed for use by private networks. *Compare with: ICD.*

DCE   Data communications equipment (as defined by the EIA) or data circuit-terminating equipment (as defined by the ITU-T): The mechanisms and links of a communications network that make up the network portion of the user-to-network interface, such as modems. The DCE supplies the physical connection to the network, forwards traffic, and provides a clocking signal to synchronize data transmission between DTE and DCE devices. *Compare with: DTE.*

D channel   (1) Data channel: A full-duplex, 16Kbps (BRI) or 64Kbps (PRI) ISDN channel. *Compare with: B channel, E channel,* and *H channel.* (2) In SNA, anything that provides a connection between the processor and main storage with any peripherals.

DDP   Datagram Delivery Protocol: Used in the AppleTalk suite of protocols as a connection-less protocol that is responsible for sending datagrams through an internetwork.

DDR   Dial-on-demand routing: A technique that allows a router to automatically initiate and end a circuit-switched session per the requirements of the sending station. By mimicking keep-alives, the router fools the end station into treating the session as active. DDR permits routing over ISDN or telephone lines via a modem or external ISDN terminal adapter.

DE   Discard Eligibility: Used in Frame Relay networks to tell a switch that a frame can be preferentially discarded if the switch is too busy. The DE is a field in the frame that is turned on by transmitting routers if the committed information rate (CIR) is oversubscribed or set to 0.

dedicated line   Point-to-point connection that does not share any bandwidth.

de-encapsulation   The technique used by layered protocols in which a layer removes header information from the Protocol Data Unit (PDU) from the layer below. *See: encapsulation.*

default route   The static routing table entry used to direct frames whose next hop is not otherwise spelled out in the routing table.

delay   The time elapsed between a sender's initiation of a transaction and the first response they receive. Also, the time needed to move a packet from its source to its destination over a path. *See also: latency.*

demarc   The demarcation point between the customer premises equipment (CPE) and the telco's carrier equipment.

demodulation   A series of steps that return a modulated signal to its original form. When receiving, a modem demodulates an analog signal to its original digital form (and, conversely, modulates the digital data it sends into an analog signal). *See also: modulation.*

demultiplexing   The process of converting a multiplexed signal comprising more than one input stream back into separate output streams. *See also: multiplexing.*

designated bridge   In the process of forwarding a frame from a segment to the root bridge, the bridge with the lowest root path cost.

designated port   Used with the Spanning Tree Protocol (STP) to designate forwarding ports. If there are multiple links to the same network, STP will shut a port down to stop network loops.

designated router (DR)   An OSPF router that creates LSAs for a multi-access network and is required to perform other special tasks in OSPF operations. Multi-access OSPF networks that maintain a minimum of two attached routers identify one router that is chosen by the OSPF Hello protocol, which makes possible a decrease in the number of adjacencies necessary on a multi-access network. This in turn reduces the quantity of routing protocol traffic and the physical size of the database.

desktop layer   The access layer is sometimes referred to as the desktop layer. The access layer controls user and workgroup access to internetwork resources.

destination address   The address for the network device(s) that will receive a packet.

DHCP   Dynamic Host Configuration Protocol: DHCP is a superset of the BootP protocol. This means that it uses the same protocol structure as BootP, but it has enhancements added. Both of these protocols use servers that dynamically configure clients when requested. The two major enhancements are address pools and lease times.

dial backup   Dial backup connections are typically used to provide redundancy to Frame Relay connections. The backup link is activated over an analog modem or ISDN.

directed broadcast   A data frame or packet that is transmitted to a specific group of nodes on a remote network segment. Directed broadcasts are known by their broadcast address, which is a destination subnet address with all the host bits turned on.

discovery mode   Also known as dynamic configuration, this technique is used by an Apple-Talk interface to gain information from a working node about an attached network. The information is subsequently used by the interface for self-configuration.

distance-vector protocols   The distance-vector protocols find the best path to a remote network by judging distance. Each time a packet goes through a router, that's called a hop. The route with the least number of hops to the network is determined to be the best route. However, Cisco's IGRP is considered distance vector and uses a composite metric of bandwidth and delay of the line to determine the best path to a remote network.

distance-vector routing algorithm   In order to find the shortest path, this group of routing algorithms reports on the number of hops in a given route, requiring each router to send its complete routing table with each update, but only to its neighbors. Routing algorithms of this type tend to generate loops, but they are fundamentally simpler than their link-state counterparts. *See also: link-state routing algorithm* and *SPF*.

distribution layer   Middle layer of the Cisco three-layer hierarchical model, which helps you design, install, and maintain Cisco hierarchical networks. The distribution layer is the point where access layer devices connect. Routing is performed at this layer.

DLCI   Data Link Connection Identifier: Used to identify virtual circuits in a Frame Relay network.

DLSw   Data Link Switching: IBM developed Data Link Switching (DLSw) in 1992 to provide support for SNA (Systems Network Architecture) and NetBIOS protocols in router-based networks. SNA and NetBIOS are nonroutable protocols that do not contain any logical layer 3 network information. DLSw encapsulates these protocols into TCP/IP messages that can be routed and is an alternative to Remote Source-Route Bridging (RSRB).

DLSw+   Cisco's implementation of DLSw. In addition to support for the RFC standards, Cisco added enhancements intended to increase scalability and to improve performance and availability.

DNS   Domain Name System: Used to resolve hostnames to IP addresses.

DSAP   Destination Service Access Point: The service access point of a network node, specified in the destination field of a packet. *See also: SSAP and SAP.*

DSR   Data Set Ready: When a DCE is powered up and ready to run, this EIA/TIA-232 interface circuit is also engaged.

DSU   Data service unit: This device is used to adapt the physical interface on a data terminal equipment (DTE) mechanism to a transmission facility such as T1 or E1 and is also responsible for signal timing. It is commonly grouped with the channel service unit and referred to as the CSU/DSU. *See also: CSU.*

DTE   Data terminal equipment: Any device located at the user end of a user-network interface serving as a destination, a source, or both. DTE includes devices such as multiplexers, routers, protocol translators, and computers. The connection to a data network is made through data communication equipment (DCE) such as a modem, using the clocking signals generated by that device. *See also: DCE.*

DTR   Data Terminal Ready: An activated EIA/TIA-232 circuit communicating to the DCE the state of preparedness of the DTE to transmit or receive data.

DUAL   Diffusing Update Algorithm: Used in Enhanced IGRP, this convergence algorithm provides loop-free operation throughout an entire route's computation. DUAL grants routers involved in a topology revision the ability to synchronize simultaneously, while routers unaffected by this change are not involved. *See also: Enhanced IGRP.*

DVMRP   Distance Vector Multicast Routing Protocol: Based primarily on the Routing Information Protocol (RIP), this Internet gateway protocol implements a common, condensed-mode IP multicast scheme, using IGMP to transfer routing datagrams between its neighbors. *See also: IGMP.*

DXI   Data Exchange Interface: DXI defines the effectiveness of a network device such as a router, bridge, or hub to act as an FEP to an ATM network by using a special DSU that accomplishes packet encapsulation.

dynamic entries   Used in layer 2 and layer 3 devices to dynamically create a table of either hardware addresses or logical addresses dynamically.

dynamic routing   Also known as "adaptive routing," this technique automatically adapts to traffic or physical network revisions.

dynamic VLAN An administrator will create an entry in a special server with the hardware addresses of all devices on the internetwork. The server will then report the associated VLAN to a switch that requests it based on the new device's hardware address.

E1 Generally used in Europe, a wide-area digital transmission scheme carrying data at 2.048Mbps. E1 transmission lines are available for lease from common carriers for private use.

E.164 (1) Evolved from standard telephone numbering system, the standard recommended by ITU-T for international telecommunication numbering, particularly in ISDN, SMDS, and BISDN. (2) Label of field in an ATM address containing numbers in E.164 format.

eBGP External Border Gateway Protocol: Used to exchange route information between different autonomous systems.

E channel Echo channel: A 64Kbps ISDN control channel used for circuit switching. Specific description of this channel can be found in the 1984 ITU-T ISDN specification, but it was dropped from the 1988 version. *See also: B channel, D channel,* and *H channel.*

edge device A device that enables packets to be forwarded between legacy interfaces (such as Ethernet and Token Ring) and ATM interfaces based on information in the Data Link and Network layers. An edge device does not take part in the running of any Network layer routing protocol; it merely uses the route description protocol in order to get the forwarding information required.

EEPROM Electronically erasable programmable read-only memory: Programmed after their manufacture, these nonvolatile memory chips can be erased if necessary using electric power and reprogrammed. *See also: EPROM* and *PROM.*

EFCI Explicit Forward Congestion Indication: A congestion feedback mode permitted by ABR service in an ATM network. The EFCI may be set by any network element that is in a state of immediate or certain congestion. The destination end system is able to carry out a protocol that adjusts and lowers the cell rate of the connection based on value of the EFCI. *See also: ABR.*

EIGRP *See: Enhanced IGRP.*

EIP Ethernet Interface Processor: A Cisco 7000 series router interface processor card, supplying 10Mbps AUI ports to support Ethernet Version 1 and Ethernet Version 2 or IEEE 802.3 interfaces with a high-speed data path to other interface processors.

ELAN Emulated LAN: An ATM network configured using a client/server model in order to emulate either an Ethernet or Token Ring LAN. Multiple ELANs can exist at the same time on a single ATM network and are made up of a LAN emulation client (LEC), a LAN emulation server (LES), a broadcast and unknown server (BUS), and a LAN emulation configuration server (LECS). ELANs are defined by the LANE specification. *See also: LANE, LEC, LECS,* and *LES.*

ELAP EtherTalk Link Access Protocol: In an EtherTalk network, the link-access protocol constructed above the standard Ethernet Data Link layer.

encapsulation   The technique used by layered protocols in which a layer adds header information to the Protocol Data Unit (PDU) from the layer above. As an example, in Internet terminology, a packet would contain a header from the Data Link layer, followed by a header from the Network layer (IP), followed by a header from the Transport layer (TCP), followed by the application protocol data.

encryption   The conversion of information into a scrambled form that effectively disguises it to prevent unauthorized access. Every encryption scheme uses some well-defined algorithm, which is reversed at the receiving end by an opposite algorithm in a process known as decryption.

endpoints   *See: BGP neighbors.*

end-to-end VLANs   VLANs that span the switch fabric from end to end; all switches in end-to-end VLANs understand about all configured VLANs. End-to-end VLANs are configured to allow membership based on function, project, department, and so on.

Enhanced IGRP (EIGRP)   Enhanced Interior Gateway Routing Protocol: An advanced routing protocol created by Cisco combining the advantages of link-state and distance-vector protocols. Enhanced IGRP has superior convergence attributes, including high operating efficiency. *See also: IGP, OSPF,* and *RIP.*

enterprise network   A privately owned and operated network that joins most major locations in a large company or organization.

EPROM   Erasable programmable read-only memory: Programmed after their manufacture, these nonvolatile memory chips can be erased if necessary using high-power light and reprogrammed. *See also: EEPROM* and *PROM.*

ESF   Extended Superframe: Made up of 24 frames with 192 bits each, with the 193rd bit providing other functions including timing. This is an enhanced version of SF. *See also: SF.*

Ethernet   A baseband LAN specification created by the Xerox Corporation and then improved through joint efforts of Xerox, Digital Equipment Corporation, and Intel. Ethernet is similar to the IEEE 802.3 series standard and, using CSMA/CD, operates over various types of cables at 10Mbps. Also called DIX (Digital/Intel/Xerox) Ethernet. *See also: 10BaseT, Fast Ethernet,* and *IEEE.*

EtherTalk   A data-link product from Apple Computer that permits AppleTalk networks to be connected by Ethernet.

excess burst size   The amount of traffic by which the user may exceed the committed burst size.

excess rate   In ATM networking, traffic exceeding a connection's insured rate. The excess rate is the maximum rate less the insured rate. Depending on the availability of network resources, excess traffic can be discarded during congestion episodes. *Compare with: maximum rate.*

EXEC session   Cisco term used to describe the command-line interface. The EXEC session exists in user mode and privileged mode.

expansion   The procedure of directing compressed data through an algorithm, restoring information to its original size.

expedited delivery   Specified by one protocol layer communicating either with other layers or with the identical protocol layer in a different network device, an option that requires that identified data be processed faster.

explorer frame   Used with source route bridging to find the route to the remote bridged network before a frame is transmitted.

explorer packet   An SNA packet transmitted by a source Token Ring device to find the path through a source-route-bridged network.

extended IP access list   IP access list that filters the network by logical address, protocol field in the Network layer header, and even the port field in the Transport layer header.

extended IPX access list   IPX access list that filters the network by logical IPX address, protocol field in the Network layer header, or even socket number in the Transport layer header.

Extended Setup   Used in setup mode to configure the router with more detail than Basic Setup mode. Allows multiple-protocol support and interface configuration.

external EIGRP route   Normally, the administrative distance of an EIGRP route is 90, but this is true only for what is known as an internal EIGRP route. These are routes originated within a specific autonomous system by EIGRP routers that are members of the same autonomous system. The other type of route is called an external EIGRP route and has an administrative distance of 170, which is not so good. These routes appear within EIGRP route tables courtesy of either manual or automatic redistribution, and they represent networks that originated outside of the EIGRP autonomous system.

failure domain   The region in which a failure has occurred in a token ring. When a station gains information that a serious problem, such as a cable break, has occurred with the network, it sends a beacon frame that includes the station reporting the failure, its NAUN and everything between. This defines the failure domain. Beaconing then initiates the procedure known as autoreconfiguration. *See also: autoreconfiguration* and *beacon.*

fallback   In ATM networks, this mechanism is used for scouting a path if it isn't possible to locate one using customary methods. The device relaxes requirements for certain characteristics, such as delay, in an attempt to find a path that meets a certain set of the most important requirements.

Fast Ethernet   Any Ethernet specification with a speed of 100Mbps. Fast Ethernet is 10 times faster than 10BaseT while retaining qualities such as MAC mechanisms, MTU, and frame format. These similarities make it possible for existing 10BaseT applications and management tools to be used on Fast Ethernet networks. Fast Ethernet is based on an extension of IEEE 802.3 specification (IEEE 802.3u). *Compare with: Ethernet. See also: 100BaseT, 100BaseTX,* and *IEEE.*

fast switching   A Cisco feature that uses a route cache to speed packet switching through a router. *Contrast with: process switching.*

fault tolerance   The extent to which a network device or a communication link can fail without communication being interrupted. Fault tolerance can be provided by added secondary routes to a remote network.

FDDI   Fiber Distributed Data Interface: A LAN standard, defined by ANSI X3T9.5, that can run at speeds up to 200Mbps and uses token-passing media access on fiber-optic cable. For redundancy, FDDI can use a dual-ring architecture.

FDM   Frequency-Division Multiplexing: A technique that permits information from several channels to be assigned bandwidth on one wire based on frequency. *See also: TDM, ATDM, and statistical multiplexing.*

FECN   Forward Explicit Congestion Notification: A bit set by a Frame Relay network that informs the DTE receptor that congestion was encountered along the path from source to destination. A device receiving frames with the FECN bit set can ask higher-priority protocols to take flow-control action as needed. *See also: BECN.*

FEIP   Fast Ethernet Interface Processor: An interface processor employed on Cisco 7000 series routers, supporting up to two 100Mbps 100BaseT ports.

filtering   Used to provide security on the network with access lists. LAN switches filter the network by MAC (hardware) address.

firewall   A barrier purposefully erected between any connected public networks and a private network—made up of a router or access server or several routers or access servers—that uses access lists and other methods to ensure the security of the private network.

fixed configuration router   A router that cannot be upgraded with any new interfaces.

flapping   Term used to describe a serial interface that is going up and down.

Flash   Electronically erasable programmable read-only memory (EEPROM). Used to hold the Cisco IOS in a router by default.

flash memory   Developed by Intel and licensed to other semiconductor manufacturers, it is nonvolatile storage that can be erased electronically and reprogrammed, physically located on an EEPROM chip. Flash memory permits software images to be stored, booted, and rewritten as needed. Cisco routers and switches use flash memory to hold the IOS by default. *See also: EPROM and EEPROM.*

flat network   Network that is one large collision domain and one large broadcast domain.

floating routes   Used with dynamic routing to provide backup routes (static routes) in case of failure.

flooding   When traffic is received on an interface, it is then transmitted to every interface connected to that device except the interface from which the traffic originated. This technique can be used for traffic transfer by bridges and switches throughout the network.

flow control A methodology used to ensure that receiving units are not overwhelmed with data from sending devices. Pacing, as it is called in IBM networks, means that when buffers at a receiving unit are full, a message is transmitted to the sending unit to temporarily halt transmissions until all the data in the receiving buffer has been processed and the buffer is again ready for action.

forward/filter decisions When a frame is received on an interface, the switch looks at the destination hardware address and finds the exit interface in the MAC database. The frame is only forwarded out the specified destination port.

FQDN Fully qualified domain name: Used within the DNS domain structure to provide name-to-IP-address resolution on the Internet. An example of an FQDN is `bob.acme.com`.

FRAD Frame Relay access device: Any device affording a connection between a LAN and a Frame Relay WAN. *See also: Cisco FRAD and FRAS.*

fragment Any portion of a larger packet that has been intentionally segmented into smaller pieces. A packet fragment does not necessarily indicate an error and can be intentional. *See also: fragmentation.*

fragmentation The process of intentionally segmenting a packet into smaller pieces when sending data over an intermediate network medium that cannot support the larger packet size.

FragmentFree LAN switch type that reads into the data section of a frame to make sure fragmentation did not occur. Sometimes called modified cut-through.

frame A logical unit of information sent by the Data Link layer over a transmission medium. The term often refers to the header and trailer, employed for synchronization and error control, that surround the data contained in the unit.

frame filtering Frame filtering is used on a layer 2 switch to provide more bandwidth. A switch reads the destination hardware address of a frame and then looks for this address in the filter table, built by the switch. It then sends the frame out only the port where the hardware address is located, and the other ports do not see the frame.

frame identification (frame tagging) VLANs can span multiple connected switches, which Cisco calls a switch fabric. Switches within this switch fabric must keep track of frames as they are received on the switch ports, and they must keep track of the VLAN they belong to as the frames traverse this switch fabric. Frame tagging performs this function. Switches can then direct frames to the appropriate port.

Frame Relay A more efficient replacement of the X.25 protocol (an unrelated packet relay technology that guarantees data delivery). Frame Relay is an industry-standard, shared-access, best-effort, switched Data Link layer encapsulation that services multiple virtual circuits and protocols between connected mechanisms.

Frame Relay bridging Defined in RFC 1490, this bridging method uses the identical spanning-tree algorithm as other bridging operations but permits packets to be encapsulated for transmission across a Frame Relay network.

Frame Relay switching   Packet switching for Frame Relay packets that is provided by a service provider.

frame tagging   *See: frame identification.*

frame types   Used in LANs to determine how a packet is put on the local network. Ethernet provides four different frame types. These are not compatible with each other, so for two hosts to communicate, they must use the same frame type.

framing   Encapsulation at the Data Link layer of the OSI model. It is called framing because the packet is encapsulated with both a header and a trailer.

FRAS   Frame Relay Access Support: A feature of Cisco IOS software that enables SDLC, Ethernet, Token Ring, and Frame Relay-attached IBM devices to be linked with other IBM mechanisms on a Frame Relay network. *See also: FRAD.*

frequency   The number of cycles of an alternating current signal per time unit, measured in hertz (cycles per second).

FSIP   Fast Serial Interface Processor: The Cisco 7000 routers' default serial interface processor, it provides four or eight high-speed serial ports.

FTP   File Transfer Protocol: The TCP/IP protocol used for transmitting files between network nodes, it supports a broad range of file types and is defined in RFC 959. *See also: TFTP.*

full duplex   The capacity to transmit information between a sending station and a receiving unit at the same time. *See also: half duplex.*

full mesh   A type of network topology where every node has either a physical or a virtual circuit linking it to every other network node. A full mesh supplies a great deal of redundancy but is typically reserved for network backbones because of its expense. *See also: partial mesh.*

global command   Cisco term used to define commands that are used to change the router configuration and that affect the whole router. In contrast, an interface command only affects the interface on which it's configured.

GMII   Gigabit MII: Media Independent Interface that provides 8 bits at a time of data transfer.

GNS   Get Nearest Server: On an IPX network, a request packet sent by a customer for determining the location of the nearest active server of a given type. An IPX network client launches a GNS request to get either a direct answer from a connected server or a response from a router disclosing the location of the service on the internetwork to the GNS. GNS is part of IPX and SAP. *See also: IPX and SAP.*

grafting   A process that activates an interface that has been deactivated by the pruning process. It is initiated by an IGMP membership report sent to the router.

GRE   Generic Routing Encapsulation: A tunneling protocol created by Cisco with the capacity for encapsulating a wide variety of protocol packet types inside IP tunnels, thereby generating a virtual point-to-point connection to Cisco routers across an IP network at remote points. IP tunneling using GRE permits network expansion across a single-protocol backbone environment by linking multiprotocol subnetworks in a single-protocol backbone environment.

guardband The unused frequency area found between two communications channels, furnishing the space necessary to avoid interference between the two.

half duplex The capacity to transfer data in only one direction at a time between a sending unit and receiving unit. *See also: full duplex.*

handshake Any series of transmissions exchanged between two or more devices on a network to ensure synchronized operations.

H channel High-speed channel: A full-duplex, ISDN primary rate channel operating at a speed of 384Kbps. *See also: B channel, D channel,* and *E channel.*

HDLC High-Level Data-Link Control: Using frame characters, including checksums, HDLC designates a method for data encapsulation on synchronous serial links and is the default encapsulation for Cisco routers. HDLC is a bit-oriented synchronous Data Link layer protocol created by ISO and derived from SDLC. However, most HDLC vendor implementations (including Cisco's) are proprietary. *See also: SDLC.*

helper address The unicast address specified, which configures the Cisco router to change the client's local broadcast request for a service into a directed unicast to the server.

hierarchical addressing Any addressing plan employing a logical chain of commands to determine location. IP addresses are made up of a hierarchy of network numbers, subnet numbers, and host numbers to direct packets to the appropriate destination.

hierarchy Term used in defining IP addressing; in hierarchical addressing, some bits are used for networking and some bits for host addressing. Also used in the DNS structure and the Cisco design model.

HIP HSSI Interface Processor: An interface processor used on Cisco 7000 series routers, providing one HSSI port that supports connections to ATM, SMDS, Frame Relay, or private lines at speeds up to T3 or E3.

holddown The state a route is placed in so that routers can neither advertise the route nor accept advertisements about it for a defined time period. Holddowns are used to avoid accepting bad information. The actual information might be good, but it is not trusted. A route is generally placed in holddown when one of its links fails.

hop The movement of a packet between any two network nodes. *See also: hop count.*

hop count A routing metric that calculates the distance between a source and a destination based on the number of routers in the path. RIP employs hop count as its sole metric. *See also: hop* and *RIP.*

host address Logical address configured by an administrator or server on a device. Logically identifies this device on an internetwork.

Host-to-Host layer Layer in the Internet Protocol suite that is equal to the Transport layer of the OSI model.

HSCI High-Speed Communication Interface: Developed by Cisco, a single-port interface that provides full-duplex synchronous serial communications capability at speeds up to 52Mbps.

HSRP Hot Standby Router Protocol: A protocol that provides high network availability and nearly instantaneous hardware fail-over without administrator intervention. It generates a Hot Standby router group, including a lead router that lends its services to any packet being transferred to the Hot Standby address. If the lead router fails, it will be replaced by any of the other routers—the standby routers—that monitor it.

HSSI High-Speed Serial Interface: A network standard physical connector for high-speed serial linking over a WAN at speeds of up to 52Mbps.

hubs Physical layer devices that are really just multiple port repeaters. When an electronic digital signal is received on a port, the signal is reamplified or regenerated and forwarded out all segments except the segment from which the signal was received.

hybrid routing protocol Routing protocol that uses the attributes of both distance-vector and link-state. Enhanced Interior Gateway Routing Protocol (Enhanced IGRP).

ICD International Code Designator: Adapted from the subnetwork model of addressing, this assigns the mapping of Network layer addresses to ATM addresses. ICD is one of two ATM formats for addressing created by the ATM Forum to be utilized with private networks. *See also: DCC.*

ICMP Internet Control Message Protocol: Documented in RFC 792, it is a Network layer Internet protocol for the purpose of reporting errors and providing information pertinent to IP packet procedures.

IEEE Institute of Electrical and Electronics Engineers: A professional organization that, among other activities, defines standards in a number of fields within computing and electronics, including networking and communications. IEEE standards are the predominant LAN standards used today throughout the industry. Many protocols are commonly known by the reference number of the corresponding IEEE standard.

IEEE 802.1 The IEEE committee specification that defines the bridging group. The specification for STP (Spanning Tree Protocol) is IEEE 802.1D. The STP uses STA (spanning-tree algorithm) to find and prevent network loops in bridged networks. The specification for VLAN trunking is IEEE 802.1Q.

IEEE 802.3 The IEEE committee specification that defines the Ethernet group, specifically the original 10Mbps standard. Ethernet is a LAN protocol that specifies physical layer and MAC sublayer media access. IEEE 802.3 uses CSMA/CD to provide access for many devices on the same network. Fast Ethernet is defined as 802.3U, and Gigabit Ethernet is defined as 802.3Q. *See also: CSMA/CD.*

IEEE 802.5 IEEE committee that defines Token Ring media access.

IGMP   Internet Group Management Protocol: Employed by IP hosts, the protocol that reports their multicast group memberships to an adjacent multicast router.

IGP   Interior gateway protocol: Any protocol used by an internetwork to exchange routing data within an independent system. Examples include RIP, IGRP, and OSPF.

IGRP   Interior Gateway Routing Protocol: Cisco proprietary distance-vector routing algorithm. Upgrade from the RIP protocol.

ILMI   Integrated (or Interim) Local Management Interface. A specification created by the ATM Forum, designated for the incorporation of network-management capability into the ATM UNI. Integrated Local Management Interface cells provide for automatic configuration between ATM systems. In LAN emulation, ILMI can provide sufficient information for the ATM end station to find an LECS. In addition, ILMI provides the ATM NSAP (Network Service Access Point) prefix information to the end station.

in-band management   In-band management is the management of a network device "through" the network. Examples include using Simple Network Management Protocol (SNMP) and Telnet directly via the local LAN. *Compare with: out-of-band management.*

in-band signaling   In-band signaling is the use of the bearer channel to deliver signaling, as call waiting in analog POTS lines. This is as opposed to out-of-band signaling, as in the case of the D channel being used to present a second active call in an ISDN circuit.

inside network   In NAT terminology, the inside network is the set of networks that are subject to translation. The outside network refers to all other addresses—usually those located on the Internet

insured burst   In an ATM network, it is the largest, temporarily permitted data burst exceeding the insured rate on a PVC and not tagged by the traffic policing function for being dropped if network congestion occurs. This insured burst is designated in bytes or cells.

interarea routing   Routing between two or more logical areas. *Contrast with: intra-area routing. See also: area.*

interface configuration mode   Mode that allows you to configure a Cisco router or switch port with specific information, such as an IP address and mask.

interface processor   Any of several processor modules used with Cisco 7000 series routers. *See also: AIP, CIP, EIP, FEIP, HIP, MIP, and TRIP.*

Intermediate System to Intermediate System (IS-IS)   Intermediate System–to–Intermediate System: An OSI link-state hierarchical routing protocol.

internal EIGRP route   These are routes originated within a specific autonomous system by EIGRP routers that are members of the same autonomous system.

Internet   The global "network of networks," whose popularity has exploded starting in the mid 1990s. Originally a tool for collaborative academic research, it has become a medium for exchanging and distributing information of all kinds. The Internet's need to link disparate computer platforms and technologies has led to the development of uniform protocols and standards that have also found widespread use within corporate LANs. *See also: TCP/IP and MBONE.*

internet   Before the rise of the Internet, this lowercase form was shorthand for "internetwork" in the generic sense. Now rarely used. *See also: internetwork.*

Internet layer   Layer in the Internet Protocol suite of protocols that provides network addressing and routing through an internetwork.

Internet protocol (IP)   Any protocol belonging to the TCP/IP protocol stack. *See also: TCP/IP.*

internetwork   Any group of networks interconnected by routers and other mechanisms, typically operating as a single entity.

internetworking   Broadly, anything associated with the general task of linking networks to each other. The term encompasses technologies, procedures, and products. When you connect networks to a router, you are creating an internetwork.

intra-area routing   Routing that occurs within a logical area. *Contrast with: interarea routing.*

Inverse ARP   Inverse Address Resolution Protocol: A technique by which dynamic mappings are constructed in a network, allowing a device such as a router to locate the logical network address and associate it with a permanent virtual circuit (PVC). Commonly used in Frame Relay to determine the far-end node's TCP/IP address by sending the Inverse ARP request across the local DLCI.

IP   Internet Protocol: Defined in RFC 791, it is a Network layer protocol that is part of the TCP/IP stack and offers connectionless service. IP furnishes an array of features for addressing, type-of-service specification, fragmentation and reassembly, and security.

IP address   Often called an Internet address, this is an address uniquely identifying any device (host) on the Internet (or any TCP/IP network). Each address consists of four octets (32 bits), represented as decimal numbers separated by periods (a format known as "dotted-decimal"). Every address is made up of a network number, an optional subnetwork number, and a host number. The network and subnetwork numbers together are used for routing, while the host number addresses an individual host within the network or subnetwork. The network and subnetwork information is extracted from the IP address using the subnet mask. There are five classes of IP addresses (A–E), in which classes A through C allocate different numbers of bits to the network, subnetwork, and host portions of the address. *See also: CIDR, IP,* and *subnet mask.*

IPCP   IP Control Program: The protocol used to establish and configure IP over PPP. *See also: IP* and *PPP.*

IP multicast   A technique for routing that enables IP traffic to be reproduced from one source to several endpoints or from multiple sources to many destinations. Instead of transmitting one packet to each individual point of destination, one packet is sent to a multicast group specified by only one IP endpoint address for the group.

IPX   Internetwork Packet eXchange: Network layer protocol (layer 3) used in Novell NetWare networks for transferring information from servers to workstations. Similar to IP and XNS.

IPXCP   IPX Control Protocol: The protocol used to establish and configure IPX over PPP. *See also: IPX* and *PPP.*

IPXWAN   Protocol used for new WAN links to provide and negotiate line options on the link using IPX. After the link is up and the options have been agreed upon by the two end-to-end links, normal IPX transmission begins.

ISDN   Integrated Services Digital Network: Offered as a service by telephone companies, a communication protocol that allows telephone networks to carry data, voice, and other digital traffic. *See also: BISDN, BRI,* and *PRI.*

IS-IS   *See: Intermediate System–to–Intermediate System (IS-IS)*

ISL routing   Inter-Switch Link routing: A Cisco proprietary method of frame tagging in a switched internetwork. Frame tagging is a way to identify the VLAN membership of a frame as it traverses a switched internetwork.

isochronous transmission   Asynchronous data transfer over a synchronous data link, requiring a constant bit rate for reliable transport. *Compare with: asynchronous transmission* and *synchronous transmission.*

ITU-T   International Telecommunication Union-Telecommunication Standardization Sector: This is a group of engineers that develops worldwide standards for telecommunications technologies.

Kerberos   An authentication and encryption method that can be used by Cisco routers to ensure that data cannot be "sniffed" off of the network. Kerberos was developed at MIT and was designed to provide strong security using the Data Encryption Standard (DES) cryptographic algorithm.

LAN   Local area network: Broadly, any network linking two or more computers and related devices within a limited geographical area (up to a few kilometers). LANs are typically high-speed, low-error networks within a company. Cabling and signaling at the Physical and Data Link layers of the OSI are dictated by LAN standards. Ethernet, FDDI, and Token Ring are among the most popular LAN technologies. *Compare with: MAN.*

LANE   LAN emulation: The technology that allows an ATM network to operate as a LAN backbone. To do so, the ATM network is required to provide multicast and broadcast support, address mapping (MAC-to-ATM), and SVC management, in addition to an operable packet format. Additionally, LANE defines Ethernet and Token Ring ELANs. *See also: ELAN.*

LAN switch   A high-speed, multiple-interface transparent bridging mechanism, transmitting packets between segments of data links, usually referred to specifically as an Ethernet switch. LAN switches transfer traffic based on MAC addresses. *See also: multilayer switch* and *store-and-forward packet switching.*

LAPB Link Accessed Procedure, Balanced: A bit-oriented Data Link layer protocol that is part of the X.25 stack and has its origin in SDLC. *See also: SDLC and X.25.*

LAPD Link Access Procedure on the D channel: The ISDN Data Link layer protocol used specifically for the D channel and defined by ITU-T Recommendations Q.920 and Q.921. LAPD evolved from LAPB and is created to comply with the signaling requirements of ISDN basic access.

latency Broadly, the time it takes a data packet to get from one location to another. In specific networking contexts, it can mean either (1) the time elapsed (delay) between the execution of a request for access to a network by a device and the time the mechanism actually is permitted transmission, or (2) the time elapsed between when a mechanism receives a frame and the time that frame is forwarded out of the destination port.

layer Term used in networking to define how the OSI model works to encapsulate data for transmission on the network.

layer 3 switch *See: multilayer switch.*

layered architecture Industry standard way of creating applications to work on a network. Layered architecture allows the application developer to make changes in only one layer instead of the whole program.

LCP Link Control Protocol: The protocol designed to establish, configure, and test data-link connections for use by PPP. *See also: PPP.*

leaky bucket An analogy for the generic cell rate algorithm (GCRA) used in ATM networks for checking the conformance of cell flows from a user or network. The bucket's "hole" is understood to be the prolonged rate at which cells can be accommodated, and the "depth" is the tolerance for cell bursts over a certain time period.

learning bridge A bridge that transparently builds a dynamic database of MAC addresses and the interfaces associated with each address. Transparent bridges help to reduce traffic congestion on the network.

LE ARP LAN Emulation Address Resolution Protocol: The protocol providing the ATM address that corresponds to a MAC address.

leased line Permanent connection between two points leased from the telephone companies.

LEC LAN emulation client: Software providing the emulation of the link layer interface that allows the operation and communication of all higher-level protocols and applications to continue. The LEC runs in all ATM devices, which include hosts, servers, bridges, and routers. *See also: ELAN and LES.*

LECS LAN emulation configuration server: An important part of emulated LAN services, providing the configuration data that is furnished upon request from the LES. These services include address registration for Integrated Local Management Interface (ILMI) support, configuration support for the LES addresses and their corresponding emulated LAN identifiers, and an interface to the emulated LAN. *See also: LES and ELAN.*

LES   LAN emulation server: The central LANE component that provides the initial configuration data for each connecting LEC. The LES typically is located on either an ATM-integrated router or a switch. Responsibilities of the LES include configuration and support for the LEC, address registration for the LEC, database storage and response concerning ATM addresses, and interfacing to the emulated LAN. *See also: ELAN, LEC,* and *LECS.*

link   A link is a network or router interface assigned to any given network. When an interface is added to the OSPF process, it's considered by OSPF to be a link. This link, or interface, will have state information associated with it (up or down) as well as one or more IP addresses.

link-state protocols   In link-state protocols, also called shortest-path-first protocols, the routers each create three separate tables. One of these tables keeps track of directly attached neighbors, one determines the topology of the entire internetwork, and one is used as the routing table. Link-state routers know more about the internetwork than any distance-vector routing protocol.

link-state routing algorithm   A routing algorithm that allows each router to broadcast or multicast information regarding the cost of reaching all its neighbors to every node in the internetwork. Link-state algorithms provide a consistent view of the network and are therefore not vulnerable to routing loops. However, this loop-free network is achieved at the cost of somewhat greater difficulty in computation and more widespread traffic (compared with distance-vector routing algorithms). *See also: distance-vector routing algorithm.*

LLAP   LocalTalk Link Access Protocol: In a LocalTalk environment, the data link–level protocol that manages node-to-node delivery of data. This protocol provides node addressing and management of bus access, and it also controls data sending and receiving to ensure packet length and integrity.

LLC   Logical Link Control: Defined by the IEEE, the higher of two Data Link layer sublayers. LLC is responsible for error detection (but not correction), flow control, framing, and software-sublayer addressing. The predominant LLC protocol, IEEE 802.2, defines both connectionless and connection-oriented operations. *See also: Data Link layer* and *MAC.*

LMI   Local Management Interface: An enhancement to the original Frame Relay specification. Among the features it provides are a keepalive mechanism, a multicast mechanism, global addressing, and a status mechanism.

LNNI   LAN Emulation Network-to-Network Interface: In the Phase 2 LANE specification, an interface that supports communication between the server components within one ELAN.

load   Like IGRP, EIGRP uses only bandwidth and delay of the line to determine the best path to a remote network by default. However, EIGRP can use a combination of bandwidth, delay, load, and reliability in its quest to find the best path to a remote network. Load refers to the amount of data on the link.

load balancing   The act of balancing packet load over multiple links to the same remote network.

local explorer packet   In a Token Ring SRB network, a packet generated by an end system to find a host linked to the local ring. If no local host can be found, the end system will produce one of two solutions: a spanning explorer packet or an all-routes explorer packet.

local loop Connection from a demarcation point to the closest switching office.

LocalTalk Utilizing CSMA/CD, in addition to supporting data transmission at speeds of 230.4Kbps, LocalTalk is Apple Computer's proprietary baseband protocol, operating at the Data Link and Physical layers of the OSI reference model.

logical address Network layer address that defines how data is sent from one network to another. Examples of logical addresses are IP and IPX.

loop avoidance If multiple connections between switches are created for redundancy purposes, network loops can occur. Spanning Tree Protocol (STP) is used to stop network loops while still permitting redundancy.

loopback address The IP address 127.0.0.1 is called the diagnostic or loopback address, and if you get a successful ping to this address, your IP stack is then considered to be initialized. If it fails, then you have an IP stack failure and need to reinstall TCP/IP on the host.

loopback interface Loopback interfaces are logical interfaces, which means they are not real router interfaces. They can be used for diagnostic purposes as well as OSPF configuration.

LPD Line Printer Daemon: Used in the Unix world to allow printing to an IP address.

LSA Link-State Advertisement: Contained inside of link-state packets (LSPs), these advertisements are usually multicast packets, containing information about neighbors and path costs, that are employed by link-state protocols. Receiving routers use LSAs to maintain their link-state databases and, ultimately, routing tables.

LUNI LAN Emulation User-to-Network Interface: Defining the interface between the LAN emulation client (LEC) and the LAN emulation server (LES), LUNI is the ATM Forum's standard for LAN emulation on ATM networks. *See also: LES and LECS.*

MAC Media Access Control: The lower sublayer in the Data Link layer, it is responsible for hardware addressing, media access, and error detection of frames. *See also: Data Link layer and LLC.*

MAC address A Data Link layer hardware address that every port or device needs in order to connect to a LAN segment. These addresses are used by various devices in the network for accurate location of logical addresses. MAC addresses are defined by the IEEE standard and their length is six characters, typically using the burned-in address (BIA) of the local LAN interface. Variously called hardware address, physical address, burned-in address, or MAC layer address.

MacIP In AppleTalk, the Network layer protocol encapsulating IP packets in Datagram Delivery Protocol (DDP) packets. MacIP also supplies substitute ARP services.

MAN Metropolitan area network: Any network that encompasses a metropolitan area; that is, an area typically larger than a LAN but smaller than a WAN. *See also: LAN.*

Manchester encoding A method for digital coding in which a mid-bit-time transition is employed for clocking, and a 1 (one) is denoted by a high voltage level during the first half of the bit time. This scheme is used by Ethernet and IEEE 802.3.

maximum burst   Specified in bytes or cells, the largest burst of information exceeding the insured rate that will be permitted on an ATM permanent virtual connection for a short time and will not be dropped even if it goes over the specified maximum rate. *Compare with: insured burst. See also: maximum rate.*

maximum hop count   Number of routers a packet is allowed to pass before it is terminated. This is created to prevent a packet from circling a network forever.

maximum rate   The maximum permitted data throughput on a particular virtual circuit, equal to the total of insured and uninsured traffic from the traffic source. Should traffic congestion occur, uninsured information may be deleted from the path. Measured in bits or cells per second, the maximum rate represents the highest throughput of data the virtual circuit is ever able to deliver and cannot exceed the media rate. *Compare with: excess rate. See also: maximum burst.*

MBONE   The multicast backbone of the Internet, it is a virtual multicast network made up of multicast LANs, including point-to-point tunnels interconnecting them.

MBS   Maximum Burst Size: In an ATM signaling message, this metric, coded as a number of cells, is used to convey the burst tolerance.

MCDV   Maximum Cell Delay Variation: The maximum two-point CDV objective across a link or node for the identified service category in an ATM network.

MCLR   Maximum Cell Loss Ratio: The maximum ratio of cells in an ATM network that fail to transit a link or node compared with the total number of cells that arrive at the link or node. MCLR is one of four link metrics that are exchanged using PTSPs to verify the available resources of an ATM network. The MCLR applies to cells in VBR and CBR traffic classes whose CLP bit is set to zero. *See also: CBR, CLP, and VBR.*

MCR   Minimum cell rate: A parameter determined by the ATM Forum for traffic management of the ATM networks. MCR is specifically defined for ABR transmissions and specifies the minimum value for the allowed cell rate (ACR). *See also: ACR and PCR.*

MCTD   Maximum Cell Transfer Delay: In an ATM network, the total of the maximum cell delay variation and the fixed delay across the link or node. MCTD is one of four link metrics that are exchanged using PNNI topology state packets to verify the available resources of an ATM network. There is one MCTD value assigned to each traffic class. *See also: MCDV.*

media translation   A router property that allows two different types of LAN to communicate—for example, Ethernet to Token Ring.

MIB   Management Information Base: Used with SNMP management software to gather information from remote devices. The management station can poll the remote device for information, or the MIB running on the remote station can be programmed to send information on a regular basis.

MII   Media Independent Interface: Used in Fast Ethernet and Gigabit Ethernet to provide faster bit transfer rates of 4 and 8 bits at a time. Contrast to AUI interface, which is 1 bit at a time.

MIP   Multichannel Interface Processor: The resident interface processor on Cisco 7000 series routers, providing up to two channelized T1 or E1 connections by serial cables connected to a CSU. The two controllers are capable of providing 24 T1 or 30 E1 channel groups, with each group being introduced to the system as a serial interface that can be configured individually.

mips   Millions of instructions per second: A measure of processor speed.

MLP   Multilink PPP: A technique used to split, recombine, and sequence datagrams across numerous logical data links.

MMP   Multichassis Multilink PPP: A protocol that supplies MLP support across multiple routers and access servers. MMP enables several routers and access servers to work as a single, large dial-up pool with one network address and ISDN access number. MMP successfully supports packet fragmenting and reassembly when the user connection is split between two physical access devices.

modem   Modulator-demodulator: A device that converts digital signals to analog and vice versa so that digital information can be transmitted over analog communication facilities such as voice-grade telephone lines. This is achieved by converting digital signals at the source to analog for transmission and reconverting the analog signals back into digital form at the destination. *See also: modulation* and *demodulation.*

modem eliminator   A mechanism that makes possible a connection between two DTE devices without modems by simulating the commands and physical signaling required.

modulation   The process of modifying some characteristic of an electrical signal, such as amplitude (AM) or frequency (FM), in order to represent digital or analog information. *See also: AM.*

MOSPF   Multicast OSPF: An extension of the OSPF unicast protocol that enables IP multicast routing within the domain. *See also: OSPF.*

MPOA   Multiprotocol over ATM: An effort by the ATM Forum to standardize how existing and future Network layer protocols such as IP, IPv6, AppleTalk, and IPX run over an ATM network with directly attached hosts, routers, and multilayer LAN switches.

MTU   Maximum transmission unit: The largest packet size, measured in bytes, that an interface can handle.

multicast   Broadly, any communication between a single sender and multiple receivers. Unlike broadcast messages, which are sent to all addresses on a network, multicast messages are sent to a defined subset of the network addresses; this subset has a group multicast address, which is specified in the packet's destination address field. *See also: broadcast* and *directed broadcast.*

multicast address   A single address that points to more than one device on the network by specifying a special nonexistent MAC address transmitted in that particular multicast protocol. Identical to group address. *See also: multicast.*

multicast group   Multicast works by sending messages or data to IP multicast group addresses. The group is a defined set of users or hosts that are allowed to read or view the data sent via multicast.

multicast send VCC   A two-directional point-to-point virtual control connection (VCC) arranged by an LEC to a BUS, it is one of the three types of informational links specified by phase 1 LANE. *See also: control distribute VCC and control direct VCC.*

multilayer switch   A highly specialized, high-speed, hardware-based type of LAN router, the device filters and forwards packets based on their layer 2 MAC addresses and layer 3 network addresses. It's possible that even layer 4 can be read. Sometimes called a layer 3 switch. *See also: LAN switch.*

multilink   Used to combine multiple async or ISDN links to provide combined bandwidth.

multiplexing   The process of converting several logical signals into a single physical signal for transmission across one physical channel. *Contrast with: demultiplexing.*

NAK   Negative acknowledgment: A response sent from a receiver, telling the sender that the information was not received or contained errors. *Compare with: acknowledgment.*

named access list   Used in both standard and extended lists to help with administration of access lists by allowing you to name the lists instead of using numbers. This also allows you to change a single line of an access list, which isn't possible in regular, numbered access lists.

NAT   Network Address Translation: An algorithm instrumental in minimizing the requirement for globally unique IP addresses, permitting an organization whose addresses are not all globally unique to connect to the Internet nevertheless by translating those addresses into globally routable address space.

native VLAN   Cisco switches all have a native VLAN called VLAN 1. This cannot be deleted or changed in any way. All switch ports are in VLAN 1 by default.

NBP   Name Binding Protocol: In AppleTalk, the transport-level protocol that interprets a socket client's name, entered as a character string, into the corresponding DDP address. NBP gives AppleTalk protocols the capacity to discern user-defined zones and names of mechanisms by showing and keeping translation tables that map names to their corresponding socket addresses.

neighboring routers   Two routers in OSPF that have interfaces to a common network. On networks with multi-access, these neighboring routers are dynamically discovered using the Hello protocol of OSPF.

neighbors   EIGRP and OSPF routers become neighbors when each router sees the other's Hello packets.

neighborship table   In OSPF and EIGRP routing protocols, each router keeps state information about adjacent neighbors. When newly discovered neighbors are learned, the address and interface of the neighbor is recorded. This information is stored in the neighbor data structure and the neighbor table holds these entries. Neighborship table can also be referred to as neighbor table or neighborship database.

NetBEUI   NetBIOS Extended User Interface: An improved version of the NetBIOS protocol used in a number of network operating systems including LAN Manager, Windows NT, LAN Server, and Windows for Workgroups, implementing the OSI LLC2 protocol. NetBEUI formalizes the transport frame not standardized in NetBIOS and adds more functions. *See also: OSI.*

NetBIOS   Network Basic Input/Output System: The API employed by applications residing on an IBM LAN to ask for services, such as session termination or information transfer, from lower-level network processes.

NetView   A mainframe network product from IBM used for monitoring SNA (Systems Network Architecture) networks. It runs as a VTAM (Virtual Telecommunications Access Method) application.

NetWare   A widely used NOS created by Novell, providing a number of distributed network services and remote file access.

Network Access layer   Bottom layer in the Internet Protocol suite that provides media access to packets.

network address   Used with the logical network addresses to identify the network segment in an internetwork. Logical addresses are hierarchical in nature and have at least two parts: network and host. An example of a hierarchical address is 172.16.10.5, where 172.16 is the network and 10.5 is the host address.

network control protocol   A method of establishing and configuring different Network layer protocols. NCP is designed to allow the simultaneous use of multiple Network layer protocols. Some examples of protocols here are IPCP (Internet Protocol Control Protocol) and IPXCP (Internetwork Packet Exchange Control Protocol).

Network layer   In the OSI reference model, it is layer 3—the layer in which routing is implemented, enabling connections and path selection between two end systems. *See also: Application layer, Data Link layer, Physical layer, Presentation layer, Session layer,* and *Transport layer.*

network segmentation   Breaking up a large network into smaller networks. Routers, switches, and bridges are used to create network segmentation.

NFS   Network File System: One of the protocols in Sun Microsystems's widely used file system protocol suite, allowing remote file access across a network. The name is loosely used to refer to the entire Sun protocol suite, which also includes RPC, XDR (External Data Representation), and other protocols.

NHRP   Next Hop Resolution Protocol: In a nonbroadcast multi-access (NBMA) network, the protocol employed by routers in order to dynamically locate MAC addresses of various hosts and routers. It enables systems to communicate directly without requiring an intermediate hop, thus facilitating increased performance in ATM, Frame Relay, X.25, and SMDS systems.

NHS   Next Hop Server: Defined by the NHRP protocol, this server maintains the next-hop resolution cache tables, listing IP-to-ATM address maps of related nodes and nodes that can be reached through routers served by the NHS.

nibble   Four bits.

NIC   Network interface card: An electronic circuit board placed in a computer. The NIC provides network communication to a LAN.

NLSP   NetWare Link Services Protocol: Novell's link-state routing protocol, based on the IS-IS model.

NMP   Network Management Processor: A Catalyst 5000 switch processor module used to control and monitor the switch.

node address   Used to identify a specific device in an internetwork. Can be a hardware address, which is burned into the network interface card, or a logical network address, which an administrator or server assigns to the node.

non-broadcast multi-access (NBMA) networks   Non-broadcast multi-access (NBMA) networks are types such as Frame Relay, X.25, and Asynchronous Transfer Mode (ATM). These networks allow for multi-access, but have no broadcast ability like Ethernet. So, NBMA networks require special OSPF configuration to function properly and neighbor relationships must be defined.

non-designated port   A switch port that will not forward frames in order to prevent a switching loop. Spanning Tree Protocol (STP) is responsible for deciding whether a port is designated (forwarding) or non-designated (blocking).

non-stub area   In OSPF, a resource-consuming area carrying a default route, intra-area routes, interarea routes, static routes, and external routes. Non-stub areas are the only areas that can have virtual links configured across them and exclusively contain an autonomous system border router (ASBR). *Compare with: stub area. See also: ASBR and OSPF.*

NRZ   Nonreturn to zero: One of several encoding schemes for transmitting digital data. NRZ signals sustain constant levels of voltage with no signal shifting (no return to zero-voltage level) during a bit interval. If there is a series of bits with the same value (1 or 0), there will be no state change. The signal is not self-clocking. *See also: NRZI.*

NRZI   Nonreturn to zero inverted: One of several encoding schemes for transmitting digital data. A transition in voltage level (either from high to low or vice versa) at the beginning of a bit interval is interpreted as a value of 1; the absence of a transition is interpreted as a 0. Thus, the voltage assigned to each value is continually inverted. NRZI signals are not self-clocking. *See also: NRZ.*

NT   Network termination: A point in an ISDN network. *See: NT1 and NT2.*

NT1   NT1 is the device that converts the two-wire "U" interface to the four-wire "S/T."

NT2   NT2 is an ISDN-compliant switching device, like a PBX, that splits the "S/T" bus into two separate, but electrically equivalent, interfaces. The "T" interface connects to the NT1, while the "S" interface connects to TE1 devices.

NVRAM   Nonvolatile RAM: Random-access memory that keeps its contents intact while power is turned off.

OC   Optical Carrier: A series of physical protocols, designated as OC-1, OC-2, OC-3, and so on, for SONET optical signal transmissions. OC signal levels place STS frames on a multi-mode fiber-optic line at various speeds, of which 51.84Mbps is the lowest (OC-1). Each subsequent protocol runs at a speed divisible by 51.84. *See also: SONET.*

octet   Base-8 numbering system used to identify a section of a dotted decimal IP address. Also referred to as a byte.

ones density   Also known as pulse density, this is a method of signal clocking. The CSU/DSU retrieves the clocking information from data that passes through it. For this scheme to work, the data needs to be encoded to contain at least one binary 1 for each 8 bits transmitted. *See also: CSU and DSU.*

OSI   Open Systems Interconnection: International standardization program designed by ISO and ITU-T for the development of data networking standards that make multivendor equipment interoperability a reality.

OSI reference model   Open Systems Interconnection reference model: A conceptual model defined by the International Organization for Standardization (ISO), describing how any combination of devices can be connected for the purpose of communication. The OSI model divides the task into seven functional layers, forming a hierarchy with the applications at the top and the physical medium at the bottom, and it defines the functions each layer must provide. *See also: Application layer, Data Link layer, Network layer, Physical layer, Presentation layer, Session layer,* and *Transport layer.*

OSPF   Open Shortest Path First: A link-state, hierarchical routing algorithm derived from an earlier version of the IS-IS protocol, whose features include multipath routing, load balancing, and least-cost routing. OSPF is the suggested successor to RIP in the Internet environment. *See also: Enhanced IGRP, IGP,* and *IP.*

OSPF area   An OSPF area is a grouping of contiguous networks and routers. All routers in the same area share a common Area ID. Because a router can be a member of more than one area at a time, the Area ID is associated with specific interfaces on the router. This would allow some interfaces to belong to area 1, while the remaining interfaces can belong to area 0. All of the routers within the same area have the same topology table.

OUI   Organizationally unique identifier: Code assigned by the IEEE to an organization that makes network interface cards. The organization then puts this OUI on each and every card it manufactures. The OUI is 3 bytes (24 bits) long. The manufacturer then adds a 3-byte identifier to uniquely identify the host. The total length of the address is 48 bits (6 bytes) and is called a hardware address or MAC address.

out-of-band management   Management "outside" of the network's physical channels—for example, using a console connection not directly interfaced through the local LAN or WAN or a dial-in modem. *Compare to: in-band management.*

out-of-band signaling   Within a network, any transmission that uses physical channels or frequencies separate from those ordinarily used for data transfer.

outside network   In NAT terminology, the inside network is the set of networks that are subject to translation. The outside network refers to all other addresses—usually those located on the Internet.

packet   In data communications, the basic logical unit of information transferred. A packet consists of a certain number of data bytes, wrapped or encapsulated in headers and/or trailers that contain information about where the packet came from, where it's going, and so on. The various protocols involved in sending a transmission add their own layers of header information, which the corresponding protocols in receiving devices then interpret.

packet switch   A physical device that makes it possible for a communication channel to share several connections; its functions include finding the most efficient transmission path for packets.

packet switching   A networking technology based on the transmission of data in packets. Dividing a continuous stream of data into small units—packets—enables data from multiple devices on a network to share the same communication channel simultaneously but also requires the use of precise routing information.

PAP   Password Authentication Protocol: In Point-to-Point Protocol (PPP) networks, a method of validating connection requests. The requesting (remote) device must send an authentication request, containing a password and ID, to the local router when attempting to connect. Unlike the more secure CHAP (Challenge Handshake Authentication Protocol), PAP sends the password unencrypted and does not attempt to verify whether the user is authorized to access the requested resource; it merely identifies the remote end. *See also: CHAP.*

parity checking   A method of error checking in data transmissions. An extra bit (the parity bit) is added to each character or data word so that the sum of the bits will be either an odd number (in odd parity) or an even number (even parity).

partial mesh   A type of network topology in which some network nodes form a full mesh (where every node has either a physical or a virtual circuit linking it to every other network node), but others are attached to only one or two nodes in the network. A typical use of partial-mesh topology is in peripheral networks linked to a fully meshed backbone. *See also: full mesh.*

passive state   Regarding an EIGRP routing table, a route is considered to be in the passive state when a router is not performing a route convergence.

PAT   Port Address Translation: This process allows a single IP address to represent multiple resources by altering the source TCP or UDP port number.

PCM   Pulse code modulation: Process by which an analog signal is converted into digital information.

PCR   Peak cell rate: As defined by the ATM Forum, the parameter specifying, in cells per second, the maximum rate at which a source may transmit.

PDN   Public data network: Generally for a fee, a PDN offers the public access to a computer communication network operated by private concerns or government agencies. Small organizations can take advantage of PDNs, aiding them to create WANs without investing in long-distance equipment and circuitry.

PDU   Protocol Data Unit: The processes at each layer of the OSI model. PDUs at the Transport layer are called segments; PDUs at the Network layer are called packets or datagrams; and PDUs at the Data Link layer are called frames. The Physical layer uses bits.

PGP   Pretty Good Privacy: A popular public-key/private-key encryption application offering protected transfer of files and messages.

phantom router   Used in a Hot Standby Routing Protocol (HSRP) network to provide an IP default gateway address to hosts.

Physical layer   The lowest layer—layer 1—in the OSI reference model, it is responsible for converting data frames from the Data Link layer (layer 2) into electrical signals. Physical layer protocols and standards define, for example, the type of cable and connectors to be used, including their pin assignments and the encoding scheme for signaling 0 and 1 values. *See also: Application layer, Data Link layer, Network layer, Presentation layer, Session layer*, and *Transport layer.*

PIM   Protocol Independent Multicast: A multicast protocol that handles the IGMP requests as well as requests for multicast data forwarding.

PIM-DM   Protocol Independent Multicast Dense Mode: PIM-DM utilizes the unicast route table and relies on the source root distribution architecture for multicast data forwarding.

PIM-SM   Protocol Independent Multicast Sparse Mode: PIM-SM utilizes the unicast route table and relies on the shared root distribution architecture for multicast data forwarding.

Ping   Packet Internet Groper: A Unix-based Internet diagnostic tool consisting of a message sent to test the accessibility of a particular device on the IP network. The term's acronym reflects the underlying metaphor of submarine sonar. Just as the sonar operator sends out a signal and waits to hear it echo ("ping") back from a submerged object, the network user can ping another node on the network and wait to see if it responds.

pinhole congestion   A problem associated with distance-vector routing protocols if more than one connection to a remote network is known, but they are different bandwidths.

plesiochronous   Nearly synchronous, except that clocking comes from an outside source instead of being embedded within the signal as in synchronous transmissions.

PLP   Packet Level Protocol: Occasionally called X.25 level 3 or X.25 Protocol, a Network layer protocol that is part of the X.25 stack.

PNNI   Private Network-Network Interface: An ATM Forum specification for offering topology data used for the calculation of paths through the network, among switches and groups of switches. It is based on well-known link-state routing procedures and allows for automatic configuration in networks whose addressing scheme is determined by the topology.

point-to-multipoint connection   In ATM, a communication path going only one way, connecting a single system at the starting point, called the "root node," to systems at multiple points of destination, called "leaves." *See also: point-to-point connection.*

point-to-point connection   In ATM, a channel of communication that can be directed either one way or two ways between two ATM end systems. Also refers to a point-to-point WAN serial connection. *See also: point-to-multipoint connection.*

poison reverse updates   These update messages are transmitted by a router back to the originator (thus ignoring the split-horizon rule) after route poisoning has occurred. Typically used with DV routing protocols in order to overcome large routing loops and offer explicit information when a subnet or network is not accessible (instead of merely suggesting that the network is unreachable by not including it in updates). *See also: route poisoning.*

polling   The procedure of orderly inquiry used by a primary network mechanism to determine if secondary devices have data to transmit. A message is sent to each secondary, granting the secondary the right to transmit.

POP   (1) Point of presence: The physical location where an interexchange carrier has placed equipment to interconnect with a local exchange carrier. (2) Post Office Protocol: A protocol used by client e-mail applications for recovery of mail from a mail server.

port security   Used with layer 2 switches to provide some security. Not typically used in production because it is difficult to manage. Allows only certain frames to traverse administrator-assigned segments.

port numbers   Used at the transport layer with TCP and UDP to keep track of host-to-host virtual circuits.

positive acknowledgment with retransmission   A connection-oriented session that provides acknowledgment and retransmission of the data if it is not acknowledged by the receiving host within a certain time frame.

POTS   Plain old telephone service: This refers to the traditional analog phone service that is found in most installations.

PPP   Point-to-Point Protocol: The protocol most commonly used for dial-up Internet access, superseding the earlier SLIP. Its features include address notification, authentication via CHAP or PAP, support for multiple protocols, and link monitoring. PPP has two layers: the Link Control Protocol (LCP) establishes, configures, and tests a link; and then any of various Network Control Protocols (NCPs) transport traffic for a specific protocol suite, such as IPX. *See also: CHAP, PAP, and SLIP.*

prefix routing   Method of defining how many bits are used in a subnet and how this information is sent in a routing update. For example, RIP version 1 does not send subnet mask information in the route updates. However, RIP version 2 does. This means that RIP v2 updates will send /24, /25, /26, etc., with a route update, which RIP v1 will not.

Presentation layer   Layer 6 of the OSI reference model, it defines how data is formatted, presented, encoded, and converted for use by software at the Application layer. *See also: Application layer, Data Link layer, Network layer, Physical layer, Session layer, and Transport layer.*

PRI   Primary Rate Interface: A type of ISDN connection between a PBX and a long-distance carrier, which is made up of a single 64Kbps D channel in addition to 23 (T1) or 30 (E1) B channels. *See also: ISDN.*

priority queuing   A routing function in which frames temporarily placed in an interface output queue are assigned priorities based on traits such as packet size or type of interface.

privileged mode   Command-line EXEC mode used in Cisco routers and switches that provides both viewing and changing of configurations.

Process/Application layer   Upper layer in the Internet Protocol stack. Responsible for network services.

process switching   As a packet arrives on a router to be forwarded, it's copied to the router's process buffer, and the router performs a lookup on the layer 3 address. Using the route table, an exit interface is associated with the destination address. The processor forwards the packet with the added new information to the exit interface, while the router initializes the fast-switching cache. Subsequent packets bound for the same destination address follow the same path as the first packet.

PROM   Programmable read-only memory: ROM that is programmable only once, using special equipment. *Compare with: EPROM.*

propagation delay   The time it takes data to traverse a network from its source to its destination.

protocol   In networking, the specification of a set of rules for a particular type of communication. The term is also used to refer to the software that implements a protocol.

protocol-dependent modules   The protocol-dependent modules, used in the EIGRP routing protocol, are responsible for network layer, protocol-specific requirements that allow multiple protocol support for IP, IPX and AppleTalk.

protocol stack   A collection of related protocols.

Proxy Address Resolution Protocol   Proxy ARP: Used to allow redundancy in case of a failure with the configured default gateway on a host. Proxy ARP is a variation of the ARP protocol in which an intermediate device, such as a router, sends an ARP response on behalf of an end node to the requesting host.

pruning   The act of trimming down the shortest-path tree. This deactivates interfaces that do not have group participants.

PSE   Packet switching exchange: The X.25 term for a switch.

PSN   Packet-switched network: Any network that uses packet-switching technology. Also known as packet-switched data network (PSDN). *See also: packet switching.*

PSTN   Public switched telephone network: Colloquially referred to as "plain old telephone service" (POTS). A term that describes the assortment of telephone networks and services available globally.

PVC   Permanent virtual circuit: In a Frame Relay or ATM network, a logical connection, defined in software, that is maintained permanently. *Compare with: SVC. See also: virtual circuit.*

PVP   Permanent virtual path: A virtual path made up of PVCs. *See also: PVC.*

PVP tunneling   Permanent virtual path tunneling: A technique that links two private ATM networks across a public network using a virtual path, wherein the public network transparently trunks the complete collection of virtual channels in the virtual path between the two private networks.

QoS   Quality of service: A set of metrics used to measure the quality of transmission and service availability of any given transmission system.

queue   Broadly, any list of elements arranged in an orderly fashion and ready for processing, such as a line of people waiting to enter a movie theater. In routing, it refers to a backlog of information packets waiting in line to be transmitted over a router interface.

R reference point   Used with ISDN networks to identify the connection between an NT1 and an S/T device. The S/T device converts the four-wire network to the two-wire ISDN standard network.

RADIUS   Remote Authentication Dial-In User Service: A protocol that is used to communicate between the remote access device and an authentication server. Sometimes an authentication server running RADIUS will be called a RADIUS server.

RAM   Random-access memory: Used by all computers to store information. Cisco routers use RAM to store packet buffers and routing tables, along with the hardware addresses cache.

RARP   Reverse Address Resolution Protocol: The protocol within the TCP/IP stack that maps MAC addresses to IP addresses. *See also: ARP.*

RARP server   A Reverse Address Resolution Protocol server is used to provide an IP address from a known MAC address.

rate queue   A value, assigned to one or more virtual circuits, that specifies the speed at which an individual virtual circuit will transmit data to the remote end. Every rate queue identifies a segment of the total bandwidth available on an ATM link. The sum of all rate queues should not exceed the total available bandwidth.

RCP   Remote Copy Protocol: A protocol for copying files to or from a file system that resides on a remote server on a network, using TCP to guarantee reliable data delivery.

redundancy   In internetworking, the duplication of connections, devices, or services that can be used as a backup in the event that the primary connections, devices, or services fail.

reference model   Used by application developers to create applications that work on any type of network. The most popular reference model is the Open Systems Interconnection (OSI) model.

reliability   Like IGRP, EIGRP uses only bandwidth and delay of the line to determine the best path to a remote network by default. However, EIGRP can use a combination of bandwidth, delay, load and reliability in its quest to find the best path to a remote network. Reliability refers to the reliability of the link to each remote network.

reliable multicast   When EIGRP sends multicast traffic it uses the Class D address 224.0.0.10. As I said, each EIGRP router is aware of who its neighbors are, and for each multicast it sends out, it maintains a list of the neighbors who have replied. If EIGRP doesn't get a reply from a neighbor, it will switch to using unicasts to resend the same data. If it still doesn't get a reply after 16 unicast attempts, the neighbor is declared dead. People often refer to this process as reliable multicast.

Reliable Transport Protocol (RTP)   The reliable transport protocol, used in the EIGRP routing protocol, is responsible for guaranteed, ordered delivery of EIGRP packets to all neighbors.

reload   An event or command that causes Cisco routers to reboot.

RIF   Routing Information Field: In source-route bridging, a header field that defines the path direction of the frame or token. If the Route Information Indicator (RII) bit is not set, the RIF is read from source to destination (left to right). If the RII bit is set, the RIF is read from the destination back to the source, so the RIF is read right to left. It is defined as part of the token ring frame header for source-routed frames, which contains path information.

ring   Two or more stations connected in a logical circular topology. In this topology, which is the basis for Token Ring, FDDI, and CDDI, information is transferred from station to station in sequence.

ring topology   A network logical topology comprising a series of repeaters that form one closed loop by connecting unidirectional transmission links. Individual stations on the network are connected to the network at a repeater. Physically, ring topologies are generally organized in a closed-loop star. *Compare with: bus topology* and *star topology.*

RIP   Routing Information Protocol: The most commonly used interior gateway protocol in the Internet. RIP employs hop count as a routing metric. *See also: Enhanced IGRP, IGP, OSPF,* and *hop count.*

RJ connector   Registered jack connector: Used with twisted-pair wiring to connect the copper wire to network interface cards, switches, and hubs.

rolled cable   Type of wiring cable that is used to connect a PC's COM port to a router or switch console port.

ROM   Read-only memory: Chip used in computers to help boot the device. Cisco routers use a ROM chip to load the bootstrap, which runs a power-on self-test, and then find and load the IOS in flash memory by default.

root bridge   Used with Spanning Tree Protocol to stop network loops from occurring. The root bridge is elected by having the lowest bridge ID. The bridge ID is determined by the priority (32,768 by default on all bridges and switches) and the main hardware address of the device.

route flap   A route that is being announced in an up/down fashion.

route poisoning   Used by various DV routing protocols in order to overcome large routing loops and offer explicit information about when a subnet or network is not accessible (instead of merely suggesting that the network is unreachable by not including it in updates). Typically, this is accomplished by setting the hop count to one more than maximum. *See also: poison reverse updates.*

route summarization   In various routing protocols, such as OSPF, EIGRP, and IS-IS, the consolidation of publicized subnetwork addresses so that a single summary route is advertised to other areas by an area border router.

routed protocol   Routed protocols (such as IP and IPX) are used to transmit user data through an internetwork. By contrast, routing protocols (such as RIP, IGRP, and OSPF) are used to update routing tables between routers.

router   A Network layer mechanism, either software or hardware, using one or more metrics to decide on the best path to use for transmission of network traffic. Sending packets between networks by routers is based on the information provided on Network layers. Historically, this device has sometimes been called a gateway.

Router ID (RID)   The Router ID (RID) is an IP address used to identify the router. Cisco chooses the Router ID by using the highest IP address of all configured loopback interfaces. If no loopback interfaces are configured with addresses, OSPF will choose the highest IP address of all active physical interfaces.

routing   The process of forwarding logically addressed packets from their local subnetwork toward their ultimate destination. In large networks, the numerous intermediary destinations a packet might travel before reaching its destination can make routing very complex.

routing domain   Any collection of end systems and intermediate systems that operate under an identical set of administrative rules. Every routing domain contains one or several areas, all individually given a certain area address.

routing metric   Any value that is used by routing algorithms to determine whether one route is superior to another. Metrics include such information as bandwidth, delay, hop count, path cost, load, MTU, reliability, and communication cost. Only the best possible routes are stored in the routing table, while all other information may be stored in link-state or topological databases. *See also: cost.*

routing protocol   Any protocol that defines algorithms to be used for updating routing tables between routers. Examples include IGRP, RIP, and OSPF.

routing table   A table kept in a router or other internetworking mechanism that maintains a record of only the best possible routes to certain network destinations and the metrics associated with those routes.

RP   Route processor: Also known as a supervisory processor; a module on Cisco 7000 series routers that holds the CPU, system software, and most of the memory components used in the router.

RSP   Route/Switch Processor: A processor module combining the functions of RP and SP used in Cisco 7500 series routers. *See also: RP and SP.*

RTS   Request To Send: An EIA/TIA-232 control signal requesting permission to transmit data on a communication line.

S reference point   ISDN reference point that works with a T reference point to convert a four-wire ISDN network to the two-wire ISDN network needed to communicate with the ISDN switches at the network provider.

sampling rate   The rate at which samples of a specific waveform amplitude are collected within a specified period of time.

SAP   (1) Service Access Point: A field specified by IEEE 802.2 that is part of an address specification. (2) Service Advertising Protocol: The Novell NetWare protocol that supplies a way to inform network clients of resources and services availability on network, using routers and servers. *See also: IPX.*

SCR   Sustainable cell rate: An ATM Forum parameter used for traffic management, it is the long-term average cell rate for VBR connections that can be transmitted.

SDH   Synchronous Digital Hierarchy: One of the standards developed for Fiber Optics Transmission Systems (FOTS).

SDLC   Synchronous Data Link Control: A protocol used in SNA Data Link layer communications. SDLC is a bit-oriented, full-duplex serial protocol that is the basis for several similar protocols, including HDLC and LAPB. *See also: HDLC and LAPB.*

seed router   In an AppleTalk network, the router that is equipped with the network number or cable range in its port descriptor. The seed router specifies the network number or cable range for other routers in that network section and answers to configuration requests from nonseed routers on its connected AppleTalk network, permitting those routers to affirm or modify their configurations accordingly. Every AppleTalk network needs at least one seed router physically connected to each network segment.

sequencing   Used in virtual circuits and segmentation to number segments so they can be put back together again in the correct order.

serial transmission   WAN serial connectors use serial transmission, which takes place one bit at a time, over a single channel.

server   Hardware and software that provide network services to clients.

Session layer   Layer 5 of the OSI reference model, responsible for creating, managing, and terminating sessions between applications and overseeing dataexchange between presentation layer entities. *See also: Application layer, Data Link layer, Network layer, Physical layer, Presentation layer, and Transport layer.*

set-based   Set-based routers and switches use the `set` command to configure devices. Cisco is moving away from set-based commands and is using the command-line interface (CLI) on all new devices.

setup mode   Mode that a router will enter if no configuration is found in nonvolatile RAM when the router boots. Allows the administrator to configure a router step-by-step. Not as robust or flexible as the command-line interface.

SF   A super frame (also called a D4 frame) consists of 12 frames with 192 bits each, and the 193rd bit providing other functions including error checking. SF is frequently used on T1 circuits. A newer version of the technology is Extended Super Frame (ESF), which uses 24 frames. *See also: ESF.*

shared tree   A method of multicast data forwarding. Shared trees use an architecture in which multiple sources share a common rendezvous point.

Shortest Path First (SPF)   A type of routing algorithm. The only true SPF protocol is Open Shortest Path First (OSPF).

signaling packet   An informational packet created by an ATM-connected mechanism that wants to establish connection with another such mechanism. The packet contains the QoS parameters needed for connection and the ATM NSAP address of the endpoint. The endpoint responds with a message of acceptance if it is able to support the desired QoS, and the connection is established. *See also: QoS.*

silicon switching   A type of high-speed switching used in Cisco 7000 series routers, based on the use of a separate processor (the Silicon Switch Processor, or SSP). *See also: SSE.*

simplex   A mode at which data or a digital signal is transmitted. Simplex is a way of transmitting in only one direction. Half duplex transmits in two directions but only one direction at a time. Full duplex transmits both directions simultaneously.

sliding window   The method of flow control used by TCP, as well as several Data Link layer protocols. This method places a buffer between the receiving application and the network data flow. The "window" available for accepting data is the size of the buffer minus the amount of data already there. This window increases in size as the application reads data from it and decreases as new data is sent. The receiver sends the transmitter announcements of the current window size, and it may stop accepting data until the window increases above a certain threshold.

SLIP   Serial Line Internet Protocol: An industry standard serial encapsulation for point-to-point connections that supports only a single routed protocol, TCP/IP. SLIP is the predecessor to PPP. *See also: PPP.*

SMDS   Switched Multimegabit Data Service: A packet-switched, datagram-based WAN networking technology offered by telephone companies that provides high speed.

SMTP   Simple Mail Transfer Protocol: A protocol used on the Internet to provide electronic mail services.

SNA   System Network Architecture: A complex, feature-rich, network architecture similar to the OSI reference model but with several variations; created by IBM in the 1970s and essentially composed of seven layers.

SNAP   Subnetwork Access Protocol: SNAP is a frame used in Ethernet, Token Ring, and FDDI LANs. Data transfer, connection management, and QoS selection are three primary functions executed by the SNAP frame.

snapshot routing   Snapshot routing takes a point-in-time capture of a dynamic routing table and maintains it even when the remote connection goes down. This allows the use of a dynamic routing protocol without requiring the link to remain active, which might incur per-minute usage charges.

SNMP   Simple Network Management Protocol: This protocol polls SNMP agents or devices for statistical and environmental data. This data can include device temperature, name, performance statistics, and much more. SNMP works with MIB objects that are present on the SNMP agent. This information is queried, then sent to the SNMP server.

socket   (1) A software structure that operates within a network device as a destination point for communications. (2) In AppleTalk networks, an entity at a specific location within a node; AppleTalk sockets are conceptually similar to TCP/IP ports.

software address   Also called a logical address. This is typically an IP address, but can also be an IPX address.

SOHO   Small office/home office: A contemporary term for remote users.

SONET   Synchronous Optical Network: The ANSI standard for synchronous transmission on fiber-optic media, developed at Bell Labs. It specifies a base signal rate of 51.84Mbps and a set of multiples of that rate, known as Optical Carrier levels, up to 2.5Gbps.

source tree   A method of multicast data forwarding. Source trees use the architecture of the source of the multicast traffic as the root of the tree.

SP   Switch processor: Also known as a ciscoBus controller, it is a Cisco 7000 series processor module acting as governing agent for all CxBus activities.

span   A full-duplex digital transmission line connecting two facilities.

SPAN   Switched Port Analyzer: A feature of the Catalyst 5000 switch, offering freedom to manipulate within a switched Ethernet environment by extending the monitoring ability of the existing network analyzers into the environment. At one switched segment, the SPAN mirrors traffic onto a predetermined SPAN port, while a network analyzer connected to the SPAN port is able to monitor traffic from any other Catalyst switched port.

spanning explorer packet   Sometimes called limited-route or single-route explorer packet, it pursues a statically configured spanning tree when searching for paths in a source-route bridging network. *See also: all-routes explorer packet, explorer packet,* and *local explorer packet.*

spanning tree   A subset of a network topology, within which no loops exist. When bridges are interconnected into a loop, the bridge, or switch, cannot identify a frame that has been forwarded previously, so there is no mechanism for removing a frame as it passes the interface numerous times. Without a method of removing these frames, the bridges continuously forward them—consuming bandwidth and adding overhead to the network. Spanning trees prune the network to provide only one path for any packet. *See also: Spanning Tree Protocol* and *spanning-tree algorithm.*

spanning-tree algorithm (STA) An algorithm that creates a spanning tree using the Spanning Tree Protocol (STP). *See also: spanning tree* and *Spanning Tree Protocol.*

Spanning Tree Protocol (STP) The bridge protocol (IEEE 802.1D) that enables a learning bridge to dynamically avoid loops in the network topology by creating a spanning tree using the spanning-tree algorithm. Spanning-tree frames called Bridge Protocol Data Units (BPDUs) are sent and received by all switches in the network at regular intervals. The switches participating in the spanning tree don't forward the frames; instead, they're processed to determine the spanning-tree topology itself. Cisco Catalyst series switches use STP 802.1D to perform this function. *See also: BPDU, learning bridge, MAC address, spanning tree,* and *spanning-tree algorithm.*

SPF Shortest Path First algorithm: A routing algorithm used to decide on the shortest-path. Sometimes called Dijkstra's algorithm and frequently used in link-state routing algorithms. *See also: link-state routing algorithm.*

SPID Service Profile Identifier: A number assigned by service providers or local telephone companies and configured by administrators to a BRI port. SPIDs are used to determine subscription services of a device connected via ISDN. ISDN devices use SPID when accessing the telephone company switch that initializes the link to a service provider.

split horizon Useful for preventing routing loops, a type of distance-vector routing rule where information about routes is prevented from leaving the router interface through which that information was received.

spoofing (1) In dial-on-demand routing (DDR), where a circuit-switched link is taken down to save toll charges when there is no traffic to be sent, spoofing is a scheme used by routers that causes a host to treat an interface as if it were functioning and supporting a session. The router pretends to send "spoof" replies to keepalive messages from the host in an effort to convince the host that the session is up and running. *See also: DDR.* (2) The illegal act of sending a packet labeled with a false address, in order to deceive network security mechanisms such as filters and access lists.

spooler A management application that processes requests submitted to it for execution in a sequential fashion from a queue. A good example is a print spooler.

SPX Sequenced Packet Exchange: A Novell NetWare transport protocol that augments the datagram service provided by Network layer (layer 3) protocols, it was derived from the Switch-to-Switch Protocol of the XNS protocol suite.

SQE Signal Quality Error: In an Ethernet network, a message sent from a transceiver to an attached machine that the collision-detection circuitry is working.

SRB Source-Route Bridging: Created by IBM, the bridging method used in Token Ring networks. The source determines the entire route to a destination before sending the data and includes that information in routing information fields (RIF) within each packet. *Contrast with: transparent bridging.*

SRT Source-Route Transparent bridging: A bridging scheme developed by IBM, merging source-route and transparent bridging. SRT takes advantage of both technologies in one device, fulfilling the needs of all end nodes. Translation between bridging protocols is not necessary. *Compare with: SR/TLB.*

SR/TLB Source-Route Translational Bridging: A bridging method that allows source-route stations to communicate with transparent bridge stations aided by an intermediate bridge that translates between the two bridge protocols. Used for bridging between Token Ring and Ethernet. *Compare with: SRT.*

SSAP Source Service Access Point: The SAP of the network node identified in the Source field of the packet identifying the Network layer protocol. *See also: DSAP and SAP.*

SSE Silicon Switching Engine: The software component of Cisco's silicon switching technology, hard-coded into the Silicon Switch Processor (SSP). Silicon switching is available only on the Cisco 7000 with an SSP. Silicon-switched packets are compared to the silicon-switching cache on the SSE. The SSP is a dedicated switch processor that offloads the switching process from the route processor, providing a fast-switching solution, but packets must still traverse the backplane of the router to get to the SSP and then back to the exit interface.

standard IP access list IP access list that uses only the source IP addresses to filter a network.

standard IPX access list IPX access list that uses only the source and destination IPX address to filter a network.

star topology A LAN physical topology with endpoints on the network converging at a common central device (known as a hub) using point-to-point links. A logical ring topology can be configured as a physical star topology using a unidirectional closed-loop star rather than point-to-point links. That is, connections within the hub are arranged in an internal ring. *See also: bus topology and ring topology.*

startup range If an AppleTalk node does not have a number saved from the last time it was booted, then the node selects from the range of values from 65,280 to 65,534.

state transitions Digital signaling scheme that reads the "state" of the digital signal in the middle of the bit cell. If it is five volts, the cell is read as a one. If the state of the digital signal is zero volts, the bit cell is read as a zero.

static route A route whose information is purposefully entered into the routing table by an administrator and takes priority over those chosen by dynamic routing protocols.

static VLAN A VLAN that is manually configured port-by-port. This is the method typically used in production networks.

statistical multiplexing Multiplexing in general is a technique that allows data from multiple logical channels to be sent across a single physical channel. Statistical multiplexing dynamically assigns bandwidth only to input channels that are active, optimizing available bandwidth so that more devices can be connected than with other multiplexing techniques. Also known as statistical time-division multiplexing or stat mux.

STM-1   Synchronous Transport Module Level 1. In the European SDH standard, one of many formats identifying the frame structure for the 155.52Mbps lines that are used to carry ATM cells.

store-and-forward packet switching   A technique in which the switch first copies each packet into its buffer and performs a cyclic redundancy check (CRC). If the packet is error-free, the switch then looks up the destination address in its filter table, determines the appropriate exit port, and sends the packet.

STP   (1) Shielded twisted-pair: A wiring scheme, used in many network implementations, that has a layer of shielded insulation to reduce EMI. (2) Spanning Tree Protocol.

straight-through cable   Type of Ethernet cable that connects a host to a switch, host to a hub, or router to a switch or hub.

stub area   An OSPF area carrying a default route, intra-area routes, and interarea routes, but no external routes. Configuration of virtual links cannot be achieved across a stub area, and stub areas are not allowed to contain an ASBR. *See also: non-stub area, ASBR,* and *OSPF.*

stub network   A network having only one connection to a router.

STUN   Serial Tunnel: A technology used to connect an HDLC link to an SDLC link over a serial link.

subarea   A portion of an SNA network made up of a subarea node and its attached links and peripheral nodes.

subarea node   An SNA communications host or controller that handles entire network addresses.

subchannel   A frequency-based subdivision that creates a separate broadband communications channel.

subinterface   One of many virtual interfaces available on a single physical interface.

subnet   *See: subnetwork.*

subnet address   The portion of an IP address that is specifically identified by the subnet mask as the subnetwork. *See also: IP address, subnetwork,* and *subnet mask.*

subnet mask   Also simply known as mask, a 32-bit address mask used in IP to identify the bits of an IP address that are used for the subnet address. Using a mask, the router does not need to examine all 32 bits, only those indicated by the mask. *See also: address mask* and *IP address.*

subnetting   Used in IP networks to break up larger networks into smaller subnetworks.

subnetwork   (1) Any network that is part of a larger IP network and is identified by a subnet address. A network administrator segments a network into subnetworks in order to provide a hierarchical, multilevel routing structure, and at the same time protect the subnetwork from the addressing complexity of networks that are attached. Also known as a subnet. *See also: IP* *address, subnet mask,* and *subnet address.* (2) In OSI networks, the term specifically refers to a collection of ESs and ISs controlled by only one administrative domain, using a solitary network connection protocol.

summarization   Term used to describe the process of summarizing multiple routing table entries into one entry.

supernetting   *See: summarization.*

SVC   Switched virtual circuit: A dynamically established virtual circuit created on demand and dissolved as soon as transmission is over and the circuit is no longer needed. In ATM terminology, it is referred to as a switched virtual connection. *See also: PVC.*

switch   (1) In networking, a device responsible for multiple functions such as filtering, flooding, and sending frames. It works using the destination address of individual frames. Switches operate at the Data Link layer of the OSI model. (2) Broadly, any electronic/mechanical device allowing connections to be established as needed and terminated if no longer necessary.

switch block   A combination of layer 2 switches and layer 3 routers. The layer 2 switches connect users in the wiring closet into the access layer and provide 10 or 100Mbps dedicated connections. 1900/2820 and 2900 Catalyst switches can be used in the switch block.

switch fabric   Term used to identify a layer 2 switched internetwork with many switches. More commonly, it is a term used to identify the inner workings of a switch itself. Thus, it is the matrix of pathways that any frame or cell might be able to traverse as it is switched from input port to output port.

switched LAN   Any LAN implemented using LAN switches. *See also: LAN switch.*

synchronous transmission   Signals transmitted digitally with precision clocking. These signals have identical frequencies and contain individual characters encapsulated in control bits (called start/stop bits) that designate the beginning and ending of each character. *See also: asynchronous transmission* and *isochronous transmission.*

syslog   A protocol used to monitor system log messages by a remote device.

T reference point   Used with an S reference point to change a 4-wire ISDN network to a two-wire ISDN network.

T1   Digital WAN that uses 24 DS0s at 64Kbps each to create a bandwidth of 1.536Mbps, minus clocking overhead, providing 1.544Mbps of usable bandwidth.

T3   Digital WAN that can provide bandwidth of 44.763Mbps.

TACACS+   Terminal Access Controller Access Control System Plus: An enhanced version of TACACS, this protocol is similar to RADIUS. *See also: RADIUS.*

tagged traffic   ATM cells with their cell loss priority (CLP) bit set to 1. Also referred to as Discard Eligible (DE) traffic in Frame Relay networks. Tagged traffic can be eliminated in order to ensure trouble-free delivery of higher priority traffic, if the network is congested. *See also: CLP.*

TCP   Transmission Control Protocol: A connection-oriented protocol that is defined at the transport layer of the OSI reference model. Provides reliable delivery of data.

TCP/IP   Transmission Control Protocol/Internet Protocol. The suite of protocols underlying the Internet. TCP and IP are the most widely known protocols in that suite. *See also: IP* and *TCP*.

TDM   Time Division Multiplexing: A technique for assigning bandwidth on a single wire, based on preassigned time slots, to data from several channels. Bandwidth is allotted to each channel regardless of a station's intent to send data. *See also: ATDM, FDM,* and *multiplexing*.

TE   Terminal equipment: Any peripheral device that is ISDN-compatible and attached to a network, such as a telephone or computer. TE1s are devices that are ISDN-ready and understand ISDN signaling techniques. TE2s are devices that are not ISDN-ready and do not understand ISDN signaling techniques. A terminal adapter must be used with a TE2.

TE1   Terminal Equipment Type 1. A device with a four-wire, twisted-pair digital interface is referred to as terminal equipment type 1. Most modern ISDN devices are of this type.

TE2   Terminal Equipment Type 2. Devices known as terminal equipment type 2 do not understand ISDN signaling techniques, and a terminal adapter must be used to convert the signaling.

telco   A common abbreviation for the telephone company.

Telnet   The standard terminal emulation protocol within the TCP/IP protocol stack. Method of remote terminal connection, enabling users to log in on remote networks and use those resources as if they were locally connected. Telnet is defined in RFC 854.

terminal adapter (TA)   A hardware interface between a computer without a native ISDN interface and an ISDN line. In effect, a device to connect a standard async interface to a non-native ISDN device, emulating a modem.

terminal emulation   The use of software, installed on a PC or LAN server, that allows the PC to function as if it were a "dumb" terminal directly attached to a particular type of mainframe.

TFTP   Trivial File Transfer Protocol: Conceptually, a stripped-down version of FTP; it's the protocol of choice if you know exactly what you want and where it's to be found. TFTP doesn't provide the abundance of functions that FTP does. In particular, it has no directory browsing abilities; it can do nothing but send and receive files.

TFTP host/server   A host or server on which Trivial File Transfer Protocol is used to send files using IP at the Network layer and UDP at the Transport layer, which makes it unreliable.

thicknet   Also called 10Base5. Bus network that uses a thick coaxial cable and runs Ethernet up to 500 meters.

thinnet   Also called 10Base2. Bus network that uses a thin coax cable and runs Ethernet media access up to 185 meters.

three-way handshake   Term used in a TCP session to define how a virtual circuit is set up. It is called a "three-way" handshake because it uses three data segments.

token   A frame containing only control information. Possessing this control information gives a network device permission to transmit data onto the network. *See also: token passing.*

token bus   LAN architecture that is the basis for the IEEE 802.4 LAN specification and employs token-passing access over a bus topology. *See also: IEEE.*

token passing   A method used by network devices to access the physical medium in a systematic way based on possession of a small frame called a token. *See also: token.*

Token Ring   IBM's token-passing LAN technology. It runs at 4Mbps or 16Mbps over a ring topology. Defined formally by IEEE 802.5. *See also: ring topology and token passing.*

toll network   WAN network that uses the public switched telephone network (PSTN) to send packets.

topology database   A topology database (also called a topology table) contains all destinations advertised by neighboring routers. Associated with each entry is the destination address and a list of neighbors that have advertised the destination.

Traceroute   Also Trace; IP command used to trace the path a packet takes through an internetwork.

transparent bridging   The bridging scheme used in Ethernet and IEEE 802.3 networks, it passes frames along one hop at a time, using bridging information stored in tables that associate end-node MAC addresses with bridge ports. This type of bridging is considered transparent because the source node does not know it has been bridged, because the destination frames are addressed directly to the end node. *Contrast with: SRB.*

Transport layer   Layer 4 of the OSI reference model, used for reliable communication between end nodes over the network. The transport layer provides mechanisms used for establishing, maintaining, and terminating virtual circuits, transport fault detection and recovery, and controlling the flow of information. *See also: Application layer, Data Link layer, Network layer, Physical layer, Presentation layer,* and *Session layer.*

trap   Used to send SNMP messages to SNMP managers.

TRIP   Token Ring Interface Processor: A high-speed interface processor used on Cisco 7000 series routers. The TRIP provides two or four ports for interconnection with IEEE 802.5 and IBM media with ports set to speeds of either 4Mbps or 16Mbps set independently of each other.

trunk link   Link used between switches and from some servers to the switches. Trunk links carry traffic for many VLANs. Access links are used to connect host devices to a switch and carry only VLAN information that the device is a member of.

TTL   Time to live: A field in an IP header, indicating the length of time a packet is valid.

TUD   Trunk Up-Down: A protocol used in ATM networks for the monitoring of trunks. Should a trunk miss a given number of test messages being sent by ATM switches to ensure trunk line quality, TUD declares the trunk down. When a trunk reverses state and comes back up, TUD recognizes that the trunk is up and returns the trunk to service.

tunneling   A method of avoiding protocol restrictions by wrapping packets from one protocol in another protocol's frame and transmitting this encapsulated packet over a network that supports the wrapper protocol. *See also: encapsulation.*

U reference point   Reference point between a TE1 and an ISDN network. The U reference point understands ISDN signaling techniques and uses a 2-wire connection.

UDP   User Datagram Protocol: A connectionless transport layer protocol in the TCP/IP protocol stack that simply allows datagrams to be exchanged without acknowledgments or delivery guarantees, requiring other protocols to handle error processing and retransmission. UDP is defined in RFC 768.

unicast   Used for direct host-to-host communication. Communication is directed to only one destination and is originated only from one source.

unidirectional shared tree   A method of shared tree multicast forwarding. This method allows only multicast data to be forwarded from the RP.

unnumbered frames   HDLC frames used for control-management purposes, such as link startup and shutdown or mode specification.

user mode   Cisco IOS EXEC mode that allows an administrator to perform very few commands. You can only verify statistics in user mode; you cannot see or change the router or switch configuration.

UTP   Unshielded twisted-pair: Copper wiring used in small-to-large networks to connect host devices to hubs and switches. Also used to connect switch to switch or hub to hub.

VBR   Variable bit rate: A QoS class, as defined by the ATM Forum, for use in ATM networks that is subdivided into real time (RT) class and non–real time (NRT) class. RT is employed when connections have a fixed-time relationship between samples. Conversely, NRT is employed when connections do not have a fixed-time relationship between samples, but still need an assured QoS.

VCC   Virtual channel connection: A logical circuit that is created by VCLs (virtual channel links). VCCs carry data between two endpoints in an ATM network. Sometimes called a virtual circuit connection.

VIP   (1) Versatile Interface Processor: An interface card for Cisco 7000 and 7500 series routers, providing multilayer switching and running the Cisco IOS software. The most recent version of VIP is VIP2. (2) Virtual IP: A function making it possible for logically separated switched IP workgroups to run Virtual Networking Services across the switch port.

virtual circuit (VC)   A logical circuit devised to assure reliable communication between two devices on a network. Defined by a virtual path identifier/virtual channel (really the only time "channel" is used) identifier (VPI/VCI) pair, a virtual circuit can be permanent (PVC) or switched (SVC). Virtual circuits are used in Frame Relay and X.25. Known as virtual channel in ATM. *See also: PVC and SVC.*

virtual ring   In an SRB network, a logical connection between physical rings, either local or remote.

VLAN   Virtual LAN: A group of devices on one or more logically segmented LANs (configured by use of management software), enabling devices to communicate as if attached to the same physical medium, when they are actually located on numerous different LAN segments. VLANs are based on logical instead of physical connections and thus are tremendously flexible.

VLAN ID   Sometimes referred to as VLAN color, the VLAN ID is tagged onto a frame to tell a receiving switch which VLAN the frame is a member of.

VLSM   Variable Length Subnet Mask: Helps optimize available address space and specify a different subnet mask for the same network number on various subnets. Also commonly referred to as "subnetting a subnet."

VMPS   VLAN Management Policy Server: Used to dynamically assign VLANs to a switch port.

VPN   Virtual private network: A method of encrypting point-to-point logical connections across a public network, such as the Internet. This allows secure communications across a public network.

VTP   VLAN Trunking Protocol: Used to update switches in a switch fabric about VLANs configured on a VTP server. VTP devices can be a VTP server, client, or transparent device. Servers update clients. Transparent devices are only local devices and do not share information with VTP clients. VTP devices send VLAN information down trunked links only.

VTP transparent mode   Switch mode that receives VLAN Trunking Protocol VLAN information and passes it on, but doesn't read the information.

WAN   Wide area network: Is a designation used to connect LANs together across a DCE (data communications equipment) network. Typically, a WAN is a leased line or dial-up connection across a PSTN network. Examples of WAN protocols include Frame Relay, PPP, ISDN, and HDLC.

wildcard   Used with access lists and OSPF configurations. Wildcards are designations used to identify a range of subnets.

windowing   Flow-control method used with TCP at the Transport layer of the OSI model.

WINS   Windows Internet Name Service: Name resolution database for NetBIOS names to TCP/IP address.

WinSock   Windows Socket Interface: A software interface that makes it possible for an assortment of applications to use and share an Internet connection. The WinSock software consists of a dynamic link library (DLL) with supporting programs such as a dialer program that initiates the connection.

workgroup layer   The distribution layer is sometimes referred to as the workgroup layer and is the communication point between the access layer and the core. The primary functions of the distribution layer are to provide routing, filtering, and WAN access and to determine how packets can access the core, if needed.

workgroup switching   A switching method that supplies high-speed (100Mbps) transparent bridging between Ethernet networks as well as high-speed translational bridging between Ethernet and CDDI or FDDI.

X Window A distributed multitasking windowing and graphics system originally developed by MIT for communication between X terminals and Unix workstations.

X.25 An ITU-T packet-relay standard that defines communication between DTE and DCE network devices. X.25 uses a reliable Data Link layer protocol called LAPB. X.25 also uses PLP at the Network layer. X.25 has mostly been replaced by Frame Relay.

ZIP Zone Information Protocol: A Session layer protocol used by AppleTalk to map network numbers to zone names. NBP uses ZIP in the determination of networks containing nodes that belong to a zone. *See also: ZIP storm* and *zone*.

ZIP storm A broadcast storm occurring when a router running AppleTalk reproduces or transmits a route for which there is no corresponding zone name at the time of execution. The route is then forwarded by other routers downstream, thus causing a ZIP storm. *See also: broadcast storm* and *ZIP*.

zone A logical grouping of network devices in AppleTalk. Also used in DNS. *See also: ZIP*.

Index

Note to the Reader: Throughout this index **boldfaced** page numbers indicate primary discussions of a topic. *Italicized* page numbers indicate illustrations.

D

F

O

X

Z

Wiley Publishing, Inc.
End-User License Agreement

The Absolute Best CCNA Package on the Market!

Get ready for Cisco's new CCNA exam (640-802) with the most comprehensive and challenging sample tests anywhere!

The Sybex Test Engine features:

- All the review questions, as covered in each chapter of the book

- Four full-length bonus exams with challenging questions representative of those you'll find on the real exam, available only on the CD

- An Assessment Test to narrow your focus to certain objective groups

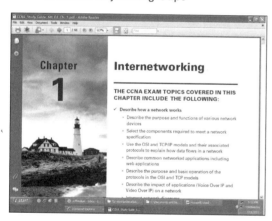

Search through the complete book in PDF!

- Access the entire *CCNA: Cisco Certified Network Associate Study Guide,* complete with figures and tables, in electronic format.

- Search the *CCNA: Cisco Certified Network Associate Study Guide* chapters to find information on any topic in seconds.

Use the electronic flashcards for PCs or Palm devices to jog your memory and prep last minute for the exam!

- Reinforce your understanding of key concepts with these hardcore flashcard-style questions.

- Download the flashcards to your Palm device and go on the road. Now you can study for the CCNA exam any time, anywhere.

- Reinforce what you've learned with over an hour's worth of useful audio and video files designed to enhance your learning experience.

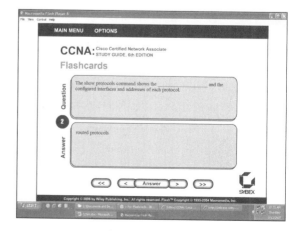